ATLA BIBLIOGRAPHY SERIES
edited by Dr. Kenneth E. Rowe

1. *A Guide to the Study of the Holiness Movement*, by Charles Edwin Jones. 1974.
2. *Thomas Merton: A Bibliography*, by Marquita E. Breit. 1974.
3. *The Sermon on the Mount: A History of Interpretation and Bibliography*, by Warren S. Kissinger. 1975.
4. *The Parables of Jesus: A History of Interpretation and Bibliography*, by Warren S. Kissinger. 1979.
5. *Homosexuality and the Judeo-Christian: An Annotated Bibliography*, by Thom Horner. 1981.
6. *A Guide to the Study of the Pentecostal Movement*, by Charles Edwin Jones. 1983.
7. *The Genesis of Modern Process Thought: A Historical Outline with Bibliography*, by George R. Lucas, Jr. 1983.
8. *A Presbyterian Bibliography*, by Harold B. Prince. 1983.
9. *Paul Tillich: A Comprehensive Bibliography . . .*, by Richard C. Crossman. 1983.
10. *A Bibliography of the Samaritans*, by Alan David Crown. 1984 (see no. 32).
11. *An Annotated and Classified Bibliography of English Literature Pertaining to the Ethiopian Orthodox Church*, by Jon Bonk. 1984.
12. *International Meditation Bibliography, 1950 to 1982*, by Howard R. Jarrell. 1984.
13. *Rabindranath Tagore: A Bibliography*, by Katherine Henn. 1985.
14. *Research in Ritual Studies: A Programmatic Essay and Bibliography*, by Ronald L. Grimes. 1985.
15. *Protestant Theological Education in America*, by Heather F. Day. 1985.
16. *Unconscious: A Guide to Sources*, by Natalino Caputi. 1985.
17. *The New Testament Apocrypha and Pseudepigrapha*, by James H. Charlesworth. 1987.
18. *Black Holiness*, by Charles Edwin Jones. 1987.
19. *A Bibliography on Ancient Ephesus*, by Richard Oster. 1987.
20. *Jerusalem, the Holy City: A Bibliography*, by James D. Purvis. Vol. I, 1988; vol. II, 1991.
21. *An Index to English Periodical Literature on the Old Testament and Ancient Near Eastern Studies*, by William G. Hupper. Vol. I, 1987; Vol. II, 1988; Vol. III, 1990; Vol. IV, 1990; Vol. V, 1992; Vol. VI, 1994; Vol. VII, 1998; Vol. VIII, 1999.
22. *John and Charles Wesley: A Bibliography*, by Betty M. Jarboe. 1987.
23. *A Scholar's Guide to Academic Journals in Religion*, by James Dawsey. 1988.
24. *An Oxford Movement and Its Leaders: A Bibliography of Secondary and Lesser Primary Sources*, by Lawrence N. Crumb. 1988; Supplement, 1993.
25. *A Bibliography of Christian Worship*, by Bard Thompson. 1989.

26. *The Disciples and American Culture: A Bibliography of Works by Disciples of Christ Members, 1866–1984*, by Leslie R. Galbraith and Heather F. Day. 1990.
27. *The Yogacara School of Buddhism: A Bibliography*, by John Powers. 1991.
28. *The Doctrine of the Holy Spirit: A Bibliography Showing Its Chronological Development* (2 vols.), by Esther Dech Schandorff. 1995.
29. *Rediscovery of Creation: A Bibliographical Study of the Church's Response to the Environmental Crisis*, by Joseph K. Sheldon. 1992.
30. *The Charismatic Movement: A Guide to the Study of Neo-Pentecostalism with Emphasis on Anglo-American Sources*, by Charles Edwin Jones. 1995.
31. *Cities and Churches: An International Bibliography* (3 vols.), by Loyde H. Hartley. 1992.
32. *A Bibliography of the Samaritans*, 2nd ed., by Alan David Crown. 1993.
33. *The Early Church: An Annotated Bibliography of Literature in English*, by Thomas A. Robinson. 1993.
34. *Holiness Manuscripts: A Guide to Sources Documenting the Wesleyan Holiness Movement in the United States and Canada*, by William Kostlevy. 1994.
35. *Of Spirituality: A Feminist Perspective*, by Clare B. Fischer. 1995.
36. *Evangelical Sectarianism in the Russian Empire and the USSR: A Bibliographic Guide*, by Albert Wardin, Jr. 1995.
37. *Hermann Sasse: A Bibliography*, by Ronald R. Feuerhahn. 1995.
38. *Women in the Biblical World: A Study Guide. Vol. I: Women in the World of Hebrew Scripture*, by Mayer I. Gruber. 1995.
39. *Women and Religion in Britain and Ireland: An Annotated Bibliography from the Reformation to 1993*, by Dale A. Johnson. 1995.
40. *Emil Brunner: A Bibliography*, by Mark G. McKim. 1996.
41. *The Book of Jeremiah: An Annotated Bibliography*, by Henry O. Thompson. 1996.
42. *The Book of Amos: An Annotated Bibliography*, by Henry O. Thompson. 1997.
43. *Ancient and Modern Chaldean History: A Comprehensive Bibliography of Sources*, by Ray Kamoo. 1999.

An Index to
English Periodical Literature
on the Old Testament
and
Ancient Near Eastern Studies

Volume VIII

Compiled and Edited by

William G. Hupper

ATLA Bibliography Series, No. 21

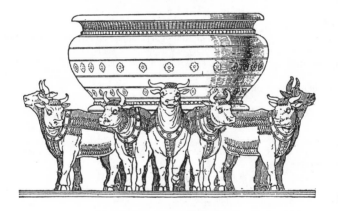

It is the way of the world that some people put errors into circulation while others try then to eradicate these same errors. This keeps everyone busy.
...*Levned og Skrifter, 1, 24*

The American Theological Library Association, and
The Scarecrow Press, Inc.
Lanham, MD, & London 1999

SCARECROW PRESS, INC.

Published in the United States of America
by Scarecrow Press, Inc.
4720 Boston Way
Lanham, Maryland 20706

4 Pleydell Gardens, Folkestone
Kent CT20 2DN, England

Cover illustration: H. von Ritgen's rendition of the brazen laver at Solomon's Temple after Bernhard Stade's *Geschichte des Volkes Israel, Erster Band* (Berlin, 1887); Citation on the title page from Jón Helgason, *Handritaspjall* (Reykjavík, 1958) as quoted in Theodore M. Andersson's *The Problem of Icelandic Saga Origins: A Historical Survey* (New Haven, Yale University Press, 1964), p. 6

British Library Cataloguing in Publication Information Available

Library of Congress Cataloging-in-Publication Data (Revised for volume 8)

Hupper, William G.
    An index to English periodical literature on the Old Testament and ancient Near Eastern studies.
        p.   cm.   —   (ATLA bibliographical series : no. 21)
        1. Bible. O.T.—Periodicals—Indexes. 2. Middle East—Periodicals—Indexes. I. American Theological Library Association. II. Title. III. Series.
    Z7772.A1H86   1987 [BS1171.2]   016.221   86-31448
ISBN 0-8108-1984-8 (v. 1)
ISBN 0-8108-2126-5 (v. 2)
ISBN 0-8108-2319-5 (v. 3)
ISBN 0-8108-2393-4 (v. 4)
ISBN 0-8108-2618-6 (v. 5)
ISBN 0-8108-2822-7 (v. 6)
ISBN 0-8108-3493-6 (v. 7)
ISBN 0-8108-3645-9 (v. 8)

©™The paper used in this publication meets the minimum requirements of American National Standard for Information Sciences—Permanence of Paper for Printed Library Materials, ANSI/NISO Z39.48–1992.
Manufactured in the United States of America.

This volume is dedicated to the memory of
Dr. William L. Lane
1931-1999
teacher, mentor, friend, and colleague

Table of Contents

v

Table of Contents

Table of Contents

Table of Contents

Table of Contents

Table of Contents

Table of Contents

xi

Table of Contents

Table of Contents

Table of Contents

Table of Contents

xv

Table of Contents

Table of Contents

Preface

Contrary to the self-imposed restriction of adding more references, this volume incorporates two additional journals that were not previously included in the index. *Irish Church Quarterly* was discovered only recently and then only six of the ten volumes could be found locally. Garrett Theological Library, Evanston, IL, was kind enough to provide copies of several articles from volumes one to four, to allow for the indexing of this series. *Zeitschrift für Religions und Geistesgeschichte* contains only a few articles in English (one of which was included in Volume VII, unfortunately without the necessary journal reference in the abbreviation section). Articles from these journals that fall into sections not covered in Volume VIII will be included in the forthcoming Author and Subject Index under the section "Additions and Corrections," which will complete the series. Additionally, a complete and corrected list of journals and abbreviations will be supplied in the index volume.

Continued thanks go to Mrs. Florence Hall, who was concerned that my moving to the West Coast would not allow her to complete the proofreading of the entire series. She has been resolute in her commitment of donated time in reading 4700+ pages of text and comparing it with over 100,000 file cards. Additional thanks go to my daughter, Susan Witt, who took many excursions to various libraries in the Boston area to supply photocopied articles which needed rechecking, and to my son, Adam, who patiently located numerous 3 x 5 cards among the many file drawers left on the East Coast that needed to be reexamined. Their assistance made the completion of this volume possible.

Finally, on a more personal note, I wish to dedicate this volume to Dr. William L. Lane, teacher, friend, mentor, and colleague. It was his encouragement to a somewhat naïve undergraduate over 28 years ago that first inspired me to undertake such an overly ambitious project. He was the one person who always believed that I would finish this task, and I rejoice that he lived long enough to know of its completion. His passing this year from this life to his eternal reward leaves a void in the hearts of all who knew him. He will always be remembered by those fortunate enough to have heard his lectures, and by the legacy of his writings. He now knows fully what we only perceive "through a glass darkly." שלום my dear friend.

Vernal Equinox 1999
Torrance, CA

Periodical Abbreviations*

A

A&A   *Art and Archaeology; the arts throughout the ages* (Washington, DC, Baltimore, MD, 1914-1934)

A/R   *Action/Reaction* (San Anselmo, CA, 1967ff.)

A&S   *Antiquity and Survival* (The Hague, 1955-1962)

A(A)   *Anadolu (Anatolia)* (Ankara, 1956ff.) [Subtitle varies; Volume 1-7 as: *Anatolia: Revue Annuelle d'Archeologie*]

AA   *Acta Archaeologica* (Copenhagen, 1930ff.)

AAA   *Annals of Archaeology and Anthropology* (Liverpool, 1908-1948; Suspended, 1916-1920)

AAAS   *Annales archéologiques arabes Syriennes. Revue d'Archéologie et d'Histoire* (Damascus, 1951ff.) [Volumes 1-15 as: *Les Annales archéologiques de Syrie* - Title Varies]

AAASH   *Acta Antiqua Academiae Scientiarum Hungaricae* (Budapest, 1951ff.)

AAB   *Acta Archaeologica* (Budapest, 1951ff.)

AAI   *Anadolu Araştirmalari Istanbul Üniversitesi Edebiyat Fakültesi eski Önasya Dilleri ve Kültürleri Kürsüsü Tarafindan Čikarilir* (Istanbul, 1955ff.) [Supersedes: *Jahrbuch für Kleinasiatische Forschungen*]

AAOJ   *American Antiquarian and Oriental Journal* (Cleveland, Chicago 1878-1914)

AASCS   *Antichthon. The Australian Society for Classical Studies* (Sydney, 1967ff.)

ABBTS   *The Alumni Bulletin [of] Bangor Theological Seminary* (Bangor, ME; 1926ff.)

ABenR   *The American Benedictine Review* (St. Paul, 1950ff.)

ABR   *Australian Biblical Review* (Melbourne, 1951ff.)

Abr-N   *Abr-Nahrain, An Annual Published by the Department of Middle Eastern Studies, University of Melbourne* (Melbourne, 1959ff.)

ACM   *The American Church Monthly* (New York, 1917-1939) [Volumes 43-45 as: *The New American Church Monthly*]

*All the journals indexed are listed in the Periodical Abbreviations even though no specific citation may appear in the present volume. Although the titles of many foreign language journals have been listed, only English language articles are included in this index (except as noted). Articles from modern Hebrew language journals are referred to by their English summary page.

ACQ	*American Church Quarterly* (New York, 1961ff.) [From Volume 7 on as: *Church Theological Review*]
ACQR	*The American Catholic Quarterly Review* (Philadelphia, 1876-1929)
ACR	*The Australasian Catholic Record* (Sydney, 1924ff.)
ACSR	*American Catholic Sociological Review* (Chicago, 1940ff.) [From Volume 25 on as: *Sociological Analysis*]
ADAJ	*Annual of the Department of Antiquities of Jordan* (Amman, 1957ff.) [Volume 14 not published—destroyed by fire at the publishers]
AE	*Annales d'Ethiopie* (Paris, 1955ff.)
AEE	*Ancient Egypt and the East* (New York, London, Chicago, 1914-1935; Suspended, 1918-1919)
Aeg	*Aegyptus: Rivista Italiana di Egittologia e di Papirologia* (Milan,1920ff.)
AER	*American Ecclesiastical Review* (Philadelphia, New York, Cincinnati, Baltimore, 1889ff.) [Volumes 11-19 as: *Ecclesiastical Review*]
AfER	*African Ecclesiastical Review: A Quarterly for Priests in Africa* (Masaka, Uganda, 1959ff.)
Aff	*Affirmation* (Richmond, VA, 1966ff.) [Volume 1 runs from 1966 to 1980 inclusive]
AfO	*Archiv für Orientforschung; Internationale Zeitschrift für Wissenschaft vom Vorderen Orient* (Berlin, 1923ff.)
AfRW	*Archiv für Religionswissenschaft* (Leipzig, 1898-1941)
AHDO	*Archives d'histoire du droit oriental et Revue internationale des droits de l'antiquité* (Brussels, 1937-38, 1947-1951, N.S., 1952-53)
AHR	See *AmHR*
AIPHOS	*Annuaire de l'institut de philologie et d'histoire orientales et slaves* (Brussels, 1932ff.)
AJ	*The Antiquaries Journal. Being the Journal of the Society of Antiquaries of London* (London, 1921ff.)
AJA	*The American Journal of Archaeology* (Baltimore, 1885ff.) [Original Series, 1885-1896 shown with *O. S;* Second Series shown without notation]
AJBA	*The Australian Journal of Biblical Archaeology* (Sydney, 1968ff.) [Volume 1 runs from 1968 to 1971 inclusive]
AJP	*The American Journal of Philology* (Baltimore, 1880ff.)
AJRPE	*The American Journal of Religious Psychology and Education* (Worcester, MA, 1904-1915)
AJSL	*The American Journal of Semitic Languages and Literatures* (Chicago, 1884-1941) [Volumes 1-11 as: *Hebraica*]
AJT	*American Journal of Theology* (Chicago, 1897-1920)

Periodical Abbreviations

AL	*Archivum Linguisticum: A Review of Comparative Philology and General Linguistics* (Glasgow, 1949-1962)
ALUOS	*The Annual of the Leeds University Oriental Society* (Leiden,1958ff.)
Amb	*The Ambassador* (Wartburg Theological Seminary, Dubuque, IA, 1952ff.)
AmHR	*American Historical Review* (New York, Lancaster, PA, 1895ff.)
AmSR	*American Sociological Review* (Washington, DC, 1936ff.)
Anat	*Anatolica: Annuaire International pour les Civilisations de l'Asie Antérieure* (Leiden, 1967ff.)
ANQ	*Newton Theological Institute Bulletin* (Newton, MA, 1906ff.) [Title varies as: *Andover-Newton Theological Bulletin; Andover-Newton Quarterly, New Series,* beginning 1960ff.]
Anthro	*Anthropos; ephemeris internationalis ethnologica et linguistica* (Salzburg, Vienna, 1906ff.)
Antiq	*Antiquity: A Quarterly Review of Archaeology* (Gloucester, England, 1927ff.)
Anton	*Antonianum. Periodicum Philosophico-Theologicum Trimestre* (Rome, 1926ff.)
AO	*Acta Orientalia ediderunt Societates Orientales Bœtava Donica, Norvegica* (Lugundi Batavorum, Havniæ, 1922ff.)
AOASH	*Acta Orientalia Academiae Scientiarum Hungaricae* (Budapest, 1950ff.)
AOL	*Annals of Oriental Literature* (London, 1820-21)
APST	*Aberdeen Philosophical Society, Transactions* (Aberdeen, Scotland, 1840-1931)
AQ	*Augustana Quarterly* (Rock Island, IL, 1922-1948)
AQW	*Anthropological Quarterly* (Washington, DC, 1928ff.) [Volumes1-25 as: *Primitive Man*]
AR	*The Andover Review* (Boston, 1884-1893)
Arch	*Archaeology* (Cambridge, MA, 1948ff.)
Archm	*Archaeometry. Bulletin of the Research Laboratory for Archaeology and the History of Art, Oxford University* (Oxford,1958ff.)
ARL	*The Archæological Review* (London, 1888-1890)
ArOr	*Archiv Orientální. Journal of the Czechoslovak Oriental Institute, Prague* (Vlašska, Czechoslovakia, 1929ff.)
AS	*Anatolian Studies: Journal of the British Institute of Archaeology at Ankara* (London, 1951ff.)
ASAE	*Annales du service des antiquités de l'Égypte* (Cairo, 1899ff.)

ASBFE *Austin Seminary Bulletin. Faculty Edition* (Austin, TX; begins with volume 71*[sic]*, 1955ff.)

ASR *Augustana Seminary Review* (Rock Island, IL, 1949-1967) [From Volume 12 on as: *The Seminary Review*]

ASRB *Advent Shield and Review* (Boston, 1844-45)

ASRec *Auburn Seminary Record* (Auburn, NY, 1905-1932)

ASSF *Acta Societatis Scientiarum Fennicae* (Helsinki, 1842-1926) [Suomen tideseura]

ASTI *Annual of the Swedish Theological Institute (in Jerusalem)* (Jerusalem, 1962ff.)

ASW *The Asbury Seminarian* (Wilmore, KY, 1946ff.)

AT *Ancient Times: A Quarterly Review of Biblical Archaeology* (Melbourne, 1956-1961)

ATB *Ashland Theological Bulletin* (Ashland, OH, 1968ff.)

ATG *Advocate for the Testimony of God* (Richmond, VA, 1834-1839)

AThR *The American Theological Review* (New York, 1859-1868) [*New Series* as: *American Presbyterian and Theological Review,* 1863-1868]

'Atiqot *'Atiqot: Journal of the Israel Department of Antiquities* (Jerusalem, 1955ff.)

ATJ *Africa Theological Journal* (Usa River, Tanzania, 1968ff.)

ATR *Anglican Theological Review* (New York, Lancaster, PA; 1918ff.)

AubSRev *Auburn Seminary Review* (Auburn, NY, 1897-1904)

Aug *Augustinianum* (Rome, 1961ff.)

AULLUÅ *Acta Universitatis Lundensis. Lunds Universitets Årsskrift. Första Avdelningen. Teologi, Juridik och Humanistika Ämnen* (Lund, 1864-1904; *N. S.,* 1905-1964)

AUSS *Andrews University Seminary Studies* (Berrien Springs, MI, 1963ff.)

AusTR *The Australasian Theological Review* (Highgate, South Australia, 1930-1966)

B

B *Biblica* (Rome, 1920ff.)

BA *The Biblical Archaeologist* (New Haven; Cambridge, MA; 1938ff.)

Baby *Babyloniaca Etudes de Philologie Assyro-Babylonienne* (Paris, 1906-1937)

BASOR   *Bulletin of the American Schools of Oriental Research* (So.
             Hadley, MA; Baltimore, New Haven, Philadelphia,
             Cambridge, MA;1919ff.)
BASP   *Bulletin of the American Society of Papyrologists*
             (New Haven, 1963ff.)
BAVSS   *Beiträge zur Assyriologie und vergleichenden semitischen
             Sprachwissenschaft* (Leipzig, 1889-1927)
BBC   *Bulletin of the Bezan Club* (Oxford, 1925-1936)
BC   *Bellamine Commentary* (Oxon., England; 1956-1968)
BCQTR   *British Critic, Quarterly Theological Review and Ecclesiastical
             Record* (London, 1793-1843) [Superseded by: *English
             Review*]
BCTS   *Bulletin of the Crozer Theological Seminary* (Upland, PA,
             1908-1934)
Bery   *Berytus. Archaeological Studies* (Copenhagen, 1934ff.)
BETS   *Bulletin of the Evangelical Theological Society* (Wheaton, IL,
             1958ff.)
BFER   *British and Foreign Evangelical Review, and Quarterly Record
             of Christian Literature* (Edinburgh, London, 1852-1888)
BH   *Buried History. Quarterly Journal of the Australian Institute
             of Archaeology* (Melbourne, 1964-65; 1967ff.)
BibR   *Biblical Repertory* (Princeton, NJ; New York, 1825-1828)
BibT   *The Bible Today* (Collegeville, MN, 1962ff.)
BIES   *Bulletin of the Israel Exploration Society* (Jerusalem,
             1937-1967) [*Yediot-* ידיעות בחקידת
             ארץ־ישראל ועתיקותיה-Begun as: *Bulletin of the
             Jewish Palestine Exploration Society* through volume
             15. English summaries discontinued from volume 27 on
             as translations published in: *Israel Exploration Journal*]
BIFAO   *Bulletin de l'institut français d'archéologie orientale au Caire*
             (Cairo, 1901ff.)
BJ   *Biblical Journal* (Boston, 1842-1843)
BJRL   *Bulletin of the John Rylands Library* (Manchester, 1903ff.)
BM   *Bible Magazine* (New York, 1913-1915)
BMB   *Bulletin du Musée de Byrouth* (Paris, 1937ff.)
BN   *Bible Numerics: a Periodical Devoted to the Numerical
             Study of the Scriptures* (Grafton, MA; 1904)
BO   *Bibliotheca Orientalis* (Leiden, 1944ff.)
BofT   *Banner of Truth* (London, 1955ff.)
BOR   *The Babylonian and Oriental Record: A Monthly Magazine of
             the Antiquities of the East* (London, 1886-1901)
BQ   *Baptist Quarterly* (Philadelphia, 1867-1877)
BQL   *Baptist Quarterly* (London, 1922ff.)

BQR	*Baptist Quarterly Review* (Cincinnati, New York, Philadelphia, 1879-1892)
BQRL	*The British Quarterly Review* (London, 1845-1886)
BR	*Biblical Review* (New York, 1916-1932)
BRCM	*The Biblical Review and Congregational Magazine* (London, 1846-1850)
BRCR	*The Biblical Repository and Classical Review* (Andover, MA, 1831-1850) [Title varies as: *Biblical Repository; The Biblical Repository and Quarterly Observer; The American Biblical Repository*]
BRec	*Bible Record* (New York, 1903-1912) [Volume 1, #1-4 as: *Bible Teachers Training School, New York City, Bulletin*]
BRes	*Biblical Research: Papers of the Chicago Society of Biblical Research* (Amsterdam, Chicago, 1956ff.)
BS	*Bibliotheca Sacra* (New York, Andover, Oberlin, OH; St. Louis, Dallas, 1843, 1844ff.)
BSAJB	*British School of Archaeology in Jerusalem, Bulletin* (Jerusalem, 1922-1925)
BSOAS	*Bulletin of the School of Oriental and African Studies. University of London* (London, 1917ff.)
BSQ	*Bethel Seminary Quarterly* (St. Paul, MN; 1952ff.) [From Volume 13 on as: *Bethel Seminary Journal*]
BT	*Biblical Theology* (Belfast, 1950ff.)
BTF	*Bangalore Theological Forum* (Bangalore, India, 1967ff.)
BTPT	*Bijdragen Tijdschrift voor philosophie en theologie* (Maastricht, 1938ff.) [Title varies as: *Bijdragen. Tijdschrift voor filosofie en theologie*]
BTr	*Bible Translator* (London, 1950ff.)
BUS	*Bucknell University Studies* (Lewisburg, PA; 1941ff.) [From Volume 5 on as: *Bucknell Review*]
BVp	*Biblical Viewpoint* (Greenville, SC, 1967ff.)
BW	*Biblical World* (Chicago, 1893-1920)
BWR	*Bible Witness and Review* (London, 1877-1881)
BWTS	*The Bulletin of the Western Theological Seminary* (Pittsburgh, 1908-1931)
BZ	*Biblische Zeitschrift* (Paderborn, 1903-1939; *New Series,* 1957ff.) [*N.S.* shown without notation]

C

C&C	*Cross and Crown. A Thomistic Quarterly of Spiritual Theology* (St. Louis, 1949ff.)
CAAMA	*Cahiers archéologiques fin de l'antiquité et moyen age* (Paris, 1961ff.)

CAAST   *Connecticut Academy of Arts and Sciences, Transactions*
(New Haven, 1866ff.)

Carm   *Carmelus. Commentarii ab instituto carmelitano editi*
(Rome, 1954ff.)

CBQ   *Catholic Biblical Quarterly* (Washington, DC; 1939ff.)

CC   *Cross Currents* (West Nyack, NY; 1950ff.)

CCARJ   *Central Conference of American Rabbis Journal*
(New York,1953ff.)

CCBQ   *Central Conservative Baptist Quarterly* (Minneapolis, 1958ff.)
[From Volume 9, #2 on as: *Central Bible Quarterly*]

CCQ   *Crisis Christology Quarterly* (Dubuque, IA; 1943-1949)
[Volume 6 as: *Trinitarian Theology*]

CD   *Christian Disciple* (Boston, 1813-1823) [Superseded by:
Christian Examiner]

CdÉ   *Chronique d'Égypte* (Brussels, 1925ff.)

CE   *Christian Examiner* (Boston, New York, 1824-1869)

Cent   *Centaurus. International Magazine of the History of
Science and Medicine* (Copenhagen, 1950ff.)

Center   *The Center* (Atlanta, 1960-1965)

CFL   *Christian Faith and Life* (Columbia, SC, 1897-1939) [Title
varies: Original Series as: *The Bible Student and
Religious Outlook,* volumes 1 & 2 as: *The Religious
Outlook;* New Series as: *The Bible Student;* Third Series
as: *The Bible Student and Teacher;* several volumes as:
Bible Champion]

ChgoS   *Chicago Studies* (Mundelein, IL; 1962ff.)

CJ   *Conservative Judaism* (New York, 1945ff.)

CJL   *Canadian Journal of Linguistics* (Montreal, 1954ff.)

CJRT   *The Canadian Journal of Religious Thought* (Toronto,
1924-1932)

CJT   *Canadian Journal of Theology* (Toronto, 1955ff.)

ClR   *Clergy Review* (London, 1931ff.)

CM   *The Clergyman's Magazine* (London, 1875-1897)

CMR   *Canadian Methodist Review* (Toronto, 1889-1895) [Volumes
1-5 as: *Canadian Methodist Quarterly*]

CNI   *Christian News from Israel* (Jerusalem, 1949ff.)

CO   *Christian Opinion* (New York, 1943-1948)

Coll   *Colloquium. The Australian and New Zealand Theological
Review* (Auckland, 1964ff.) [Volume 1 through
Volume 2, #1 as: *The New Zealand Theological Review*]

CollBQ   *The College of the Bible Quarterly* (Lexington, KY, 1909-
1965) [Break in sequence between 1927 and 1937,
resumes in 1938 with volume 15 duplicated in number]

ColTM   *Columbus Theological Magazine* (Columbus, OH; 1881-1910)

CongL   *The Congregationalist* (London, 1872-1886)

CongML	*The Congregational Magazine* (London, 1818-1845)
CongQB	*The Congregational Quarterly* (Boston, 1859-1878)
CongQL	*The Congregational Quarterly* (London, 1923-1958)
CongR	*The Congregational Review* (Boston, Chicago, 1861-1871) [Volumes 1-6 as: *The Boston Review*]
CongRL	*The Congregational Review* (London, 1887-1891)
ConstrQ	*The Constructive Quarterly. A Journal of the Faith, Work, and Thought of Christendom* (New York, London, 1913-1922)
Cont	*Continuum* (St. Paul, 1963-1970)
ContextC	*Context (Journal of the Lutheran School of Theology at Chicago)* (Chicago, 1967-1968)
ContR	*Contemporary Review* (London, New York, 1866ff.)
CovQ	*The Covenant Quarterly* (Chicago, 1941ff.) [Volume 1, #1 as: *Covenant Minister's Quarterly*]
CQ	*Crozer Quarterly* (Chester, PA; 1924-1952)
CQR	*Church Quarterly Review* (London, 1875-1968)
CR	*The Church Review* (New Haven, 1848-1891) [Title varies; Volume 62 not published]
CraneR	*The Crane Review* (Medford, MA; 1958-1968)
CRB	*The Christian Review* (Boston, Rochester; 1836-1863)
CRDSB	*Colgate-Rochester Divinity School Bulletin* (Rochester, NY; 1928-1967)
Crit	*Criterion* (Chicago, 1962ff.)
CRP	*The Christian Review: A Quarterly Magazine* (Philadelphia, 1932-1941)
CS	*The Cumberland Seminarian* (McKenzie, TN; Memphis; 1953-1970)
CSQ	*Chicago Seminary Quarterly* (Chicago, 1901-1907)
CSQC	*The Culver-Stockton Quarterly* (Canton, MO; 1925-1931)
CSSH	*Comparative Studies in Society and History: An International Quarterly* (The Hague, 1958ff.)
CT	*Christian Thought* (New York, 1883-1894)
CTJ	*Calvin Theological Journal* (Grand Rapids, 1966ff.)
CTM	*Concordia Theological Monthly* (St. Louis, 1930ff.)
CTPR	*The Christian Teacher [and Chronicle]* (London, 1835-1838; N.S., 1838-1844 as: *A Theological and Literary Journal*) [Continues as: *The Prospective Review; A Quarterly Journal of Theology and Literature*]
CTSB	*Columbia Theological Seminary Bulletin* (Columbia, SC; Decatur, GA; 1907ff.) [Title varies]
CTSP	*Catholic Theological Society, Proceedings* (Washington, DC; Yonkers, NY; 1948ff.)
CTSQ	*Central Theological Seminary Quarterly* (Dayton, OH; 1923-1931)

CUB   *Catholic University Bulletin* (Washington, DC; 1895-1914)
           [Volumes 1-20 only]

D

DDSR   *Duke Divinity School Review* (Durham, NC; 1936ff.)
           [Volumes 1-20 as: *The Duke School of Religion Bulletin;*
           Volumes 21-29 as: *Duke Divinity School Bulletin*]
DG   *The Drew Gateway* (Madison, NJ; 1930ff.)
DI   *Diné Israel. An Annual of Jewish Law and Israeli Family
           Law* דיני ישראל, שנתון למשפט עברי ולדיני
           משפחה בישראל (Jerusalem, 1969ff.)
DJT   *Dialogue: A Journal of Theology* (Minneapolis, 1962ff.)
DownsR   *Downside Review* (Bath, 1880ff.)
DQR   *Danville Quarterly Review* (Danville, KY; Cincinnati;
           1861-1864)
DR   *Dublin Review* (London, 1836-1968) [Between 1961 and 1964
           as: *Wiseman Review*]
DS   *Dominican Studies. A Quarterly Review of Theology and
           Philosophy* (Oxford, 1948-1954)
DSJ   *The Dubuque Seminary Journal* (Dubuque, IA; 1966-1967)
DSQ   *Dubuque Seminary Quarterly* (Dubuque, IA; 1947-1949)
           [Volume 3, #3 not published]
DTCW   *Dimension: Theology in Church and World* (Princeton, NJ;
           1964-1969) [Volumes 1 & 2 as: *Dimension* ; New
           format beginning in 1966 with full title, beginning again
           with Volume 1]
DTQ   *Dickinson's Theological Quarterly* (London, 1875-1883)
           [Superseded by *John Lobb's Theological Quarterly*]
DUJ   *The Durham University Journal* (Durham, 1876ff.; *N.S.,*
           1940ff.) [Volume 32 of *O.S.* = Volume 1 of *N.S.*]
DUM   *Dublin University Magazine* (Dublin, London, 1833-1880)
DunR   *The Dunwoodie Review* (Yonkers, NY; 1961ff.)

E

EgR   *Egyptian Religion* (New York, 1933-1936)
EI   *Eretz-Israel. Archaeological, Historical and Geographical
           Studies* (Jerusalem, 1951ff.) ,ארץ־ישראל
           מחקרים בידיעת הארץ ועתיקותיה
           [English Summaries from Volume 3 on]

xxix

EJS	*Archives européennes de Sociologie / European Journal of Sociology / Europäisches Archiv für Soziologie* (Paris, 1960ff.)
EN	*The Everlasting Nation* (London, 1889-1892)
EQ	*Evangelical Quarterly* (London, 1929ff.)
ER	*Evangelical Review* (Gettysburg, PA; 1849-1870) [From Volume 14 on as: *Evangelical Quarterly Review*]
ERCJ	*Edinburgh Review, or Critical Journal* (Edinburgh, London, 1802-1929)
ERG	*The Evangelical Repository: A Quarterly Magazine of Theological Literature* (Glasgow, 1854-1888)
ERL	*The English Review, or Quarterly Journal of Ecclesiastical and General Literature* (London, 1844-1853) [Continues *British Critic*]
ESS	*Ecumenical Study Series* (Indianapolis, 1955-1960)
ET	*The Expository Times* (Aberdeen, Edinburgh, 1889ff.)
ETL	*Ephemerides Theologicae Lovanienses* (Notre Dame, 1924ff.)
Eud	*Eudemus. An International Journal Devoted to the History of Mathematics and Astronomy* (Copenhagen, 1941)
Exp	*The Expositor* (London, 1875-1925)
Exped	*Expedition* (Philadelphia, 1958ff.) [Continues: *The University Museum Bulletin*]

F

F&T	*Faith and Thought* (London, 1958ff.) [Supersedes: *Journal of the Transactions of the Victoria Institute, or Philosophical Society of Great Britain*]
FBQ	*The Freewill Baptist Quarterly* (Providence, London, Dover, 1853-1869)
FDWL	*Friends of Dr. Williams's Library (Lectures)* (Cambridge, Oxford, 1948ff.)
FLB	*Fuller Library Bulletin* (Pasadena, CA; 1949ff.)
FO	*Folia Orientalia* (Kraków, 1960ff.)
Focus	*Focus. A Theological Journal* (Willowdale, Ontario, 1964-1968)
Folk	*Folk-Lore: A Quarterly Review of Myth, Tradition, Institution & Custom being The Transactions of the Folk-Lore Society And Incorporating the Archæological Review and the Folk-Lore Journal* (London, 1890ff.)
Found	*Foundations (A Baptist Journal of History and Theology)* (Rochester, NY; 1958ff.)
FUQ	*Free University Quarterly* (Amsterdam-Centrum, 1950-1965)

G

GBT	Ghana Bulletin of Theology (Legon, Ghana; 1957ff.)
GJ	Grace Journal (Winona Lake, IN; 1960ff.)
GOTR	Greek Orthodox Theological Review (Brookline, MA; 1954ff.)
GR	Gordon Review (Boston; Beverly Farms, MA; Wenham, MA; 1955ff.)
GRBS	Greek, Roman and Byzantine Studies (San Antonio; Cambridge, MA; University, MS; Durham, NC; 1958ff.) [Volume1 as: Greek and Byzantine Studies]
Greg	Gregorianum; Commentarii de re theologica et philosophica (Rome, 1920ff.) [Volume 1 as: Gregorianum; rivista trimestrale di studi teologici e filosofici]
GUOST	Glasgow University Oriental Society, Transactions (Glasgow, 1901ff.)

H

H&T	History and Theory: Studies in the Philosophy of History (The Hague, 1960ff.)
HA	Hebrew Abstracts (New York, 1954ff.)
HDSB	Harvard Divinity School Bulletin (Cambridge, MA; 1935-1969)
Herm	Hermathena; a Series of Papers on Literature, Science and Philosophy by Members of Trinity College, Dublin (Dublin, 1873ff.) [Volumes 1-20; changes to issue number from #46 on]
HeyJ	The Heythrop Journal (New York, 1960ff.)
HJ	Hibbert Journal (London, Boston, 1902-1968)
HJAH	Historia. Zeitschrift für alte Geschichte / Revue d'Histoire Ancienne / Journal of Ancient History / Rivista di Storia Antica (Baden, 1950ff.)
HJud	Historia Judaica. A Journal of Studies in Jewish History Especially in the Legal and Economic History of the Jews (New York, 1938-1961)
HQ	The Hartford Quarterly (Hartford, CT; 1960-1968)
HR	Homiletic Review (New York, 1876-1934)
HRel	History of Religions (Chicago, 1961ff.)
HS	Ha Sifrut. Quarterly for the Study of Literature הספרות, רבעון למדע הספרות (Tel-Aviv, 1968ff.)
HSR	Hartford Seminary Record (Hartford, CT; 1890-1913)
HT	History Today (London, 1951ff.)

HTR	*Harvard Theological Review* (Cambridge, MA; 1908ff.)
HTS	*Hervormde Teologiese Studien* (Pretoria, 1943ff.)
HUCA	*Hebrew Union College Annual* (Cincinnati, 1904, 1924ff.)

I

IA	*Iranica Antiqua* (Leiden, 1961ff.)
IALR	*International Anthropological and Linguistic Review* (Miami, 1953-1957)
IAQR	*Asiatic Quarterly Review* (London, 1886-1966) [1st Series as: *Asiatic Quarterly Review,* (1886-1890); 2nd Series as: *The Imperial and Asiatic Quarterly and Oriental and Colonial Record,* (1891-1895); 3rd Series, (1896-1912); New Series, Volumes 1 & 2 as: *The Asiatic Quarterly Review* (1913); Volumes 3-48 (1914-1952) as: *Asiatic Review, New Series;* Volumes 49-59 (1953-1964) as: *Asian Review, New Series;* continued as: *Asian Review, Incorporating Art and Letters [and] the Asiatic Review, New Series,* Volumes 1-3 (1964-1966)]
ICHR	*Indian Church History Review* (Serampore, West Bengal, 1967ff.)
ICMM	*The Interpreter. A Church Monthly Magazine* (London, 1905-1924)
ICQ	*Irish Church Quarterly* (Dublin, 1908-1917)
IEJ	*Israel Exploration Journal* (Jerusalem, 1950ff.)
IER	*Irish Ecclesiastical Record (A Monthly Journal under Episcopal Sanction)* (Dublin, 1864-1968)
IES	*Indian Ecclesiastical Studies* (Bangalore, India, 1962ff.)
IJA	*International Journal of Apocrypha* (London, 1905-1917) [Issues #1-7 as: *Deutero-Canonica,* pages unnumbered]
IJT	*Indian Journal of Theology* (Serampore, West Bengal, 1952ff.)
ILR	*Israel Law Review* (Jerusalem, 1966ff.)
Inter	*Interchange: Papers on Biblical and Current Questions* (Sydney, 1967ff.)
Interp	*Interpretation; a Journal of Bible and Theology* (Richmond, 1947ff.)
IPQ	*International Philosophical Quarterly* (New York, 1961ff.)
IR	*The Iliff Review* (Denver, 1944ff.)
Iran	*Iran: Journal of the British Institute of Persian Studies* (London, 1963ff.)
Iraq	*Iraq. British School of Archaeology in Iraq* (London, 1934ff.)
IRB	*International Reformed Bulletin* (London, 1958ff.)

IRM	*International Review of Missions* (Edinburgh, London, Geneva, 1912ff.)
Isis	*Isis. An International Review devoted to the History of Science and Civilization* (Brussels; Cambridge, MA; 1913ff.)
ITQ	*Irish Theological Quarterly* (Dublin, Maynooth, 1906ff.)

J

JAAR	*Journal of the American Academy of Religion* (Wolcott, NY; Somerville, NJ; Baltimore; Brattleboro, VT) [Volumes 1-4 as: *Journal of the National Association of Biblical Instructors;* Volumes 5-34 as: *Journal of Bible and Religion*]
JANES	*Journal of the Ancient Near Eastern Society of Columbia University* (New York, 1968ff.)
Janus	*Janus; Archives internationales pour l'Histoire de la Médecine et pour la Géographie Médicale* (Amsterdam; Haarlem; Leiden; 1896ff.)
JAOS	*Journal of the American Oriental Society* (Baltimore, New Haven, 1843ff.)
JAOSS	*Journal of the American Oriental Society, Supplements* (Baltimore, New Haven, 1935-1954)
JARCE	*Journal of the American Research Center in Egypt* (Gluckstadt, Germany; Cambridge, MA; 1962ff.)
JASA	*Journal of the American Scientific Affiliation* (Wheaton, IL, 1949ff.)
JBL	*Journal of Biblical Literature* (Middletown, CT; New Haven; Boston; Philadelphia; Missoula, MT; 1881ff.)
JC&S	*The Journal of Church and State* (Fresno, CA; 1965ff.)
JCE	*Journal of Christian Education* (Sydney, 1958ff.)
JCP	*Christian Philosophy Quarterly* (New York, 1881-1884) [From Volume 2 on as: *The Journal of Christian Philosophy*]
JCS	*Journal of Cuneiform Studies* (New Haven; Cambridge, MA;1947ff.)
JCSP	*Journal of Classical and Sacred Philology* (Cambridge, England, 1854-1857)
JEA	*Journal of Egyptian Archaeology* (London, 1914ff.)
JEBH	*Journal of Economic and Business History* (Cambridge, MA;1928-1932)
JEOL	*Jaarbericht van het Vooraziatisch-Egyptisch Gezelschap Ex Oriente Lux* (Leiden, 1933ff.)
JES	*Journal of Ethiopian Studies* (Addis Ababa, 1963ff.)

Periodical Abbreviations

JESHO	*Journal of the Economic and Social History of the Orient* (Leiden, 1958ff.)
JHI	*Journal of the History of Ideas. A Quarterly Devoted to Intellectual History* (Lancaster, PA; New York;1940ff.
JHS	*The Journal of Hebraic Studies* (New York; 1969ff.)
JIQ	*Jewish Institute Quarterly* (New York, 1924-1930)
JJLP	*Journal of Jewish Lore and Philosophy* (Cincinnati, 1919)
JJP	*Rocznik Papirologii Prawniczej-Journal of Juristic Papyrology* (New York, Warsaw, 1946ff.) [Suspended 1947 & 1959-60]
JJS	*Journal of Jewish Studies* (London, 1948ff.)
JKF	*Jahrbuch für Kleinasiatische Forschungen* (Heidelberg, 1950-1953) [Superseded by *Anadolu Araştirmalari Istanbul Üniversitesi Edebiyat Fakültesi eski Önasya Dilleri ve Kültürleri Kürsüsü Tarafindan Čikarilir*]
JLTQ	*John Lobb's Theological Quarterly* (London, 1884)
JMTSO	*Journal of the Methodist Theological School in Ohio* (Delaware, OH; 1962ff.)
JMUEOS	*Journal of the Manchester Egyptian and Oriental Society* (Manchester, 1911-1953) [Issue #1 as: *Journal of the Manchester Oriental Society*]
JNES	*Journal of Near Eastern Studies* (Chicago, 1942ff.)
JP	*The Journal of Philology* (Cambridge, England; 1868-1920)
JPOS	*Journal of the Palestine Oriental Society* (Jerusalem, 1920-1948) [Volume 20 consists of only one fascicle]
JQR	*Jewish Quarterly Review* (London, 1888-1908; *N.S.,* Philadelphia, 1908ff.) [Includes 75th Anniversary Volume as: *JQR, 75th*]
JR	*Journal of Religion* (Chicago, 1921ff.)
JRAI	*Journal of the Royal Anthropological Institute of Great Britain and Ireland* (London, 1872-1965) [Volumes 1-69 as: *Journal of the Anthropological Institute* Continued as: *Man, N.S.*]
JRAS	*Journal of the Royal Asiatic Society of Great Britain and Ireland* (London, 1827ff.) [*Transactions,* 1827-1835 as *TRAS; Journal* from 1834 on: (Shown without volume numbers)]
JRASCS	*Centenary Supplement of the Journal of the Royal Asiatic Society, being a Selection of papers read to the society' during the celebrations of July, 1923* (London, 1924)
JRelH	*Journal of Religious History* (Sydney, 1960ff.)
JRH	*Journal of Religion and Health* (Richmond, 1961ff.)
JRT	*Journal of Religious Thought* (Washington, DC; 1943ff.)
JSL	*Journal of Sacred Literature and Biblical Record* (London,1848-1868)

Periodical Abbreviations

JSOR	*Journal of the Society of Oriental Research* (Chicago, 1917-1932)
JSP	*The Journal of Speculative Philosophy* (St. Louis, 1868-1893)
JSS	*Journal of Semitic Studies* (Manchester, 1956ff.)
JTALC	*Journal of Theology of the American Lutheran Conference* (Minneapolis, 1936-1943) [Volumes 1-5 as: *American Lutheran Conference Journal;* continued from volume 8, #3 as: *Lutheran Outlook* (not included)]
JTC	*Journal for Theology and the Church* (New York, 1965ff.)
JTLC	*Journal of Theology: Church of the Lutheran Confession* (Eau Claire, WI; 1961ff.)
JTS	*Journal of Theological Studies* (Oxford, 1899-1949; *N.S.,* 1950ff.)
JTVI	*Journal of the Transactions of the Victoria Institute, or Philosophical Society of Great Britain* (London, 1866-1957) [Superseded by *Faith & Thought*]
Jud	*Judaism. A Quarterly Journal of Jewish Life and Thought* (New York, 1952ff.)
JWCI	*Journal of the Warburg and Courtauld Institutes* (London,1937ff.)
JWH	*Journal of World History-Cahiers d'Histoire Mondiale -Cuadernos de Historia Mundial* (Paris, 1953ff.)

K

Kêmi	*Kêmi. Revue de philologie et d'archéologie égyptiennes et coptes* (Paris, 1928ff.)
Klio	*Klio. Beiträge zur alten Geschichte* (Leipzig, 1901ff.)
Kobez	*Kobez (Qobeş);* קובץ החברה העברית לחקירת ארץ־ישראל ועתיקתיה (Jerusalem, 1921-1945)
KSJA	*Kedem; Studies in Jewish Archaeology* (Jerusalem, 1942, 1945)
Kuml	*Kuml. Årbog for Jysk Arkæologisk Selskab* (Århus, 1951ff.)
Kush	*Kush. Journal of the Sudan Antiquities Service* (Khartoum, Sudan, 1953-1968)
KZ	*Kirchliche Zeitschrift* (St. Louis; Waverly, IA; Chicago; Columbus; 1876-1943)
KZFE	*Kadmos. Zeitschrift für vor-und frühgriechische Epigraphik* (Berlin, 1962ff.)

L

L	*Levant (Journal of the British School of Archaeology in Jerusalem)* (London, 1969ff.)
Lang	*Language. Journal of the Linguistic Society of America* (Baltimore, 1925ff.)
LCQ	*Lutheran Church Quarterly* (Gettysburg, PA; 1928-1949)
LCR	*Lutheran Church Review* (Philadelphia, 1882-1927)
Lĕš	*Lĕšonénu. Quarterly for the Study of the Hebrew Language and Cognate Subjects* לשוננו (Jerusalem, 1925ff.) [English Summaries from Volume 30 onward]
LIST	*Lown Institute. Studies and Texts* (Brandeis University. Lown School of Near Eastern and Judaic Studies. Cambridge, MA; 1963ff.)
Listen	*Listening* (Dubuque, IA; 1965ff.) [Volume numbers start with "zero"]
LofS	*Life of the Spirit* (London, 1946-1964)
LQ	*The Quarterly Review of the Evangelical Lutheran Church* (Gettysburg, PA; 1871-1927; revived in1949ff.) [From 1878 on as: *The Lutheran Quarterly*]
LQHR	*London Quarterly and Holborn Review* (London, 1853-1968)
LS	*Louvain Studies* (Louvain, 1966ff.)
LSQ	*Lutheran Synod Quarterly* (Mankato, MN, 1960ff.) [Formerly *Clergy Bulletin* (Volume 1 of *LSQ* as *Clergy Bulletin,* Volume 20, #1 & #2)]
LTJ	*Lutheran Theological Journal* (North Adelaide, South Australia, 1967ff.)
LTP	*Laval Theologique et Philosophique* (Quebec, 1945ff.)
LTQ	*Lexington Theological Quarterly* (Lexington, KY; 1966ff.)
LTR	*Literary and Theological Review* (New York; Boston, 1834-1839)
LTSB	*Lutheran Theological Seminary Bulletin* (Gettysburg, PA; 1921ff.)
LTSR	*Luther Theological Seminary Review* (St. Paul, MN; 1962ff.)
LWR	*The Lutheran World Review* (Philadelphia, 1948-1950)

M

Man	*Man. A Monthly Record of Anthropological Science* (London,1901-1965; *N. S.,* 1966ff.) [Articles in original series referred to by *article* number not by *page* number - New Series subtitled: *The Journal of the Royal Anthropological Institute*]
ManSL	*Manuscripta* (St. Louis, 1957ff.)
MB	*Medelhavsmuseet Bulletin* (Stockholm, 1961ff.)
MC	*The Modern Churchman* (Ludlow, England; 1911ff.)
McQ	*McCormick Quarterly* (Chicago, 1947ff.) [Volumes 1-13 as: *McCormick Speaking*]
MCS	*Manchester Cuneiform Studies* (Manchester, 1951-1964)
MDIÄA	*Mitteilungen des deutsches Instituts für ägyptische Altertumskunde in Kairo* (Cairo, 1930ff.)
Mesop	*Mesopotamia* (Torino, Italy, 1966ff.)
MH	*The Modern Humanist* (Weston, MA; 1944-1962)
MHSB	*The Mission House Seminary Bulletin* (Plymouth, WI; 1954-1962)
MI	*Monthly Interpreter* (Edinburgh, 1884-1886)
MidS	*Midstream (Council on Christian Unity)* (Indianapolis, 1961ff.)
Min	*Ministry. A Quarterly Theological Review for South Africa* (Morija, Basutolan, 1960ff.)
Minos	*Minos. Investigaciones y Materiales Para el Estudio de los Textos Paleocretenses Publicados Bajo la Dirección de Antonio Tovar y Emilio Peruzzi* (Salamanca, 1951ff.) [From Volume 4 on as: *Minos Revista de Filología Egea*]
MIO	*Mitteilungen des Instituts für Orientforschung [Deutsche Akademie der Wissenschaften zu Berlin Institut für Orientforschung]* (Berlin, 1953ff.)
Miz	*Mizraim. Journal of Papyrology, Egyptology, History of Ancient Laws, and their Relations to the Civilizations of Bible Lands* (New York, 1933-1938)
MJ	*The Museum Journal. Pennsylvania University* (Philadelphia,1910-1935)
MMBR	*The Monthly Magazine and British Register* (London, 1796-1843) [*1st Ser.,* 1796-1826, Volumes 1-60; *N.S.,* 1826-1838, Volumes 1-26; *3rd Ser.,* 1839-1843, Volumes 1-9, however, Volumes 7-9 are marked 95-97*[sic]*]

ModR	*The Modern Review* (London, 1880-1884)
Monist	*The Monist. An International Quarterly Journal of General Philosophical Inquiry* (Chicago; La Salle, IL; 1891ff.)
Mosaic	*Mosaic* (Cambridge, MA; 1960ff.)
MQ	*The Minister's Quarterly* (New York, 1945-1966)
MQR	*Methodist Quarterly Review (South)* (Louisville, Nashville, 1847-1861; 1879-1886; 1886-1930) [*3rd Ser.* as: *Southern Methodist Review;* Volume 52 (1926) misnumbered as 53; Volume 53 (1927) misnumbered as 54; and the volume for 1928 is also marked as 54]
MR	*Methodist Review* (New York, 1818-1931) [Volume 100 not published]
MTSB	*Moravian Theological Seminary Bulletin* (Bethlehem, PA; 1959-1970) [Volume for 1969 apparently not published]
MTSQB	*Meadville Theological School Quarterly Bulletin* (Meadville, PA;1906-1933) [From Volume 25 on as: *Meadville Journal*]
Muséon	*Le Muséon. Revue d'Études Orientales* (Louvain, 1882-1915;1930/32ff.)
MUSJ	*Mélanges de l'Université Saint-Joseph. Faculté orientale* (Beirut, 1906ff.) [Title varies]
Mwa-M	*Milla wa-Milla. The Australian Bulletin of Comparative Religion* (Parkville, Victoria, 1961ff.)

N

NB	*Blackfriars. A Monthly Magazine* (Oxford, 1920ff.) [From Volume 46 on as: *New Blackfriars*]
NBR	*North British Review* (Edinburgh, 1844-1871)
NCB	*New College Bulletin* (Edinburgh, 1964ff.)
NEAJT	*Northeast Asia Journal of Theology* (Kyoto, Japan, 1968ff.)
NEST	*The Near East School of Theology Quarterly* (Beirut, 1952ff.)
Nexus	*Nexus* (Boston, 1957ff.)
NGTT	*Nederduitse gereformeerde teologiese tydskrif* (Kaapstad, N.G., Kerk-Uitgewers, 1959ff.)
NOGG	*Nihon Orient Gakkai geppo* (Tokyo, 1955-1959) [Being the *Bulletin of the Society for Near Eastern Studies in Japan*-Continued as: *Oriento*]
NOP	*New Orient* (Prague, 1960-1968)

Periodical Abbreviations

NPR	*The New Princeton Review* (New York, 1886-1888)
NQR	*Nashotah Quarterly Review* (Nashotah, WI; 1960ff.)
NT	*Novum Testamentum* (Leiden, 1955ff.)
NTS	*New Testament Studies* (Cambridge, England; 1954ff.)
NTT	*Nederlandsch Theologisch Tijdschrift* (Wageningen, 1946ff.)
NTTO	*Norsk Teologisk Tidsskrift* (Oslo, 1900ff.)
Numen	*Numen; International Review for the History of Religions* (Leiden, 1954ff.)
NW	*The New World. A Quarterly Review of Religion, Ethics and Theology* (Boston, 1892-1900)
NYR	*The New York Review. A Journal of The Ancient Faith and Modern Thought (St. John's Seminary)* (New York, 1905-1908)
NZJT	*New Zealand Journal of Theology* (Christchurch, 1931-1935)

O

OA	*Oriens Antiquus* (Rome, 1962ff.)
OBJ	*The Oriental and Biblical Journal* (Chicago, 1880-1881)
OC	*Open Court* (Chicago, 1887-1936)
ONTS	*The Hebrew Student* (Morgan Park, IL; New Haven; Hartford; 1881-1892) [Volumes 3-8 as: *The Old Testament Student;* Volume 9 onwards as: *The Old and New Testament Student*]
OOR	*Oriens: The Oriental Review* (Paris, 1926)
OQR	*The Oberlin Quarterly Review* (Oberlin, OH; 1845-1849)
Or	*Orientalia commentarii de rebus Assyri-Babylonicis, Arabicis, and Aegyptiacis, etc.* (Rome 1920-1930)
Or, N.S.	*Orientalia: commentarii, periodici de rebus orientis antiqui* (Rome, 1932ff.)
Oriens	*Oriens. Journal of the International Society of Oriental Research* (Leiden, 1948ff.)
Orient	*Orient. The Reports of the Society for Near Eastern Studies in Japan* (Tokyo, 1960ff.)
Orita	*Orita. Ibadan Journal of Religious Studies* (Ibadan, Nigeria, 1967ff.)
OrS	*Orientalia Suecana* (Uppsala, 1952ff.)
OSHTP	*Oxford Society of Historical Theology, Abstract of Proceedings* (Oxford, 1891-1968) [Through 1919 as: *Society of Historical Theology, Proceedings*]
Osiris	*Osiris* (Bruges, Belgium; 1936-1968) *[Subtitle varies]*
OTS	*Oudtestamentische Studiën* (Leiden, 1942ff.)

OTW	*Ou-Testamentiese Werkgemeenskap in Suid-Afrika, Proceedings of die* (Pretoria, 1958ff.) [Volume 1 in Volume 14 of: *Hervormde Teologiese Studies*]

P

P	*Preaching: A Journal of Homiletics* (Dubuque, IA; 1965ff.)
P&P	*Past and Present* (London, 1952ff.) *[Subtitle varies]*
PA	*Practical Anthropology* (Wheaton, IL; Eugene, OR; Tarrytown, NY; 1954ff.)
PAAJR	*Proceedings of the American Academy for Jewish Research* (Philadelphia, 1928ff.)
PAOS	*Proceedings of the American Oriental Society* (Baltimore, New Haven; 1842, 1846-50, 1852-1860) [After 1860 all proceedings are bound with *Journal*]
PAPA	*American Philological Association, Proceedings* (Hartford, Boston, 1896ff.) *[Transactions* as: *TAPA. Transactions* and *Proceedings* combine page numbers from volume 77 on]
PAPS	*Proceedings of the American Philosophical Society* (Philadelphia, 1838ff.)
PBA	*Proceedings of the British Academy* (London, 1903ff.)
PEFQS	*Palestine Exploration Fund Quarterly Statement* (London, 1869ff.) [From Volume 69 (1937) on as: *Palestine Exploration Quarterly*]
PEQ	*Palestine Exploration Quarterly* [See: *PEFQS*]
PER	*The Protestant Episcopal Review* (Fairfax, Co., VA; 1886-1900) [Volumes 1-5 as: *The Virginian Seminary Magazine*]
Person	*Personalist. An International Review of Philosophy, Religion and Literature* (Los Angeles, 1920ff.)
PF	*Philosophical Forum* (Boston, 1943-1957; *N.S.,* 1968ff.)
PHDS	*Perspectives. Harvard Divinity School* (Cambridge, MA; 1965-1967)
PIASH	*Proceedings of the Israel Academy of Sciences and Humanities* (Jerusalem, 1967ff.)
PICSS	*Proceedings of the International Conference on Semitic Studies held in Jerusalem, 19-23 July 1965* (Jerusalem, 1969)
PIJSL	*Papers of the Institute of Jewish Studies, London* (Jerusalem,1964)
PJT	*Pacific Journal of Theology* (Western Samoa, 1961ff.)

PJTSA	*Jewish Theological Seminary Association, Proceedings* (New York, 1888-1902)
PP	*Perspective* (Pittsburgh, 1960ff.) [Volumes 1-8 as: *Pittsburgh Perspective*]
PQ	*The Presbyterian Quarterly* (New York, 1887-1904)
PQL	*The Preacher's Quarterly* (London, 1954-1969)
PQPR	*The Presbyterian Quarterly and Princeton Review* (New York, 1872-1877)
PQR	*Presbyterian Quarterly Review* (Philadelphia, 1852-1862)
PR	*Presbyterian Review* (New York, 1880-1889)
PRev	*The Biblical Repertory and Princeton Review* (Princeton, Philadelphia, New York, 1829-1884) [Volume 1 as: *The Biblical Repertory, New Series;* Volumes 2-8 as: *The Biblical Repertory and Theological Review*]
PRR	*Presbyterian and Reformed Review* (New York, Philadelphia, 1890-1902)
PSB	*The Princeton Seminary Bulletin* (Princeton, 1907ff.)
PSTJ	*Perkins School of Theology Journal* (Dallas, 1947ff.)
PTR	*Princeton Theological Review* (Princeton, 1903-1929)
PUNTPS	*Proceedings of the University of Newcastle upon Tyne Philosophical Society* (Newcastle upon Tyne, 1964-70)

Q

QCS	*Quarterly Christian Spectator* (New Haven, 1819-1838) *[1st Series* and *New Series* as: *Christian Spectator]*
QDAP	*The Quarterly of the Department of Antiquities in Palestine* (Jerusalem, 1931-1950)
QRL	*Quarterly Review* (London, 1809-1967)
QTMRP	*The Quarterly Theological Magazine, and Religious Repository* (Philadelphia, 1813-1814)

R

R&E	*[Baptist] Review and Expositor* (Louisville, 1904ff.)
R&S	*Religion and Society* (Bangalore, India, 1953ff.)
RAAO	*Revue d'Assyriologie et d'Archéologie Orientale* (Paris, 1886ff.)

Periodical Abbreviations

RChR   *The Reformed Church Review* (Mercersburg, PA;
        Chambersburg, PA; Philadelphia; 1849-1926)
        [Volumes 1-25 as: *Mercersburg Review;*
        Volumes 26-40 as: *Reformed Quarterly Review;*
        4th Series on as: *Reformed Church Review*]
RCM   *Reformed Church Magazine* (Reading, PA; 1893-1896)
        [Volume 3 as: *Reformed Church Historical Magazine*]
RdQ   *Revue de Qumran* (Paris, 1958ff.)
RDSO   *Rivista degli Studi Orientali* (Rome, 1907ff.)
RÉ   *Revue Égyptologique* (Paris, 1880-1896; *N.S.,*
        1919-1924)
RefmR   *The Reformation Review* (Amsterdam, 1953ff.)
RefR   *The Reformed Review. A Quarterly Journal of the
        Seminaries of the Reformed Church in America*
        (Holland, MI; New Brunswick, NJ; 1947ff.)
        [Volumes 1-9 as: *Western Seminary Bulletin*]
RÉg   *Revue d'Égyptologie* (Paris, 1933ff.)
RelM   *Religion in the Making* (Lakeland, FL; 1940-1943)
Resp   *Response—in worship—Music—The arts* (St. Paul, 1959ff.)
RestQ   *Restoration Quarterly* (Austin, TX; Abilene, TX; 1957ff.)
RFEASB *The Hebrew University / Jerusalem: Department of
        Archaeology. Louis M. Rabinowitz Fund for the
        Exploration of Ancient Synagogues, Bulletin*
        (Jerusalem, 1949-1960)
RHA   *Revue Hittite et Asianique* (Paris, 1930ff.)
RIDA   *Revue internationale des droits de l'antiquité* (Brussels,
        1948ff.)
RJ   *Res Judicatae. The Journal of the Law Students' Society
        of Victoria* (Melbourne, 1935-1957)
RL   *Religion in Life* (New York, 1932ff.)
RO   *Rocznik Orjentalistyczny. (Wydaje Polskie towarzystwo
        orjentalisyczne)* (Kraków, Warsaw, 1914ff.)
RP   *Records of the Past* (Washington, DC; 1902-1914)
RR   *Review of Religion* (New York, 1936-1958)
RS   *Religious Studies* (London, 1965ff.)
RTP   *Review of Theology and Philosophy* (Edinburgh,
        1905-1915)
RTR   *Recueil de travaux relatifs à la philologie et à
        l'archéologie egyptiennes et assyriennes* (Paris,
        1870-1923)
RTRM   *The Reformed Theological Review* (Melbourne, 1941ff.)

S

SAENJ	*Seminar. An Annual Extraordinary Number of the Jurist* (Washington, DC; 1943-1956)
SBAP	*Society of Biblical Archæology, Proceedings* (London, 1878-1918)
SBAT	*Society of Biblical Archæology, Transactions* (London, 1872-1893)
SBE	*Studia Biblica et Ecclesiastica* (Oxford, 1885-1903) [Volume 1 as: *Studia Biblica*]
SBFLA	*Studii (Studium) Biblici Franciscani. Liber Annuus* (Jerusalem, 1950ff.)
SBLP	*Society of Biblical Literature & Exegesis, Proceedings* (Baltimore, 1880)
SBO	*Studia Biblica et Orientalia* (Rome 1959) [Being Volumes 10-12 respectively of *Analecta Biblica. Investigationes Scientificae in Res Biblicas*]
SBSB	*Society for Biblical Studies Bulletin* (Madras, India, 1964ff.)
SCO	*Studi Classici e Orientali* (Pisa, 1951ff.)
Scotist	*The Scotist* (Teutopolis, IL; 1939-1967)
SCR	*Studies in Comparative Religion* (Bedfont, Middlesex, England, 1967ff.)
Scrip	*Scripture. The Quarterly of the Catholic Biblical Association* (London, 1944-1968)
SE	*Study Encounter* (Geneva, 1965ff.)
SEÅ	*Svensk Exegetisk Årsbok* (Uppsala-Lund, 1936ff.)
SEAJT	*South East Journal of Theology* (Singapore, 1959ff.)
Sefunim	*Sefunim (Bulletin)* [היפה] ספונים (Haifa, 1966-1968)
SGEI	*Studies in the Geography of Eretz-Israel* מחקרים בגיאוגרפיה של ארץ־ישראל (Jerusalem, 1959ff.) [English summaries in Volumes 1-3 only; continuing the *Bulletin of the Israel Exploration Society (Yediot)*]
SH	*Scripta Hierosolymitana* (Jerusalem, 1954ff.)
Shekel	*The Shekel* (New York, 1968ff.)
SIR	*Smithsonian Institute Annual Report of the Board of Regents* (Washington, DC; 1846-1964; becomes: *Smithsonian Year* from 1965 on]
SJH	*Seminary Journal* (Hamilton, NY; 1892)
SJT	*Scottish Journal of Theology* (Edinburgh, 1947ff.)
SL	*Studia Liturgica. An International Ecumenical Quarterly for Liturgical Research and Renewal* (Rotterdam, 1962ff.)

SLBR	*Sierra Leone Bulletin of Religion* (Freetown, Sierra Leone; 1959-1966)
SMR	*Studia Montes Regii* (Montreal, 1958-1967)
SMSDR	*Studi e Materiali di Storia Delle Religioni* (Rome, Bologna, 1925ff.
SO	*Studia Orientalia* (Helsinki, 1925ff.)
SOOG	*Studi Orientalistici in Onore di Giorgio Levi Della Vida* (Rome, 1956)
Sophia	*Sophia. A Journal for Discussion in Philosophical Theology* (Parkville, N.S.W., Australia, 1962ff.)
SP	*Spirit of the Pilgrims* (Boston, 1828-1833)
SPR	*Southern Presbyterian Review* (Columbia, SC; 1847-1885)
SQ/E	*The Shane Quarterly* (Indianapolis, 1940ff.) [From Volume 17 on as: *Encounter*]
SR	*The Seminary Review* (Cincinnati, 1954ff.)
SRL	*The Scottish Review* (London, Edinburgh, 1882-1900; 1914-1920)
SS	*Seminary Studies of the Athenaeum of Ohio* (Cincinnati, 1926-1968) [Volumes 1-15 as: *Seminary Studies*]
SSO	*Studia Semitica et Orientalia* (Glasgow, 1920, 1945)
SSR	*Studi Semitici* (Rome, 1958ff.)
ST	*Studia Theologica* (Lund, 1947ff.)
StEv	*Studia Evangelica* (Berlin, 1959ff.) [Being miscellaneous volumes of: *Text und Untersuchungen zur Geschichte der altchristlichen Literatur,* beginning with Volume 73]
StLJ	*The Saint Luke's Journal* (Sewanee, TN; 1957ff.) [Volume 1, #1 as: *St. Luke's Journal of Theology*]
StMR	*St. Marks Review: An Anglican Quarterly* (Canberra, A.C.T., Australia, 1955ff.)
StP	*Studia Patristica* (Berlin, 1957ff.) [Being miscellaneous volumes of: *Text und Untersuchungen zur Geschichte der altchristlichen Literatur,* beginning with Volume 63]
StVTQ	*St. Vladimir's Theological Quarterly* (Crestwood, NY; 1952ff.) [Volumes 1-4 as: *St. Vladimir's Seminary Quarterly*]
Sumer	*Sumer. A Journal of Archaeology in Iraq* (Bagdad, 1945ff.)
SWJT	*Southwestern Journal of Theology* (Fort Worth, 1917-1924; *N.S.,* 1950ff.)
Syria	*Syria, revue d'art oriental et d'archéologie* (Paris, 1920ff.)

T

T&C	*Theology and the Church / SÎN-HÁK kap kàu-Hōe (Tainan Theological College)* (Tainan, Formosa, 1957ff.)
T&L	*Theology and Life* (Lancaster, PA; 1958-1966)
TAD	*Türk tarih, arkeologya ve etnoğrafya dergisi* (Istanbul, 1933-1949; continued as: *Türk arkeoloji Dergisi,* Ankara, 1956ff.)
TAPA	*American Philological Society, Transactions* (See: *PAPA*)
TAPS	*Transactions of the American Philosophical Society* (Philadelphia, 1789-1804; *N.S.,* 1818ff.)
Tarbiz	*Tarbiz. A quarterly review of the humanities;* תרביץ רבעון למדעי היהדות (Jerusalem, 1929ff.) [English summaries from Volume 24 on only]
TB	*Tyndale Bulletin* (London, 1956ff.) [Numbers 1-16 as: *Tyndale House Bulletin*]
TBMDC	*Theological Bulletin: McMaster Divinity College* (Hamilton, Ontario, 1967ff.)
TD	*Theology Digest* (St. Mary, KS, 1953ff.)
TE	*Theological Education* (Dayton, 1964ff.)
Tem	*Temenos. Studies in Comparative Religion* (Helsinki, 1965ff.)
TEP	*Theologica Evangelica. Journal of the Faculty of Theology, University of South Africa* (Pretoria, 1968ff.)
Text	*Textus. Annual of the Hebrew University Bible Project* (Jerusalem, 1960ff.)
TF	*Theological Forum* (Minneapolis, 1929-1935)
TFUQ	*Thought. A Quarterly of the Sciences and Letters* (New York, 1926ff.) [From Volume 15 on as: *Thought. Fordham University Quarterly*]
ThE	*Theological Eclectic* (Cincinnati; New York, 1864-1871)
Them	*Themelios, International Fellowship of Evangelical Students* (Fresno, CA; 1962ff.)
Theo	*Theology; A Journal of Historic Christianity* (London, 1920ff.)
ThSt	*Theological Studies* (New York; Woodstock, MD; 1940ff.)
TLJ	*Theological and Literary Journal* (New York, 1848-1861)
TM	*Theological Monthly* (St. Louis, 1921-1929)
TML	*The Theological Monthly* (London, 1889-1891)
TPS	*Transactions of the Philological Society* (London, 1842ff.) [Volumes 1-6 as: *Proceedings*]
TQ	*Theological Quarterly* (St. Louis, 1897-1920)

Tr	*Traditio. Studies in Ancient and Medieval History, Thought and Religion* (New York, 1943ff.)
Trad	*Tradition, A Journal of Orthodox Jewish Thought* (New York, 1958ff.)
TRep	*Theological Repository* (London, 1769-1788)
TRFCCQ	*Theological Review and Free Church College Quarterly* (Edinburgh, 1886-1890)
TRGR	*The Theological Review and General Repository of Religious and Moral Information, Published Quarterly* (Baltimore, 1822)
TRL	*Theological Review: A Quarterly Journal of Religious Thought and Life* (London, 1864-1879)
TT	*Theology Today* (Lansdowne, PA; Princeton, NJ; 1944ff.)
TTCA	*Trinity Theological College Annual* (Singapore, 1964-1969) [Volume 5 apparently never published]
TTD	*Teologisk Tidsskrift* (Decorah, IA; 1899-1907)
TTKB	*Türk Tarih Kurumu Belleten* (Ankara, 1937ff.)
TTKF	*Tidskrift för teologi och kyrkiga frågor (The Augustana Theological Quarterly)* (Rock Island, IL; 1899-1917)
TTL	*Theologisch Tijdschrift* (Leiden, 1867-1919) [English articles from Volume 45 on only]
TTM	*Teologisk Tidsskrift* (Minneapolis, 1917-1928)
TUSR	*Trinity University Studies in Religion* (San Antonio, 1950ff.)
TZ	*Theologische Zeitschrift* (Basel, 1945ff.)
TZDES	*Theologische Zeitschrift (Deutsche Evangelische Synode des Westens, North America)* (St. Louis, 1873-1934) [Continued from Volumes 22 through 26 as: *Magazin für Evangel. Theologie und Kirche;* and from Volume 27 on as: *Theological Magazine*]
TZTM	*Theologische Zeitblätter, Theological Magazine* (Columbus, 1911-1919)

U

UC	*The Unitarian Christian* (Boston, 1947ff.) [Volumes 1-4 as: *Our Faith*]
UCPSP	*University of California Publications in Semitic Philology* (Berkeley, 1907ff.)
UF	*Ugarit-Forschungen. Internationales Jahrbuch für die Altertumskunde Syrien-Palästinas* (Neukirchen, West Germany; 1969ff.)
ULBIA	*University of London. Bulletin of the Institute of Archaeology* (London, 1958ff.)

UMB	*The University Museum Bulletin (University of Pennsylvania)* (Philadelphia, 1930-1958)
UMMAAP	*University of Michigan. Museum of Anthropology. Anthropological Papers* (Ann Arbor, 1949ff.)
UnionR	*The Union Review* (New York, 1939-1945)
UPQR	*The United Presbyterian Quarterly Review* (Pittsburgh, 1860-1861)
UQGR	*Universalist Quarterly and General Review* (Boston, 1844-1891)
URRM	*The Unitarian Review and Religious Magazine* (Boston, 1873-1891)
USQR	*Union Seminary Quarterly Review* (New York, 1945ff.)
USR	*Union Seminary Review* (Hampden-Sydney, VA; Richmond; 1890-1946) [Volumes 1-23 as: *Union Seminary Magazine*]
UTSB	*United Theological Seminary Bulletin* (Dayton, 1905ff.) [Including: *The Bulletin of the Evangelical School of Theology; Bulletin of the Union Biblical Seminary,* later, *Bonebrake Theological Bulletin*]
UUÅ	*Uppsala Universitets Årsskrift* (Uppsala, 1861-1960)

V

VC	*Virgiliae Christianae: A Review of Early Christian Life and Language* (Amsterdam, 1947ff.)
VDETF	*Deutsche Vierteljahrsschrift für englisch-theologische Forschung und Kritik / herausgegeben von M. Heidenheim* (Leipzig, Zurich, 1861-1865) [Continued as: *Vierteljahrsschrift für deutsch – englisch- theologische Forschung und Kritik...* 1866-1873]
VDI	*Vestnik Drevnei Istorii. Journal of Ancient History* (Moscow, 1946ff.) [English summaries from 1967 on only]
VDR	*Koinonia* (Nashville, 1957-1968) [Continued as: *Vanderbilt Divinity Review,* 1969-1971]
VE	*Vox Evangelica. Biblical and Historical Essays by the Members of the Faculty of the London Bible College* (London, 1962ff.)
Voice	*The Voice* (St. Paul, 1958-1960) [Subtitle varies]
VR	*Vox Reformata* (Geelong, Victoria, Australia, 1962ff.)
VT	*Vetus Testamentum* (Leiden, 1951ff.)
VTS	*Vetus Testamentum, Supplements* (Leiden, 1953ff.)

W

Way	*The Way. A Quarterly Review of Christian Spirituality* (London, 1961ff.)
WBHDN	*The Wittenberg Bulletin (Hamma Digest Number)* (Springfield, OH; 1903ff.) [Volumes 40-60 (1943-1963) only contain *Hamma Digest Numbers*]
WesTJ	*Wesleyan Theological Journal. Bulletin of the Wesleyan Theological Society* (Lakeville, IN; 1966ff.)
WLQ	*Wisconsin Lutheran Quarterly* (Wauwatosa, WI; Milwaukee;1904ff.) [Also entitled: *Theologische Quartalschrift*]
WO	*Die Welt des Orients . Wissenschaftliche Beiträge zur Kunde des Morgenlandes* (Göttingen, 1947ff.)
Word	*Word: Journal of the Linguistic Circle of New York* (New York, 1945ff.)
WR	*The Westminster Review* (London, New York, 1824-1914)
WSQ	*Wartburg Seminary Quarterly* (Dubuque, IA; 1937-1960) [Volumes 1-9, #1 as: *Quarterly of the Wartburg Seminary Association*]
WSR	*Wesleyan Studies in Religion* (Buckhannon,WV; 1960-1970) [Volumes 53-62 only[sic]]
WTJ	*Westminster Theological Journal* (Philadelphia, 1938ff.)
WW	*Western Watch* (Pittsburgh, 1950-1959) [Superseded by: *Pittsburgh Perspective*]
WZKM	*Wiener Zeitschrift für die Kunde des Morgenlandes* (Vienna, 1886ff.)

Y

YCCAR	*Yearbook of the Central Conference of American Rabbis* (Cincinnati, 1890ff.)
YCS	*Yale Classical Studies* (New Haven, 1928ff.)
YDQ	*Yale Divinity Quarterly* (New Haven, 1904ff.) [Volumes 30-62 as: *Yale Divinity News,* continued as: *Reflections*]
YR	*The Yavneh Review. A Religious Jewish Collegiate Magazine* (New York, 1961ff.) [Volume 2 never published]

Z

Z   *Zygon. Journal of Religion and Science* (Chicago, 1966ff.)

ZA   *Zeitschrift für Assyriologie und verwandte Gebiete* [Volumes 45 on as: *Zeitschrift für Assyriologie und vorderasiatische Archäologie]* (Leipzig, Strassburg, Berlin, 1886ff.)

ZÄS   *Zeitschrift für ägyptische Sprache und Altertumskunde* (Leipzig, Berlin, 1863ff.)

ZAW   *Zeitschrift für die alttestamentliche Wissenschaft* (Giessen, Berlin, 1881ff.)

ZDMG   *Zeitschrift der Deutschen Morgenländischen Gesellschaft* (Leipzig, Wiesbaden, 1847ff.)

ZDPV   *Zeitschrift des Deutschen Palästina-Vereins* (Leipzig, Wiesbaden, 1878ff.) [English articles from Volume 82 on only]

ZfRG   *Zeitschrift für Religions und Geistesgeschichte* (Marburg, Köln, Leiden-Heideberg, 1948ff.)

Zion   *Zion. A Quarterly for Research in Jewish History, New Series* ציון, רבעין לחורתולדוה ישראל (Jerusalem, 1935ff.) [English summaries from Volume 3 on only]

ZK   *Zeitschrift für Keilschriftforschung* (Leipzig, 1884-1885)

ZNW   *Zeitschrift für die neutestamentliche Wissenschaft und die Kunde des Urchristentums (...Kunde der älteren Kirche, 1921—)* (Giessen, Berlin, 1900ff.)

ZS   *Zeitschrift für Semitistik und verwandte Gebiete* (Leipzig, 1922-1935)

Sigla[1]

*   Indicates article is additionally listed in other sections of the index.

†   Indicates that title is from the table of contents; from the header; or a composite if title is completely lacking as in early journals.

‡   Indicates a bibliographical article on a specific subject.

(§###)   Section numbers in parentheses in the table of contents and in the headers are included for sake of outline continuity, but no articles are referenced in that section.

---

1.   Complete information may be found in Volume I, page xxiii.

§955   5. *Theological Studies - General Studies*

†(   ) C., "Bauer's Theology of the Old Testament," *CTPR, N.S.,* 1 (1838-39) 193-198. *(Review)*

Edward A. Parks, "Theological Encyclopedia and Methodology," *BS* 1 (1844) 332-367. (From the unpublished Lectures of Prof. Tholuck) [The Science of writing History; Sciences Auxiliary to Practical Theology, Anthropology and Psychology, Rhetoric; Part II. Theological Sciences, On the importance of Exegetical Study, and the distinctive character of the Sacred Scriptures, The Biblical Hermeneutics, Biblical Philology of the Old and New Testaments, Biblical History and Antiquities, Biblical Introduction and Criticism, Literatures and Exegesis]

Edward A. Parks, "Theological Encyclopedia and Methodology," *BS* 1 (1844) 552-578. [I. The arrangement of Proof-texts and the Dogmatic Theology of the Bible; II. Dogmatic Theology of the Church; III. The Scientific Dogmatical Theology; IV. The History of Doctrines; V. Apologetic Theology; Characteristics of the chief tendencies of Systematic Theology; The Science of Morals; The true Idea and the various Departments of Church History; What is required in the treatment of the History of the Church; Various Departments of Ecclesiastical History; The Literature of Ecclesiastical History, also the Method of Pursuing the Study]

Edward A. Parks, "Theological Encyclopedia and Methodology," *BS* 1 (1844) 726-735. [The Object of Practical Theology (and its Literature); The various Departments of Practical Theology]

†Anonymous, "The Theology of the Old Testament," *BQRL* 16 (1852) 444-479. *(Review)*

†Anonymous, "Theology of the Old Testament," *BFER* 2 (1853) 383-399. *(Review)*

Edward Hitchcock, "The Relations and Consequent Mutual Duties Between the Philosopher and the Theologian," *BS* 10 (1853) 166-194.

*(   ) M., "Theology, Philology, Geology," *JSL, 3rd Ser.,* 2 (1855-56) 66-81; 3 (1856) 184-188.

*Benjamin F. Hosford, "Geological and Theological Analogies," *BS* 15 (1858) 300-314.

1

†Anonymous, "Kurtz on the History of the Old Covenant," *LQHR* 12 (1859) 447-462. *(Review)*

Leonard Withington, "Is Theology an Improvable Science?" *BS* 21 (1864) 787-815.

*D. H. Hitchcock, "Relations of Geology to Theology," *BS* 24 (1867) 363-388, 429-481.

J. R. Herrick, "The Claims of Theology," *BS* 25 (1868) 49-68.

*C. A. Row, "On the Relation of Reason to Philosophy, Theology, and Revelation," *JTVI* 3 (1868-69) 472-502. (Discussion pp. 502-516)

S. D. F. S., "The Distinctive Character of Old Testament Scripture," *BFER* 19 (1870) 18-40. *(Review)*

Lemuel S. Potwin, "Destructive Analysis in Theology," *BS* 29 (1872) 419-426.

Charles A. Briggs, "Exegetical Theology, Especially of the Old Testament," *PQPR* 6 (1877) 5-29.

A. Duff Jr., "Method of the Theological Use of the Bible, Especially the Old Testament," *BS* 37 (1880) 77-98.

Nathaniel West, "The Old Hebrew Theology," *ONTS* 3 (1883-84) 14-19. *(Review)*

George H. Schodde, "The Theological Study of the Old Testament," *ONTS* 3 (1883-84) 304-308.

Edward L. Curtis, "Old Testament Theology," *ONTS* 5 (1885-86) 32-33.

A. B. Davidson, "Old Testament Theology," *ET* 4 (1892-93) 210-211. *(Review)*

W. P. McKee, "Schultz's Old Testament Theology," *BW* 2 (1893) 123-129, 363-369. *(Review)*

*James Ten Broeke, "Biblical Criticism in some of its Theological and Philosophical Relations," *BW* 2 (1893) 330-342, 444-451.

W. Sanday, "The Historical Method in Theology," *ET* 9 (1897-98) 84-87.

W. T. Davison, "The Bible and Modern Theology," *MQR, 3rd Ser.,* 23 (1897-98) 351-362.

Edward Lewis Curtis, "The Outlook in Theology," *BS* 56 (1899) 1-11.

John Burton, "Old Testament Theology," *CMR* 4 (1892) 177-184.

A. F. Kirkpatrick, "Modern Criticism and Its Influence on Theology," *ET* 14 (1902-03) 172-175.

W. Cunningham, "The Reaction of Modern Scientific Thought on Theological Study," *JTS* 5 (1903-04) 161-173.

George H. Schodde, "Theology and the Scriptures," *ColTM* 24 (1904-158-165.

Karl Budde, "On the Relation of Old Testament Science to the Allied Departments and to Science in General," *AJT* 9 (1905) 76-90.

Lewis B. Paton, "Theology of the Old Testament," *BW* 25 (1905) 283-291.

W. E. Frey, "The Theology of the Old Testament," *LCR* 27 (1908) 84-90.

*F. R. Tennant, "The Influence of Darwinism upon Theology," *QRL* 211 (1909) 418-440. *(Review)*

Gerald Birney Smith, "Theology and the History of Religion," *BW* 40 (1912) 173-183.

Alban G. Widgery, "The Study of Theology," *ET* 26 (1914-15) 392-398.

W. E. Barnes, "Jewish Theology Systematically and Historically Considered," *JTS* 20 (1918-19) 184-185. *(Review)*

*C. Sprenger, "The Evolution Theory and its Bearing on Theology and Ethics," *TZDES* 46 (1918) 281-285.

George Cross, "The Motive of Theology," *JR* 2 (1922) 380-401.

E. O. James, Science and Theology," *Theo* 4 (1922) 339-348.

C. Theodore Benze, "Theology of the Old Testament," *LCR* 42 (1923) 24-29.

*Samuel S. Cohon, "Palestine in Jewish Theology," *HUCA, Jubilee Volume,* (1925) 171-210.

S. P. T. Prideaux, "A Plea for the Study of Theology," *ET* 39 (1927-28) 394-397.

G. A. Barton, "Were the Biblical Foundations of Christian Theology Derived from Babylonia?" *JBL* 40 (1921) 87-103.

Eduard König, "The Present Ills of Old Testament Theology and Their Remedy," *BS* 80 (1923) 465-470.

*T. Crouther Gordon, "Theology and Archaeology," *ET* 37 (1925-26) 425-428.

Eduard König, "The Latest History of 'Old Testament Theology'," *BS* 86 (1929) 446-457. *(Trans by E. W. Hammer)*

*H. J. Lewis, "Theology in Relation to Preaching," *ET* 41 (1929-30) 458-462.

Felix A. Levy, "The Nature and Scope of Jewish Theology and Its Bearing on Modern Thought," *YCCAR* 41 (1931) 338-364.

*G. F. Barbour, "Punishment in Ethics and Theology," *ET* 46 (1934-35) 33-36, 74-78.

F. H. Durnford, "Theology and Seismology," *ET* 51 (1939-40) 333-338.

Joseph Jaroutunian, "Recent Theology and the Biblical Mind," *JAAR* 8 (1940) 18-23.

*C. A. Cook, "Biblical Criticism, Theology, and Philosophy," *JTS* 41 (1940) 225-237.

Leonard G. Oakey, "Theology and Seismology," *ET* 52 (1940-41) 38-39.

J. M. Shaw, "The Place of Theology Among the Sciences," *ET* 52 (1940-41) 143-146.

*Fred Plocher, "Biblical Criticism and Theology," *UnionR* 3 (1941-42) #1, 25-30.

James D. Smart, "The Death and Rebirth of Old Testament Theology," *JR* 23 (1943) 1-11, 125-136.

William A. Irwin, "Old Testament Theology—Criticism of Dr. Smart's Article," *JR* 23 (1943) 286-287.

Robert C. Dentan, "The Old Testament and a Theology for Today," *ATR* 27 (1945) 17-26.

William A. Irwin, "The Reviving Theology of the Old Testament," *JR* 25 (1945) 235-246.

Robert C. Dentan, "The Nature and Function of Old Testament Theology," *JAAR* 14 (1946) 16-21.

*G. R. Driver, "Theological and Philological Problems in the Old Testament," *JTS* 47 (1946) 156-166. [I. Theological Problems (i) *The god* Ym *in proper names;* (ii) *Cain's warning;* II. Philological Problems (i) *Words misread;* (ii) *Roots confused; Dr. Guillaume's Comments*]

Richard Kroner, "Science, Philosophy and Theology," *USQR* 2 (1946-47) #3, 9-14.

Charles M. Cooper, "The Place of the Old Testament in Theology," *LCQ* 20 (1947) 164-172.

George A. F. Knight, "The New theological emphasis in Old Testament studies," *RTRM* 6 (1947) #2, 3-6.

Paul L. Lehmann, "The Direction of Theology Today," *USQR* 3 (1947-48) #1, 3-10.

Norman W. Porteous, "Towards a Theology of the Old Testament," *SJT* 1 (1948) 136-149.

*C. R. North, "Old Testament Theology and the History of Hebrew Religion," *SJT* 2 (1949) 113-126.

A. S. Herbert, "Living Issues in Biblical Scholarship. Is there a Theology of the Old Testament," *ET* 61 (1949-50) 361-363.

*B. D. Napier, "Community Under Law. *On Hebrew Law and Its Theological Implications,*" *Interp* 7 (1953) 404-417.

Victor R. Gold, "H. H. Rowley's Old Testament Theology," *LQ, N.S.,* 11 (1959) 159-169. *(Review)*

*N[orman] W. Porteous, "Semantics and Old Testament Theology," *OTS* 8 (1950) 1-14.

‡H. H. Rowley, "Recent Foreign Theology. Old Testament Theology," *ET* 62 (1950-51) 318-319. *(Review)*

August J. Englebrecht, "Prolegomena to Old Testament Theology," *WSQ* 14 (1950-51) #4, 3-11.

*Aage Bentzen, "Biblical Criticism, History of Israel, and Old Testament Theology," *EQ* 23 (1951) 85-88.

William A. Irwin, "Trends in Old Testament Theology," *JAAR* 19 (1951) 183-190.

Stanley Brice Frost, "The Christian Theology of the Old Testament," *LQHR* 177 (1952) 185-191.

Isaac Heinemann, "The Idea of the Jewish Theological Seminary in the Light of Modern Thought," *HJud* 16 (1954) 71-80.

Norman W. Porteous, "The Old Testament and Some Theological Thought-Forms," *SJT* 7 (1954) 153-169.

T. S. Garrett, "Recent Biblical Studies and Their Doctrinal Implications," *SJT* 7 (1954) 225-232.

*Lawrence E. Toombs, "O.T. Theology and the Wisdom Literature," *JAAR* 23 (1955) 193-196.

John Baker, "The Construction of an O.T. Theology," *Theo* 58 (1955) 252-257.

Eugene R. Fairweather, "Christian Theology and the Bible," *CJT* 2 (1956) 65-75.

*James Barr, "The Problem of Old Testament Theology and the History of Religion," *CJT* 3 (1957) 141-149.

Charles Homer Giblin, "'As It is Written...'—A Basic Problem in Noematics and its Relevance to Biblical Theology," *CBQ* 20 (1958) 327-353, 477-498.

Delbert R. Hillers, "An Historical Survey of Old Testament Theology Since 1922," *CTM* 29 (1958) 571-594, 664-677.

Jakob J. Petuchowski, "The Question of Jewish Theology," *Jud* 7 (1958) 49-55.

Monford Harris, "Interim Theology," *Jud* 7 (1958) 302-308.

Ralph L. Smith, "The Revival of Old Testament Theology," *SWJT, N.S.,* 1 (1958-59) #2, 35-42.

*Donald Mathers, "Biblical and Systematic Theology," *CJT* 5 (1959) 15-24.

Norman W. Porteous, "Old Testament Theology," *LQHR* 184 (1959) 27-31.

T. A. M. Barnett, "Trends in Old Testament Theology," *CJT* 6 (1960) 91-101.

Howard M. Teeple, "Notes on Theologians' Approach to the Bible," *JBL* 79 (1960) 164-166.

*John Bowman, "The Doctrine of Creation, Fall of Man and Original Sin in Samaritan and Pauline Theology," *RTR* 19 (1960) 65-72.

*James A. Wharton, "'Smitten of God...' A Theological investigation of the enemies of Yahweh in the Old Testament," *ASBFE* 76 (1960-61) #1, 3-36.

P. Wernberg-Möller, "Is There an Old Testament Theology?" *HJ* 59 (1960-61) 21-29.

Roland E. Murphy, "A New Theology of the Old Testament," *CBQ* 23 (1961) 217-223. *(Review)*

Frederick Ferré, "The Use and Abuse of Theological Arguments," *JR* 41 (1961) 182-193.

Z. M. Schachter, "A Contemporary Attempt at the Perennial Questions," *Jud* 10 (1961) 112-118.

Emanuel Rackman, "Truth and Wisdom: An Orthodox Approach," *Jud* 10 (1961) 142-150.

*Lawrence E. Toombs, "Archaeology and Theological Studies," *DG* 32 (1961-62) 26-34.

James F. Ross, "Recent Trends in Old Testament Theology," *DG* 32 (1961-62) 35-45.

Christoph Barth, "The Significance of von Rad's 'Theology of the Old Testament'," *McQ* 15 (1961-62) #4, 24-29.

Walter C. Klein, "What is Old Testament Theology?" *ACQ* 2 (1962) 153-156.

*Claus Westermann, "The Meaning of Hermeneutics in Theology," *DG* 33 (1962-63) 127-141.

*John Gray, "Towards a Theology of the Old Testament: The Contribution of Archaeology," *ET* 74 (1962-63) 347-351.

John Macquarrie, "How is Theology Possible?" *USQR* 18 (1962-63) 295-305.

John Murray, "Systematic Theology—I," *WTJ* 25 (1962-63) 133-142.

*Ludwig R. Dewitz, "Old Testament Theology and Missions," *CTSB* 56 (1963) #2, 1-12.

J. C. Calhoun, "Old Testament Theologies: A Comparative Analysis," *DunR* 3 (1963) 155-193.

Leroy Runde, "Recent Directions in Old Testament Theology," *Scotist* 19 (1963) 18-29.

Norman W. Porteous, "Second Thoughts. II. The Present State of Old Testament Theology," *ET* 75 (1963-64) 70-74.

John Murray, "Systematic Theology—II," *WTJ* 26 (1963-64) 33-46.

*Arlis John Ehlen, "Old Testament Theology as *Heilsgeschichte,*" *CTM* 35 (1964) 517-544.

Sten H. Stenson, "Prophecy, Theology, and Philosophy," *JR* 44 (1964) 17-28.

Leo Baeck, "Theology and History," *Jud* 13 (1964) 274-284.

Eugene B. Borowitz, "Theological Issues in the New Torah Translation," *Jud* 13 (1964) 335-345.

*F. Hecht, "The Theological Interpretation of the Old Testament: An Act of Deliberation," *NGTT* 5 (1964) 93-98.

*Walther Zimmerli, "The Place and Limit of the Wisdom in the Framework of the Old Testament Theology," *SJT* 17 (1964) 146-158.

Rudolf Bultmann, "On the Question of a Philosophical Theology," *USQR* 20 (1964-65) 261-263.

Paul Holmer, "Language and Theology: Some Critical Notes," *HTR* 58 (1965) 241-261.

Roland E. Clements, "The Problem of Old Testament Theology," *LQHR* 190 (1965) 11-17.

Arnold C. Schultz, "Frontier Issues in Contemporary Theology in Evangelical Perspective. The Old Testament," *BETS* 9 (1966) 63-68.

Marten H. Woudstra, "The Religious Problem-Complex of Prophet and Priest in Contemporary Thought," *CTJ* 1 (1966) 39-66. *[OT Refs., pp. 42-47]*

G. Fohrer, "The Centre of a Theology of the Old Testament," *NGTT* 7 (1966) 198-206.

Paul L. Watson, "Old Testament Theology," *RestQ* 9 (1966) 261-274.

*J. Cartmell, "'Dogmatic Versus Biblical Theology'," *Scrip* 18 (1966) 77-83. *(Review) [OT Refs., p. 82]*

Leonard Hodgson, "Exegesis and Exposition," *CJT* 13 (1967) 42-49.

Bernhard Erling, "Theology as Science and Art," *JR* 47 (1967) 233-243.

Patrick Fannon, "A Theology of the Old Testament," *Scrip* 19 (1967) 46-53.

Shubert Spero, "'Is there an indigenous Jewish Theology?'" *Trad* 9 (1967-68) #1/2, 52-69.

J. Barton Payne, "Faith and History in the Old Testament," *BETS* 11 (1968) 111-120.

*Dennis J. McCarthy, "Theology and Covenant in the Old Testament," *BibT* #42 (1969) 2904-2908.

*F. N. Jasper, "Old Testament theology: a problem of ministerial training," *Min* 9 (1969) #2, 58-61.

*Alan D. Crown, "Theology, Eschatology and Law in Samaritan Funeral Rites and Liturgy," *GUOST* 23 (1969-70) 86-101.

Peter R. Ackroyd, "Theology of Tradition—An Approach to Old Testament Theological Problems," *BTF* 3 (1969-71) #2, 49-64.

§956 **5.1 Biblical Theology - General Studies**

*Anonymous, "Storr's Biblical Theology," *CRB* 1 (1836) 69-82. *(Review)*

Charles A. Briggs, "Biblical Theology," *DTQ, N.S.,* 1 (1882) 433-455.

Charles A. Briggs, "Biblical Theology," *PR* 3 (1882) 503-528.

Charles A. Briggs, "The Place of Biblical Theology," *ONTS* 3 (1883-84) 200-201.

Albert H. Newman, "Biblical Theology—Its Nature, Presuppositions, Methods, and Perils," *BQR* 6 (1884) 240-256.

Anonymous, "Shall We Study Biblical Theology?" *ONTS* 4 (1884-85) 89-90.

W. S. Bean, "A Plea for Biblical Theology," *PQ* 3 (1889) 598-606.

Philip Schaff, "Biblical Theology," *HR* 25 (1893) 401-403.

George Stockton Burroughs, "The Present Status of the Biblical Theology of the Old Testament," *BS* 57 (1900) 512-531.

Gurhardus*[sic]* Vos, "The Nature and Aims of Biblical Theology," *USR* 13 (1901-02) 194-199.

N. Forsander, "A Study in Biblical Theology," *TTKF* 6 (1904) 248-255.

Luther Kuhlman, "Biblical Theology: Its Relation to Ministerial Training," *LQ* 35 (1905) 21-35.

Frank C. Porter, "Crucial Problems in Biblical Theology," *JR* 1 (1921) 78-81.

James Oscar Boyd, "Biblical Theology in the Study and in the Pulpit," *EQ* 2 (1930) 70-112.

*John Vernon McGee, "Theology of the Tabernacle," *BS* 94 (1937) 153-175, 295-320, 409-429; 95 (1938) 22-39.

F. N. Davey, "Biblical Theology," *Theo* 38 (1939) 166-176.

Clarence T. Craig, "Biblical Theology and the Rise of Historicism," *JBL* 62 (1943) 281-294.

John A. McFadden, "A Plea of Biblical Theology," *EQ* 17 (1945) 204-211.

Ralph M. Earle Jr., "The Revival of Biblical Theology," *ASW* 2 (1947) 59-69.

Rolland Emerson Wolfe, "The Terminology of Biblical Theology," *JAAR* 15 (1947) 143-147.

C. R. North, "The Redeemer God. The Historical Basis of Biblical Theology," *Interp* 2 (1948) 3-16.

R. Lansing Hicks, "Present-Day Trends in Biblical Theology," *ATR* 32 (1950) 137-153.

Ernest R. Lacheman, "The Renaissance of Biblical Theology. A Review-Article," *JAAR* 19 (1951) 71-75. *(Review)*

E. C. Rust, "The Nature and Problems of Biblical Theology," *R&E* 50 (1953) 463-487.

Kenneth Grayston, "The Rise and Significance of Biblical Theology," *LQHR* 179 (1954) 96-101.

R. A. F. MacKenzie, "The Concept of Biblical Theology," *CTSP* 10 (1955) 48-67. (Discussion, pp. 67-73)

Gerhard Ebeling, "The Meaning of 'Biblical Theology'," *JTS, N.S.,* 6 (1955) 210-225.

Russell F. Aldwinckle, "Biblical Theology and Philosophy," *RL* 24 (1955) 395-407.

A. P. Leary, "Biblical Theology and History," *CQR* 157 (1956) 402-414.

R. A. F. MacKenzie, "Biblical Theology," *TD* 4 (1956) 131-135.

Peter Hackett, "A Note on the Nature of Biblical Theology," *BC* 1 (1956-58) 113-116.

James Muilenburg, "Is There a Biblical Theology?" *USQR* 12 (1956-57) #4, 29-37.

E. L. Allen, "The Limits of Biblical Theology," *JAAR* 25 (1957) 13-18.

*George Eldon Ladd, "Biblical Theology, History, and Revelation," *R&E* 54 (1957) 195-204.

James R. Branton, "Our Present Situation in Biblical Theology," *RL* 26 (1957) 5-18.

J. K. S. Reid, "Biblical Theology," *LQHR* 183 (1958) 93-98.

Winston L. King, "Some Ambiguities in Biblical Theology," *RL* 27 (1958) 95-104.

*Henry Joe Cadbury, "The Exegetical Conscience," *Nexus* 2 (1958-59) 3-6.

Samuel Sandmel, "'Biblical Theology'—A Dissent," *CCARJ* #24 (1959) 15-20.

*Donald Mathers, "Biblical and Systematic Theology," *CJT* 5 (1959) 15-24.

Edward J. Young, "What Is Old Testament Biblical Theology?" *EQ* 31 (1959) 136-142.

Ceslaus Spicq, "The work of biblical theology," *TD* 7 (1959) 29-34.

Robert L. Horn, "Biblical Theology and a Scientific World View," *ESS* 5 (1960-61) 32-46.

‡William L. Reed (*in cooperation with* Roscoe M. Pierson and William R. Barr), "A Selected Bibliography on Biblical Theology," *ESS* 5 (1960-61) 121-126.

C. A. Simpson, "An Inquiry into the Biblical Theology of History," *JTS, N.S.,* 12 (1961) 1-13.

G. W. Anderson, "Recent Biblical Theologies. V. Th. C. Vriezen's 'Outline of Old Testament Theology'," *ET* 73 (1961-62) 113-116. *(Review)*

James Barr, "Recent Biblical Theologies. VI. Gerhard von Rad's Theologie des Alten Testaments," *ET* 73 (1961-62) 142-146. *(Review)*

Peter R. Ackroyd, "Recent Biblical Theologies. VII. G. A. F. Knight's 'A Christian Theology of the Old Testament'," *ET* 73 (1961-62) 164-168. *(Review)*

Philip S. Watson, "The Nature and Function of Biblical Theology," *ET* 73 (1961-62) 195-200.

Hubert Cunliffe-Jones, "The 'Truth' of the Bible," *ET* 72 (1961-62) 287. *[Biblical Theology]*

John Bright, "Recent Biblical Theologies. VIII. Edmond Jacob's 'Theology of the Old Testament'," *ET* 73 (1961-62) 304-305. *(Review)*

Norman K. Gottwald, "Recent Biblical Theologies. IX. Walther Eichrodt's 'Theology of the Old Testament'," *ET* 74 (1962-63) 209-212. *(Review)*

David H. Wallace, "Biblical Theology: Past and Future," *TZ* 19 (1963) 88-105.

Joseph Bourke, "A Survey of Biblical Theology," *LofS* 18 (1963-64) 51-68.

Frederick Sontag, "Philosophy and Biblical Theology: A Prologue," *RL* 33 (1963-64) 224-237.

David Hill, "What is Biblical Theology?" *BT* 15 (1965) #3, 17-22.

G. Van Groningen, "Conservative and Neo-Orthodox Biblical Theology—A Review Article," *VR* #5 (1965) 13-25. *(Review)*

*J. Cartmell, "'Dogmatic Versus Biblical Theology'," *Scrip* 18 (1966) 77-83. *(Review) [OT Refs., p. 82]*

James Arthur Walther, "The Significance of Methodology for Biblical Theology," *PP* 10 (1969) 217-234.

§957 *5.2 Natural Theology - General Studies*

*Anonymous, "The Testimony of Natural Theology to Christianity," *QRL* 21 (1819) 41-66. *(Review)*

†Anonymous, "Crombie's *Natural Theology,*" *QRL* 51 (1834) 213-228. *(Review)*

†Anonymous, "Lord Brougham's Discourse on Natural Theology," *DUM* 6 (1835) 448-466. *(Review)*

†Anonymous, "Paley's *Natural Theology Illustrated,*" *QRL* 55 (1835-36) 387-416. *(Review)*

†Anonymous, "Dr. Chambers on Natural Theology," *DUM* 7 (1836) 597-610. *(Review)*

*Anonymous, "Geology considered with Reference to Natural Theology," *QRL* 56 (1836) 31-64. *(Review)*

Anonymous, "On the Study and the Spirit of Natural Theology," *CTPR* 3 (1837) 384-397.

†J. H. T., "The Connexion of Natural and Divine Truth," *CTPR, N.S.,* 1 (1838-39) 160-177. *(Review)*

Henry Ziegler, "Natural Theology," *ER* 16 (1865) 480-499.

*G. Henslow, "On Certain Analogies between the Methods of Deity in Nature and in Revelation," *JTVI* 4 (1869-70) 262-273. (Discussion, pp. 273-293)

George D'Oyly Snow, "Natural Theology," *ContR* 21 (1872-73) 573-596.

Thomas Hill, "Theology a Possible Science," *BS* 31 (1874) 1-29.

J. Macbride Sterrett, "Natural Realism: Or, Faith, the Basis of Science and Religion," *BS* 31 (1874) 74-97.

Thomas Hill, "The Foundations of Theology Sure," *BS* 31 (1874) 209-234.

Thomas Hill, "The Natural Foundations of Theology," *BS* 31 (1874) 436-458.

Thomas Hill, "The Testimony of Organic Life," *BS* 31 (1874) 593-615.

Thomas Hill, "The Natural Sources of Theology," *BS* 32 (1875) 1-18.

Thomas Hill, "The Natural Foundations of Theology," *DTQ* 1 (1875) 54-66.

Thomas Hill, "Organic Forms," *BS* 36 (1879) 1-22.

Frederic Gardiner, "The Persistence of Force; a Point in the Argument of Natural Theology," *BS* 38 (1881) 1-25.

Thomas Hill, "Necessity and Infinity," *BS* 39 (1882) 344-366.

*Thomas Hill, "Theism and Ethics," *BS* 40 (1883) 643-654.

*Frederic Perry Noble, "Natural Religion Prophetic of Revelation," *BS* 48 (1891) 52-73.

*R. M. Wenley, "Philosophy of Religion and the Endowment of Natural Theology," *Monist* 12 (1901-02) 21-48.

Henry W. Warren, "The Pre-Biblical Bible," *MR* 90 (1908) 177-185.

James Bissett Pratt, "Natural Religion: Consciousness and Its Implications," *HTR* 16 (1923) 287-304.

C. J. Wright, "Wanted—A Revived Natural Theology," *ET* 43 (1931-32) 328-333.

J. S. Boys Smith, "Hume's Dialogues Concerning Natural Religion," *JTS* 37 (1936) 337-349.

J. M. Shaw, "Can We Have Religion Without God?" *ET* 48 (1936-37) 246-252.

Gwilym O. Griffith, "Natural Theology and the Ministry of the Word," *SJT* 1 (1948) 258-271.

*Sam M. Hamilton, "Natural Theology and the Ontological Argument. Part I," *SR* 7 (1960-61) #2, 1-46.

*Sam M. Hamilton, "Natural Theology and the Ontological Argument. Part II," *SR* 7 (1960-61) 47-88.

G. Douglas Young, "The Values and Limitations of Natural Theology," *JASA* 16 (1964) 65-67.

Peter G. Berkhout, "The Bible of Nature," *JASA* 19 (1967) 111-114.

Arthur W. Munk, "The Biblical Basis of Natural Theology," *LQHR* 193 (1968) 43-50. [In the Old Testament, pp. 44-46]

(§958) **5.3 Theological Studies Classified According to Old Testament Books**

§959   **5.3.1 Theological Studies in the Pentateuch**

*Anonymous, "Christ in the Book of Genesis," *CR* 24 (1872) 397-417.

*B. F. Wilson, "The Christology of Genesis," *PQ* 3 (1889) 212-232. [I. Gen. 3:14, 15. Exegetical argument; II. Gen. 3:14, 15. The Internal Messianic Element; III. Gen. 3:14, 15. The Historico-Messianic Element; IV. Gen. 9:25-27. Exegetical Argument; V. Gen. 9:25-27. The Internal Messianic Element; VI. Gen. 9:25-27. The Historico-Messianic Element]

J. A. Kelso, "The Gospel in Genesis," *CFL, N.S.,* 4 (1901) 15-22.

*Howard Osgood, "Christ in the Pentateuch," *CFL, N.S.,* 6 (1902) 83-90.

F. R. Tennant, "The Theological Significance of the Early Chapters of Genesis," *ET* 30 (1918-19) 297-300.

*C. T. Fritsch, "Anti-Anthropomorphisms in the First Five Books of the Septuagint," *JBL* 61 (1942) ix.

Samuel L. Terrien, "The Theological Significance of Genesis," *JAAR* 14 (1946) 29-32.

*Lester J. Kuyper, "Deuteronomy, a Source Book for Theology," *HTS* 7 (1950-51) 181-190.

Lester J. Kuyper, "Theology in Deuteronomy," *RefR* 4 (1950-51) #1, 1-4.

*Gilmore H. Guyot, "Messianism in the Book of Genesis," *CBQ* 13 (1951) 415-421.

*Roderick A. F. MacKenzie, "The Messianism of Deuteronomy," *CBQ* 19 (1957) 299-305.

Walter Harrelson, "Guidance in the Wilderness. *The Theology of Numbers,*" *Interp* 13 (1959) 24-36.

Elizabeth R. Achtemeier, "The Exodus and the Gospel in the Old Testament," *T&L* 3 (1960) 188-197.

Jacob M. Myers, "The Requisites for Response. *On the Theology of Deuteronomy,*" *Interp* 15 (1961) 14-31.

Ralph L. Smith, "Theological Concepts in the Book of Deuteronomy," *SWJT, N.S.,* 7 (1964-65) #1, 17-32.

Moshe Weinfield, "Theological Currents in Pentateuchal Literature," *PAAJR* 37 (1969) 117-139.

(§960) *5.3.2 Theological Studies in the Prophets*

§961   *5.3.2.1 Theological Studies in the*
                      Former Prophets

*A. D. Crown, "Some Traces of Heterodox Theology in the Samaritan Book of Joshua," *BJRL* 50 (1967-68) 178-198.

§962 *5.3.2.2 Theological Studies in the Latter Prophets*

Anonymous, "The Doctrine of the Prophets," *CQR* 36 (1893) 424-439. *(Review)*

§963   *5.3.2.2.1 Theological Studies in the Major Prophets*

Hinckley G. Mitchell, "The Theology of Jeremiah," *JBL* 20 (1901) 56-76.

A. B. Davidson, "The Theology of Isaiah: Preliminary," *ET* 5 (1893-94) 296-298.

A. B. Davidson, "The Theology of Isaiah: II.," *ET* 5 (1893-94) 369-374.

A. B. Davidson, "The Theology of Isaiah: III.," *ET* 5 (1893-94) 391-396.

A. B. Davidson, "The Theology of Isaiah: V.," *ET* 5 (1893-94) 488-492.

A. B. Davidson, "The Theology of Isaiah. VI.," *ET* 6 (1894-95) 9-13.

Geerhardus Vos, "Some Doctrinal Features of the Earlier Prophecies of Isaiah," *PRR* 8 (1897) 444-463.

William C. Schaeffer, "The Historic Purpose of the Divine Election; The Doctrine Viewed from the Standpoint of Isaiah," *RChR, 4th Ser.,* 1 (1897) 40-51.

Henry S. Gehman, "The Ruler of the Universe. *The Theology of First Isaiah,*" *Interp* 11 (1957) 269-281.

*Carroll Stuhlmueller, "The Theology of Creation in Second Isaias," *CBQ* 21 (1959) 429-467.

Walther Eichrodt, "'The Holy One in Your Midst'. *The Theology of Isaiah,*" *Interp* 15 (1961) 259-273. *(Trans. by Lloyd Gaston)*

*A. van Selms, "Literary Criticism of Ezekiel as a Theological Problem," *OTW* 4 (1961) 24-37.

*Gerald R. Haemmerle, "Jeremiah's Concept of Sin," *SS* 19 (1967-68) #1, 62-83.

P. Kyle McCarter Jr., "Literary Considerations Relating to the Theology of Jeremiah," *McQ* 23 (1969-70) 130-141.

§964 *5.3.2.2.2 Theological Studies in the Minor Prophets*

*Hinckley G. Mitchell, "The Idea of God in Amos," *JBL* 7 (1887), Part 2, 33-42.

*Edward Mack, "The Theology of Hosea and Amos, as a Witness to the Age of the Pentateuch," *PQ* 8 (1894) 512-530.

J. T. Marshall, "The Theology of Malachi," *ET* 7 (1895-96) 16-19, 73-75, 125-127.

William Caldwell, "The Theology of the Book of Jonah," *BW* 19 (1902) 378-383.

*Arvid S. Kapelrud, "God as a Destroyer in the Preaching of Amos and in the Ancient Near East," *JBL* 71 (1952) 33-38.

*Alphonsus Benson, "'... From the Mouth of the Lion'. The Messianism of Amos," *CBQ* 19 (1957) 199-212.

*Eugene H. Maly, "Messianism in Osee," *CBQ* 19 (1957) 213-225.

*Robert T. Siebeneck, "The Messianism of Aggeus and Proto-Zacharias," *CBQ* 19 (1957) 312-328.

Eric C. Rust, "The Theology of Hosea," *R&E* 54 (1957) 510-521.

Carl G. Howie, "Expressly for Our Time. *The Theology of Amos,*" *Interp* 13 (1959) 273-285.

*C. J. Labuschagne, "Amos' conception of God and the Popular theology of his time," *OTW* 7&8 (1964-65) 122-133.

Donald L. Williams, "The Theology of Amos," *R&E* 63 (1966) 393-404.

Ralph L. Smith, "The Theological Implications of the Prophecy of Amos," *SWJT, N.S.,* 9 (1966-67) #1, 49-56.

*Donald C. Horrigan, "The Concept of Sin as Adultery in the Prophecy of Hosea," *SS* 19 (1967-68) #1, 84-95.

*A. H. van Zyl, "Messianic scope in the Book of Micah," *OTW* 11 (1968) 62-72.

(§965) *5.3.3 Theological Studies in the Hagiographa*

§966   *5.3.3.1 Theological Studies in the*
                    Poetic Books

Henry M. Harman, "The Divine names of the book of Job," *JBL* 6 (1886)
Part 1, 119.

W. T. Davison, "The Theology of the Psalms," *ET* 7 (1895-96) 200-204,
249-253, 347-352, 392-396, 535-539.

*Samuel Plantz, "Doctrine of the Future Life in the Book of Job," *MR* 78
(1896) 45-59.

Patrick V. Higgins, "Some Theological Aspects of the Psalms," *IER, 4th
Ser.,* 28 (1911) 175-185.

*Ralph Rogers Hawthorne, "Jobine Theology," *BS* 101 (1944), 64-75, 173-
186, 290-303, 417-433; 102 (1945) 37-54.

*Henry S. Gehman, "The Theological Approach of the Greek Translator of
Job 1-15," *JBL* 68 (1949) 231-240.

*Donald H. Gard, "The Concept of the Future Life According to the
Translator of the Book of Job," *JBL* 73 (1954) 137-143.

Harold Knight, "Job (Considered as a Contribution to Hebrew Theology),"
SJT 9 (1956) 63-76.

*William L. Reed, "Symbolism and Theology of the Psalms," *CollBQ* 37
(1960) #3, 35-43.

*Alfred von Rohr Sauer, "Salvation by Grace: The Heart of Job's
Theology," *CTM* 37 (1966) 259-270.

*John Carmody, "The Theology of Psalm 145," *BibT* #43 (1969) 2972-2979.

§967   *5.3.3.2 Theological Studies in the Megilloth*

Paschal P. Parente, "The Canticle of Canticles in Mystical Theology," *CBQ*
6 (1944) 142-158.

§968   **5.3.3.3 Theological Studies in
the Historical Books**

C. Umhau Wolf, "Daniel and the Lord's Prayer. *A Synthesis of the Theology of the Book of Daniel,*" *Interp* 15 (1961) 398-410.

Robert North, "Theology of the Chronicler," *JBL* 82 (1963) 369-381.

*Peter R. Ackroyd, "History and Theology in the Writings of the Chronicler," *CTM* 38 (1967) 501-515.

(§969) **5.4 Theological Studies Classified According to Topic**

§970   **5.4.1 Studies on the Doctrine of the Word of God**

Anonymous, "Revelation and Inspiration," *SPR* 9 (1855-56) 555-581.

J. F. Smith, "The Bible as the Word of God," *JSL, 4th Ser.,* 3 (1863) 99-106.

D. A., "Inspiration and Revelation," *JSL, 4th Ser.,* 9 (1866) 167-179.

E. P. Barrows, "Revelation and Inspiration," *BS* 24 (1867) 593-628; 25 (1868) 316-346; 28 (1871) 637-654; 29 (1872) 427-458, 640-665.

*E. P. Barrows, "Revelation and Inspiration. XII. The Quotations of the New Testament in their Relation to the Question of Inspiration," *BS* 30 (1873) 305-322.

F[rancis] D[ana] Hemenway, "The Divine Origin of the Bible," *MR* 59 (1877) 667-678.

[Francis Dana] Hemenway, "The Divine Origin of the Bible. An Argument in Outline," *DTQ* 4 (1878) 161-167.

Anonymous, "Inspiration and Revelation," *BWR* 3 (1881) 57-100.

D. W. Faunce, "God's Method in the Bible," *JCP* 3 (1883-84) 459-469.

George Harris, "The Doctrine of Sacred Scripture," *AR* 1 (1884) 46-61. *(Review)*

George T. Ladd, "The Interpretation of the Bible and the Doctrine of Sacred Scripture," *AR* 2 (1884) 18-34.

George T. Ladd, "The Question Restated," *AR* 4 (1885) 1-16.

Herrick Johnson, "The Silence of Scripture a Proof of Its Divine Origin," *PR* 7 (1886) 209-230. *[OT Refs., pp. 219-222]*

E. F. Burr, "Infallible Scripture," *BFER* 36 (1887) 740-761.

T. W. Hooper, "The Unchangeable Word," *PQ* 2 (1888) 208-216.

C. G. Montefiore, "Many Moods in the Hebrew Scriptures," *JQR* 2 (1889-90) 142-165.

Anonymous, "The Human Quantity in the Holy Scriptures," *MR* 72 (1890) 586-595.

Llewelyn J. Evans, "The Inerrancy of Scripture," *HR* 22 (1891) 99-108.

Alfred Cave, "The Inerrancy of Scripture," *HR* 23 (1892) 99-107.

[G. B. Strickler], "The Divine Origin of the Scriptures," *USR* 8 (1896-97) 71-77.

A. G., "Bibliology," *TQ* 1 (1897) 129-144, 257-270, 385-400.

Calvin S. Gerhard, "The Bible and the Word of God," *RChR, 4th Ser.,* 2 (1898) 1-12.

*D. S. Margoliouth, "Lines of Defence of the Biblical Revelation. V. The Bible of the Jews," *Exp, 6th Ser.,* 2 (1900) 229-240, 262-277.

Charles William Pearson, "Open Inspiration Versus a Closed Canon and Infallible Bible," *OC* 16 (1902) 175-181. [Remarks by Paul Carus, p. 152]

G. B. Strickler, "The Divine Origin of the Sacred Scriptures," *USR* 16 (1904-05) 331-342.

G. L. Young, "The Israelitish Scriptures," *CFL, 3rd Ser.,* 2 (1905) 474-476.

William Henry Burns, "The Holy Spirit and the Holy Scriptures. The Holy Spirit in the Production, Interpretation and Preservation of the Scriptures," *CFL, 3rd Ser.,* 6 (1907) 30-34.

A. H. M'Neile, "What is the Bible?" *ET* 19 (1907-08) 18-21.

James Orr, "Need and Basis of a Doctrine of Holy Scripture," *R&E* 6 (1909) 379-393.

*Willis J. Beecher, "Some Problems Concerning the Bible," *CFL, 3rd Ser.,* 12 (1910) 417-420. [I. The Processes by Which God Gave the Scriptures, pp. 417-418]

R. A. Webb, "Revelation: Inspiration: The Record," *USR* 24 (1912-13) 194-201.

D. S. Margoliouth, "The Bible of the Jews," *TZTM* 3 (1913) 544-567.

J. M. Buckley, "Inspiration and Revelation," *CFL, 3rd Ser.,* 20 (1915) 107-110. *[marked as "continued" but was not]*

William Jennings Bryan, "The Bible, the Word of God," *CFL, 3rd Ser.,* 27 (1921) 431-433.

H. E. Dana, "The Authenticity of the Holy Scriptures," *SWJT* 6 (1922) 40-78. *[OT Refs., pp. 47-60]*

George Johnson, "The Perfection of Scripture," *PTR* 23 (1925) 529-543.

Emil E. Fischer, "Apologetics and Modern Trends in Religious Thought. II. Revelation and Inspiration," *LCR* 45 (1926) 17-36.

Arthur C. Headlam, "Christian Theology. The Bible," *CQR* 13 (1931-32) 71-107.

*Sigmund Mowinckel, "'The Spirit' and the 'Word' in the Pre-exilic Reforming Prophets," *JBL* 53 (1935) 199-227.

R. Moehring, "Holy Writ IS God's Word," *KZ* 60 (1936) 527-530.

Lewis Sperry Chafer, "Introduction to Bibliology," *BS* 94 (1937) 132-152.

John A. W. Haas, "The Word of God," *LCQ* 10 (1937) 276-283.

J. P. Milton, "The Bible as the Word of God," *JTALC* 3 (1938) #11, 24-38; #12, 21-35.

M. Reu, "What is Scripture and How Can We Become Certain of Its Divine Origin?" *KZ* 63 (1939) 399-429, 473-478.

Anonymous, "The Inerrancy of the Scriptures," *CTM* 16 (1945) 116-118.

Richard Kehoe, "The Scriptures as the Word of God," *NB* 27 (1946) 453-460.

George W. Anderson, "The Idea of the Word of God in the Old Testament," *LQHR* 172 (1947) 123-129. [I. The Word as Power; II. The Word as Revelation; III. The Word as 'Hypostasis']

G. S. Hendry, "The Exposition of the Holy Scriptures," *SJT* 1 (1948) 29-46.

Arendj Nijk, "The Word of Jahweh in the Old Testament," *RefR* 3 (1949-50) #2, 8-10.

Hans Urs von Balthasar, "Scripture as the Word of God," *DownsR* 68 (1950) 1-20. *(Trans. by Donald Nicholl)*

E. La B. Cherbonnier, "The Theology of the Word of God," *JR* 33 (1953) 16-30.

J. W. D. Smith, "Religious Education. The Words of Scripture or the Word of God?" *ET* 65 (1953-54) 81-82.

B. J. Oosterhoff, "The Old Testament as the Word of God," *RefmR* 1 (1953-54) #3, 6-10.

W. B. Streufert, "The Appeal to Scripture as the Living Voice of God," *CTM* 25 (1954) 537-541.

William F. Orr, "The Bible as the Word of God," *WW* 5 (1954) #1, 8-13.

*T. Worden, "Questions and Answers. Similarities with Pagan Religions. What attitude ought we to adopt to the parallels so frequently adduced from extra-biblical sources in support of a denial that the Bible is the revealed word of God?" *Scrip* 10 (1958) 58-60.

J. L. McKenzie, "The Word of God in the Old Testament," *ThSt* 21 (1960) 183-206.

Vernon H. Kooy, "The Word of God and the Words of Scripture," *RefR* 14 (1960-61) #3, 29-42.

Walter R. Roehrs, "The Theology of the Word of God in the Old Testament," *CTM* 32 (1961) 261-273.

*William G. Young, "The Holy Spirit and the Word of God," *SJT* 14 (1961) 34-59. [1. The Authority of the Bible—The Need for a New Approach; 2. The Spirit and the Word—Inspiration, Communication, Illumination; 3. Particular Applications: A. 'Original Documents'. NT use of LXX, B. Authorship and 'Authenticity', C. Historical Criticism, D. Historical and Scientific Accuracy, E. Moral and Spiritual Infallibility]

*A. G. Errey, "The Book about God," *PQL* 8 (1962) 320-326. [The Word and the Deed, pp. 321-322; The Word in the Old Testament, pp. 322-324]

H. J. Richards, "Inerrant Errors," *Scrip* 14 (1962) 97-109.

Richard H. Bube, "A Perspective on Scriptural Inerrancy," *JASA* 15 (1963) 86-92.

Frank L. Benz, "What Is the Word of God?" *Amb* 12 (1963-64) #3, 4-12.

James Russell, "The Bible: The Infallible, Inerrant Word of God," *RefmR* 12 (1964-65) 65-77.

Francis J. Houdek, "The Word of God: Types and Meaning," *Focus* 2 (1965) #2, 56-69.

Gilbert B. Weaver, "The Doctrine of Revelation and Inspiration in the Old Testament," *GJ* 6 (1965) #1, 16-28.

Werner E. Lemke, "The Bible as the Word of God," *CovQ* 24 (1966) #1, 29-44.

Edward J. Young, "The God-Breathed Scripture," *GJ* 6 (1966) #3, 3-45. [I. Scripture—God Breathed and Profitable; II. What is the God-Breathed Scripture? III. The Bible and the Christian Faith; IV. A Modern View of the Bible]

Marten H. Woudstra, "Prophecy, Magic, and the Written Word," *CTJ* 2 (1967) 53-56.

Robert Preus, "Notes on the Inerrancy of Scripture," *CTM* 38 (1967) 363-375.

George I. Mavrodes, "Science and the Infallibility of the Bible," *JASA* 19 (1967) 90-92.

*Walther Zimmerli, "The Word of God in the Book of Ezekiel," *JTC* 4 (1967) 1-13.

Hermon N. Ridderbos, "An Attempt at the Theological Definition of Inerrancy, Infallibility, and Authority," *IRB* #32&33 (1968) 27-41.

*G. Gerald Harrop, "The Bible Cover to Cover," *TBMDC* #4 (1968) 1-19. [Foreword; The Problem of Authority in the Christian Faith; The Problem of the Old Testament as Christian Scripture; The Rehabilitation of the Old Testament in the Church; The Whole Bible as Divine Revelation]

K. Runia, "The Words of God and the Words of Scripture," *VR* #11 (1968) 1-8.

W. Ralph Thompson, "Facing Objections Raised Against Biblical Inerrancy," *WestTJ* 3 (1968) 21-29.

Wilber T. Dayton, "Theology and Biblical Inerrancy," *WestTJ* 3 (1968) 30-37.

‡Ronald Scharfe, "Select Bibliography of Periodical Articles on Revelation, Inspiration and Authority of Scripture: 1960 to 1969," *Them* 6 (1968-69) #3/4, 54-56.

William G. Heidt, "Points toward a more precise appreciation of the Bible as The Word of God," *BibT* #45 (1969) 3131-3139.

William R. Eischhorst, "The Issue of Biblical Inerrancy in Definition and Defense," *GJ* 10 (1969) #1, 3-17.

*Bernard Ramm, "The Relationship of Science, Factual Statements and the Doctrine of Biblical Inerrancy," *JASA* 21 (1969) 98-104.

§971 *5.4.1.1 Studies on the Authority of the Bible, especially the Old Testament [See also: The Historical Reliability of the Old Testament (includes Studies on Authority) §291 ←]*

†Anonymous, "The Divine Authority of the Holy Scripture asserted, from its Adaptation to the real State of Human Nature," *BCQTR, N.S.,* 10 (1818) 361-378. *(Review)*

*Anonymous, "Storr's Biblical Theology," *CRB* 1 (1836) 69-82. [§13. Divine authority of the Old Testament, p. 79] *(Review)*

B. B. Edwards, "The Imprecations in the Scriptures," *BS* 1 (1844) 97-110.

*Anonymous, "Of Sabbaths, as observed by the Jews; and of the authority of the Jewish Scriptures," *WR* 54 (1850-51) 179-206.

Hiram Carleton, "Has the Divine Authority of the Bible been established irrespective of the Facts of Science or the Opinion of Men relative to Moral Truth?" *TLJ* 12 (1859-60) 632-663. *(Review)*

Edmond de Pressensé, "The Authority of Holy Scripture," *CongL* 1 (1872) 98-103, 149-156.

William Henry Green, "The Perpetual Authority of the Old Testament," *PQPR* 6 (1877) 221-255.

W. A. E., "The Bible: Its Design and Authority," *ERG, 7th Ser.,* 1 (1878-79) 274-285.

S. S. Martyn, "The Bible as a Final Authority for Religious Truth," *JCP* 1 (1881-82) #4, Article #3, 1-18.

D. W. Simon, "The Authority of the Bible," *BQRL* 80 (1884) 364-377.

J. G. Murphy, "The Authority of Holy Scripture," *ONTS* 5 (1884-85) 145-150, 203-207.

A. A. Berle, "The Bible as Authority and Index," *BS* 51 (1894) 361-385.

*Frank Hugh Foster, "The Authority and Inspiration of the Scriptures," *BS* 52 (1895) 69-96, 232-258.

David Foster Estes, "The Authority of Scripture," *BS* 55 (1898) 414-443.

W. M. Lisle, "The Authority of the Bible," *CFL, 3rd Ser.,* 3 (1905) 54-63.

J. A. Rimbach, "Three of the Principal Proofs for the Divine Authority of the Bible," *TQ* 9 (1905) 32-47, 103-116.

A. vC. P. Huizinga, "Some Thoughts Concerning Bible-Authority," *CFL, 3rd Ser.,* 7 (1907) 192-198.

Arthur Metcalf, "The Authority of the Bible," *HR* 58 (1909) 130-133.

R. W. Moss, "The Religious Authority of the Old Testament," *LQHR* 112 (1909) 331-332.

George H. Schodde, "The Basis of Biblical Authority," *BM* 1 (1913) 90-100.

George Johnson, "The Authority of the Holy Scripture," *PTR* 12 (1914) 454-481.

Joseph Agar Beet, "The Inspiration and Authority of the Bible," *LQHR* 126 (1916) 251-270.

W. T. Conner, "The Nature of the Authority of the Bible," *SWJT* 2 (1918) #4, 11-17.

E. Klotsche, "The Divine Authority of the Holy Scriptures," *LQ* 51 (1921) 190-206.

Frank Grant Lewis, "The Bible as Authority. I.," *HR* 83 (1922) 97-101.

A. T. Robinson, "The Bible as Authority. II.," *HR* 83 (1922) 101-105.

*Clarence Edward Macartney, "The Authority of the Holy Scriptures," *PTR* 23 (1925) 389-396.

*Clarence Edward Macartney, "The Authority of the Holy Scriptures," *TM* 5 (1925) 294-300.

C[larence] E[dward] Macartney, "The Authority of the Holy Scriptures," *WLQ* 23 (1926) 21-28. [Note by M., pp. 36-37]

J. Vernon Bartlet, "The Bible as Authority. I," *CongQL* 6 (1928) 537-541.

John Bevan, "The Bible as Authority. II," *CongQL* 6 (1928) 541-547.

Julius A. Bewer, "The Authority of the Old Testament," *JR* 16 (1936) 1-9.

Hedley Hodkin, "The Authority of the Bible Today," *ET* 49 (1937-38) 231-234.

Werner Elert, "The Authority of the Bible in the Church," *LCQ* 20 (1947) 392-416. [The Authority of the Old Testament, pp. 407-412] *(Trans. by Gustav K. Wiencke)*

Otto A. Piper, "The Authority of the Bible," *TT* 6 (1949-50) 159-173. *[OT Refs., pp. 169f.]*

Burton H. Throckmorton Jr., "The Authority of the Bible," *ABBTS* 29 (1954) #4, 1-11.

Stanley Brice Frost, "The Authority of the Bible," *LQHR* 179 (1954) 90-95.

H. H. Rowley, "The Authority of the Bible. *An Apologetic Appealing to Objective Evidence,*" *SQ/E* 18 (1957) 3-20.

Peter Brunner, "A Doctrine of Biblical Authority. *Proposed in Outline,*" *SQ/E* 18 (1957) 21-27. *(Trans. by Ralph W. Wilburn)*

*Martin J. Heinecken, "The Authority of the Word of God," *Voice* 1 (1958) 1-49. [I. History and Myth; II. The Meaning of Revelation; III. The Word of God, the Bible, Propositional Truth]

Martin H. Franzmann, "The Posture of the Interpreter," *CTM* 31 (1960) 149-164. ['Mimesis' and the Authority of the Old Testament, pp. 160-161]

R. Buick Knox, "The Bible in the Church," *ET* 73 (1961-62) 372-374.

James R. Branton, "The Authority of the Bible," *Found* 5 (1962) 100-111.

Patrick Fannon, "The Council and the Bible. 2. Scripture and Tradition," *ClR* 48 (1963) 623-632.

Robert Preus, "The Power of God's Word," *CTM* 34 (1963) 453-465.

Diego Arenhoevel, "Does the Bible Suffice as a Source of Faith," *LofS* 19 (1964) 68-78.

Wesley W. Nelson, "The Authority of the Written Word," *CovQ* 24 (1966) #1, 18-28.

*Hermon N. Ridderbos, "An Attempt at the Theological Definition of Inerrancy, Infallibility, and Authority," *IRB* #32&33 (1968) 27-41.

Klaas Runia, "The Authority of Scripture," *CTJ* 4 (1969) 165-194.

‡*Ronald Scharfe, "Select Bibliography of Periodical Articles on Revelation, Inspiration and Authority of Scripture: 1960 to 1969," *Them* 6 (1968-69) #3/4, 54-56.

*Graeme Goldsworthy, "The Old Testament—A Christian Book," *Inter* 2 (1969-70) 24-33. [IV. The Authority of the Old Testament, pp. 27-28]

§972 *5.4.1.2 Studies on Divine Revelation and the Old Testament*

†Anonymous, "Jones on Divine Revelation," *BCQTR, N.S.,* 16 (1821) 561-584. *(Review)*

*†Anonymous, "Penrose on the Use of Miracles," *BCQTR, N.S.,* 22 (1824) 138-143. *[Revelation] (Review)*

Anonymous, "Logic, Reason, and Revelation," *CTPR, N.S.,* 6 (1844) 365-375.

Anonymous, "Divine Revelation," *CTPR, 3rd Ser.,* 3 (1847) 585-593. *(Review)*

Anonymous, "Conscience and Revelation," *BRCM* 6 (1849-50) 453-481.

E. P. Barrows, Jr., "The Indivisible Nature of Revelation," *BS* 10 (1853) 764-788.

Alexander W. McLeod, "Divine Revelation Practically Considered and Applied," *MQR* 9 (1855) 370-383.

W. A. McSwain, "On Divine Revelation," *MQR* 9 (1855) 557-566.

*Anonymous, "Mythology and Revelation," *CRB* 21 (1856) 603-611.

*Anonymous, "Conflicts of Revelation and Science—The Science of the Bible Phenomenal," *DQR* 4 (1864) 339-361.

*C. A. Row, "On the Relation of Reason to Philosophy, Theology, and Revelation," *JTVI* 3 (1868-69) 472-502. (Discussion pp. 502-516)

*G. Henslow, "On Certain Analogies between the Methods of Deity in Nature and in Revelation," *JTVI* 4 (1869-70) 262-273. (Discussion, pp. 273-293)

P. Kleinert, "Holy Scripture a Divine Revelation," *MR* 52 (1870) 45-65. *(Trans. by J. F. Hurst[sic])*

J. C. Murphy, "What is Truth?" *BS* 29 (1872) 289-309. *[Revelation]*

Anonymous, "Have We a Revelation from God?" *BWR* 1 (1877) 101-192.

C. A. Row, "God's Threefold Revelation of Himself; in the Universe, in Man's Conscience and Moral Nature, and in the Incarnation," *PR, 4th Ser.,* 1 (1878) 702-732.

*†Anonymous, "Colenso's Last Volume and Supernatural Religion," *LQHR* 53 (1879-80) 104-151. *[Revelation] (Review)*

*H. E. D[ennehy], "Revelation, Geology, and the Antiquity of Man," *IER, 3rd Ser.,* 1 (1880) 185-193, 260-272.

P. Thomson, "God in Nature and in History. Contributions Toward a True Theory of Revelation," *Exp, 2nd Ser.,* 1 (1881) 161-179, 241-252.

*J. H. McIlvaine, "Science and Revelation," *JCP* 1 (1881-82) #3, Article #2, 1-24.

S. Crane, "Revelations of God," *UQGR, N.S.,* 18 (1881) 55-72.

George T. Ladd, "Revelation," *JCP* 2 (1882-83) 156-178.

J. A. Quarles, "The Bible a Divine Revelation," *SPR* 34 (1883) 30-54.

C. Walker, "Scriptural Evolution," *CR* 44 (1884) 147-161. *[Revelation]*

Anonymous, "Revelation Corroborated," *MQR, 2nd Ser.,* 7 (1885) 76-81.

John Kirk, "Divine Revelation," *ERG, 9th Ser.,* 2 (1887) 322-328.

*John L. Girardeau, "The Miracle, The Principle of Unity in the Evidences of a Divine Revelation," *PQ* 2 (1888) 369-387.

'Philo', "What is a Revelation?" *URRM* 32 (1889) 289-309.

E. Benj. Andrews, Washington Gladden, E. H. Johnson, I. E. Dwinell, Alvah Hovey, Newman Smyth, and R. B. Welch, "A 'Symposium' on the 'Gradualness of Revelation'," *ONTS* 11 (1890) 177-185.

*Frederic Perry Noble, "Natural Revelation Prophetic of Revelation," *BS* 48 (1891) 52-73.

J. B. Shearer, "The Object and Scope of Written Revelation," *PQ* 6 (1892) 329-340.

D. Witton Jenkins, "Horton's 'Revelation and the Bible'," *ET* 4 (1892-93) 209-313. *(Review)*

J. E. Spilman, "God's Method in Divine Revelation," *PQ* 7 (1893) 560-570.

G. S. Rollins, "The Principle of Adaptation in Revelation," *BW* 16 (1900) 259-271.

*D. S. Margoliouth, "Lines of Defence of the Biblical Revelation. V. The Bible of the Jews," *Exp, 6th Ser.,* 2 (1900) 229-240, 262-277.

J. E. M'Ouat, "Divine Revelation in the Light of Old Testament Criticism," *ET* 12 (1900-01) 487-494.

Charles P. Grannan, "Divine Element in Scripture—Revelation," *ACQR* 26 (1901) 353-374.

*W[illiam] Ewing, "Palestine and Revelation," *GUOST* 2 (1901-07) 18-20.

C. J. Södergren, "Reason and Revelation," *TTKF* 5 (1903) 91-100.

William Ewing, "Palestine and Revelation," *BW* 24 (1904) 86-93.

G. L. Young, "What is Biblical Revelation?" *CFL, 3rd Ser.,* 1 (1904) 617-626.

John Kunze, "Revelation a Certainty," *LCR* 24 (1905) 668-681. *(Trans. by C. Theodore Benze)*

*S. M'Comb, "Immortality and Revelation," *LQHR* 103 (1905) 305-321. *(Review)*

John Kunze, "Revelation a Certainty. Part II," *LCR* 25 (1906) 45-53. *(Trans. by C. Theodore Benze)*

John Kunze, "Revelation a Certainty. Part III," *LCR* 25 (1906) 311-317. *(Trans. by C. Theodore Benze)*

John Kunze, "Revelation a Certainty. Part IV," *LCR* 25 (1906) 511-517.

John Kunze, "Revelation a Certainty. V," *LCR* 25 (1906) 695-698.

E. G. King, "Criticism and Revelation," *ICMM* 6 (1909-10) 379-383. *[OT Refs., pp.379-381]*

Henry Proctor, "The Unity of Revelation," *AAOJ* 32 (1910) 93-96.

A. H. McNeil, "God's Self-Revelation to Israel," *ICMM* 8 (1911-12) 255-262.

Henry Proctor, "The Evolution of Revelation," *AAOJ* 34 (1912) 34-36, 93-95.

A. E. Garvie, "Can the Literature of a Divine Revelation be Dealt with by Historical Science?" *ET* 25 (1913-14) 156-161.

Anonymous, "The Permanent Value of the Old Testament Revelation," *MR* 97 (1915) 477-481.

R. P. Lippincott, "God's Supreme Revelation a Growth," *BWTS* 8 (1915-16) 65-79.

Henry William Rankin, "Philosophy and the Problem of Revelation," *PTR* 13 (1915) 409-460; 14 (1916) 265-311.

*J. S. Ross, "Methodist Higher Criticism Arm-in-Arm with Infidelity," *CFL, 3rd Ser.,* 21 (1916) 116-118. [I. Revelation, pp. 116-117]

A. L. Vail, "Is Written Revelation from God Reasonable?" *SWJT* 3 (1919) #2, 22-26.

J. A. Singmaster, "The Bible, a Divine Revelation. (An Outline of the Doctrine)," *LQ* 50 (1920) 330-350.

Horace M. Ramsey, "Progressive Revelation of the Bible," *ACM* 13 (1923) 220-225.

W. R. Matthews, "The Idea of Revelation," *MC* 14 (1924-25) 83-88.

V. F. Storr, "Revelation," *JTVI* 58 (1926) 113-125, 133-136. (Discussion, pp. 125-133) [Communications by R. P. Hadden, p. 136; W. E. Leslie, pp. 136-137; Avary H. Forbes, pp. 137-138; William C. Edwards, pp. 138-139; F. C. Wood, pp. 139-141; Lewis M. Davies, pp. 141-144; John Tuckwell, pp. 144-146; William Fisher, pp. 146-147; W. Hoste, pp. 147-149; G. B. Michell, pp. 149-151]

Hugh Ross Mackintosh, "The Idea of Revelation," *USR* 39 (1927-28) 325-341.

*George Boddis, "Prophecy as an Evidence of Divine Revelation," *CFL, 3rd Ser.,* 34 (1928) 483-489.

G. Ch. Aalders, "The Reality of Prophetical Revelation," *EQ* 1 (1929) 113-120, 233-240.

D. S. Cairns, "The Three Levels of Revelation in the Bible," *BR* 14 (1929) 508-520.

Leander S. Keyser, "The Reasonableness of a Special Divine Revelation," *EQ* 2 (1930) 127-136.

W. E. Hough, "The Necessity of Christ for Revelation," *BQL* 5 (1930-31) 338-346. *[OT Refs., pp. 342-345]*

*W. Bell Dawson, "Science and the Divine Revelation," *BR* 16 (1931) 77-96.

John A. W. Hass, "What is Revelation?" *LCQ* 9 (1936) 18-26.

Lewis Sperry Chafer, "Revelation (Continuing the Series on Bibliology)," *BS* 94 (1937) 264-280.

Otto W. Heick, "Revelation and the Bible," *LCQ* 10 (1937) 125-132.

H. Wheeler Robinson, "The Philosophy of Revelation as Illustrated in the Old Testament," *OSHTP* (1937-38) 26-28.

John M. Graham, "After Fifty Years. X. Revelation and the Bible," *ET* 50 (1938-39) 537-540.

Charles M. Jacobs, "The Idea of Revelation," *LCQ* 12 (1939) 62-73.

C. H. Dodd, "Constructive Theology. X. Revelation," *ET* 51 (1939-40) 446-449.

*Harold C. Rowse, "Symbolism and Revelation," *BQL* 10 (1940-41) 5-11.

*R. H. Fuller, "The Word of God," *Theo* 47 (1944) 267-271.

John W. Bowman, "The Bible as Revelation," *TT* 1 (1944-45) 455-469. [I. The Formal Nature of the Revelation: Act and Word; II. The Content of the Revelation: The Gospel; III. The Instrument of the Revelation: The Prophet]

G. W. Bromiley, "The Biblical Doctrine of Divine Revelation," *JTVI* 77 (1945) 81-95, 97-100. (Communications by P. W. Evans, pp. 95-96; Alexander Fraser, pp. 96-97)

*F. W. Dillistone, "Wisdom, Word, and Spirit. Revelation in the Wisdom Literature," *Interp* 2 (1948) 275-287.

J. N. Sanders, "The Problem of Revelation," *Theo* 51 (1948) 89-95.

Conrad Bergendoff, "The Sphere of Revelation," *LWR* 1 (1948-49) #2, 38-53.

H. S. Curr, "Progressive Revelation," *JTVI* 83 (1951) 1-11, 22-23. (Discussion, pp. 11-15) [Communications by F. F. Bruce, pp. 15-17; W. E. Filmer, pp. 17-18; R. S. Timberlake, pp. 18-19; L. D. Ford, pp. 19-22]

Geo. O. Lillegard, "'Progressive Revelation'," *WLQ* 48 (1951) 45-58.

Allan A. MacRae, "The Scientific Approach to the Old Testament," *BS* 110 (1953) 18-24, 130-138, 234-241, 309-320.

*George E[ldon] Ladd, "The Revelation and Jewish Apocalyptic," *EQ* 29 (1957) 94-128.

*George E[ldon] Ladd, "Revelation, History, and the Bible," *JASA* 9 (1957) #3, 15-18.

*George Eldon Ladd, "Biblical Theology, History, and Revelation," *R&E* 54 (1957) 195-204.

*C. A. Simpson, "Old Testament Historiography and Revelation," *HJ* 56 (1957-58) 319-332.

Wesley J. Fuerst, "The Word of God in the Old Testament," *LQ, N.S.,* 10 (1958) 315-326.

*Martin J. Heinecken, "The Authority of the Word of God," *Voice* 1 (1958) 1-49. [I. History and Myth; II. The Meaning of Revelation; III. The Word of God, the Bible, Propositional Truth]

Albert Gilin, "To see God," *TD* 7 (1959) 171-174.

E. F. Osborn, "Realism and Revelation," *ABR* 8 (1960) 29-37.

*Zvi E. Kurzweil, "Three Views on Revelation and Law," *Jud* 9 (1960) 291-298.

D. Glenn Rose, "The Biblical Idea of Revelation. *Its Relevance for Constructive Theology Today,*" *SQ/E* 21 (1960) 201-217.

I. F. Church, "The Bible and Revelation," *Theo* 63 (1960) 491-497.

*Martin H. Scharlemann, "God's Acts As Revelation," *CTM* 32 (1961) 209-216.

Jakob J. Petuchowski, "Revelation and the Modern Jew," *JR* 41 (1961) 28-37.

Joseph H. Gumbiner, "Revelation and Liberal Jewish Faith," *Jud* 10 (1961) 119-128.

*R. H. Altus, "God's Revelation and History," *AusTR* 33 (1962) 3-7.

*G. Van Groningen, "Old Testament Historicity and Divine Revelation," *VR* #1 (1962) 3-23.

Patrick Fannon, "The Council and the Bible: I. Divine Revelation," *CIR* 48 (1963) 539-549.

John C. Whitcomb Jr., "Biblical Inerrancy and the Double-Revelation Theory," *GJ* 4 (1963) #1, 3-20.

Moses Mendelssohn, "On Reason and Revelation," *Jud* 12 (1963) 476-478.

*James Barr, "Revelation Through History in the Old Testament and in Modern Theology," *PSB* 56 (1963) #3, 4-14.

Donald Evans, "Protestant and Roman Views of Revelation: 1. Protestant Views," *CJT* 10 (1964) 258-264.

Jean Martucci, "Protestant and Roman Views of Revelation: 2. A Roman Catholic Commentary," *CJT* 10 (1964) 265-270.

Edmund Hill, "Revelation in the Bible. III. In the Old Testament," *Scrip* 16 (1964) 16-21.

Henry Babcock Adams, "Revelation in the Light of Communication Theory. *A Dialogue of Perception and Response*," *SQ/E* 25 (1964) 470-475.

Louis Rabinowitz, "Torah Min ba-Shamayim," *Trad* 7 (1964-65) #1, 34-45.

Jacob M. Chinitz, "The Elusive Revelation," *Jud* 14 (1965) 187-204.

Thomas H. Olbricht, "The Bible As Revelation," *RestQ* 8 (1965) 211-232.

Jakob J. Petuchowski, "Reflections on Revelation," *CCARJ* 13 (1965-66) #6, 4-11.

Robert Preus, "The Doctrine of Revelation in Contemporary Theology," *BETS* 9 (1966) 111-124.

N.C.W.C. Translation, "Dogmatic Constitution on Divine Revelation (Chapters 3, 4, 5 and 6)," *BTr* 17 (1966) 139-144. *[Chap. 4 on OT]*

*G. Gerald Harrop, "'But Now Mine Eye Seeth Thee'," *CJT* 12 (1966) 80-84. *[Hebrew and Greek idea of Revelation compared]*

*A. Malamat, "Prophetic Revelations in New Documents from Mari and the Bible," *EI* 8 (1967) 75*.

*William R. Murdock, "History and Revelation in Jewish Apocalypticism," *Interp* 21 (1967) 167-187.

Kevin McNamara, "Divine Revelation," *ITQ* 34 (1967) 3-19.

Bruce Vawter, "God Spoke," *Way* 7 (1967) 171-179.

Eugene H. Maly, "Constitution on Divine Revelation: Chapter I," *BibT* #35 (1968) 2418-2425.

Walter J. Burghardt, "Constitution on Divine Revelation: Chapter II," *BibT* #35 (1968) 2426-2432.

Frederick L. Mariarty, "Constitution on Divine Revelation: Chapter III," *BibT* #35 (1968) 2433-2440.

Joseph Grassi, "Constitution on Divine Revelation: Chapter IV," *BibT* #35 (1968) 2441-2446.

Joseph Grassi, "Constitution on Divine Revelation: Chapter IV," *BibT* #35 (1968) 2441-2446.

*Herbert C. Brichto, "On Faith and Revelation in the Bible," *HUCA* 39 (1968) 35-53.

Charles J. Galloway, "Revelation as Event," *Scrip* 20 (1968) 10-19.

§973 *5.4.1.3 Studies on Inspiration and the Old Testament*

†'Pyrrho', "Observations concerning Inspiration," *TRep* 2 (1770) 462-464.

†'Pamphilus', "Observations on Inspiration," *TRep* 4 (1784) 17-26.

Anonymous, "An Argument against the Reasoning found in the Scriptures being inspired," *TRep* 4 (1784) 364-370.

†Anonymous, "Professor Findlay on the Jewish Scriptures," *BCQTR* 24 (1804) 294-295. *(Review)*

Anonymous, "On the Study of Divinity. Chapter VIII. On the Inspiration of the Sacred Scriptures," *MR* 2 (1819) 401-403.

Anonymous, "The Inspiration of the Scriptures. No. I.," *SP* 1 (1828) 402-406.

Anonymous, "The Inspiration of the Scriptures. No. II. *Mistakes to be avoided, and cautions to be observed,*" *SP* 1 (1828) 474-480.

Anonymous, "The Inspiration of the Scriptures. No. III. *Mistakes to be avoided, and cautions to be observed,*" *SP* 1 (1828) 624-629.

Anonymous, "The Inspiration of the Scriptures. No. IV. *Inspiration of the Scriptures of the Old Testament proved,*" *SP* 2 (1829) 9-15. *[Part V on NT]*

Anonymous, "The Inspiration of the Scriptures. No. VI. *What views are we to entertain respecting the nature and extent of divine inspiration?*" *SP* 2 (1829) 185-195.

Anonymous, "The Inspiration of the Scriptures. No. VII. *Application of the Doctrine to different parts of Scriptures.–Perfection of the Bible,*" *SP* 2 (1829) 237-242.

†Anonymous, "Truth, Inspiration and Interpretation of the Scriptures," *BCQTR, 4th Ser.,* 21 (1837) 76-131. *(Review)*

A. P. P., "On Inspiration," *CE* 32 (1842) 204-218.

E. H. S., "Inspiration of the Scriptures," *CE* 35 (1843-44) 340-366.

Leonard Woods, "The Inspiration of the Scriptures," *CRB* 9 (1844) 1-20.

Anonymous, "The Inspiration of Scripture," *CTPR, N.S.,* 6 (1844) 387-400.

(   ) F., "Theopneusty; or the Plenary Inspiration of the Holy Scriptures," *MR* 27 (1845) 594-625. *(Review)*

M. S., "Inspiration of the Scriptures," *CRB* 12 (1847) 219-238.

Anonymous, "Review of the Bible," *CTPR, 3rd Ser.,* 4 (1848) 150-151. *(Review)*

J. S. L., "The Inspiration of the Scriptures," *UQGR* 5 (1848) 343-357.

E. T., "Inspiration of the Scriptures," *UQGR* 6 (1849) 382-391.

Brewin Grant, "The Doctrine of Inspiration, as Maintained in the Scriptures Themselves," *BRCM* 6 (1849-50) 289-302.

Anonymous, "On the Inspiration of the Authors of the Scriptures," *JSL, 1st Ser.,* 5 (1850) 437-495.

Anonymous, "The Plenary Inspiration of the Scriptures," *SPR* 4 (1850-51) 457-498.

W. M. T., "Inspiration," *JSL, 1st Ser.,* 7 (1851) 315-333.

T. V. Moore, "Inspiration of the Scriptures: Morell's Theory Discussed and Refuted," *MQR* 5 (1851) 20-57.

Anonymous, "Theories of Inspiration," *ER* 3 (1851-52) 492-520.

Anonymous, "The Credibility and Plenary Inspiration of the Scriptures," *SPR* 5 (1851-52) 73-92.

Anonymous, "The Spirit of the Old Testament," *BFER* 1 (1852) 115-152.

†Anonymous, "Infallibility of the Bible and Recent Theories of Inspiration," *NBR* 18 (1852-53) 138-185. *(Review)*

J. W. Hall, "The Inspiration of the Sacred Scriptures," *TLJ* 6 (1853-54) 459-478. *(Review)*

A. A. L., "The Bible, Inspired and Inspiring," *CE* 56 (1854) 165-188.

F. A. D. Tholuck, "The Doctrine of Inspiration," *JSL, 2nd Ser.,* 6 (1854) 331-369.

J. T. G., "Inspiration and Infallibility," *JSL, 2nd Ser.,* 7 (1854-55) 141-155.

Eleaszar T. Fitch, "The True Doctrine of Divine Inspiration," *BS* 12 (1855) 217-263.

*Anonymous, "The Bearing of the Geological Theory of the Age of the World on the Inspiration of the Bible," *TLJ* 9 (1856-57) 251-270.

†Anonymous, "Mr. Lee of Dublin on the Inspiration of the Scriptures," *TLJ* 9 (1856-57) 609-621. *(Review)*

M. Kalisch, "Jewish Ideas of Inspiration," *JSL, 3rd Ser.,* 5 (1857) 178.

†Anonymous, "Inspiration," *NBR* 27 (1957) 215-253. *(Review)*

†Anonymous, "The Inspiration of the Scriptures, its Nature and Extent," *TLJ* 10 (1857-58) 1-45, 177-203. *(Review)*

Anonymous, "The Inspiration of the Scriptures: Objections to it," *TLJ* 10 (1857-58) 353-371.

Anonymous, "The Inspiration of the Scriptures: Objections to it Refuted," *TLJ* 10 (1857-58) 528-547.

†Anonymous, "The Inspiration of the Holy Scripture, its Nature and Proof," *BFER* 7 (1858) 253-285. *(Review)*

Joseph Torrey, "Essay on Inspiration," *BS* 15 (1858) 314-336.

†Anonymous, "Inspiration of Scripture—Current Theories," *LQHR* 10 (1858) 285-343. *(Review)*

Daniel Curry, "Inspiration of the Holy Scriptures," *MR* 40 (1858) 256-272. *(Review)*

M. N., "Biblical Criticism," *JSL, 4th Ser.,* 2 (1862-63) 189-191. *[Inspiration of the OT]*

J. C., "Inspiration," *BFER* 13 (1864) 466-482. *(Review)*

Anonymous, "The Inspiration of the Scriptures," *CongR* 4 (1864) 429-449.

[Hermann] Zeller, "Inspiration.—Translated from Zeller's 'Biblisches Wörterbuch.'," *ER* 15 (1864) 293-298. *(Trans. by Charles F. Schaeffer)*

Anonymous, "The Relation between the Divine and Human Elements in Holy Scripture," *LQHR* 22 (1864) 408-428. *(Review)*

D. A., "On the Nature and Extent of Divine Inspiration: Illustrated by Extracts from Various Authors," *JSL, 4th Ser.,*6 (1864-65) 257-294.

W. R. Coxwell Rogers, "Verbal Inspiration Defended," *JSL, 4th Ser.,* 7 (1865) 184-205.

I. M. Atwood, "Inspiration," *UQGR, N.S.,* 2 (1865) 285-292.

D. A., "Inspiration of Scripture," *JSL, 4th Ser.,* 8 (1865-66) 274-282.

Anonymous, "Inspiration," *JSL, 4th Ser.,* 8 (1865-66) 463-465.

*†Anonymous, "Smith's Book of Prophecy," *LQHR* 25 (1865-66) 392-409.

Edward Biley, "Inspiration," *JSL, 4th Ser.,* 9 (1866) 216-217.

D. A., "Theory of Inspiration Drawn from Scripture," *JSL, 4th Ser.,* 9 (1866) 322-333.

D. A., "Limitation of Inspiration," *JSL, 4th Ser.,* 10 (1866-67) 104-122.

Anonymous, "Inspiration," *JSL, 4th Ser.,* 10 (1866-67) 184-185.

*J. L., "Inspiration," *BFER* 16 (1867) 537-556. *(Review)*

Edward Biley, "Inspiration," *JSL, 5th Ser.,* 1 (1867) 242-243.

Gilbert Haven, "Scripture Inspiration," *MR* 49 (1867) 325-352.

Lemuel Moss, "Dr. Curtis on Inspiration," *BQ* 2 (1868) 83-117. *(Review)*

Gilbert Haven, "The Divine Element in Inspiration," *MR* 50 (1868) 5-16. *(Review)*

*B. Gildersleeve, "Canonicity and Inspiration of the Sacred Scriptures," *SPR* 19 (1868) 370-394. *(Review)*

Geo. Hill, "Inspiration of the Scriptures," *UQGR, N.S.,* 5 (1868) 302-318.

Walter Mitchell, "On the Unphilosophical Character of some Objections to the Divine Inspiration of Scripture," *JTVI* 3 (1868-69) 63-86. (Discussion, pp. 86-96)

D. F. S. S., "The Distinctive Character of the Old Testament Scripture," *BFER* 19 (1870) 18-40.

D. F. S. S., "The Distinctive Character of the Old Testament Scripture," *ThE* 7 (1871) 83-109.

James A. Lyon, "The Contrast Between Man and the Brute Creation Establishes the Divine Origin of the Scriptures," *PQPR* 2 (1873) 726-737.

A. D. Go., "Inspiration," *ERG, 6th Ser.,* 4 (1877-78) 190-195.

Francis Roubiliac Conder, "On the Religious Imagination in the East," *DUM* 91 (1878) 345-357, 468-477.

G. W. Lasher, "Inspiration," *BQR,* 1 (1879) 100-118, 246-260.

A. H. Kremer, "The Plenary Inspiration of the Bible," *RChR* 26 (1879) 562-571.

Ezra P. Gould, "The Extent of Inspiration," *BS* 35 (1878) 326-352.

Mary J. De Long, "Inspiration and the Bible," *UQGR, N.S.,* 16 (1879) 186-197.

James MacGregor, "Nature of the Divine Inspiration of Scripture," *BFER* 29 (1880) 201-219.

R. A. Redford, "Inspiration," *BQRL* 72 (1880) 99-122.

A. A. Hodge and B. B. Warfield, "Inspiration," *BFER* 30 (1881) 569-604.

O. P. Eaches, "What Latitude of Belief is Allowed by the Doctrine of Inspiration," *BQR* 3 (1881) 185-201.

Charles Elliott, "Subjective Theory of Inspiration," *PRev, 4th Ser.,* 8 (1881) 192-204.

A. A. Hodge and Benjamin B. Warfield, "Inspiration," *PR* 2 (1881) 225-260.

Charles Elliott, "Subjective Theory of Inspiration," *DTQ, N.S.,* 1 (1882) 236-244.

J. H. Potts, "Inspiration of the Scriptures," *MQR, 2nd Ser.,* 4 (1882) 51-58.

George T. Ladd, "Inspiration," *JCP* 2 (1882-83) 225-249.

Isaac Errett, "Leading Theories of Inspiration," *CT* 1 (1883-84) 353-380.

Alvah Hovey, "Theories of Inspiration," *BFER* 33 (1884) 343-361.

Alvah Hovey, "Theories of Inspiration," *BQR* 6 (1884) 26-46.

I. P. Warren, "The Inspiration of the Old Testament," *BS* 41 (1884) 310-326.

George N. Boardman, "Inspiration;—with Remarks on the Theory Presented in Ladd's Doctrine of Sacred Scripture," *BS* 41 (1884) 506-549.

G[eorge] H. S[chodde], "The Inspiration of Scripture," *ColTM* 4 (1884) 360-372.

John Healy, "Cardinal Newman on the Inspiration of Scripture," *IER, 3rd Ser.,* 5 (1884) 137-149.

Andrew Wallace, "The Inspiration of Scriptures. An Essay for Young Men," *ERG, 8th Ser.,* 3 (1884-85) 203-214, 233-246.

C. H. L. S[chuette], "Some Objections to the Doctrine of Inspiration Answered," *ColTM* 5 (1885) 321-340.

Geo. H. McKnight, "The Inspiration of the Bible. Article III.," *CR* 45 (1885) 531-539.

S. Crane, "Inspiration," *UQGR, N.S.,* 23 (1886) 389-399.

Charles Jerdan, "The Plenary Inspiration of Holy Scripture," *BFER* 36 (1887) 75-91.

George Davies, "Divine Inspiration of Scripture," *ERG, 9th Ser.,* 2 (1887) 30-33.

J. Coleman Adams, "Aspiration and Inspiration," *UQGR, N.S.,* 24 (1887) 40-49.

S. Crane, "Inspiration.   Part II," *UQGR, N.S.,* 24 (1887) 326-337.

Anonymous, "Mr. Horton on Inspiration," *CongRL* 2 (1888) 934-941. *(Review)*

John Cuthbert Hedley, "Can the Scriptures Err?" *DR, 3rd Ser.,* 20 (1888) 144-165. *[Original numbering as Volume 103]*

Anonymous, "Some Recent Views of Inspiration," *CongRL* 3 (1889) 333-348. *(Review)*

Henry A. Rogers, "Cave's 'The Inspiration of the Old Testament Inductively Considered'," *ONTS* 9 (1889) 264-278. *(Review)*

Robert Watts, "The Question of Inspiration," *TML* 1 (1889) 231-241.

Robert Watts, "The Question of Inspiration. Paper No. II," *TML* 2 (1889) 247-257.

Robert Watts, "Professor Memerie on Inspiration," *TML* 2 (1889) 398-410. *(Review)*

James W. Morris, "Inspiration," *PER* 3 (1889-90) 64-70.

Anonymous, "The Mechanism of Inspiration," *MR* 72 (1890) 746-756.

John D. Davis, E. Mix, James R. Boise, Thos. Scott Bacon, James Strong, Reuen Thomas, Lewis F. Stearns, "A 'Symposium' on Some Great Biblical Questions, Especially Inspiration," *ONTS* 11 (1890) 303-309.

[W.T.] Davison, "Inspiration and Biblical Criticism," *ET* 2 (1890-91) 173-178.

George H. Schodde, "The Sacred Scriptures," *LQ* 21 (1891) 465-495.

Benjamin B. Warfield, "The Present Problem of Inspiration," *HR* 21 (1891) 410-416.

H. C. Alexander, "The Doctrine of Inspiration Considered on Its Divine and Human Side," *PQ* 5 (1891) 190-208.

J. A. Quarles, "Inspiration," *PQ* 5 (1891) 332-349.

John Pym Carter, "The Inspiration of the Scriptures," *PQ* 5 (1891) 525-535.

M. Loy, "The Inspiration of the Holy Scripture," *ColTM* 11 (1891) 65-88, 129-151.

J. J. Lias, "The Nature and Limits of Inspiration. *I.—Theories of Inspiration,*" *TML* 5 (1891) 217-229.

J. J. Lias, "The Inspiration of the Scriptures. *II.—Doctrine of the Churches,*" *TML* 5 (1891) 343-352.

J. J. Lias, "The Inspiration of the Scriptures. *III.—Discussion of the Question,*" *TML* 5 (1891) 386-401.

*James H. Fairchild, "Authenticity and Inspiration of the Scriptures," *BS* 49 (1892) 1-29.

J. R. Purcell, "The Inspiration of Holy Scripture," *EN* 4 (1892) 193-201.

Charles S. Albert, "Theories of Inspiration," *LQ* 22 (1892) 87-97.

W. Rupp, "The Inspiration of the Bible," *RChR* 39 (1892) 34-63.

Talbot W. Chambers, "The Inspiration of the Scriptures," *RChR* 39 (1892) 437-460.

Martin R. Vincent, "The Personal Factor in Biblical Inspiration," *NW* 2 (1893) 103-121.

Benjamin B. Warfield, "The Real Problem of Inspiration," *PRR* 4 (1893) 177-221. [The Biblical Doctrine of Inspiration Clear; I. Modifications of the Biblical Doctrine Undermine the Authority of the Scriptures, Christ Versus the Apostles, Accommodation or Ignorance? Teaching Versus Opinion, Fact Versus Doctrine; II. Immense Weight of Evidence for the Biblical Doctrine; III. Immense Presumption Against Alleged Facts Contradictory of the Biblical Doctrine]

*H. C. Alexander, "The Doctrine of Inspiration as Affected by the Essential Relation Between Thought and Language," *PQ* 7 (1893) 157-186.

Benjamin B. Warfield, "The Bible Doctrine of Inspiration," *CT* 11 (1893-94) 163-181.

G. H. Mitchell, "Inspiration and the Old Testament," *CT* 11 (1893-94) 182-194.

J. J. Lampe, S. G. Law, H. G. Mitchell, W. W. McLane, "Inspiration Under Review," *CT* 11 (1893-94) 195-200.

Benjamin B. Warfield, "Dr. B. B. Warfield Replies to His Critics," *CT* 11 (1893-94) 215-219.

James G. Patterson, "Verbal Inspiration," *CT* 11 (1893-94) 356-369.

C. G. Montefiore, "A Note on Inspiration," *JQR* 6 (1893-94) 586-595.

Benjamin B. Warfield, "The Inspiration of the Bible," *BS* 51 (1894) 614-640.

Robert A. Webb, "The Testimony of God," *PQ* 8 (1894) 1-18.

W. Dieckhoff, "The Inspiration and Inerrancy of Scripture," *LCR* 13 (1894) 66-74.

Anonymous, "Modern Views of Inspiration," *LQHR* 82 (1894) 64-83. *(Review)*

Benjamin B. Warfield, "Prof. Henry Preserved Smith on Inspiration," *PRR* 5 (1894) 600-653.

Maurice G. Hansen, "Has the Theory of Plenary Inspiration Been Invalidated by the Latest Investigations of Biblical Criticism?" *RChR* 41 (1894) 171-195.

D. Van Horne, "Are there Different Degrees of Authority in the Different Parts of the Holy Scripture?" *RCM* 2 (1894-95) #2, 8-12.

*Frank Hugh Foster, "The Authority and Inspiration of the Scriptures," *BS* 52 (1895) 69-96, 232-258.

M. A. Willcox, "Theories of Inspiration," *BW* 5 (1895) 169-180.

*H. C. Hatcher, "The language and literature of the Old Testament," *CMR* 7 (1895) 20-29. [V. The inspiration is claimed for the Old Testament writings, pp. 28-29]

Joseph MacRory, "The Divine Authorship and Inspiration of the Bible," *IER, 3rd Ser.,* 16 (1895) 26-43.

Joseph MacRory, "The Nature and Extent of Inspiration," *IER, 3rd Ser.,* 16 (1895) 193-208.

James, Monroe, "The Divine Origin of the Religion of the Bible; or, How a Layman Thought Out His Evidences," *BS* 53 (1896) 205-230, 429-443.

John J. Young, "The Lutheran Church in Relation to the Inspiration of the Holy Scriptures," *LQ* 26 (1896) 153-170.

Charles A. Webster, "Inspiration," *CM, 3rd Ser.,* 14 (1897) 100-107.

J. C. Jacoby, "Inspiration of the Scriptures," *LQ* 27 (1897) 217-232.

Joseph A. Vance, "Inspiration," *PQ* 12 (1898) 491-509.

E. Fitch Burr, "Christus Probator," *HR* 38 (1899) 305-309.

*M. Coover, "Biblical Quotations in the New Testament and Their Relation to Inspiration," *LQ* 30 (1900) 315-325.

G[eorge] H. Schodde, "The Inspiration Argument," *ColTM* 21 (1901) 34-40.

George H. Schodde, "Theses on the Inspiration of the Scriptures, with Special Reference to Modern Doubts," *ColTM* 21 (1901) 321-339.

Milton S. Terry, "Biblical Inspiration Inductively Considered," *MQR, 3rd Ser.,* 28 (1902) 338-348.

Clarence K. Crawford, "The Inspiration of the Old Testament," *PQ* 17 (1903-04) 370-383.

E. E. Smith, "The Proof of Inspiration," *PQ* 17 (1903-04) 504-511.

J. P. Sheraton, "The Product of Inspiration—The Inspired Scriptures," *CFL, 3rd Ser.,* 1 (1904) 84-95.

W[illiam] R[alph] Inge, "The Mystical Element in the Bible," *LCR* 23 (1904) 266-279. *[OT Refs., pp. 266-269]*

Leander S. Keyser, "The Plenary Inspiration of the Bible," *LCR* 23 (1904) 471-488.

J. E. Godbey, "Inspiration," *MQR, 3rd Ser.,* 30 (1904) 326-332.

*Hector Hall, "Grounds for Maintaining the Integrity and Inspiration of the Scriptures," *CFL, 3rd Ser.,* 2 (1905) 179-189.

Luther T. Townsend, "'Inspiration of the Bible from the Orthodox Point of View'," *CFL, 3rd Ser.,* 2 (1905) 405-423.

Henry A. Poels, "History and Inspiration," *CUB* 11 (1905) 19-67, 152-194.

*C. H. W. Johns, "Assyriology and Inspiration," *ICMM* 1 (1905) 38-52, 125-132.

A. H. Keane, "The Moral Argument Against the Inspiration of the Old Testament," *HJ* 4 (1905-06) 147-162, 666.

Charles T. Ovenden, "'The Moral Argument Against the Inspiration of the Old Testament'," *HJ* 4 (1905-06) 430-432.

James F. Driscoll, "Recent Views on Biblical Inspiration. (I)," *NYR* 1 (1905-06) 81-88.

James F. Driscoll, "Recent Views on Biblical Inspiration. (II)," *NYR* 1 (1905-06) 198-205.

William H. Bates, "The Bible's Doctrine of Its Own Inspiration," *CFL, 3rd Ser.,* 4 (1906) 343-354.

*Henry A. Poels, "History and Inspiration. Saint Jerome," *CUB* 12 (1906) 182-218.

W. A. Jarrel, "The Bible Verbally Inspired," *BS* 64 (1907) 109-134.

Anonymous, "A Neglected Analogy," *BS* 64 (1907) 179-182.

W. A. Jarrel, "Extracts from 'The Bible Verbally Inspired'," *CFL, 3rd Ser.,* 7 (1907) 218-225.

[G. Frederick Wright], "A Neglected Analogy: Suggestion by Rev. Dr. Jarrel's Article," *CFL, 3rd Ser.,* 7 (1907) 225-227.

Richard Brook, "The Bible and Religion," *ICMM* 5 (1908-09) 296-305, 408-418.

*Herbert Pentin, "The Inspiration of the Apocrypha," *ICMM* 5 (1908-09) 310-315.

J. C. Ryle, "'Plenary Verbal Inspiration'," *CFL, 3rd Ser.,* 11 (1909) 82.

Gerald Birney Smith, "Testing the Doctrine of Inspiration," *BW* 36 (1910) 152-165.

G. Henslow, "The Scientific Meaning of Inspiration," *HR* 60 (1910) 25-28.

James Orr, William Newton Clark, and C. S. Beardslee, "The Scientific Meaning of Inspiration," *HR* 60 (1910) 261-264.

*J. F. Pollock, "The Inspiration and Interpretation of the Scriptures," *LQ* 40 (1910) 479-498.

Hugh Pope, "The Scholastic View of Inspiration," *ITQ* 6 (1911) 275-298.

*Charles Edward Smith, "The Wonders of Divine Inspiration in the First Chapter of the Bible," *CFL, 3rd Ser.,* 14 (1911-12) 12-15.

Caspar Wistar Hodge, "The Witness of the Holy Spirit to the Bible," *PTR* 11 (1913) 41-84.

T. Herbert Bindley, "What Ought We to Understand by the Inspiration of the Bible?" *ICMM* 10 (1913-14) 268-277.

*J. Agar Beet, "The Inspiration and Authority of the Bible," *LQHR* 126 (1916) 251-270.

Leander S. Keyser, "A Liberal Critic's View of Biblical Inspiration," *TZTM* 7 (1917) 365-378.

H. E. Wheeler, "The Inspiration of the Bible," *MQR, 3rd Ser.,* 44 (1918) 233-251.

H. C. Ackerman, "The Nature of Spirit and Its Bearing upon Inspiration," *BW* 53 (1919) 145-148.

Maurice Pryke, "The Danger of Biblical Infallibility," *MC* 10 (1920-21) 339-345.

L. T. Townsend, "Verbal Inspiration," *CFL, 3rd Ser.,* 28 (1922) 3-11.

Abbot Ford, "On Inspiration," *DownsR* 40 (1922) 78-88. *(Review)*

A. Ryland, "The Inspiration of Scripture," *ACQR* 48 (1923) 118-129.

W. B. Riley, "The Bible—Is it an Evolution or an Inspiration?" *CFL, 3rd Ser.,* 29 (1923) 274-280.

John A. Rice, "Why I Believe the Whole Bible as the Inspired Word of God," *MQR, 3rd Ser.,* 50 (1924) 247-256.

W. D. Schermerhorn, "The Inspiration of the Bible," *MR* 107 (1924) 711-722.

William Brenton Greene Jr., "The Inspiration of the Bible," *PTR* 22 (1924) 235-276.

I. D. Ylvisaker, "A Restatement of the Inspiration of the Bible," *TTM* 8 (1924-25) 291-304.

W. R. Henderson, "Verbal Inspiration," *CFL, 3rd Ser.,* 31 (1925) 26-33.

Alvah J. McClain, "The Inspiration of the Bible," *CFL, 3rd Ser.,* 31 (1925) 260-265.

W. H. T. Dau., "'The Pure, Clear Foundation of Israel'," *TM* 5 (1925) 1-8.

T. T. Page, "The Inspiration of the Bible," *CFL, 3rd Ser.,* 32 (1926) 39-40.

S. G. Woodrow, "The Present Inspiration of the Bible," *BQL* 3 (1926-27) 49-55.

Leonard Kendall, "The Plenary Inspiration of the Bible," *TTM* 11 (1927-28) 1-51.

J. Newton Parker, "Inspiration of the Scriptures," *CFL, 3rd Ser.,* 34 (1928) 137-148.

P. E. Kretzmann, "Modern Views about Inspiration—and the Truth of Scriptures," *PTR* 27 (1929) 227-244.

Francis L. Patton, "The Inspiration of the Bible," *USR* 41 (1929-30) 243-252.

*R. Birch Hoyle, "Philo on Inspiration," *BR* 15 (1930) 23-39.

Michael Mar Yosip, "Inspiration and Inerrancy," *USR* 42 (1930-31) 306-313.

E. E. Bigger, "Verbal Inspiration of the Scriptures," *USR* 43 (1931-32) 329-344.

J. E. Cousar Jr., "The Bible—Through Discovery or Through Inspiration?" *USR* 44 (1932-33) 352-363.

*Charles E. Raven, "Inspiration and Prophecy," *MC* 24 (1934-35) 385-396.

John Aberly, "The Bible—The Word of God," *LCQ* 8 (1935) 113-125.

*H. Wheeler Robinson, "Some Outstanding Old Testament Problems. II. Canonicity and Inspiration," *ET* 47 (1935-36) 119-123.

George Drach, "The Inspiration of the Sacred Scriptures," *LCQ* 9 (1936) 244-252.

Lewis Sperry Chafer, "Bibliology. II. Inspiration," *BS* 94 (1937) 389-409; 95 (1938) 7-21.

C. D. Matthews, "Ibn Taimiyya's Theory of Inspiration," *JBL* 56 (1937) xiii.

William H. Bates, "Inspiration," *CFL, 3rd Ser.,* 44 (1938) 27-35.

Hjalmar W. Johnson, "Some Thoughts on Inspiration," *JTALC* 4 (1939) #5, 11-40.

John Murray, "The Inspiration of the Scripture," *WTJ* 2 (1939-40) 73-104.

Victor J. Tengwald, "The Verbal Inspiration of the Bible," *AQ* 19 (1940) 125-129.

H. H. Rowley, "The Inspiration of the Old Testament," *CongQL* 18 (1940) 164-177.

Th. Engelder, "Verbal Inspiration—a Stumbling-Block to the Jews and Foolishness to the Greeks," *CTM* 12 (1941) 241-265, 340-362, 401-427, 481-510, 561-588, 801-827, 881-913; 13 (1942) 8-39, 161-183, 241-264, 414-441, 481-510, 561-590, 731-757, 811-833, 888-926.

H. S. Curr, "An Argument for the Verbal Inspiration of the Bible," *JTVI* 73 (1941) 29-37, 41 [Discussion and communications, pp. 37-40]

Carl O. Nelson, "The Inspiration of the Scriptures," *CovQ* 4 (1944) #3, 12-18.

P. E. Kretzmann, "The Christocentric Theory of Inspiration," *CTM* 15 (1944) 187-192.

*Carl Eberhard, "Geography of the Bible in Relation to Inspiration (A Conference Paper)," *CTM* 15 (1944) 736-747.

*Harry F. Baughman, "Jeremiah and the Word of the Lord," *LCQ* 18 (1945) 223-240.

William Young, "The Inspiration of Scripture in Reformation and in Barthian Theology," *WTJ* 8 (1945-46) 1-38.

F. F. Bruce, "What Do We Mean by Biblical Inspiration?" *JTVI* 78 (1946) 121-128, 136-138. (Discussion, pp. 128-136)

Joseph Haroutunian, "The Bible and the Word of God," *Interp* 1 (1947) 291-308.

Merrill F. Unger, "The Inspiration of the Old Testament," *BS* 107 (1950) 430-449.

*John A. O'Flynn, "'Humani Generis' and Sacred Scripture," *ITQ* 19 (1952) 25-32, 163-174.

K. Smyth, "The Inspiration of the Scriptures," *Scrip* 6 (1953-54) 67-75.

H. L. Ellison, "Some Thoughts on Inspiration," *EQ* 26 (1954) 210-217.

J. R. C. Perkin, "The Inspiration of the Bible," *BQL* 16 (1955-56) 220-227, 271-276.

F. W. Schwarz, "Verbal Inspiration," *RefmR* 3 (1955-56) 205-210.

W. J. Dalton, "St. Jerome on the Inspiration and Inerrancy of Scripture," *ACR* 33 (1956) 313-320.

Kenneth S. Kantzer, "The Importance of Inspiration," *JASA* 8 (1956) #4, 8-10.

Ralph M. Dornette, "The Inspiration of the Scriptures," *SR* 3 (1956-57) 1-9.

R. A. F. MacKenzie, "Some Problems in the Field of Inspiration," *CBQ* 20 (1958) 1-8.

*J. T. Forestell, "The Limitation of Inerrancy," *CBQ* 20 (1958) 9-18.

Francis J. Schroeder, "Pere Lagrange: Record and Teaching in Inspiration," *CBQ* 20 (1958) 206-217.

Warren Vanhetloo, "Various Evidences of Verbal Inspiration," *CCBQ* 1 (1958) #4, n.p.n.

Merrill F. Unger, "The Inspiration of the Old Testament," *CCBQ* 1 (1958) #4, n.p.n.

David Michael Stanley, "The Concept of Biblical Inspiration," *CTSP* 13 (1958) 65-89. (Discussion, pp. 89-95)

*T. Worden, "Inerrancy in the O.T. Teaching on Life After Death...." *Scrip* 10 (1958) 28-29.

Paul Auvray, "Scripture and tradition in the Hebrew community," *TD* 6 (1958) 31-32.

Karl Rahner, "The Inspiration of Scripture," *TD* 8 (1960) 8-12.

Richard P. C. Hanson, "The Inspiration of Holy Scripture," *ATR* 43 (1961) 145-152.

Eugene Heideman, "The Inspiration of the Bible," *RefR* 15 (1961-62) #1, 18-29.

D. J. B. Hawkins, "A Suggestion About Inspiration," *DownsR* 80 (1962) 197-202, 212-213. (Remarks by the Abbot of Downside, pp. 202-211)

Wilfrid Harrington, "The Inspiration of Scripture," *ITQ* 29 (1962) 3-24.

Gordon H. Clark, "Holy Scripture," *BETS* 6 (1963) 3-6.

Ralph Earle, "Further Thoughts on Biblical Inspiration," *BETS* 6 (1963) 7-17.

John Murray, "The Infallibility of Scripture," *BofT* #30 (1963) 8-13.

Edward J. Young, "The Only Approach to the Bible," *BofT* #31 (1963) 39-40.

J. T. Forestell, "'Hear, O Israel, the Word of the Lord!'" *BibT* #13 (1964) 838-844.

Edward J. Young, "The Bible and Rome," *BS* 121 (1964) 117-124.

Edward J. Young, "The Bible and Protestantism," *BS* 121 (1964) 236-242.

John A. Witmer, "The Biblical Evidence for the Verbal Plenary Inspiration of the Bible," *BS* 121 (1964) 243-252.

*Edward J. Young, "The Bible and Error," *BS* 121 (1964) 303-310.

Siegbert W. Becker, "The Verbal Inspiration of the Holy Scriptures," *WLQ* 61 (1964) 5-32, 81-106.

Roger Nicole, "The Inspiration of Scripture," *GR* 8 (1964-65) 93-109.

E. P. Kauffeld, "The Doctrine of the Verbal and Plenary Inspiration of Scripture," *LSQ* 5 (1964-65) #3, 2-22.

Paul R. Jackson, "The Lord of the Scriptures," *RefmR* 12 (1964-65) 143-147.

*Edward J. Young, "The Bible and History," *BS* 122 (1965) 16-22.

Joseph Blenkinsopp, "The Bible and the People.   Rethinking Biblical Inspiration," *CIR* 51 (1966) 40-46.

Joseph Blenkinsopp, "The Bible and the People.   Rethinking Biblical Inerrancy," *CIR* 51 (1966) 130-135.

*Robert Murray, "The Inspiration and Interpretation of Scripture," *HeyJ* 7 (1966) 428-434.

Kevin Condon, "Word and Logos.   Reflections on the Problem of Inspiration," *ITQ* 33 (1966) 114-132.

Millard J. Erickson, "A New Look at Various Aspects of Inspiration," *BSQ* 15 (1966-67) 16-26.

Stanley N. Gundry, "The Inspiration of Scripture," *RefmR* 14 (1966-67) 138-144.

John O'Flynn, "The Inspirations of the Scriptures," *IER, 5th Ser.,* 107 (1967) 362-373.

Lewis Foster, "The Issue of the Inspiration of Scripture," *SR* 14 (1968) 33-40.

§974 **5.4.2 Studies on the Doctrine of God [See also: Studies on Monolatry and Monotheism §420 ←]**

Joseph Cottle, "On the Being of God," *CongML* 15 (1832) 401-406.

(   ) Davies, "God Himself the Ultimate End of All Things," *PRev* 4 (1832) 94-115.

J. W. Ward, "The Authority of God," *BS* 2 (1844) 437-451.

W. P. A., "The Hebrew Ideas of God," *CE* 45 (1848) 27-48.

J. S. Maginnis, "Translations from Anselm, Proslogion, or an Allocution concerning the Existence of God," *BS* 8 (1851) 534-553.

J. S. Maginnis, "Proofs of the Existence of God. A Reply to Anselm, and Anselm's Rejoinder," *BS* 8 (1851) 699-715.

George Duffield, "The True God known only by Faith," *TLJ* 5 (1852-53) 79-94.

Daniel P. Noyes, "An Essay Towards a Demonstration of the Divine Existence," *BS* 13 (1856) 388-437.

J. R. Keiser, "The Incomprehensibility of God," *ER* 8 (1856-57) 153-171.

Enoch Pond, "God the Supreme Disposer, and a Moral Governor," *TLJ* 10 (1857-58) 624-635.

Anonymous, "The Fatherhood of God," *ERG, 2nd Ser.,* 1 (1858-59) 1-3.

J. Few Smith, "God seen in his Works," *ER* 11 (1859-60) 83-96.

*H. C., "Ancient Atheism and Superstition," *JSL, 4th Ser.,* 1 (1862) 24-55.

J. A. Dorner, "Dorner on the Immutability of God. On the Right Conception of the Dogmatic Idea of the Immutability of God, with special reference to the mutual relation between God's supra-historical and historical existence," *BFER* 12 (1863) 348-377. *[OT Refs., pp. 373-375] (Translated and Abridged from the German)*

Benjamin W. Dwight, "The Doctrine of God's Providence, in Itself, and Its Relations and Uses," *BS* 21 (1864) 584-634.

Enoch Pond, "God the Supreme Disposer and Moral Governor," *BS* 21 (1864) 838-855.

*Anonymous, "The Name, and the Idea, of God," *CE* 78 (1865) 198-206.

S. D. Simonds, "The Doctrine Concerning God," *MR* 47 (1865) 412-430.

S. Cobb, "The Infinity of God," *UQGR, N.S.,* 2 (1865) 28-35.

Anonymous, "The Idea of God; Its Origin, and Its Validity," *ERG, 3rd Ser.,* 4 (1865-66) 117-130.

Miles P. Squier, "The Being of God," *AThR, N.S.,* 4 (1866) 357-375.

*Tayler Lewis, "The Bible Idea of Truth, as Inseparable from the Divine Personality," *AThR, N.S.,* 4 (1866) 199-213.

Anonymous, "The Being and Character of God," *ERG, 4th Ser.,* 2 (1867-68) 215-223. *(Review)*

Charles B. Rice, "The Self-Existence of God," *CongR* 8 (1868) 222-230.

D. E. Snow, "God in the Old Testament," *CongQB* 12 (1870) 545-551.

A. M. Fairbairn, "The Idea of God: Its Genesis and Development," *ContR* 18 (1871) 416-442.

J. B. Dalgairns, "The Personality of God," *ContR* 24 (1874) 321-338.

M. P. L., "Morning Hours with the Bible. II. The God of the Prophets," *URRM* 1 (1874) 257-262.

*Francis Bowen, "The Idea of God in the Soul of Man," *BS* 33 (1876) 740-754.

George T. Ladd, "The Origin of the Conception of God," *BS* 24 (1877) 1-36.

J. H. McIlvaine, "Revelation and Science," *BS* 34 (1877) 259-283.

George T. Ladd, "The Difficulties of the Concept of God," *BS* 34 (1877) 593-631.

George T. Ladd, "The Concept of God as the Ground of Progress," *BS* 35 (1878) 619-655.

[J. A.] Dorner, "The Unchangeableness of God," *BS* 36 (1879) 28-60, 209-225. *(Trans. by D. W. Simon)*

[James(?)] Morison, "The Idea of God," *ERG, 7th Ser.,* 2 (1879-80) 114-119.

George T. Ladd, "History and the Concept of God," *BS* 37 (1880) 593-639.

E. V. Gerhart, "The Christian Doctrine of God," *BS* 37 (1880) 686-728.

J. Ming, "The Existence of God Demonstrated," *ACQR* 6 (1881) 92-111, 229-248, 643-667.

Charles F. Thwing, "The Fundamental Laws of Belief," *BS* 38 (1881) 303-316.

John J. Tigert, "God in History," *MQR, 2nd Ser.,* 3 (1881) 252-270.

B. N. Martin, "Recent Physical Theories in Their Bearing on the Theistic Argument," *JCP* 1 (1881-82) #4, Article #2, 1-30.

J. Ming, "The Existence of God Demonstrated. On What Grounds does the Atheist Deny the Existence of God? (Fourth and Concluding Article," *ACQR* 7 (1882) 223-244.

George P. Fisher, "The Arguments for the Being of God," *JCP* 2 (1882-83) 113-134.

Francis L. Patton, "The Genesis of the Idea of God," *JCP* 2 (1882-83) 283-307.

Joseph Agar Beet, "The Holiness of God," *Exp, 2nd Ser.,* 6 (1883) 147-159.

*R. V. Foster, "The Names and Doctrine of God," *ONTS* 3 (1883-84) 369-376.

H. J. Schuh, "Attributes of Divinity," *ColTM* 4 (1884) 305-309.

William T. Shedd, "The Ontological Argument for the Divine Existence," *PR* 5 (1884) 213-227.

*Edward L. Curtis, "The Advent of Jehovah," *PR* 6 (1885) 606-612.

Harriet M. Snell, "The Origin of the Concept of God. Part I," *UQGR, N.S.,* 22 (1885) 5-16.

Harriet M. Snell, "The Origin of the Concept of God. Part II," *UQGR, N.S.,* 22 (1885) 133-145.

S. R. Calthrop, "God," *URRM* 26 (1886) 481-497.

Anonymous, "The Immanence of God," *MQR, 3rd Ser.,* 1 (1886-87) 53-63.

S. W. Howland, "The Relation of God to His Universe," *BS* 44 (1887) 693-706.

Jas. M. Campbell, "God a Consuming Fire," *ERG, 9th Ser.,* 2 (1887) 137-144.

Charles S. Robinson, "Where was the Creator Before the Creation?" *HR* 13 (1887) 405-409.

*Hinckley G. Mitchell, "The Idea of God in Amos," *JBL* 7 (1887) Part 2, 33-42.

John W. Chadwick, "The Revelation of God," *URRM* 27 (1887) 489-507.

James Douglas, "The Divine Immanency," *BS* 45 (1888) 329-355, 487-505, 567-584; 46 (1889) 50-72; 48 (1891) 400-419.

Anonymous, "The Self-Revelation of God," *LQHR* 71 (1888-89) 67-90. *(Review)*

*R. Travers Hereford, "A Unitarian Minister's View of the Talmudic Doctrine of God," *JQR* 2 (1889-90) 454-464.

John S. Vaughan, "Thoughts of the Simplicity of God," *IER, 3rd Ser.,* 11 (1890) 686-699.

Anonymous, "God," *OC* 4 (1890-91) 2305-2306.

George T. Ladd, "The Biblical and the Philosophical Conception of God," *ONTS* 12 (1891) 20-27, 79-85, 148-154.

A. B. Curtis, "The Idea of God," *UQGR, N.S.,* 28 (1891) 152-162.

John W. Smith, "Man's Conception of God from an Historical Standpoint," *BW* 4 (1894) 338-348.

A. G. Voigt, "The Wrath of God," *LQ* 24 (1894) 506-516.

*Hamilton M. Bartlett, "Evolution and the Idea of God," *PER* 8 (1894-95) 563-570.

Jacob Cooper, "A Priori or Ontological Proof of the Existence of God," *PRR* 5 (1894) 592-599.

Adolph Moses, "The Reasons Why We Believe in God," *YCCAR* 6 (1895-96) 120-133.

Cornelius Walker, "Proofs of Divine Existence," *BS* 55 (1898) 459-484.

A. G., "Theology," *TQ* 2 (1898) 1-13, 129-141, 257-278, 385-397.

E. Caird, "St. Anselm's Argument for the Being of God," *JTS* 1 (1899-1900) 23-39.

Kerr D. Macmillan, "'God as Father in the Old Testament'," *CFL, N.S.,* 1 (1900) 54-55.

J[ohn] D. D[avis], "Editorial Notes," *CFL, N.S.,* 2 (1900) 65-67. [The Idea of God As Commonly Expressed by the Hebrews; The Plural Expressed God's Exaltation; The Plural Used by the Canaanites Before the Hebrew Occupation, The Plural Used Similarly In Other Words]

H. Osgood, "The Tender, Loving God of the Old Testament," *CFL, N.S.,* 2 (1900) 78-89.

J. A. Auarles, "The Idea of God of Biblical Origin," *CFL, N.S.,* 2 (1900) 106-112.

George Ricker Berry, "The Old Testament Teaching Concerning God," *AJT* 5 (1901) 254-278.

W. D. Kerswill, "Jehovah, the God of Redemption," *CFL, N.S.,* 5 (1902) 318-325.

W. McDonald, "God: Known or Unknown?" *IER, 4th Ser.,* 11 (1902) 328-339.

J. J. Lias, "Modifications in the Idea of God, Produced by Modern Thought and Scientific Discovery," *JTVI* 34 (1902) 42-64, 80-82. (Discussion, pp. 64-73) [Communications by Rev. Prof. Caldecott, pp. 73-75; W. F. Kimm, pp. 75-76; J. Logan Lobley, pp. 76-77; L. G. Bomford, pp. 77-80]

W. H. Freemantle, "The Witness of the Old Testament to the Immanence of God," *OSHTP* (1903-04) 39-41.

William H. Hodge, "The Infinite, Contradictory and Faith," *PTR* 2 (1904) 592-598. *[Arguments for Man's capability to know God]*

A. B. Sharpe, "The Morality of the Creator," *DR* 136 (1905) 146-167.

Robert C. Cockerill, "Definition of God," *Monist* 15 (1905) 637-638.

D. Barry, "The Witness of Conscience to the Existence of God," *ACQR* 31 (1906) 331-342.

*Grey Hubert Skipwith, "The Lord of Heaven (The Fire of God; The Mountain Summit; The Divine Chariot; and The Vision of Ezekiel)," *JQR* 19 (1906-07) 688-703.

M. E. Welch, "'Scientific Criticism Can not Discover God in the Old Testament'," *CFL, 3rd Ser.,* 6 (1907) 414-416.

Samuel Z. Beam, "The Old Testament Conception of God," *RChR, 4th Ser.,* 11 (1907) 519-533.

Arthur C. McGiffert, "Modern Ideas of God," *HTR* 1 (1908) 10-27.

William Hayes Ward, "A Fragment of the Cosmological Argument," *AJT* 13 (1909) 229-237.

D. Gath Whitley, "The Scientific Foundations of Belief in God," *BS* 66 (1909) 606-638.

J. H. Levy, "The God of Israel," *WR* 171 (1909) 16-29.

*Thomas W. Galloway, "Does Evolutionary Philosophy Offer Any Argument for the Reality of God?" *HTR* 3 (1910) 500-510.

Edouard Montet, "Thought on the Idea of a First Cause," *AJT* 15 (1911) 238-249.

John Bascom, "Basis of Theism," *BS* 68 (1911) 132-153.

Edward P. Gardner, "Nature and the Supernatural as Together Constituting the One System of God," *BS* 68 (1911) 584-599.

J. C. Quinn, "The Silence of Holy Scripture a Proof of Its Inspiration," *CFL, 3rd Ser.,* 14 (1911-12) 145-146.

*Henry A. Stimson, "The Development of the Doctrine of God and Man," *BS* 70 (1913) 193-201.

*A. Noordtzij, "The Old Testament Revelation of God and the Ancient-Oriental Life," *BS* 70 (1913) 622-652. *(Trans. by John H. deVries)*

Ferrand E. Corley, "The Poverty of God," *LQHR* 120 (1913) 284-305.

W. Watson, "The Fear of God," *ET* 25 (1913-14) 234-235.

*Eduard König, "The Idea of God in Babylonia and in Israel," *HR* 68 (1914) 3-7.

Maurice Henry Fitzgerald Collis, "The Argument from Design," *ICQ* 7 (1914) 300-315.

*John S. Banks, "The Idea of God in Israel and Babylon," *LQHR* 122 (1914) 129-131.

James Mudge, "To What Extent Does God Reign?" *BS* 72 (1915) 446-463.

Andrew C. Zenos, "Apocryphal Literature and Bible Study. II. God, Sin, and Salvation," *HR* 69 (1915) 22-23.

*G. H. Box, "The Doctrine of God in the Jewish Apocryphal and Apocalyptic Literature," *IJA* #41 (1915) 37-39. *(Review)*

George H. Schodde, "The God of Moses a Revelation," *TZTM* 5 (1915) 569-575.

*J. M. Powis Smith, "The Effect of the Disruption of the Hebrew Thought of God," *AJSL* 32 (1915-16) 261-269.

Richard Brook, "The Passivity of God," *ICMM* 12 (1915-16) 41-54.

G. A. Frank Knight, "A New Setting for the Teleological Argument," *ET* 29 (1917-18) 66-70.

Leander S. Keyser, "The Jehovah of Israel. Was He the Universal God or Only a National God?" *BR* 3 (1918) 352-374.

David Foster Estes, "The Divine Immanence," *BS* 75 (1918) 399-428.

L. Franklin Gruber, "The Theory of a Finite and Developing Deity Examined," *BS* 75 (1918) 475-526.

H. J. R. Marston, "The Reserved Rights of God," *JTVI* 50 (1918) 74-81.

F. R. Tennant, "Moral Arguments for the Existence of God," *ET* 30 (1918-19) 358-360.

Frank Hugh Foster and L. Franklin Gruber, "The Theory of a Finite and Developing Deity," *BS* 76 (1919) 125-132.

*Anonymous, "Job's Conception of God," *CFL, 3rd Ser.,* 25 (1919) 289.

J. Dick Fleming, "Belief in God and Its Rational Basis," *ET* 31 (1919-20) 535-539.

*Leslie J. Walker, "Time, Eternity and God," *HJ* 18 (1919-20) 36-48.

Edward Scribner Ames, "The Validity of the Idea of God," *JR* 1 (1921) 462-481.

John Edwards LeBosquet, "The Unconventional God," *JR* 1 (1921) 578-591.

*T. Nicklin, "The Angel of God, or God the King?" *ET* 33 (1921-22) 378-379.

William Phillips Hall, "The God who Created Heaven and Earth," *CFL, 3rd Ser.,* 28 (1922) 15-16.

*Leander S. Keyser, "I Believe in God and Creation," *CFL, 3rd Ser.,* 28 (1922) 357-362.

J. Scott Lidgett, "The Sovereignty of God," *ContR* 122 (1922) 707-715.

Eugene W. Lyman, "The Rationality of Belief in the Reality of God," *JR* 2 (1922) 449-465.

*Edmond G. A. Holmes, "The Idea of Evolution and the Idea of God," *HJ* 21 (1922-23) 227-247.

*N. H. Williams, "'The Idea of Evolution and the Idea of God'," *HJ* 21 (1922-23) 386-388.

Bowyer M. Stewart, "The Definition of God," *HTR* 16 (1923) 259-266.

A. Eustance Haydon, "The Quest of God," *JR* 3 (1923) 590-597.

Walter M. Horton, "Reasons for Believing in God," *JR* 3 (1923) 598-615.

Hugo Gressman, "The Development of the Idea of God in the Old Testament," *MR* 106 (1923) 924-936.

Dudley Wright, "The Mysteries of Merkabah," *OC* 37 (1923) 402-407. *[The Chariot-Throne of Yahweh]*

George A. Barrow, "The God of Realism," *ATR* 6 (1923-24) 1-13.

H. D. A. Major, "The Self-Limitation of God," *ICMM* 20 (1923-24) 35-41.

*Samuel Nirenstein, "The Problem of the Existence of God in Maimonides, Alanus and Averroes: A Study in the Religious Philosophy of the Twelfth Century," *JQR, N.S.* 14 (1923-24) 395-454.

*James H. Grier, "Israel's Vision of God," *BS* 81 (1924) 116-125.

*A. Marmorstein, "The Unity of God in Rabbinic Literature," *HUCA* 1 (1924) 467-502.

*Harry A. Wolfson, "Notes on Proofs of the Existence of God in Jewish Philosophy," *HUCA* 1 (1924) 575-596.

John Wright Buckham, "Professor Howison's Idea of God. A Criticism and Reply," *JR* 4 (1924) 411-412.

Clarence A. Beckwith, "Professor Howison's Idea of God. A Criticism and a Reply," *JR* 4 (1924) 412-413.

Henry Nelson Wieman, "How Do We Know God?" *JR* 5 (1925) 113-129.

F. M. Bennett, "The Personal God," *Person* 6 (1925) 114-120.

Clement C. J. Webb, "Recent Thought on the Doctrine of God," *ET* 37 (1925-26) 359-366.

*F. Herbert Stead, "The Idea of God in the Psalms. I.," *ET* 37 (1925-26) 547-551.

D. M. M'Intyre, "The Silence of God: How is it to be Explained," *JTVI* 58 (1926) 258-273, 287. (Discussion, pp. 273-282) [Communications by F. C. Wood, pp. 282-284; Sydney T. Klein, pp. 284-285; Theodore Roberts, pp. 285-286; William Hoste, pp. 286-287]

*F. Herbert Stead, "The Idea of God in the Psalms. II.," *ET* 38 (1926-27) 18-20.

E. O. James, "The idea of God in Early Religions," *Antho* 22 (1927) 793-802.

Walter Marshall Horton, "The Objective Element in the Experience of God," *JR* 7 (1927) 540-560.

*T. O. Rorie, "Isaiah's Conception of God," *MQR, 3rd Ser.,* 53 (1927) 130-132.

*M[oses] Marcus, "Space and Time in Relation to the Existence of God According to the Talmud," *JIQ* 4 (1927-28) #1, 7-9.

*A. L. Williams, "The Old Rabbinic Doctrine of God," *JTS* 29 (1927-28) 440-441. *(Review)*

Leonard Hodgson, "Compromise, Tension, and Personality," *ATR* 11 (1928-29) 233-241.

J. E. Boodin, "God," *HJ* 27 (1928-29) 577-594.

Bernard Bamberger, "Fear and Love of God in the Old Testament," *HUCA* 6 (1929) 39-53.

[Ralph Tyler Flewelling], "Highbrowing God," *Person* 10 (1929) 5-11.

C. Van Til, "God and the Absolute," *EQ* 2 (1930) 358-388.

Barnet R. Brickner, "The God-Idea in the Light of Modern Thought and Its Pedagogic Implications," *YCCAR* 40 (1930) 304-322. *[Table of Contents Title:* "Teaching the God Concept in the Light of the New Knowledge of Our Day"]

Shailer Mathews, "Social Patterns and the Idea of God," *JR* 11 (1931) 159-178.

G. H. Langley "Knowledge of God," *Monist* 41 (1931) 339-351.

Alfred E. Garvie, "The Problem of God," *ET* 43 (1931-32) 41-42. *(Review)*

*Fleming James, "Was There Monotheism in Israel Before Amos?" *ATR* 14 (1932) 130-142.

H. J., "Does God Develop?" *HJ* 31 (1932-33) 384-389.

A. E. Silverstone, "God as King," *JMUEOS* #17 (1932) 47-51.

J. M. Powis Smith, "The Growth of the Hebrew Idea of God," *JR* 12 (1932) 24-39.

Arthur C. Wickenden, "The Effect of the College Experience upon Student's Concepts of God," *JR* 12 (1932) 242-267.

Edgar Sheffield Brightman, "A Temporalist View of God," *JR* 12 (1932) 544-555.

Harold H. Titus, "A Neo-Realist's Idea of God," *JR* 13 (1933) 127-138.

W. A. Irwin, "An Examination of the Progress of Thought in the Dialogue of Job," *JR* 13 (1933) 150-164.

Barnard Heller, "The Concept of God in Jewish Literature and Life," *YCCAR* 43 (1933) 242-289. [Discussion by: [Samuel] Schulman, pp. 289-290; [David] Philipson, p. 290; [Emanuel] Gamoran, p. 290; [Theodore] Lewis, pp. 290-291; [Samuel Sale] p. 291; [Morton M.] Berman, p. 291; [Abraham J.] Feldman, p. 291; [Leon] Fram, pp. 291-292; [Mauris] Ranson, p. 292; [Efraim] Rosenzweig, pp. 292-293; [Samuel] Goldenson, p. 293]

Arthur C. Headlam, "The Doctrine of God," *CQR* 118 (1934) 1-22, 163-187.

Andrew Banning, "Professor Brightman's Theory of a Limited God. A Criticism," *HTR* 27 (1934) 145-168.

Harold L. Creager, "The Jealous God," *LCQ* 7 (1934) 271-282.

Samuel S. Cohon, "The Idea of God in Judaism," *YCCAR* 45 (1935) 207-228.

*Felix A. Levy, "God and Reform Judaism," *YCCAR* 45 (1935) 229-245.

William Fulton, "Divine Personality," *ET* 47 (1935-36) 199-203.

E. O. James, "Some Outstanding Old Testament Problems. III. The Development of the Idea of God in the Old Testament," *ET* 47 (1935-36) 150-154.

Wilhelm Schmidt, "The Origin of the Idea of God," *USR* 47 (1935-36) 116-126.

*James Bissett Pratt, "God and the Moral Law," *HTR* 29 (1936) 153-170.

*E. Bikerman, "Anonymous Gods," *JWCI* 1 (1937-38) 187-196. [4. The Anonymous God of the Jews, pp. 195-196]

*Lewis Sperry Chafer, "Theology Proper," *BS* 95 (1938) 260-290.

*Lewis Sperry Chafer, "Biblical Theism," *BS* 95 (1938) 390-416.

*Edward J. Young, "The God of Horeb," *EQ* 10 (1938) 10-29.

Peter A. Bertocci, "An Empirical Critique for the Moral Argument of God," *JR* 18 (1938) 275-288.

L. H. Brockington, "The Voice of God," *BQL* 9 (1938-39) 102-108.

L. H. Brockington, "The 'Face of God' in the Old Testament," *ET* 50 (1938-39) 557-560.

*Lewis Sperry Chafer, "Biblical Theism," *BS* 96 (1939) 5-37, 138-163, 264-284, 390-404.

C. D. Broad, "Arguments for the Existence of God," *JTS* 40 (1939) 16-30, 156-167.

James Wood, "The Living God in the Old Testament," *ET* 51 (1939-40) 548-550.

Alfred E. Garvie, "Is God Impersonal, Personal, or Supra-Personal?" *RR* 4 (1939-40) 17-22.

*H. P. Hamann, "The Evolutionistic Error with Regard to the God of Israel," *AusTR* 11 (1940) 42-48, 65-70.

Edward J. Young, "The God of the Fathers," *WTJ* 3 (1940-41) 25-40.

*H. P. Hamann, "The Appearance of God in the Old Testament, and The Angel of the Lord," *AusTR* 12 (1941) 97-108; 13 (1942) 9-12.

Paul Weiss, "Sources of the Idea of God," *JR* 22 (1942) 156-172.

G. Parrinder, "A Reasoned Approach to Religion," *ET* 54 (1942-43) 124-127. [I. Creative Mind; II. Personality in God]

Stephen J. Brown, "Theology and the Study of God," *IER, 5th Ser.,* 62 (1943) 295-305, 374-382.

*Julian Morgenstern, "Deutero-Isaiah's Terminology for 'Universal God'," *JBL* 62 (1943) 269-280.

Henry Nelson Wieman, "Can God be Perceived?" *JR* 23 (1943) 23-32.

*Peter C. Young, "Has Man Made God in His Own Image?" *ET* 55 (1943-44) 105-108.

*H. Wheeler Robinson, "The Council of Yahweh," *JTS* 45 (1944) 151-157.

*W. Norman Pittenger, "God and the World: Their Relationship as Seen in Jewish Prophecy," *ATR* 29 (1947) 57-61.

G. Ernest Wright, "The God of Biblical Faith," *McQ* 1 (1947-48) #3, 7-10.

*Joseph L. Mihelic, "The Concept of God in the Book of Nahum," *Interp* 2 (1948) 199-207.

*John Newton Thomas, "'What is Man?' The Biblical Doctrine of the Image of God," *Interp* 3 (1949) 154-163.

*H. H. Rowley, "Living Issues in Biblical Scholarship. The Antiquity of Israelite Monotheism," *ET* 61 (1949-50) 333-338.

Laurence J. Lafleur, "If God Were Eternal," *JR* 20 (1940) 382-389.

Herbert Gordon May, "The Patriarchal Idea of God," *JBL* 60 (1941) 113-128.

Edward Scribner Ames, "New Trends in Thinking About God," *JR* 21 (1941) 373-384.

E. L. Mascall, "Professor Broad and the Cosmological Argument," *JTS* 43 (1942) 200-204.

J. Philip Hyatt, "The Old Testament Idea of God and Its Modern Relevance," *RL* 11 (1942) 350-358.

*John Derby, "God and History," *Theo* 44 (1942) 24-31.

William H. Bernhardt, "The Cognitive Quest For God," *JR* 23 (1943) 91-102.

William H. Bernhardt, "God As Dynamic Determinant," *JR* 23 (1943) 276-285.

Peter C. Young, "Has Man Made God in His Own Image?" *ET* 55 (1943-44) 105-108.

Charles A. Hartshorne, "A Mathematical Analysis of Theism," *RR* 8 (1943-44) 14-19.

C. H. Kaiser, "The Formal Fallacy of the Cosmological Argument," *JR* 24 (1944) 155-161.

Edwin Lewis, "The Question Concerning God," *TT* 1 (1944-45) 441-454.

M. Aloysia, "The God of Wrath?" *CBQ* 8 (1946) 407-415.

*L. H. Brockington, "The Hebrew Conception of Personality in Relation to the Knowledge of God," *JTS* 47 (1946) 1-11.

John Baillie, "Why I Believe in God," *USQR* 3 (1947-48) #3, 3-6.

William A. Christian, "God and the World," *JR* 28 (1948) 255-262.

*L. H. Brockington, "Audition in the Old Testament," *JTS* 49 (1948) 1-8. *[God's communication with man]*

*John Newton Thomas, "'What is Man?' The Biblical Doctrine of the Image of God," *Interp* 3 (1949) 154-163.

O. Herrlin, "Philosophy and the Foundation of Belief in God," *ST* 2 (1949-50) 103-109.

Fredrich Horst, "Face to Face. *The Biblical Doctrine of the Image of God,*" *Interp* 4 (1950) 259-270. *(Trans. by John Bright)*

*Samuel Sandmel, "Abraham's Knowledge of the Existence of God," *HTR* 44 (1951) 137-139.

Huston Smith, "The Operational View of God: A Study in the Impact of Metaphysics on Religious Thought," *JR* 31 (1951) 94-113.

George W. Frey Jr., "Some Aspects of the Hebrew Idea of God," *UTSB* 26 (1951-52) #1, 2-8.

John L. McKenzie, "God and Nature in the Old Testament," *CBQ* 14 (1952) 18-39, 124-145.

D. J. B. Hawkins, "What do the Proofs of the Existence of God purport to do?" *ClR* 37 (1952) 321-332.

H. Cunliffe-Jones, "Central Perspective. *The Bible is a Book about God,*" *Interp* 6 (1952) 27-38.

Jacob B. Agus, "The Idea of God," *Jud* 1 (1952) 203-217.

*Jacob Kohn, "God and the Reality of Evil," *Person* 33 (1952) 117-130.

*F[rank] M[oore] Cross Jr., "The Council of Yahweh in Second Isaiah," *JBL* 71 (1952) xi.

*Frank M[oore] Cross Jr., "The Council of Yahweh in Second Isaiah," *JNES* 12 (1953) 274-277.

F. B. Julian, "The Maleness of God," *HJ* 52 (1953-54) 343-348. [O.T. related studies, pp. 344-345]

Abraham J. Heschel, "The Divine Pathos. *The Basic Category of Prophetic Theology,*" *Jud* 2 (1953) 61-67.

August Brunner, "The Jealous God," *TD* 1 (1953) 147-150.

Alastair McKinnon, "God, Humanity and Sexual Polarity," *HJ* 52 (1953-54) 337-342. [O.T. related studies, pp. 339-341]

E. W. Price Evans, "But God Only is Great," *ET* 66 (1954-55) 125.

R. J. Zwi Werblowsky, "The Male God and the God of Males," *HJ* 53 (1954-55) 334-342.

Geddes MacGregor, "Does Scripture Limit the Power of God?" *HJ* 53 (1954-55) 382-386.

*Sheldon H. Blank, "'Doest Thou Well to be Angry?' A Study in Self-Pity," *HUCA* 26 (1955) 29-41.

*Samuel S. Cohon, "The Unity of God. A Study in Hellenistic and Rabbinic Theology," *HUCA* 26 (1955) 425-479.

R[obert] H. Pfeiffer, "The Fear of God," *IEJ* 5 (1955) 41-48.

*Michael Leahy, "The Popular Idea of God in Amos," *ITQ* 22 (1955) 68-73.

David S. Shapiro, "The Existence of God," *Jud* 4 (1955) 333-338.

Ted R. Clark, "The Doctrine of a Finite God," *R&E* 52 (1955) 21-43.

A. W. Pink, "'The Godhood of God'," *BofT* 1 (1955-59) #10, 24-26.

Edward Burnley, "The Impassibility of God," *ET* 67 (1955-56) 90-91.

John F. Gates, "The Ontological Witness," *GR* 2 (1956) 54-60.

*P. Ronflette, "Biological finality and God's existence," *TD* 4 (1956) 13-16.

J. Gray, "The Hebrew conception of the Kingship of God," *VT* 6 (1956) 268-285.

Norman H. Snaith, "Expository Problems. God: Transcendent and Immanent," *ET* 68 (1956-57) 68-71.

*William Connoly, "God and History in the Old Testament," *MH* 12 (1956-56) #1, 11-18.

Samuel K. Mikolaski, "Some Reflections on the Christian Doctrine of God," *EQ* 29 (1957) 85-93.

E. L. Allen, "God Hidden and God Revealed," *PQL* 3 (1957) 139-149.

Eugene B. Borowitz, "The Idea of God," *YCCAR* 67 (1957) 174-186.

William Bowman Piper, "Berkeley's Demonstration of God," *HTR* 51 (1958) 275-287.

Frank B. Dilley, "Is There 'Knowledge' of God?" *JR* 38 (1958) 116-126.

*B. Gemser, "God in Genesis," *OTS* 12 (1958) 1-21.

John D. W. Watts, "The Knowledge of God in the Old Testament," *R&E* 55 (1958) 155-164.

Pieter De Jong, "The Doctrine of God," *CJT* 5 (1959) 242-250.

*J. Benjamin Bedenbaugh, "The Doctrine of God in Deutero-Isaiah," *LQ*, *N.S.*, 11 (1959) 154-158.

Frederick Ferre, "Is Language About God Fraudulent?" *SJT* 12 (1959) 337-360.

Wallace Gray, "Is God Supernatural?" *HJ* 58 (1959-60) 347-349.

*H. A. Wolfson, "The Philonic God of Revelation and His Latter-day Deniers," *HTR* 53 (1960) 101-124.

*Joseph H. Golner, "God, Satan and Atonement," *Jud* 9 (1960) 299-306.

John L. McKenzie, "Vengeance is Mine," *Scrip* 12 (1960) 33-39. *[The anger of God]*

*W. Peter Boyd, "The Mystery of God and Revelation," *SJT* 13 (1960) 178-182.

*James A. Wharton, "'Smitten of God...' A Theological Investigation of the Enemies of Yahweh in the Old Testament," *ASBFE* 86 (1960-61) #1, 3-36.

*Sam M. Hamilton, "Natural Theology and the Ontological Argument. Part I," *SR* 7 (1960-61) #2, 1-46.

*Sam M. Hamilton, "Natural Theology and the Ontological Argument. Part II," *SR* 7 (1960-61) #3, 47-88.

Frederick Holmgren, "The Concept of God as Redeemer in the Old Testament," *CovQ* 19 (1961) #2, 9-18.

Martin J. Buss, "The Language of the Divine 'I'," *JAAR* 29 (1961) 102-107.

Paul L. Brown, "Is God a Person or Personal Being?" *Person* 42 (1961) 320-336.

Paul J. W. Miller, "The Ontological Argument for God," *Person* 42 (1961) 337-351.

Alex. Jones, "God's Choice: Its Nature and Consequences," *Scrip* 13 (1961) 35-43.

J. Gray, "The Kingship of God in the Prophets and Psalms," *VT* 11 (1961) 1-29.

Bernard Heller, "The Reality of God," *CCARJ* 9 (1961-62) #1, 16-17, 44.

Charles Hartshorne, "What did Anselm Discover?" *USQR* 17 (1961-62) 213-222. *[Ontological Proof of God]*

J. MacDonald Smith, "Can Science Prove that God Exists?" *HeyJ* 3 (1962) 126-138.

Robert T. Fauth, "The Image of God," *T&L* 5 (1962) 267-272.

J. C. Murray, "On the Structure of the Problem of God," *ThSt* 23 (1962) 1-26. *[OT Refs., pp. 2-5]*

*E. C. B. MacLaurin, "The Development of the Idea of God in Ancient Canaan," *JRelH* 2 (1962-63) 277-294.

Cyril C. Richardson, "The Strange Fascination of the Ontological Argument," *USQR* 18 (1962-63) 1-21.

*Claus Westermann, "God and His Creation," *USQR* 18 (1962-63) 197-209.

Charles Hartshorne, "Further Fascination of the Ontological Argument," *USQR* 18 (1962-63) 244-245.

Jovan Brkić, "Further Fascination of the Ontological Argument," *USQR* 18 (1962-63) 246-249.

W. Richard Comstock, "Further Fascination of the Ontological Argument," *USQR* 18 (1962-63) 250-255.

J. A. Sanders, "God is God," *Found* 6 (1963) 343-361.

*Martin P. Nilsson, "The High God and the Mediator," *HTR* 56 (1963) 101-120.

Elwyn A. Smith, "The Historicity of God," *JR* 43 (1963) 20-34.

Mary Edith Runyan, "The Relationship Between Ontological and Cosmological Arguments," *JR* 43 (1963) 56-58.

*Henry Cohen, "The Idea of God in Jewish Education," *Jud* 12 (1963) 165-178.

*J. Prescott Johnson, "The Ontological Argument in Plato," *Person* 44 (1963) 24-34.

*Shemuel Yeiven, "The Age of the Patriarchs," *RDSO* 38 (1963) 277-302. [II. - *The God of Abraham*, pp. 285-290]

A. W. Argyle, "God's 'Repentance' and the LXX," *ET* 75 (1963-64) 367.

George I. Mavrodes, "God and Verification," *CJT* 10 (1964) 187-191.

Jeanette C. Stevenson, "Contemporary Views on the Doctrine of God," *CJT* 10 (1964) 237-246.

Heywood J. Thomas, "The Transcendence of God," *LQHR* 189 (1964) 184-189.

*Lester J. Kuyper, "Grace and Truth. *An Old Testament Description of God, and its Use in the Johannine Gospel,*" *Interp* 18 (1964) 3-19.

*Edwin C. Kingsbury, "The Prophets and the Council of Yahweh," *JBL* 83 (1964) 279-286.

Anthony Hanson, "Symbolism and the Doctrine of God," *LQHR* 189 (1964) 178-183.

G. T. Manley, "The God of Abraham," *TB* #14 (1964) 3-7.

Bruce Vawter, "The Ways of God," *Way* 4 (1964) 167-175.

*C. J. Labuschagne, "Amos' conception of God and the popular theology of his time," *OTW* 7&8 (1964-65) 122-133.

Lester J. Kuyper, "The Repentance of God," *RefR* 18 (1964-65) #4, 3-16.

Charles Hartshorne, "The Theistic Proofs," *USQR* 20 (1964-65) 115-129.

Charles Hartshorne, "Abstract and Concrete Approaches to Deity," *USQR* 20 (1964-65) 265-270.

Leonard Hodgson, "The Word 'God'," *CJT* 11 (1965) 83-92.

H. C. McDonald, "Monopolar Theism and the Ontological Argument," *HTR* 58 (1965) 387-416.

Charles G. Werner, "The Ontological Argument for the Existence of God," *Person* 46 (1965) 269-283.

J. E. Fishon, "God," *PQL* 2 (1965) 310-316.

David Polish, "The God of Nature and the God of Existence," *CCARJ* 13 (1965-66) #3, 4-12.

R. G. Crawford, "The Image of God," *ET* 77 (1965-66) 233-236.

*Joseph L. Mihelic, "The Concept of God in Deutero-Isaiah," *BRes* 11 (1966) 29-41.

Gordon D. Kaufman, "On the Meaning of 'God': Transcendence without Mythology," *HTR* 59 (1966) 105-132.

J. Brenton Sterns, "On the Impossibility of God's Knowing That He Does Not Exist," *JR* 46 (1966) 1-8.

*Walter Gerhardt Jr., "The Hebrew/Israelite Weather-Deity," *Numen* 13 (1966) 128-143.

Bruce Vawter, "The God of Israel," *Way* 6 (1966) 5-14.

*A. Capell, "God is the Plaintiff," *Coll* 2 (1966-68) 195-203.

*F. H. Cleobury, "God, Creation and Evolution," *MC, N.S.,* 10 (1966-67) 7-18.

J. Murtagh, "'Under the Shadow of thy Wings'," *BibT* #32 (1967) 2229-2232.

Leslie Zeigler, "The Problem of God," *ABBTS* 42 (1967) #4, 1-11.

Edwin C. Kingsbury, "The Theophany of *Topos* and the Mountain of God," *JBL* 86 (1967) 205-210.

Mordecai M. Kaplan, "The Evolution of the Idea of God in Jewish Religion," *JQR, 75th* (1967) 332-346.

Norbert Samuelson, "On Proving God's Existence: I," *Jud* 16 (1967) 21-36.

Monford Harris, "On Proving God's Existence: II," *Jud* 16 (1967) 37-41.

*André [A.] Neher, "A Reflection on the Silence of God. 'I Will Not Be Inquired of by You' (*Ezekiel* 20:3)," *Jud* 16 (1967) 434-442. *(Trans. by Minnette Grunmann)*

John G. Levack, "The Private Life of God," *SJT* 20 (1967) 272-281.

Dennis J. McCarthy, "A Great and Terrible God," *Way* 7 (1967) 259-269.

*Samuel Amirtham, "To be near to and far away from Yahweh: The Witness of the individual psalms of lament to the concept of the presence of God," *BTF* 2 (1968) #2, 31-55.

Samuel Atlas, "Man And The Ethical Idea of God," *CCARJ* 15 (1968) #1, 40-53.

Robert C. Neville, "Can God Create Men and Address Them Too?" *HTR* 61 (1968) 603-623.

Donald M. Mackay, "The Sovereignty of God in the Natural World," *SJT* 21 (1968) 13-26.

James   Quinn,   "The   Living   God,"   *Way*   8   (1968)   87-96.

John   L.   McKenzie,   "No   Idle   God,"   *Way*   8   (1968)   171-180.

*James Barr, "The Image of God in the Book of Genesis—A Study in Terminology," *BJRL* 51 (1968-69) 11-26.

J. O. Rymer, "The Problem of the Mystery of God," *Coll* 3 (1968-70) 11-22.

John [H.] Williamson, "The Transcendence of God," *Coll* 3 (1968-70) 23-36.

Herbert Bronstein, "Yahveh as Father in Hebrew Scripture," *Crit* 8 (1968-69) #1, 8-11.

*Albert Plotkin, "The Nature of God According to Jeremiah," *CCARJ* 16 (1969) #1, 21-31.

James Wm. McClendon Jr., "Can There be Talk About God-and-the-World?" *HTR* 62 (1969) 33-49.

Michael McLain, "On Theological Models," *HTR* 62 (1969) 155-187.

A. S. Hebert, "The Sovereignty of God in a Changing World," *Orita* 3 (1969) 93-99.

Bernhard Erling, "Motif Research Analysis and the Existence and Nature of God," *PP* 10 (1969) 155-167.

Lester J. Kuyper, "The Suffering and the Repentance of God," *SJT* 22 (1969) 257-277. [The Suffering of God; The Repentance and Non-Repentance of God; History of Interpretation; Questions on God's Repentance]

M. Treves, "The Reign of God in the Old Testament," *VT* 19 (1969) 230-243.

John L. McKenzie, "The Newness of God," *Way* 9 (1969) 267-277.

*Fritz A. Rothschild, "The Concept of God in Jewish Education," *CJ* 24 (1969-70) #2, 2-20.

§975 **5.4.2.1 *Studies on Creation / Cosmogony***

†Anonymous, "The Scripture Theory of the Earth," *BCQTR* 14 (1799) 113-115. *(Review)*

†Anonymous, "A Treatise on the Records of the Creation, and on the Moral Attitudes of the Creator, with particular Reference to the Jewish History," *QRL* 16 (1816-17) 37-69. *(Review)*

†Anonymous, "Vestiges of the Natural History of Creation," *CTPR, 3rd Ser.,* 1 (1845) 49-82. *(Review)*

Anonymous, "Explanations. A Sequel to the Vestiges of the Natural History of Creation. By the Author of that Work," *CTPR, 3rd Ser.,* 2 (1846) 33-44. *(Review)*

C. F. L. F., "Lessons of Theology taught in the Works of Creation," *UQGR* 3 (1846) 413-421.

George I. Chance, "Of the Divine Agency in the Production of Material Phenomena," *BS* 5 (1848) 342-357.

W. C. Wisner, "The End of God in Creation," *BRCR, 3rd Ser.,* 6 (1850) 430-456.

*E. P. Barrows, "The Mosaic Narrative of the Creation Considered Grammatically and in Its Relations to Science," *BS* 13 (1856) 743-789.

*James D. Dana, "Thoughts on Species," *BS* 14 (1857) 854-874.

C. Gooch, "The Record of Creation," *JSL, 4th Ser.,* 1 (1862) 339-350.

J. Challis, "The Scripture Cosmogony," *JSL, 4th Ser.,* 2 (1862-63) 200-206.

( ) Blackie, "The Mosaic Account of Creation contrasted with the Heathen Mythologies and Philosophies," *ThE* 1 (1864) 77-87.

W. H. Darnell, "The Creation," *SPR* 18 (1867-68) 473-482.

Russell Martineau, "The Creation," *TR* 5 (1868) 1-25, 224-243, 334-356.

G. Warington, "On the Biblical Cosmogony scientifically considered," *JTVI* 3 (1868-69) 337-366. (Discussion, pp. 366-384)

Edward A. Lawrence, "The Creative Period in History," *BS* 27 (1870) 454-468.

W. Profeit, "The Doctrine of Creation proved from the Relations Subsisting between Internal and External Nature," *BFER* 22 (1873) 317-324.

*B. W. Savile, "Heathen Cosmogonies Compared with the Hebrew," *JTVI* 10 (1876-77) 251-301. (Discussion, pp. 301-315)

John F. Hurst, "Creation," *DTQ* 3 (1877) 419-425.

Theodore Appel, "Creation and Cosmogony," *RChR* 24 (1877) 123-180.

J. H. McIlvaine, "The Miracle of Creation," *PR, 4th Ser.,* 1 (1878) 830-850.

A. S. A., "The Genesaic Theory of Creation," *ERG, 7th Ser.,* 1 (1878-79) 255-266.

I. E. Graeff, "Divine Origin of the Universe," *RChR* 28 (1881) 304-321.

Henry W. Crosskey, "The Mosaic Cosmogony," *ModR* 4 (1883) 675-696.

M. S. Terry, "The Biblical Creation," *ONTS* 5 (1885-86) 365-369.

R. F. Clarke, "A Skeptical Difficulty Against Creation," *ACQR* 12 (1887) 278-293.

Charles S. Robinson, "Creation Learned by Faith," *HR* 13 (1887) 492-496.

Geo. D. Armstrong, "Creation as a Doctrine of Science," *PQ* 1 (1887-88) 106-128.

*James D. Dana, "On the Cosmogony of Genesis," *AR* 9 (1888) 197-200.

L. H. Schuh, "The Doctrine of Creation," *ColTM* 8 (1888) 35-56.

*Chas. S. Robinson, "Evolution as a Theory of Creation," *HR* 16 (1888) 123-127.

Thomas Hill, "Creation is Revelation," *URRM* 30 (1888) 1-15.

S. H. Kellogg, "The Creative Laws and the Scripture Revelation," *BS* 46 (1889) 393-424.

Charles Caverno, "The Intellectual Element in Matter," *BS* 46 (1889) 425-442.

Joseph   Parker,   "Creation,"   *CT*   7   (1889-90)   147-150.

James D. Dana, "The Genesis of the Heavens and the Earth and All the Host of Them," *ONTS* 11 (1890) 12-23, 84-97.

Orlando Dana Miller, "The Abyss, or Chaos, of the Ancient Cosmogonies," *UQGR, N.S.,* 27 (1890) 79-91.

Anonymous, "Mr. Gladstone's Forthcoming Book on the Old Testament," *ET* 2 (1890-91) 29-32. *(Review)*

*John Coleman Adams, "The Christ and the Creation," *AR* 17 (1892) 225-237.

J. N. Wythe, "The True Idea of Creation," *MR* 74 (1892) 559-569.

John D. Davis, "The Semitic Tradition of Creation," *PRR* 3 (1892) 448-461.

C. B. Warring, "Hebrew Cosmogony," *BS* 53 (1896) 50-67.

C. B. Warring, "The Hebrew Cosmogony Again," *BS* 53 (1896) 522-539.

W. A. Lambert, "Hebrew 'Cosmogony'," *LCR* 19 (1900) 519-529; 20 (1901) 129-137.

W. L. Davidson, "The Bible Story of Creation: a Phase of the Theistic Argument," *Exp, 6th Ser.,* 9 (1904) 286-300.

*George Macloskie, "Creation as Illustrated by Evolution," *USR* 17 (1905-06) 89-100.

*Anonymous, "Professor Driver's 'Assured Results', and His 'Scientific' Method," *CFL, 3rd Ser.,* 5 (1906) 371-374. [Critique on *The Cosmogony of Genesis*]

*F. R. Tennant, "The Origin of Life," *ET* 19 (1907-08) 352-355.

*Stephen D. Peet, "The Cosmogony of the Bible Compared with that of the Ancient Pagans," *AAOJ* 30 (1908) 145-160.

Anonymous, "The Shape of the Earth," *AAOJ* 30 (1908) 224.

*W. M. Patton, "Cosmogonies in the Apocrypha and in Genesis," *IJA* #17 (1909) 33-37.

A. E. Whatham, "The Yahweh-Tehom Myth," *BW* 36 (1910) 329-333.

*E. G. King, "The Covenant of Creation in the Psalms," *ICMM* 8 (1911-12) 410-421.

Benjamin B. Warfield, "Calvin's Doctrine of Creation," *PTR* 13 (1915) 190-255.

*F. R. Tennant, "Creation, and the Origin of the Soul," *ET* 31 (1919-20) 185-187.

Samuel A. B. Mercer, "A New Turning Point in the Study of Creation," *ATR* 3 (1920-21) 1-17.

*Leander S. Keyser, "I Believe in God and Creation," *CFL, 3rd Ser.,* 28 (1922) 357-362.

John Wright Buckman, "Bible Teaching Concerning Creation," *HR* 84 (1922) 183-185.

*William Jennings Bryan, "God and Evolution. I. Moses vs. Darwin," *HR* 83 (1922) 446-452.

L[eander] S. K[eyser], "The Bible Doctrine of Creation," *CFL, 3rd Ser.,* 30 (1924) 4-6.

L[eander] S. Keyser, "The Great Problem of Origins," *CFL, 3rd Ser.,* 30 (1924) 35-38.

Frank R. Buckalwe, "The Mosaic Cosmogony," *CFL, 3rd Ser.,* 31 (1925) 555-557; 32 (1926) 37-39.

W. Maslin Frysinger, "The Argument from Design," *CFL, 3rd Ser.,* 33 (1927) 419-420.

*Herbert W. Magoun, "The Cosmogony Problem and the Meaning of Hebrew 'Yom'," *CFL, 3rd Ser.,* 34 (1928) 604-611.

Melvin Grove Kyle, "The Bible in Its Setting. III. The Creation of Inanimate Things," *BS* 86 (1929) 290-318, 406-431.

Dudley Joseph Whitney, "Divine Creation a Reasonable View," *CFL, 3rd Ser.,* 36 (1930) 377-378.

Dudley Joseph Whitney, "Conclusions About Creation," *CFL, 3rd Ser.,* 36 (1930) 596-600.

Ambrose Fleming, "Modern Cosmogony," *EQ* 2 (1930) 113-119.

Ambrose Fleming, "Creation and Modern Cosmogony," *JTVI* 62 (1930) 266-282.

H. J. Schick, "The Origin of Life," *TZDES* 58 (1930) 411-419.

J. Parton Milum, "The Story of Creation Read Again," *LQHR* 156 (1931) 38-49.

Otto   Lock,   "Creation   of   Matter,"   *TF*   3   (1931)   37-54.

Otto   Lock,   "Creation   of   Life,"   *TF*   3   (1931)   217-224.

Dyson Hague, "No Creation Without a Creator," *CFL, 3rd Ser.,* 41 (1935) 55-58.

Arthur   C.   Headlam,   "Creation,"   *CQR*   127   (1938-39)   185-226.

John Macleod, "Constructive Theology. IV. Creation," *ET* 51 (1939-40) 167-171.

*C. F. Russell, "God and Nature—Creation and Miracle," *MC* 29 (1939-40) 313-325.

*G. Ernest Wright, "How Did Early Israel Differ from Her Neighbors," *BA* 6 (1943) 1-10, 13-20. [IX. Early Israelite Traditions of the Beginning of the World, p. 20]

*Harry Wolfson, "The Kalam Problem of Nonexistence and Saadia's Second Theory of Creation," *JQR, N.S.,* 36 (1945-46) 371-391.

*Edward McCrady, "Genesis and Pagan Cosmogonies," *JTVI* 72 (1940) 44-64, 68-71. (Communications by E. J. G. Titterington, p. 64; H. S. Curr, pp. 64-66; L. M. Davies, pp. 66-68)

Michael J. Gruenthaner, "The Scriptural Doctrine on First Creation," *CBQ* 9 (1947) 48-58, 206-219, 307-320.

*W. S. Boycott, "Creation and Christology," *Theo* 52 (1949) 443-448.

Henry Bett, "The Doctrine of Creation," *LQHR* 175 (1950) 212-216.

E.   Ehrhardt,   "Creatio   ex   Nihilo,"   *ST*   4   (1950)   13-43.

*E. L. Allen, "The Hebrew View of Nature," *JJS* 2 (1950-51) 100-104.

J. Heywood Thomas, "The Idea of Creation," *HJ* 50 (1951-52) 153-161.

Edwin Lewis, "The Creative Conflict," *RL* 21 (1952) 390-400.

Henry W. Reimann, "Luther on Creation. A Study in Theocentric Theology," *CTM* 24 (1953) 26-40.

Walter E. Lammerts, "Creation in Terms of Modern Concepts of Genetics and Physics," *JASA* 5 (1953) #3, 7-10.

G. Lambert, "Creation in the Bible," *TD* 2 (1954) 159-162.

John Murray, "Calvin's Doctrine of Creation," *WTJ* 17 (1954-55) 21-44.

*E[phraim] A. Speiser, "'ED in the Story of Creation," *BASOR* #140 (1955) 9-11.

Jaroslav Pelikan, "The Doctrine of Creation in Lutheran Confessional Theology," *CTM* 26 (1955) 569-579.

Bernhard W. Anderson, "The Earth is the Lord's. *An Essay on the Biblical Doctrine of Creation*," *Interp* 9 (1955) 3-20.

Valens Kieffer, "Creation," *Scotist* 11 (1955) 65-70.

*A. Altmann, "A Note on the Rabbinic Doctrine of Creation," *JJS* 7 (1956) 195-206.

*Ethan Mengers, "The Creation Doctrine of Isaiah 40-66," *WSQ* 20 (1956-57) #3, 2-14.

*Merrill F. Unger, "The Old Testament Revelation of the Creation of Angels and Earth," *BS* 114 (1957) 206-212.

L. C. Birch, "Creation and the Creator," *JR* 37 (1957) 85-98. [Two Concepts of God's Creativity; Metaphysics as the Meeting Ground of Theology and Science; Critique of Brunner's Conception of Creation; The Relevance of Modern Studies of Evolution to the Christian Doctrine of Creation, *The Continuity of the Creative Process, Chance and the Order of Nature;* The Travail of Creation]

Laurence Bright, "Creation: A Philosopher's Point of View," *DownsR* 76 (1958) 150-159.

John Wren-Lewis, "Science and the Doctrine of Creation," *ET* 71 (1958-59) 80-82.

I. Baer, "On the Problem of Eschatological Doctrine During the Period of the Second Temple. Dialectics and Mysticism in the Founding of the Halacha," *Zion* 23&24 (1958-59) #3/4, II-III. [Appendix I. Remarks on the Doctrine of Creation, pp. III-IV]

*Carroll Stuhlmueller, "The Theology of Creation in Second Isaias," *CBQ* 21 (1959) 429-467.

A. Seidenberg, "The Separation of Sky and Earth at Creation," *Folk* 70 (1959) 477-482.

Meyrick H. Carré, "Doctrines of Creation and the Rise of Science," *LQHR* 184 (1959) 54-59.

William Strawson, "The Doctrine of Creation," *PQL* 5 (1959) 114-122.

*Glen Cavaliero, "Christology and Creation," *Theo* 62 (1959) 136-141. *[OT Refs., pp. 136-138]*

Bruce Vawter, "A Note on 'The Waters Beneath the Earth'," *CBQ* 22 (1960) 71-73.

Jaroslav Pelikan, "Creation and Causality in the History of Christian Thought," *JR* 40 (1960) 246-255.

William J. Tinkle, "Creation, a Finished Work," *JASA* 13 (1961) 15-17.

Heywood J. Thomas, "Some Comments on Tillich's Doctrine of Creation," *SJT* 14 (1961) 113-118.

Dan L. Deegan, "The Christological Determinant in Barth's Doctrine of Creation," *SJT* 14 (1961) 119-135.

*Ruth Amiran, "Myths of the Creation of Man and the Jericho Statues," *BASOR* # 167 (1962) 23-25.

R. Laird Harris, "The Bible and Cosmology," *BETS* 5 (1962) 11-17.

R. Rossignol, "Was The World Created in Time?" *IES* 1 (1962) 20-36.

R. Rossignol, "Was The World Created in Time? II," *IES* 1 (1962) 139-143.

B. D. Napier, "On Creation—Faith in the Old Testament. *A Survey,"* *Interp* 16 (1962) 21-42.

J. H. Kroeze, "Remarks and Questions regarding some creation-passages in the O.T.," *OTW* 5 (1962) 15-26.

P. de Letter, "The Roman Catholic Doctrine of Creation," *R&S* 9 (1962) #2, 42-49.

T. S. Garrett, "Creation—A Modern Christian Viewpoint," *R&S* 9 (1962) #3, 59-65.

Robert W. Gleason, "Creation in the Old Testament," *TFUQ* 37 (1962) 527-542.

Wilbert R. Gawrisch, "The Biblical Account of Creation and Modern Theology," *WLQ* 59 (1962) 161-202.

*Claus Westermann, "God and His Creation," *USQR* 18 (1962-63) 197-209.

*Vilmos Vajta, "Creation and Worship," *SL* 2 (1963) 29-46.

*Regin Prenter, "Worship and Creation," *SL* 2 (1963) 82-95.

*Lucien Legrand, "Creation as cosmic victory of Yahweh," *TD* 11 (1963) 154-158.

W[illiam] R. Lane, "The Initiation of Creation," *VT* 13 (1963) 63-73.

Thorleif Bowman, "The Biblical Doctrine of Creation," *CQR* 165 (1964) 140-151.

Harold H. Ditmanson, "The Call for a Theology of Creation," *DJT* 3 (1964) 264-273. [V. The Biblical Root of Belief in Creation, pp. 270-272]

*G. Gary Cohen, "Hermeneutical Principles and Creation Theories," *GJ* 5 (1964) #3, 17-29.

M. L. Kretzmann, "The Lutheran View of Creation," *IJT* 13 (1964) 67-73, 135-144.

Danton B. Sailor, "Moses and Atomism," *JHI* 25 (1964) 3-16.

Milos Bic, "The Theology of the Biblical Creation Epic," *SEÅ* 28&29 (1964) 9-38.

A. D. Matthews, "The Prophetic Doctrine of Creation," *CQR* 166 (1965) 141-149.

Paul   Evdokimov,   "Nature,"   *SJT*   18   (1965)   1-22.

*W. Dantine, "Creation and Redemption: Attempt at Theological Interpretation in the Light of Contemporary Understanding of the World," *SJT* 18 (1965) 129-147. [A. The Key Position of Anthropology; B. Cosmic Christology? C. The Lordship of Christ in Creation]

Loran R. Fisher, "From Chaos to Cosmos," *SQ/E* 26 (1965) 183-197. [I. Biblical Creation; II. The Exodus-Sinai Tradition and its Relation to Creation; III. Deutero-Isaiah and his Disciples; IV. Conclusion]

*L[oran] R. Fisher, "Creation at Ugarit and in the Old Testament," *VT* 15 (1965) 313-324.

William Winn, "The Doctrine of Creation," *SEAJT* 7 (1965-66) #4, 22-27.

Robert M. Page, "Cosmogony-Science, Myth, and Genesis," *JASA* 18 (1966) 12-14.

Walter R. Hearn, "Reports on the Sessions of the International Conference on Science and Christian Faith, Oxford, England July 22, 1965: The Meaning of Creation," *JASA* 18 (1966) 25-28.

Clarence E. Harms, "A Perspective on Creation," *JC&S* 2 (1966) #2, 3-21.

John   Ashton,   "Creator   of   All   Things,"   *Way*   6   (1966)   89-103.

H.   B.   Phillips,   "Creation,"   *Z*   1   (1966)   401.

*F. H. Cleobury, "God, Creation and Evolution," *MC, N.S.,* 10 (1966-67) 7-18.

*Dennis J. McCarthy, "'Creation' Motifs in Ancient Hebrew Poetry," *CBQ* 29 (1967) 393-406.

D. Gareth Jones, "Some Byways of Creation," *F&T* 96 (1967) #3, 13-26.

*John C. Whitcomb Jr., "The Creation of the Heavens and the Earth," *GJ* 8 (1967) #2, 27-32.

*J. Philip Hyatt, "Was Yahweh Originally a Creator Deity?" *JBL* 86 (1967) 369-377.

Leroy T. Howe, "Is the World ex Nihlio?" *Sophia* 6 (1967) #1, 21-29.

H. Dermot McDonald, "The Idea of Creation in Historical Perspective," *VE* 5 (1967) 27-48.

*Ph B. Harner, "Creation Faith in Deutero-Isaiah," *VT* 17 (1967) 298-306.

*Moshe Weinfeld, "God the Creator in Gen. I and in the Prophecy of Second Isaiah," *Tarbiz* 37 (1967-68) #2, I-II.

A. Seidenberg, "The Separation of Sky and Earth at Creation (II)," *Folk* 80 (1969) 188-196.

*Mary K. Wakeman, "The Biblical Earth Monster in the Cosmogonic Combat Myth," *JBL* 88 (1969) 313-320.

David Foyt, "Creation and the Second Law of Thermodynamics," *RestQ* 12 (1969) 181-190.

*Michael Negus, "Man, Creation and the Fossil Record," *SCR* 3 (1969) 49-55.

*Jefim Schirmann, "The Battle Between Behemoth and Leviathan According to an Ancient Hebrew *Piyyuṭ*," *PIASH* 4 (1969-70) 327-369.

§976 **5.4.2.2 *Studies on Cosmography***

T. C., "The Idea of the Jews, respecting the Form of the Universe," *QCS* 1 (1819) 400-401.

*T. G. P[inches], "Talmudische und midrashische Parallelen zum Babylonischen Weltschöpfungsepos," *JRAS* (1904) 369-370. *[English text]*

Leon Gry, "The Idea of Light in the Old Testament," *NYR* 2 (1906-07) 70-85.

William H. Cobb, "Note on a Hebrew Conception of the Universe," *JBL* 29 (1910) 24-28.

Lawrence Parmly Brown, "The Cosmic Madness," *OC* 33 (1919) 610-633.

Austin Ralph Middleton, "The Creator's Plan of the Universe," *MQR, 3rd Ser.,* 49 (1923) 258-287.

Harold L. Creager, "The Great Conflict of Good and Evil," *LCQ* 11 (1938) 275-281.

Francis I. Andersen, "The Modern Conception of the Universe in Relation to the Conception of God," *JTVI* 82 (1950) 79-100, 107-111. (Discussion, pp. 100-103) (Communications by D. Dewar, pp. 103-105; L. Merson Davies, p. 105; P. W. Petty, pp. 105-106; W. E. Leslie, p. 106; H. K. Airy Shaw, pp. 106-107)

John L. McKenzie, "God and Nature in the Old Testament," *TD* 1 (1953) 79-80.

G. A. F. Knight, "The Concept of Chaos," *GUOST* 16 (1955-56) 14-17.

Merrill F. Unger, "Old Testament Revelation Concerning Eternity Past," *BS* 114 (1957) 133-140.

*Joseph Bourke, "'Leviathan Which Yahweh Made to Laugh At'," *LofS* 13 (1958-59) 122-129.

John J. McGovern, "The Waters of Death," *CBQ* 21 (1959) 350-358.

A. L. Burns, "Some Biblical Sources of Concepts in International Theory," *ABR* 11 (1963) 24-32.

*Elizabeth R. Achtemeier, "Jesus Christ, the Light of the World. *The Biblical Understanding of Light and Darkness*," *Interp* 17 (1963) 439-449.

Robert M. Grant, "Causation and 'The Ancient World View'," *JBL* 83 (1964) 34-40.

*G. Sarfatti, "Talmudical Cosmography," *Tarbiz* 35 (1965-66) #2, V-VII.

Frederick Sontag, "What Leibniz' God Cannot Do," *USQR* 21 (1965-66) 227-231.

Lester J. Kuyper, "The Biblical View of Nature," *RefR* 22 (1968-69) #3, 12-17.

§977 *5.4.2.3 Studies on Cosmology*

*Anonymous, "The Testimony of Natural Theology to Christianity," *QRL* 21 (1819) 41-66. *(Review)*

Anonymous, "The Scripture Cosmology, Illustrated and Confirmed by the Discoveries and Conclusions of Geology," *CongML* 20 (1837) 496-502, 569-573, 624-627, 706-710.

†Anonymous, "Professor Lewis's Scriptural Cosmology," *TLJ* 8 (1855-56) 271-342. *(Review)*

W. F. Warren, "Biblical Cosmology and the Doctrine of the Fall of the World," *BS* 20 (1863) 752-778.

E. V. Gerhart, "The Complement of Genesis," *RChR* 24 (1877) 265-272.

J. L. Challis, "On the Metaphysics of Scripture," *JTVI* 11 (1877-78) 196-223. (Discussion, pp. 223-237)

M. C. Read, "Genesis and Abiogenesis," *OBJ* 1 (1880) 121-123.

J. E. Howard, "The Supernatural in Nature," *JTVI* 16 (1882-83) 291-316. (Discussion, pp. 316-319)

*James D. Dana, "Creation; or, the Biblical Cosmology in the Light of Modern Science," *BS* 42 (1885) 201-224. *(Review)*

Robert Watts, "The Huxleyan Kosmology," *BFER* 35 (1886) 401-424.

Anonymous, "Dana's Tribute to Guyot," *BS* 43 (1886) 586-589.

*S. R. Driver, "The Cosmology of Genesis," *Exp, 3rd Ser.,* 3 (1886) 23-45.

Anonymous, "The Cosmology of Genesis, Rejoinder to Professor Driver's Critique of Professor Dana," *BS* 45 (1888) 356-365. *[Subtitle of article reads:* Professor Driver's Critique of Professor Dana]

C. M. Mead, "Is Space a Reality? Observations on Professor Bowne's Doctrine of Space, Motion, and Change," *BS* 47 (1890) 415-444.

H. B. Fry, "Finite and Infinite," *BS* 50 (1893) 668-695.

S. R. Driver, "Magna est Veritas et Prævalet," *Exp, 5th Ser.,* 7 (1898) 464-469.

J. William Dawson, "Note on Canon Driver's Article, 'Magna est Veritas, et Prævalet'," *Exp, 5th Ser.,* 8 (1898) 306-308.

*Duncan B. Macdonald, "Job and Muslim Cosmology," *AJSL* 15 (1898-99) 168-169.

A. G., "Cosmology," *TQ* 3 (1899) 1-20, 129-163.

*S. A. B Mercer, "The Cosmology of the Apocrypha and Pseudepigrapha," *IJA* #32 (1913) 3-5.

*Adam C. Welch, "The Prophets and the World-Order," *Exp, 8th Ser.,* 18 (1919) 81-99.

John Elliott Wishart, "Is the Doctrine of an Intelligent First Cause Out of Date?" *HJ* 38 (1939-40) 449-456.

*Julian Obermann, "Wind, Water, and Light in an Archaic Inscription from Shechem," *JBL* 57 (1938) 239-254.

*David Cains, "Aldous Huxley—Cosmology and Ethnic," *ET* 50 (1938-39) 55-60.

Arthur Stanley Pease, "Caeli Enarrant," *HTR* 34 (1941) 163-200.

*Sabatino Moscati, "The Wind in Biblical and Phoenician Cosmology," *JBL* 66 (1947) 305-310.

Robert Rendall, "The Note of Crisis in Biblical History," *EQ* 22 (1950) 83-94.

Delbert Eggenberger, "Methods of Dating the Earth and the Universe," *JASA* 3 (1951) #1, 1-3.

Carl Gaenssle, "Velikovsky and the Hebrew Bible," *CTM* 23 (1952) 105-114.

C[arl] Gaenssle, "A Look at Current Biblical Cosmologies," *CTM* 23 (1952) 738-749.

Paul A. Zimmermann, "Some Observations on Current Cosmological Theories," *CTM* 24 (1953) 490-515.

*H[erbert] G. May, "Cosmic Connotations of Mayim Rabbim," *JBL* 72 (1953) v.

*Herbert G. May, "Some Cosmic Connotations of *Mayim Rabbîm,* 'Many Waters'," *JBL* 74 (1955) 9-21.

Edmond LaB. Cherbonnier, "Is There a Bible Metaphysic?" *TT* 15 (1958-59) 454-469.

Robert S. Ellwood, "The Creation of Time, A Study of the Theological Implications of Certain Modern Theories of Cosmology," *ATR* 41 (1959) 215-229.

David W. Hay, "Christianity and Cosmology," *CJT* 5 (1959) 231-241.

Claude Tresmontant, "Biblical Metaphysics," *CC* 10 (1960) 229-250. *(Trans. by Ronald Koshoshek)*

*James A.Wharton, "'Smitten of God...' A Theological Investigation of the Enemies of Yahweh in the Old Testament," *ASBFE* 86 (1960-61) #1, 3-36.

Langdon B. Gilkey, "Cosmology, Ontology, and the Travail of Biblical Language," *JR* 41 (1961) 194-205.

Elmer G. Suhr, "The Column of the Cosmos," *AJA* 66 (1962) 200.

Langdon B. Gilkey, "Cosmology, Ontology, and the Travail of Biblical Language," *CTM* 33 (1962) 143-154.

*Robley Edward Whiton, "The Concept of Origins," *TFUQ* 37 (1962) 245-268.

*Clark Hopkins, "The Canopy of Heaven and the Aegis of Zeus," *AJA* 67 (1963) 212.

*Rem Edwards, "Is There a Metaphysics of Genesis?" *Cont* 1 (1963-64) 368-372.

*James Quigley, "A Catholic Response," *Cont* 1 (1963-64) 373-384.

*Clark Hopkins, "The Canopy of Heaven and the Aegis of Zeus," *BUS* 12 (1964) #3, 1-16.

Roland Puccetti, "Before Creation," *Sophia* 3 (1964) #3, 24-36.

John King-Farlow, "Precosmological Hypotheses," *Sophia* 4 (1965) #1, 22-26.

*James Quigley, "Is There a Metaphysics of Genesis? II," *Cont* 2 (1966) 105-118.

John M. Dougherty, "Holy War as Cosmic," *Focus* 3 (1966-67) #2, 38-50.

*Gene Rice, "Cosmological Ideas and Religious Truth in Genesis i," *JRT* 23 (1966-67) 15-30.

*Mircea Eliade, "Cosmic Myth and 'Sacred History'," *RS* 2 (1966-67) 171-184.

§978 *5.4.2.4 Studies on the Works, Will, and Providence of God*

*Anonymous, "Divine Providence in its Relation to Sin," *ERG, 1st Ser.,* 1 (1854-55) 268-277.

Anonymous, "The Relation of Divine Providence to Physical Laws," *BS* 12 (1855) 179-205.

D. T. Fiske, "The Divine Decrees," *BS* 19 (1862) 400-431.

George F. Magoun, "Are the Natural and Spiritual Worlds One in Law?" *BS* 42 (1885) 270-290.

William Tucker, "The Doctrine of Providence as Held by the Orientalists in Ancient Times," *AAOJ* 9 (1887) 356-359.

Joseph B. West, "The Equity of Providence," *MQR, 3rd Ser.,* 10 (1891) 132-147.

Minot J. Savage, "The Origin of Goodness," *NW* 3 (1894) 78-89.

Jacob Cooper, "Theodicy," *BS* 60 (1903) 401-421, 649-671.

Charles F. Dole, "The Divine Providence," *HTR* 1 (1908) 112-125.

W. T. Davison, "God and Man in Human History," *LQHR* 110 (1908) 193-212. *(Review)*

A. D. Belden, "The Problem of Divine Protection," *R&E* 18 (1921) 161-169.

*D. S. Cairns, "The Divine Providence Illustrated from the Life of Moses," *BR* 7 (1922) 31-47.

J. H. Horstmann, "The Will of God. Shall It, Can It Be Done on Earth as It Is in Heaven?" *TZDES* 52 (1924) 344-351. [Moses and the Will of God, pp. 345-348; The Prophets and the Will of God, pp. 348-349]

William Manson, "The Work of God," *CJRT* 2 (1925) 164.

J. Scott Lidgett, "The Activity of God," *ContR* 130 (1926) 736-745.

Abraham Cronbach, "Divine Help as a Social Phenomenon," *HUCA* 5 (1928) 583-620.

*Arvid S. Kapelrud, "God as Destroyer in the Preaching of Amos and in the Ancient Near East," *JBL* 71 (1952) 33-38.

Frank B. Dilley, "Does the 'God Who Acts' Really Act?" *ATR* 47 (1965) 66-80. [I. The 'Action' of the God Who Acts; II. Alternative Ways of Conceiving God's Action]

Charles Hatfield, "Probability and God's Providence," *JASA* 17 (1965) 16-22.

William R. Foster," The Acts of God," *GJ* 6 (1966) #1, 25-34.

Gordon D. Kaufman, "On the Meaning of 'Act of God'," *HTR* 61 (1968) 175-201.

Louis Jacobs, "Providence," *Jud* 17 (1968) 197-202.

§979 *5.4.2.5 Studies concerning Miracles*

*†Anonymous, "Penrose on the Use of Miracles," *BCQTR, N.S.,* 22 (1824) 138-143. *(Review)*

†Anonymous, "Penrose—On the Evidence of the Scripture Miracles," *BCQTR, 4th Ser.,* 1 (1827) 60-92. *(Review)*

S. C. L., "Miracles," *UQGR* 1 (1844) 233-256.

Anonymous, "The Miracles of Moses and the Apostles contrasted with the Incantations of the Egyptian Magicians," *BJ* 2 (1843) 59-70.

†Anonymous, "Modern Opinions on Ecclesiastical Miracles," *ERL* 5 (1846) 395-436. *(Review)*

Enoch Pond, "Miracles," *BRCR, 3rd Ser.,* 3 (1847) 304-323.

George I. Chace, "Of the Divine Agency in the Production of Material Phenomena," *BS* 5 (1848) 342-357.

S. P. T., "Definitions of Miracles," *JSL, 1st Ser.,* 5 (1850) 511-512.

Edward Hitchcock, "Special Divine Interpositions in Nature," *BS* 11 (1854) 776-800.

D. H. Focht, "Miracles," *ER* 9 (1857-58) 530-563.

*†G. B., "P.S.," *JSL, 3rd Ser.,* 4 (1856-57) 161-164. *[The Dial of Ahaz]*

J. M. Manning, "The Denial of the Supernatural," *BS* 20 (1863) 256-278.

Edward Hitchcock, "The Law of Nature's Consistancy Subordinate to the Higher Law of Change," *BS* 20 (1863) 489-561.

Anonymous,   "Miracles,"   *WR*   80   (1863)   352-370.

W. W. English, "On Miracles; their Compatibility with Philosophical Principles," *JTVI* 1 (1866-67) 256-276; 301-302. (Discussion, pp. 279-301)

E. B. Penny, "Thoughts on Miracles," *JTVI* 1 (1866-67) 276-279. (Discussion, pp. 279-301)

F. R. Conder,   "On   Miracle,"   *DUM*   91   (1878)   64-79.

George H. Schodde, "The Nature and Purpose of Old Testament Miracles," *LQ* 10 (1880) 422-431.

Joseph Lear,   "Miracles,"   *MQR, 2nd Ser.,*   3   (1881)   271-287.

Almoni Peloni, "Miracles—The Problem Stated," *Exp, 2nd Ser.,* 4 (1882) 241-264.

W. Steadman Aldis, "Is the Belief in Miracles Reasonable?" *BQRL* 76 (1882) 339-357.

*Leonard W. Bacon, "Prayer and Miracle in Relation to Natural Law," *JCP* 3 (1883-84) 319-343.

Francis W. Ryder, "Miracles *Versus* the Continuity of Nature," *JCP* 3 (1883-84) 491-510.

R. R. Howison, "The Pseudo-Scientific View of Miracles," *PQ* 1 (1887-88) 343-349.

*John L. Girardeau, "The Miracle, the Principle of Unity in the Evidences of a Divine Revelation," *PQ* 2 (1888) 369-387.

*O.P. Eaches, "Fulfilled Prophecy—A Standing Miracle," *BQR* 11 (1889) 468-482.

T. G. Selby, "Brevia: Second Twilights and Old Testament Miracles," *Exp, 3rd Ser.,* 9 (1889) 317-320.

Walter Lloyd, "Miracles," *WR* 132 (1889) 168-184.[I Miracles and Natural Causes, pp. 168-174; II Miracles and Science, pp. 174-176; III. Old Testament Miracles, pp. 177-180; IV. The Periodic Theory, pp. 181-184]

Walter Lloyd, "Miracles and Doctrine," *WR* 132 (1889) 394-403.

Abel H. Huizinga, "The Miracles of the Bible," *BS* 49 (1892) 129-142.

G. Frederick Wright, "The Credibility of the Supernatural in the Old Testament," *BS* 49 (1892) 149-153.

J. A. Selbie, "Miracles," *ET* 8 (1896-97) 560.

John Stevens, "The Miracles of the Bible," *MR* 79 (1897) 65-70.

Anonymous, "The Nature of Miracles," *BS* 55 (1898) 360-361.

Willard W. Wadsworth, "A Study in Miracles," *MQR, 3rd Ser.,* 24 (1898) 228-238.

*G. Frederick Wright, "Physical Preparation for Israel in Palestine," *BS* 58 (1901) 360-369.

*Charles B. Warring, "Miracle, Law, Evolution," *BS* 60 (1903) 750-764.

George Frederick Wright, "Mediate Miracles," *HR* 45 (1903) 18-23.

William Dewar, "What is a Miracle?" *AJT* 8 (1904) 240-255.

F. J. Lamb, "Miracle—Testimony of God," *BS* 62 (1905) 126-145.

William Brenton Greene Jr., "The Relation of the Miracle to Nature," *BS 63* (1906) 542-557.

G. Frederick Wright, "The Place of the 'Mediate' Miracle—An Explanation," *CFL, 3rd Ser.,* 4 (1906) 361-363.

A. Allen Brockington, "Some Characteristics of Old Testament Miracles," *ET* 18 (1906-07) 299-302.

R. B. Gridlestone, "The Spiritural Idea of Miracles," *JTVI* 39 (1907) 61-75. (Discussion, pp. 75-82)

John D. Davis, "The Article 'Miracle', from 'A Dictionary of the Bible'," *CFL, 3rd Ser.,* 12 (1910) 145-146. *(Review)*

P. Borden Bowne, "Concerning Miracle," *HTR* 3 (1910) 143-166.

George T. Knight, "The Definition of the Supernatural," *HTR* 3 (1910) 310-324.

John Edwards Le Bosquet, "The Classification and Evolution of Miracle," *AJT* 15 (1911) 569-583.

F. J. Lamb, "Miracle and the Christian Religion," *BS* 68 (1911) 557-583. *(Review)*

*A. B. Leonard, "The Value of Prophecy and Miracles," *MR* 95 (1913) 730-734.

Herbert Pakenham-Walsh, "Divine Healing," *ICQ* 7 (1914) 148-162. *[OT Refs., p. 154]*

R. L. Marshall, "The Attitude of the Historical Student Towards Miraculous Records," *ET* 28 (1916-17) 149-152.

E. C. Gordon, "Credibility of Biblical Miracles," *CFL, 3rd Ser.,* 23 (1917) 70-73.

T. Robinson, "Bible Miracles," *CFL, 3rd Ser.,* 23 (1917) 269-271.

*J. B. Tannehill, "Unbelievable Stores," *CFL, 3rd Ser.,* 23 (1917) 312-314.

T. R. R. Stebbing, "Thaumaturgy in the Bible. A Protest from within the Church of England," *HJ* 18 (1919-20) 345-360.

John T. Marriott, "'Thaumaturgy in the Bible. A Protest from within the Church of England'," *HJ* 18 (1919-20) 593-594.

Anonymous, "The Miraculous in the Bible," *TZDES* 48 (1920) 112-126.

*Walter F. Adeney, "Miracle and Prophecy," *HJ* 19 (1920-21) 133-142.

B. W. Bacon, "Miracle and Scripture," *MC* 10 (1920-21) 286-295.

Edwin Lewis, "The Question of Miracle," *MR* 104 (1921) 369-378. [II. Miracle in the Old Testament, pp. 371-373]

John E. McFadyen, "Miracle in the Old Testament," *HJ* 21 (1922-23) 739-753.

H. C. Ackerman, "Miracle and the Natural," *ATR* 6 (1923-24) 124-131.

Roderick J. F. MacDonald, "'Miracle in the Old Testament'," *HJ* 22 (1923-24) 180-181.

A. H. Finn, "The Miraculous in the Holy Scripture," *JTVI* 60 (1928) 99-111, 120-121. (Discussion, pp. 111-117) (Communication by F. C. Wood, pp. 117-118)

J. H. Morrison, "Natural Law and Miracles," *ET* 41 (1929-30) 154-160.

Harold Paul Sloan, "A Study of the Biblical Supernatural," *BR* 16 (1931) 5-10.

W. Bell Dawson, "Miracles and the Laws of Nature," *EQ* 5 (1933) 225-245.

W. H. Boulton, "Miracle; a Necessary Adjunct of Revelation," *JTVI* 69 (1937) 273-285, 291-292. (Discussion, pp. 285-291)

*E. Ehnmark, "Anthropomorphis and Miracle," *UUÅ* (1939), Band 2, #12, i-viii, 1-230.

*C. F. Russell, "God and Nature—Creation and Miracle," *MC* 29 (1939-40) 313-325.

Henry S. Curr, "The Intrinsic Credibility of Biblical Miracles," *BS* 98 (1941) 469-478.

H. Wheeler Robinson, "The Nature-Miracles of the Old Testament," *JTS* 45 (1944) 1-12.

*Alexander Guttmann, "The Significance of Miracles for Talmudic Judaism," *HUCA* 20 (1947) 363-406.

*Michael J. Greunthaner, "Two Sun Miracles of the Old Testament," *CBQ* 10 (1948) 271-290.

*Philip E. Hughes, "Miracle and Myth," *EQ* 20 (1948) 184-195.

James B. Pritchard, "Motifs of Old Testament Miracles," *CQ* 27 (1950) 97-109.

Harold Knight, "The Old Testament Concept of Miracle," *SJT* 5 (1952) 355-361.

Russell Maatman, "Science and Biblical Miracles," *JASA* 7 (1955) #1, 7-8.

François Taymans, "Miracles, signs of the supernatural," *TD* 5 (1957) 18-23.

C. J. Mullo Weir, "Some Thought on Old Testament Miracles," *ALUOS* 1 (1958-59) 25-42.

Michael C. Perry, "Believing and Commending the Miracles," *ET* 83 (1961-62) 340-343.

William Jurgens, "Toward an Understanding of Old Testament Miracles," *Amb* 11 (1962-63) #4, 1-7.

Stephen Bertman, "A Note on the Reversible Miracle," *HRel* 3 (1963-64) 323-327.

*George F. Howe, "Miracles and the Study of Origins," *JASA* 17 (1965) 93-96.

Eldon R. Hay, "A Contranatural View of Miracle," *CJT* 13 (1967) 266-280.

*Graeme Goldsworthy, "The Old Testament—A Christian Book," *Inter* 2 (1969-70) 24-33. [II. Exegesis and miracles, pp. 25-26]

§980 *5.4.2.6 Studies on the Attributes of God*

George I. Chace, "Of Moral Attributes of the Divine Being," *BS* 7 (1840) 668-696.

R. A., "The Sovereignty of God," *BRCM* 4 (1847-48) 322-334.

Enoch Pond, "The Justice of God," *BRCR, 3rd Ser.,* 4 (1848) 586-594.

Anonymous, "The Truth of God," *MQR* 2 (1848) 287-293.

George I. Chace, "Of the Existence and Natural Attributes of the Divine Being," *BS* 7 (1850) 328-352.

Austin Phelps, "The Oneness of God in Revelation and in Nature," *BS* 16 (1859) 836-863.

G. C. B., "Divine Sovereignty—What is its Nature?" *ERG, 3rd Ser.,* 2 (1863-64) 249-255.

Robert G. Vermilye, "The Suffering of God," *CongR* 5 (1865) 1-31.

*Tayler Lewis, "The Bible Idea of Truth, as Inseparable from the Divine Personality," *AThR, N.S.,* 4 (1866) 199-213.

*Henry Cowles, "Sin and Suffering in the Universe, as Related to the Power, Wisdom and Love of God," *BS* 30 (1873) 729-763.

J. P. Lacroix, "Rothe on the Limitations of Divine Foreknowledge," *BS* 32 (1875) 137-160.

Robert L. Dabney, "God's Indiscriminate Proposals of Mercy as Related to His Power, Wisdom, and Sincerity," *PRev,* 54 (1878) Part 2, 33-66.

Francis L. Patton, "Retribution, in Relation to the Justice, Goodness and Purpose of God," *PRev* 54 (1878) Part 1, 1-23.

L. A. Fox, "God's Sovereignty," *LQ* 10 (1880) 484-511.

Wm. Henry Cobb, "Recent Theories on the Divine Foreknowledge," *BS* 40 (1883) 655-694.

*James Watson, "Evil and the Divine Attributes," *ERG, 8th Ser.,* 2 (1883-84) 105-107.

William H. Dallinger, "God's True Glory, and Man's Knowledge of It," *JCP* 3 (1883-84) 140-144.

H. P. Smith, "The Scriptural Conception of the Glory of God," *ONTS* 3 (1883-84) 325-329.

James H. Fairchild, "The Divine Personality," *BS* 41 (1884) 217-233.

James S. Candlish, "The Personality of God," *PRev* 60 (1884) Part 2, 133-152.

Edward Lewis Curtis, "Divine Love in the Old Testament," *PR* 9 (1888) 199-207.

John Milton Williams, "Divine Limitation," *BS* 47 (1890) 253-266.

John S. Vaughan, "Thoughts on the Nature of God," *IER, 3rd Ser.,* 12 (1891) 308-318.

John S. Vaughan, "Thoughts on the Wisdom of God," *IER, 3rd Ser.,* 12 (1891) 815-823.

E. H. Blakeney, "The Righteousness of God," *ET* 6 (1894-95) 45-46.

Henry C. Sheldon, "The Problem of Divine Foreknowledge," *MQR, 3rd Ser.,* 20 (1896) 323-332.

Cyrus L. Sulzberger, "Unity of God," *JQR* 9 (1896-97) 723.

Joel Hedgepeth, "The Problem of Divine Foreknowledge," *MQR, 3rd Ser.,* 24 (1898) 62-69.

E. C. Gordon, "The Love of God as Revealed in the Old Testament. (A Bible Study)," *CFL, O.S.,* 3 (1899) 96-102.

P. T. Forsyth, "The Slowness of God," *ET* 11 (1899-1900) 218-222.

C. C. J. Webb, "The Idea of Personality as Applied to God," *JTS* 2 (1900-01) 49-65.

W. D. Kerswill, "The Mercy of God According to Moses," *CFL, N.S.,* 4 (1901) 87-94.

Geerhardus Vos, "The Scriptural Doctrine of the Love of God," *PRR* 13 (1902) 1-37.

*J. H. Ropes, "'Righteousness' and 'The Righteousness of God' in the Old Testament and St. Paul," *JBL* 22 (1903) 211-227.

James Hendry, "The Beauty of the Lord," *ET* 22 (1910-11) 346-349.

*Harry Austryn Wolfson, "Crescas on the Problem of Divine Attributes," *JQR, N.S.,* 7 (1916-17) 1-44, 175-221.

James H. Snowden, "The Personality of God," *BR* 2 (1917) 330-368, 551-585; 4 (1919) 191-225.

William Fairfield Warren, "The Beauty of God," *MR* 101 (1918) 20-28.

*George McCready Price, "God as Revealed by Modern Science," *CFL, 3rd Ser.,* 27 (1921) 243-254. [Does God Really Care? pp. 250-254]

George Galloway, "The Problem of the Personality of God," *JR* 1 (1921) 296-306.

*Elihu Grant, "Oracle in the Old Testament," *AJSL* 39 (1922-23) 257-281. *[Ability of God to 'Speak']*

A. D. Belden, "The Reticence of God," *ET* 34 (1922-23) 504-506.

Edwyn Bevan, "The Anger of God," *QRL* 239 (1923) 290-306. *(Review)*

W. H. T. Dau, "The Laughter of God," *TM* 4 (1924) 193-201.

W. R. Inge, "The Justice of God," *ET* 36 (1924-25) 170-173.

R. O. Hall, "The Courtesy of God," *IRM* 18 (1925) 400-411.

A. G. Widgery, "The Attributes of God," *JTS* 28 (1926-27) 75-78. *(Review)*

George L. Richardson, "The Jealousy of God," *ATR* 10 (1927-28) 47-50.

Leslie H. Bunn, "Divine Sovereignty in Revision," *ET* 40 (1928-29) 364-366.

*Ralph Marcus, "Divine Names and Attributes in Hellenistic Jewish Literature," *PAAJR* 3 (1931-32) 43-120.

Everett F. Harrison, "Have We a God of Destruction?" *BS* 91 (1934) 24-33.

H. Ellis Lininger, "The Personality of God," *CFL, 3rd Ser.,* 40 (1934) 312-314.

*Lewis Sperry Chafer, "Biblical Theism," *BS* 95 (1938) 390-416. [II. The Attributes of God, pp. 399-416; *BS* 96 (1939) 5-37]

W. F. Lofthouse, "The Righteousness of Jahveh," *ET* 50 (1938-39) 341-345, 441-445.

J. C. Hardwick, "The Wrath of God and the Wrath of Man," *HJ* 39 (1940-41) 251-256. *[OT Refs., pp. 251-254]*

John Newton Thomas, "The Sovereignty of God," *USR* 52 (1940-41) 222-236.

Francis E. Barker, "The Fatherhood of God," *CQR* 132 (1941) 174-196.

A. Gordon James, "The Immutability of God," *ET* 53 (1941-42) 35-37.

Henry Nelson Wieman, "Power and Goodness of God," *JR* 23 (1943) 266-275.

Arthur C. Cochrane, "The Patience and Wisdom of God," *CCQ* 2 (1944-45) #4, 46-53.

*Dom Illtyd Trethowan, "Original Sin and the Justice of God," *DR* 217 (1945) 10-24.

R. P. C. Hanson, "The Wrath of God," *ET* 58 (1946-47) 216-218.

*Titus Ludes, "Job and the Wisdom of God," *Scotist* 6 (1947) 43-48.

*Joseph O. Eckelkamp, "Jonas and the Will of God," *Scotist* 6 (1947) 58-63.

*J. Gray, "The Wrath of God in Canaanite and Hebrew Literature," *JMUEOS* #25 (1947-53) 9-19.

T. C. Smith, "The Wrath of God," *R&E* 45 (1948) 193-208.

George A. Turner, "Ideas of Transcendence and Immanence in Early Judaism," *JBL* 69 (1950) xv.

Israel Efros, "Holiness and Glory in the Bible. An approach to the history of Jewish thought," *JQR, N.S.,* 41 (1950-51) 363-377.

James Muilenburg, "A Mediation on Divine Fatherhood," *UQSR* 6 (1950-51) #1, 3-5.

Leon Morris, "The Wrath of God," *ET* 63 (1951-52) 142-145.

H[arry] A[ustryn] Wolfson, "Albinus and Plotinus on Divine Attributes," *HTR* 45 (1952) 115-130.

Roland Potter, "The Love of God in the Old Testament," *LofS* 8 (1953-54) 58-66.

*John A. Bollier, "The Righteousness of God. *A Word Study,*" *Interp* 8 (1954) 404-413.

Edward J. Kilmartin, "The Jealousy of God," *MH* 11 (1954-55) #1, 28-32.

*Cecil S. Emden, "The Psalmist's Emphasis on God's Kindness," *CQR* 156 (1955) 233-235.

T. E. Pollard, "The Impassibility of God," *SJT* 8 (1955) 353-364.

David Noel Freedman, "God Compassionate and Gracious," *WW* 6 (1955) #1, 6-21.

*A. M. Dubarle, "Original Sin and God's Justice," *Scrip* 9 (1957) 97-108. *(Trans. by B. Dickinson)*

Frank Benz, "The Fatherhood of God in the Old Testament," *Amb* 6 (1957-58) #4, 20-24.

*A. M. Dubarle, "Original Sin and God's Justice," *TD* 6 (1958) 139-142.

Martin H. Scharlemann, "God is One," *LQ, N.S.,* 11 (1959) 230-236.

William H. Poteat, "Foreknowledge and Foreordination: A Critique of Models of Knowledge," *JR* 40 (1960) 18-26.

*Z. W. Falk, "Two Symbols of Justice," *VT* 10 (1960) 72-74.

*H. K. Moulton, "The Names and Attributes of God," *BTr* 13 (1962) 71-80.

Paul Hinnebusch, "With Outstretched Arm," *C&C* 14 (1962) 390-404. *[The Mercy of God]*

Harry A[ustryn] Wolfson, "Joseph Ṣaddiḳ on Divine Attributes," *JQR, N.S.,* 55 (1964-65) 277-289. [Corr. *JQR, N.S.,* 56 (1965-66) p. 247]

S. M. Houghton, "The Sovereignty of God," *RefmR* 12 (1964-65) 133-142.

Harry A[ustryn] Wolfson, "Maimonides on the Unity and Incoporeality of God," *JQR, N.S.,* 56 (1965-66) 112-136. (Corr. p. 247)

Alexander Altmann, "The Divine Attributes. An Historical Survey of the Jewish Discussion," *Jud* 15 (1966) 40-60.

Kenneth J. Woollcombe, "The Pain of God," *SJT* 20 (1967) 129-148.

John R. Edwards, "God's Covenant Wrath," *SS* 19 (1967-68) #1, 24-38.

§981 *5.4.2.7 Studies on the Nature of God (specifically Omnipotence, Omniscience, and Omnipresence)*

E. K., "On the Divine Omnipresence," *QCS* 2 (1820) 229-323, 343-346.

S. I., "The Omnipotence of God," *JSL, 3rd Ser.,* 14 (1861-62) 432-436.

W. L. Browne, "The Omnipotence of God," *JSL, 4th Ser.,* 1 (1862) 443-448.

Robert Thomas Byrn, "Creative Limitations," *ICQ* 9 (1916) 47-58.

F. R. Tennant, "Divine Omnipotence," *ET* 31 (1919-20) 34-36.

F. R. Tennant, "The Conception of a Finite God," *ET* 31 (1919-20) 89-91.

C. W. Hodge, "Dr. Tennant on the Divine Omnipotence and the Conception of a Finite God," *PTR* 18 (1920) 337-342.

W[illia]m Hallock Johnson, "Is God Almighty?" *PTR* 20 (1922) 562-584. [I. The Biblical Data]

W[illia]m Hallock Johnson, "Is God Almighty? II. Omnipotence and Religious Experience," *PTR* 21 (1923) 202-222.

W[illia]m Hallock Johnson, "Is God Almighty? III. Omnipotence and Philosophy," *PTR* 21 (1923) 521-540.

F. D. Jenkins, "Modern Philosophical Views of Space in Relation to Omnipresence, Part I," *PTR* 22 (1924) 614-637.

F. D. Jenkins, "Modern Philosophical Views of Space in Relation to Omnipresence, Part II," *PTR* 23 (1925) 19-50.

Alfred E. Garvie, "The Omnipotence of God," *ET* 42 (1930-31) 526.

Frederick Bronkema, "The Omnipotence of God," *CCQ* 1 (1943-44) #4, 22-29; 2 (1944-45) #1, 38-42; 2 (1944-45) #2, 37-42.

Arthur C. Conchrane, "The Omnipresence of God," *CCQ* 3 (1945-46) #1, 22-35.

*Herbert Gordon May, "Prometheus and Job: The Problem of the God of Power and the Man of Worth," *ATR* 34 (1952) 240-246.

Richard L. Rubenstein, "God's Omnipotence in Rabbinic Judaism," *Jud* 9 (1960) 120-128.

*Paul R. Clifford, "Omnipotence and the Problem of Evil," *JR* 41 (1961) 118-128.

John T. Wilcox, "A Question from Physics for Certain Theists," *JR* 41 (1961) 293-300. *[Omniscience]*

*Emil L. Fackenheim, "Human Freedom and Divine Power. Philosophical Reflections on a Religious Issue," *Jud* 12 (1963) 338-343.

*Kathryn Sullivan, "The God of All Power," *Way* 3 (1963) 247-256.

John Lachs, "Two Concepts of God," *HTR* 59 (1966) 227-240. *[Omniscience]*

Lewis S. Ford, "John Lachs' Two Concepts of God: A Rejoinder," *HTR* 61 (1968) 498-499.

J. P. Versteeg, "The Almighty God," *RefmR* 17 (1969-70) 147-157.

§982 *5.4.2.8 Studies on the Glory of God (The Shekinah)*

*T. T. Titus, "The Shekinah," *ER* 11 (1859-60) 344-369.

Ashley Carus-Wilson, "The Vision of the Divine Glory," *ICMM* 6 (1909-10) 81-91.

*George Foot Moore, "Intermediates in Jewish Theology. Memra, Shekinah, and Metatron," *HTR* 15 (1922) 41-85. [I. Memra, Shekinah, pp. 41-61]

*F. C. Burkitt, "Memra, Shekinah, Metatron," *JTS* 24 (1923) 158-159.

*G. H. Box, "The Idea of Intermediation in Jewish Theology. A Note on Memra and Shekinah," *JQR, N.S.,* 23 (1932-33) 103-119.

*G. R. Berry, "The Glory of Yahweh and the Temple," *JBL* 56 (1937) 115-117.

*Herbert Gordon May, "The Departure of the Glory of Yahweh," *JBL* 56 (1937) 309-321.

Harold L. Creager, "The Glory of God in the Old Testament," *LCQ* 13 (1940) 392-401.

A. F. Knight, "The Shekhinah in Jewish and Christian Thinking," *GUOST* 12 (1944-46) 1-3.

Max Kadushin, "On the Meaning of Shekinah," *CJ* 1 (1945) #2, 9-14. *[Treats only post-Biblical aspects]*

*L. H. Brockington, "The Presence of God. (A Study of the Use of the Term 'Glory of Yahweh.')," *ET* 57 (1945-46) 21-25.

*Herbert Parzen, "The Shekinah in Tannaitic Literature," *CJ* 3 (1946-47) #1, 12-20.

George I. Laurenson, "Is God Really Omniscient?" *RL* 20 (1950-51) 180-184. [Comments by Edwin Lewis, pp. 184-186 and Carl F. H. Henry, pp. 186-189]

August Pieper, "'The Glory of God'," *WLQ* 52 (1955) 104-126, 168-183, 247-259; 53 (1956) 1-13, 139-151; 54 (1957) 27-38; 55 (1958) 1-15. *(Trans. by John Schaadt and Carl Lawrenz)*

Howard P. Hanko, "The Glory of God," *RefR* 9 (1955-56) #1, 8-10.

Joseph Bourke, "Encounter with God—III: from Tabernacle to Temple," *LofS* 16 (1961-62) 182-1197.

Christopher Kiesling, "The Glory of God," *C&C* 14 (1962) 421-431.

Raphael Patai, "The Shekhina," *JR* 44 (1964) 275-288.

*F. X. Sheehan, "The Glory of God: Doxa-Kavodh," *BibT* #26 (1966) 1815-1821.

§983 5.4.2.9 Studies concerning Anthropomorphism and Theophanies

Joshua Frederick Denham, "On the Philosophy of Anthropomorphism," *JSL, 1st Ser.,* 1 (1848) 9-21.

*Anonymous, "The Theophany Celebrated Psalm XVIII. 6-16. Real, not Figurative," *TLJ* 4 (1851-52) 91-116.

E. H. Plumptre, "Anthropomorphic Religion," *Exp, 1st Ser.,* 1 (1875) 44-61.

M. Stuart Phelps, "Anthropomorphism," *PR, 4th Ser.,* 8 (1881) 120-144.

S. J. Morris, "Anthropopathy," *MQR, 2nd Ser.,* 7 (1885) 545-556.

Alexander Winchell, "Anthropomorphism," *MR* 67 (1885) 510-535.

R. H. H., "Professor Winchell on 'Anthropomorphism'," *MR* 67 (1885) 764-766. (Remarks by the editor [Daniel Curry], pp. 766-770)

Frank Fairfield, "Anthropomorphism," *ERG, 9th Ser.,* 2 (1887) 57-65.

*A. W. Burr, "The Theophanies of Homer and the Bible," *BS* 44 (1887) 521-549.

William Hayes Ward, "Light on Scriptural Texts from Recent Discoveries. I. The Divine Wings," *HR* 25 (1893) 117-119. *[Anthropomorphism]*

Julian Morgenstern, "Biblical Theophanies," *ZA* 28 (1913) 15-60.

Herbert H. Gowen, "'The Out-Streched Arm'," *ATR* 3 (1920-21) 74-77.

*F. C. Burkitt, "Memra, Shekinah, Metatron," *JTS* 24 (1922-23) 158-159.

L[eander] S. K[eyser], "The Striking Anthropomorphisms of the Bible," *CFL, 3rd Ser.,* 32 (1926) 62-63.

*[W. M.] Flinders Petrie, "A Portrait Head," *AEE* 17 (1932) 69. *[The Finger of God]*

Herbert H. Gowen, "Manuum Impositio," *ATR* 19 (1937) 288-296.

*E. Ehnmark, "Anthropomorphism and Miracle," *UUÅ* (1939) Band 2, #12, i-viii, 1-230.

L. H. Brockington, "The Hand of Man and the Hand of God," *BQL* 10 (1940-41) 191-197.

*C. T. Fritsch, "Anti-Anthropomorphisms in the First Five Books of the Septuagint," *JBL* 61 (1942) ix.

*G. Ernest Wright, "How Did Early Israel Differ from Her Neighbors?" *BA* 6 (1943) 1-10, 13-20. [III. The Significance of Anthropomorphism, pp. 8-9]

Wilhelm Vischer, "Words and the Word. *The Anthropomorphisms of the Biblical Revelation,*" *Interp* 3 (1949) 3-18.

‡H. H. Rowley, "Recent Foreign Theology. Anthropomorphism in the Old Testament," *ET* 62 (1950-51) 318. *(Review)*

Raphael Loewe, "Jerome's Treatment of an Anthropomorphism," *VT* 2 (1952) 261-272.

*Harry M. Orlinsky, "The Treatment of Anthropomorphisms and Anthropopathisms in the LXX of Isaiah," *EI* 3 (1954) IX-X.

*Roderick A. F. MacKenzie, "The Divine Soliloquies in Genesis," *CBQ* 17 (1955) 277-286. *[Anthropomorphism]*

*Harry M. Orlinsky, "The Treatment of Anthropomorphisms and Antropopathisms in the Septuagint of Isaiah," *HUCA* 27 (1956) 193-200.

*Arthur Soffer, "The Treatment of Anthropomorphisms and Anthropopathisms in the Septuagint of Psalms," *HUCA* 28 (1957) 85-107.

James Barr, "Theophany and anthropomorphism in the Old Testament," *VTS* 7 (1960) 31-38.

Joseph Bourke, "Encounter with God in the Old Testament," *LofS* 15 (1960-61) 398-405.

Joseph Bourke, "Encounter with God in the Old Testament–II," *LofS* 15 (1960-61) 490-497.

G. Ch. Aalders, "The theophanies of the Old Testament," *FUQ* 8 (1961-62) 3-15.

*Joseph Bourke, "From Temple to Heavenly Court," *LofS* 16 (1961-62) 407-420.

E. LaB. Cherbonnier, "The Logic of Biblical Anthropomorphism," *HTR* 55 (1962) 187-206.

*J. Shunary, "Avoidance of Anthropomorphism in the Targum of Psalms," *Text* 5 (1966) 133-144.

*Edwin M. Yamauchi, "Anthropomorphism in the Ancient Religions," *BS* 125 (1968) 29-44.

A. L. Oppenheim, "'The Eyes of the Lord'," *JAOS* 88 (1968) 173-180.

*Murray Lichtenstein, "Dream-Theophany and the E Document," *JANES* 1 (1968-69) #2, 45-54.

§984 *5.4.2.10 Studies on the Doctrine of the Trinity*

Anonymous, "Judaism and the Trinity," *CR* 6 (1853-54) 219-233. *(Review)*

Anonymous, "Objections to the Doctrine of the Trinity from the Unity of God, as Taught in Scripture, Answered," *SPR* 8 (1854-55) 305-328.

*Anonymous, "The Elohim as a Title of God, and as Implying a Plurality of the Godhead," *SPR* 8 (1854-55) 545-559.

Anonymous, "The Nature and Origin of the Pagan Doctrine of Triads, or a Trinity," *SPR* 8 (1854-55) 560-579.

Anonymous, "Further Objections to the Doctrine of the Trinity Answered. *A Consideration of the Heathen Doctrine of the Trinity, the opinions of the ancient Jews, and the almost universal testimony of the Christian world, both ancient and modern,*" *SPR* 9 (1855-56) 1-32.

Thomas Smyth, "The Testimony of the Ancient Jews to the Plurality and Trinity of the Godhead," *SPR* 10 (1857-58) 94-105.

Anonymous, "The Trinity of the Godhead, the Doctrine of the Scriptures," *SPR* 11 (1858-59) 68-91, 175-194.

W. A. P., "The Divine Three-in-One," *ERG, 2nd Ser.,* 2 (1859-60) 249-257. *[Parts I & II related to the Old Testament]*

Robert Balgarnie, "Imago Dei," *HR* 23 (1892) 296-302.

H. B. Swete, "Requests and Replies," *ET* 10 (1898-99) 511. *[The Trinity in the OT]*

Justus Newton Brown, "What is the Trinity," *BS* 59 (1902) 85-107.

Joseph E. Walker, "Polytheism, Tritheism, and the Trinity," *BS* 62 (1905) 455-473.

P. P. Sandford, "On the Trinity," *MR* 16 (1934) 65-67.

N. Friedmann, "The Mystery of the Trinity," *CTM* 15 (1944) 721-729.

*Julian Morgenstern, "The Divine Triad in Biblical Mythology," *JBL* 64 (1945) 15-37.

†H. F. Davis, "The Introit for the Mass of Trinity Sunday," *Scrip* 2 (1947) 48-49. *[Trinity in the OT]*

R. C. Fuller, "Questions and Answers. Is there any reference in the Old Testament to the doctrine of the Blessed Trinity, or was Christ the first to reveal to us the truth of God being Three-in-One?" *Scrip* 5 (1952-53) 102-103.

Jacob W. Heikkinen, "The Doctrine of the Trinity. 4. The Doctrine of the Trinity and the Bible," *RL* 29 (1959-60) 42-51.

Reginald H. Fuller, "On Demythologizing the Trinity," *ATR* 43 (1961) 121-131.

L. S. Albright, "The Doctrine of the Trinity. A Question of Meaning and Mission," *RL* 33 (1963-64) 275-285.

R. G. Crawford, "Is the Doctrine of the Trinity Scriptural?" *SJT* 20 (1967) 282-294.

*Robert C. Neville, "Creation and the Trinity," *ThSt* 30 (1969) 3-26.

§985 *5.4.2.11 Studies on the Names of God*

†R. M., "Answer to G. W.," *MMBR* 3 (1797) 336-337. *[Names of God]*

G. B. K., "On the Divine Name שַׁדַּי Shaddai, 'The Almighty'," *BRCM* 5 (1848-49) 304-315.

[Pliny E.] Chase, "On Certain Primitive Names of the Supreme Being," *PAPS* 9 (1862-64) 420-424.

*Anonymous, "The Name, and the Idea, of God," *CE* 78 (1865) 198-206.

J. M. Johnson, "The Name of the Lord," *AThR, N.S.,* 4 (1866) 465-474.

Eleazer Lord, "The Divine Names in the Hebrew Scriptures," *AThR, N.S.,* 5 (1867) 268-298.

[Edward Hayes] Plumptre, "The Lord of Sabaoth. A Biblical Study," *ThE* 6 (1869) 85-92.

J. B. Walker, "The Doctrine of the Divine Name," *CongR* 10 (1870) 343-353.

W. M. Thomson, "The Natural Basis of Our Spiritual Language: Divine Names and Titles," *BS* 31 (1874) 136-158.

W. M. Thomson, "The Natural Basis of Our Spiritual Language," *DTQ* 1 (1875) 373-385. [Divine Names and Titles]

*John Urquhart, "The Divine Names in Genesis," *BFER* 30 (1881) 227-242.

*John Urquhart, "Jehovistic and Elohistic Theories," *BFER* 31 (1882) 205-238.

F. Frothingham, "The God of Abraham, Isaac, and Jacob," *URRM* 20 (1883) 62-70.

James Foote, "Hebrew Names of God," *ERG, 8th Ser.,* 2 (1883-84) 33-39.

*Talbot W. Chambers, "The Occurrence of the Divine Names in Genesis," *ONTS* 3 (1883-84) 91-92.

*R. V. Foster, "The Names and Doctrine of God," *ONTS* 3 (1883-84) 369-376.

*Barnard C. Taylor, "The Divine Names as They Occur in the Prophets," *AJSL* 2 (1885-86) 109-110.

*Henry M. Harman, "The Divine Names in the Book of Job," *JBL* 6 (1886) part 1, 119.

*S. R. Calthrop, "'Jehovah of Hosts.'," *URRM* 25 (1886) 540-551.

*Thomas Laurie, "The Name of God and the Cuneiform Inscriptions," *BS* 45 (1888) 515-518.

Anonymous, "The Names of God," *CQR* 27 (1888-89) 280-296. *(Review)*

*Thomas Laurie, "El Shaddai," *BS* 47 (1890) 360-362.

*F. Tilney Bassett, "Requests and Replies," *ET* 3 (1891-92) 555. *[Jehovah of Hosts]*

A. J. Maas, "A Chapter in Mosaic Theodicy," *AER* 7 (1892) 106-120.

*Thos. Stoughton Potwin, "The Divine Names in the Book of Genesis, in the Light of Recent Discoveries," *BS* 50 (1893) 348-357.

J. A. Selbie, "Jah," *ET* 7 (1895-96) 470.

Morris Jastrow Jr., "The Origin of the Form יה of the Divine Name," *ZAW* 16 (1896) 1-16.

Stanley A. Cook, "The Divine Name Ša in the Old Testament," *ET* 10 (1898-99) 525-526.

A. C. Zenos, "The Self-Revelation of God in His Names," *CFL, O.S.,* 3 (1899) 300-305.

*F. J. Coffin, "Third commandment," *JBL* 19 (1900) 166-188. [V. The Use and Abuse of the Divine Name in the Old Testament, pp. 180-183]

*James A. Kelso, "The Antiquity of the Divine Title עליון אל in Gen. 14," *JBL* 20 (1901) 50-55.

*Robert Kilgour, "Old Testament Names for God: Their Rendering into Hindi and Cognate Languages. A Plea for the Transliterations of the Sacred Name," *GUOST* 2 (1901-07) 50-52.

108 Studies on the Names of God §985 cont.

George Drach, "The Names of God in the Old Testament," *LCR* 21 (1902) 375-387. [The Primitive Period and the Name "El"; "El-Eljon" and the second stage; "El-schaddai" and the third stage; Summary]

*Julius Boehmer, "כָּבוֹד a Divine Name? A Note on Ps. CXLIX. 5," *ET* 14 (1902-03) 334-336.

James A. Montgomery, "'The Place' as an Appelation of Deity," *JBL* 24 (1905) 17-26.

R. B. de Bary, "The Word 'Father' as Applied to God," *HR* 52 (1906) 368-369.

*John Taylor, "Jahweh and Non-Israelites," *ET* 18 (1906-07) 502-503. *(Review)*

Ephraim M. Epstein, "The Mosaic Names of God, and What They Denote," *Monist* 17 (1907) 389-414.

*Andrew Craig Robinson, "Lord of Hosts," *ET* 19 (1907-08) 188-189.

X., "The Lord of Hosts," *ET* 19 (1907-08) 235-236.

*A. P. Cox, "The Name of God in Genesis. I.," *ET* 20 (1908-09) 378.

*John Skinner, "The Name of God in Genesis. II.," *ET* 20 (1908-09) 378-379.

*Harold M. Wiener, "The Name of God in Genesis," *ET* 20 (1908-09) 473-475.

*Nivard Johann Schlögl, "The Name of God in Genesis," *ET* 20 (1908-09) 563.

*C. F. Burney, "Four and Seven as Divine Titles," *JTS* 12 (1910-11) 118-120.

*T. K. Cheyne, "New God Names," *JBL* 30 (1911) 104-105.

T. K. Cheyne, "Eshmun and Other Divine Names," *ET* 23 (1911-12) 136.

Eb. Nestle, "'Lord' in the A.V.," *ET* 23 (1911-12) 184.

*John Skinner, "The Divine Names in the Genesis," *Exp, 8th Ser.,* 6 (1913) 289-313, 400-420, 494-514.

*Johannes Dashe, "Divine Appelations, Textual Criticism and Documentary Theory. My Reply to Dr. Skinner," *Exp, 8th Ser.,* 6 (1913) 481-510.

*John Skinner, "The Divine Names in the Pentateuch," *ET* 25 (1913-14) 472-473. *(Review)*

*Robert C. Thomson, "The Names of God in Genesis," *GUOST* 4 (1913-14) 7-9.

M. Gaster, "'The Lord of Hosts'," *ET* 26 (1914-15) 475-461.

*Anonymous, "The Elephantine Papyri and the Old Testament," *HR* 69 (1915) 368. *[Name of God]*

*Robert Dick Wilson, "The Use of 'God' and 'Lord' in the Koran," *PTR* 21 (1919) 644-650.

*Robert Dick Wilson, "Use of the Words for God in the Apocryphal and Pseudepigraphal Literature of the Jews," *PTR* 18 (1920) 103-122.

Robert Dick Wilson, "The Names of God in the Old Testament," *PTR* 18 (1920) 460-492.

W. H. Langdon, "What's in a Name?" *CFL, 3rd Ser.,* 28 (1922) 209-210.

Maurice Canney, "Shaddai," *ET* 34 (1922-23) 332.

F. C. Burkitt, "Memra, Shekinah, Metatron," *JTS* 24 (1922-23) 158-159.

John G. Reid, "What is His Name?" *CFL, 3rd Ser.,* 33 (1927) 207-208.

*R[obert] D[ick] Wilson, "The Names of God in the Psalms," *PTR* 25 (1927) 1-39.

*J. M. Powis Smith, "The Use of Divine Names as Superlatives," *AJSL* 45 (1928-29) 212-213.

H. W. Magoun, "'The Name' of God According to the Scriptures," *CFL, 3rd Ser.,* 35 (1929) 416-417.

*A. McCaig, "The Use of the Divine Names in the Pentateuch," *EQ* 2 (1930) 14-31.

*A. Marmorstein, "Philo and the Names of God," *JQR, N.S.,* 22 (1931-32) 295-306.

*Ralph Marcus, "Divine Names and Attributes in Hellenistic Jewish Literature," *PAAJR* 3 (1931-32) 43-120.

*E. L. Sukenik, "Potsherds from Samaria, Inscribed with the Divine Name," *PEFQS* 68 (1936) 34-37.

*W. E. Staples, "A Note on an Inscribed Potsherd," *PEFQS* 68 (1936) 155.

*James A. Montgomery, "The Highest, Heaven, Aeon, Time, etc., in Semitic Religion," *HTR* 31 (1938) 143-150.

*G. R. Driver, "Hebrew *'al* ('High One') as a Divine Title,' *ET* 50 (1938-39) 92-93.

*Lewis Sperry Chafer, "Biblical Theism. The Names of God," *BS* 96 (1939) 390-404.

William H. McClellan, "'Dominus Deus Sabaoth'," *CBQ* 2 (1940) 300-307.

E. Burrows, "The Meaning of El Šaddai," *JTS* 41 (1940) 152-161.

*Norval Gerhard Hegland, "Sermons in Hebrew Words," *JTALC* 6 (1941) 817-835, 935-944. [Part I. Chief Names for God, pp. 820-835]

*C. M. Cooper, "The Divine Personal Pronoun in the Psalms," *JBL* 64 (1945) iii.

‡H. H. Rowley, "Recent Foreign Theology. The Lord of Hosts," *ET* 60 (1948-49) 109. *(Review)*

*Samuel S. Cohon, "The Name of God, A Study in Rabbinic Theology," *HUCA* 23 (1950-51) Part 1, 579-604.

*A. Murtonen, "A Philological and Literary Treatise on the Old Testament Divine Names אל, אלוה, אלהים, and יהוה," *SO* 18 (1952) #1, 1-105.

*Mitchell Dahood, "The Divine Name 'Ēlî in the Psalms," *ThSt* 14 (1953) 452-457.

N.   H.   Tur-Sinai,   "El   Shaddai,"   *EI*   3   (1954)   II.

M. H. Segal, "El, Elohim, and YHWH in the Bible," *JQR, N.S.,* 46 (1955-56) 89-115.

J. A. Martin Jr., "St. Thomas and Tillich on the Names of God," *JR* 37 (1957) 253-259.

Walter Lowrie, "The Proper Name of God," *ATR* 46 (1959) 245-252.

*M[itchell] Dahood, "Is *'Eben Yiśrāēl* a Divine Title? (Gen. 49, 24)," *B* 40 (1959) 1002-1007.

Norman Walker, "A new Interpretation of the Divine Name 'Shaddai'," *ZAW* 72 (1960) 64-66.

Sigmund Mowinckel, "The Name of the God of Moses," *HUCA* 32 (1961) 121-133.

Avraham Haltz, "Kiddush and Hillul Hashem," *Jud* 10 (1961) 360-367.

E. C. B. MacLaurin, "Shaddai," *ABR-N* 3 (1961-62) 99-118.

*H. K. Moulton, "The Names and Attributes of God," *BTr* 13 (1962) 71-80.

F. Zimmerman, "*'El* and *Adonai*," *VT* 12 (1962) 190-195.

*A. F. Knight, "Ego Eimi," *Coll* 1 (1964-66) 219-224.

*Roland E. Clements, "Divine Titles as a Problem of Old Testament Translation," *BTr* 17 (1966) 81-84.

*A. Crepin, "The Names of God in the Church Fathers and in Old English Poetry," *StP* 9 (1966) 525-531.

*J. Murtagh, "The 'Name' in Egypt and Israel," *BibT* #37 (1968) 2585-2589.

*F. G. Smith, "Observations on the Greek Use of the Names and Titles of God in Genesis," *EQ* 40 (1968) 103-110.

*Lloyd R. Bailey, "Israelite *'Ēl Šadday* and Amorite *Bêl Šadê*," *JBL* 87 (1968) 434-438.

§986 *5.4.2.11.1 Studies concerning El and Elohim*

*Anonymous, "On Elohim as a Title of God, and as Implying a Plurality of the Godhead," *SPR* 8 (1854-55) 545-559.

Francis Brown, "The Divine Name, El," *PR* 3 (1882) 404-407.

*William Aikman, "The Word Elohim and Jehovah in Genesis," *MR* 59 (1877) 616-626.

*William Aikman, "The Word Elohim and Jehovah in Genesis," *DTQ* 5 (1879) 292-302.

*R. V. Foster, "The Word Elohim in Genesis I," *ONTS* 6 (1886-87) 241-243.

*Thomas Laurie, "El Shaddai," *BS* 47 (1890) 360-362.

J. G. Tasker, "Elohim," *ET* 10 (1898-99) 219-221.

Henry Proctor, "Elohim: The Object of Primeval Worship," *AAOJ* 27 (1905) 33-34.

*William Henry Green, "The Use of 'Elohim' and 'Jehovah' in the Pentateuch," *CFL, 3rd Ser.,* 4 (1906) 258-265, 337-343.

*J. F. C. Fuller, "Elohim and the Number π," *Monist* 17 (1907) 110-111.

*J. Battersby Harford, "Since Wellhausen," *Exp, 9th Ser.,* 4 (1925) 4-26. [Supplementary Note on the Use of Elohim in the Pentateuch, pp. 20-26]

Harold M. Wiener, "Elohim Outside of the Pentateuch and Baumgaertäel's Investigation," *BS* 72 (1915) 308-333.

W. H. Griffith Thomas, "'Elohim'," *ET* 27 (1915-16) 45.

R. H. Pfeiffer, "Three Assyriological Footnotes to the Old Testament," *JBL* 47 (1928) 184-187. [1. Ilāni = Elohim, pp. 184-185]

*John L. McKenzie, "The Appellative use of *El* and *Elohim*," *CBQ* 10 (1948) 170-181.

*Otto Eissfeldt, "El and Yahweh," *JSS* 1 (1956) 25-37.

Norman Walker, "Elohim and Eloah," *VT* 6 (1956) 214-215.

Anne E. Draffkorn, "*Ilāni/Elohim*," *JBL* 76 (1957) 216-224.

*Patrick D. Miller Jr., "El the Warrior," *HTR* 60 (1967) 411-431.

§987 *5.4.2.11.2 Studies concerning Yahweh, Jehovah, and Jah*

†M. R., "On the Appellation 'Jehovah'," *MMBR* 6 (1798) 247-248.

(   ) Simpson, "The Name of Jehovah," *MMBR* 6 (1798) 419-422.

Joseph Wise, "The Name of Jehovah," *MMBR* 6 (1798) 425.

†Anonymous, "Jehovah, Origin of the word," *MMBR* 27 (1809) 51.

*E. Ballantine, "Interpretation of Exodus VI. 2, 3.," *BRCR* 3 (1833) 730-748.

[Frederic August Grottreu] Tholuck, "On the Hypothesis of the Egyptian or Indian Origin of the Name Jehovah," *BRCR* 4 (1834) 89-108. *(Trans. by Edward Robinson)*

T. J., "The Septuagint Translation of Jehovah," *JSL, 2nd Ser.,* 6 (1854) 519.

Alexander MacWhorter*[sic]*, "Jehovah Considered as a Memorial Name," *BS* 14 (1857) 98-124.

T. T., "The Divine Name Jehovah," *JSL, 3rd Ser.,* 8 (1858-59) 436-437.

*A[lexander] Mc[Whorter],"Yav in Assyrian; or 'Jehovah' on the Bricks and Inscribed Cylinders of 'Ur of the Chaldees'," *JSL, 3rd Ser.,* 9 (1859) 174-175.

*W[illiam] H[enry] Green, "The Name Jehovah," *ER* 16 (1865) 86-103.

Thomas Tyler, "The Memorial Name," *JSL, 4th Ser.,* 7 (1865) 206-213; 8 (1865-66) 197-200.

Alexander MacWhorter*[sic]*, "Mr. Tyler on the Memorial Name," *JSL, 4th Ser.,* 7 (1865) 454-455; 8 (1865-66) 465.

*W. R[obertson] Smith, "On the Name Jehovah (Jahve) and the Doctrine of Exodus III. 14," *BFER* 25 (1876) 153-165.

*William Aikman, "The Word Elohim and Jehovah in Genesis," *MR* 59 (1877) 610-626.

*William Aikman, "The Word Elohim and Jehovah in Genesis," *DTQ* 5 (1879) 292-302.

Charles Elliott, "The Name Jehovah," *OBJ* 1 (1880) 199-201.

*Samuel Cox, "The Tetragrammaton. Exodus iii. 14," *Exp, 2nd Ser.,* 1 (1881) 12-24.

A. H. Sayce, "The Origin of the Name 'Jehovah.'," *ModR* 3 (1882) 855-857.

114   *Studies concerning Yahweh, Jehovah, and Jah*   §987 cont.

Thomas Tyler, "The Origin of the Name 'Jehovah.',," *ModR* 3 (1882) 608-613; 4 (1883) 177-179.

O. D. Miller, "The Name of God Revealed to Moses," *UQGR, N.S.,* 21 (1884) 445-464.

Ed. König, "On the Source of the Name יהוה," *AJSL* 1 (1884-85) 255-257.

*S. R. Calthrop, "'Jehovah of Hosts.'," *URRM* 25 (1886) 540-551.

Andrew Lang, "Was Jehovah a Fetish Stone?" *ContR* 57 (1890) 353-365.

*J. A. MacDonald, "The name of Jehovah in the Book of Esther," *CMR* 2 (1890) 174-181.

*F. Tilney Bassett, "Requests and Replies," *ET* 3 (1891-92) 555. *[Jehovah of Hosts]*

*Theo. G. Pinches, "Ya and Yawa (Jah and Jahweh) in Assyro-Babylonian Inscriptions," *SBAP* 15 (1892-93) 13-15.

William Hayes Ward, "Light on Scriptural Texts from Recent Discoveries. IV. The Ineffable Name," *HR* 25 (1893) 410-412.

John W. Primrose, "'May Know that I am Jehovah.'—A Bible Study," *PQ* 11 (1897) 523-530.

*A. H. Sayce, "Yahveh in Early Babylonia," *ET* 9 (1897-98) 522.

*Fritz Hommel, "Yahveh in Early Babylonia," *ET* 10 (1898-99) 42.

*Fritz Hommel, "The Etymology of יהוה," *ET* 10 (1898-99) 48.

Fritz Hommel, "Jahve, Ea, and Sin," *ET* 10 (1898-99) 144.

Ed. König, "The Origin of the Name יהוה," *ET* 10 (1898-99) 189-192.

*Paul Carus, "Yahveh and Manitou," *Monist* 9 (1898-99) 382-415.

J. Cleveland Hall, "Yahweh," *PER* 12 (1898-99) 399-403.

William Ashmore, "The Kingship of Jehovah," *R&E* 4 (1907) 47-70.

John E. McFadyen, "Who was Jehovah?" *HR* 54 (1907) 127-130.

D. G. Brinton, "The origin of the sacred name Jahva," *AfRW* 2 (1899) 226-236.

William W. McLane, "The Natural History of Yahweh," *HR* 37 (1899) 119-124.

R. M. Spence, "Yah, Yahve," *ET* 11 (1899-1900) 94-95.

*Fritz Hommel, "Yahweh in Early Babylonia: A Supplementary Note," *ET* 11 (1899-1900) 270.

E. Riggs, "Pronunciation of the Sacred Name Jehovah," *CFL, N.S.,* 3 (1901) 175-176.

*L. B. Paton, "Deborah's Conception of Yahweh," *BW* 19 (1902) 197-198.

John D. Davis, "Jehovah: A Name Descriptive of the Divine Character," *CFL, 3rd Ser.,* 6 (1902) 68-70.

*A. H. Keane, "Ea; Yahweh: Dyaus; ΖΕΥΣ; Jupiter," *JQR* 15 (1902-03) 559-582.

John C. Granberry, "Jehovah," *CFL, N.S.,* 7 (1903) 107-110.

C. H. W. Johns, "The Name Jehovah in the Abrahamic Age," *Exp, 6th Ser.,* 8 (1903) 282-293.

George Drach, "The Names of God in the Old Testament. II," *LCR* 22 (1903) 507-514. [The Name Yahwe (Jehova)]

*C. R. Conder, "Notes and Queries. *The Name of Jehovah on Seals,*" *PEFQS* 35 (1903) 96.

C. Gaenssle, "Was Jehovah in Preprophetic Times a National Deity?" *TQ* 8 (1904) 25-46.

*William R. Arnold, "The Divine Name in Exodus iii. 14," *JBL* 24 (1905) 107-165.

Anonymous, "Derivation of Yahveh," *RP* 4 (1905) 156.

*Ed. König, "Has the Name 'Jahweh' Been Found Among the Canaanites?" *ET* 17 (1905-06) 331-333.

Cornelius Walker, "The Real Meaning of 'Jehovah'," *CFL, 3rd Ser.,* 5 (1906) 30-34.

John Urquhart, "'The Jehovah Name'," *CFL, 3rd Ser.,* 5 (1906) 34-35.

*William Henry Green, "The Use of 'Elohim' and 'Jehovah' in the Pentateuch," *CFL, 3rd Ser.,* 4 (1906) 258-265, 337-343.

A. H. Sayce, "The Name of Yeho, Yahveh," *ET* 18 (1906-07) 26-27.

Eb. Nestle, "Deus Abraham," *ET* 18 (1906-07) 143.

*Wm. B. Stevenson, "Was the Ark Jehovah's Throne?" *ET* 18 (1906-07) 379-380.

*Ed. König, "Has the Name 'Jahweh' Been Discovered in the Babylonian Monuments?" *ET* 18 (1906-07) 429-430.

L. A. Pooler, "The Name 'Jahweh'," *ET* 18 (1906-07) 525.

John T. McFarland, "Did the Patriarchs Know the Name 'Jehovah'?" *CFL, 3rd Ser.,* 7 (1907) 251-253.

A. H. Sayce, "The Name יהוה," *ET* 19 (1907-08) 525-526.

Eb. Nestle, "Remarks, #3," *ET* 19 (1907-08) 475. *[Ref. Sayce (above)]*

Eb. Nestle, "The Divine Name 'Jhv' or 'Jhvh'," *ET* 19 (1907-08) 564-565.

George F. Moore, "Notes on the Name יהוה," *AJT* 12 (1908) 34-52.

*J. Glentworth Butler, "Scriptural Identification of the Christ with Jehovah," *CFL, 3rd Ser.,* 9 (1908) 112-114.

*E. J. Pilcher, "A Coin of Gaza, and the Vision of Ezekiel," *SBAP* 30 (1908) 45-52. *[YHWH]*

W. R. W. Gardner, "The Name 'Yahweh'," *ET* 20 (1908-09) 91-92.

H. F. B. Compston, "YAHÛ or YAHW," *ET* 20 (1908-09) 231-232.

*Francis J. Lamb, "'Exodus' An 'Ancient Document', Proof of Jehovah's Existence and Character 'Once for All'," *CFL, 3rd Ser.,* 11 (1909) 157-167.

*W. Max Müller, "The Semitic God of Tahpanhes. Probably an Ancient Relief of Yahveh," *OC* 23 (1909) 1-5.

P[aul] C[arus], "An Image of Yahveh," *OC* 23 (1909) 189-190.

*[Paul Carus], "A Yahveh Picture and What it Teaches," *OC* 24 (1910) 391-404.

Eb.   Nestle,   "Jah,"   *ET*   22   (1910-11)   90.

*Stephen Langdon, "Concerning 'Jahweh' in Lexicographical Babylonian Tablets," *ET* 22 (1910-11) 139-140.

H.   F.   B.   Compston,   "Jah,"   *ET*   22   (1910-11)   140.

*A. H. Sayce, "Yahweh and Jerusalem," *ET* 22 (1910-11) 226-229.

Anonymous, "Origin and Meaning of 'Jehovah' the Key to the Scriptures," *CFL, 3rd Ser.,* 15 (1912) 12-15. [I. Did the Patriarchs Know the Name "Jehovah?"; II. Misleading Etymological Speculations Concerning the Origin of the Name]

George C. Alborn, "Meaning and Use of the Name 'Jehovah'," *CFL, 3rd Ser.,* 15 (1912) 71-73.

*J[ohn] Skinner, "The Divine Names in Genesis," *Exp, 8th Ser.,* 5 (1913) 289-313, 400-420, 494-514. [I. Exodus VI. 2, 3; II. The Pericope-Hypothesis; III. Recensions in the Septuagint]

*John Skinner, "The Divine Names in Genesis," *Exp, 8th Ser.,* 6 (1913) 23-45, 97-116, 266-288. [IV. The Hebrew Text, 1. Hebrew Manuscripts, 2. The Samaritan Pentateuch; V. The Limits of Textual Uncertainty]

Thos. Torrance, "An Illustration," *ET* 28 (1916-17) 425-426. *[Dread of the Jews to pronounce the name YHWH]*

*James A. Montgomery, "Babylonian *niš* 'oath' in West-Semitic," *JAOS* 37 (1917) 329-330. [(?) יהוה נסי]

John A. Maynard, "The Bearing of the Change from Yahu to Yahweh in Mosaic Times," *ATR* 1 (1918-19) 93-95.

Joseph   D.   Wilson,   "Jehovah,"   *BS*   76   (1919)   221-227.

Joseph Offord, "The Mountain Throne of Jahveh," *PEFQS* 51 (1919) 39-45.

*Alexander M'Nair, "'Thus Saith Jahweh'," *ET* 32 (1920-21) 508-509.

*W[illiam] H. B[ates], "Jehovah—Not know yet known," *CFL, 3rd Ser.,* 27 (1921) 400.

*J. E. Walker, "The Supreme Object of Worship in Ancient China, Was It Jehovah?" *BS* 79 (1922) 23-42.

*William Phillips Hall, "A Biblical Study of 'The Name' of God, and Its Relation to the Lord Jesus Christ," *CFL, 3rd Ser.,* 29 (1923) 600-607.

Anonymous, "The Meaning of Jehovah," *Exp, 9th Ser.,* 2 (1924) 467.

*W[illiam] F[oxwell] Albright, "Contributions of Biblical Archaeology and Philology," *JBL* 43 (1924) 363-393. [2. The Name *Yahweh,* pp. 370-378]

W[illiam] F[oxwell] Albright, "Further Observations on the Name *Yahweh* and Its Modifications in Proper Names," *JBL* 44 (1925) 158-162.

F. C. Burkitt, "On the Name Yahweh," *JBL* 44 (1925) 353-356.

*R. H. Pfeiffer, "Images of Yahweh," *JBL* 45 (1926) 211-222.

F. B. Denio, "On the Use of the Word Jehovah in Translating the Old Testament," *JBL* 46 (1927) 146-149.

G. R. Driver, "The original form of the name 'Yahweh': evidence and conclusions," *ZAW* 46 (1928) 7-25.

*Wm. C. Robinson, "Jesus Christ is Jehovah," *USR* 44 (1932-33) 278-292, 380-400.

*W. C. Robinson, "Jesus Christ is Jehovah," *EQ* 5 (1933) 144-155, 271-290.

James D. Smart, "A New Approach to the 'Ebed-Yahweh Problem," *ET* 45 (1933-34) 168-172.

*B. D. Eerdmans, "The Name Jahu," *OTS* 5 (1948) 1-29.

*William A. Irwin, "Images of Yahweh," *CQ* 19 (1942) 292-301.

A. Lincoln Shute, "Jehovah," *R&E* 39 (1942) 321-332.

*C. T. Fritsch, "The Translation of Yahweh by *(ho) Theos* in the Greek Pentateuch," *JBL* 63 (1944) iv-v.

*J. A. Montgomery, "The Hebrew Divine Name and the Personal Pronoun *hū*," *JBL* 63 (1944) 161-163.

Raymond A. Bowman, "Yahweh the Speaker," *JNES* 3 (1944) 1-8.

Julian Obermann, "The Divine Name *YHWH* in the Light of Recent Discoveries," *JBL* 68 (1949) 301-323. [1. Hebrew *'ănî yahwê* and Phoenician *yqtl'nk;* 2. *YHWH* as a Proper Name; 3. *YHWH* as a Nomen Agentis; 4. Theophorous Formations; 5. Evolution of the Epithet]

A. Murtonen, "The Appearance of the Name *YHWH* Outside Israel," *SO* 16 (1951) #3, 1-11.

*P. Peters, "The Divine Name YHWH in the Dead Sea Scrolls," *WLQ* 48 (1951) 148.

R. A. Barclay, "The Origin of the Name *'YHWH'*," *GUOST* 15 (1953-54) 44-47.

Charles R. A. Cunliffe, "The Divine Name of Yahweh," *Scrip* 6 (1953-54) 112-115.

*G. R. Driver, "Reflections on Recent Articles," *JBL* 73 (1954) 125-136. [I. The Interpretation of YHWH as a Participal Form from a Causative Theme of the Verb, pp. 125-131]

Jeremiah O'Connell, "The Name Yahweh," *ITQ* 22 (1955) 355-358.

J. Philip Hyatt, "Yahweh as 'The God of My Father'," *VT* 5 (1955) 130-136.

*Otto Eissfeldt, "El and Yahweh," *JSS* 1 (1956) 25-37.

S. D. Goitein, "*YHWH* the Passionate. The Monotheistic Meaning and Origin of the Name *YHWH*," *VT* 6 (1956) 1-9.

Immanuel Lewy, "The Beginnings of the Worship of Yahweh, Conflicting Biblical Views," *VT* 6 (1956) 429-435.

Norman Walker, "Yahwism and the Divine Name 'Yhwh'," *ZAW* 70 (1958) 262-265.

Myles M. Bourke, "Yahweh, the divine name," *TD* 7 (1959) 174-176.

Raymond Abba, "The Divine Name Yahweh," *JBL* 80 (1961) 320-328.

Frank Moore Cross Jr., "Yahweh and the God of the Patriarchs," *HTR* 55 (1962) 225-259.

Hans Kosmala, "The Name of God (YHWH and HU')," *ASTI* 2 (1963) 103-106.

Roy A. Rosenberg, "Yahweh Becomes King," *JBL* 85 (1966) 297-307.

*Walter Gerhardt Jr., "The Hebrew/Israelite Weather-Deity," *Numen* 13 (1966) 128-143. *[YHWH]*

*J. Philip Hyatt, "Was Yahweh Originally a Creator Deity?" *JBL* 86 (1967) 369-377.

*P. C. Craigie, "'Yahweh is a Man of Wars'," *SJT* 22 (1969) 183-188.

*J. L. Crenshaw, "*YHWH Ṣeba'ôt Šemô:* A Form-Critical Analysis," *ZAW* 81 (1969) 156-175.

§988 *5.4.2.11.3 Studies on the Tetragrammaton*

*B., "The Septuagint and the New Testament Rendering of 'Jehovah:' or, the Reasons why the New Testament seems to Sanction the Septuagint in Rendering יהוה by κυριος," *BRCM* 3 (1847) 21-28.

†Anonymous, "McWhorter on the Memorial Name," *PQR* 6 (1857-58) 86-105. *(Review)*

[Reginal Stuart Poole], "On the Antiquity of the Name Jehovah," *JSL, 4th Ser.,* 3 (1863) 180-181.

Paul De Lagarde, "The Meaning of יהוה," *BS* 35 (1878) 544-551.

John P. Peters, "Professor Friedrich Delitzsch and the Word יהוה," *ONTS* 2 (1882-83) 129-142.

*J. F. Garrison, "The Theology of the Lost Word and the Manifestation of the Divine Name," *JLTQ* 1 (1884) 1-28.

*S. T. Anderson, "I Am That I Am," *ONTS* 4 (1884-85) 310-313.

S. R. Driver, "Recent Theories on the Origin and Nature of the Tetragrammaton," *SBE* 1 (1885) 1-20.

Charles Rufus Brown, "Pronunciation of יהוה," *AJSL* 4 (1887-88) 54.

C. J. Ball, "The true Name of the God of Israel," *BOR* 3 (1888-89) 49-56.

*Frederic Gardiner, "On the Duplication of the Tetragrammaton in Isaiah 12:2; 26:4," *ONTS* 9 (1889) 219-223.

B. C. Taylor, "A Note on the Pronunciation of יהוה," *AJSL* 8 (1891-92) 103.

G. Margoliouth, "The Divine Name יהוה," *SBAP* 17 (1895) 57-63.

G. H. Skipwith, "The Tetragrammaton: Its Meaning and Origin," *JQR* 10 (1897-98) 662-677.

Geo. G. Cameron, "Requests and Replies," *ET* 11 (1899-1900) 60. *[The Tetragrammaton]*

*F. J. Coffin, "Third commandment," *JBL* 19 (1900) 166-188. [IV. The Name of Yahweh (שם יהוה), pp. 177-180]

Thomas Tyler, "The Origin of the Tetragrammaton," *JQR* 13 (1900-01) 581-593.

Hans H. Spoer, "The Origin and Interpretation of the Tetragrammaton," *AJSL* 18 (1901-92) 9-35.

*James A. Kelso, "Is the Divine Name in Hebrew Ever Equivalent to the Superlative?" *AJSL* 19 (1902-03) 152-158.

J. H. Levy, "The Tetra(?)grammaton," *JQR* 15 (1902-03) 97-99.

*W. F. Warren, "Beginnings of Hebrew Monotheism—The Ineffable Name," *MR* 84 (1902) 24-35.

*Dom Adalbert Amadolini, "The Nomen Tetragrammaton in Genesis IV. 1," *DR* 132 (1903) 336-340.

*James A. Montgomery, "Notes from the Samaritan," *JBL* 25 (1906) 49-54. [I. A Nineteenth Century Witness to the Pronunciation of YHWH, pp. 49-51]

Anonymous, "YHWH," *MR* 90 (1908) 136-140.

George F. Moore, "Notes on the Name יהוה," *AJSL* 25 (1908-09) 312-318.

J. A. Montgomery, "Babylonian Section. The Pronunciation of the 'Ineffable Name' According to a Jewish Text in the Museum," *MJ* 1 (1910) 28-30.

*Eb. Nestle, "The Tetragramm on the Title-Pages of the Authorized Version, 1611," *ET* 22 (1910-11) 423.

*Eb. Nestle, "The Pointing of the Tetragrammaton. I.," *ET* 22 (1910-11) 524.

A. R. S. Kennedy, "The Pointing of the Tetragrammaton. II.," *ET* 22 (1910-11) 524-525.

George F. Moore, "Notes on the Name יהוה," *AJSL* 28 (1911-12) 56-62.

W. St. Clair Tisdall, "A New Solution of an Old Problem," *BS* 70 (1913) 587-598. *[The Tetragrammaton]*

K. Kohler, "The Tetragrammaton (Shem ham-M'forash) and Its Uses," *JJLP* 1 (1919) 19-32.

*A. Cowley, "A Passage in the Mesha Inscription, and the Early Form of the Israelitish Divine Name," *JRAS* (1920) 175-184.

*James A. Montgomery, "The Survival of the Tetragrammaton in Daniel," *JBL* 40 (1921) 86.

D. D. Luckenbill, "The Pronunciation of the Name of the God of Israel," *AJSL* 40 (1923-24) 277-283.

*James Edward Hogg, "Exegetical Notes. IV. The Translation of יהוה," *AJSL* 41 (1924-25) 272-274.

*G. R. Driver, "The Aramaic Language," *JBL* 45 (1926) 323-325. *[The Tetragrammaton]*

Leroy Waterman, "Method in the Study of the Tetragrammaton," *AJSL* 43 (1926-27) 1-7.

A. L. Williams, "Yāhōh," *JTS* 28 (1926-27) 276-282.

F. C. Burkitt, "Yahweh or Yahoh: Additional Note," *JTS* 28 (1926-27) 407-409.

*James A. Montgomery, "The *hemzah-h* in the Semitic," *JBL* 46 (1927) 144-146.

Jacob Z. Lauterbach, "Substitutes for the Tetragrammaton," *PAAJR* 2 (1930-31) 39-67.

A. Lukyn Williams, "The Tetragrammaton—Jahweh, Name or Surrogate?" *ZAW* 54 (1936) 262-269.

*E. L. Sukenik, "A Further Note on an Inscribed Potsherd," *PEQ* 69 (1937) 140-141.

*Cyrus H. Gordon, "The Pointing of יְהֹוָה," *ZAW* 56 (1938) 174.

Ralph Marcus, "The Name *YHWH*," *JBL* 58 (1938) vi.

A. Spiro, "Corruption of the Tetragrammaton," *JBL* 60 (1941) x.

William A. Irwin, "The Tetragrammaton: An Overlooked Interpretation," *JNES* 3 (1944) 257-259.

*W. G. Waddell, "The Tetragrammaton in the LXX," *JTS* 45 (1944) 158-161.

*Harry Torczyner, "Abbreviation or Haplography?" *JBL* 64 (1945) 399.

Harry M. Orlinsky, "A Rejoinder," *JBL* 64 (1945) 400-402.

Harry Torczyner, "Yes, Haplography!" *JBL* 64 (1945) 545-546. [Editorial Note by Robert H. Pfeiffer, p. 546]

*B. D. Eerdmans, "The Name Jahu," *OTS* 5 (1948) 1-29.

G. J. Thierry, "The Pronunciation of the Tetragrammaton," *OTS* 5 (1948) 30-42.

S. Edward Tesh, "The Emergence and the Nature of the Tetragrammaton," *SQ/E* 9 (1948) 181-193.

Charles C. Torrey, "The Magic of 'Lotapes'," *JBL* 68 (1949) 325-327.

*S. M. Stern, "Notes on the New Manuscript Find," *JBL* 69 (1950) 19-30. [The Tetragrammaton, pp. 29-30]

Norman Walker, "The Writing of the Divine Name in the Mishna," *VT* 1 (1951) 309-310.

*A. Murtonen, "A Philological and Literary Treatise on the Old Testament Divine Names אֵל, אֱלוֹהַ, אֱלֹהִים, and יהוה," *SO* 18 (1952) #1, 1-105.

Norman Walker, "The Writing of the Divine Name in Aquila and the Ben Asher Text," *VT* 3 (1953) 103-104.

Z. Ben-Hayyim, "On the Pronunciation of the Tetragrammaton by the Samaritans," *EI* 3 (1954) IX.

S. Talmon, "A Case of Abbreviation Resulting in Double Readings," *VT* 4 (1954) 206-208.

*C. R. A. Cunliffe, "'I am who am'," *TD* 4 (1956) 23.

*John MacDonald, "The Tetragrammaton in Samaritan Liturgical Compositions," *GUOST* 17 (1957-58) 37-47.

David Noel Freedman, "The Name of the God of Moses," *JBL* 79 (1960) 151-156.

E. C. B. MacLaurin, "YHWH, the Origin of the Tetragrammaton," *VT* 12 (1962) 439-463.

*Howard R. Bailey, "On Naming," *IR* 20 (1963) #1, 43-50. [Tetragrammaton, p. 44]

*Norman Walker, "The Riddle of the Ass's Head and the Question of a Trigram," *ZAW* 75 (1963) 225-227.

Eliyahu Rose-Pinnah, "The Sefer Yetzirah and the Original Tetragrammaton," *JQR, N.S.,* 57 (1967-68) 212-226.

§989 *5.4.2.11.4 Studies concerning Compound Names*

Wm. Crowell, "Jehovah Jireh," *CRB* 22 (1857) 492-506.

J. A. Selbie, "The Lord of Hosts (יהוה צְבָאוֹת)," *ET* 8 (1896-97) 31-32.

*George A. Barton, Western Semitic Deities with Compound Names," *JBL* 20 (1901) 22-27. [1. Yahweh-Elohim, pp. 22-23]

Nathaniel Schmidt, "Yahwe Elohim," *JBL* 33 (1914) 25-47.

F. M. Behymer, "On the Origin of the Hebrew Deity-Name El Shaddai," *Monist* 25 (1915) 269-275.

*N[orman] Walker, "Do Plural Names of Majesty Exist in Hebrew?" *VT* 7 (1957) 208.

A. Lukyn Williams, "The Lord of Hosts," *JTS* 38 (1937) 50-56.

*Hugo McCord, "The Meaning of YHWH *Tsidhkēnu* ('The Lord Our Righteousness') in Jeremiah 23:6 and 33:16," *RestQ* 6 (1962) 114-121.

*S. B. Gurewicz, "Some Examples of Modern Hebrew Exegeses of the OT," *ABR* 11 (1963) 15-23. [2. The Biblical Expression ה' אלהים, pp. 18-22]

*Matitahu Tsevat, "Studies in the Book of Samuel," *HUCA* 36 (1965) 49-58. [IV. Yahweh Ṣeba'oṭ]

J. P. Ross, " Yahweh Ṣebā'oṭ in Samuel and Psalms," *VT* 17 (1967) 76-92.

§990 **5.4.3 Studies on the Doctrine of Christ**

Anonymous, "Christ in the Old Testament," *CRB* 21 (1856) 204-219.

A. K. Moulton, "Jesus Christ," *FBQ* 16 (1868) 297-335; 17 (1869) 28-59, 170-204. *[OT Refs., pp. 28-52, 194]*

*Anonymous, "Was Jesus the Subject of Old Testament Prophecy?" *MR* 73 (1891) 270-280.

J. C. Simmons, "Christ in the Old and New Testament," *MQR, 3rd Ser.,* 6 (1889) 362-375.

*Prescott F. Jernagan, "Christological Implications of the Higher Criticism," *BW* 3 (1894) 420-428.

*J. Glentworth Butler, "Scriptural Identification of the Christ with Jehovah," *CFL, 3rd Ser.,* 9 (1908) 112-114.

Gilbert T. Sadler, "The Pre-Christian Idea of Christ," *MC* 11 (1921-22) 117-119.

*William Phillips Hall, "A Biblical Study of 'The Name' of God, and Its Relation to the Lord Jesus Christ," *CFL, 3rd Ser.,* 29 (1923) 600-607.

Wilbert F. Howard, "Christ—Lord of the Scriptures," *MR* 114 (1931) 418-423.

S[tanley] A. Cook, "From the Old Testament to the New," *OSHTP* (1938-39) 57-59.

Daniel G. Finestone, "The Vicarious Death of Christ in the Light of the Old Testament," *BS* 97 (1940) 34-62. [I. The Covenants; II. Old Testament Types; III. Prophecy]

Reginald Glanville, "Jesus in the Old Testament," *LQHR* 169 (1944) 35-41.

Brevard S. Childs, "Christ in the Old Testament: A Study of Glory," *MHSB* 2 (1955) #2, 34-43.

G. Ch. Aalders, "Christ Reflected in the Old Testament," *RefmR* 4 (1956-57) 158-164.

A. J. B. Higgins, "The Old Testament and Some Aspects of New Testament Christology," *CJT* 6 (1960) 200-210.

Francis E. Elmo, "Christ—The Fulfillment of the Old Testament," *DunR* 3 (1963) 5-38.

§991 *5.4.4 Studies on Old Testament Christology*

Anonymous, "Christologie des Alten Testaments, und Commentar über die Messianschen Weissagungen der Propheten. Von E. W. Hengstenberg, &c. Christology of the Old Testament and Commentary upon the Prophecies relating to the Messiah. By Dr. E. W. Hengstenberg," *CE* 16 (1834) 321-364. *(Review)*

*M. Stuart, "Christology of the Book of Enoch; *With an account of the Book itself, and Critical Remarks upon it,*" BRCR, N.S.,* 3 (1840) 86-137.

H. P., "The Image of God," *JSL, 3rd Ser.,* 6 (1857-58) 168-170.

R. R. Coon, "Yahveh Christ," *CRB* 23 (1858) 127-147. *(Review)*

Howard Crosby, "The Jewish Christian's Notion of a Redeemer," *AThR* 2 (1860) 288-294.

*Anonymous, "Christ in the Book of Genesis," *CR* 24 (1872) 397-417.

*B. F. Wilson, "The Christology of Genesis," *PQ* 3 (1889) 212-232.

*John Coleman Adams, "The Christ and the Creation," *AR* 17 (1892) 225-237.

Anonymous, "Christ in the Old Testament," *RChR, 4th Ser.,* 5 (1901) 382-394.

W. D. Kerswill, "The Old Testament Saviour," *CFL, N.S.,* 5 (1902) 165-171.

*Howard Osgood, "Christ in the Pentateuch," *CFL, N.S.,* 6 (1902) 83-90.

C. J. Södergren, "Glimpses of the face of Christ in the Old Testament mirror," *TTKF* 4 (1902) 116-123.

*Henry T. Sell, "Christ in the Old Testament; or, the Development of the Messianic Idea," *BS* 60 (1903) 737-749.

W. L., "The Resurrection of Christ as Prophesied," *TQ* 9 (1905) 145-148.

F. W. Stellhorn, "The Christology of the Old Testament," *ColTM* 27 (1907) 1-12, 65-74, 129-138, 193-203, 321-329; 28 (1908) 1-12, 65-71.

*J. Glentworth Butler, "Scriptural Identification of the Christ with Jehovah," *CFL, 3rd Ser.,* 9 (1908) 112-114.

James Orr, "The Resurrection of Jesus. 9. Neo-Babylonian Theories— Jewish and Apocryphal Ideas," *Exp, 7th Ser.,* 6 (1908) 306-325.

Harry Austryn Wolfson, "How the Jews will Reclaim Jesus," *JIQ* 1 (1924-25) 66-71.

William Benjamin Smith, "Milk or Meat?" *HJ* 31 (1932-33) 372-383.

H. H. Rowley, "The Hope of Christ in the Old Testament," *ET* 60 (1948-49) 290. *(Review)*

*W. S. Boycott, "Creation and Christology," *Theo* 52 (1949) 443-448.

Markus Barth, "The Christ in Israel's History," *TT* 11 (1954-55) 342-353.

Abraham J. Klausner, "Wolfson on Reclaiming Jesus," *CCARJ* 12 (1956) 18-21.

*Glen Cavaliero, "Christology and Creation," *Theo* 62 (1959) 136-141. *[OT Refs., pp. 136-138]*

Noel C. Schultz, "The Deity of Christ in the Old Testament," *AusTR* 32 (1961) 7-14.

§992 *5.4.4.1 Studies on Theophanies and the Pre-Incarnate Christ*

"Josephus," "Of the Pre-existence of the Messiah," *TRep* 4 (1784) 477-483.

E. Noyes, "Theophanies of the Old Testament," *BRCR, 3rd Ser.,* 5 (1849) 282-289.

J. O. S., "The Pre-existence of Christ," *UQGR* 19 (1862) 41-59.

A. R. Abbott, "The Pre-existence of Jesus Christ,"*UQGR, N.S.,* 1 (1864) 448-466.

Anonymous, "'The God of Glory,' with Abraham; and 'The Son of Man,' in the Glory of God," *BWR* 2 (1878) 351-388.

*J. F. Garrison, "The Theology of the Lost Word and the Manifestation of the Divine Name," *JLTQ* 1 (1884) 1-28.

T. W. Hooper, "The Pre-incarnate Christ," *PQ* 6 (1892) 399-409.

A. H. Huizinga, "A Collation of Some Passages which Speak of Seeing God," *PQ* 10 (1896) 501-515.

George A. Barton, "On the Jewish-Christian Doctrine of the Preëxistence of the Messiah," *JBL* 21 (1902) 78-91.

Julian Morgenstern, "Biblical Theophanies," *ZA* 25 (1911) 139-193; 28 (1913-14) 15-60.

L[eander] S. K[eyser], "The Pre-existence of Our Lord," *CFL, 3rd Ser.,* 33 (1927) 11-13.

Nelson Glueck, "The Theophany of the God of Sinai," *JAOS* 56 (1936) 462-471.

Anthony Hanson, "Theophanies in the Old Testament and the Second Person of the Trinity," *Herm* #65 (1945) 67-73.

John F. Walvoord, "The Preincarnate Son of God," *BS* 104 (1947) 25-34, 154-169, 282-289, 415-425.

Johannes Lindblom, "Theophanies in Holy Places in Hebrew Religion," *HUCA* 32 (1961) 91-106.

*W. Dantine, "Creation and Redemption: Attempt at a Theological Interpretation in the Light of Contemporary Understanding of the World," *SJT* 28 (1965) 129-147. [A. The Key Position of Anthropology; B. Cosmic Christology? C. The Lordship of Christ in Creation]

E. C. John, "Divine Manifestations," *BTF* 3 (1969-71) #2, 1-9. *[OT Refs.: pp. 1-3]*

§993 *5.4.4.2 Studies on the Incarnation*

F. C. Conybeare, "The Philosophical Aspects of the Doctrine of Divine Incarnation," *JQR* 7 (1894-95) 607-629.

John Laird, "The Philosophy of the Incarnation," *HTR* 33 (1940) 131-149.

Dale Moody, "The Miraculous Conception. The Old Testament," *R&E* 51 (1954) 495-507.

Balmer H. Kelly, "Word of Promise. *The Incarnation in the Old Testament,*" *Interp* 10 (1956) 3-15.

T. F. Torrance, "The Israel of God. *Israel and the Incarnation,*" *Interp* 10 (1956) 305-320.

Charles L. Feinberg, "The Virgin Birth in the Old Testament," *BS* 117 (1960) 313-324.

Aloysius M. Ambrozic, "Incarnation in the Bible," *BibT* #27 (1966) 1874-1879.

§994 *5.4.4.3 Studies concerning the Logos*

*†Anonymous, "Bryant on Philo Judæus," *BCQTR* 11 (1798) 13-17, 141-148. *(Review)*

J. F. Denham, "On the Doctrine of the Logos," *JSL, 1st Ser.,*3 (1849) 107-135.

*John A. Reubelt, "The Logos of Philo Judæus and that of St. John," *MR* 40 (1858) 110-129.

Anonymous, "The Palestinian Word," *CE* 74 (1863) 44-61.

*Franz Delitzsch, "The Logos in John and Philo," *AThR, N.S.,* 2 (1864) 506-515.

Ludwig Noire, "The Logos Theory," *OC* 4 (1890-91) 2194-2197.

*Paton J. Gloag, "The Logos of Philo and St. John," *PRR* 2 (1891) 46-57.

B. D. Hahn, "The Origin and Doctrine of the Logos," *BQR* 14 (1892) 176-201, 300-321. [I. Alexandrianism; II. The Alexandrian Logos; III. The Alexandrian Logos and the Logos of John; IV. The Logos of John and Jewish Literature]

*W. St. C[had] Boscawen, "The Creative Power of the Divine Word and Name," *BOR* 8 (1895-1900) 271-276.

*Lawrence [H.] Mills, "Was Vohu Manah Philo's Logos?" *IAQR, 3rd Ser.,* 9 (1900) 351-352.

Lawrence [H.] Mills, "The False Philoian Logos," *IAQR, 3rd Ser.,* 12 (1901) 109-119.

*M. Gaster, "The Logos Ebraikes in the Magical Papyri of Paris, and the Book of Enoch," *JRAS* (1901) 109-117. [Hebrew Logos, pp. 111ff.]

*Fritz Hommel, "The Logos in the Chaldean Story of Creation," *ET* 14 (1902-03) 103-109.

Herbert Baynes, "The History of the Logos," *JRAS* (1906) 373-385.

*Lawrence [H.] Mills, "The 'Ahuna-Vairya' and the Logos," *IAQR, 3rd Ser.,* 24 (1907) 92-97.

A. K. Reischauer, "Japanese Buddhism and the Doctrine of the Logos," *BW* 41 (1913) 245-251. [2. The Hebrew Logos, pp. 246-247]

*Stephen Langdon, "A Sumerian Liturgy Containing an Ode to the Word," *MJ* 9 (1918) 158-163.

*S[tephen] Langdon, "The Babylonian Conception of the Logos," *JRAS* (1918) 433-449.

W[illiam] F[oxwell] Albright, "The Supposed Babylonian Derivation of the Logos," *JBL* 39 (1920) 143-151.

*Francis Clarke, "Sources of St. John's Logos Doctrine," *IER, 5th Ser.,* 20 (1922) 390-397, 602-615; 21 (1923) 50-68, 481-502. [Philo Judæus on Logos, 21 (1923) pp. 50-68]

George N. Mendenhall, "The *Logos* Idea in Philosophy and Theology," *LQ* 52 (1922) 191-197.

*J. Rendel Harris, "Athena, Sophia and the Logos," *BJRL* 7 (1922-23) 56-72.

*W[illiam] F[oxwell] Albright, "The Sumerian Conception of *Giš-Xar*—A Correction," *JSOR* 7 (1923) 79. [cf. *JBL* 39 (1920) 143-151]

Francis Clarke, "The Logos of St. John in Holy Writ," *IER, 5th Ser.,* 24 (1924) 177-202. [The Logos in the Old Testament, pp. 188-196]

*G. H. Dix, "The Heavenly Wisdom and the Divine Logos in Jewish Apocalyptic," *JTS* 26 (1924-25) 1-12.

*J. S. Boughton, "Conscience and Logos in Philo," *LCQ* 4 (1931) 121-133.

*R. E. Wolfe, "Continuity of Thought between Proverbs and Fourth Gospel as regards the *Logos,*" *JBL* 64 (1945) x.

Eric May, "The Logos in the Old Testament," *CBQ* 8 (1946) 438-447.

*Warren C. Young, "The Logos Doctrine of Philo Judaeus," *PF* 4 (1946) 14-22.

Otto W. Heick, "Christ, the Word in the New Testament," *AQ* 26 (1947) 10-18. [The Word in the Old Testament, pp. 12-13]

*Richard R. Caemmerer, "A Concordance Study on the Concept 'Word of God'," *CTM* 22 (1951) 170-185.

*A. W. Argyle, "The Logos of Philo: Personal or Impersonal?" *ET* 66 (1954-55) 13-14.

*A. E. Errey, "The Book about God," *PQL* 8 (1962) 320-326. [The Incarnate Word, pp. 325-326]

*Martin McNamara, "*Logos* of the Fourth Gospel and *Memra* of the Palestinian Targum (Ex 12^{42})," *ET* 79 (1967-68) 115-117.

*Abdel-Aziz Saleh, "Plural Sense and Cultural Aspects of the Ancient Egyptian *mdw-nṯr,*" *BIFAO* 68 (1969) 15-38. ["Word of God']

§995 **5.4.4.4 Studies on Messianic Prophecy [See also: Messianic Expectation in Israel §459 ←]**

† 'Pamphilus', "Observations on the Prophets of the Old Testament," *TRep* 4 (1784) 97-122.

'Pamphilus', "Observations on the Prophecies relating to the Messiah, and the future Glory of the House of David," *TRep* 5 (1786) 210-242, 301-316.

E. F., "Old Testament Prophecies Concerning Christ," *UQGR* 6 (1849) 129-143.

F. W. C. Umbreit, "The Gospel in the Old Testament," *ER* 1 (1849-50) 39-54. *(Trans. by Charles F. Schaeffer)*

*B. B. Edwards, "Messianic Prophecies. A Popular Lecture on the One Hundred and Tenth Psalm" *BS* 9 (1852) 609-622.

S. C. Bartlett, "Theories of Messianic Prophecy," *BS* 18 (1861) 724-772.

*†Anonymous, "Smith's Book of Prophecy," *LQHR* 25 (1865-66) 392-409. *(Review)*

*Henry M. Harman, "The Prophecy of Jacob Respecting the Messiah," *MR* 51 (1869) 411-422.

H. Louis Baugher, "Christ's Prophecy of his Sufferings," *ER* 21 (1870) 128-134.

*Wolcott Calkins, "The Great Messianic Prophecy," *DTQ* 4 (1878) 19-30.

A. B. Davidson, "The Various Kinds of Messianic Prophecy," *Exp, 1st Ser.,* 8 (1878) 241-257, 379-390.

Henry M. Stuart, "Messianic Prophecy," *CR* 31 (1879) 341-348.

*Edward L. Curtis, "Some Features of Messianic Prophecy as Illustrated by the Book of Joel," *ONTS* 3 (1883-84) 97-102, 141-145.

C. Von Orelli, "The Fulfillment of Prophecy in the New Covenant," *ONTS* 4 (1884-85) 66-71. *(Trans. by George H. Schodde)*

*A. F. Kirkpatrick, "The Messianic Interpretation of Nathan's Prophecy to David," *ONTS* 5 (1884-85) 276-277.

*R. P. Stebbins, "Criticism of Some Passages in Isaiah Interpreted by J. A. Alexander, as Predicting the Messiah," *JBL* 5 (1885) 79-82.

B. Pick, "Old Testament Passages Messianically Applied," *AJSL* 2 (1885-86) 24-32.

B. Pick, "Old Testament Passages Messianically Applied. II.," *AJSL* 2 (1885-86) 129-139.

Alfred Edersheim, "Prophecy Referring to Christ," *ONTS* 6 (1885-86) 34.

B. Pick, "Old Testament Passages Messianically Applied by the Ancient Synagogue," *AJSL* 3 (1886-87) 30-38, 265-268.

B. Pick, "Old Testament Passages Messianically Applied by the Ancient Synagogue," *AJSL* 4 (1887-88) 46-51, 176-185, 247-249.

O. Cone, "Messianic Prophecy," *UQGR, N.S.,* 25 (1888) 5-26.

W. G. Ballantine, "Messianic Prophecy," *ONTS* 12 (1891) 262-266.

*Joseph William Reynolds, "Messianic Prophecy, *or Reasoning with the Jews,*" *TML* 5 (1891) 73-84.

Andrew W. Archibald, "Minute Prediction and Modern Doubt," *BS* 49 (1892) 546-559.

W. M. Olyphant, "Messianic Prophecy," *ONTS* 15 (1892) 29-30.

*E. L. Curtis, "Messianic Prophecy in the Book of Job," *BW* 1 (1893) 119-121.

Arthur D. Pierson, "Prophecy," *HR* 25 (1893) 69-70.

James C. Quinn, "The Witness of Prophecy to Christ," *PER* 8 (1894-95) 99-115.

*W. J. Beecher, "Messianic Prophecy; Its Apologetic Value," *AubSRev* 1 (1897) 13-27.

‡George S. Goodspeed, "Some Books on Messianic Prophecy," *BW* 12 (1898) 444-447. *[Short Bibliography]*

*H. L. Wayland, "The Interpretation of Prophecy," *HR* 35 (1898) 261.

*G. H. Gwilliam, "Interpretation of Messianic Prophecy. A Sermon Preached at the Church of St. Mary-the-Virgin, Oxford, on Sunday Afternoon, 11th, March, 1900," *ET* 11 (1899-1900) 392-398.

T. E. Schmauk, "Huehn's Messianic Prophecies," *LCR* 19 (1900) 37-41. *(Review)*

Rayner, Winterbotham, "Nazareth and Bethlehem in Prophecy," *Exp, 6th Ser.*, 3 (1901) 14-26.

Hartley Dewart, "The Higher Criticism and Messianic Prophecy," *BS* 59 (1902) 305-324.

R. Bruce Taylor, "Messianic Prophecy," *ET* 16 (1904-05) 488-493.

James Todd, "Christ and the Old Testament," *HR* 47 (1904) 131-136.

*C. F. Burney, "The Christian Interpretation of Messianic Prophecy," *ICMM* 2 (1905-06) 256-272.

Henry A. Redpath, "Christ, the Fulfilment of Prophecy," *Exp, 7th Ser.*, 3 (1907) 1-20.

S. Lawrence Brown, "Messianic Interpretation," *ICMM* 5 (1908-09) 273-286.

H. S. Gedge, "Correspondence and Discussions. Messianic Prophecy," *ICMM* 5 (1908-09) 440.

Charles Plater, "A Plea for the Prophets," *ITQ* 5 (1910) 433-443.

A. H. McNeil, "Messianic Interpretations," *ICMM* 7 (1910-11) 248-259.

Ed. König, "The Consummation of the Old Testament in Jesus Christ," *Exp, 8th Ser.*, 4 (1912) 1-19, 97-119.

*E. C. Selwyn, "An Oracle of the Lord in Isaiah xxxii," *Exp, 8th Ser.*, 5 (1913) 167-177.

W. B. Stevenson, "The Influence of 'Court Style' on the Messianic Phraseology of the Old Testament," *GUOST* 4 (1913-22) 18-19.

*A. M. Haggard, "A Difficult Messianic Prophecy," *BS* 72 (1915) 154-158.

Eduard König, "Suffering as an Element in Messianic Prophecy," *HR* 70 (1915) 185-190.

L. H. Dorchester, "Messianic Prophecy—Old and New Views," *MR* 97 (1915) 873-883.

*David Capell Simpson, "Messianic Prophecy and the Jewish Problem," *CQR* 88 (1919) 109-122.

G. Hartford, "The Prince of Peace," *Exp, 8th Ser.,* 17 (1919) 81-99.

*F. A. Molony, "Predictions and Expectation of the First Coming of Christ," *JTVI* 53 (1921) 79-92, 101-102. (Discussion, pp. 92-98) (Communications by James Gossett-Tanner, p. 98; J. E. H. Thomson, pp. 98-99; Alfred T. Schofield, p. 99; M. A. Alves, pp. 99-101)

*Douglas Hilary Corley, "Messianic Prophecy in First Isaiah," *AJSL* 39 (1922-23) 220-224.

*Ed. König, "The Messianic Prophecies and Popular Eschatology," *MR* 106 (1923) 963-968.

*Paul Morris, "Christianity and Prophecy Fulfilment," *OC* 37 (1923) 230-242.

Ed. König, "Are There Any Messianic Predictions?" *Theo* 9 (1924) 6-13.

G. R. Berry, "Messianic Predictions," *JBL* 45 (1926) 232-237.

George Lindley Young, "Messianic Prophecy and Its Fulfillment," *BS* 86 (1929) 218-239.

J. Ridderbos, "The Messianic Promise of Salvation and the Later Discoveries," *EQ* 1 (1929) 252-267.

J. S. Bezzant, "Messianic Prophecy," *MC* 19 (1929-30) 653-664. *(Sermon)*

*T. C. Skinner, "The Significance of the Old Testament Scriptures to Our Lord Jesus Christ," *JTVI* 62 (1930) 134-144, 161-163. [(Discussion, pp. 145-155) (Communications by L. M. Davies; pp. 155-157, William Hoste; pp. 157-158; J. J. B. Coles, p. 158; A. G. Secrett, pp. 158-160; W. R. Rowlatt-Jones, pp. 160-161)]

Elmer E. Flack, "The Messianic Mind and the Ministry Today," *LCQ* 5 (1932) 57-72.

David L Cooper, "The Prince of the Prophetic Word," *BS* 91 (1934) 420-432.

J. W. Bailey, "The Temporary Messianic Reign in the Literature of Early Judaism," *JBL* 53 (1934) 170-187.

W. O. E. Oesterley, "Messianic Prophecy and Extra-Israelite Beliefs," *CQR* 119 (1934-35) 1-11.

*Gilmore H. Guyot, "The Prophecy of Balaam," *CBQ* 2 (1940) 330-340.

L. L. Nash, "Messianic prophecy," *RTRM* 4 (1945) #1, 27-34.

John F. Walvoord, "The Incarnation of the Son of God," *BS* 105 (1948) 36-43, 145-153.

*P. P. Saydon, "Old Testament Prophecy and Messias Prophecies," *Scrip* 4 (1949-51) 335-339.

Clyde T. Francisco, "Things Old and New," *R&E* 47 (1950) 311-323.

*Gilmore H. Guyot, "Messianism in the Book of Genesis," *CBQ* 13 (1951) 415-421.

Austin Farrer, "Messianic Prophecy," *Theo* 54 (1951) 335-342.

Leon Morris, "The Idea of redemption in the Old Testament," *RTRM* 11 (1952) #3, 94-102.

*Harold L. Craeger, "The Immanuel Passage as Messianic Prophecy," *LQ, N.S.,* 7 (1955) 339-343.

*Roland E. Murphy, "Notes on Old Testament Messianism and Apologetics," *CBQ* 19 (1957) 5-15.

*Alphonsus Benson, "'... From the Mouth of the Lion' The Messianism of Amos," *CBQ* 19 (1957) 199-212.

*Eugene H. Maly, "Messianism in Osee," *CBQ* 19 (1957) 213-225.

*Roderick A. F. MacKenzie, "The Messianism of Deuteronomy," *CBQ* 19 (1957) 299-305.

Antonine DeGuglielmo, "The Fertility of the Land in the Messianic Prophecies," *CBQ* 19 (1957) 306-311.

*Robert T. Siebeneck, "The Messianism of Aggeus and Proto-Zacharias," *CBQ* 19 (1957) 312-328.

*Neal Flanagan, "Messianic Fulfillment in St. Paul," *CBQ* 19 (1957) 474-484.

*Bruce Vawter, "In Many Fragmentary and Varying Utterances: The Use of Messianic Prophecy in Apologetics," *CTSP* 14 (1959) 97-119.

Andre Chouraqui, "The Messiah of Israel," *CC* 11 (1961) 331-343. *(Trans. by Richard T. DeGeorge)*

Robert D. Culver, "The Old Testament as Messianic Prophecy," *BETS* 7 (1964) 91-97.

William J. Hassold, "Rectilinear or Typological Interpretation of Messianic Prophecy?" *CTM* 38 (1967) 155-167.

§996 *5.4.4.5 Studies on Christological Titles and Predicates*

Anonymous, "Christ: Prophet, Priest and King," *AThR* 1 (1859) 292-305.

R. B. Drummond, "The 'Son of God' Considered as a Title of the Messiah," *TRL* 3 (1866) 465-485.

W. M. Thomson, "Natural Basis of Our Spiritual Language, VI.—The Sun of Righteousness," *BS* 34 (1877) 139-157.

George Henderson, "The Names and Titles of Christ," *PTR* 20 (1922) 475-536.

F. C. Burkitt, "Memra, Shekinah, Metatron," *JTS* 24 (1922-23) 158-159.

*Wm. C. Robinson, "Jesus Christ is Jehovah," *USR* 44 (1932-33) 278-292, 380-400.

*W. Childs Robinson, "Jesus Christ is Jehovah," *EQ* 5 (1933) 144-155, 271-290.

Erminie Huntress, "'Son of God' in Jewish Writings Prior to the Christian Era," *JBL* 54 (1935) 117-123.

*Edwin E. Le Bas, "Was the Corner-Stone of Scripture a Pyramidion?" *PEQ* 78 (1946) 103-115.

J. G. S. S. Thomson, "The Shepherd-Ruler Concept in the OT and Its Application in the NT," *SJT* 8 (1955) 406-418.

S. Herbert Bess, "The Term 'Son of God' in the Light of Old Testament Idiom," *GJ* 6 (1965) #2, 16-23.

John   Dresse,   "Maranatha!"   *BibT*   #33   (1967)   2296-2304.

§997 *5.4.4.5.1 Studies concerning the "Messiah"*

†Anonymous, "Bloomfield's Dissertation of a Promised Redeemer," *BCQTR, N.S.,* 12 (1819) 652-660. *(Review)*

*Geo. Chr. Knapp, "Dissertation of 2 Pet. I. 19-21; as Exhibiting the Nature and Use of Old Testament Prophecies; Especially Those which Relate to the Messiah," *BibR* 2 (1826) 207-238. *(Trans. by E. N. K.)*

[Ernst Wilhelm] Hengstenberg, "Godhead of the Messiah in the Old Testament," *BRCR* 3 (1833) 652-683. *(Trans. by George Howe)*

G. R. N., "Whether the Deity of the Messiah be a Doctrine of the Old Testament," *CE* 19 (1835) 273-302.

*W. F., "Scripture Parallelisms. The Messias Prophet: with Remarks on the Parallelistic Form of His Discourses," *JSL, 1st Ser.,* 6 (1850) 179-188.

T. M., "Jesus Christ the True Messiah. Examined a Posteriori, or a View of the Claims of Jesus Christ to the Character of God's Messiah," *MQR* 4 (1850) 449-476.

O. B. F., "The Christ of the Jews," *CE* 51 (1851) 161-185.

E. P. Barrows, "The Relation of David's Family to the Messiah," *BS* 11 (1854) 306-328.

*S. P. Tregelles, "Dr. S. P. Davidson and Horne's Introduction," *JSL, 3rd Ser.,* 4 (1856-57) 424-439. [Eternal Sonship of the Messiah, pp. 435-439]

Anonymous, "The Prophetic Messiah," *MQR,* 14 (1860) 213-222.

Anonymous, "The Sceptre of Judah," *PQR* 9 (1860-61) 595-610.

T. B. Thayer, "Ancient and Modern Unbelief," *UQGR, N.S.,* 1 (1864) 149-162. [I. Jesus not the Messiah of the Old Testament Prophecies, pp. 148-153]

W. R. Coxwell Rogers, "'The Coming One'" a Meditation," *JSL, 4th Ser.,* 10 (1866-677) 350-371.

Samuel Davidson, "The Jewish Messiah.—I.," *TRL* 6 (1869) 516-536.

Samuel Davidson, "The Jewish Messiah.—II.," *TRL* 7 (1870) 1-30.

Samuel Davidson, "The Relation of the New Testament Messiah to His Jewish Prototype.—III.," *TRL* 8 (1871) 1-30.

Samuel Davidson, "The Relation of the New Testament Messiah to His Jewish Prototype.—IV.," *TRL* 8 (1871) 342-360.

*J. Colver Wightman, "הַמָּשִׁיחַ, The Messiah," *BQ* 10 (1876) 302-311.

Claude R. Conder, "Note on Various Traditions as to the Place Where Messias Should be Born," *PEFQS* 8 (1876) 98-99.

*J. H. Allen, "The Messiah and the Christ in History," *URRM* 8 (1877) 608-625.

T. K. Chyene, "Mr. Drummond's 'Jewish Messiah'," *TRL* 15 (1878) 205-215. *(Review)*

*B. Pick, "Talmudic Notices Concerning the Messiah," *PR* 5 (1884) 505-510.

Daniel Van Pelt, "Was the Messiah to be Divine?" *RChR* 29 (1882) 232-251.

Anonymous, "The Jewish and the Christian Messiah: A Study and an Argument," *LQHR* 68 (1887) 1-25. *(Review)*

F. F. M., "Religion and the Messiah," *ACQR* 13 (1888) 706-720.

Anonymous, "The Messiah in the Old Testament," *CQR* 26 (1888) 95-123.

*G. B. Gary, "The References to the 'King' in the Psalter in their Bearing on (A) Questions of Date, (B) Messianic Belief," *OSHTP* (1894-95) 27-29.

A. Cowley, "The Samaritan Doctrine of the Messiah," *Exp, 5th Ser.,* 1 (1895) 161-174.

*Nathaniel Schmidt, "Was בר נשא a Messianic Title?" *JBL* 15 (1896) 36-53.

C[harles] A. Briggs, "The Wisdom of Jesus the Messiah," *ET* 8 (1896-97) 393-398, 452-455, 492, 496; 9 (1897-98) 69-75.

R. H. Charles, "The Messiah of Old Testament Prophecy and Apocalyptic and the Christ of the New Testament," *Exp, 6th Ser.,* 5 (1902) 241-259.

*Jas. C. Morris, "The Book of Job and the Revelation of the Messiah," *MQR, 3rd Ser.,* 29 (1903) 498-506.

*A. Smythe Palmer, "Michael the Messiah," *ET* 16 (1904-05) 287.

*Jacob ben Aaron, "The Messianic Hope of the Samaritans," *OC* 21 (1907) 272-296. *[Trans. by Abdullah Ben Kori]*

*William E. Barton, "The Samaritan Messiah. Further Comments of the Samaritan High Priest," *OC* 21 (1907) 528-538.

Sigmund Frey, "Messiah—Christos," *OC* 22 (1908) 562-566.

Edward A. Wicher, "Ancient Jewish Views on the Messiah," *BW* 34 (1909) 317-325, 404-409.

*G. Margoliouth, "The Two Zadokite Messiahs," *JTS* 12 (1910-11) 446-450.

*G. H. Box, "The Christian Messiah in the Light of Judaism Ancient and Modern," *JTS* 13 (1911-12) 321-338.

George C. Peck, "Jesus—Messiah," *MR* 94 (1912) 264-270.

Elmer L. Coblentz, "Jesus' Messianic Consciousness," *RChR, 4th Ser.,* 19 (1915) 287-302. [II. The Various Jewish Ideas, pp. 289-292]

*H. J. Wicks, "The Doctrine of the Messiah in Jewish Apocrypha and Apocalyptic," *IJA* # 46 (1916) 34-36.

Benjamin B. Warfield, "The Divine Messiah in the Old Testament," *PTR* 14 (1916) 369-416.

L. P. Smith, "The Messianic Ideal of Isaiah," *JBL* 36 (1917) 158-212.

*John Gamble, "The Messiahs of Virgil and Isaiah," *MC* 8 (1918-19) 386-389. *(Review)*

A. Kampmeier, "A Pre-Christian Jewish Christ," *OC* 33 (1919) 296-310.

D. S. Margoliouth, "The Messiah," *Exp, 8th Ser.,* 25 (1923) 1-21.

*Archibald Duff, "The Rise of the Title 'Messiah'," *Exp, 8th Ser.,* 25 (1923) 205-215.

*Lawrence D. Murphy, "Messiah the Priest-King (Psalm CIX.)," *IER, 5th Ser.,* 21 (1923) 174-180.

G. H. Dix, "The Messiah ben-Joseph," *JTS* 27 (1926) 130-143.

Henry J. Allen, "Our Lord's Conception of His Messiahship in Relation to Old Testament Prophecy," *ET* 40 (1928-29) 563-567.

*Wm. Weber, "Jesus, the Prophet and Messiah," *OC* 43 (1929) 294-304.

Herbert W. Magoun, "The Real Jewish Crux To-day," *CFL, 3rd Ser.,* 37 (1931) 645-649.

T. F. Royds, "Jesus the Messiah," *MC* 23 (1933-34) 128-134. *(Sermon)*

F. B. Lovell, "Early Christian Interpretation of Jesus as Messiah," *JBL* 53 (1934) iv.

A. Lukyn Williams, "A Modern Jewish Philosopher on the Doctrine of the Messiah," *CQR* 122 (1936) 61-73.

*S. V. McCasland, "The Pre-Christian Messiah and Demons," *JBL* 55 (1936) viii.

Jacob Gartenhaus, "The Virgin Birth of the Messiah," *CRP* 7 (1938) 84-94.

*W. M. Mackay, "Messiah in the Psalms," *EQ* 11 (1939) 153-164.

C[harles] C. Torrey, "The Two Messiahs," *JBL* 61 (1941) ii.

Charles C. Torrey, "The Messiah Son of Ephraim," *JBL* 66 (1947) 253-277.

*G. R. Beasley-Murray, "The Two Messiahs in the Testament of the Twelve Patriarchs," *JTS* 48 (1947) 1-12.

*J. R. Porter, "The Messiah in the Testament of Levi XVIII," *ET* 61 (1949-50) 90-91.

*Matthew Black, "The Messiah in the Testament of Levi xviii," *ET* 60 (1948-49) 321-322.

*Matthew Black, "Contributions and Comments. The Messiah in the Testament of Levi xviii," *ET* 61 (1949-50) 157-158.

*H. H. Rowley, "The Suffering Servant and the Davidic Messiah," *OTS* 8 (1950) 100-136.

O. S. Rankin, "The Messianic Office in the Literature of Judaism and in the New Testament," *ZAW* 63 (1950-51) 259-270.

*Abram Spiro, "Pseudo-Philo's Saul and the Rabbis' Messiah ben Ephraim," *PAAJR* 21 (1952) 119-137.

*A. J. B. Higgins, "Priest and Messiah," *VT* 3 (1953) 321-336.

*Cecil Roth, "Messianic Symbols in Palestine Archaeology," *PEQ* 87 (1955) 151-164.

*Wallace I. Wolverton, "The King's 'Justice' in Pre-Exilic Israel," *ATR* 41 (1959) 276-286. [*Mishpaṭ* and Messiah, pp. 284-285]

*Morton Smith, "'God's Begetting the Messiah' in 1QSa," *NTS* 5 (1959-60) 218-224.

Reidar B. Bjornard, "Jesus and the Messiah of the Old Testament," *Found* 3 (1960) 172-175.

*W. Wirgin, "On King Herod's Messianism" *IEJ* 11 (1961) 153-154.

*E[dward] L. Bode, "The Baptist, the Messiah and the Monks of Qumran," *BibT* #17 (1965) 1111-1116.

A. J. B. Higgins, "The Priestly Messiah," *NTS* 13 (1966-67) 211-239.

Gerald L. Ceranowski, "Messiah-King," *SS* 18 (1966-67) #1, 39-56. *[OT Refs., pp. 40-47]*

Roy A. Rosenberg, "Who is the Moreh haṣṢedeq?" *JAAR* 36 (1968) 118-122.

Donald MacLeod, "The Divine Messiah," *BofT* #74 (1969) 25-33; #75 (1969) 33-39.

§998 *5.4.4.5.2 Studies concerning "The Angel of the Lord"*

Anonymous, "The Angel Jehovah," *CRB* 24 (1859) 594-606.

*H. C. Ackerman, "The Principle of Differentiation Between 'The Word of the Lord' and 'The Angel of the Lord'," *AJSL* 37 (1920-21) 145-149.

Herbert Crossland, "The Angel of God," *ET* 34 (1922-23) 91.

Daniel Finestone, "Is the Angel of Jehovah in the Old Testament the Lord Jesus Christ?" *BS* 95 (1938) 372-377.

R. W. Frank, "The Angel of the Lord," *RL* 5 (1936) 124-131.

C. Goodspeed, "The Angel of Jehovah," *BS* 36 (1879) 593-615.

*H. P. Hamann, "The Appearance of God in the Old Testament, and the Angel of the Lord," *AusTR* 12 (1941) 97-108; 13 (1942) 9-12.

Paul E. Kretzmann, "The 'Angel of the Lord' in the Old Testament," *TM* 2 (1922) 33-36.

G. R. N., "Meaning of the Title, 'Angel of Jehovah,' as used in Scripture; being in continuation of the Article on the 'Deity of the Messiah not a Doctrine of the Old Testament'," *CE* 20 (1836) 207-240.

G. R. N., "The 'Angel of Jehovah,' mentioned in the Old Testament, not identical with the Messiah; being the Conclusion of the Article on the 'Deity of the Messiah not a Doctrine of the Old Testament'," *CE* 20 (1836) 329-342.

*T. Nicklin, "The Angel of God, or God the King?" *ET* 33 (1921-22) 378-379.

Henry A. Sawtelle, "The Angel of Jehovah," *BS* 16 (1859) 805-835.

Θ, "Messiah, the Angel of Jehovah," *CongML* 26 (1843) 886-892.

B. B. Warfield, "The Angel of Jehovah and Critical Views," *CFL, N.S.,* 8 (1903) 59-60.

§999 *5.4.4.5.3 Studies concerning "Priest"*

Rendel Harris, "The Sinless High Priest," *ET* 33 (1921-22) 217-218.

*A. J. B. Higgins, "Priest and Messiah," *VT* 3 (1953) 321-336.

§1000 *5.4.4.5.4 Studies concerning "Prophet"*

*E. P. Barrows Jr., "The Prophet like unto Moses," *BRCR, 3rd Ser.,* 3 (1847) 645-655.

Anonymous, "Jesus as Prophet and Messiah," *CE* 88 (1867) 79-99. *(Review)*

*Wm. Weber, "Jesus, The Prophet and Messiah," *OC* 43 (1929) 294-304.

§1001 *5.4.4.5.5 Studies concerning "The Servant of the Lord"*
(includes Studies on the "Suffering Servant")

Ernst Wilhelm Hengstenberg, "A Suffering and Atoning Messiah taught in the Old Testament," *LTR* 1 (1834) 239-255. *(Trans. by Leonard Woods Jr.) [marked as to be continued but never was]*

William Henry Cobb, "Servant of Jahveh," *JBL* 14 (1895) 95-113.

*W. E. Barnes, "The Two Servants of Jehovah, the Conqueror and the Sufferer, in Deutero-Isaiah," *ET* 8 (1896-97) 28-31.

*J. A. Selbie, "The 'Servant of the Lord' Passages," *ET* 12 (1900-01) 170.

F. B. Denio, "The Servant of Jehovah," *AJT* 5 (1901) 322-327.

*R. M. Moffat, "The Servant of the Lord," *ET* 13 (1901-02) 7-10, 67-69, 174-178.

Geo. M. Layman, "The Servant of Jehovah as an Ideal Man," *CFL, N.S.,* 6 (1902) 16-23.

John D. Davis, "The Servant of Jehovah," *CFL, N.S.,* 8 (1903) 306-311. *(Editorial)*

Henry Nelson Bullard, "The Servant of Jehovah," *CFL, 3rd Ser.,* 1 (1904) 474-477.

*E. Cutler Shedd, "The Servant of Jehovah in the Light of the Inscriptions. A World Empire, A World Religion," *BW* 30 (1907) 464-468.

H. A. A. Kennedy, "The Self-Conciousness of Jesus and the Servant of the Lord," *ET* 19 (1907-08) 346-349, 394-397, 442-446, 487-491. [I. The Old Testament Revelation; II. The Attitude of the New Testament Writers; III. The Influence of Isaiah; IV. The Servant in the Gospels]

H. Maldwyn Hughes, "Judaism and a Suffering Messiah," *IJA* #28 (1912) 18-20.

*H. Chadwick, "The Servant of Yahweh," *ITQ* 15 (1920) 330-342.

*R. A. Aytoun, "The Servant of the Lord in the Targum," *JTS* 23 (1921-22) 172-180.

*John E. McFadyen, "A New View of the Servant of the Lord," *ET* 34 (1922-23) 294-296.

*Stanley A. Cook, "The Servant of the Lord," *ET* 34 (1922-23) 440-442.

*F. A. Farley, "Jeremiah and 'The Suffering Servant of Jehovah' in Deutero-Isaiah," *ET* 38 (1926-27) 521-524.

W. E. Wilson, "The 'Servant'," *ET* 39 (1927-28) 136-137.

*Annie E. Skemp, "'Immanuel' and 'The Suffering Servant of Jahweh': A Suggestion," *ET* 44 (1932-33) 94-95.

*Leroy Waterman, "The Martyred Servant Motif of Isaiah 53," *JBL* 56 (1937) 27-34.

*T. H. Robinson, "The Servant Songs," *ET* 50 (1938-39) 141. *(Review)*

*Christopher R. North, "Who Was the Servant of the Lord in Isaiah LIII?" *ET* 52 (1940-41) 181-184, 219-221.

J. Philip Hyatt, "The Sources of the Suffering Servant Idea," *JNES* 3 (1944) 79-86.

*Norman H. Snaith, "The So-Called Servant Songs," *ET* 56 (1944-45) 79-81.

Richard T. Murphy, "Second Isaias: The Servant of the Lord," *CBQ* 9 (1947) 262-274.

Lester J. Kuyper, "Servant of Jahweh," *RefR* 2 (1947-48) #4, 10-13.

*H. H. Rowley, "The Suffering Servant and the Davidic Messiah," *OTS* 8 (1950) 100-136.

Christopher R. North, "The Suffering Servant: Current Scandinavian Discussion," *SJT* 3 (1950) 397-408.

*Edward J. Young, "The Origin of the Suffering Servant Idea," *WTJ* 13 (1950-51) 19-34.

*Wm. H. Brownlee, "The Servant of the Lord in the Qumran Scrolls I.," *BASOR* #132 (1953) 8-15.

*H. L. Ginsberg, "The Oldest Interpretation of the Suffering Servant," *JBL* 72 (1953) xxii.

*Matthew Black, "Servant of the Lord and Son of Man," *SJT* 6 (1953) 1-11.

H. L. Ginsberg, "The Oldest Interpretation of the Suffering Servant," *VT* 3 (1953) 400-404.

*Wm. H. Brownlee, "The Servant of the Lord in the Qumran Scrolls II," *BASOR* #135 (1954) 33-38.

*Curt Lindhagen, "Important Hypothesis Reconsidered. IX. The Servant of the Lord," *ET* 67 (1955-56) 279-283, 300-302.

Vernon H. Kooy, "The Servant Image," *RefR* 12 (1958-59) #4, 30-40.

Robert Lennox, "The Servant of Yahweh in the Old Testament," *TT* 15 (1958-59) 315-320.

Reidar B. Bjornard, "The Servant of God," *Found* 3 (1960) 259-261.

Frederick L. Moriarty, "The Suffering Servant," *Way* 2 (1962) 121-134.

Margaret E. Thrall, "The Suffering Servant and the Mission of Jesus," *CQR* 164 (1963) 281-288.

*Claude Chavasse, "The Suffering Servant and Moses," *CQR* 165 (1964) 152-163.

W. M. W. Roth, "The Anonymity of the Suffering Servant," *JBL* 83 (1964) 171-179.

Roy A. Rosenberg, "Jesus, Isaac, and the 'Suffering Servant'," *JBL* 84 (1965) 381-388.

*Timothy Mitchell, "Christ as the EBED YAHWEH," *ITQ* 36 (1969) 245-250.

§1002 *5.4.4.5.6 Studies concerning the "Son of Man"*

J. J. Van Oosterzee, "The Son of Man," *PRev* 54 (1878) Part 2, 115-148.

R. H. Charles, "The Son of Man," *ET* 4 (1892-93) 504-506.

Vernon Bartlett, "The 'Son of Man': A Rejoinder," *ET* 5 (1893-94) 41-42.

David Eaton, "Professor Dalman on 'The Son of Man'," *ET* 10 (1898-99) 438-443. *(Review)*

Eb. Nestle, "The 'Son of Man' in the Old Testament," *ET* 11 (1899-1900) 238.

Fritz Hommel, "The Apocalyptic Origin of the Expression 'Son of Man'," *ET* 11 (1899-1900) 341-345.

*Nathaniel Schmidt, "'Son of Man' in the Book of Daniel," *JBL* 19 (1900) 22-28.

James Croskery, "Recent Discussions on the Meaning of the Title 'Son of Man'," *ET* 13 (1901-02) 351-355.

Hewlett Johnson, "Editorial Notes," *ICMM* 6 (1909-10) 11-16. [The Son of Man; "The Message of the Son of Man"; Dr. Abbott's Argument; The Idea Behind the Vision of Daniel and Ezekiel; The Same Idea in Genesis and Psalms; Choice of the humbler title; Our Lord a new man, rather than a new teacher]

F. P. Badham, "The Title 'Son of Man'," *TTL* 45 (1911) 395-448.

John W. Graham, "The Mind of the Son of Man," *ICMM* 8 (1911-12) 289-302. *[OT Refs., pp. 289-291]*

Walter Henry Townsend Gahan, "'The Son of Man'," *ICQ* 5 (1912) 74-76.

John Rothwell Willis, "'The Son of Man'," *ICQ* 5 (1912) 163-164.

Thomas à Kempis O'Reilly, "The 'Son of Man,' A Prophecy Unfulfilled," *CUB* 20 (1914) 523-532.

Paul Haupt, "Hidalgo and Filius Hominis," *JBL* 40 (1921) 167-169.

*A. T. Cadoux, "The Son of Man," *ICMM* 18 (1921-22) 202-214. *[OT Refs., pp. 202-203]*

J. M. Creed, "The Heavenly Man," *JTS* 26 (1924-25) 113-136. *[Son of Man, pp. 129-136]*

J. Courtenay James, "The Son of Man: Origin and Uses of the Title," *ET* 36 (1924-25) 209-314.

Nathaniel Schmidt, "Recent Study of the Term 'Son of Man'," *JBL* 45 (1926) 326-335.

Pierson Parker, "The Meaning of 'Son of Man'," *JBL* 60 (1941) 151-157.

John Bowman, "The Background of the Term 'Son of Man'," *ET* 59 (1947-48) 283-288.

Matthew Black, "Unsolved New Testament Problems. The 'Son of Man' in the Old Biblical Literature," *ET* 60 (1948-49) 11-15.

T. W. Manson, "The Son of Man in Daniel, Enoch and the Gospels," *BJRL* 32 (1949-50) 171-193.

*Matthew Black, "Servant of the Lord and Son of Man," *SJT* 6 (1953) 1-11.

L. Johnston, "The Son of Man," *Scrip* 6 (1953-54) 181-183. *[OT Refs., p. 181]*

T. J. Tinsley, "The Sign of the Son of Man," *SJT* 8 (1955) 197-306.

J. A. Emerton, "The Origin of the Son of Man Imagery," *JTS, N.S.,* 9 (1958) 225-242.

Eduard Schweizer, "The Son of Man," *JBL* 79 (1960) 119-129. [Jewish Sources, p. 122]

*James Muilenburg, "The Son of Man in Daniel and the Ethiopic Apocalypse of Enoch," *JBL* 79 (1960) 197-209.

*G. H. P. Thompson, "The Son of Man: The Evidence of the Dead Sea Scrolls," *ET* 72 (1960-61) 125.

*Joseph Bourke, "From Temple to Heavenly Court," *LofS* 16 (1961-62) 407-420. [4. The Final Personification of the Kabod in Daniel's Vision of the Son of Man, pp. 417-420]

E[duard] Schweizer, "The Son of Man Again," *NTS* 9 (1962-63) 256-261.

J. C. Hindley, "Jesus as 'The Son of Man' in the Light of Recent Discussions," *SBSB* 1 (1964) 42-60.

Howard M. Teeple, "The Origin of the Son of Man Christology," *JBL* 84 (1965) 213-250.

Norman Perrin, "The Son of Man in Ancient Judaism and Primitive Christianity: A Suggestion," *BRes* 11 (1966) 17-28.

Ransom Marlow, "The *Son of Man* in Recent Journal Literature," *CBQ* 28 (1966) 20-30.

J. B. Cortes and F. M. Gatti, "Son of Man or Son of Adam," *B* 49 (1968) 457-502. [2. The Son of Man in Hebrew and Aramaic, pp. 477-486]

J. Massingberd Ford, "'Son of Man'—A Euphemism?" *JBL* 87 (1968) 257-266.

David Stanley, "The Quest of the Son of Man," *Way* 8 (1968) 3-17. [The Symbolic figure in Daniel, pp. 6-7]

A. Gelston, "A Sidelight on the 'Son of Man'," *SJT* 22 (1969) 189-196.

§1003 *5.4.4.5.7 Studies concerning "Mediator"*

*George Foot Moore, "Intermediaries in Jewish Theology. Memra, Shekinah, Metatron," *HTR* 15 (1922) 41-85.

*F. C. Burkitt, "Memra, Shekinah, Metatron," *JTS* 24 (1923) 158-159.

*G. H. Box, "The Idea of Intermediation in Jewish Theology, a Note on Memra and Shekinah," *JQR, N.S.,* 23 (1932-33) 103-119.

M. Black, "The Origin of the Name Metatron," *VT* 1 (1951) 217-219.

A. Murtonen, "The Figure of *Meṭaṭrôn*," *VT* 3 (1953) 409-411.

*Martin P. Nilsson, "The High God and the Mediator," *HTR* 56 (1963) 101-120.

§1004   **5.4.4.5.8 Studies concerning "Wisdom"**

*E. P. Barrows, "Wisdom as a Person in the Book of Proverbs," *BS* 15 (1858) 353-381.

*E. P. Barrows, "Wisdom as a Person in the Book of Proverbs," *JSL, 3rd Ser.,*7 (1858) 346-368.

*J. Rendel Harris, "Athena, Sophia, and the Logos," *BJRL* 7 (1922-23) 56-72.

*G. H. Dix, "The Heavenly Wisdom and the Divine Logos in Jewish Apocalyptic," *JTS* 26 (1924-25) 1-12.

*C. F. Burney, "Christ as the APXH of Creation. (Prov. viii 22, Col. i 15-19, Rev. iii 14)," *JTS* 27 (1925-26) 160-177.

W. L. Knox, "The Divine Wisdom," *JTS* 38 (1937) 230-237.

Ralph Marcus, "On Biblical Hypostases of Wisdom," *HUCA* 23 (1950-51) 157-171.

*H. Jaeger, "The Patristic Conception of Wisdom in the Light of Biblical and Rabbinic Research," *StP* 4 (1961) 90-106.

Roland E. Murphy, "The Incarnational Aspects of Old Testament Wisdom," *BibT* #9 (1963) 560-566.

§1005 **5.4.5 Studies on the Doctrine of the Holy Spirit**

*Anonymous, "What is the Scriptural Meaning of the Phrase *'The Spirit of God?'*," *CD* 1 (1813) 178-180, 206-210.

†Anonymous, "Biddulph—Operation of the Holy Spirit," *QRL* 31 (1824-25) 111-125. *(Review)*

Anonymous, "Scripture Doctrine of the Spirit," *CTPR, 3rd Ser.,* 4 (1848) 426-432. *(Review)*

Anonymous, "Doctrine of the Holy Spirit," *CE* 81 (1866) 217-233. *(Review)* *[OT Refs., pp. 221-222]*

W. W. English, "On Biblical Pneumatology and Psychology," *JTVI* 6 (1872-73) 166-180, 198-199. (Discussion pp. 180-198)

Thomas Kelly Cheyne, "The Progressive Revelation of the Personality of the Holy Spirit," *CM* 10 (1880) 129-143.

Frederick Chalmers, "The Holy Spirit in the Old Testament and the New," *CM* 12 (1881) 379-383.

P. A. Nordell, "The Old Testament Doctrine of the Spirit of God," *ONTS* 4 (1884-85) 433-444.

Charles F. Thwing, "The Scriptural Doctrine of the Holy Spirit," *BS* 46 (1889) 262-292. *[Major OT Refs., pp. 264-265]*

J. Tomlinson, "The Holy Spirit," *LQ* 20 (1890) 446-456.

*John Robson, "The Holy Spirit in Creation," *ET* 5 (1893-94) 467-470.

Benjamin B. Warfield, "The Spirit of God in the Old Testament," *PRR* 6 (1895) 665-687.

F. B. Denio, "Scriptural teaching respecting the Holy Spirit," *JBL* 15 (1896) 135-150. *[OT Refs. pp. 135-138]*

A. B. Davidson, "The Spirit of God in the Old Testament," *ET* 11 (1899-1900) 21-24.

*Dunlop Moore, "The Significance of the Different Printing of a Letter in Two Versions of the Bible," *CFL, N.S.,* 7 (1903) 354-357.

H. Douglas Spaeth, "The Doctrine of the Holy Spirit, I," *LCR* 22 (1903) 263-279.

H. Douglas Spaeth, "The Doctrine of the Holy Spirit. II," *LCR* 22 (1903) 469-492.

Anonymous, "The Old Testament Doctrine of the Spirit," *ET* 21 (1909-10) 276-278.

*John P. Peters, "The Wind of God," *JBL* 30 (1911) 44-54.

E. Y. Mullins, "The Holy Spirit in the Old Testament," *R&E* 9 (1912) 246-257.

A. E. Garvey, "The Development of the Doctrine of the Holy Spirit," *OSHTP* (1923-25) 5-33. *[OT Refs., pp. 7-10]*

Alphes S. Mowbray, "The Doctrine of the Holy Spirit. I. The Holy Spirit Revealed in the Old and New Testaments," *MR* 107 (1924) 355-357.

H. Wheeler Robinson, "The Holy Spirit in the Bible," *ET* 39 (1927-28) 3-8.

Anonymous, "The Creative Spirit," *MR* 111 (1928) 459-460.

Owen Phillips Eaches, "God, the Holy Spirit," *CQ* 7 (1930) 159-168.

Horace Millard DuBose, "The Holy Spirit in the Old Testament," *MR* 113 (1930) 209-221.

R. S. Cripps, "The Holy Spirit in the Old Testament," *Theo* 24 (1932) 272-280.

Carl Armerding, "The Holy Spirit in the Old Testament," *BS* 92 (1935) 277-291, 433-441.

*Sigmund Mowinckel, "'The Spirit' and the 'Word' in the Pre-Exilic Reforming Prophets," *JBL* 53 (1935) 199-227.

Reginald Tribe, "The Spirit in the Old Testament Writings," *Theo* 32 (1936) 256-269.

Harvie Branscomb, "The Biblical Doctrine of the Holy Spirit," *RL* 8 (1939) 195-199.

*J. W. Hunkin, "The Spirit of Man and the Spirit of God (I)," *MC* 29 (1939-40) 473-484.

John F. Walvoord, "The Person of the Holy Spirit," *BS* 97 (1940) 166-188.

John F. Walvoord, "The Work of the Holy Spirit in the Old Testament," *BS* 97 (1940) 289-317, 410-434.

*John F. Walvoord, "The Eschatology of the Holy Spirit," *BS* 99 (1942) 418-427.

George Stock, "The Old Testament and the Holy Spirit," *CQR* 135 (1942-43) 206-224.

F. W. Dillistone, "The Biblical Doctrine of the Holy Spirit," *TT* 3 (1946-47) 486-497.

Geoffrey F. Nuttall, "Spirit of Power and Love. The Biblical Doctrine of the Holy Spirit," *Interp* 4 (1950) 24-35.

Montgomery J. Shroyer, "'The Lord Is the Spirit'," *RL* 20 (1950-51) 35-21. [I. The Old Testament, pp. 21-24]

Edwin Lewis, "God with Man. The Biblical Doctrine of the Holy Spirit," *Interp* 7 (1953) 281-298.

C. L. Mitton, "The Teaching of the Bible about the Holy Spirit," *LQHR* 180 (1955) 168-173. *[OT Refs., pp. 168-170]*

L. Johnston, "The Spirit of God," *Scrip* 8 (1956) 65-74.

*Lester J. Kuyper, "The Holy One and the Holy Spirit," *RefR* 11 (1957-58) #3, 1-10.

Joseph Bourke, "The Spirit of God in the Old Testament," *LofS* 13 (1958-59) 538-550. [I. Primitive Salvific History: *RUACH* as Wind; II. 'Presence Theology': *RUACH* as Charism; III. The New Humanistic Movement: the *RUACH* as the Breath of God]

Monroe Parker, "The Holy Spirit in the Old Testament," *CCBQ* 3 (1960) #1, 25-28.

*William G. Young, "The Holy Spirit and the Word of God," *SJT* 14 (1961) 34-59.

Earl C. Scott, "The 'Spirit' in the Old and New Testaments," *ASBFE* 79 (Nov., 1963) #3, 26-62.

William A. Barry, "Spirit as the Source of Life in the Old Testament," *BibT* #17 (1965) 1103-1110.

Th. C. Vriezen, "Ruach Yahweh (Elohim) in the Old Testament," *OTW* 9 (1966) 50-61.

G. Henton Davies, "The Holy Spirit in the Old Testament," *R&E* 63 (1966) 129-134.

Frederick [L.] Moriarty, "The Spirit of the Lord," *Way* 6 (1966) 175-183.

Paul Younger, "A New Start Towards the Doctrine of the Spirit," *CJT* 13 (1967) 123-133.

R. G. Crawford, "The Holy Spirit," *EQ* 40 (1968) 165-172.

John Navone, "The Holy Spirit," *Scrip* 20 (1968) 80-95. [1. The *Creator Spiritus* in the Old Testament, pp. 80-81]

§1006 *5.4.6 Studies on the Unseen World - General Studies*

George I. Chace, "Of Spirit and the Constitution of Spiritual Beings," *BS* 5 (1848) 633-650.

*P. A. Nordell, "Old Testament Word Studies: 9. Angels, Demons, etc.," *ONTS* 8 (1888-89) 341-345.

R. Bruce Boswell, "The Evolution of Angels and Demons in Christian Theology," *OC* 14 (1900) 483-501.

*George A. Barton, "The Origin of the Names of Angels and Demons in the Extra-Canonical Literature to 100 A.D.," *JBL* 31 (1912) 156-167.

*Robert North, "Separated Spiritual Substances in the Old Testament," *CBQ* 29 (1967) 419-449.

§1007   *5.4.6.1 Studies on Angelology*

'Philalethes', "Of the Prince Michael," *TRep* 6 (1788) 216-217.

I. I. F., "On Angelic Guardianship," *CongML* 1 (1818) 527-531.

Anonymous, "Angels," *MMBR* 49 (1820) 536.

Anonymous, "On the Cherubim of the Sacred Scriptures," *QCS, 3rd Ser.,* 8 (1836) 368-388.

Lewis Mayer, "The Scriptural Idea of Angels," *BRCR* 12 (1838) 356-388.

Moses Stuart, "Sketches of Angelology in the Old and New Testament," *BS* (1843) 88-154.

A. D. C. Twesten, "The Doctrine Respecting Angels," *BS* 1 (1844) 769-793. [1. The Nature of Angels, 2. The State (status) of Angels, 3. Good and Evil Angels] *(Trans. by H. B. Smith)*

T[homas] J[efferson] S[awyer], "Fallen Angels," *UQGR* 1 (1844) 294-324.

A. D. C. Twesten, "The Doctrine Respecting Angels," *BS* 2 (1845) 108-123. [The employment of Angels; Objections to the Existence of Angels considered] *(Trans. by H. B. Adams)*

H., "Sketches on the Doctrine of Angels," *BRCM* 4 (1847-48) 289-312. *[OT Refs., pp. 291-293]*

[Hans(?)] Bahr, "The Cherubim," *CRB* 14 (1849) 592-610.

†Anonymous, "Modern Angelology," *ERL* 12 (1849) 272-287. *(Review)*

P. Q., "The Ministry of Angels," *JSL, 2nd Ser.,* 1 (1851-52) 283-319.

J. H. C., "The Origin of the Cherubic Forms Mentioned in the Holy Scriptures, Considered in Connection with Some of the Discoveries of Layard at Nineveh," *JSL, 2nd Ser.,* 3 (1852-53) 154-167.

J. H. C., "On the Existence and Characteristics of Angels," *JSL, 2nd Ser.,* 5 (1853-54) 122-137.

J. H. C., "On the Existence and Characteristics of Angels (From the Journal of Sacred Literature, London; October, 1853.)," *MQR* 8 (1854) 109-129.

S. Patton, "'The Existence and Characteristics of Angels'," *MQR* 8 (1854) 357-368.

*†Anonymous, "Religious History of Mankind," *LQHR* 5 (1855-56) 289-334. [Cherubim, pp. 314-315] *(Review)*

T. V. Moore, "The Cherubic Symbol," *MQR* 11 (1857) 73-90.

W[illiam] Hurlin, "Angels," *CRB* 24 (1859) 18-31.

H. D., "Scriptural Account of the Cherubim," *JSL, 3rd Ser.,* 9 (1859) 88-95.

*R. C. G., "The Cherubim of Eden," *ERG, 4th Ser.,* 3 (1868-69) 35-43.

H. Louis Gaugher, "The Good Angels," *ER* 20 (1869) 221-233.

C. G. B., "The Ministry of Angels," *ERG, 4th Ser.,* 4 (1869-70) 270-282.

Edward Riehm, "The Cherubim," *CongR* 10 (1870) 1-19. *(Trans. by C. M. Mead)*

J. A. Brown, "Angelology," *LQ* 3 (1873) 374-397.

Malcolm White, "The Cherubim," *BFER* 25 (1876) 539-546.

E. Nesbit, "Angels," *BQ* 10 (1876) 1-18.

George T. Ladd, "Biblical Notes: The Cherubim," *DTQ* 2 (1876) 453-463.

George T. Ladd, "Cherubim," *BS* 33 (1876) 32-51.

John Crawford, "The Cherubim," *BS* 35 (1879) 225-247.

*Stephen H. Stackpole, "Sons of God. A Study of the Scriptural Uses of the Title," *BQR* 2 (1880) 315-333. [I. Uses of the Title in the Old Testament. 1. Angels, pp. 316-318]

*Francis Brown, "The Cherubim in Babylonian Mythology," *PR* 3 (1882) 168-169.

T. K. Cheyne, "The Seraphim," *Exp, 3rd Ser.,* 1 (1885) 319.

E. A. Wallis Budge, "The Seraphim," *Exp, 3rd Ser.,* 1 (1885) 320.

T. K. Cheyne, "The Cherubim," *Exp, 3rd Ser.,* 1 (1885) 400.

E. A. Wallis Budge, "The Cherubim," *Exp, 3rd Ser.,* 1 (1885) 400.

J. M. McNulty, "The Cherubim," *HR* 14 (1887) 299-305.

Howard Crosby, "Michael and Gabriel," *HR* 19 (1890) 160-162.

G. C. M. Douglas, "Archangels," *ET* 3 (1891-92) 545-549.

*Lawrence Mills, "Philo's δυνάμεις and the Amesha Spenta," *JRAS* (1901) 553-568.

*A. Smythe Palmer, "Michael the Messiah," *ET* 16 (1904-05) 287.

*James A. Montgomery, "Notes from the Samaritan," *JBL* 25 (1906) 49-54. [V. Angels Attendant at the Sacrifices, p. 54]

A. L. Williams, "The Cult of the Angels at Colossae," *JTS* 10 (1908-09) 413-438. [I. The Doctrine of Angels among the Jews; 2. The Worship of Angels among the Jews]

*Rayner Winterbotham, "The Angel-Princes of Daniel," *Exp, 8th Ser.,* 1 (1911) 50-58.

*L. H. Gray, "Iranian Miscellanies. c) The Iranian Name בגדאנא," *JAOS* 33 (1913) 285.

J. H. Wade, "The Doctrine of Angels," *MC* 3 (1913-14) 417-423.

*A. H. Sayce, "Assyriological Notes," *SBAP* 39 (1917) 207-212. [The Cherubim, pp. 207-208]

*Harry Pressfield, "Angels—and the Problem of Evil," *MQR, 3rd Ser.,*47 (1921) 535-537.

R. H. Pfeiffer, "Cherubim," *JBL* 41 (1922) 249-250.

Maurice A. Canney, "Sky Folk in the Old Testament," *JMUEOS* #10 (1923) 53-58.

Marinus James, "Angelology," *R&E* 20 (1923) 84-93.

Leo Jung, "Fallen Angels in Jewish, Christian and Mohammedan Literature (Chapters 1 & 2)," *JQR, N.S.,* 15 (1924-25) 467-502.

H. M. Selby, "The Attendants of Yahveh," *OC* 39 (1925) 1-6.

Leo Jung, "Fallen Angels in Jewish, Christian and Mohammedan Literature (Chapters 3-7 and Appendices)," *JQR, N.S.,* 16 (1925-26) 45-88, 171-205, 287-336.

*G. H. Dix, "The Seven Archangels and the Seven Spirits: A Study in the Origin, Development, and Messianic Associations of the Two Themes," *JTS* 28 (1926-27) 233-250.

Ellen Conroy McCaffery, "The Names of the Archangels," *OC* 41 (1927) 278-287.

*C. Kaplan, "Angels in the Book of Enoch," *ATR* 12 (1929-30) 423-437.

Chaim Kaplan, "The Angel of Peace, Uriel, Metatron," *ATR* 13 (1931) 306-313.

*J. W. Crowfoot, "The Ivories from Samaria," *PEFQS* 65 (1933) 7-26. *[Cherubim]*

*Herbert G. May, "A Supplementary Note on the Ivory Inlays from Samaria," *PEFQS* 65 (1933) 88-89. *[Cherubim]*

Alan Rowe, "Winged Monsters, Etc.—Some Tentative Suggestions," *PEFQS* 65 (1933) 97-99.

W[illiam] F[oxwell] Albright, "What Were the Cherubim?" *BA* 1 (1938) 1-3.

*W[illiam] F[oxwell] Albright, "The Golden Calf and the Cherubim," *JBL* 57 (1938) xviii.

Lewis Sperry Chafer, "Angelology," *BS* 98 (1941) 389-420, 99 (1942) 6-25, 135-156, 262-296, 391-417.

*John L. McKenzie, "The Divine Sonship of Angels," *CBQ* 5 (1943) 293-300.

B. J. Bamberger, "The Rebel Angels," *JBL* 63 (1944) iv.

Harold B. Kuhn, "The Angelology of the Non-Canonical Jewish Apocalypses," *JBL* 67 (1948) 217-232.

Ilona E. Ellinger, "Winged Figures," *AJA* 54 (1950) 265. *[Angels]*

*A. F. L. Beeston, "Angels in Deuteronomy 33^1, *JTS, N.S.,* 2 (1951) 30-31.

Charles C. Torrey, "Alexander Jannaeus and the Archangel Michael," *VT* 4 (1954) 208-211.

Gordon Chilvers, "Angels," *EQ* 27 (1955) 108-128.

*Merrill F. Unger, "The Old Testament Revelation of the Creation of Angels and Earth," *BS* 114 (1957) 206-212.

*Menahem Mansoor, "Studies in the *Hodayot*—IV,' *JBL* 76 (1957) 139-148.

Rosemary Heddon, "Angels in Scripture," *LofS* 12 (1957-58) 112-118.

George M. Landes, "Shall We Neglect the Angels?" *USQR* 14 (1958-59) #4, 19-25.

*M. Haran, "The Ark and the Cherubim: Their Symbolic Significance in Biblical Ritual," *IEJ* 9 (1959) 30-38, 89-94.

*H[arry] A. Wolfson, "The Pre-Existent Angel of the Magharians and Al-Nahāwandī," *JQR, N.S.,* 51 (1960-61) 89-106.

S. G. F. Brandon, "Angels: The History of an Idea," *HT* 13 (1963) 655-665.

*Bernard J. Bamberger, "The Sadducees and the Belief in Angels," *JBL* 82 (1963) 433-435.

Eric F. F. Bishop, "Angelology in Judaism, Islam and Christianity," *ATR* 46 (1964) 142-154.

*Solomon Zeitlin, "The Sadducees and the Belief in Angels," *JBL* 83 (1964) 67-71.

*Gerald Cooke, "The Sons of (the) God(s)," *ZAW* 76 (1964) 22-47.

*L. Thunberg, "Early Christian Interpretation of the Three Angels in Gen. 18," *StP* 7 (1966) 560-570.

Masashi Takahashi, "An Oriental's Approach to the Problems of Angelology," *ZAW* 78 (1966) 343-350.

*Samuel Belkin, "Some Obscure Tradition Mutually Clarified in Philo and Rabbinic Literature," *JQR* 75th (1967) 80-103. [4. Heavenly Birds, pp. 88-90]

*E. W. Hengstenberg, "The Cherubim and Their Symbolical Meaning," *ThE* 5 (1968) 168-198. *[Article XIII - pages misnumbered] (Trans. by S. O. Allen)*

*E. Lacheman, "The Seraphim of Isaiah 6," *JQR, N.S.,* 59 (1968-69) 71-72.

§1008 *5.4.6.2 Studies on Demonology, Demon Possession, and Exorcism*

*J. H. Young, "The Existence and Fall of Satan and His Angels," *MR* 20 (1838) 100-117.

*S. Comfort, "Calm Review of Article on the 'Existence and Fall of Satan,' &c.," *MR* 20 (1838) 303-308.

*J. H. Young, "Defence of the Existence and Fall of Satan and His Angels," *MR* 20 (1838) 464-467.

*S. Comfort, "Review of the Defence of the Existence of Satan and His Angels," *MR* 21 (1839) 105-112.

Anonymous, "Pythonic and Demonic Possessions in India and Judea. Part I," *DUM* 32 (1848) 262-275.

Anonymous, "Pythonic and Demonic Possessions in India and Judea. Part II," *DUM* 32 (1848) 421-443.

William Elfe Tayler, "The Scriptural Doctrine of Demonical Possession," *JSL, 1st Ser.,* 4 (1849) 1-19.

*S. I. L. Rapport, "Asmodai," *MQR* 7 (1853) 500-513. *(Trans. by H. Bear)*

*Wm. Hurlin, "The Devil and his Angels," *CRB* 23 (1858) 38-49.

E. L. Belkinsopp, "Demonism," *JSL, 3rd Ser.,* 14 (1861-62) 186-191.

S. Louis, "Palestinian Demonology," *SBAP* 9 (1886-87) 217-228.

*William Hayes Ward, "Notes on Oriental Antiquities. X. Tiamat and Other Evil Spirits, as Figured on Oriental Seals," *AJA, O.S.,* 6 (1890) 291-298.

Crawford H. Toy, "Evil Spirits in the Bible," *JBL* 9 (1890) 17-30.

F. C. Conybeare, "Christian Demonology," *JQR* 9 (1896-97) 59-114, 444-470, 581-603.

*J. A. Selbie, "Demonology, Magic, etc.," *ET* 10 (1898-99) 326-328.

*W. O. E. Oesterley, "The Demonology of the Apocrypha," *IJA* #7 (1906) 8-9.

W. O. E. Oesterley, "The Demonology of the Old Testament," *Exp, 7th Ser.,* 3 (1907) 316-332.

W. O. E. Oesterley, "The Demonology of the Old Testament Illustrated from the Prophetical Writings," *Exp, 7th Ser.,* 3 (1907) 527-544.

*W. O. E. Oesterley, "The Demonology of the Old Testament, Illustrated by Psalm XCI," *Exp, 7th Ser.,*4 (1907) 132-151.

Allan H. Godbey, "Field-Spirits in the Old Testament," *AJSL* 41 (1924-25) 280.

Maximilian Rudwin, "The Loves of Demons," *OC* 44 (1930) 599-619.

*S[tephen] Langdon, "Babylonian and Hebrew Demonology with reference to the supposed borrowing of Persian Dualism in Judaism and Christianity," *JRAS* (1934) 45-56.

Wilfred Lawrence Knox, "Jewish Liturgical Exorcism," *HTR* 31 (1938) 191-203.

*S. V. McCasland, "The Pre-Christian Messiah and Demons," *JBL* 55 (1936) viii.

Campbell Bonner, "The Technique of Exorcism," *HTR* 36 (1943) 39-49.

Michael J. Gruenthaner, "The Demonology of the Old Testament," *CBQ* 6 (1944) 6-27.

Campbell Bonner, "The Violence of Departing Demons," *HTR* 37 (1944) 334-336.

*H. Torczyner, "A Hebrew Incantation Against Night-Demons from Biblical Times," *JNES* 6 (1947) 18-29.

Lyman S. Johnson, "Demons and Magic: A Study in Metatechnology," *IR* 6 (1949) 115-126. *[Refs. to OT and comparative religion, pp. 115-119]*

Edward Langton, "What are Demons?" *LQHR* 179 (1954) 26-32. *[OT Refs., pp. 27-29]*

Don Altmann, "Demonology," *Amb* 7 (1958-59) #3, 11-19, #5, 22-28.

*Bernard Goldman, "A Snake Goddess, Asiatic Demonology and the Gorgon," *AJA* 65 (1961) 189.

Leon E. Wright, "Are Demons Outmoded?" *JRT* 18 (1961-62) 5-21.

*Lloyd Gaston, "Beelzebul," *TZ* 18 (1962) 247-255. *[OT Refs., pp. 247-250]*

G. Scholem, "Some Sources of Jewish-Arabic Demonology," *JJS* 16 (1965) 1-13.

Wesley D. Smith, "So-called Possession in Pre-Christian Greece," *TAPA* 96 (1965) 403-426.

H. A. Kelly, "Demonology and Diabolical Temptation," *TFUQ* 40 (1965) 165-194.

*Timothy McDermott, "The Devil and his Angels," *NB* 48 (1966-67) 16-25.

H. A. Kelly, "Demonology and Diabolical Temptation," *TD* 14 (1966) 131-136.

*Susan Lee Sherman and John Briggs Curtis, "Divine-Human Conflicts in the Old Testament," *JNES* 28 (1969) 231-242. [Demonology, pp. 233-235]

§1009 **5.4.6.2.1 Studies concerning Satan**

*J. H. Young, "The Existence and Fall of Satan and His Angels," *MR* 20 (1838) 100-117.

*S. Comfort, "Calm Review of Article on the 'Existence and Fall of Satan,' &c.," *MR* 20 (1838) 303-308.

*J. H. Young, "Defence of the Existence and Fall of Satan and His Angels," *MR* 20 91838) 464-467.

*S. Comfort, "Review of the Defence of the Existence of Satan and His Angels," *MR* 21 (1839) 105-112.

Anonymous, "The Personality of Satan," *CRB* 9 (1844) 349-357.

W. R. F., "Scripture Doctrine of Satan, or the Devil," *UQGR* 9 (1857) 395-404.

*Wm. Hurlin, "The Devil and his Angels," *CRB* 23 (1858) 38-49.

Anonymous, "The History and Doctrine of the Devil," *CE* 66 (1859) 351-381. *(Review)*

Thomas Woodward, "The Bible History of Satan: Is He a Fallen Angel?" *DUM* 53 (1859) 421-437.

T. B. T., "Did Jesus Sanction the Jewish Belief in regard to the Devil?" *UQGR* 17 (1860) 291-308.

G. L. C., "The Doctrine of the Personality of the Devil Historically Considered," *UQGR* 17 (1860) 401-423.

Anonymous, "The Theory of a Personal Devil," *CE* 71 (1861) 157-180. *(Review)*

*John Duns, "The Serpent of Eden, from the Point of View of Advanced Science," *BS* 21 (1864) 163-179.

P. H. Wicksteed, "Roskoff's History of the Devil," *TRL* 8 (1871) 30-52. *(Review)*
Anonymous, "History of the Devil," *UQGR, N.S.,* 8 (1871) 335-359.

E. Compton, "The History, Power, and Destiny of the Devil, as Revealed in the Word of God," *DTQ* 5 (1879) 282-292.

Philip H. Wicksteed, "Histories of the Devil," *TRL* 16 (1879) 398-415. *(Review)*

George Hill, "A Personal Devil—Does he Exist?" *UQGR, N.S.,* 16 (1879) 286-302.

*Maurice G. Hansen, "The Name Lucifer," *ONTS* 4 (1884-85) 71-73.

M. Linday Kellner, "Satan: an Old Testament Study," *CR* 50 (1887) 736-742.

Talbot W. Chambers, "Satan in the Old Testament," *PRR* 3 (1892) 22-34.

J. T Gladhill, "The Devil, the Prince of this World. A Bible Study," *LQ* 23 (1893) 402-420.

C. C. Everett, "The Devil," *NW* 4 (1895) 1-22.

*Paul Carus, "Azazel and Satan," *OC* 9 (1895) #44, 4692-4693.

*N. A. Koenig, "Lucifer," *ET* 18 (1906-07) 479.

F. W. Fitzpatrick, "The Devil," *OC* 21 (1907) 69-84.

*J. A. F. Gregg, "The Identification of the Serpent with Satan in the Book of Wisdom," *IJA* #23 (1910) 77-78.

C. F. Sparkman, "Satan and his Ancestors, from a Psychological Standpoint," *AJRPE* 5 (1912) 52-86, 163-194. [Part I. Historical Development, pp. 52-86; Part II. Rise, Growth and Death of Satan, pp. 163-194]

John Edwards Le Bosquet, "The Evil One: A Development," *HTR* 5 (1912) 371-384.

A. Smythe Palmer, "The Fall of Lucifer," *HJ* 11 (1912-13) 766-786.

William Caldwell, "The Doctrine of Satan. I. In the Old Testament," *BW* 41 (1913) 29-33.

*William Caldwell, "The Doctrine of Satan. II. Satan in Extra-Biblical Apocalyptic Literature," *BW* 41 (1913) 98-102.

Perovsky Petrovo-Solovovo, "The Fall of Lucifer," *HJ* 12 (1913-14) 193-194.

Anonymous, "Who Was 'Satan'," *HR* 68 (1914) 456.

Robert H. Kennett, "Satan," *ICMM* 11 (1914-15) 26-33.

C. Wesley Hutchinson, "A Human Original for 'Satan'," *ET* 32 (1920-21) 425-426.

H. H. B. Ayles, "The Biblical Doctrine of Satan," *ICMM* 18 (1921-22) 115-119.

George Wilson Brent, "Seven Appearances of the Devil in Scriptures," *CFL, 3rd Ser.,* 31 (1925) 353-354.

Robert H. Pfeiffer, "Satan," *MR* 109 (1926) 897-902.

Allen H. Godbey, "The Devil in Legend and Literature," *OC* 47 (1933) 385-397.

H. J. Flowers, "The History of the Devil," *CQ* 11 (1934) 63-79.

Harry Torczyner, "How Satan Came into the World," *ET* 48 (1936-37) 563-565.

*W. H. A. Learoyd, "The Envy of the Devil in Wisdom II. 24," *ET* 51 (1939-40) 395-396.

R. O. P. Taylor, "The Accuser," *ET* 53 (1941-42) 99-102.

Edward Langton, "The Passing of Satan," *HJ* 42 (1943-44) 152-157.

A., "A Roman View of Satan's Fall," *CTM* 16 (1945) 47.

F. F. Bruce, "The Crooked Serpent," *EQ* 20 (1948) 283-288.

Elliot Van N. Diller, "The Devil's Wisdom," *CQ* 27 (1950) 313-320.

Samuel J. Warner, "The Concept of Satan as an Aid to the Understanding of Human Destructiveness," *JRT* 13 (1955-56) 93-109.

*Joseph H. Golner, "God, Satan and Atonement," *Jud* 9 (1960) 299-306.

Kestutis A. Trimakas, "Satan: His Dedivinized Existence and Activity," *MH* 15 (1960) 12-24.

Kester Svendsen, "Satan and Science," *BUS* 9 (1960-61) #2, 130-142.

Gediminas K. Kijauskas, "Satan and the Counter Kingdom," *MH* 16 (Spring, 1961) 1-21.

Richmond Lattimore, "Why the Devil is the Devil," *PAPS* 106 (1962) 427-429.

S.G. F. Brandon, "The Devil: In Faith and History," *HT* 13 (1963) 468-478.

*Timothy McDermott, "The Devil and his Angels," *NB* 48 (1966-67) 16-25.

§1010 *5.4.6.3 Psychical Researches and Studies*

Anonymous, "Spiritism and the Bible," *SPR* 23 (1872-73) 611-654.

J. B. Gardiner, "Psychic Research and the Holy Scripture," *ICMM* 7 (1910-11) 288-302.

C. W. Emmet, "Psychical Research and Its Bearing on Some Biblical Problems," *ET* 24 (1912-13) 344-349.

J. Stafford Wright, "The Bearing of Psychical Research upon the Interpretation of the Bible," *JTVI* 80 (1948) 33-45, 52-55. [(Discussion, pp. 46-47) (Communications by L. R. Wheeler, pp. 47-49; P. W. O'Gorman, pp. 49-51; R. E. D. Clark, pp. 51-52)]

*Robert E. D. Clark, "Prophecy and Psychical Research," *JTVI* 83 (1951) 137-148, 156-157. [(Discussion pp. 149-152) (Communications by J. Stafford Wright, pp. 152-153; F. F. Bruce, pp. 153-154; L. D. Ford, pp. 154-155; L. Merson Davies, pp. 155-156)]

§1011 *5.4.7 Studies on the Doctrine of Man*

†Anonymous, "Huntingford—On the Separate Existence of the Soul," *BCQTR, 4th Ser.,* 6 (1829) 130-162. *[OT Refs., pp. 142-143] (Review)*

Anonymous, "An Inquiry into the Doctrine of the Innate Corrupton of Human Nature: being an Examination of those Parts of Scripture on which it has been founded," *CTPR, N.S.,* 3 (1841) 46-66.

*J. W. Ward, "The Consistency of the Eternal Purposes of God with the Free Agency of Men," *BS* 4 (1847) 77-95.

George I. Chace, "Of the Independence of the Mental Powers upon Bodily Organization," *BS* 6 (1849) 534-558.

Edward Beecher, "Man the Image of God," *BS* 7 (1850) 409-425.

[Fréd. de] Rougemont, "Historical Geography and Ethnography," *BS* 11 (1854) 217-254. *(Trans. by E. C. Tracy)*

C. F. Keil, "The Preexistence of the Soul," *BS* 12 (1855) 156-178.

*James G. Frazer, "On Certain Burial Customs as illustrative of the Primitive Theory of the Soul," *JRAI* 15 (1885-86) 64-101. (Discussion, 101-104)

Joseph Haven, "The Moral Faculty," *BS* 13 (1856) 229-272. *(Conscience)*

*James D. Dana, "Thoughts on Species," *BS* 14 (1857) 854-874.

J. Fr. Bruch, "The Pre-existence of the Soul," *BS* 20 (1863) 681-733. *[A Paraphrase from the German]*

Geo. D. Boardman, "The Scriptural Anthropology," *BQ* 1 (1867) 177-190, 325-340, 428-444.

John Bascom, "Conscience, its Relations and Office," *BS* 24 (1867) 150-175.

O. D. Miller, "Biblical Psychology," *UQGR, N.S.,* 6 (1869) 297-315.

Charles Graham, "Some Scriptural Aspects of Man's Tripartite Nature," *JTVI* 6 (1872-73) 202-219. (Discussion, pp. 220-231)

Anonymous, "Man Made in the Image of God," *ERG, 5th Ser.,* 4 (1873-74) 216-227.

James Macgregor," The Place of Man Theologically Regarded," *BFER* 24 (1875) 113-137.

*Geo. S. Morris, "The Immortality of the Human Soul," *BS* 33 (1876) 695-715.

*Francis Bowen, "The Idea of God in the Soul of Man," *BS* 33 (1876) 740-754.

J. Williamson Nevin, "Bible Anthropology," *RChR* 24 (1877) 329-365.

Joseph Le Conte, "Man's Place in Nature," *PRev* 54 (1878) Part 2, 776-803.

†Anonymous, "Heard's Tripartite Nature of Man," *LQHR* 52 (1879) 109-149. *(Review)*

F. A. Gast, "Old Testament Doctrine of the Spirit of Man," *RChR* 26 (1879) 391-412.

E. R. Conder, "The Bible a Revelation of Man," *CongL* 11 (1882) 186-196.

[M.] L[oy], "Soul and Spirit," *ColTM* 3 (1883) 133-148.

[F. W.] St[ellhorn], "Are There Any Remnants of the Image of God in Natural Man?" *ColTM* 4 (1884) 95-106.

[M.] L[oy], "The Nature of the Will," *ColTM* 4 (1884) 129-242.

[M.] L[oy], "Liberty of the Will," *ColTM* 4 (1884) 257-305.

[M.] L[oy], "The Bondage of the Will," *ColTM* 4 (1884) 321-348.

[M.] L[oy], "The Discipline of the Will," *ColTM* 5 (1885) 1-25.

*J. M. Hawley, "The Image of God," *MQR, 2nd Ser.,* 8 (1886) 17-40.

Chas. S. Robinson, "Man Created as a Living Soul," *HR* 14 (1887) 312-316.

Chas. S. Robinson, "God's Image in Man," *HR* 14 (1887) 400-403.

J. D. Gold, "Man: What is He?" *ERG, 9th Ser.,* 3 (1887-88) 209-219.

S. H. Kellogg, "Trichotomy: A Biblical Study," *BS* 47 (1890) 461-490.

Marshall Randles, "Requests and Replies," *ET* 2 (1890-91) 156-157. [The Spiritual Nature of Man]

Arthur T. Pierson, "The Brute in Man," *HR* 25 (1893) 158.

*Frank Cramer, "The Theological and Scientific Theories of the Origin of Man," *BS* 48 (1891) 510-516.

Charles F. Deems, "Soul and Spirit: A Study in Biblical Psychology," *CT* 11 (1893-94) 406-418.

Smith B. Goodenow, "Primeval Man," *BS* 51 (1894) 158-164.

George A. Barton, "The Kinship of gods and men among the early Semites," *JBL* 15 (1896) 168-182.

L. H. Schuh, "The Origin of the Soul," *ColTM* 18 (1898) 47-56.

A. G., "Anthropology," *TQ* 3 (1899) 257-286, 385-451.

J. W. Dawson, "The Origin and Antiquity of Man," *ET* 11 (1899-1900) 149-152.

Samuel Wittlesey, "The Tripartite Nature of Man," *BS* 58 (1901) 692-704.

Joseph Agar Beet, "The Immortality of the Soul. 1. Immortality before Christ," *Exp, 6th Ser.,* 3 (1901) 50-61.

J. W. Ross, "The Divine Fatherhood," *BS* 62 (1905) 666-684.

*Frank Chamberlin Porter, "The Pre-Existence of the Soul in the Book of Wisdom and in the Rabbinical Writings," *AJT* 12 (1908) 53-115.

Norman S. Wolf, "The Biblical Doctrine of the Heart," *LQ* 38 (1908) 197-209.

James Lindsay, "Psychology of the Soul," *PTR* 6 (1908) 437-454.

*G. Elliot Smith, "'Heart and Reins' in Mummification," *JMUEOS* #1 (1911) 41-44. [Supplementary note, pp. 45-48]

*Hope W. Hogg, "'Heart and Reins' in the Ancient Literatures of the Nearer East," *JMUEOS* #1 (1911) 49-91.

*M. A. Canney, "'Heart and Reins.' Further Notes on Hebrew Idioms," *JMUEOS* #1 (1911) 93-94.

*Leonard W. King, "'Heart and Reins' in Relation to Babylonian Liver Divination," *JMUEOS* #1 (1911) 95-98.

L. C. Casartelli, "'Heart and Reins' in Ancient Irān," *JMUEOS* #1 (1911) 99-101.

T. W. Rhys Davids, "'Hearts and Reins' in India," *JMUEOS* #1 (1911) 103-106.

J. G. Frazer, "'Heart and Reins' and Ideas of Uncultured Races," *JMUEOS* #1 (1911) 107-108.

Benjamin B. Warfield, "On the Antiquity and Unity of the Human Race," *PTR* 9 (1911) 1-25.

*Frank Chamberlin Porter, "The Pre-Existence of the Soul in the Book of Wisdom and in the Rabbinical Writings," *IJA* #29 (1912) 33-34. (with note by W. B. Stevenson)

*Henry A. Stimson, "The Development of the Doctrine of God and Man," *BS* 70 (1913) 193-201.

*S. A. B. Mercer, "The Pre-existence of the Soul in the Apocrypha and Pseudepigrapha," *IJA* #45 (1916) 19-22.

*Louis L. Mann, "Freedom of the Will in Talmudic Literature," *YCCAR* 27 (1917) 301-337.

*F. R. Tennant, "Creation, and the Origin of the Soul," *ET* 31 (1919-20) 185-187.

Francis J. Hall, "This Miserable and Naughty World," *ATR* 3 (1920-21) 97-113.

E. O. James, "The Origin and the Fall of Man," *Theo* 3 (1921) 16-22, 78-89.

F. D. Jenkins, "The Problem of Mental Evolution," *PTR* 22 (1924) 46-71, 277-303.

Leander S. Keyser, "The Problem of Man's Origin," *BS* 82 (1925) 146-157.

Herbert C. Alleman, "The Old Testament and the New Psychology," *LQ* 56 (1926) 159-169.

P[hilip] M[auro], "'What is Man?'," *CFL, 3rd Ser.,* 35 (1929) 573-576.

Mary E. McDonough, "The Biological Status of the First and Last Adam," *CFL, 3rd Ser,.* 35 (1929) 654-657.

Duncan McNeill, "What is Man?" *CFL, 3rd Ser.,* 36 (1930) 491-493.

J. H. Morrison, "Man's Place in the Physical Universe," *ET* 42 (1930-31) 502-508.

Anonymous, "Notes and Comments. How Old is Man's Conscience?" *A&A* 32 (1931) 187.

Walter Ovid Kinsolving, "Have I a Soul?" *ATR* 13 (1931) 388-404.

*J. H. Morrison, "Man's Origin and Fall," *ET* 44 (1932-33) 182-188.

John S. Axtell, "What is Man?" *CFL, 3rd Ser.,* 39 (1933) 243-247.

J. H. Morrison, "Physical Indeterminancy and Human Free Will," *ET* 45 (1933-34) 318-323.

R. H. Altus, "The Immortality of the Soul of Man," *AusTR* 5 (1934) 41-52.

*Harry Austryn Wolfson, "The Internal Senses in Latin, Arabic, and Hebrew Philosophic Texts," *HTR* 28 (1935) 69-133.

Campbell Bonner, "Palladas and Jewish Reflection upon the Beginnings of Man," *JAOS* 55 (1935) 196-199.

Preston M. Evans, "Man—A Living Soul," *CFL, 3rd Ser.,* 42 (1936) 306-307.

W. R. Matthews, "What is Man?" *MC* 26 (1936-37) 148-154. *(Sermon)*

Arthur C. Headlam, "The Doctrine of Man," *CQR* 128 (1939) 1-39.

L. M. Davies, "Man in the Image of God," *JTVI* 71 (1939) 170-181, 190-193. (Discussion, pp. 181-190)

*J. W. Hunkin, "The Spirit of Man and the Spirit of God (I)," *MC* 29 (1939-40) 473-484.

T. W. Rosmarin, "The Old Testament on Freedom of Will," *JBL* 59 (1940) xiv-xv.

*Norval Garhard Hogland, "Sermons in Hebrew Words," *JTALC* 6 (1941) 817-855, 935-944. [Part II. Chief Words for Man]

James Muilenburg, "Imago Dei," *RR* 6 (1941-42) 392-406.

William Matheson, "Conscience," *WTJ* 4 (1941-42) 97-122.

Herbert Pierrepont Houghton, "On the Immortality of the Soul," *ATR* 24 (1942) 63-70.

Lewis Sperry Chafer, "Anthropology," *BS* 100 (1943) 220-243, 354-373, 479-496; 101 (1944) 8-29, 132-148, 264-282, 391-402.

J. Philip Hyatt, "The Old Testament View of Man," *RL* 14 (1944-45) 526-534.

Otto A. Pipper, "The Biblical Understanding of Man," *TT* 1 (1944-45) 188-203.

Roger Douglass Congdon, "The Doctrine of Conscience," *BS* 102 (1945) 226-232, 346-359, 474-489. [The Problem; Introduction/Extra-Biblical Theories, Ancient Theories: 1. Babylonian and Assyrian, 2. Egyptian, 3. Hebrew, 4. Greek, 5. Roman; More Recent Theories: Current Definitions; Theories Based on the Bible. 1. From Christ to the Middle Ages, 2. The Middle Ages and Reformation; Ignorance of the Doctrine; Summary; Source Material, Lexicographical and historical study, Use of the Term in the New Testament. Use of the Term in the Septuagint, Other Passages and Uses in the New Testament, Summary]

Roger Douglass Congdon, "The Doctrine of Conscience," *BS* 103 (1946) 68-81. [Doctrinal Study; 1. Definition; 2. The Acquisition and Development of Conscience; 3. Scope of the Doctrine, a. The Conscience of the Saved, b. The Conscience of the Unsaved; 4. Summary of the Doctrine, a. Ideas Excluded, b. Ideas Included]

*L. H. Brockington, "The Hebrew Conception of Personality in Relation to the Knowledge of God," *JTS* 47 (1946) 1-11.

*Julian O. Krusling, "Evolution and Man," *SS* 15 (June, 1946) 38-47.

Levi A. Olan, "On the Nature of Man," *YCCAR* 58 (1948) 255-271, 277-278. [Discussion by: Samuel S. Cohon, pp. 271-273; Julius Leibert, pp. 273-274; Max Kaufman, pp. 274-275; Melvin S. Sands, p. 275; Allen S. Green, p. 275; William Silverman, pp. 275-276; Leon Fram, p. 276; Philip S. Bernstein, p. 278; Abba Hillel Silver, pp. 278-284]

John Marsh, "Doctrine of Man. Man in the Old Testament," *ET* 60 (1948-49) 335-337.

*John Newton Thomas, "'What is Man?' *The Biblical Doctrine of the Image of God," Interp* 3 (1949) 154-163.

John Henderson, "The Biblical doctrine of the Imago Dei," *RTRM* 8 (1949) #4, 1-8.

Klaus Hoffman, "Man and His Call," *Scrip* 4 (1949-51) 162-168.

H. F. Lovell Cocks, "Doctrine in Man. The Divine Image in Man," *ET* 61 (1949-50) 43-46.

Philip B. Marquart, "Basic Anxiety and Adamic Motivation," *JASA* 2 (1950) #3, 1-6.

C. Umhau Wolf, "The Unity of Man in the Old Testament," *LWR* 3 (1950) 42-50.

Lester J. Kuyper, "The Biblical Doctrine of Man," *RefR* 4 (1950-51) #3, 7-10.

Ernest White, "A Preface to Biblical Psychology," *JTVI* 83 (1951) 51-65, 75-77. [(Discussion, pp. 65-66) (Communications by F. F. Bruce, pp. 66-67; J. Stafford Wright, pp. 67-68; Basil F. C. Atkinson, pp. 68-70; Douglas Dewar, pp. 70-71; John Byrt, pp. 71-72; H. K. Airy Shaw, pp. 72-75)]

Robert Gordis, "The Nature of Man in the Judeo-Christian Tradition," *Jud* 2 (1953) 101-109.

Zachary C. Xintaras, "Man—The Image of God," *GOTR* 1 (1954-55) 48-62.

*H. Hamann, "Some Neo-Orthodox Voices on Anthropology," *AusTR* 26 (1955) 69-85.

*Sheldon H. Blank, "'Doest Thou Well to be Angry?' A Study in Self-Pity," *HUCA* 26 (1955) 29-41.

L. B. Cross, "The Bible and the Understanding of Man," *MC* 45 (1955) 191-203.

James G. S. S. Thomson, "Sleep: An Aspect of Jewish Anthropology," *VT* 5 (1955) 421-433.

John Wren-Lewis, "The Continuous Fall. A Study in the Necessity of Taking Transcendence Seriously," *HJ* 54 (1955-56) 358-368.

Samuel J. Schultz, "The Unity of the Race," *BS* 113 (1956) 46-52.

Humphrey J. T. Johnson, "The Origin of Man. Theological Considerations," *ClR* 41 (1956) 534-543.

*Herbert G. Wood, "Expository Problems. Man Created in the Image of God," *ET* 68 (1956-57) 165-168.

A. W. Argyle, "'Outward' and 'Inward' in Biblical Thought," *ET* 68 (1956-57) 196-199.

*Peter May, "The Self and the Spirit," *IJT* 6 (1957) 131-142.

Samuel E. Loewenstamm, "Man as Image and Son of God," *Tarbiz* 27 (1957-58) #1, I.

H. Hamann, "Has Man a Soul?" *AusTR* 29 (1958) 101-116.

*Mary Francis Thelen, "*J.B.*, Job, and the Biblical Doctrine of Man," *JAAR* 27 (1959) 201-205.

C. Everett Tilson*[sic(?)]*, "Brute or Angel," *VDR* 3 (1959) #2, 2-6.

D. M. MacKay, "Man as a Mechanism," *F&T* 91 (1959-60) 145-156, 157. (Communication by C. H. Hume, pp. 156-157) (The Three-fold Emphasis of the Bible, p. 146)

William Young, "The Nature of Man in the Amsterdam Philosophy," *WTJ* 22 (1959-60) 1-12.

Glenn E. Witlock, "The Structure of Personality in Hebrew Psychology. *The Implications of the Hebrew View of Man for Psychology of Religion*," *Interp* 14 (1960) 3-13.

Michael Baily, "Biblical Man and some Formulae of Christian Teaching," *ITQ* 27 (1960) 173-200.

Emerson W. Shideler, "Darwin and the Doctrine of Man," *JR* 40 (1960) 198-211.

J. R. Chandran, "Man in the Bible," *R&S* 7 (1960) #3, 17-26.

Robert Laurin, "The Concept of Man as a Soul," *ET* 72 (1960-61) 131-134.

W. David Stacey, "Man as a Soul," *ET* 72 (1960-61) 349-350.

H.-J. Kraus, "The dignity of man in the light of the Bible," *Min* 1 (1960-61) #2, 4-11.

Herbert H. Rose, "The Relevancy of A. D. Gordon's View of Man," *Jud* 10 (1961) 40-48.

P.   Vittoz,   "Man,"   *BTr*   13   (1962)   121-123.

C. S. Thoburn, "The Biblical Understanding of Man's Origin Nature and Destiny," *IJT* 11 (1962) 17-28.

David S. Shapiro, "The Doctrine of the Image of God and *Imitatio Dei,*" *Jud* 12 (1963) 57-77.

*Emil L. Fackenheim, "Human Freedom and Divine Power. Philosophical Reflections on a Religious Issue," *Jud* 12 (1963) 338-343.

Gershon Weiler, "The Hebrew Concept of Man," *Mwa-M* #3 (1963) 47-65.

John E. Skinner, "What Is a Man?" *JRH* 3 (1963-64) 90-96.

*H. A. Theiste, "The Scriptural Doctrine of the Body and Soul with Special Reference to Death and Resurrection," *LSQ* 4 (1963-64) #3, 2-9. *[OT Refs., pp. 3-5]*

Jean R. Zurcher, "The Christian View of Man: I," *AUSS* 2 (1964) 156-168.

E. W. Marter, "The Hebrew Concept of 'Soul' in Pre-Exilic Writings," *AUSS* 2 (1964) 97-108.

Jean R. Zurcher, "The Christian View of Man: II," *AUSS* 3 (1964) 66-83.

S. G. F. Brandon, "The Idea of the Soul: The History of Mankind's Most Fundamental Concept. Part One: In the West," *HT* 14 (1964) 181-191.

Heinrich J. Vogel, "The Old Testament Concept of the Soul," *WLQ* 61 (1964) 33-56, 107-129, 191-203.

Vasilios M. Vellas, "The Spiritual Man According to the Old Testament," *GOTR* 10 (1964-65) 107-120.

Norman Lamm, "Man's Position in the Universe. A Comparative Study of the Views of Saadia Gaon and Maimonides," *JQR, N.S.,* 55 (1964-65) 208-234.

*W. Dantine, "Creation and Redemption: Attempt at a Theological Interpretation in the Light of Contemporary Understanding of the World," *SJT* 18 (1965) 129-147. [A. The Key Position of Anthropology; B. Cosmic Christology? C. The Lordship of Christ in Creation]

D. Lys, "The Israelite Soul According to the LXX," *VT* 16 (1966) 181-228.

Brian S. Mawhinney, "Man—His Origin, His Nature and His God," *F&T* 95 (1966-67) 54-71.

*Anthony T. Padavano, "Original Sin and Christian Anthropology," *CTSP* 22 (1967) 93-131. *[OT Refs., pp. 95-99]*

*Harry Neumann, "Kierkegaard and Socrates on the Dignity of Man," *Person* 48 (1967) 453-460.

*Thomas W. Cebula, "The Role of the Heart in the Old Testament Psychology of Sin," *SS* 19 (1967-68) #1, 11-23.

William L. Holladay, "God's Crowning Self-Expression," *ABBTS* 43 (1968) #1, 6-10.

Alexander Altmann, "*Homo Imago Dei* in Jewish and Christian Theology," *JR* 48 (1968) 235-259.

D. J. A. Clines, "The Image of God in Man," *TB* #19 (1968) 53-103.

S. Vernon McCasland, "Man in the Biblical Perspective," *LTQ* 3 (1968) 107-116.

Samuel J. Mikolaski, "On the Nature of Man," *F&T* 97 (1968-69) #2, 3-32.

*Leo Landman, "Law and Conscience: The Jewish View," *Jud* 18 (1969) 17-29.

Henry Wansbrough, "Corporate Personality in the Bible: Adam and Christ —a biblical use of the concept of personality," *NB* 50 (1969) 798-804.

*T. Francis Glasson, "'Visions of Thy Head' (Daniel 2^{28}) The Heart and the Head in Bible Psychology," *ET* 81 (1969-70) 247-248.

§1012 *5.4.8 Studies on the Doctrine of Sin, Temptation, Evil,
         and the Fall*

†'Oxoniensis', "An Essay on the Origin of Evil," *TRep* 1 (1769) 443-448.

†Anonymous, "On the Introduction of Sin," *SP* 5 (1832) 273-276.

William Tucker, "Introduction of Moral Evil," *SP* 6 (1833) 605-606.

*M. Stuart, "Have the Sacred Writers any where asserted that the Sin or
Righteousness of one is imputed to another," *BRCR* 7 (1836) 241-330.

M. Stuart, "What is Sin?   Translation of a passage from Vitringa's
Observationes Sacrae in relation to this question, with introductory and
other Remarks," *BRCR, N.S.,* 1 (1839) 261-294.

†Anonymous, "Man and His Moral Relations," *BQRL* 3 (1846) 1-33.
(Review)

Anonymous, "Miscellanies and Correspondence," *BRCM* 4 (1847-48) 120-
125. [I. Original Sin, p. 120, II. (by G.), pp. 121-125]

C. G. Bretschneider, "History of the Doctrine of Original Sin," *OQR* 3
(1847-48) 350-361. *(Trans. by H. Cowles)*

*J. Pye Smith, "On Death, as Connected with the Fall," *JSL, 1st Ser.,* 1
(1848) 167-171.

J. F. C., "The Christian Review on Original Sin," *CE* 53 (1852) 93-104.

Anonymous, "The Doctrine of Original Sin," *CRB* 17 (1852) 1-32. *(Review)*

C. D., "The Nature of Sin, and its Earliest Developments," *JSL, 2nd Ser.,* 4
(1853) 80-100. *(Review)*

*Anonymous, "Divine Providence in its Relation to Sin," *ERG, 1st Ser.,* 1
(1854-55) 268-277.

Anonymous, "Thoughts on Original Sin," *SPR* 9 (1855-56) 425-462.

L. P. Hickok, "Perpetual Sin and Omnipotent Goodness," *BS* 13 (1856) 48-
80.

E. F., "Heathen Views of the Punishment of Sin," *UQGR* 13 (1856) 84-95.

Anonymous, "The Origin of Sin," *ERG, 1st Ser.,* 3 (1856-57) 221-225.

Anonymous, "Original Sin," *ERG, 2nd Ser.,* 1 (1858-59) 270-277.

*Anonymous, "The Atonement as related to Sin, and to a Divine Lawgiver," *AThR* 1 (1859) 141-151.

Anonymous, "The Relation of Adam to his Posterity," *BFER* 12 (1863) 252-260.

Joseph Haven, "Sin, as Related to Human Nature and to the Divine Purpose," *BS* 20 (1863) 445-488.

J. F. Fairchild, "The Nature of Sin," *BS* 25 (1868) 30-48.

A. C. Thomas, "The Origin of Sin," *UQGR, N.S.,* 6 (1869) 149-158.

Anonymous, "Original Sin," *ERG, 5th Ser.,* 1 (1870-71) 298-304. *(Review)*

A. H. Kremer, "Original Sin," *RChR* 19 (1872) 50-60.

L. P. Hickok, "Temptation No Excuse for Transgression," *BS* 30 (1873) 648-671.

*William Adamson, "Did Adam Excuse or Confess His Sin?" *ERG, 7th Ser.,* 3 (1880-81) 233-244.

[M.] L[oy], "Original Sin," *ColTM* 2 (1882) 321-329.

James Atkinson, "The Existence of Evil," *ERG, 8th Ser.,* 2 (1883-84) 80-89.

*James Watson, "Evil and the Divine Attributes," *ERG, 8th Ser.,* 2 (1883-84) 105-107.

W. Rupp, "What is Original Sin?" *RChR* 32 (1885) 173-204.

Charles A. Salmond, "The Biblical Doctrine of Sin," *BFER* 35 (1886) 601-626.

*Louis M. Flocken, "Physical Evil: Its Sources and Office According to Amos," *ONTS* 12 (1891) 28-33.

*Moncure D. Conway, "Solomonic Literature," *OC* 12 (1898) 385-410. [Solomonic Antijahvism, pp. 385-390]

Milton S. Terry, "Biblical Doctrine of Human Sinfulness," *MQR, 3rd Ser.,* 25 (1899) 337-348.

*F. R. Tennant, "The Teaching of Ecclesiasticus and Wisdom on the Introduction of Sin and Death," *JTS* 2 (1900-01) 207-223.

B. B. Warfield, "The Problem of Evil in Later Judaism," *CFL, N.S.,* 6 (1902) 177-178.

Cornelius Walker, "The First Sin, Its Consequences, and the Remedy," *BS* 60 (1903) 315-333.

W. Mackintosh Mackay, "Mr. Tennant's Theory of the Origin of Sin," *ET* 15 (1903-04) 324-346.

*Albert G. Mackinnon, "An Impressionist Sketch of Sin," *ET* 15 (1903-04) 380-381.

C. Bigg, "The Doctrines of the Fall and Original Sin," *JTS* 5 (1903-04) 466-469. *(Review)*

J. A. Mason, "A Modern Theory of the Fall," *JTS* 5 (1903-04) 481-498.

James Denney, "Relations of Sin and Death," *LCR* 23 (1904) 192-194.

A. F. Rohr, "The Doctrines of the Scriptures Concerning Original Sin," *ColTM* 25 (1905) 76-99, 160-186.

*H. R. Mackintosh, "Sin and Grace in Early Judaism," *ET* 17 (1905-06) 348-349. *(Review)*

Walter Quincy Scott, "Some Reflections on Biblical Ideas of Sin," *BRec* 3 (1906) 389-390.

George Barker Stevens, "The Prophetic Teaching Concerning Sin," *BW* 27 (1906) 423-440.

R. E. McDaniel, "Origin of Sin," *LCR* 25 (1906) 744-752.

*Charles Reed Zahnister, "Evolution and the Fall," *BW* 29 (1907) 41-44.

William Ashmore, "But How Could Perfect Beings Fall into Sin?" *CFL, 3rd Ser.,* 6 (1907) 379-384.

Theodore C. Foote, "Visiting the Sins upon the Innocent," *JAOS* 28 (1907) 309-316.

George S. Patton, "Beyond Good and Evil," *PTR* 6 (1908) 392-436.

Sanford N. Carpenter, "Original Sin," *LQ* 39 (1909) 396-409.

Robert H. Kennett, "The Sin of the Righteous," *ICMM* 6 (1909-10) 349-361.

W. Emery Barnes, "Nathan and David. The Knowledge of Sin under the Old Covenant," *Exp, 7th Ser.,* 9 (1910) 449-456.

James Orr, "Sin as a Problem of To-day. VI. Sin and Evolutionary Theory —The Origins," *Exp, 7th Ser.,* 10 (1910) 6-25.

Henry Preserved Smith, "The Hebrew View of Sin," *AJT* 15 (1911) 525-545.

Caroline M. Breyfogle, "The Hebrew Sense of Sin in the Pre-Exilic Period," *AJT* 16 (1912) 542-560.

Edward L. Schaub, "The Consciousness of Sin," *HTR* 5 (1912) 121-138.

A. H. McNeil, "Law, Sin, and Sacrifice, in the Old Testament," *ICMM* 9 (1912-13) 376-383.

J. M. T. Winther, "The Idea of Sin in the Old Testament," *BM* 1 (1913) 859-910.

*B. V. Miller, "The Greek Fathers and Original Sin," *IER, 5th Ser.,* 2 (1913) 113-132.

*A. Van Hoonacker, "The Connexion of Death with Sin according to Gen. II., III.," *Exp, 8th Ser.,* 9 (1915) 131-143.

*Andrew C. Zenos, "Apocryphal Literature and Bible Study. II. God, Sin and Salvation," *HR* 69 (1915) 22-23.

S. A. Stein, "Origin of Sin," *TZTM* 5 (1915) 461-468.

F. R. Tennant, "The Psychology of Sin," *ET* 30 (1918-19) 411-413.

F. R. Tennant, "The Problem of the Existence of Moral Evil," *ET* 30 (1918-19) 519-521.

Samuel S. Cohon, "The Origin of Death," *JJLP* 1 (1919) 371-396.

*Samuel A. B. Mercer, "Words for Sin in the Old Testament," *ATR* 2 (1919-20) 234-236.

James D. Buhrer, "The Experience of Sin, Prehistoric in Origin," *RChR, 4th Ser.,* 23 (1919) 393-401.

*George McCready Price, "God as Revealed by Modern Science," *CFL, 3rd Ser.,* 27 (1921) 243-254. [Is God the Author of Evil? pp. 247-250]

W[illiam] H. B[ates], "Is God the Author of Evil," *CFL, 3rd Ser.,* 27 (1921) 353-355. *(Editorial)*

*Harry Pressfield, "Angels—and the Problem of Evil," *MQR, 3rd Ser.,* 47 (1921) 535-537.

*A. Buchler, "Ben Sira's conception of Sin and Atonement," *JQR, N.S.,* 13 (1922-23) 303-335, 461-502; 14 (1923-34) 53-83.

F. R. Tennant, "Recent Theories as to the Cause of Universal Sinfulness," *ET* 35 (1923-24) 503-506.

James H. Snowden, "A Psychological Study of the First Human Sin," *MQR, 3rd Ser.,* 50 (1924) 95-103.

William J. Hinke, "The Central Problem in the Old Testament," *ASRec* 20 (1924-25) 161-179.

J. Hoeness, "The Bible and the Sins of the Saints," *TM* 5 (1925) 326-335, 363-369.

H. Wheeler Robinson, "Recent Thought on the Doctrine of Sin," *ET* 37 (1925-26) 152-156.

Charles B. Dawson, "The Mystery of Evil," *IER, 5th Ser.,* 29 (1927) 168-196.

T. A. Lacey, "Original Sin and the Fall," *CQR* 105 (1927-28) 65-78.

*J. S. Boys-Smith, "The Ideas of the Fall and of Original Sin," *JTS* 29 (1927-28) 305-310. *(Review)*

*B. V. Miller, "St. Irenaeus and Original Sin," *IER, 5th Ser.,* 32 (1928) 138-146.

*J. H. Morrison, "Man's Origin and Fall," *ET* 44 (1932-33) 182-188.

Lewis Sperry Chafer, "The Doctrine of Sin," *BS* 91 (1934) 390-408.

L[eander] S. K[eyser], "The Origin of Sin: The Biblical Account Justified," *CFL, 3rd Ser.,* 40 (1934) 177-181. *(Editorial)*

Lewis Sperry Chafer, "The Doctrine of Sin," *BS* 92 (1935) 7-25, 134-153, 349-411; 93 (1936) 5-25, 133-161, 263-288.

Albert T. Mollegen, "The Christian Doctrine of Sin and Salvation, Part I. The Christian Doctrine of Sin," *ATR* 20 (1938) 276-295. [I. The Uniqueness of the Christian Doctrine of Sin; II. The Form of the Doctrine of Sin in the Old Testament; III. The Christian Norm for Sin; IV. The Christian Doctrine of Sin in Context]

Thomas Hancock Grafton, "Why Do Men Suffer?" *USR* 50 (1938-39) 350-357.

J. S. Whale, "Constructive Theology. VII. Sin," *ET* 51 (1939-40) 311-317.

C. T. Fritsch, "Sin in the Septuagint," *JBL* 60 (1941) vi-vii.

Ralph D. Heim, "The Doctrine of Original Sin," *LCQ* 14 (1941) 308-324.

Herbert W. Schneider, "Sin and Society," *RR* 6 (1941-42) 407-413.

Hjalmar Sundquist, "The Origin of Evil," *CovQ* 4 (1944) #2, 3-11.

*Dom Illtyd Trethowan, "Original Sin and the Justice of God," *DR* 217 (1945) 10-24.

Israel Lebendiger, "The Problem of Evil," *CJ* 2 (1945-46) #2, 15-19.

W. E. Staples, "Some Aspects of Sin in the Old Testament," *JNES* 6 (1947) 65-79.

Samuel S. Cohon, "Original Sin," *HUCA* 21 (1948) 275-331.

*Robert A. Bartels, "Law and Sin in Fourth Esdras and Saint Paul," *LQ, N.S.,* 1 (1949) 319-330.

John M. Oesterreicher, "The Jews: Mirror of Our Sins," *C&C* 2 (1950) 32-46.

*James Thayer Addison, "Sin and Atonement," *ATR* 33 (1951) 137-148, 201-208. [I. The Nature and Origin of Sin: A Suggestion; II. Punishment and Forgiveness; III. The Place of Christ's Death in the Work of Atonement; IV. The So-Called 'Cost of Forgiveness' in the Atonement]

Alfred Von Rohr Sauer, "The Concept of Sin in the Old Testament," *CTM* 22 (1951) 705-718.

*Jacob Kohn, "God and the Reality of Evil," *Person* 33 (1952) 117-130.

J. Howard W. Rhys, "A Study of the Understanding of Sin in the Scriptures," *ATR* 35 (1953) 18-27.

Philip Marquart, "The Biblical Psychology of Conviction," *JASA* 7 (1955) #2, 13-16.

George Wesley Buchanan, "The Old Testament Meaning of the Knowledge of Good and Evil," *JBL* 75 (1956) 114-120.

*David S. Shapiro, "The Problem of Evil and the Book of Job," *Jud* 5 (1956) 46-52.

Merrill F. Unger, "The Old Testament Revelation of the Beginning of Sin," *BS* 114 (1957) 326-332.

*Robert Gordis, "The Knowledge of Good and Evil in the Old Testament and the Qumran Scrolls," *JBL* 76 (1957) 123-138.

T. Worden, "The Meaning of 'Sin'," *Scrip* 9 (1957) 44-53. *[OT Refs., pp. 45-46]*

*A. M. Dubarle, "Original Sin and God's Justice," *Scrip* 9 (1957) 97-108. *(Trans. by B. Dickinson)*

T. Worden, "The Remission of Sins—II," *Scrip* 9 (1957) 115-127. *[Part I not applicable]*

Leon Morris, "The Punishment of Sin in the Old Testament," *ABR* 6 (1958) 61-86.

A. M. Dubarle, "Original Sin in Genesis," *CC* 8 (1958) 343-362. *(Trans. by Dom John Higgens)*

R. L. Bruckberger, "Original Sin," *C&C* 10 (1958) 442-453.

William T. Burner Jr., "Dialectical Personalism and the Problem of Original Sin," *Person* 39 (1958) 249-255.

*A. M. Dubarle, "Original Sin and God's Justice," *TD* 6 (1958) 139-142.

H. S. Stern, "The Knowledge of Good and Evil," *VT* 8 (1958) 405-418.

Norman Lade, "The Concept of Sin in the Law," *ABR* 7 (1959) 54-57.

*J. Edgar Bruns, "Depth-Psychology and the Fall," *CBQ* 21 (1959) 78-82.

*D. Daube, "Concessions to Sinfulness in Jewish Law," *JJS* 10 (1959) 1-14.

Charles H. Patterson, "Concerning the Knowledge of Good and Evil," *Person* 41 (1960) 459-470.

Thomas Worden, "The remission of sins," *TD* 8 (1960) 45-50. *[OT Refs. p. 97]*

*John Wren-Lewis, "What Was the Original Sin?" *ET* 72 (1960-61) 177-180.

William B. Neenan, "Doctrine of Original Sin in Scripture," *ITQ* 28 (1961) 54-64.

*Paul R. Clifford, "Omnipotence and the Problem of Evil," *JR* 41 (1961) 118-128.

Richard L. Rubenstein, "The Meaning of Sin in Rabbinic Theology," *Jud* 10 (1961) 227-236.

L. Johnston, "Sin and Repentance," *Scrip* 13 (1961) 1-12.

Merle Brouwer, "The Fall and Original Sin in Contemporary Literature," *RefR* 15 (1961-62) #1, 30-35.

N. L. A. Tidwell, "A Biblical Concept of Sin," *CQR* 163 (1962) 411-420.

David F. Busby, "Guilt," *JASA* 14 (1962) 113-116.

Bruce Vawter, "Scriptural meaning of 'sin'," *TD* 10 (1962) 223-226.

Bernard Ramm, "The Fall and Natural Evil," *SWJT, N.S.,* 5 (1962-63) #2, 21-32.

*J. Z. Baruch, "The Relation between Sin and Disease in the Old Testament," *Janus* 51 (1964) 295-302.

*Pierre Smulders, "Evolution and original sin," *TD* 13 (1965) 172-176.

*Cyrus H. Gordon, "Leviathan: Symbol of Evil," *LIST* 3 (1966) 1-9.

Kenneth Kinghorn, "Biblical Concepts of Sin," *WestTJ* 1 (1966) 21-26.

James M. Reese, "Current Thinking on Original Sin," *AER* 157 (1967) 92-100. *[OT Refs., pp. 93-95]*

Lionel Swain, "The Bible and the Origin of Sin," *ClR* 52 (1967) 337-344.

*Anthony T. Padovano, "Original Sin and Christian Anthropology," *CTSP* 22 (1967) 93-131. *[OT Refs., pp. 95-99]*

Franz Rosenzweig, "On Temptation," *Jud* 16 (1967) 90-96.

Piet Schoonenberg, "Original sin and man's situation," *TD* 15 (1967) 203-208.

*J. K. Zink, "Uncleanness and Sin. A Study of Job XIV 4 and Psalm LI 7," *VT* 17 (1967) 354-361.

*H. Mowvley, "Health and Salvation in the Old Testament," *BQL* 22 (1967-68) 100-133.

Timothy McDermott, "Original Sin (I)," *NB* 49 (1967-68) 180-189.

Timothy McDermott, "Original Sin (II)," *NB* 49 (1967-68) 237-243.

Joseph Blenkinsopp, "The original meaning of Original Sin," *BibT* #31 (1967) 2183-2190.

Michael J. Cantley, "The Biblical Doctrine of Original Sin," *CTSP* 22 (1967) 133-171.

Kevin Condon, "The Biblical Doctrine of Original Sin," *ITQ* 34 (1967) 20-36.

Zoltan Alszeghy and Maurizio Flick, "A peronalistic view of original sin," *TD* 15 (1967) 190-196.

Zoltan Alszeghy and Maurizio Flick, "A evolutionary view of original sin," *TD* 15 (1967) 197-202.

Robert E. Bathalter, "The Old Testament's Emphasis on Sin as a Personal Offense Against God," *SS* 19 (1967-68) #1, 3-10.

*Thomas W. Cebula, "The Role of the Heart in the Old Testament Psychology of Sin," *SS* 19 (1967-68) #1, 11-23.

*Gerald R. Haemmerle, "Jeremiah's Concept of Sin," *SS* 19 (1967-68) #1, 62-83.

*Donald C. Horrigan, "The Concept of Sin as Adultery in the Prophecy of Hosea," *SS* 19 (1967-68) #1, 84-95.

*Walter Harrelson, "Guilt and Rites of Purification related to the Fall of Jerusalem in 587 B.C.," *Numen* 15 (1968) 218-221.

*James L. Connor, "Original Sin: Contemporary Approaches," *ThSt* 29 (1968) 215-240.

Bruce Milina, "Some Observations on the Origin of Sin in Judaism and St. Paul," *CBQ* 31 (1969) 18-34.

John H. Johansen, "The Fall and Original Sin," *CovQ* 27 (1969) #1, 18-26.

*Gnana Robinson, "A Terminological Study of the Idea of Sin in the Old Testament," *IJT* 18 (1969) 112-123.

*R. Vande Walle, "The Sin in the Garden and the Sinfulness of the World," *IJT* 18 (1969) 124-164. [I. The Sin in the Garden, pp. 124-140; II. The Sin of the World, pp. 140-148; III. Recent Attempts at a New Formulation, pp. 148-162; General Conclusion, pp. 162-164]

*Bezalel Safran, "The Problem of Theodicy in the Book of Psalms," *YR* 7 (1969) 63-68.

§1013 *5.4.8.1 Studies on Suffering*

Henry Cowles, "Sin and Suffering in the Universe, as Related to the Power, Wisdom, and Love of God," *BS* 30 (1873) 729-763.

Harlan Creelman, "The Problem of Well-Being and Suffering in the Old Testament," *BW* 7 (1896) 255-263, 325-338.

*James A. Craig, "A Study of Job and the Jewish Theory of Suffering," *Monist* 19 (1898-99) 481-523.

A. H. McNeil, "The Problem of Suffering in the Old Testament," *ICMM* 6 (1909-10) 371-378.

*T. F. Royds, "Job and the Problem of Suffering," *ICMM* 11 (1914-15) 378-387.

H. Hamilton, "The Problem of Suffering in the Old Testament," *JTS* 18 (1916-17) 242-243. *(Review)*

J. M. Powis Smith, "The Problem of Suffering in the Old Testament," *BW* 49 (1917) 194-200, 259-264, 323-328, 386-390; 50 (1917) 58-64.

Paul Humbert, "The Old Testament and the Problem of Suffering," *BW* 52 (1918) 115-135.

F. R. Tennant, "The Problem of Pain and Suffering," *ET* 30 (1918-19) 473-475.

*Ed. König, "The Problem of Suffering in the Light of the Book of Job," *ET* 32 (1920-21) 361-363.

J. O. Leath, "The Problem of Suffering in the Old Testament," *MQR, 3rd Ser.,* 50 (1924) 300-307.

*L B. Paton, "The Problem of Suffering in the Pre-Exilic Prophets," *JBL* 46 (1927) 111-131.

*Eduard König, "The Problem of Suffering and the Book of Job," *MR* 110 (1927) 582-586.

John E. McFayden, "The Problem of Suffering. Suffering in the Old Testament," *HR* 105 (1933) 15-17.

*E. Brennecke, "The Place of Suffering in the Plan of God as Debated in the Book of Job," *LCQ* 7 (1934) 165-180.

*William R. Seaman, "The Book of Job and the Problem of Suffering," *LCQ* 14 (1941) 52-60.

*A. A. Jones, "The Problem of Suffering in the Book of Job," *EQ* 16 (1944) 282-293.

Donald Fay Robinson, "Suffering as the Proof of Sin," *ATR* 28 (1946) 203-208.

Donald De Young, "The Problem of Suffering in the Old Testament," *RefR* 8 (1954-55) #4, 9-12.

*Jim Alvin Sanders, "Suffering as Divine Discipline in the Old Testament and Post-Biblical Judaism," *CRDSB* 28 (1955 Special Issue), 1-135. [I. Introduction; II. Lexical Study of *yasar* in the Bible; III. Suffering as Divine Discipline in the Life and Message of Jeremiah; IV. Suffering as Divine Discipline in the Old Testament; V. Suffering as Divine Discipline in Post-Biblical Judaism; VI. Conclusions]

*Edgar Jones, "Suffering in the Psalter: A Study of the Problem of Suffering in the Book of Psalms," *CongQL* 34 (1956) 53-63.

Hugh Stevenson Tigner, "The Prospective of Victory. *The Problem of Human Suffering in the Old and New Testaments*," *Interp* 12 (1958) 399-406.

Bill   Adix,   "Suffering,"   *Amb*   7   (1958-59)   #2,   4-9.

*David S. Shapiro, "The Book of Job and the Trial of Abraham," *Trad* 4 (1961-62) 210-220.

Douglas Straton, "God, Freedom and Pain," *HTR* 55 (1962) 143-159.

*Robert Hillis Goldsmith, "The Healing Scourge. *A Study in Suffering and Meaning*," *Interp* 17 (1963) 271-279.

*A. R. C. Leaney, "The Eschatological Significance of Human Suffering in the Old Testament and the Dead Sea Scrolls," *SJT* 16 (1963) 286-296.

Lester J. Kuyper, "How Long, O Lord, How Long?" *RefR* 17 (1963-64) #4, 3-10. *[Suffering]*

*Albert Plotkin, "The Nature of Suffering in Jeremiah," *CCARJ* 16 (1969) #2, 13-19.

§1014 *5.4.8.2 Studies on Death*

*J. Pye Smith, "On Death, as Connected with the Fall," *JSL, 1st Ser.,* 1 (1848) 167-171.

*F. R. Tennant, "The Teaching of Ecclesiasticus and Wisdom on the Introduction of Sin and Death," *JTS* 2 (1900-01) 207-223.

James Denney, "Relations of Sin and Death," *LCR* 23 (1904) 192-194.

*A. Van Hoonacher, "Connexion of Death with Sin according to Gen. II., III.," *Exp, 8th Ser.,* 9 (1915) 131-143.

Samuel S. Cohon, "The Origin of Death," *JJLP* 1 (1919) 371-396.

*R. M. Montgomery, "Midrash Genesis Rabbah on 'Death'," *JBL* 68 (1949) xvi.

*M. D. Goldman, "Lexicographical Notes on the Hebrew Text of the Bible: Euphemism for Dying and its Implications," *ABR* 1 (1951) 64-65.

Reuven Yaron, "Hellenistic Influences in *Deyatiqi* and *Mattan*," *Tarbiz* 27 (1957-58) #4, v. *[Death]*

§1015 *5.4.9 Studies on the Doctrine of Salvation and Reconciliation*

†Anonymous, "Universal Salvation Out of Inherent Depravity," *CTPR, 3rd Ser.,* 2 (1846) 58-72.

Andrew Lang, "Myths of the Origin of Death," *PRev* 60 (1884) Part 2, 56-67.

Conrad Mascol, "The Scripture Idea of Salvation," *URRM* 29 (1888) 1-11.

*George B. Stevens, "Weber on the Soteriology of the Talmud," *ONTS* 9 (1889) 15-24, 79-86.

William Hayes Ward, "The Biblical Condition of Salvation," *AR* 16 (1891) 545-557.

J. H., "How the Children of God Before the Flood were Saved," *TQ* 4 (1900) 412-431.

W. D. Kerswill, "Salvation by Grace in the Old Testament," *CFL, N.S.,* 7 (1903) 101-107.

W. D. Kerswill, "Old Testament Salvation—Through Faith," *CFL, N.S.,* 8 (1903) 147-153.

*C. G. Montefiore, "Rabbinic Conceptions of Repentance," *JQR* 16 (1903-04) 209-257.

*H. R. Mackintosh, "Sin and Grace in Early Judaism," *ET* 17 (1905-06) 348-349. *(Review)*

*Andrew C. Zenos, "Apocryphal Literature and Bible Study. II. God, Sin, and Salvation," *HR* 69 (1915) 22-23.

*J. B. McClellan, "Redemption, Salvation and Atonement in the Old and New Testaments," *Exp, 8th Ser.,* 11 (1916) 107-122.

Charles Edward Smith, "The Way of the Tree of Life," *BS* 85 (1928) 461-468.

*Will Herberg, "Judaism and Christianity: Their Unity and Difference. The Double Covenant in the Divine Economy of Salvation," *JAAR* 21 (1943) 67-78.

Lewis Sperry Chafer, "Soteriology," *BS* 102 (1945) 8-26, 135-152; 103 (1946) 4-16, 140-160, 261-282; 104 (1947) 3-24, 135-153, 263-281, 393-414.

T. F. Torrance, "The Doctrine of Grace in the Old Testament," *SJT* 1 (1948) 55-64.

Alan Richardson, "Instrument of God. The Unity of the Biblical Doctrine of Salvation," *Interp* 3 (1949) 273-285.

Anonymous, "The New Song," *Interp* 3 (1949) 308-313.

Paul Lehmann, "Deliverance and Fulfillment. *The Biblical View of Salvation,*" *Interp* 5 (1951) 387-400.

William Manson, "The Biblical Doctrine of Mission," *IRM* 42 (1953) 257-265.

*William L. Reed, "Some Implications of Ḥēn for Old Testament Religion," *JBL* 73 (1954) 36-41.

Robert Dobbie, "The Biblical Foundation of the Mission of the Church: I. Old Testament," *IRM* 51 (1962) 196-205.

James K. Zink, "Salvation in the Old Testament. *A Central Theme,*" *SQ/E* 25 (1964) 405-414.

*Aloys Dirksen, "Metanoeite!" *BibT* #19 (1965) 1261-1269. [The Old Testament "Conversion"; Old Testament Vocabulary of Conversion, pp. 1263-1265]

Lindsey P. Pherigo, "Christian and Jewish Concepts of Salvation," *RL* 35 (1965-66) 553-560.

John E. Wrigley, "An Old Testament Ecumenical Message," *BibT* #25 (1966) 1763-1769.

*Alfred von Rohr Sauer, "Salvation by Grace: The Heart of Job's Theology," *CTM* 37 (1966) 259-270.

James Montgomery Boice, "What Do We Mean by Salvation? 2. Perspectives on Biblical Salvation," *RL* 36 (1967) 181-190.

Geoffrey W. Grogan, "The Experience of Salvation in the Old and New Testaments," *VE* 5 (1967) 4-26.

J. F. A. Sawyer, "Spaciousness. (An important feature of language about salvation in the Old Testament)," *ASTI* 6 (1967-68) 20-34.

*H. Mowvley, "Health and Salvation in the Old Testament," *BQL* 22 (1967-68) 100-113.

Leo Lieberman, "A Psychological Commentary on the Biblical Doctrine of Salvation," *Z* 3 (1968) 85-91.

P. Victor Prema Sagar, "'Salvation' in the Old Testament," *IJT* 18 (1969) 197-205.

A. van Selms, "God's election in the Old Testament," *Min* 9 (1969) #2, 51-57.

§1016 *5.4.9.1 Studies on "Heilsgeschichte" (The History of Salvation), includes the Individual in Salvitic History*

George D. Armstrong, "The Old Testament Church. An Examination of Several Particulars in the Constitution of the Church, as it Existed under the Old Testament Dispensation," *MQR* 7 (1853) 540-554.

Geo. H. Schodde, "The Christianity of the Old Testament," *ONTS* 5 (1884-85) 293-295.

D. S. Gregory, "Old Testament.—Divine Religion of Salvation in Old and Typical Form," *HR* 32 (1896) 352-353. *[Outline of OT]*

John Merlin Powis Smith, "The Rise of Individualism Among the Hebrews," *AJT* 10 (1906) 251-266.

John E. McFadyen, "Communion with God in the Bible," *BW* 33 (1909) 85-95, 249-259. [I. In the Old Testament Prophets; II. In the Historical Books of the Old Testament]

*Theron H. Rice, "The House of God in the History of Redemption," *USR* 35 (1913-14) 305-312.

*J[ohn] E. McFadyen, "The Mosaic Origin of the Decalogue," *Exp, 8th Ser.,* 12 (1916) 37-59, 105-117, 210-221. [VI. The Decalogue and Individualism, pp. 110-117]

*Theodore Woods Noon, "The Idea of Individualism in Jeremiah and Ezekiel," *MQR, 3rd Ser.,* 52 (1926) 659-665.

W. O. E. Oesterley, "History and Belief in the Old Testament," *Theo* 26 (1933) 123-135.

John L. McKenzie, "Divine Sonship and Individual Religion," *CBQ* 7 (1945) 32-47.

L. H. Brockington, "The Hebrew Conception of Personality in Relation to the Knowledge of God," *OSHTP* (1945-46) 27-30.

Henry S. Gehman, "The Covenant—The Old Testament Foundation of the Church," *TT* 7 (1950-51) 26-41.

D. Broughton Knox, "The Church and the people of God in the Old Testament," *RTRM* 10 (1951) #1, 12-20.

W. Stanford Reid, "The New Testament Belief in an Old Testament Church," *EQ* 24 (1952) 194-205.

Will Herberg, "Judaism and Christianity: Their Unity and Difference. The Double Covenant in the Divine Economy of Salvation," *JAAR* 21 (1953) 67-78.

O. R. Sellers, "Seeking God in the Old Testament," *JAAR* 21 (1953) 234-237.

O. [R.] Sellers, "Seeking God in the Old Testament," *JBL* 72 (1953) v-vi.

Samuel Lucien Terrien, "A Currently Neglected Aspect of Biblical Theology," *USQR* (Jan., 1954, Special Issue) 3-13. [The importance of the individual in the *Heilsgeschichte*]

*Robert Gordis, "The Temptation of Job—Tradition Versus Experience in Religion," *Jud* 4 (1955) 195-208.

H. Neil Richardson, "God's Search for Man in Biblical Thought," *JAAR* 23 (1955) 9-16.

H. H. Rowley, "Individual and Community in the Old Testament," *TT* 12 (1955-56) 491-510.

Jack Boozer, "A Biblical Understanding of Religious Experience," *JAAR* 26 (1958) 291-297.

Roger Mehl, "The Biblical Understanding of Community and Person," *CJT* 5 (1959) 221-230.

*O. H. M. Lehmann, "Religious Experience in the Gospels and in Contemporary Rabbinic Literature," *StEv* 1 (1959) 557-561.

James Muilenburg, "The Biblical Understanding of What God Requires," *ABBTS* 35 (1960) #2, 6-11.

*J. A. Sanders, "The Grace of God in the Prophets," *Found* 4 (1961) 262-265.

*J. A. Sanders, "The Grace of God in the Prophets. (Part II)," *Found* 4 (1961) 363-365.

Eric C. Rust, "The Destiny of the Individual in the Thought of the Old Testament," *R&E* 58 (1961) 296-311.

*Page H. Kelley, "Jeremiah's Concept of Individual Religion," *R&E* 58 (1961) 452-463.

Vincent M. Novak, "Teaching Salvation-History," *BibT* #2 (1962) 115-119.

*J. A. Sanders, "The Grace of God in the Prophets. (Part III)," *Found* 5 (1962) 74-77.

Jerome D. Quinn, "'The Word of the Lord Came...' (Jer. 1:4)," *BibT* #9 (1963) 567-572.

Claus Westermann, "God and His People. *The Church in the Old Testament,*" *Interp* 17 (1963) 259-270.

*G. W. Anderson, "Israel's Creed: Sung, not Signed," *SJT* 16 (163) 277-285.

*Paul Connors, "Haggadic History," *BC* 3 (1962-64) 162-167.

*Arlis John Ehlen, "Old Testament Theology as *Heilsgeschichte,*" *CTM* 35 (1964) 517-544.

Robert Davidson, "Faith and History in the Old Testament," *ET* 77 (1965-66) 100-104.

D. Glenn Rose, "The Meaning of Confession in the Life of Israel," *MidS* 6 (1966-67) #2, 1-16.

H. D. Beeby, "Confessing the Faith in the Old Testament," *SEAJT* 8 (1966-67) #1, 21-36.

*Bruce Vawter, "History and the Word," *CBQ* 29 (1967) 512-523.

*Robert C. Hill, "The Dimensions of Salvation History in the Wisdom Books," *Scrip* 19 (1967) 97-106.

Stephen S. Yonick, "The Rejection of Saul: A Study of Sources," *AJBA* 1 (1968-71) #4, 29-50.

R. Davidson, "Some Aspects of the Theological Significance of Doubt in the Old Testament," *ASTI* 7 (1968-69) 41-52.

Gary Schoubourg, "The Individual and the People of God," *BibT* #41 (1969) 2832-2838.

Norman C. Habel, "The Gospel Promise to Abraham," *CTM* 40 (1969) 346-355.

*E. C. John, "Forgiveness in the Prophecy of Judgment," *IJT* 18 (1969) 206-218.

§1017 *5.4.9.2 Studies on Atonement*

*E. C. Wines, "The Doctrine of Atonement as taught in Isaiah LII. LIII.," *TLJ* 6 (1853-54) 404-417.

*Anonymous, "The Atonement as related to Sin, and to a Divine Lawgiver," *AThR* 1 (1859) 141-151.

Anonymous, "The Atonement, as set forth in the Old Testament," *BWR* 2 (1878) 53-88.

*Willis J. Beecher, "The idea of atonement, as found in the piel verb כִּפֶּר and the nouns כִּפֻּרִים and כַּפֹּרֶת," *JBL* 4 (1884) 144.

*J. Max Hark, "Blood-Covenanting and Atonement," *AR* 5 (1886) 375-389.

H. Clay Trumbull and Edmund M. Vittum, "Correspondence," *AR* 5 (1886) 559-563. *[Blood-Covenanting and Atonement]*

Henry Preserved Smith, "The Old Testament Theory of Atonement," *AJT* 10 (1906) 412-422.

John Merlin Powis Smith, "The Biblical Doctrine of Atonement: I. Atonement in Preprophetic Israel," *BW* 31 (1908) 22-31.

John Merlin Powis Smith, "The Biblical Doctrine of Atonement: II. Atonement in Prophets and Deuteronomy," *BW* 31 (1908) 113-121.

John Merlin Powis Smith, "The Biblical Doctrine of Atonement: III. Atonement in the Later Priestly Literature," *BW* 31 (1908) 207-217.

Ernest D[eWitt] Burton, "The Biblical Doctrine of Atonement: IV. Atonement in Non-Canonical Jewish Literature," *BW* 31 (1908) 276-289.

John L. Darby, "Is There No Atonement?" *ET* 21 (1909-10) 224-225.

*J. B. McClellan, "Redemption, Salvation and Atonement in the Old and New Testaments," *Exp, 8th Ser.,* 11 (1916) 107-122.

H. H. B. Ayles, "The Old Testament Doctrine of the Atonement," *ICMM* 14 (1917-18) 206-209.

Andrew Keogh, "Correspondence. 'The Old Testament Doctrine of the Atonement'," *ICMM* 14 (1917-18) 341.

M. G. Glazebrook, "Hebrew Conceptions of Atonement and Their Influence upon Early Christian Doctrine," *JTS* 20 (1918-19) 109-126.

*A. Buchler, "Ben Sira's conception of Sin and Atonement," *JQR, N.S.,* 13 (1922-23) 303-335, 461-502; 14 (1923-24) 53-83.

Royden Keith Yerkes, "Atonement," *ATR* 29 (1947) 28-33.

*James Thayer Addison, "Sin and Atonement," *ATR* 33 (1951) 137-148, 201-208. [I. The Nature and Origin of Sin: A Suggestion; II. Punishment and Forgiveness; III. The Place of Christ's Death in the Work of Atonement; IV. The So-Called 'Cost of Forgiveness' in the Atonement]

*Leon Morris, "The Biblical Idea of Atonement," *ABR* 2 (1952) 83-95. [The Non-cultic Use of כפר; The Cultic use of כפר; Other Considerations, Atonement in the New Testament]

Cuthbert Lattey, "Vicarious Solidarity in the OT," *VT* 1 (1951) 267-274.

S. H. Hooke, "The Theory and Practice of Substitution," *VT* 2 (1952) 2-17.

Otto J. Baab, "The God of Redeeming Grace. *Atonement in the Old Testament,*" *Interp* 10 (1956) 131-143.

Charles W. Perkins, "Old Testament Background for a Christian Doctrine of the Atonement," *UTSB* 56 (1956-57) #2, 23-26.

*Eric S. Gabe, "Atonement in Judaism and the Missionary Approach," *IRM* 46 (1957) 276-282, 394-400.

*Joseph H. Golner, "God, Satan and Atonement," *Jud* 9 (1960) 299-306.

Ralph H. Elliott, "Atonement in the Old Testament," *R&E* 59 (1962) 11-26.

*Hobart E. Freeman, "The Problem of the Efficacy of Old Testament Sacrifices," *GJ* 4 (1963) #1, 21-28.

Kenneth F. Dougherty, "Atonement and Scripture," *CTSP* 19 (1964) 15-39. [Atonement in the Old Testament, pp. 19-25]

*David R. Dilling, "The Atonement and Human Sacrifice," *GJ* 5 (1964) #1, 24-43.

*Yehudi Moshe Felman, "Repentance and Atonement in the Hebrew Bible," *YR* 5 (1966) 82-122.

Roy B. Ward, "Special Study in Judaism," *RestQ* 11 (1968) 184-189. *(Review)*

§1018 *5.4.9.3 Studies on Redemption, Forgiveness, and Repentance*

†Anonymous, "Hamilton's Dissertation on Human Redemption," *BCQTR, N.S.,* 12 (1819) 75-89. *(Review)*

Charles Short, "Pardon and Punishment," *Exp, 1st Ser.,* 9 (1879) 150-159.

George W. McSherry, "Regeneration Under the Old Testament," *LQ* 26 (1896) 523-533.

E. C. Gordon, "The Biblical History of Redemption: Notes and Outline," *CFL, O.S.,* 3 (1899) 222-226.

R. A. Torrey, "A Biblical Study on Repentance," *LCR* 19 (1900) 601-610.

*C. G. Montefiore, "Rabbinic Conceptions of Repentance," *OSHTP* (1903-04) 5-38.

D. S. Gregory, "Outline View of the Bible as God's Revelation of Redemption," *CFL, 3rd Ser.,* 1 (1904) 45-55.

*Anonymous, "Editorial Notes. Teaching on Forgiveness in the Testament of Gad," *ICMM* 4 (1907-08) 242-243.

*J. B. McClellan, "Redemption, Salvation and Atonement in the Old and New Testaments," *Exp, 8th Ser.,* 11 (1916) 107-122.

H. A. Kent, "The Forgiveness of Sins in the Old Testament," *Exp, 8th Ser.,* 21 (1921) 365-386.

Victor Monod, "The Relation Between Travel and Conversion," *ET* 50 (1938-39) 183-187. *(Trans. by Hugh Thomson Kerr Jr.)*

Richard T. Du Brau, "Forgiveness in the LXX," *CTM* 16 (1945) 249-256.

*Norman H. Snaith, "The Prophets and Sacrifice and Salvation," *ET* 58 (1946-47) 152-153.

*Alcuin Kirberg, "Saul and the Grace of God," *Scotist* 6 (1947) 84-93.

Felix Aber, "Merit and Unearned Mercy," *CJ* 8 (1951-52) #2, 1-8.

Walter R. Roehrs, "The Grace of God in the Old Testament," *CTM* 23 (1952) 895-910; 24 (1953) 41-52.

Leon Morris, "The Idea of redemption in the Old Testament," *RTRM* 11 (1952) #3, 94-102.

Zeev W. Falk, "Gestures Expressing Affirmation," *JSS* 4 (1959) 268-269.

Roland Potter, "Redemption in the Old Testament," *LofS* 14 (1959-60) 452-460.

C. J. de Catanzaro, "Forgiveness in the Old Testament," *ACQ* 2 (1962) 26-39.

*Henry McKeating, "Divine Forgiveness in the Psalms," *SJT* 18 (1965) 69-83.

*Yehudi Moshe Felman, "Repentance and Atonement in the Hebrew Bible," *YR* 5 (1966) 82-122.

*William G. Most, "A Biblical Theology of Redemption in a Covenant Framework," *CBQ* 29 (1967) 1-19.

*Theodore Friedman, "The Sabbath: Anticipation of Redemption," *Jud* 16 (1967) 445-452.

*Kalonomos Kalman Epstein, "Sexual Purity and Redemption," *Jud* 17 (1968) 65-67.

*Jakob J. Petuchowski, "The Concept of Teshuvah in the Bible and in the Talmud," *Jud* 17 (1968) 175-185.

Kevin G. O'Connell, "Grace in the Old Testament," *Scrip* 20 (1968) 42-48.

*E. C. John, "Forgiveness in the Prophecy of Judgment," *IJT* 18 (1969) 206-218.

§1019 *5.4.9.4 Studies on Justification*

Gerrit H. Hospers, "The Doctrine of Justification by Faith and the Old Testament," *BS* 85 (1928) 435-451.

Paul Jacobs, "Theodicy in the Old Testament," *EQ* 9 (1937) 371-382.

Philip S. Watson, "Constructive Theology. XI. Justification," *ET* 51 (1939-40) 499-502.

*Leon L. Morris, "Justification by Faith: The Old Testament and Rabbinic Anticipation," *EQ* 24 (1952) 24-36.

*Walter R. Roehrs, "Covenant and Justification in the Old Testament," *CTM* 35 (1964) 583-602.

*Horace D. Hummel, "Law and Grace in Judaism and Lutheranism," *LQ, N.S.,* 21 (1969) 416-429.

§1020 *5.4.9.5 Studies on Sanctification, Righteousness,*
and Holiness

*M. Stuart, "Have the Sacred Writers any where asserted that the Sin or Righteousness of one is imputed to another?" *BRCR* 7 (1836) 241-330.

Anonymous, "Legal Holiness, and not Gracious, that which God has Determined to Establish Throughout His Universe," *PQR* 1 (1852-53) 275-289.

E. Johnson, "The Saintly Life. The Old Testament Idea of Holiness and the Holy," *BFER* 36 (1887) 349-359.

E. Johnson, "Definitions of the Old Testament Idea of Holiness," *BFER* 36 (1887) 641-653.

J. T. Gladhill, "A Biblical View of Sanctification," *LQ* 20 (1890) 600-613. *[OT Refs., pp. 600-602]*

Edward B. Coe, "The Biblical Meaning of Holiness," *PRR* 1 (1890) 42-47.

*S. Schechter, "The Rabbinical Conception of Holiness," *JQR* 10 (1897-98) 1-12. (Correction by W. Bacher, p. 382)

John P. Peters, "The Hebrew Idea of Holiness," *BW* 14 (1899) 344-355.

Israel Aaron, "The Holiness of a Peculiar People," *YCCAR* 8*[sic]* (1899) 202-208. *(Sermon) [Bound between vols. 9 and 10]*

Philip Stafford Moxom, "Personal Righteousness," *BS* 57 (1900) 54-67.

James Orr, "The Reality of Individual Piety in the Old Testament," *R&E* 9 (1912) 471-486.

I. Abrahams, "The Imitation of God," *OSHTP* (1920-22) 34-37.

J. Oman, "The Idea of the Holy," *JTS* 25 (1923-24) 275-286.

H. G. Enelow, "A Note on a Spiritual Healing in Jewish Tradition," *YCCAR* 37 (1927) 362-368.

D. M. McIntyre, "The Hebrew Creed," *EQ* 9 (1937) 271-278.

John W. Lambert, "The Idea of Holiness in the Old Testament," *SQ/E* 7 (1946) 86-96.

Helmer Ringgren, "The Prophetical Conception of Holiness," *UUÅ* (1948) #12, 1-30.

*Norman Porteous, "Ritual and Righteousness. *The Relation of Ethics to Religion in the Prophetic Literature,*" *Interp* 3 (1949) 400-414.

*H. H. Rowley, "Holiness in the Prophets," *ET* 61 (1949-50) 61. *(Review)*

Bruno Italiener, "The Mussaf-Kedushah," *HUCA* 26 (1955) 413-424.

R. A. Letch, "Sanctification in the Old Testament," *LQHR* 180 (1955) 129-131.

*L. Jacobs, "The Concept of Ḥasid in the Biblical and Rabbinic Literatures," *JSS* 8 (1957) 143-154.

*Lester J. Kuyper, "The Holy One and the Holy Spirit," *RefR* 11 (1957-58) #3, 1-10.

J. Robinson, "The Prophetic Teaching on Righteousness and Our Preaching," *CQR* 161 (1960) 14-23.

C. J. de Catanzaro, "Fear, Knowledge, and Love: A Study in Old Testament Piety," *CJT* 9 (1963) 166-173.

*U. Milo Kaufmann, "Expostulation with the Divine. *Contrasting Attitudes in Greek and Hebrew Piety,*" *Interp* 18 (1964) 171-182.

John J. Lewis, "Righteousness Between the Testaments," *Coll* 1 (1964-66) 141-148.

David S. Shapiro, "The Meaning of Holiness in Judaism," *Trad* 7 (1964-65) #1, 46-80.

J. N. Schofield, "'Righteousness' in the Old Testament," *BTr* 16 (1965) 112-116.

Larry R. Thornton, "God's Standards for the Kings of Judah," *CCBQ* 11 (1968) #3, 16-30.

Bernard Cooke, "Holiness in the World. 1. Holiness and the Bible," *RL* 37 (1968) 8-17.

Saphir P. Athyal, "Cultic Holiness and its Moral Content in the Old Testament," *IJT* 18 (1969) 165-179.

§1021 *5.4.10 Studies on Faith*

Mark Hopkins, "Faith," *PRev* 54 (1878) Part 2, 511-540.

Oswald John Simon, "The Position of Faith in the Jewish Religion," *JQR* 2 (1889-90) 53-61.

W. Emery Barnes, "Divine Guidance in the Old Testament," *ICMM* 7 (1910-11) 23-29.

*John S. Banks, "Old Testament Reasons for Faith in Answers to Prayer," *LQHR* 121 (1914) 123-126.

‡H. H. Rowley, "Recent Foreign Theology. Faith and Society in the Old Testament," *ET* 61 (1949-50) 190-191. *(Review)*

Thomas F. Torrance, "One Aspect of the Biblical Conception of Faith," *ET* 68 (1956-57) 111-114.

C. F. D. Moule, "The Biblical Conception of 'Faith'," *ET* 68 (1956-57) 157, 222.

T[homas] F. Torrance, "The Biblical Conception of 'Faith'," *ET* 68 (1956-57) 221-222.

Frank R. Neff Jr., "The Unity of the Biblical Doctrine of Faith in God," *TUSR* 6 (1958-60) 132-145.

Floyd V. Filson, "The Nature of Biblical Faith," *JAAR* 27 (1959) 223-227.

*Samuel L. Terrien, "Faith and Ritual in the Old Testament," *ABBTS* 38 (1963) #2, 13-23.

Geoffrey Francis Wood, "Man's Response to God's Word," *BibT* #9 (1963) 573-579. [Abraham, pp. 575-577; Israel, pp. 577-578]

Joseph Cahill, "Faith in the Old Testament," *BibT* #15 (1964) 959-967.

*Eliezer Berkovits, "Faith and Law," *Jud* 13 (1964) 422-430.

Fredrick L. Moriarty, "Faith in Israel," *Way* 4 (1964) 3-12.

Georg Fohrer, "Action of God and decision of man in the Old Testament," *OTW* 9 (1966) 31-39.

*Herbert C. Brichto, "On Faith and Revelation in the Bible," *HUCA* 39 (1968) 35-53.

W. J. A. Power, "The Jackson Lectures, 1969: The Concept of Faith in the Early Tradition of Israel," *PSTJ* 22 (1969) #2/3, 7-13.

§1022 *5.4.11 Studies on Prayer*

Anonymous, "Prayer as a Means of Grace," *MQR* 8 (1854) 340-357.

William Winans, "Prayer," *MQR* 9 (1855) 21-37, 218-228.

J. Wofford Tucker, "Prayer," *MQR* 9 (1855) 544-556.

J. E. Wells, "The Physical Value of Prayer," *BS* 32 (1875) 62-97.

'Carpus', "The Biblical Conception of Prayer," *Exp, 1st Ser.,* 5 (1877) 321-335.

'Carpus', "The Reasonableness of Prayer," *Exp, 1st Ser.,* 5 (1877) 406-421.

'Carpus', "The Reign of Law an Incentive to Prayer," *Exp, 1st Ser.,* 6 (1877) 36-50.

'Carpus', "The Limits of Prayer," *Exp, 1st Ser.,* 6 (1877) 113-129.

George Matheson, "Science and the Christian Idea of Prayer," *Exp, 1st Ser.,* 9 (1879) 1-23.

*Leonard W. Bacon, "Prayer and Miracle in Relation to Natural Law," *JCP* 3 (1883-84) 319-343.

*B. Pick, "The Rites, Ceremonies and Customs of the Jews," *HR* 17 (1889) 199-206. [VII. Daily Prayers and Confession of Faith, pp. 202-203]

William W. Kinsley, "Science and Prayer," *BS* 48 (1891) 128-143, 218-229, 439-455; 49 (1892) 89-108, 199-212.

Waldo S. Pratt, "The Prayers of the Old Testament," *HSR* 2 (1891-92) 87-102.

(   ) G., "A History of Biblical Prayer," *ONTS* 14 (1892) 243.

Donald MacRae, "Answers to Prayer," *ET* 11 (1899-1900) 302-305.

*Archibald Farily Carr, "Elijah as an Illustration of Prayer," *CFL, N.S.,* 4 (1901) 111-117.

J. Cromarty Smith, "Intercession in the Old Testament," *GUOST* 2 (1901-07) 49-50.

Frank Orman Beck, "Prayer: A Study in its History and Psychology," *AJRPE* 2 (1906-07) 107-121. [I. 4. In Jewish Polytheism—later in monotheism, p. 110]

*I. Abrahams, "Some Rabbinic Ideas on Prayer," *JQR* 20 (1907-08) 272-293.

Wm. W. Guth, "Prayer in Scripture," *MR* 90 (1908) 602-610.

W. Hope Davidson, "The First Recorded Prayer in the Bible," *ET* 23 (1911-12) 332.

Mary Whiton Calkins, "The Nature of Prayer," *HTR* 4 (1911) 489-500.

*John S. Banks, "Old Testament Reasons for Faith in Answers to Prayer," *LQHR* 121 (1914) 123-126.

Edward Metcalfe, "Thoughts on Prayer," *ET* 26 (1914-15) 565-566.

*J. W. Hunkin, "Judas Maccabaeus and Prayers for the Dead," *Exp, 8th Ser.,* 9 (1915) 361-365.

Edward Chauncey Baldwin, "Prayer Ancient and Modern," *HR* 69 (1915) 277-282.

R. H. Coats, "The School of Prayer," *ET* 27 (1915-16) 105-107.

Alfred E. Garvie, "Prayer in Relation to Human Freedom," *ET* 27 (1915-16) 420-423.

Albert Clarke Wyckoff, "The Science of Prayer," *BR* 1 (1916) 507-532; 2 (1917) 52-74.

*Sidney S. Tedesche, "Prayers of the Apocrypha and their Importance in the Study of Jewish Liturgy," *YCCAR* 26 (1916) 376-398.

James Donald, "Prayer in War-Time," *ET* 28 (1916-17) 122-123. *[Psa. 55:17]*

John Bretherton, "Is the Weather a Legitimate Subject for Prayer?" *ET* 29 (1917-18) 519-520.

Geo. C. Walker, "'For Thy Name's Sake'," *ET* 30 (1918-19) 234.

J.   Ritchie   Smith,   "Prayer,"   *PTR*   17   (1919)   87-97.

Abraham Cronbach, "The Social Implication of Prayer," *HUCA, Jubilee Volume* (1925) 483-512.

Cyril E. Hudson, "On Prayer," *ATR* 9 (1926-27) 355-364.

H. C. Alleman, "Prayer in the Old Testament," *LCQ* 1 (1928) 147-155.

John W. Clayton, "Wanted—A Science of Prayer," *ET* 44 (1932-33) 124-128.

R. K. Orchard, "Prayers of the Bible," *CongQL* 16 (1938) 292-299.

G. H Parbrook, "With the Jew at Prayer," *CongQL* 18 (1940) 271-282.

L. Paul Moore Jr., "Prayer in the Pentateuch," *BS* 98 (1941) 329-350, 479-488; 99 (1942) 108-113.

Abraham Heschel, "Prayer," *RR* 9 (1944-45) 153-168. [I. Prayer as an Answer; II. Prayer and the Spiritual Life; III. Suffering—The Source of Prayer? IV. The Nature of Kawwana; V. The Essence of Prayer; VI. The Two Main Types of Prayer; VII. The Vision of Prayer]

Eugen Rosentock-Huessy, "Hitler and Israel, or on Prayer. A Chapter from 'Letters to Cynthia'," *JR* 25 (1945) 129-139.

*Walter G. Williams, "Prayer in the Life of Jeremiah," *RL* 15 (1946) 436-445.

*Sheldon H. Blank, "The Confessions of Jeremiah and the Meaning of Prayer," *HUCA* 21 (1948) 331-354.

Julian N. Hartt, "Some Metaphysical Gleanings from Prayer," *JR* 31 (1951) 254-263.

Sheldon H. Blank, "Men Against God—The Promethean Element in Biblical Prayer," *JBL* 72 (1953) 1-14.

Otto A. Piper, "Praise of God and Thanksgiving. *The Biblical Doctrine of Prayer. 1*," *Interp* 8 (1954) 3-20.

Floyd V. Filson, "Petition and Intercession. *The Biblical Doctrine of Prayer. 2*," *Interp* 8 (1954) 21-34.

D. R. Ap-Thomas, "Some Notes on the Old Testament Attitude to Prayer," *SJT* 9 (1956) 422-429.

D. R. Ap-Thomas, "Notes on Some Terms Relating to Prayer," *VT* 6 (1956) 225-241.

J. G. Weiss, "The Kavvanoth of Prayer in Early Hasidism," *JJS* 9 (1958) 163-192.

*Eugene Mihaly, "Jewish Prayer and Synagogue Architecture," *Jud* 7 (1958) 309-319.

Abraham J. Heschel, "Prayer and Theological Discipline," *USQR* 14 (1958-59) #4, 3-8.

D. Daube, "A Prayer Pattern in Judaism," *StEv* 1 (1959) 539-545.

Eugene Bradford, "Intercessory Prayer: A Ministerial Task," *WJT* 20 (1959-60) 13-48.

J. G. Weiss, "Via passiva in early Hasidism," *JJS* 11 (1960) 137-155.

Sheldon H. Blank, "Some Observations Concerning Biblical Prayer," *HUCA* 32 (1961) 75-90.

Steven S. Schwarzschild, "Speech and Silence Before God," *Jud* 10 (1961) 195-204.

Anonymous, "Hellenistic Jewish Prayers," *Jud* 11 (1962) 268-270.

*Julien Harvey, "The Prayer of Jeremias," *Way* 3 (1963) 165-173. *(Trans. by Peter Hebblethwaite)*

David Stacey, "Clues from the Old Testament," *PQL* 11 (1965) 267-274. [V. Prayer]

J. W. Bowker, "Intercession in the Qur'ān and the Jewish Tradition," *JSS* 11 (1966) 69-82.

Gerald J. Blidstein, "The Limits of Prayer: A Rabbinic Discussion," *Jud* 15 (1966) 164-170.

Patrick J. Ryan, "The Pattern of Biblical Prayer," *BibT* #31 (1967) 2155-2162.

Henry McKeating, "Prayer in the Old Testament," *PQL* 15 (1969) #4, 38-42.

§1023 *5.4.11.1 Studies on Specific Prayers*

[Alfred] Edersheim, "The Hymnody of the Jewish Temple," *DTQ* 1 (1875) 475-478.

D. W. Fisher, "A Jewish Prayer Book," *PQPR* 6 (1877) 495-506.

E. N. Calisch, "The Kaddīsh," *EN* 3 (1891) 90-92.

E. N. Adler, "MS. of Haftaras of the Triennial Cycle," *JQR* 8 (1895-96) 528-529.

M. Friedlander, "A Fragment of a Shorthand Hagadah," *JQR* 9 (1896-97) 520-521. [Bodleian Library (Heb. MSS. e68)]

George Alexander Kohut, "Prayers for Rain," *AJSL* 15 (1898-99) 105-108.

G. H. Box, "St. Peter in the Jewish Liturgy," *ET* 15 (1903-04) 93-95.

*†[I. Schwab], "'The Kaddish'," *YCCAR* 15 (1905) 205-222. [I. The Origin of the Kaddish; II. The Kaddish and the Lord's Prayer; III. The Kedushah a Messianic Eulogy]

*I. Elbogen, "Studies in the Jewish Liturgy," *JQR* 19 (1906-07) 229-249. [I. B, C, פרס על שמע]

*I. Elbogen, "Studies in the Jewish Liturgy," *JQR* 19 (1906-07) 704-720. [II. A, B, C עבר לפני התיבה]

A. L. Emanuel, "The Jewish Prayer Book," *ContR* 113 (1918) 88-92.

*K. Kohler, "Shema Yisroel. *Origin and Purpose of its Daily Recital*," *JJLP* 1 (1919) 255-264.

K. Kohle, "The Origin and Composition of the Eighteen Benedictions with a Translation of the Corresponding Essene Prayers in the Apostolic Constitutions," *HUCA* 1 (1924) 387-426.

Solomon B. Freehof, "The Origin of the Taḥanun," *HUCA* 2 (1925) 339-350.

A. Lukyn Williams, "Spiritual Elements in the Hebrew Prayer Book," *IRM* 15 (1926) 205-207.

Millar Burrows, "A Contemporary Document of Palestinian Folk-Religion," *BASOR* #60 (1935) 9-11. *[Prayer]*

M. Wallenstein, "The Hebrew Piyyuṭ," *JMUEOS* #19 (1935) 45-47.

*J. Wahrhaftig, "A Jewish Prayer in a Greek Papyrus," *JTS* 40 (1939) 376-381.

*Louis I. Rabinowitz, "The Psalms in Jewish Liturgy," *HJud* 6 (1944) 109-122.

Solomon Zeitlin, "An Historical Study of the First Canonization of the Hebrew Liturgy," *JQR, N.S.,* 36 (1945-46) 211-229; 38 (1947-48) 289-316.

*M. Wallenstein, "A Piyyuṭ from the Cairo Genizah (Bodley MS. 2716/6, fol. 16b 6-17a 6)," *JMUEOS* #25 (1947-53) 20-24.

M. Liber, "Structure and History of the *Tefilah*," *JQR, N.S.,* 40 (1949-50) 331-357.

*Philip Kieval, "The Decalogue and Our Liturgy," *CJ* 7 (1950-51) #4, 20-24.

Leon J. Liebreich, "The *Pesuke De-Zimra* Benedictions," *JQR, N.S.,* 41 (1950-51) 195-206.

Leon J. Liebreich, "The Intermediate Benedictions of the *Amidah*," *JQR, N.S.,* 42 (1951-52) 423-426.

N. Wieder, "The Old Palestinian Ritual—New Sources," *JJS* 4 (1953) 30-37, 65-73. [I. The *Habhdalah* in the Festival *'Amidah,* According to the Palestinian Rite. II. *(untitled);* III. Doxological Prologue and Epilogue to the Festival Psalm; IV. The Original Form of the Doxology יהללון; V. The Text of MS. Cambridge, T-S. H.8/61]

Solomon Gandz, "The Benediction over the Luminaries and the Stars," *JQR, N.S.,* 44 (1953-54) 305-325.

Solomon Zeitlin, "The Morning Benediction and the Readings in the Temple," *JQR, N.S.,* 44 (1953-54) 330-336.

S. Esh, "*Parshiyyot* and *Haftarot*," *Tarbiz* 26 (1956-57) #2, VII.

Solomon Zeitlin, "Historical Studies of the Hebrew Liturgy," *JQR, N.S.,* 49 (1958-59) 169-178.

*J. G. Weiss, "On the formula melekh ha-'olam as anti-Gnostic protest," *JJS* 10 (1959) 169-171.

Cecil Roth, "Melekh ha-'olam: Zealot influence in the Liturgy?" *JJS* 11 (1960) 173-175.

Joseph Heinemann, "The Formula melekh ha-'olam," *JJS* 11 (1960) 177-179.

*Joseph Heinemann, "Prayers of Beth Midrash Origin," *JSS* 5 (1960) 264-280.

Joseph Heinemann, "The *Hosha'not*—Remnants of Ancient Piyyutim," *Tarbiz* 30 (1960-61) #4, I-II.

C. P. Price, "Jewish Morning Prayer and Early Christian Anaphoras," *ATR* 43 (1961) 153-168.

Elias J. Bickerman, "The Civic Prayer of Jerusalem," *HTR* 55 (1962) 163-185.

*Solomon Zeitlin, "The Hallel: A Historical Study of Canonization of the Hebrew Liturgy," *JQR, N.S.,* 53 (1962-63) 22-29.

*Leon J. Liebreich, "Aspects of the New Year Liturgy," *HUCA* 34 (1963) 125-176. [I. The Two Recensions of the Ya-'aleh we-Yavo' Prayers, pp. 125-131]

Aaron Mirsky, "The Origin of 'The Eighteen Benedictions' of the Daily Prayer," *Tarbiz* 33 (1963-64) II-III. *[Megilla]*

Avraham Holtz, "The Concept of *Qiddush Hashem* in the Jewish Prayer Book," *HTR* 57 (1964) 137-140.

*E. J. Weisenberg, "The Liturgical Term melekh ha-'olam," *JJS* 15 (1964) 1-56.

J. Heinemann, "Once Again Melekh Ha-'Olam," *JJS* 15 (1964) 149-154.

N. Wieder, "The Form of the Third Benediction of the *'Amida* on *Rosh Hashshana* and *Yom Kippur*," *Tarbiz* 34 (1964-65) #1, III-IV.

Aharon Mirsky, "The Earlier and Later Versions of the Third Benediction of the 'Amida," *Tarbiz* 34 (1964-65) #3, VI.

Leon J. Liebreich, "The Insertions in the Third Benediction of the Holy Day 'Amidoth," *HUCA* 36 (1965) 79-101.

Jakob J. Petuchowski, "Reform Benedictions for Rabbinic Ordinances," *HUCA* 37 (1966) 175-189.

*D. Flusser, "Qumran and Jewish 'Apotropaic' Prayers," *IEJ* 16 (1966) 194-205.

*E. Wiesenberg, "Gleanings of the Liturgical Term *Melekh Ha-'Olam*," *JJS* 17 (1966) 47-72.

Ezra Fleischer, "*Havdalah-Shiv'atot* according to Palestinian Ritual," *Tarbiz* 36 (1966-67) #4, III-IV.

*N Wieder, "A Controversial Mishnaic and Liturgical Expression," *JJS* 18 (1967) 1-8. [וכל באי (ה)עולם עוברים לפניו כבני מרון]

§1024 *5.4.12 Studies on Proselytizing and Missionary Activities*

E. P. Barrows, "The Missionary Spirit of the Psalms and Prophets," *BS* 17 (1860) 457-494.

L. H. Schuh, "The Missionary Period of the Old Testament," *ColTM* 19 (1899) 361-366.

Alphaeus W. Wilson, "The Attitude of the Old Testament Toward Missions," *USR* 17 (1905-06) 144-149.

W. G. Jordan, "The Growth of the Missionary Idea in the Old Testament," *BW* 35 (1910) 177-185, 259-266.

George H. Schodde, "Israel and Missions," *TZTM* 6 (1916) 91-93. *(Editorial)*

George Drach, "Old Testament Foundations of Foreign Missions," *LCR* 37 (1918) 151-155.

A. H. McNeil, "The Missionary Idea in the Old Testament," *ICMM* 15 (1918-19) 274-278.

Newport J. D. White, "The Missionary Spirit of the Old Testament," *Exp, 8th Ser.,* 19 (1920) 140-148.

William Manson, "The Biblical Doctrine of Mission," *IRM* 42 (1953) 257-265.

Virgil H. Todd, "Evangelism in the Old Testament," *CS* 5 (1957-58) #1, 1-4.

John Allen Moore, "The Light that Failed: Missions in the Old Testament," *CongQL* 36 (1958) 36-43.

*Ben Zion Wacholder, "Attitudes Towards Proselytizing in the Classical Halakah," *HJud* 20 (1958) 77-96.

Robert Dobbie, "The Biblical Foundation of the Mission of the Church: I. Old Testament," *IRM* 51 (1962) 196-205.

§1025 *5.4.13 Studies on Israel as the "Chosen People" and the Restoration of Israel*

*Luther F. Dimmick, "The Spirit of Prophecy in Relation to the Future Condition of the Jews," *BS* 4 (1847) 337-369.

W. L. Brown, "The Israel of Unfulfilled Prophecy," *JSL, 3rd Ser.,* 14 (1861-62) 437-443.

Edwin Martin, "The Conversion and Restoration of the Jews," *SPR* 31 (1880) 70-92.

Barnard C. Taylor, "God's Purpose in Choosing Israel," *ONTS* 12 (1891) 86-90.

Wilbur Fletcher Steele, "A Divine Romance," *MR* 80 (1898) 213-230.

Pollock, J.F., "The Covenant People and Their Part in the Promises," *LQ,* 30 (1900) 518-533.

J. Edwin Hartman, "Israel's Idea of Heredity," *RChR, 4th Ser.,* 5 (1901) 317-328.

Benjamin B. Warfield, "God's Revelation of Himself to Israel," *CFL, 3rd Ser.,* 7 (1907) 289-292.

William C. Heyer, "The Relation of God to His People," *LCR* 29 (1910) 87-97.

George W. Gilmore, "A Critical Note—The Marks of Possession," *HR* 67 (1914) 400-401.

R. L. Marshall, "The Isolation of the Jew," *ET* 29 (1917-18) 420-424.

*G. A. Cooke, "Palestine and the Restoration of Israel: A Study in Prophecy," *Exp, 8th Ser.,* 15 (1918) 81-90.

*Anonymous, "The Restoration of Palestine to the Jews and Prophecy," *MR* 103 (1920) 651-657.

J. M. Powis Smith, "The Chosen People," *AJSL* 45 (1928-29) 73-82.

Arno Clemens Gaebelien, "The Future Fulfillment of the Promises to Israel," *BR* 15 (1930) 379-393.

Herbert Parzen, "Israel in Palestine—The Prophetic View," *JQR, N.S.,* 24 (1933-34) 217-231.

K. B. Aikman, "Eugenics and the Chosen People," *EQ* 7 (1935) 225-231.

Charles Lee Feinberg, "What Israel Means to God," *BS* 93 (1936) 301-314.

*Charles Lee Feinberg, "Job and the Nation of Israel. First Study: In the Hands of the Enemy," *BS* 96 (1939) 405-411.

*Charles Lee Feinberg, "Job and the Nation of Israel. Second Study: At the Mercy of the Critics," *BS* 97 (1940) 27-33.

*Charles Lee Feinberg, "Job and the Nation of Israel. Third Study: Face to Face with the Lord," *BS* 97 (1940) 211-216.

Iver Olson, "The Chosen People," *JTALC* 6 (1941) 368-370.

*H. D. W., "'The Hope of Israel;' or, the Restoration of Israel identified with the Resurrection of the Dead," *MR* 24 (1942) 192-220.

Alexander J. Burnstein, "The conception of Israel in the Kusari," *CJ* 1 (1945) #2, 19-26. [II. The Spiritual Relationship Between God and Israel, pp. 20-26]

Julius H. Greenstone, "The Election of Israel," *CJ* 1 (1945) #2, 27-30.

Ben Zion Bokser, "The Election of Israel," *CJ* 3 (1946-47) #4, 17-25.

Solomon Zeitlin, "Jewish Rights in Palestine," *JQR, N.S.,* 38 (1947-48) 119-134.

Bert C. Kreller, "Palestine and the Jew," *BS* 105 (1948) 82-88, 198-212.

Jakob Jocz, "The Jewish-Christian Controversy Concerning Israel," *IRM* 37 (1948) 382-392.

*Merrill F. Unger, "Ezekiel's Vision of Israel's Restoration," *BS* 106 (1949) 312-324, 432-445.

*Merrill F. Unger, "Ezekiel's Vision of Israel's Restoration (Concluded)," *BS* (107) 1950) 51-63.

T. F. Torrance, "Salvation is of the Jews," *EQ* 22 (1950) 164-173.

J. C. Campbell, "God's People and the Remnant," *SJT* 3 (1950) 78-85.

*E. W. Heaton, "The Root שאר and the Doctrine of the Remnant," *JTS, N.S.,* 3 (1952) 27-41.

Will Herberg, "Jewish Existence and Survival: A Theological View," *Jud* 1 (1952) 19-26.

Abraham F. Citron, "'Chosen People'?" *Jud* 1 (1952) 274-276. (Reply by Will Herberg, pp. 276-277)

Norman Snaith, "The People of God. The Beginning: A People Saved by Grace," *PQL* 1 (1954-55) 15-20.

Norman Snaith, "The People of God. A Kingdom of Priests, an Holy Nation," *PQL* 1 (1954-55) 113-118.

Charles Lee Feinberg, "The State of Israel," *BS* 112 (1955) 311-319.

Milton R. Konvitz, "Many are Called and Many are Chosen," *Jud* 4 (1955) 58-64.

*D. W. Watts, "The People of God. A Study of the Doctrine in the Pentateuch," *ET* 67 (1955-56) 232-237.

Jacob L. Halevi, "The Lord's Elect and Peculiar Treasure," *Jud* 5 (1956) 22-30.

Anonymous, "The People of God in the Old Testament," *GBT* 1 (1957-61) #10, 19-35.

Richard L. Twomey, "The Purpose of the Election of Israel," *MH* 13 (1957-58) #3, 1-9.

Eyvind Sivertsen, "The Scriptures and Israel," *RefmR* 5 (1957-58) 222-232.

*S. du Toit, "Relevant Principles in Connection with the Exegesis of the Old Testament Prophecies, with special reference to the Future of Israel," *OTW* 2 (1959) 1-5.

*James Muilenburg, "Father and Son," *T&L* 3 (1960) 177-187. [The Father-Son Relation in the Old Testament, pp. 179-183] *[Israel's Relation to God]*

Arthur A. Cohen, "The God of Israel—Pursuer and Pursued," *Jud* 10 (1961) 296-297.

Daniel J. Elazar, "The People Israel and Responsibility," *Jud* 10 (1961) 297-300.

Maurice Friedman, "Biblical Dialogue, Covenant and Hassidic Fervor," *Jud* 10 (1961) 300-303.

Irwin Weil, "Israel—The Wrestler With God," *Jud* 10 (1961) 347-349.

Michael Wyschogrod, "Divine Election and Commandment," *Jud* 10 (1961) 350-352.

Yves M.-J. Congar, "Modern Israel: fulfillment of God's promise?" *TD* 9 (1961) 95-96.

Frederick A. Doppelt, "A Reappraisal of the Chosen People Concept," *CCARJ* 9 (1961-62) #2, 11-15, 21.

Emanuel Rackman, "Israel and God: Reflections on Their Encounter," *Jud* 11 (1962) 233-241.

J. R. Porter, "The Israel of God," *CQR* 164 (1963) 138-147.

Leon I. Fever, "The Meaning of Israel," *CCARJ* 11 (1963-64) #3, 6-9.

John M. Oesterreicher, "Speaking of the Jews," *BibT* #13 (1964) 864-868.

Robert Myrant, "Captivity and Restoration—Israel's History," *CCBQ* 7 (1964) #1, 29-43.

*Charles L. Feinberg, "God's Message to Man Through the Prophets. II. The Prophetic Word and Israel," *GJ* 5 (1964) #2, 10-15.

*Eugene Milhaly, "A Rabbinic Defense of the Election of Israel, An Analysis of Sifre Deuteronomy 32:9, Pisqa 312," *HUCA* 35 (1964) 103-143.

Arthur Hertzberg, "The Secularity of Israel's Election," *Jud* 13 (1964) 387-392.

*A. Cody, "When is the Chosen People Called a gôy?" *VT* 14 (1964) 1-16.

Virgil H. Todd, "The Relation of the Child to the Covenant People According to the Old Testament," *CS* 11 (1964-70) #2, 2-7, 10-14.

E. Clancy, "The Election Tradition of the Old Testament," *ACR* 42 (1965) 96-112.

Richard Batey, "The Biblical Doctrine of the People of God," *RestQ* 8 (1965) 2-9.

David C. Pellett, "Election or Selection? *The Historical Basis for the Doctrine of Election of Israel,*" *SQ/E* 26 (1965) 155-169.

Dennis [J.] McCarthy, "Israel, My First-Born Son," *Way* 5 (1965) 183-191.

James A. Sanders, "Promise and Providence," *USQR* 21 (1965-66) 295-303.

John J. Dougherty, "The People of God," *BibT* #26 (1966) 1804-1807. [Israel as God's People, p. 1806]

R. E. Clements, "The Relation of Children to the People of God in the Old Testament," *Found* 9 (1966) 131-144.

Ernst Simon, "The Jew as God's Witness in the World," *Jud* 15 (1966) 306-318.

*Henri Cazelle, "The Unity of the Bible and the People of God," *Scrip* 18 (1966) 1-10.

Claus Westermann, "God and his people," *TD* 14 (1966) 24-28.

John F. Walvoord, "The Resurrection of Israel," *BS* 124 (1967) 3-15.

*Harry M. Orlinsky, "'A Light of the Nations': A Problem in Biblical Theology," *JQR, 75th* (1967) 409-428.

Simon Rawidowicz, "Israel: The Ever-Dying People," *Jud* 16 (1967) 423-433.

Frank M. Cross Jr. "A Christian Understanding of the Election of Israel," *ANQ, N.S.,* 8 (1967-68) 237-240.

Sheldon H. Blank, "The Theology of Jewish Survival According to Biblical Sources," *CCARJ* 15 (1968) #4, 22-31, 104.

A. van Selms, "God's election in the Old Testament," *Min* 9 (1969) 51-57.

G. W. Anderson, "Some Observations on the Old Testament Doctrine of the Remnant," *GUOST* 23 (1969-70) 1-10.

§1026 *5.4.14 Studies on Covenants [See also: Studies concerning Covenants, Contracts, Curses, Oaths, Treaties, and Vows §138 ←]*

†'Paulinus', "Observations on the Abrahamic Covenant," *TRep* 2 (1770) 306-411.

Anonymous, "The Abrahamic Covenant," *SPR* 2 (1848-49) 81-94.

Anonymous, "The Abrahamic Covenant and the New Testament," *PQR* 3 (1854-55) 529-571.

A. G. G., "The Promise to Abraham," *UQGR* 13 (1856) 375-400.

W. R. F., "The Promise to Abraham," *UQGR* 18 (1861) 361-372.

Anonymous, "The Covenants of Scripture," *DQR* 2 (1862) 35-57.

Henry Dana Ward, "The Everlasting Covenant of Promise to David," *ER* 17 (1866) 426-447.

T. R. Palmer, "The Abrahamic Covenant," *BQ* 5 (1871) 314-334.

Robert G. Balfour, "The Sinai Covenant," *BFER* 26 (1877) 511-527.

James Scott, "The Correlation of the Old and New Covenants," *ONTS* 4 (1884-85) 252-257.

*C. J. Bredenkamp, "God's Covenant in the Prophets," *ONTS* 4 (1884-85) 353-357. *(Trans. by H. M. Douglas)*

Geo. H. Schodde, "The Old Testament Covenant," *BS* 42 (1885) 401-430.

G[eorge] H. S[chodde], "The Character of the Old Testament Covenant," *ColTM* 5 (1885) 35-57.

J. S. Candlish, "The Notion of Divine Covenants in the Bible," *ET* 4 (1892-93) 19-23, 65-68.

J. A Selbie, "The Old Testament Conception of a Covenant," *ET* 8 (1896-97) 448-449.

*Stephen D. Peet, "The Bow in the Cloud; The Token of a Covenant," *AAOJ* 28 (1906) 65-80.

G. A. Cooke, "The Covenant in Israel," *OSHTP* (1910-11) 14-19.

*Duncan Cameron, "Covenant Loyalty," *ET* 27 (1915-16) 26-29.

C. A. Blomgren, "The Blood Covenant," *TTKF* 19 (1917) 190-198, 259-266.

*James Oscar Boyd, "The Davidic Dynasty," *PTR* 25 (1927) 215-239.

James Oscar Boyd, "The Davidic Covenant: The Oracle," *PTR* 25 (1927) 417-443.

James Oscar Boyd, "Echoes of the Covenant with David," *PTR* 25 (1927) 587-609.

Alfred D. Miller, "Old Testament Covenants and the Lord's Supper. An Interpretation," *CJRT* 7 (1930) 197-204.

Theodore H. Robinson, "'Covenant' in the Old Testament," *ET* 53 (1941-42) 298-299.

Richard W. Gray, "A Comparison Between the Old Covenant and the New Covenant," *WTJ* 4 (1941-42) 1-30.

Charles Fred Lincoln, "The Biblical Covenants," *BS* 100 (1943) 309-323, 442-449, 565-573.

*Will Herberg, "Judaism and Christianity: Their Unity and Difference. The Double Covenant in the Divine Economy of Salvation," *JAAR* 21 (1943) 67-78.

*P. E. Kretzmann, "The Chronology of the Two Covenants," *CTM* 15 (1944) 767-771.

Helen Silving, "The State Contract in the Old Testament," *JR* 24 (1944) 17-32.

John F. Walvoord, "The Fulfillment of the Abrahamic Covenant," *BS* 102 (1945) 27-36.

John F. Walvoord, "The Fulfillment of the Davidic Covenant," *BS* 102 (1945) 153-166.

Matthew Black, "The Covenant of People," *ET* 57 (1945-46) 277-278.

John F. Walvoord, "The New Covenant with Israel," *BS* 103 (1946) 16-27.

John L. McKenzie, "The Divine Sonship of Israel and the Covenant," *CBQ* 8 (1946) 320-331.

A. W. Argyle, "Grace and the Covenant," *ET* 60 (1948-49) 26-27.

*Paul Ramsey, "Elements of a Biblical Political Theory," *JR* 29 (1949) 258-283. [I. Covenant; II. Justice]

George E. Mendenhall, "Covenant Forms in Israelite Tradition," *BA* 17 (1954) 50-76. [The Nature of Covenant; The Structure of the Covenant; Other Factors in the Covenant; Covenant Forms in Israel; The Covenant of Joshua 24; The Breakdown of the Covenant Form; The Rediscovery of Moses; Epilogue]

James Freeman Rand, "Old Testament Fellowship with God," *BS* 108 (1951) 227-236, 323-333, 423-433; 109 (1952) 47-54, 151-163, 226-238.

*James F. Walvoord, "The Abrahamic Covenant and Premillennialism," *BS* 108 (1951) 414-422; 109 (1952) 37-46, 136-150, 217-225, 293-303.

John F. Walvoord, "The Kingdom Promises to David," *BS* 110 (1953) 97-110.

John F. Walvoord, "The New Covenant with Israel," *BS* 110 (1953) 193-205.

Conald Foust, "The Covenant Message of the Prophets," *Scotist* [9] (1953) 42-59.

*E. F. Kevan, "The Covenants and the Interpretation of the Old Testament," *EQ* 26 (1954) 19-28.

J. A. Thompson, "Non-Biblical Covenants in the Ancient Near East and Their Relevance for Understanding the Covenant Motif in the Old Testament," *ABR* 8 (1960) 39-45.

R[osemary] S[heed], "Justice in Israel: Key to the Covenant," *LofS* 15 (1960-61) 57-70.

Meredith G. Kline, "Dynastic Covenant," *WTJ* 23 (1960-61) 1-15.

D. F. Payne, "The Everlasting Covenant," *TB* #7&8 (1961) 10-16.

*Helmer Ringgren, "Enthronement Festival or Covenant Renewal?" *BRes* 7 (1962) 45-48.

*J. C. Hindley, "The Meaning and Translation of Covenant," *BTr* 13 (1962) 90-101.

Leonard Bushinski, "Striking a Covenant," *BibT* #4 (1963) 218-223.

*R. F. Collins, "The Berîth-Notion of the Cairo Damascus Covenant and its Comparison with the New Testament," *ETL* 39 (1963) 555-594.

C. F. Whitley, "Covenant and Commandment in Israel," *JNES* 22 (1963) 37-48.

*Edward Heppenstall, "The Law and the Covenant at Sinai," *AUSS* 2 (1964) 18-26.

*Walter R. Roehrs, "Covenant and Justification in the Old Testament," *CTM* 35 (1964) 583-602.

Meredith G. Kline, "Law Covenant," *WTJ* 27 (1964-65) 1-20.

*Frederick L. Moriarty, "Prophet and Covenant," *Greg* 46 (1965) 817-853.

Erhard Gerstenberger, "Covenant and Commandment," *JBL* 84 (1965) 38-51.

*G. M. Tucker, "Covenant Forms and Contract Forms," *VT* 15 (1965) 487-503.

Joseph Klein, "The Covenant and Confirmation," *CCARJ* 13 (1965-66) #6, 24-30.

*D. A. Hubbard, "The Wisdom Movement and Israel's Covenant Faith," *TB* #17 (1966) 3-34.

*M. J. Buss, "The Covenant Theme in Historical Perspective," *VT* 16 (1966) 502-504.

*William G. Most, "A Biblical Theology of Redemption in a Covenant Framework," *CBQ* 29 (1967) 1-19.

*E. D. Stockton, "The Fortress Temple of Shechem and Joshua's Covenant," *AJBA* 1 (1968-71) #1, 24-28.

*Dennis J. McCarthy, "Theology and Covenant in the Old Testament," *BibT* #42 (1969) 2904-2908.

*Robert Polzin, "*HWQY*ᶜ and Covenantal Institutions in Early Israel," *HTR* 62 (1969) 227-240.

John J. Mitchell, "Abram's Understanding of the Lord's Covenant," *WTJ* 32 (1969-70) 24-48.

*Meredith G. Kline, "Canon and Covenant," *WTJ* 32 (1969-70) 49-67, 179-200.

§1027 *5.4.15 Studies on Ethics*

Tayler Lewis, "Bible Ethics," *BRCR, 3rd Ser.,* 4 (1848) 554-564. *(Review)*

*D., "The Canaanitish Wars. How are the Canaanitish Wars to be Reconciled with the Principles of Christianity?" *CRB* 13 (1848) 345-365.

Samuel D. Cochrane, "God's Positive Moral Government Over Moral Agents, Additional to that which is Merely Natural," *BS* 11 (1854) 254-277.

†Anonymous, "The Ethical System of the Bible," *TLJ* 7 (1854-55) 666-680. *(Review)*

Anonymous, "The Universal Fatherhood of God and the Universal Brotherhood of Man, God's Argument Against Oppression," *ER* 14 (1862-63) 578-599.

Anonymous, "The Ethics of Aristotle," *WR* 87 (1867) 24-63. *(Review)*

Anonymous, "The Attitude of the Ancient Mind with respect to Truth," *SPR* 19 (1868) 502-517.

*Joseph P. Thompson, "Notes on Egyptology," *BS* 28 (1871) 397-402. *(Review) [Morals]*

*Anonymous, "The Bible and Strong Drink," *WR* 103 (1875) 50-64. *[OT Refs. pp. 55-59]*

J. H. McIlvaine, "The Moral Difficulties of the Old Testament," *BS* 34 (1877) 672-707.

Robert M'Cheyne Edgar, "Old Testament Morality," *BFER* 27 (1878) 1-32.

Henry Wace, "The Bible and Morality," *CM* 7 (1878) 52-63.

*Keningale Cook, "Theism and Ethics in Ancient Greece," *DUM* 92 (1878) 584-592, 641-655.

*George Rawlinson, "Duties of Higher Towards Lower Races," *PRev* 54 (1878) Part 2, 804-847.

*Henry Hayman, "The Teaching of Holy Scripture regarding fermented Liquors," *CM* 9 (1879) 65-81.

*Anonymous, "The Scriptural View of Wine and Strong Drink," *CQR* 8 (1879) 413-436.

*[Stephen D. Peet], "Was the Jewish Religion Ethical?" *AAOJ* 2 (1879-80) 157-159.

*A. B. Rich, "Doe the Scriptures Prohibit the Use of Alcoholic Beverages?" *BS* 37 (1880) 99-133, 305-327, 401-418. *[Word Studies of Old Testament Terms]*

*Anonymous, "Was the Jewish Religion Ethical," *OBJ* 1 (1880) 3-5.

*Reginald Stuart Poole, "Hebrew Ethics in Evidence of the Date of Hebrew Documents," *ContR* 39 (1881) 629-636.

H. C. Mabie, "Hebrew Manhood," *ONTS* 1 (1882) #1, 9.

*Thomas Hill, "Theism and Ethics," *BS* 50 (1883) 643-654.

*E. P. Evans, "Biblical Exegesis and Historical Criticism," *URRM* 24 (1885) 237-254. *[Ethics of the Destruction of the Canaanites]*

Robert Lorimer, "The Relation of the Gentile Nations in the Old Testament Times to the Moral Government of God," *BFER* 35 (1886) 651-667.

A. P. Peabody, "Classic and Semitic Ethics," *AR* 10 (1888) 561-576.

R. L. Dabney, "Anti-Biblical Theories of Rights," *PQ* 2 (1888) 217-242.

George Dana Broadman, "Immoralities of the Old Testament Heroes," *AR* 11 (1889) 278-285.

Anonymous, "Ethics of the Old Testament," *MR* 71 (1889) 273-277.

Eugene Revillout, "Egyptian Ethics," *BS* 47 (1890) 390-414. *(Trans. by Florence Osgood)*

*Anthony Maas, "The Mosaic Law in the Light of Ethics," *ACQR* 17 (1892) 123-136.

*Charles A. Hobbs, "The Alleged Cruelty of God to the Canaanites," *BQR* 14 (1892) 455-496.

*William H. Arnoux, "The Influence of the Bible on Modern Jurisprudence," *CT* 10 (1892-93) 21-30.

*Anson P. Atterbury, "Ethical Teaching of the Book of Job Concerning the Conduct of God Toward Man," *CT* 10 (1892-93) 123-136.

John Milton Williams, "The Supreme Law of the Moral World," *BS* 50 (1893) 640-655.

*John Taylor, "A Prophet's View of International Ethics," *Exp, 4th Ser.,* 8 (1893) 96-109.

W. L. Sheldon, "The Ethics of Greece," *OC* 7 (1893) 3521-3525.

*Ernest D. Burton, "The Ethical Teachings of Jesus in Relation to the Ethics of the Pharisees and of the Old Testament," *BW* 10 (1897) 198-208.

*J. Cheston Morris, "The Ethics of Solomon," *PAPS* 33 (1894) 310-332.

A. J. Heller, "The Moral Difficulties of the Old Testament," *RChR* 41 (1894) 225-249.

James Frederick McCurdy, "The Moral Evolution of the Old Testament," *AJT* 1 (1897) 658-691.

*Howard Osgood, "Morals before Moses," *PRR* 8 (1897) 267-278.

J. E. Rankin, "The Influence of the Bible upon the Human Conscience," *BS* 57 (1900) 336-365.

Henry A. Stimson, "The Ethics of the Old Testament," *BW* 16 (1900) 87-97.

*D. S. Margoliouth, "Lines of Defence of the Biblical Revelation. 4. The Argument from Silence," *Exp, 6th Ser.,* 2 (1900) 129-154.

Walter M. Patton, "The Bible and Temperance," *BW* 18 (1901) 361-366.

*W. Brenton Greene Jr., "The Ethics of the Book of Proverbs," *CFL, N.S.,* 4 (1901) 136-141.

Joseph J. Lampe, "Manners and Morals in Israel and in the Times of Isaiah," *CFL, N.S.,* 4 (1901) 259-267.

*Jas. A. Quarles, "The Sociology of Joseph's Day. Ethical," *CFL, N. S.,* 6 (1902) 110-116.

George R. Berry, "The Ethical Teaching of the Old Testament," *BW* 21 (1903) 108-114, 197-205.

William C. Wilkinson, "The Divine 'Cruelty' in Nature and in Scripture," *HR* 46 (1903) 419-423.

J. F. McCurdy, "The Morality of the Old Testament," *BW* 23 (1904) 408-416.

J. F. McCurdy, "The Morality of the Old Testament. II," *BW* 24 (1904) 15-21.

T. C. Todd, "On the 'Aristocratic' Character of the Old Testament," *Exp, 6th Ser.,* 9 (1904) 129-132.

*Charles Callaway, "The Prophet and the Priest in Hebrew Ethics," *WR* 161 (1904) 533-539.

Theodore Gerald Soares, "What is the Ethical Value of the Old Testament in Modern Life?" *BW* 27 (1906) 23-31.

William Henry George*[sic]*, "Unique Excellence of Old Testament Ethics," *CFL, 3rd Ser.,* 4 (1906) 420-427.

Ira M. Price, "Some Phases of the Ethical Character of the Old Testament and the Ethics of Ancient Oriental Peoples," *R&E* 3 (1906) 368-384.

Friedrich Giesebrecht, "The Moral Level of the Old Testament Scriptures," *AJT* 11 (1907) 31-55.

Benedict Steuart, "Divine Morality in the Old Testament," *IER, 4th Ser.,* 21 (1907) 486-506.

*Anonymous, "Editorial Notes. Ethical Thoughts in Our Lord's Day," *ICMM* 4 (1907-08) 241-242.

*R[obert] H[enry] Charles, "Man's Forgiveness of his Neighbour: a Study in Religious Development," *Exp, 7th Ser.,* 6 (1908) 492-505.

James Orr, "Autonomy in Ethics," *PTR* 6 (1908) 269-277.

A. v. C. P. Huizinga, "The Function of Authority in Life and Its Relation to Legalism in Ethics and Religion," *PTR* 6 (1908) 588-636.

J. Edward Mercer, "Is the Old Testament a Suitable Basis for Moral Instruction?" *HJ* 7 (1908-09) 333-345.

*Charles Edward Smith, "Ethics of the Mosaic Law," *BS* 76 (1909) 267-277.

*H. T. Andrews, "The Ethical Teaching of the Testaments of the XII Patriarchs," *IJA* #18 (1909) 63-65.

*H. Maldwyn Hughes, "The Apocrypha and Pseudepigrapha and Christian Ethics," *IJA* #19 (1909) 77-79.

*Willis J. Beecher, "Some Problems Concerning the Bible," *CFL, 3rd Ser.,* 12 (1910) 417-420. [III. A Study in Bible Ethics—David and Jacob, pp. 419-420]

*M. Gaster, "The Ethics of Jewish Apocryphal Literature," *IJA* #20 (1910) 17-19. *(Review)*

Edward Day, "The Humanitarianism of the Deuteronomists," *BW* 38 (1911) 113-125.

*H. G. Enelow, "The Ethical Element in the Talmud," *MQR, 3rd Ser.,* 37 (1911) 469-483, 745-757.

George Melville Bolling, "The Greek View of the Relation Between Poetry and Morality," *CUB* 19 (1913) 268-286.

George W. Gilmore, "Morality in Ancient Egypt," *HR* 66 (1913) 286-287.

*Jacob Z. Lauterbach, "The Ethics of the Halakah," *YCCAR* 23 (1913) 249-287.

Hilda Flinders Petrie, "Notes on the Ethics of the Egyptians," *AEE* 1 (1914) 55-58. [Notes on an address by Alan H. Gardiner]

John Mullins Aldridge, "Jewish and Christian Ethics," *ICQ* 7 (1914) 139-147.

*Shirley Jackson Case, "Religion and War in the Graeco-Roman World," *AJT* 19 (1915) 179-199.

*Charles Caverno, "The Rule in Cain's Case: A Study in Ethics," *BS* 72 (1915) 235-245.

C. J. Cadoux, "The Ethics of a Hebrew Lawyer," *ICMM* 12 (1915-16) 158-169.

*E. W. Winstanley, "The Testaments of the Twelve Patriarchs as a Guide to Conduct," *IJA* #43 (1915) 61-65.

*Eduard König, "Israel's Attitude Respecting Alien-Right and Usages of War in Antiquity," *HR* 72 (1916) 184-189.

Arthur J. Westermayr, "Moral Law and the Bible," *OC* 30 (1916) 531-546.

W. C. Taylor, "Moral Difficulties in the Old Testament," *R&E* 13 (1916) 388-396.

*Anonymous, "Jael. A Study in Early Ethics," *ET* 28 (1916-17) 349-354.

*Robert A. Aytoun, "The Ethics of the Jael Narratives," *ET* 28 (1916-17) 520-522.

*J. P. Robertson, "Genesis a Miracle in Morals," *USR* 28 (1916-17) 187-200.

Samuel A. B. Mercer, "Sumerian Morals," *JSOR* 1 (1917) 47-84.

A. Kampmeier, "Comments on 'Moral Law and the Bible'," *OC* 31 (1917) 238-245.

J. W. H., "Some Aspects of the Treatment of Ingratitude in Greek and English Literature," *TAPA* 48 (1917) 37-48.

Samuel S. Cohon, "Love, Human and Divine, in Post-Biblical Literature," *YCCAR* 27 (1917) 244-300.

G. Buchanan Gray, "Profane Nations," *ET* 29 (1917-18) 250-254. *[Ethics and Warfare]*

G. C. Montefiore, "The Old Testament and its Ethical Teaching," *HJ* 16 (1917-18) 234-250.

*Robert H. Kennett, "Plunder and Punishment," *ICMM* 14 (1917-18) 47-51.

Samuel A. B. Mercer, "Early Egyptian Morals," *JSOR* 2 (1918) 3-27.

Samuel A. B. Mercer, "Early Babylonian Morals," *JSOR* 2 (1918) 55-75.

*C. Sprenger, "The Evolution Theory and its Bearing on Theology and Ethics," *TZDES* 46 (1918) 281-285.

Samuel A. B. Mercer, "Morals of Israel, I. Pre-prophetic Morals," *ATR* 1 (1918-19) 24-41, 288-303.

Thomas Adamson, "Kaiseriana," *ET* 30 (1918-19) 374-376. [Adoni-Bezek and Justice (Judges 1:7); Agag—Judgment (1 Sam. 15:33); Oded—Judgment and Mercy (2 Chron. 28:9)

Samuel A. B. Mercer, "Egyptian Morals of the Middle Kingdom," *JSOR* 3 (1919) 1-13.

Samuel A. B. Mercer, "Morals of Israel, II. Early Prophetic Morals," *ATR* 2 (1919-20) 126-140.

George A. Barrow, "The Morality of Religion," *ATR* 2 (1919-20) 175-194.

Samuel A. B. Mercer, "Assyrian Morals," *JSOR* 4 (1920) 1-15.

Samuel A. B. Mercer, "Morals of Israel, III. Late Prophetic and Priestly Morals," *ATR* 3 (1920-21) 211-227.

*G. A. Cooke, "Some Principles of Reconstruction from the Old Testament Prophets," *ICMM* 17 (1920-21) 17-26.

Samuel A. B. Mercer, "Egyptian Morals of the Empire," *JSOR* 5 (1921) 36-50.

Samuel A. B. Mercer, "Late Babylonian Morals," *JSOR* 5 (1921) 84-95.

Edward Mack, "The Ethical Message of the Old Testament," *USR* 34 (1922-23) 240-254.

*I. G. Matthews, "The Hebrew Bondage and Its Influence on Hebrew Morals," *CJRT* 1 (1924) 300-306.

H. F. B. Compston, "Jewish Humanism," *CQR* 99 (1924-25) 40-58.

H. Slonimsky, "A Word Towards the Re-Awakening of Interest in Jewish Ethics," *JIQ* 1 (1924-25) 102-105.

*G. M. Bruce, "The Prophets as a Moral Code," *TTM* 9 (1925-26) 285-297.

*V. Aptowitzer, "The Rewarding and Punishing of Animals and Inanimate Objects. On the Aggadic View of the World," *HUCA* 3 (1926) 117-155.

A. R. Gordon, "The Ethics of Jewish Apocalypse," *CJRT* 4 (1927) 19-27.

Edward*[sic]* König, "The Origin of the Sense of Decency according to the Bible," *MR* 111 (1928) 135-138.

W[illiam] A. Irwin, "Truth in Ancient Israel," *JR* 9 (1929) 357-388.

R. E. Page, "Justice as Expressed in the Old Testament," *MR* 112 (1929) 925-927.

Wm. Brenton Greene Jr., "The Ethics of the Old Testament," *PTR* 27 (1929) 153-192, 313-366. [The General Characteristics of Old Testament Ethics; The Fundamentals of Old Testament Ethics; The Objections to Old Testament Ethics]

*Gerson S. Englemen, "The Ethics of Isaiah," *CTSQ* 7 (1929-30) #3, 2-6.

*Edward A. Arbez, "The Relations Between Religion and Morality Among the Early Semites," *AQW* 4 (1931) #1/2, 1-11.

*Martin R. P. McGuire, "The Relations Between Religion and Morality Among the Early Greeks and Romans," *AQW* 4 (1931) #1/2, 11-22.

George L. Robinson, "The Bible Oriental in Its Standards of Morality," *BS* 89 (1932) 351-362.

*John Paterson, "Some Ethical Insights of Prophecy," *RL* 1 (1932) 540-550.

Gordon H. Clark, "Kant and Old Testament Ethics," *EQ* 7 (1933) 232-240.

*G. F. Barbour, "Punishment in Ethics and Theology," *ET* 46 (1934-35) 33-36, 74-78.

*E. David Faust, "A Prophet Attacks Profit," *JAAR* 3 (1935) #1, 29-31.

*Oscar N. Olson, "The Ethical Concepts of the Psalms," *AQ* 15 (1936) 348-361.

*James Bissett Pratt, "God and the Moral Law," *HTR* 29 (1936) 153-170.

*David Cains, "Aldous Huxley—Cosmology and Ethic," *ET* 50 (1938-39) 55-60.

L. Hodgson, "Ethics in the Old Testament," *OSHTP* (1940-41) 11-14.

Michael J. Gruenthaner, "The Old Testament and Retribution in this Life," *CBQ* 4 (1942) 101-110.

L. Hodgson, "Ethics in the Old Testament," *CQR* 134 (1942) 153-169.

Matthew P. Stapleton, "Ancient Wisdom and Modern Times," *CBQ* 4 (1942) 311-322.

Matthew P. Stapleton, "Ancient Wisdom and Modern Times II," *CBQ* 5 (1943) 47-62.

P. W. Miller, "Light from the Patriarchs for our Day," *EQ* 15 (1943) 136-160.

E. K. Simpson, "The Displacement of the Decalogue," *EQ* 16 (1944) 192-201.

*LeRoy Waterman, "The Ethical Clarity of the Prophets," *JBL* 64 (1945) 297-307.

K. J. Foreman, "Love Your Enemies—An Ancient Military Law," *Interp* 2 (1948) 465-466

Walther Eichrodt, "Revelation and Responsibility. *The Biblical Norm of Social Behavior,*" *Interp* 3 (1949) 387-399.

*Norman W. Porteous, "Ritual and Righteousness. *The Relation of Ethics to Religion in the Prophetic Literature,*" *Interp* 3 (1949) 400-414.

G. E. Mendenhall, "The Old Testament Concept of Vengeance," *JBL* 68 (1949) viii-ix.

W. G. D. MacLennan, "The New Norm of Life. *The Biblical Doctrine of Obedience,*" *Interp* 4 (1950) 284-297.

Edward Thomas Ramsdell, "The Old Testament Understanding of Truth," *JR* 31 (1951) 264-273.

*R[obert H.] Pfeiffer, "The Image of the Delian Apollo and Apolline Ethics," *JWCI* 15 (1952) 20-32.

*Joseph Klausner, "Monotheism and Ethics in Judaism," *Jud* 1 (1952) 325-333.

Joseph Klausner, "Christian and Jewish Ethics," *Jud* 2 (1953) 16-30.

*Chaim W. Reines, "The Self and the Other in Rabbinic Ethics," *Jud* 2 (1953) 123-132.

*Meredith G. Kline, "The Intrusion and the Decalogue," *WTJ* 16 (1953-54) 1-22.

Harold M. Schulweis, "The Ethics of Jewish Civilization," *Jud* 5 (1956) 136-146.

V[artan] D. Melconian, "God's Mandate for Peace," *McQ* 10 (1956-57) #3, 7-10.

Louis Jacobs, "Greater Love Hath No Man....The Jewish Point of View of Self-Sacrifice," *Jud* 6 (1957) 41-47.

*Herold S. Stern, "The Ethics of the Clean and the Unclean," *Jud* 6 (1957) 319-327.

L. Johnston, "Old Testament Morality," *CBQ* 20 (1958) 19-25.

Peter Remnant, "God and the Moral Law," *CJT* 4 (1958) 23-29.

*Samuel Noah Kramer, "Love, Hate, and Fear. Psychological Aspects of Sumerian Culture," *EI* 5 (1958) 66*-74*.

W. G. Lambert, "Morals in Ancient Mesopotamia," *JEOL* #15 (1958) 184-196.

Jack L. Cohen, "Towards a Theology of Ethics," *Jud* 7 (1958) 56-63.

*Robert Dobbie, "Sacrifice and Morality in the Old Testament," *ET* 70 (1958-59) 297-300.

*H. H. Rowley, "Sacrifice and Morality: A Rejoinder," *ET* 70 (1958-59) 341-342.

Jacob L. Halevi, "Kierkegaard's Teleological Suspension of the Ethical—Is it Jewish?" *Jud* 8 (1959) 291-302.

Ch. W. Reines, "The Jewish Conception of Work," *Jud* 8 (1959) 329-337.

*Richard L. Scheef Jr., "Worship and Ethics in the Bible," *T&L* 3 (1960) 198-207.

Peter J. Fliess, "War Guilt in the History of Thucydides," *Tr* 16 (1960) 1-17.

E. Hammershaimb, "On the ethics of the Old Testament prophets," *VTS* 7 (1960) 75-101.

Wilford O. Cross, "Current Objections to Natural Law Theory in Ethics," *ATR* 43 (1961) 32-46.

Leo Baeck, "The Meaning of Justice," *CCARJ* 9 (1961-62) #1, 6-15.

Robert M. Carson Jr., "Human Rights and Dignity under the Laws of the Pentateuch," *PP* 2 (1961) #1, 27-41.

*Marvin Tate, "Jeremiah and Social Reform," *R&E* 58 (1961) 438-451.

Ivan Engnell, "The Biblical Attitude to Work. 1. Work in the Old Testament," *SEÅ* 26 (1961) 5-12.

Meir Weiss, "Some Problems of the Biblical 'Doctrine of Retribution'," *Tarbiz* 31 (1961-62) #3, I-II; 32 (1962-63) #1, I-II.

Leon Roth, "Moralization and Demoralization in Jewish Ethics," *Jud* 11 (1962) 291-302.

*Jacob Milgorm, "The Biblical Diet Laws as an Ethical System. *Food and Faith,*" *Interp* 17 (1963) 288-301.

Solomon Simon, "Stringent Aggadah—Lenient Halachan," *Jud* 12 (1963) 296-306.

Gordon H. Clark, "Capital Punishment," *F&T* 93 (1963-64) 12-18. [Correspondence by Timothy C. F. Stunt, pp. 95-100]

Elie Benamozegh, "Judaism and Christianity in the Light of Noachism. *I. Jewish and Christian Ethics,*" *Jud* 13 (1964) 220-228.

T. Kichko, "What Does Jewish Ethics Teach," *Mosaic* 5 (1964) #1, 55-57.

*P. R. Smythe, "Our Duty to Animals," *MC, N.S.,* 8 (1964-65) 263-268. *[OT Refs., p. 265]*

*C. W. Schudder, "Ethics in Deuteronomy," *SWJT, N.S.,* 7 (1964-65) #1, 33-40.

David Stacey, "Clues from the Old Testament," *PQL* 11 (1965) 173-180. [IV. Ethics]

*Frank W. Wilson, "Thoughts on the Theology of Animal Welfare," *PQL* 11 (1965) 222-228. [I. The Old Testament, pp. 223-225]

*J. Philip Hyatt, "Moses and the Ethical Decalogue," *SQ/E* 26 (1965) 199-206.

Nicholas Crotty, "Biblical Perspectives in Moral Theology," *ThSt* 26 (1965) 574-595.

*F. B. Huey Jr., "The Ethical Teaching of Amos.   Its Content and Relevance," *SWJT, N.S.,* 9 (1966-67) #1, 57-68.

A. K. Irvine, "Homicide in Pre-Islamic South Arabia," *BSOAS* 30 (1967) 277-291. [Addenda by A. F. L. Beeston, pp. 291-292]

*Donald R. Rouse, "God's Judgment on the Canaanites," *CCBQ* 10 (1967) #4, 34-46.

Jacob Neusner, "What is Normative in Jewish Ethics?" *Jud* 16 (1967) 3-20.

*Samuel Sandmel, "The Confrontation Of Greek And Jewish Ethics: Philo, De Decalogo," *CCARJ* 15 (1968) #1, 54-63.

H. S. Smith, "A Note on Amnesty," *JEA* 54 (1968) 209-214.

*Aaron Samuel Tameret, "Passover and Non-Violence," *Jud* 17 (1968) 203-210. *(Trans. by Everett E. Gendler)*

*Reuven Kimelman, "Non-Violence in the Talmud," *Jud* 17 (1968) 316-334.

Paul E. Dinter, "A Biblical View of Peace," *DudR* 9 (1969) 122-133.

Dennis P. Keane, "A Biblical View of Change and Violence," *DunR* 9 (1969) 134-144.

David Daube, "Limitations on Self-Sacrifice in Jewish Law and Tradition," *Theo* 72 (1969) 291-304.

*Graeme Goldsworthy, "The Old Testament—A Christian Book," *Inter* 2 (1969-70) 24-33. [III. Exegesis and ethics, pp. 26-27]

§1028 *5.4.15.1 Studies on the Law and the Gospel*

Baden Powell, "The Law and the Gospel," *JSL, 1st Ser.,* 1 (1848) 326-353.

*T. P. Stafford, "The Relation of the Ethical Teaching of Jesus to that of the Old Testament," *R&E* 14 (1917) 466-478.

*Johannes Hempel, "On the Problems of Law in the Old and New Testaments," *ATR* 34 (1952) 227-231.

Paul L. Holmer, "Law and Gospel Re-Examined," *TT* 10 (1953-54) 474-481.

Alfred von Rohr Sauer, "The Message of Law and Gospel in the Old Testament," *CTM* 26 (1955) 172-187, 256-264.

Robert Davidson, "Some Aspects of the Old Testament Contribution to the Pattern of Christian Ethics," *SJT* 12 (1959) 388-399.

*Henry Piorkowski, "Law and Love in the Old Testament," *Scotist* 23 (1967) 33-46.

§1029 *5.4.15.2 Studies on Ethics and Social Implications*

*Anonymous, "Spirit of the Hebrew Scriptures.—No. III. Public Worship: Social Crime, and its Retribution," *CE* 17 (1834) 78-92.

H[osea] B[allou] 2nd, "The Biblical Argument for Capital Punishment as a Divine Ordinance," *UQGR* 6 (1849) 341-358.

*Anonymous, "The Borrowing of the Jewels from the Egyptians," *DQR* 4 (1864) 362-384.

*J. M. C., "Thoughts on Genesis IX. 6: in relation to capital punishment," *JSL, 4th Ser.,* 5 (1864) 314-320.

*J. M. C., "Capital Punishment and Genesis IX. 6," *JSL, 4th Ser.,* 6 (1864-65) 314-319.

*'Orientalist', "Slavery Not Sanctioned in the Bible," *JSL, 4th Ser.,* 8 (1865-66) 315-320.

J. C. H., "The Scriptural Argument for Capital Punishment," *DUM* 75 (1870) 414-422.

*George Bertin, "Akkadian Precepts for the Conduct of Man in his Private Life," *SBAT* 8 (1883-84) 230-270.

†Anonymous, "Bribery, Ancient and Modern," *QRL* 163 (1886) 1-33. *(Review)*

Louis Voss, "The Old Testament in Its Relation to Social Reform," *PQ* 10 (1896) 442-457.

A. G., "Paragraphs on the Ethics of War," *TQ* 2 (1898) 278-280.

George A. Barton, "Elements of Peace Doctrine in the Old Testament," *BW* 19 (1902) 426-432.

*Wilbur F. Crafts, "Social Ethics: An Outline Study of the Second Great Commandment," *HR* 46 (1903) 229-230.

Orlo J. Price, "The Biblical Teaching concerning the Hireling and the Pauper," *BW* 29 (1907) 269-283.

W. S. Scarborough, "The Greeks and Suicide," *PAPA* 39 (1907) xxii-xxiii.

W. F. Lofthouse, "The Social Teaching of the Law," *Exp, 7th Ser.,* 5 (1908) 449-469.

*R. H. Charles, "Man's Forgiveness of his Neighbour: a Study in Religious Development," *Exp, 7th Ser.,* 6 (1908) 492-505.

William Frederic Bade, "The Growth of Ethical Ideals in Old Testament Times," *BW* 33 (1909) 182-190.

William Frederic Bade, "The Growth of Ethical Ideals in Old Testament Times," *BW* 33 (1909) 326-336. [II. The Prophets of the Eighth Century B.C.]

William Frederic Bade, "The Growth of Ethical Ideals in Old Testament Times," *BW* 34 (1909) 180-186. [III. Deuteronomy and Jeremiah, *ca.* 650-586 B.C.]

Samuel Zane Batten, "The Old Testament Doctrine of Social Opportunity," *BW* 42 (1913) 284-290.

J. W. Diggle, "The Bible and War," *Exp, 8th Ser.,* 8 (1914) 538-549.

William Brenton Greene Jr., "The Bible as the Text-Book in Sociology," *PTR* 12 (1914) 1-22.

John Pinkerton, "National Hate," *ET* 26 (1914-15) 299-302.

*J[ohn] M[erlin] Powis Smith, "Religion and War in Israel," *AJT* 19 (1915) 17-31.

*G. A. Cooke, "The Prophets and War," *Exp, 8th Ser.,* 10 (1915) 214-223.

William Elliot Griffis, "Does the Bible Throw any Light on the Race Question," *HR* 70 (1915) 94-99.

J. Abelson, "The Attitude of Judaism Towards War," *ET* 27 (1915-16) 391-395.

*J. E. McFadyen, "Isaiah and War," *Exp, 8th Ser.,* 11 (1916) 161-175.

*Eduard König, "Israel's Attitude Respecting Alien-Right and Usages of War in Antiquity," *HR* 72 (1916) 184-189.

H. Pereira Mendes, "The Bible Solution of War," *HR* 72 (1916) 195-196.

Wilfred J. Moulton, "Old Testament Ideas of War and Peace," *LQHR* 125 (1916) 43-58.

J. D. Maynard, "The Old Testament and War," *ICMM* 14 (1917-18) 15-30.

Ivan Lee Holt, "The Old Testament and War," *MQR, 3rd Ser.,* 44 (1918) 670-679.

Max Reichler, "The Jewish Conception of Justice," *YCCAR* 29 (1919) 316-340. {Discussion: [Abraham] Cronbach, pp. 340-346; Clifton Harby Levy, p. 346; [Kaufman] Kohler, pp. 346-347; [Samuel] Schulman, p. 347; [Max] Heller, pp. 347-348; [Samuel] Sale, p. 348; [Max] Reichler, p. 348}

P. Whitwell Wilson, "The Bible and the Industrial Problem," *BR* 6 (1921) 104-115.

Jacob Z. Lauterbach, "The Attitude of the Jew Towards the Non-Jew," *YCCAR* 31 (1921) 186-233.

*Fleming James, "The Attitude of the Hebrew Prophets Toward War," *ACM* 17 (1925) 43-57.

Fleming James, "Is There Pacifism in the Old Testament?" *ATR* 11 (1928-29) 224-232.

Walter L. Lingle, "The Bible and War," *USR* 40 (1928-29) 159-172. *[OT Refs., pp. 160-164]*

*W. W. Cannon, "The Disarmament Passage in Isaiah ii. and Micah iv," *Theo* 24 (1932) 2-8.

*Dwight F. Putman, "War and Religion: An Unholy Alliance," *LCQ* 9 (1936) 197-205. [1. War and Religion in the Tribe of Dan, pp. 197-200]

*Cyrus H. Gordon, "Nuzi Tablets Relating to Theft," *Or, N.S.,* 5 (1936) 305-330.

*Leon Nemoy, "A Tenth Century Disquisition of Suicide According to Old Testament Law (From the *Kitāb Al-Anwār* of Yaʿqūb Al-Qirqisānī)," *JBL* 57 (1938) 411-420.

Abraham Cronbach, "War and Peace in Jewish Tradition," *YCCAR* 46 (1936) 198-221.

*T. Fish, "War and Religion in Ancient Mesopotamia," *BJRL* 23 (1939) 387-402.

*H. Hamann, "Prophecy and War," *AusTR* 11 (1940) 55-57.

*H. Hamann, "'Spoiling the Egyptians'," *AusTR* 11 (1940) 88-90.

*J. S. MacArthur, "The Pre-Exilic Prophets and Pacifism," *ET* 52 (1940-41) 97-100.

P. E. Kretzmann, "The Bible and War," *CTM* 12 (1941) 207-208.

James P. Berkley, "The Old Testament and War," *ANQ* 35 (1943) #2, 1-12.

*Pearl Louise Weber, "What Plato Said About War," *Person* 22 (1941) 376-383.

*J. Philip Hyatt, "Jeremiah and War," *CQ* 20 (1943) 52-58.

John A. Vander Waal, "The Biblical Teaching on Church and State," *RefR* 3 (1949-50) #4, 1-4. *[OT Refs., pp. 1-2]*

*Robert North, "The Biblical Jubilee and Social Reform," *Scrip* 4 (1949-51) 323-335.

*Neil G. Smith, "Family Ethics in the Wisdom Literature," *Interp* 4 (1950) 453-457.

Carlton C. Allen, "The Biblical Springs of Freedom," *TUSR* 1 (1950-51) n.p.n.

David M. Shohet, "Mercy Death in Jewish Law," *CJ* 8 (1951-52) #3, 1-15.

Simon Federbush, "The Problem of Euthanasia in Jewish Tradition," *Jud* 1 (1952) 64-68.

*Emanuel Rackman, "Talmudic Insights on Human Rights," *Jud* 1 (1952) 158-163.

Alfred Bloom, "Human Rights in Israel's Thought. *A Study of Old Testament Doctrine*," *Interp* 8 (1954) 422-432.

George Goyder, "The Relevance of Biblical Justice to Industry," *SJT* 9 (1956) 264-277.

*W. F. Leemans, "Some aspects of theft and robbery in Old-Babylonian documents," *RDSO* 32 (1957) 661-666.

W. G. Lambert, "Morals in Ancient Mesopotamia," *JEOL* #15 (1957-58) 184-196.

A. Garfield Curnow, "A Consideration of the Teaching of the Bible on Human Freedom," *F&T* 90 (1958) 46-61.

*Matitiahu Tsevat, "Marriage and Monarchical Legitimacy in Ugarit and Israel," *JSS* 3 (1958) 237-243.

T. B. Maston, "Biblical Teachings and Race Relations," *R&E* 56 (1959) 233-242.

Walter Harrelson, "The Biblical Concept of the Free Man," *R&E* 57 (1960) 263-280.

*Z. W. Falk, "Collective Responsibility in Bible and Aggada," *Tarbiz* 30 (1960-61) #1, II.

Moshe David Herr, "The Problem of War on the Sabbath and the Second Temple and the Talmudic Books," *Tarbiz* 30 (1960-61) #3, VII-IX.

Guy H. Ranson, "A Biblical Interpretation of Work," *TUSR* 7 (1960-63) 57-67.

Ch. W. Reines, "The Jewish Attitude Toward Suicide," *Jud* 10 (1961) 160-170.

Walter Rein, "The Bible Speaks on Social Relations," *VDR* 5 (1961) 3-5.

Barry Baldwin, "Crime and Criminals in Graeco-Roman Egypt," *Aeg* 43 (1963) 256-263.

*C. J. de Catanzaro, "The Godly Society—An Aspect of the Prophetic Message," *ACQ* 4 (1964) 216-224.

Gerald J. Blidstein, "Capital Punishment—The Classic Jewish Discussion," *Jud* 14 (1965) 159-171.

*Roland E. Murphy, "The Old Testament Wisdom Literature and the Problem of Retribution," *Scotist* 20 (1964) 5-18.

*Paul E. Davies, "'The Poor You Have With You Always'. *(The Biblical View of Poverty),*" *McQ* 18 (1964-65) #2, 37-48.

Lawrence H. Davis, "Attitudes and Policies toward Gentiles during the Maccabean Period," *YR* 6 (1965) 5-20.

Eugene W. Bushala, "Torture of Non-Citizens in Homicide Investigations," *GRBS* 9 (1968) 61-68.

*Frank W. Wilson, "Thoughts on the Theology of Animal Welfare," *PQL* 11 (1965) 222-228. [I. The Old Testament, pp. 223-225]

§1030 *5.4.16 Studies on Prophecy*

†Anonymous, "Levi on the Old Testament," *BCQTR* 12 (1798) 37-49. *(Review)*

†Anonymous, "Zouch on the Prophecies," *BCQTR* 17 (1801) 74-78. *(Review)*

†Anonymous, "Faber on Prophecies relative to Judah and Israel," *BCQTR* 36 (1810) 462-472. *(Review)*

J. Rofe, "The Fulfillment of Prophecy," *MR* 5 (1822) 217-219.

†Anonymous, "Davidson's Discourses on Prophecy," *BCQTR, N.S.,* 22 (1824) 368-389. *(Review)*

[Ernst Wilhelm] Hengstenberg, "On the Nature of Prophecy," *BRCR* 2 (1832) 138-173. *(Trans. by James F. Warner)*

M. Stuart, "On the Alleged Obscurity of Prophecy," *BRCR* 2 (1832) 217-245.

†Anonymous, "Keith *on the Prophecies,"* *QRL* 53 (1835) 142-174. *(Review)*

*F. M. Hubbard, "Commerce and Manufacturing of Ancient Babylon, intended to illustrate some parts of the Prophetic Scriptures," *BRCR* 7 (1836) 364-390.

E. P. Barrows Jr., "Christianity Foretold Under the Symbols of Judaism," *BRCR, 3rd Ser.,* 3 (1847) 411-422.

*Luther F. Dimmick, "The Spirit of Prophecy in Relation to the Future Condition of the Jews," *BS* 4 (1847) 337-369.

J. A. Seiss, "Remarks on the Study of Prophecy," *ER* 1 (1849-50) 104-119.

*†[David N. Lord], "Prof. McClelland's Rules for the Interpretation of Prophecy," *TLJ* 3 (1850-51) 80-102. *(Review)*

*H[iram] C[arleton], "Thoughts on the Interpretation of Prophecy," *TLJ* 3 (1850-51) 642-667.

*Anonymous, "The Chief Characteristics and Laws of Prophetic Symbols," *TLJ* 3 (1850-51) 667-695.

E. P. Barrows, "The Element of Time in Prophecy," *BS* 12 (1855) 789-821.

*†Anonymous, "Dr. Fairbairn on Prophecy and its Proper Interpretation," *TLJ* 9 (1856-57) 353-396. *(Review)*

Anonymous, "Tholuck on Prophecy," *CE* 71 (1861) 353-374. *(Review)*

Anonymous, "The Matter of Prophecy," *PRev* 34 (1862) 559-578.

Anonymous, "Prophecy: its nature, interpretation and uses," *JSL, 4th Ser.,* 2 (1862-63) 1-20.

Anonymous, "The Matter of Prophecy," *BFER* 12 (1863) 168-183.

Henry Bannister, "Fairbairn on Prophecy," *MR* 49 (1867) 182-198. *(Review)*

†Anonymous, "Prophecy in the Critical Schools of the Continent," *BQRL* 52 (1870) 313-343. *(Review)*

William Gray Elmslie, "The Perspective in Prophecy," *BFER* 21 (1872) 326-347.

*Anonymous, "Prophets and Prophecy," *SPR* 26 (1875) 138-159. [Signification of the Name; The Prophetic Order; The Prophetic Gift; Their Manner of Life; The Prophetic Inspiration; Dreams; The Vision; The Prophetic Ecstasy; As to the Mode of Prophetic Communication; The Criteria of Prophecy]

*William Henry Green, "The Prophets and Prophecy in Israel," *DTQ* 4 (1878) 544-572.

*William Henry Green, "The Prophets and Prophecy in Israel," *PRev* 54 (1878) Part 2, 281-328.

*John W. Chadwick, "Prophets and Prophecy in Israel," *URRM* 9 (1878) 361-382. *(Review)*

*†Anonymous, "Prophecies concerning Israel after the Captivity," *LQHR* 53 (1879-80) 1-23. *(Review)*

Henry Cowles, "Prophecy: Its Interpretation and Uses," *MQR, 2nd Ser.,* 3 (1881) 465-477.

Nathaniel West, "Orelli on Old Testament Prophecy," *ONTS* 2 (1882-83) 142-150. *(Review)*

Anonymous, "The Study of Prophecy," *ONTS* 4 (1884-85) 185-186.

T. K. Cheyne, "Jewish Interpretation of Prophecy," *ONTS* 4 (1884-85) 421-424.

Alfred Edersheim, "The Character of Prophecy," *ONTS* 5 (1884-85) 179-180.

*Edward L Curtis, "The Advent of Jehovah," *PR* 6 (1885) 606-612.

*R. V. Foster, "Hebrew Prophets and Prophecy," *ONTS* 6 (1886-87) 110-113, 150-153, 166-170.

*Edward L. Curtis, "Some Features of Old Testament Prophecy Illustrated by the Book of Amos," *ONTS* 6 (1886-87) 136-139.

*O. P. Eaches, "Fulfilled Prophecy—A Standing Miracle," *BQR* 11 (1889) 468-482.

Frederic Gardiner, "The Description of Spiritual Phenomena Under the Figure of Natural Convulsions," *ONTS* 9 (1889) 162-169.

C.   H.   Waller,   "Prophecy,"   *TML*   2   (1889)   83-98.

W. Frith, "Reasons for the Study of Unfulfilled Prophecy," *EN* 2 (1890) 33-34.

I. Hellmuth, "The Spirit of Prophecy," *EN* 2 (1890) 97-104.

E. W. Relton, "The Nature of Prophecy," *CM, N.S.,* 8 (1890) 1-17.

Anonymous, "The Predictive Element in Prophecy," *MR* 72 (1890) 260-270.

Richard Wheatley, "Prophecy, Fulfilled and Unfulfilled, in Jewish Experiences," *MR* 72 (1890) 347-364.

*S[ylvester] Burnham, "Conditional Element in Prophecy. Illustrated by Isaiah 66:12-24 and other Passages," *ONTS* 10 (1890) 73-77.

*Anonymous,   "Prophecy   and   History,"   *ONTS*   10   (1890)   243.

*Anonymous, "Was Jesus the Subject of Old Testament Prophecy?" *MR* 73 (1891) 270-280.

'Wellesley Students', "The Historical Element in Prophecy: Its Relation to the Divine Element," *ONTS* 12 (1891) 341-347.

Anonymous, "Generic Fulfillment of Prophecy," *ONTS* 14 (1892) 247.

S[ylvester] Burnham, "The Conditional element in prophecy," *CMR* 5 (1893) 1-10.

F. H. Woods, "Hebrew Prophecy and Modern Criticism," *ET* 5 (1893-94) 256-261, 342-346, 452-458, 543-549; 6 (1894-95) 78-80, 92-93, 127-130, 214-219, 314-319, 366-371, 404-409, 459-464, 477, 506-510, 523; 7 (1895-96) 28-32.

*Joseph Agar Beet, "New Testament Teaching on the Second Coming of Christ: 1. Preparatory: The Old Testament and the Book of Enoch," *Exp, 4th Ser.,* 9 (1894) 430-439.

Alexander B. Grosart, "Hebrew Prophecy and Modern Criticism," *ET* 6 (1894-59) 91-92.

James Hastings, "'Hebrew Prophecy and Modern Criticism'," *ET* 6 (1894-95) 476-477.

Carl Heinrich Cornill, "The Israelitish Prophecy," *OC* 9 (1895) 4417-4419.

William R. Harper, "Outline Topics in the History of Old Testament Prophecy. I. Prophecy, Its Content and Definition; Literature," *BW* 7 (1896) 39-45.

*William R. Harper, "Outline Topics in the History of Old Testament Prophecy. II. Prophetic Situations: Amos, Isaiah, Zephaniah, Deutero-Isaiah.—Principles of Prophecy," *BW* 7 (1896) 120-129.

William R. Harper, "Outline Topics in the History of Old Testament Prophecy. III. The Classification of Prophetical Material," *BW* 7 (1896) 199-206.

Sylvester Burnham, "The Ideal Element in Prophecy," *BW* 8 (1896) 211-220.

William R. Harper, "Outline Topics in the History of Old Testament Prophecy. IV. Prophecy before the Conquest of Canaan," *BW* 7 (1896) 273-279.

William R. Harper, "Outline Topics in the History of Old Testament Prophecy. V. Prophecy in the United Kingdom 1050 B.C. - 937 B.C.," *BW* 7 (1896) 352-358.

William R. Harper, "Outline Topics in the History of Old Testament Prophecy. VI. The History of the Northern Kingdom," *BW* 8 (1896) 37-45.

*William R. Harper, "Outline Topics in the History of Old Testament Prophecy. VII. Prophecy of Isaiah and His Contemporaries," *BW* 8 (1896) 221-228.

*William R. Harper, "Outline Topics in the History of Old Testament Prophecy. VIII. Prophecy of Jeremiah and His Contemporaries," *BW* 8 (1896) 280-288.

*William R. Harper, "Outline Topics in the History of Old Testament Prophecy. IX. Prophecy of the Babylonian Captivity," *BW* 8 (1896) 364-375.

Walter R. Betteridge, "The Predictive Element in Old Testament Prophecy," *BS* 54 (1897) 50-65.

*H. L. Wayland, "The Interpretation of Prophecy," *HR* 35 (1898) 261.

*Frank C. Porter, "Prophecy and Apocalypse," *BW* 14 (1899) 36-41.

Ed. König, "Prophecy and History," *ET* 11 (1899-1900) 305-310.

Lewis B. Paton, "The Origin of the Prophetic Teaching," *HSR* 10 (1899-1900) 89-116.

*(   ) Sellin, "Jeremiah of Anathoth. A Study of Old Testament Prophecy," *ColTM* 21 (1901) 112-123, 173-185. *(Trans. by D. M. Martens)*

Benjamin B. Warfield, "Dr. Davidson's Article on Prophecy," *CFL, N.S.,* 6 (1902) 121-127. [Two Contrasting Views as to the Data; Dr. Davidson's Estimate of Hebrew Prophecy; Dr. Davidson on the Predictive Element; Dr. Davidson on Messianic Prophecy; Dr. Davidson on the Origin of Prophecy; Dr. Davidson's Account of Prediction; Were There Any True Prophets? Dr. Davidson's Failure] *(Editorial)*

W. G. Moorehead, "The True Nature of Prophecy," *CFL, N.S.,* 6 (1902) 315-326.

*Wilbert Webster White, "Some distinguishing features of Old Testament prophets and prophecy," *BRec* 1 (1903-04) 221-228.

William R. Harper, "Constructive Studies in the Prophetic Element in the Old Testament. I. The General Scope of the Prophetic Element. Content and Classification," *BW* 23 (1904) 50-58.

William R. Harper, "Constructive Studies in the Prophetic Element in the Old Testament. II. The General Scope of the Prophetic Element. Definition and Principles," *BW* 23 (1904) 132-141.

William R. Harper, "Constructive Studies in the Prophetic Element in the Old Testament. III. Prophecy and Prophetism During the Period of the Patriarchs and Judges," *BW* 23 (1904) 212-223.

William R. Harper, "Constructive Studies in the Prophetic Element in the Old Testament. IV. Prophecy and Prophetism during the Davidic Period," *BW* 24 (1904) 47-58.

William R. Harper, "Constructive Studies in the Prophetic Element in the Old Testament. V. The Background of Prophecy and Prophetism in the Northern Kingdom," *BW* 24 (1904) 128-136, 201-215.

William R. Harper, "Constructive Studies in the Prophetic Element in the Old Testament. VI. The Product of Prophecy and Prophetism in the Northern Kingdom," *BW* 24 (1904) 292-300.

William R. Harper, "Constructive Studies in the Prophetic Element in the Old Testament. VII. The Messages of the Prophetic Narratives J and E," *BW* 24 (1904) 361-376.

*William R. Harper, "Constructive Studies in the Prophetic Element in the Old Testament. VIII. The Prophetic Messages of Amos," *BW* 24 (1904) 448-462.

Moses Buttenwieser, "Essence of Prophecy," *HUCA* (1904) 81-105.

*William R. Harper, "Constructive Studies in the Prophetic Element in the Old Testament. IX. The Prophetic Message of Hosea," *BW* 25 (1905) 52-61.

James Strachan, "Dr. Davidson's 'Old Testament Prophecy'," *ET* 16 (1904-05) 42.

William R. Harper, "Old Testament Prophecy," *BW* 25 (1905) 43-45. *(Review)*

John Urquhart, "The Miracle of Prophecy," *CFL, 3rd Ser.,* 3 (1905) 3-11.

G. L. Young, "The Historical Method and Its Relation to the Study of Prophecy," *CFL, 3rd Ser.,* 3 (1905) 383-393.

*Jacob H. Kaplan, "Psychology of Prophecy," *AJRPE* 2 (1906-07) 168-203.

Kempter Fullerton, "The Reformation Principle of Exegesis and the Interpretation of Prophecy," *AJT* 12 (1908) 422-442.

*Eduard König, "Relations of Babylonian and Old Testament Culture. V. *Comparison Between Babylonian and Old Testament Prophecy,*" *HR* 58 (1909) 283-286.

John Merlin Powis Smith, "Semitic Prophecy," *BW* 35 (1910) 223-233.

*G. A. Smith, "The Experience of Balaam as Symbolic of the Origins of Prophecy," *Exp, 8th Ser.,* 5 (1913) 1-11.

*A. B. Leonard, "The Value of Prophecy and Miracles," *MR* 95 (1913) 730-734.

*D. E. Thomas, "The Psychological Approach to Prophecy," *AJT* 18 (1914) 241-256.

Andrew C. Zenos, "Unfulfilled Prophecies in the Bible," *HR* 67 (1914) 487-488.

William Watson, "The Messianic Woes," *IJA* #39 (1914) 63-69.

*J. E. McFadyen, "The Mosaic Origin of the Decalogue," *Exp, 8th Ser.,* 11 (1916) 152-160, 222-231, 311-320, 384-400; 12 (1916) 37-59, 105-117, 210-221. [V. The Relation of the Decalogue to Prophecy, pp. 105-110]

*I. G. Matthews, "How to Interpret Old Testament Prophecy," *BW* 52 (1918) 326-334.

*G. A. Cooke, "Palestine and the Restoration of Israel: A Study in Prophecy," *Exp, 8th Ser.,*15 (1918) 81-90.

J[ohn] M[erlin] Powis Smith, "Southern Influences upon Hebrew Prophecy," *AJSL* 35 (1918-19) 1-19.

Elcanon Isaacs, "The Metrical Basis of Hebrew Prophecy," *AJSL* 35 (1918-19) 20-54.

J[ohn] M[erlin] Powis Smith, "The Conservatism of Early Prophecy," *AJT* 23 (1919) 290-299.

I. G. Matthews, "How to Interpret Old Testament Prophecy," *BW* 53 (1919) 87-112, 206-226, 328-336.

Anonymous, "What place has Prophecy in the Bible?" *CFL, 3rd Ser.,* 25 (1919) 16-18.

J. J. Lias, "The Evidence of Fulfilled Prophecy," *BS* 77 (1920) 23-45, 204-220.

*Anonymous, "The Restoration of Palestine to the Jews and Prophecy," *MR* 103 (1920) 651-657.

*Walter F. Adeney, "Miracle and Prophecy," *HJ* 19 (1920-21) 133-142.

James Flynn, "The Nature of Old Testament Prophecy," *IER, 5th Ser.*, 17 (1921) 271-282.

Neil E. Stevens, "Botanical Figures in Biblical Prophecy," *MR* 104 (1921) 419-425.

H. C. Ackerman, "The Nature of Hebrew Prophecy," *ATR* 4 (1921-22) 97-127.

Robert Hull, "Compenetration in Prophecy," *IER, 5th Ser.*, 20 (1922) 594-601.

J. L. Ernst, "Psychology of Prophecy," *TZDES* 50 (1922) 429-433.

*Elihu Grant, "Oracle in the Old Testament," *AJSL* 39 (1922-23) 257-281.

*J. M. T. Winther, "Prophet and Prophecy," *BR* 8 (1923) 213-228, 400-416.

*Albion R. King, "Prophet and Apocalypticism," *MR* 107 (1924) 852-866.

Kyle M. Yates, "The Supernatural in Prophecy," *R&E* 21 (1924) 3-18.

*Innes Logan, "Prophecy and Sacrifice; A Note," *Exp, 9th Ser.*, 3 (1925) 62-65.

H. Gressmann, "Foreign Influences in Hebrew Prophecy," *JTS* 27 (1925-26) 241-254.

A. H. Finn, "The Predictive Element in Holy Scripture," *JTVI* 59 (1927) 165-178, 186-187. [(Discussion, pp. 178-186) (Communications by G. Mackinlay, p. 187; L. M. Davies, pp. 187-189)]

*George Boddis, "Prophecy as an Evidence of Divine Revelation," *CFL, 3rd Ser.*, 34 (1928) 483-489.

Herbert Waldo Hines, "The Development of the Psychology Prophecy," *JR* 8 (1928) 212-224.

*John Paterson, "Some Ethical Insights of Prophecy," *RL* 1 (1932) 540-550.

W. A. Maier, "Hebrew Prophecy a Unique Divine Bestowal," *CTM* 5 (1934) 199-205.

*John Paterson, "Prophecy and Asceticism," *RL* 3 (1934) 209-211.

*Charles E. Raven, "Inspiration and Prophecy," *MC* 24 (1934-35) 385-396.

Sigmund Mowinckel, "Ecstatic Experience and Rational Elaboration in Old Testament Prophecy," *AO* 13 (1935) 264-291.

John H. Bennetch, "The Apologetic Argument from Fulfilled Prophecy," *BS* 93 (1936) 348-354.

Nelson B. Baker, "Important Considerations in the Interpretation of Old Testament Prophecy," *CRP* 6 (1937) 298-307.

Edward D. Myers, "The Psychology of Prophecy," *JAAR* 5 (1937) 55-62.

E[dward] D. Myers, "The Psychology of Prophecy," *JBL* 56 (1937) x-xi.

George W. Anderson, "A Swedish Study of Hebrew Prophecy," *ET* 50 (1938-39) 562-563.

*H. Th. Obbink, "The Forms of Prophetism," *HUCA* 14 (1939) 23-28.

*H. Hamann, "Prophecy and War," *AusTR* 11 (1940) 55-57.

J. Ribberbos, "The Nature of Prophecy," *EQ* 12 (1940) 112-122.

Harry Austryn Wolfson, "Hallevi and Maimonides on Prophecy," *JQR, N.S.,* 32 (1941-42) 345-370.

*H. Wheeler Robinson, "Hebrew Sacrifice and Prophetic Symbolism," *OSHTP* (1941-42) 26-27.

*H. Wheeler Robinson, "Hebrew Sacrifice and Prophetic Symbolism," *JTS* 43 (1942) 129-139.

Harry Austryn Wolfson, "Hallevi and Maimonides on Prophecy," *JQR, N.S.,* 33 (1942-43) 49-82. (Corrections, p. 264)

H. H. Rowley, "The Nature of Prophecy in the Light of Recent Study," *OSHTP* (1942-43) 32-35.

Lewis Sperry Chafer, "An Introduction to the Study of Prophecy," *BS* 100 (1943) 98-133. [1. The Period Represented by the Old Testament, pp. 109f.]

F. C. Synge, "Prophecy and 'Prenouncement'," *CQR* 136 (1943) 36-58.

Harold Knight, "The Problem of Divine Passibility and Prophetic Theology," *Theo* 46 (1943) 25-32.

H. H. Rowley, "The Nature of Prophecy in the Light of Recent Study," *HTR* 38 (1945) 1-38.

C. C. McCown, "In History or Beyond History," *HTR* 38 (1945) 151-175. [V. The Dilemma of the Prophets, pp. 162-166]

*Nahum Norbert Glatzer, "A Study of the Talmudic Interpretation of Prophecy," *RR* 10 (1945-46) 115-137.

J. C. Whitney, "The Origins of Prophecy," *BQL* 12 (1946-48) 173-178.

*W. Norman Pittenger, "God and the World: Their Relationship as Seen in Jewish Prophecy," *ATR* 29 (1947) 57-61.

*Claude Sauerbrei, "The Holy Man in Israel: A Study in the Development of Prophecy," *JNES* 6 (1947) 209-218.

*G. R. Beasley-Murray, "Biblical Eschatology: The Interpretation of Prophecy," *EQ* 20 (1948) 221-240.

Roderic Dunkerley, "Prophecy and Prediction," *ET* 61 (1949-50) 260-263.

*P. P. Saydon, "Old Testament Prophecy and Messias Prophecies," *Scrip* 4 (1949-51) 335-339.

*W. Glyn Evans, "Will Babylon Be Restored?" *BS* 107 (1950) 335-342, 481-487.

*John Bowman, "Prophets and Prophecy in Talmud and Midrash," *EQ* 22 (1950) 107-114, 205-220, 255-275.

William E. Hulme, "The Psychology of Religious Prophecy," *LC, N.S.,* 2 (1950) 202-206.

Merrill F. Unger, "The Character of Old Testament Prophecy," *BS* 108 (1951) 167-171.

S. B. Gurewicz, "Prophecy in Israel," *ABR* 2 (1952) 29-41.

Charles Henry Murphy, "God and the Gentiles," *BS* 109 (1952) 364-373. *[Marked as 'to be continued' but was not]*

Peter W. Stoner, "Probability in Biblical Prophecy," *JASA* 4 (1952) #4, 3-5.

*C. R. Milley, "The Word of Yahweh—Its Implications in OT Prophecy," *JBL* 71 (1952) x.

*R. J. Zwi Werblowsky, "The Rebuilding of the Temple and the Re-introduction of Sacrifice in the Light of Rabbinical Judaism," *Theo* 56 (1953) 82-88.

*Th. C. Vriezen, "Prophecy and Eschatology," *VTS* 1 (1953) 199-229.

Th. C. Vriezen, "Hope in the Old Testament," *HTS* 10 (1953-54) 145-155.

R. C. Fuller, "Prophecy in Israel," *Scrip* 6 (1953-54) 108-111.

I. H. Seeligmann, "The Problems of Prophecy in Israel. Its Development and Characteristics," *EI* 3 (1954) VII.

*R. B. Y. Scott, "Is Preaching Prophecy?" *CJT* 1 (1955) 11-18.

Robert E. Bornemann, "On Prophecy and Fulfillment," *LQ, N.S.,* 7 (1955) 329-338.

*Martin Burber, "Prophecy, Apocalyptic and the Historical Hour," *USQR* 12 (1956-57) #3, 9-21.

Robert D. Culber, "The Difficulty of Interpreting Old Testament Prophecy," *BS* 114 (1957) 201-205.

L. P. Altus, "The Psychological Viewpoint of the Visions and Dreams in the Bible," *AusTR* 29 (1958) 61-67.

Hugh B. MacLean, "True and False in Old Testament Prophecy," *RefR* 12 (1958-59) #3, 11-23.

*L. Johnston, "Prophecy and History," *CIR* 44 (1959) 602-615.

*Benjamin B. Dayton, "Numerical Codes in Bible Prophecy," *JASA* 11 (1959) #3, 6-11.

Wilhelm C. Linss, "Prediction and Fulfillment," *LQ, N.S.,* 11 (1959) 237-243.

Theodore H. Robinson, "Prophecy," *LQHR* 184 (1959) 32-37.

*S. du Toit, "Relevant Principles in Connection with the Exegesis of the Old Testament Prophecies, with special reference to the Future of Israel," *OTW* 2 (1959) 1-5.

Walter C. Klein, "A Broad Survey of Prophetism," *ATR* 42 (1960) 278-299.

*Bruce Vawter, "Apocalyptic: Its Relation to Prophecy," *CBQ* 22 (1960) 33-46.

John J. Castelot, "The Spirit of Prophecy: An Abiding Charism," *CBQ* 23 (1961) 210-217.

Ralph H. Elliott, "Old Testament Prophecy," *R&E* 58 (1961) 407-416.

*E. W. Heaton, "Prophecy and wisdom," *OSHTP* (1962-63) 4-5.

Peter L. Berger, "Charisma and Religious Innovation: The Social Location of Israelite Prophecy," *AmSR* 28 (1963) 940-950.

Charles L. Feinberg, "God's Message to Man Through the Prophets. I. The Commanding Importance of the Prophetic Scriptures," *GJ* 5 (1964) #2, 3-9.

Charles L. Feinberg, "God's Message to Man Through the Prophets. II. The Prophetic Word and Israel," *GJ* 5 (1964) #2, 10-15.

Charles L. Feinberg, "God's Message to Man Through the Prophets. III. The Prophetic Word and the Nations," *GJ* 5 (1964) #2, 16-20.

*Sten H. Stenson, "Prophecy, Theology, and Philosophy," *JR* 44 (1964) 17-28.

Aug. Pieper, "The Perspective of Old Testament Prophecy," *JTLC* 4 (1964) #2, 16-20.

*Allan A. MacRae, "Abraham and the Stars," *JASA* 17 (1965) 65-67.

G. Ernest Wright, "The Nations in Hebrew Prophecy," *SQ/E* 26 (1965) 225-237.

G. Van Groningen, "The Gift of Tongues in the Old Testament," *VR* #4 (1965) 3-19.

*Abraham Malamat, "Prophetic revelations in the new documents from Mari and the Bible," *VTS* 15 (1965) 207-227.

*E. Reim, "Seasonal Psalms and Prophecy," *JTLC* 6 (1966) #5, 1-5.

T. Miles Bennett, "Hebrew Prophecy," *SWJT, N.S.,* 9 (1966-67) #1, 7-20.

*John H. Hayes, "Prophetism at Mari and Old Testament Parallels," *ATR* 49 (1967) 397-409.

Rolf Rendtorff, "Reflections on the Early History of Prophecy in Israel," *JTC* 4 (1967) 14-34.

*Ian M. Blake, "Jericho (Ain Es-Sultan): Joshua's Curse and Elisha's Miracle—One Possible Explanation," *PEQ* 99 (1967) 86-97.

*Jimmy J. Roberts, "Antecedents to Biblical Prophecy from the Mari Archives," *RestQ* 10 (1967) 121-133.

G. M. Lee, "A Note on Old Testament Prophecies," *ET* 79 (1967-68) 22.

*John H. Hayes, "Prophetism at Mari and Old Testament Parallels," *TUSR* 9 (1967-69) 31-42.

John H. Hayes, "The Usage of Oracles Against Foreign Nations in Ancient Israel," *TUSR* 9 (1967-69) 43-58.

*George Eldon Ladd, "The Hermeneutics of Prophecy," *ASW* 22 (1968) #2, 14-18.

John H. Hayes, "The Usage of Oracles Against Foreign Nations in Ancient Israel," *JBL* 87 (1968) 81-92.

Paul Malashevitz, "The Ecstatic Element in Old Testament Prophecy," *DTCW* 6 (1968-69) #1, 81-99.

*Clyde J. Hurst, "Guidelines for Interpreting Old Testament Prophecy Applied to Isaiah 40-66," *SWJT, N.S.,* 11 (1968-69) #1, 29-44.

*P. Grech, "Interprophetic Re-interpretation and Old Testament Eschatology," *Aug* 9 (1969) 235-265.

W. L. Moran, "New Evidence from Mari on the History of Prophecy," *B* 50 (1969) 15-56.

Charles H. Miller, "The Background of Prophecy," *BibT* #40 (1969) 2757-2764.

James G. Williams, "The Social Location of Israelite Prophecy," *JAAR* 37 (1969) 153-165.

§1031 *5.4.17 Studies on Eschatology*

*F. W. Farrar, "Rabbinic Eschatology," *Exp, 1st Ser.,* 7 (1878) 295-317.

Edwin Cone Bissell, "Eschatology of the Old Testament," *BS* 36 (1879) 320-341.

Anonymous, "Brief Outline of the Scripture Eschatology," *BWR* 3 (1881) 101-104.

Philip Schaff, "Studies in Eschatology," *PR* 4 (1883) 723-743. [The Jewish Eschatology, pp. 723-726]

J. B. Bittinger, "The Eschatology of the Psalms," *AR* 2 (1884) 225-246.

Th. Kliefoth, "The Sources of Eschatology," *LCR* 7 (1888) 47-68.

*George B. Stevens, "Weber on the Eschatology of the Talmud," *ONTS* 8 (1888-89) 4-6, 45-49, 85-88, 140-143.

M. Wolkenberg, "The Eschatology of the Rabbinic contemporaries of Our Lord," *EN* 3 (1891) 49-57 145-150, 193-197.

A. W. Goodnow, "The Jews and Eschatology," *BQR* 14 (1892) 443-454.

G. Deutsch, "Eschatology of the Jews until the Close of the Talmud," *YCCAR* 4&5 (1892-95) 100-111.

A. B. Davidson, "The Eschatology of Isaiah," *ET* 5 (1893-94) 438-442.

D. H. Bolles, "The Eschatology of the Book of Job," *HR* 28 (1894) 175-180, 264-269.

Marcus Dods, "Der Antichrist in der ueberlieferung des judenthums, des Neuen Testaments, und der alten Kirche," *LCR* 18 (1899) 414-417. ["The Antichrist in Jewish Tradition, the New Testament and the Ancient Church" - *English Text*]

A. C. Watson, "Old Testament Eschatology," *GUOST* 2 (1901-07) 13-14.

John Alfred Faulkner, "The End of the World," *HR* 42 (1901) 542-545.

*S. D. F. Salmond, "The Immortality of the Soul and the Scripture Doctrine of the Last Things," *LQHR* 98 (1902) 140-160. *(Review)*

*Lewis A. Muirhead, "The Eschatology of 4 Esdras," *ET* 18 (1906-07) 406-409. *(Review)*

*L[awrence H.] Mills, "Exilic Jewish Eschatology: In How Far was it Zoroastrianism," *IAQR, 3rd Ser.*, 23 (1907) 98-105.

*G. Buchanan Gray, "The Heavenly Temple and the Heavenly Altar," *Exp, 7th Ser.*, 5 (1908) 385-402, 530-546.

Benjamin W. Bacon, "Jewish Eschatology and the Teaching of Jesus," *BW* 34 (1909) 15-25.

*Anonymous, "Eschatology and the Kingdom of Heaven," *CQR* 69 (1909-10) 84-113.

Martin O'Ryan, "Eschatology of the Old Testament," *IER, 4th Ser.*, 27 (1910) 472-486.

*W. V. Hauge, "The Eschatology of the Apocryphal Scriptures," *JTS* 12 (1910-11) 57-98.

A. C. Welch, "Old Testament Eschatology," *ET* 24 (1912-13) 208-210. *(Review)*

William Watson, "Survey of Recent Literature on Biblical Eschatology," *RTP* 9 (1913-14) 125-136.

I. Abrahams, "Pharisaic Eschatology," *OSHTP* (1914-15) 32-34.

H. R. Mackintosh, "Eschatology in the Old Testament and Judaism," *Exp, 8th Ser.*, 10 (1915) 47-65.

*William Watson, "The New Heaven and the New Earth," *Exp, 8th Ser.*, 9 (1915) 165-179.

*J. Agar Beet, "Greek Eschatology, a Needful Preparation for the Gospel of Christ," *IJA* #41 (1915) 23-26.

A. H. T. Clarke, "The Fulfillment of Prophecy," *JTVI* 48 (1916) 85-87. (Discussion, pp. 87-91)

Herbert H. Gowen, "The Eschatology of the Old Testament," *ATR* 2 (1919-20) 195-208.

Geerhardus Vos, "Eschatology of the Psalter," *PTR* 18 (1920) 1-43.

N. Schmidt, "The Origin of Jewish Eschatology," *JBL* 61 (1922) 102-114.

*L. Ginzberg, "Some Observations on the Attitude of the Synagogue Towards the Apocalyptic-Eschatological Writings," *JBL* 41 (1922) 115-136.

*A. J. Wensinck, "The Semitic New Year and the Origin of Eschatology," *AO* 1 (1922-23) 158-199.

*Ed[uard] König, "The Messianic Prophecies and Popular Eschatology," *MR* 106 (1923) 963-968.

A. N. Wilder, "The Nature of Jewish Eschatology," *JBL* 50 (1931) 201-206.

W. K. Lowther Clarke, "The Clouds of Heaven: An Eschatological Study," *Theo* 31 (1935) 63-72, 128-141. *[OT Refs., pp. 63-72]*

*C. L. E. Hoopmann, "The Meaning of the Term, 'The Last Times'," *AusTR* 7 (1936) 7-12. *[OT Refs, Deut. 4:30; Isa. 2:2; Micah 4:1; Joel 2:28-32]*

George Ricker Berry, "The Future in the Later Prophets," *JAAR* 8 (1940) 82-84. (Editorial Note, pp. 89-90)

*John F. Walvoord, "The Eschatology of the Holy Spirit," *BS* 99 (1942) 418-427.

*John Derby, "History and Eschatology," *Theo* 44 (1942) 90-99.

J. A. Thompson, "Some Elements of Jewish Eschatology in the Book of Joel," *JBL* 66 (1947) xi.

*G. R. Beasley-Murray, "Biblical Eschatology: The Interpretation of Prophecy," *EQ* 20 (1948) 221-240.

‡H. H. Rowley, "Recent Foreign Theology. The God Who Comes," *ET* 60 (1948-49) 110. *(Review)*

‡H. H. Rowley, "Recent Foreign Theology. Old Testament Eschatology," *ET* 60 (1948-49) 168. *(Review)*

John Baillie, "Beliefs About the Last Things," *CongQL* 28 (1950) 206-218.

*Robert E. D. Clark, "Prophecy and Psychical Research," *JTVI* 83 (1951) 137-148, 156-157. [(Discussion, pp. 149-152) (Communications by J. Stafford Wright, pp. 152-153; F. F. Bruce, pp. 153-154; L. D. Ford, pp. 154-155; L. Merson Davies, pp. 155-156)]

G. A. F. Knight, " Eschatology in the Old Testament," *SJT* 4 (1951) 355-362.

*M. A. C. Warren, "Eschatology and History," *IRM* 41 (1952) 337-350.

S. B. Frost, "Eschatology and Myth," *VT* 2 (1952) 70-80.

*Th. C. Vriezen, "Prophecy and Eschatology," *VTS* 1 (1953) 199-229.

Alan Champion, "The Eschatological Treatment of Time and Eternity," *CongQL* 32 (1954) 151-164.

John Bowman, "Early Samaritan Eschatology," *JJS* 6 (1955) 63-72.

F. F. Bruce, " Eschatology," *LQHR* 183 (1958) 99-103. *[OT Refs., pp. 99-100]*

I. Baer, "On the Problem of Eschatological Doctrine During the Period of the Second Temple," *Zion* 23&24 (1958-59) #1/2, I-II.

I. Baer, "On the Problem of Eschatological Doctrine During the Period of the Second Temple. Dialectics and Mysticism in the Founding of the Halacha," *Zion* 23&24 (1958-59) #3/4, II-III.

*Brevard S. Childs, "The Enemy from the North and the Chaos Tradition," *JBL* 78 (1959) 187-198.

Thomas J. J. Altizer, "The Religious Foundations of Biblical Eschatology," *JR* 39 (1959) 263-273.

*Bruce Vawter, "Apocalyptic: Its Relation to Prophecy," *CBQ* 22 (1960) 33-46. [What Is Eschatology? pp. 37-41]

*David N. Freedman, "History and Eschatology. *The Nature of Biblical Religion and Prophetic Faith*," *Interp* 14 (1960) 143-154.

*Charles De Santo, "God and Gog," *RL* 30 (1960-61) 112-117.

W. F. Stinespring, "Eschatology in Chronicles," *JBL* 80 (1961) 209-219.

George Wesley Buchanan, "Eschatology and the 'End of Days'," *JNES* 20 (1961) 188-193.

*John P. Newport, "Biblical Interpretation and Eschatological-Holy History," *SWJT, N.S.,* 4 (1961) #1, 83-110.

A. S. Kapelrud, "Eschatology in the Book of Micah," *VT* 11 (1961) 392-405.

*Arthur L. Merrill, "The Old Testament and the Future," *MHSB* 7 (1962) #1, 3-14. [Eschatology, pp. 10-13]

*H. Kosmala, "At the End of the Days," *ASTI* 2 (1963) 27-37.

*A. R. C. Leaney, "The Eschatological Significance of Human Suffering in the Old Testament and the Dead Sea Scrolls," *SJT* 16 (1963) 286-296.

Heinrich Gross, "Eschatology in the Old Testament," *TD* 12 (1964) 196-200.

*J. Licht, "Time and Eschatology in Apocalyptic Literature and in Qumran," *JJS* 16 (1965) 177-182.

*R. J. Taylor, "The Eschatological Meaning of Life and Death in the Book of Wisdom, I-IV," *ETL* 42 (1966) 72-137.

Richard H. Hiers, "Eschatology and Methodology," *JBL* 85 (1966) 170-184.

George Wesley Buchanan, "Sabbatical Eschatology," *CNI* 18 (1967) #3/4, 49-55.

*David J. Ellis, "Biblical Apocalyptic and Prophecy," *F&T* 96 (1967) #3, 27-40.

*David F. Payne, "The Place of Daniel in Old Testament Eschatology," *Them* 4 (1967) #1, 33-40.

Hershel J. Matt, "An Outline of Jewish Eschatology," *Jud* 17 (1968) 186-196.

*J. Coert Rylaarsdam, "Jewish Hope and Christian Eschatology," *LTSB* 48 (1968) #2, 24-34.

*Jacob B. Agus, "Context and Challenge—A Response to Rylaarsdam," *LTSB* 48 (1968) #2, 35-44.

*B. J. van der Merwe, "'Actualizing Eschatology' in Isaiah 40-55," *TEP* 1 (1968) 16-18.

Lloyd Neve, "Realized Eschatology in Psalm 51," *ET* 80 (1968-69) 264-266.

*P. Grech, "Interprophetic Re-interpretation and Old Testament Eschatology," *Aug* 9 (1969) 235-265.

*Alan D. Crown, "Theology, Eschatology and Law in Samaritan Funeral Rites and Liturgy," *GUOST* 23 (1969-70) 86-101.

Bruce L. Smith, "The Bible and Eschatology," *Inter* 2 (1969-70) 67-73. *[OT Refs., pp. 69-71]*

§1032 **5.4.17.1 Studies concerning "The Kingdom"**

Charles Elliott, "The Messianic Kingdom," *PR* 3 (1882) 225-240.

F. B. Denio, "The Kingdom of God in the Old Testament," *ONTS* 6 (1886-87) 55-58, 71-76.

J. W. Walden, "The Kingdom of God. Its Millennial Dispensation," *CFL, O.S.,* 2 (1898) 8-11, 31-34, 55-58.

A. Robertson, "'The Kingdom of God in the Old Testament'," *ET* 14 (1902-03) 159-160. *(Review)*

F. P. Ramsay, "The Kingdom of God in the Old Testament," *CFL, N.S.,* 8 (1903) 103-112.

George D. Castor, "The Kingdom of God in the Light of Jewish Literature," *BS* 66 (1909) 344-361.

A. Kampmeier, "The Jewish Expectation of God's Kingdom in Its Successive Stages," *OC* 25 (1911) 621-635.

William Watson, "The New Jerusalem," *ET* 25 (1913-14) 454-457.

William Watson, "The Temporal Blessings of the Messianic Kingdom," *IJA* #41 (1915) 31-36.

Hewlett Johnson, "The Editor's Notes," *ICMM* 12 (1915-16) 1-20, 111. *[The Kingdom of God]*

Norris Olson, "The Kingdom of God," *TTM* 9 (1925-26) 174-207, 264-284. [The Old Testament Conception of the Kingdom, pp. 176-185; The Jewish Conception of the Kingdom, pp. 185-188]

*Allen H. Godbey, "The Pagan Millennium," *MR* 109 (1926) 581-601, 755-773. [II. A Millennium on Earth Not an Old Testament Teaching, pp. 582-585]

Earle Bennett Cross, "The Kingdom of God in the Old Testament," *CRDSB* 6 (1933-34) 216-233.

*J. W. Bailey, "The Temporary Messianic Reign in the Literature of Early Judaism," *JBL* 53 (1934) 170-187.

Daniel Curtis Troxel, "The Kingdom of God," *CollBQ* 15 (1938) #1, 6-21.

R. T. Stamm, "On Earth, as It is in Heaven," *LCQ* 12 (1939) 168-182.

Walter H. Koenig, "New Testament Light on Old Testament 'Mellennialistic' Prophecies," *CTM* 19 (1948) 81-92.

Robert M. Grant, "The Coming of the Kingdom," *JBL* 67 (1948) 297-303.

*George E. Ladd, "The Kingdom of God in the Jewish Apocryphal Literature," *BS* 109 (1952) 55-62.

*George E. Ladd, "The Kingdom of God in Jubilees," *BS* 109 (1952) 164-174.

*George E. Ladd, "The Kingdom of God in I Enoch," *BS* 109 (1952) 318-331; 110 (1953) 32-49.

John F. Walvoord, "A Review of Crucial Questions about the Kingdom of God," *BS* 110 (1953) 1-10.

Norman Snaith, "The Kingdom of God," *PQL* 1 (1954-55) 402-407.

Alva J. McClain, "The Greatness of the Kingdom," *BS* 112 (1955) 11-27, 107-124, 209-224, 304-310.

Alphin C. Conrad, "The Kingdom Hope of Israel In The Old Testament," *BSQ* 6 (1957-58) #2, 4-12.

M. Z. Segal, "The Golden Age in the Vision of the Prophets," *Tarbiz* 27 (1957-58) #1, I-II.

G. Henton Davies, "The Clues of the Kingdom in the Bible. *A Survey,*" *Interp* 14 (1960) 155-160.

*Niel Middleton, "God's Kingdom and his Judgment," *LofS* 17 (1962-63) 162-171. *[OT Refs., pp. 162-166]*

Yonina Talmon, "Millenarian Movements," *EJS* 7 (1966) 159-200.

§1033 *5.4.17.2 Studies on the Judgment of God*

T. W. Chambers, "The Biblical Doctrine of Divine Judgment," *PR* 8 (1887) 519-525.

C. G. Montefiore, "The Doctrine of Divine Retribution in the Old Testament, the New Testament, and the Rabbinical Literature," *JQR* 3 (1890-91) 1-12. [I. The Old Testament]

*S. Schechter, "The Doctrine of Divine Retribution in the New Testament and the Rabbinical Literature," *JQR* 3 (1890-91) 34-51. [III. Rabbinical Literature]

*C. G. Montefiore, "Hebrew and Greek Ideas on Providence and Divine Retribution," *JQR* 5 (1892-93) 517-590.

Frank J. Goodwin, "The Biblical Doctrine of Divine Justice," *HR* 47 (1904) 51-56.

William L. Sullivan, "Judgment Day in Jewish Thought," *NYR* 1 (1905-06) 728-738.

William Watson, "The Last Judgment," *ET* 27 (1915-16) 316-319.

*Joseph Rauch, "Apocalypse in the Bible," *JJLP* 1 (1919) 163-195. [II. "Day of Judgment", p. 167]

Simon Blocker, "God's Redemptive Judgments," *RefR* 5 (1951-52) #1, 1-2.

*John L. McKenzie, "The Judge of All the Earth," *Way* 2 (1962) 209-218.

*Neil Middleton, "God's Kingdom and his Judgment," *LofS* 17 (1962-63) 162-171. *[OT Refs., pp. 162-166]*

S. G. F. Brandon, "The Judgment of the Dead: The Dawn of Man's Moral Consciousness," *HT* 14 (1964) 564-573.

*E. C. John, "Forgiveness in the Prophecy of Judgment," *IJT* 18 (1969) 206-218.

§1034 5.4.17.3 Studies on the Day of Yahweh

*Willis J. Beecher, "'The Day of Jehovah' in Joel," *HR* 18 (1889) 355-358.

Willis J. Beecher, "The Doctrine of the Day of Jehovah Before Joel's Time," *HR* 18 (1889) 449-451.

*Willis J. Beecher, "The Doctrine of the Day of Jehovah in Obadiah and Amos," *HR* 19 (1890) 157-160.

G. E. Ffrench, "The Day of the Lord," *ET* 4 (1892-93) 383-384.

John M. P. Smith, "The Day of Yahweh," *AJT* 5 (1901) 505-533.

A. S. Carrier, "The Day of Jehovah," *CFL, N.S.,* 5 (1902) 46-51.

*Andrew Baird, "'The Day of Jahve' in the Old Testament Prophets," *GUOST* 4 (1913-22) 35-37.

*Joseph Rauch, "Apocalypse in the Bible," *JJLP* 1 (1919) 163-195. [III. יהוה יום‎—National Aspect, pp. 168-173; IV. יהוה יום‎—Individual as Combined with National Aspect, pp. 173-176]

*W. W. Cannon, "'The Day of the Lord' in Joel," *CQR* 103 (1926-27) 32-63.

*R. E. Wolfe, "The Day of Yahweh Editor in the Book of the Twelve," *JBL* 54 (1935) iii.

Norman Snaith, "The Day of the Lord," *PQL* 1 (1954-55) 304-309.

Devlin Hutton, "'The Day of the Lord'," *Amb* 6 (1957-58) #5, 19-25. [1. 'Yom Yahweh' 'The Day of Thy Lord' in the Old Testament, pp. 20-22]

G[erhard] von Rad, "The Origin of the Concept of the Day of Yahweh," *JSS* 4 (1959) 97-108.

Warren Vanhetloo, "Old Testament Passages Referring to the Day of the Lord," *CCBQ* 5 (1962) #4, 7-16.

George Mark Elliott, "Modern Views of the Origin and Nature of the Day of Yahweh," *SR* 11 (1964-65) 35-78.

Meir Weiss, "The Origin of the 'Day of the Lord'—Reconsidered," *HUCA* 37 (1966) 29-60.

F. C. Fensham, "A possible origin of the concept of the Day of the Lord," *OTW* 9 (1966) 90-97.

John P. Comiskey, "The Day of Yahweh—divine judgment unto wrath or mercy," *BibT* #32 (1967) 2214-2220.

Ralph W. Klein, "The Day of the Lord," *CTM* 39 (1968) 517-525.

*Victor Eppstein, "The Day of Yahweh in Jeremiah 4:23-28," *JBL* 87 (1968) 93-97.

*Patrick D. Miller Jr., "The Divine Council and the Prophetic Call to War," *VT* 18 (1968) 100-107.

§1035 *5.4.18 Studies concerning the Future State, Immortality (Life after Death; The Future Life; Paradise; Future Punishment, etc.)*

'Maro', "Is the doctrine of a future state of rewards and punishments taught in the Old Testament?" *QCS* 3 (1821) 505-511.

†Anonymous, "Scripture Revelations concerning a Future State," *BCQTR, 4th Ser.,* 9 (1831) 1-43. *(Review)*

Anonymous, "Is a Future State of Happiness and Misery Revealed in the Old Testament?" *SP* 4 (1831) 305-311.

†Anonymous, "Mills, on the Belief in a Future State," *BCQTR, 4th Ser.,* 11 (1832) 90-117. *(Review)*

E. R. B., On Immortality," *CTPR, N.S.,* 1 (1838-39) 562-572.

Enoch Pond, "The Intermediate Place," *BRCR, N.S.,* 5 (1841) 464-478.

Isaac Robinson, "Did the Old Testament Saints believe in a future state of rewards and punishments?" *BJ* 1 (1842) 233-241.

*Asahal Abbot, "The Doctrine of Man's Immortality, and of the Eternal Punishment of the Wicked, as Set Forth in the Ancient Scriptures," *BRCR, 3rd Ser.,* 5 (1849) 618-635.

George I. Chace, "Doctrine of the Resurrection of the Dead," *BS* 6 (1849) 48-75.

W. R. A., "The Hebrew Doctrine of a Future Life," *CE* 60 (1856) 1-29.

E. P. Barrows, "The Scriptural Doctrine of a Future State," *BS* 15 (1858) 625-661.

S. Tuska, "Did the Ancient Hebrews Believe in the Doctrine of Immortality?" *BS* 17 (1860) 787-816.

Anonymous, "Daniel versus Zoroaster," *CR* 16 (1864-65) 355-370. *(Review)*

*Geo. S. Morris, "The Immortality of the Human Soul," *BS* 33 (1876) 695-715.

John Fenton, "Miscellanea Theologica. II. The Jewish Idea of Existence after Death, illustrated from Assyrian Mythology," *TRL* 13 (1876) 299-301.

Anonymous, "Doctrine of a Future State in the Pentateuch," *BWR* 1 (1877) 268-269.

Henry Cowles, "Future Punishment of the Wicked as Revealed in the Old Testament," *BS* 35 (1878) 514-543.

M. Gregoire, "The Belief of the Hebrews in the Immortality of the Soul," *BQR* 1 (1879) 411-439. *[Trans. with notes by W. H. H. Marsh]*

John F. Kendall, "The After-World," *PR* 1 (1880) 694-712.

H. O. Rowlands, "The Doctrine of the Future Life in the Old Testament," *ONTS* 3 (1883-84) 329-340.

A. A. Pfanstiehl, "The Old Testament and Future Life," *ONTS* 3 (1883-84) 389-392.

George F. Moore, "The Future Life in the Old Testament," *AR* 2 (1884) 433-455, 516-518.

James T. Bixby, "Immortality and Science," *BS* 41 (1884) 44-67.

Samuel Cox, "The Hope of Immortality: Jewish and Christian," *Exp, 2nd Ser.,* 8 (1884) 28-53.

Llewellyn T. Evans, "Biblical Doctrine of the Intermediate State," *PR* 8 (1887) 325-333. *[OT Refs., pp. 326-328]*

*D. Castelli, "The Future Life in Rabbinic Literature," *JQR* 1 (1888-89) 314-352.

Wm. H. Laird, "The Old Testament and the Future State," *PER* 2 (1888-89) 345-351.

Charles D. W. Bridgman, "Immortality in the Old Testament Scriptures," *CT* 7 (1889-90) 415-420.

Charles A. Briggs, "The Middle State in the Old Testament," *HR* 19 (1890) 20-26.

L. M. Simmons, "Sleep and Death," *JQR* 3 (1890-91) 366.

J. J. McElhinney, "The Intermediate State," *PER* 4 (1890-91) 221-234. [I. The Doctrine in the Holy Scripture, pp. 221-228]

*Anonymous, "The Future Life in Egypt and Israel," *ONTS* 13 (1891) 120-121.

Milton S. Terry, "The Hebrew Doctrine of the Future Life," *BWi* 2 (1893) 87-91.

*William Hayes Ward, "Light on Texts from Recent Discoveries. VII. The Immortality of the Soul in the Inscription of Panammu I," *HR* 26 (1893) 127-128.

*William Hayes Ward, "Light on Texts from Recent Discoveries. XI. The Shades of the Dead: Rephaim and Teraphim," *HR* 26 (1893) 508-510.

*J. B. Remesnyder, "Job xix. 25-27 and Immortality and Resurrection in the Old Testament," *HR* 28 (1894) 463-465.

*Nathaniel Schmidt, "Immortality and the Hadad Statue," *JBL* 13 (1894) 16-18.

*Thomas Stoughton Potwin, "Ideas of the Future Life in the Pentateuch," *BS* 52 (1895) 423-438.

A. B. Davidson, "Modern Religion and Old Testament Immortality," *Exp, 5th Ser.,* 1 (1895) 321-333.

*Samuel Plantz, "Doctrine of the Future Life in the Book of Job," *MR* 78 (1896) 45-59.

Samuel Holmes, "The Doctrine of Immortality in the Old Testament in the Light of Higher Criticism," *WR* 145 (1896) 92-97.

A. B. Davidson, "The Old Testament Doctrine of Immortality," *ET* 8 (1896-97) 10-14. *(Review)*

A. Roberts, "On the Knowledge of a Future State Possessed by the Ancient Hebrews," *Exp, 5th Ser.,* 5 (1897) 377-389.

J. C. Jacoby, "The Scripture View of Immortality," *LQ* 28 (1898) 406-419.

A[ngus] C[rawford], "Notes—Critical. Immortality," *PER* 13 (1899-1900) 113.

T. McK. Stuart, "Immortality in the Old Testament," *MR* 82 (1900) 21-33.

Arthur Metcalf, "The Evolution of the Belief in the World Beyond the Grave," *BW* 17 (1901) 339-346.

*Paul Carus, "The Babylonian and Hebrew Views of Man's Fate after Death," *OC* 15 (1901) 346-366.

C. G. Montefiore, "The Desire for Immortality," *JQR* 14 (1901-02) 96-110.

Howard Osgood, "Resurrection 3000-4000 B.C. and the Old Testament," *BS* 59 (1902) 409-433.

*S. D. F. Salmond, "The Immortality of the Soul and the Scripture Doctrine of the Last Things," *LQHR* 98 (1902) 140-160. *(Review)*

R. H. Charles, "The Rise and Development in Israel of the Belief in a Future Life," *Exp, 6th Ser.,* 7 (1903) 49-64.

H. Peters, "Immortality in the Old Testament," *LCR* 23 (1904) 514-524.

Junius B. Remensynder, "The Intermediate State," *HR* 50 (1905) 358-360.

*S. M'Comb, "Immortality and Revelation," *LQHR* 103 (1905) 305-321. *(Review)*

R. H. Bennett, "The Immortal Hope in Reason and Scripture," *MQR, 3rd Ser.,* 32 (1906) 723-733.

*C. F. Burney, "The Rise of a Belief in a Future Life in Israel," *ICMM* 3 (1906-07) 240-256, 371-387; 4 (1907-08) 41-57, 156-174.

Henry Preserved Smith, "The Prechristian Hebrew Idea of Immortality," *HR* 53 (1907) 184-188.

David Purves, "The State of the Dead," *HJ* 6 (1907-08) 90-100.

*Crawford H. Toy, "The Future in Wisdom i.-v.," *IJA* #14 (1908) 13-14.

John D. Davis, "The Future Life in Hebrew Thought During the Pre-Persian Period," *PTR* 6 (1908) 246-268.

Lewis Bayles Paton, "The Hebrew Idea of the Future Life," *BW* 35 (1910) 8-20, 80-92, 159-171, 246-258, 339-352.

*F. Y. Leggatt, "Job's Contribution to the Problem of the Future State," *Exp, 7th Ser.,* 9 (1910) 326-340.

*Anonymous, "Early Christian Vision of the Other-world," *IJA* #26 (1911) 54-55; #29 (1912) 36-37. *(Review)*

Simeon Spindle, "The Belief in Immortality," *AJRPE* 5 (1912) 5-51.

W. M. Patton, "Views of Death and the Future Life in the 2nd Century B.C.," *IJA* #33 (1913) 26-30.

J. Agar Beet, "The Hereafter in the Bible and in Modern Thought," *HJ* 12 (1913-14) 837-855.

L. W. Grensted, "Immortality in the Old Testament," *ICMM* 11 (1914-15) 169-179.

C. J. Wright, "The Old Testament Conception of Immortality," *HR* 69 (1915) 261-267.

Howard N. Brown, "Immortality," *HTR* 8 (1915) 45-61.

*Hewlett Johnson, "The Editor's Notes," *ICMM* 12 (1915-16) 1-20, 111. *[Doctrine of a Future Life]*

D. S. Margoliouth, "Arguments from the Pentateuch for the Future Life," *Exp, 8th Ser.,* 20 (1920) 104-114.

Paul Haupt, "Abraham's Bosom," *AJP* 42 (1921) 162-167.

Samuel A. B. Mercer, "The Destiny of the Righteous in Israel," *ATR* 4 (1921-22) 185-191.

*E. H. Askwith, "The Hope of Immortality in the Psalter," *Exp, 8th Ser.,* 25 (1923) 74-80.

H. Wheeler Robinson, "The Old Testament Approach to Life After Death," *CongQL* 3 (1925) 138-151.

W. R. Matthews, "Recent Thought on the Doctrine of Immortality," *ET* 37 (1925-26) 437-441.

Samuel Gardiner Ayres, "The Eternal Soul Myth, Possibly in the Bible," *MR* 109 (1926) 789-799.

Herbert G. Wood, "Modern Science and the Hope of Immortality," *ET* 40 (1928-29) 25-27.

George Lindley Young, "The Old Testament and Immortality," *BS* 87 (1930) 266-283.

Georg Bertram, "The Problem of Death in Popular Judaeo-Hellenistic Piety," *CQ* 10 (1933) 257-287. *(Trans. by Morton S. Enslin)*

*J. B. Rowell, "Immortality," *BS* 92 (1935) 154-169.

*Michael J. Gruenthaner, "The Future Life in the Psalms," *CBQ* 2 (1940) 57-63.

Leon Nemoy, "Biblical Quasi-Evidence for the Transmigration of Souls," *JBL* 59 (1940) 159-168.

*John J. Weisengoff, "Death and Immortality in the Book of Wisdom," *CBQ* 3 (1941) 104-133.

*J. A. Montgomery, "Soul Gods," *HTR* 34 (1941) 321-322.

*Ovid R. Sellers, "Israelite Belief in Immortality," *BA* 8 (1945) 1-16. [Sources of Information; Beliefs of Primitive Peoples; Immortality among the Egyptians; Babylonian Beliefs; Canaanite Concepts; Immortality in the Old Testament; Archaeological Evidence; Conclusions]

Samuel M. Segel, "The Immortality of the Soul According to Judaism," *RL* 13 (1944) 562-567.

Louis Finkelstein, "The Jewish Doctrine of Human Immortality," *HDSB* 10 (1944-45) 5-34.

Walter G. Williams, "The Conception of Life after Death in the Old Testament," *IR* 2 (1945) 218-223, 258-268.

*Erwin R. Goodenough, "Philo on Immortality," *HTR* 39 (1946) 85-108.

Norman H. Snaith, "Life After Death. The Biblical Doctrine of Immortality," *Interp* 1 (1947) 309-324.

James E. Bear, "Is Man as Man Immortal? A Reply," *Interp* 1 (1947) 493-498.

E. F. Sutcliff, "The Future Life in the Old Testament," *Scrip* 2 (1947) 93-99; 3 (1948) 7-13.

Erland Ehnmark, "The Problem of Immortality," *HTR* 44 (1951) 1-23.

G. W. Murray, "Modern Approaches to the Doctrine of Immortality," *CQR* 153 (1952) 162-170.

Norman A. Logan, "The Old Testament and a Future Life," *SJT* 6 (1953) 165-172.

T. W. Manson, "The Bible and Personal Immortality," *CongQL* 32 (1954) 7-16.

*Donald H. Gard, "The Concept of the Future Life According to the Translator of the Book of Job," *JBL* 73 (1954) 137-143.

H. H. Rowley, "The Future Life in the Thought of the Old Testament," *CongQL* 33 (1955) 116-132.

*J Pedersen, "Wisdom and immortality," *VTS* 3 (1955) 238-246.

George Mark Elliott, "Future Life in the Old Testament," *SR* 3 (1956-57) 41-93.

H. W. F. Saggs, "Some Ancient Semitic Ideas on the Afterlife," *F&T* 90 (1958) 157-182.

*T. Worden, "Inerrancy and O.T. Teaching on Life After Death. I am aware that much of the Old Testament teaching has undergone development. But it would seem that what is said about life after death in such books as Sirach, Job, Qoheleth, and some of the Psalms is not simply imperfect, but positively erroneous. I can grant that the writers were not the beneficiaries of a complete revelation on this question, but these inspired authors have made very deliberate, positive judgments on the nature of the afterlife which are incompatible with revealed truth (Cf. Is. 38:18; Bar. 2:17; Job 10:21-22; Pss. 6:6; 88:6; 115:17; Qoh. 9:10). How do you explain the inerrancy of these inspired writings in this instance?" *Scrip* 10 (1958) 28-29.

Paul J. Schwab, "Immortality—A Complex and Evolving Theory in Hebrew Literature," *TUSR* 6 (1958-60) 51-65.

*M. Dahood, "Immortality in Prv 12, 28," *B* 41 (1960) 176-181.

*J. van der Ploeg, "The Belief in Immortality in the Writings of Qumrān," *BO* 18 (1961) 118-124.

Emmanuel Gitlin, "The Experience of Death. *A Biblical Response,*" *SQ/E* 22 (1961) 3-14.

John H. Otwell, "Immortality in the Old Testament. *A Review of the Evidence,*" *SQ/E* 22 (1961) 15-27.

Hans Jonas, "Immortality and Modern Temper," *HTR* 55 (1962) 1-20.

David Daube, "Death as a Release in the Bible," *NT* 5 (1962) 82-104.

*Arthur Maltby, "The Book of Ecclesiastes and the After-Life," *EQ* 35 (1963) 39-44.

*W. Wirgin, "The *Menorah* as a Symbol of After-Life," *IEJ* 14 (1964) 102-104.

Andrew F. Key, "The Concept of Death in Early Israelite Religion," *JAAR* 32 (1964) 239-247.

Norman H. Snaith, "Justice and Immortality," *SJT* 17 (1964) 309-324.

*Robert E. Bailey, "Is 'Sleep' the Proper Biblical Term for the Intermediate State?" *ZNW* 55 (1964) 161-167.

R. J. Wilson, "The Hope of Life Hereafter in the Old Testament," *ET* 76 (1964-65) 199.

S. H. Hooke, "Life After Death: V. Israel and the After-Life," *ET* 76 (1964-65) 236-239.

*S. H. Hooke, "Life After Death: VI. The Extra-Canonical Literature," *ET* 76 (1964-65) 273-276.

Harold L. Creager, "The Biblical View of Life After Death," *LQ, N.S.,* 17 (1965) 111-121.

H. W. Huppenbauer, "Death, an Old Testament View," *GBT* 3 (1966-71) #9, 8-18.

Lionel Swain, "The Bible and the Old Testament. Eternal Life in the Old Testament," *CIR* 52 (1967) 104-109.

H. C. Thomson, "Old Testament Ideas on Life After Death," *GUOST* 22 (1967-68) 46-55.

J. Barr, "The Immortality of the Soul. Resurrection and Immortality—Old Testament," *ABR* 16 (1968) 51.

M. J. Charlesworth, "The Immortality of the Soul, The Soul," *ABR* 16 (1968) 52.

David Daube, "The Night of Death," *HTR* 61 (1968) 629-632.

Elmer Smick, "The Bearing of New Philological Data on the Subjects of Resurrection and Immortality in the Old Testament," *WTJ* 31 (1968-69) 12-21.

§1036 *5.4.18.1 Studies concerning Sheol*

*Robert Young, "Sheol, Hades; Gehenna, Tartarus," *HR* 6 (1881-82) 48-49.

*Frederick Charles Cowper, "Concerning Sheol, Hades, and Gehenna, with some Classical Myths and Traditions Therefrom," *PER* 9 (1895-96) 76-86.

Sidney Zandstra, "Sheol and the Pit in the Old Testament," *PTR* 5 (1907) 631-641.

*Joseph Offord, "Archaeological Notes on Jewish Antiquities. XVI. *Sheol and the Babylonian Land of Shades,*" *PEFQS* 48 (1916) 143-144.

*Paul Haupt, "The Original Meaning of Sheol," *JBL* 36 (1917) 258.

*(   ) D., "Sheol Passages in the Old Testament," *TQ* 10 (1906) 22-23.

*W[illiam] F[oxwell] Albright, "The Etymology of *Še'ol*," *AJSL* 34 (1917-18) 209-210.

*Arthur T. Burbridge, "Caves, Pits, and Sheol," *LQHR* 130 (1918) 75-86.

Fred B. Pearson, "Sheol and Hades in the Old and New Testament," *R&E* 35 (1938) 304-314.

Clement J. McNaspy, "Sheol in the Old Testament," *CBQ* 6 (1944) 326-333.

Charles P. Johnson, "Sheol: Its Concept and Significance," *RefR* 10 (1956-57) #2, 32-38.

C. Farnham, "Sheol—Hades," *Amb* 7 (1958-59) #1, 8-12.

D. K. Innes, "The Meaning of She'ol in the Old Testament," *EQ* 32 (1960) 196-202.

§1037 *5.4.18.2 Studies on Hell*

P. P. Sanford, "On Eternal Punishment," *MR* 10 (1827) 255-256.

*M. Stuart, "Future Punishment, as exhibited in the Book of Enoch," *BRCR, N.S.,* 4 (1840) 1-35.

*Asahal Abbot, "The Doctrine of Man's Immortality, and of the Eternal Punishment of the Wicked, as Set Forth in the Ancient Scriptures," *BRCR, 3rd Ser.,* 5 (1849) 618-635.

W. E. Manley, "If Endless Punishment is not Revealed in the Old Testament, It is not in the New," *UQGR, N.S.,* 3 (1866) 281-294.

*Robert Young, "Sheol, Hades; Gehenna, Tartarus," *HR* 6 (1881-82) 48-49.

A. Lowy, "Old Jewish Legends on Biblical Topics. II. Legendary description of Hell," *SBAP* 10 (1887-88) 333-342.

William W. McLane, "An Historical Study of Hell. Part I.—Ethnic Options," *HR* 23 (1892) 215-222.

William W. McLane, "An Historical Study of Hell. Part II.—Religious Beliefs," *HR* 24 (1892) 200-208.

William W. McLane, "An Historical Study of Hell. Part III.—Christian Doctrines," *HR* 24 (1892) 483-491. *[OT Refs., pp. 483-484]*

*Frederick Charles Cowper, "Concerning Sheol, Hades and Gehenna, with Some Classical Myths and Traditions Therefrom," *PER* 9 (1895-96) 76-86.

Aurthur J. Waugh, "The Confusion Concerning Hades, Hell, and Gehenna," *HR* 48 (1904) 197-199.

James A. Montgomery, "The Holy City and Gehenna," *JBL* 27 (1908) 24-47.

Bernard Pick, "The Punishments in the Other World. As Described in the Apocalypse of Peter, the Sibylline Oracles, the Acts of Thomas, and the Apocalypse of Paul," *OC* 32 (1918) 641-662.

A. D. Martin, "'Everlasting Punishment': An Exegetical Note," *CongQL* 3 (1925) 306-313.

George Lindley Young, "The Final Fate of the Wicked," *BS* 83 (1926) 403-426; 84 (1927) 50-74, 177-202.

*Timothy McDermott, "Hell," *NB* 48 (1966-67) 186-197. [Gehenna, pp. 191-197]

W. Lillie, "Towards a Biblical Doctrine of Punishment," *SJT* 21 (1968) 449-461.

§1038 *5.4.18.3 Studies on Heaven and Paradise*

M. Kalisch, "The Biblical View of Heaven," *ONTS* 1 (1882) #1, 16.

R. H. Charles, "The Seven Heavens, An Early Jewish and Christian Belief," *ET* 7 (1895-96) 57-61, 115-118.

*Anonymous, "Eschatology and the Kingdom of Heaven," *CQR* 69 (1909-10) 84-113.

L. S. A. Wells, "Séjours et Habitats Divins," *IJA* #25 (1911) 34. *(Review)*

*William Watson, "Paradise: according to the Apocrypha and Pseudepigrapha," *IJA* #38 (1914) 74-78.

U. E. Simon, "Heaven in the Hebrew Tradition," *JTVI* 89 (1957) 118-128.

*Bernard Goldman, "The Oriental Gate of Heaven," *AJA* 67 (1963) 211.

§1039 *5.4.19 Studies concerning the Resurrection of the Dead*

P. Rizer, "Scripture Doctrine Concerning the Resurrection of the Dead," *ER* 5 (1853-54) 60-75. *[OT Refs., pp. 60-61, 63-65, 67-68]*

Anonymous, "The Resurrection of the Body," *BWR* 1 (1877) 301-302.

*A. G. Laurie, "The Persian, Jewish and Christian Resurrections," *UQGR, N.S.,* 16 (1879) 257-271.

J. W. Deane, "The Growth of the Doctrine of the Resurrection of the Body among the Jews," *Exp, 2nd Ser.,* 7 (1884) 190-204, 292-303, 393-400.

*A. Fergus Ferguson, "Job on Life and Resurrection," *ERG, 9th Ser.,* 2 (1887) 20-25.

Howard Osgood, "The Resurrection in the Pentateuch," *BQR* 10 (1888) 425-436.

L. W. Hayhurst, "The Supposed Obscurity of the Old-Testament Treatment of Death and Resurrection," *BQR* 14 (1892) 333-348.

D. H. Geissinger, "The Biblical Doctrine of the Resurrection," *LCR* 22 (1903) 223-230.

*T. W. Kretchmann, "Job on the Resurrection of the Body," *LCR* 25 (1906) 570-579.

L. S. Alban Wells, "Jewish Parties and the Resurrection," *ICMM* 8 (1911-12) 68-82.

Fr. Schwarz, "The Resurrection of the Body in the Old Testament," *TQ* 18 (1914) 1-16.

William Watson, "The Resurrection of the Dead," *ICMM* 11 (1914-15) 295-304.

*A. Marmorstein, "The Doctrine of the Resurrection of the Dead in Rabbinical Theology," *AJT* 19 (1915) 577-591.

*J. Agar Beet, "Greek Eschatology, a Needful Preparation for the Gospel of Christ," *IJA* #41 (1915) 23-26.

*Rachel Wischnitzer-Bernstein, "The Conception of the Resurrection in the Ezekiel Panel of the Dura Synagogue," *JBL* 60 (1941) 43-55.

*H. D. W., "'The Hope of Israel;' or, the Restoration of Israel identified with the Resurrection of the Dead," *MR* 24 (1942) 192-220.

Elmer W. Fondell, "Resurrection Truth in the Old Testament," *CovQ* 6 (1946) #4, 195-207.

H. Birkeland, "The Belief in the Resurrection of the Dead in the Old Testament," *ST* 3 (1949) 60-78.

*Maximiliano Garcia Cordero, "Corporal Resurrection in the Book of Job," *TD* 2 (1954) 90-93.

J. Terence Forestell, "Christian Revelation and the Resurrection of the Wicked," *CBQ* 19 (1957) 165-189.

Charles Davis, "The Resurrection of the Body," *ClR* 43 (1958) 137-150, 205-216. *[OT Refs., pp. 142-145]*

Lawrence E. Toombs, "The Doctrine of the Resurrection in Intertestamental Judaism," *DG* 29 (1958-59) 147-159.

James J. Heller, "The Resurrection of Man," *TT* 15 (1958-59) 217-229.

*H. A. Theiste, "The Scriptural Doctrine of the Body and Soul with Special Reference to Death and Resurrection," *LSQ* 4 (1963-64) #3, 2-9. *[OT Refs., pp. 3-5]*

D. W. Cundry, "The Ghost in the Machine and the Body of the Resurrection," *SJT* 18 (1965) 164-169.

Lionel Swain, "The Bible and the People. The Resurrection in the Old Testament," *ClR* 51 (1966) 949-954.

*F. H. Drinkwater, "Jewish Apocalyptic and the Resurrection," *Cont* 6 (1968) 433-436.

§1040 5.5 The Use of the Old Testament and Other literature in the New Testament

'Scrutator', "Observations on the Prophecies of the Old Testament quoted in the New," *TRep* 5 (1786) 111-125.

(   ) R., "New Testament Interpretation.   Suggestions on the New Testament Use of the Old," *CRB* 4 (1839) 477-490.

J. T. Gray, "On the Citations of the Old Testament in the New," *JSL, 1st Ser.,* 2 (1848) 197-221.

W. Robinson, "Citations from the Old Testament in the New," *JSL, 1st Ser.,* 3 (1849) 382-389.

L. M., "Letter and Spirit in the Old Testament Scriptures," *JSL, 1st Ser.,* 7 (1851) 146-161.

F. A. G. Tholuck, "The Citations of the Old Testament in the New," *BS* 11 (1854) 568-616. *(Trans. by Charles A. Aiken)*

Anonymous, "The Old Testament Judged by the New," *CRB* 20 (1855) 409-422.

( ) A., "Quotations in the New Testament from the Old," *JSL, 3rd Ser.,* 2 (1855-56) 98-104.

*G. P., "The Septuagint Version. Part III. *The Quotations in the New Testament Considered,*" *JSL, 3rd Ser.,* 7 (1858) 35-59.

Lyman Whiting, "The Old Testament in the New," *AThR* 3 (1861) 283-290.

Anonymous, "The Old Testament in the New," *BFER* 11 (1862) 40-46.

D. A., "Quotations of Scripture," *JSL, 5th Ser.,* 1 (1867) 369-393.

*J. J. Van Oosterzee, "The Citations from the Old Testament by Our Lord and His Apostles," *ThE* 4 (1867) 45-53. *(Trans. from the Dutch)*

*E. P. Barrows, "Revelation and Inspiration. XII. The Quotations of the New Testament in their Relation to the Question of Inspiration," *BS* 30 (1873) 305-322.

*Anonymous, "The Old Testament and the New," *CongL* 2 (1873) 321-324.

*Anonymous, "On the Development of Dogmatic Teaching Regarding the Old Law in the Lifetime of the Apostles," *IER, 3rd Ser.,* 2 (1881) 455-467.

*William Burnett, "The Relation of the Old Testament to the New," *ONTS* 3 (1883-84) 115-119.

S. Burnham, "The Value of the Old Testament for A Correct Knowledge of the New," *ONTS* 5 (1884-85) 157-161, 220-222.

J. M. Stifler, "The Relation of the Gospels and the Pentateuch," *BQR* 7 (1885) 73-90.

G[eorge] H. Schodde, "The Old Testament in the Light of the New," *ColTM* 7 (1887) 107-128.

*J. Rawson Lumby, "Old Testament Criticism in the Light of New Testament Quotations," *Exp, 3rd Ser.,* 9 (1889) 337-351.

William H. Ryder, "The Fulfillment of Prophecy," *AR* 13 (1890) 20-25.

B. C. Patterson, "Some Biblical Critics," *USR* 2 (1890-91) 268-270.

*W. D. Meyer, "The Relation of the New Testament to the Mosaic System," *ONTS* 13 (1891) 143-146.

*James M. Ludlow, "The Septuagint and Old Testament Quotations in the New Testament," *HR* 24 (1892) 11-15.

*F. H. Wallace, "Relation of Extra-Canonical Jewish Literature to the New Testament," *MR* 79 (1897) 697-711.

*Henry Jayman, "The Book of Enoch in Reference to the New Testament and Early Christian Antiquity," *BW* 12 (1898) 37-46.

*R. Mackintosh, "O.T. Quotations in N.T. Speeches: What Version or What Recension of the O.T. Text do they seem to Presuppose?" *OSHTP* (1898-99) 20-26.

W. M. McPheeters, "Current Criticism and Interpretation of the Old Testament. 'It Says:' 'Scripture Says:' 'God Says.'," *CFL, O.S.,* 3 (1899) 306-307.

Benjamin B. Warfield, "'It Says:' 'Scripture Says:' 'God Says.'," *PRR* 10 (1899) 472-510.

*S. Schechter, "Some Rabbinic Parallels to the New Testament," *JQR* 12 (1899-1900) 415-433.

*M. Coover, "Biblical Quotations in the New Testament, and Their Relation to Inspiration," *LQ* 30 (1900) 315-325.

H. A. A. Kennedy, "'Judaism and the New Testament'," *ET* 12 (1900-01) 422-423. *(Review)*

*Motier A. Bullock, "Jehovah's Protest Against the Altar Service," *BS* 59 (1902) 529-536. [The New Testament Use of these Old Testament Symbols, pp. 532-536]

W. H. Bennett, "The New Testament and Jewish Literature," *Exp, 6th Ser.,* 5 (1902) 52-65, 135-148.

*Ivan Panin, "The Old Testament Women in the New," *BN* 1 (1904) #5, 139-149.

Walter F. Adeney, "The Relation of New Testament Theology to Jewish Alexandrian Thought," *BW* 26 (1905) 41-54.

Arthur Carr, "The Eclectic Use of the Old Testament in the New Testament," *Exp, 6th Ser.,* 11 (1905) 340-351.

J. B. Anderson, "The Validity of the New Testament's Discernment of Christ in the Old Testament," *R&E* 2 (1905) 489-505.

A. P. Fors, "Vetus Testamentum in Novo," *TTKF* 7 (1905) 49-56.

*C. F. Burney, "The Christian Interpretation of Messianic Prophecy," *ICMM* 2 (1905-06) 256-272.

William H. Bates, "Quotations in the New Testament from the Old Testament," *CFL, 3rd Ser.,* 4 (1906) 275-278.

*F. W. Klingensmith, "The Psalter and the New Testament. I," *LCR* 25 (1906) 457-465.

*F. W. Klingensmith, "The Psalter and the New Testament. II," *LCR* 25 (1906) 711-718.

*Alfred Plummer, "The Relation of the Testaments of the Twelve Patriarchs to the Books of the New Testament," *Exp, 7th Ser.,* 6 (1908) 481-491.

*Anonymous, "The use of the Apocrypha in the New Testament," *IJA* #13 (1908) 4-6.

*R. H. Charles, "The Testaments of the Twelve Patriarchs in Relation to the New Testament," *Exp, 7th Ser.,* 7 (1909) 111-118.

*G. Buchanan Gray, "The Virgin Birth in Relation to the Interpretation of Isaiah 7:14," *Exp, 8th Ser.,* 1 (1911) 289-308.

J. Courtenay James, "An Intermediate Aramaic Version," *ET* 25 (1913-14) 88-90.

Robert Gardner, "The Old Testament in the New: Some Illustrations," *GUOST* 4 (1913-22) 42-44.

*H. McLauchlan, "The Apocrypha and the New Testament," *IJA* #42 (1915) 44-45.

S. P. T. Prideaux, "The New Testament in the Light of the Jewish Apocrypha and Pseudepigrapha," *IJA* #51 (1917) 56-58.

George W. Gilmore, "Sources of Old-Testament Quotations in the New Testament," *HR* 76 (1918) 139-140.

William H. Bates, "Quotations in the New Testament from the Old Testament," *BS* 77 (1920) 424-428.

*Paul Morris, "Christianity and Prophecy Fulfillment," *OC* 37 (1923) 230-242.

J. Rendel Harris, "A Factor of Old Testament Influence in the New Testament," *ET* 37 (1925-26) 6-11.

*J. Rendel Harris, "The Influence of Philo upon the New Testament," *ET* 37 (1925-26) 565-566.

C. H. Turner, "Ο ΥΙΟC ΜΟΥ Ο ΑΓΑΠΗΤΟC," *JTS* 27 (1925-26) 113-129.

A. Lukyn Williams, "The Problem of the Septuagint and Quotations in the New Testament, *JTVI* 58 (1926) 152-162, 174. [(Discussion, pp. 162-170) (Communications by Miss Hamilton Law, p. 170; Miss L. M. Mackinlay, pp. 170-171; J. M. Pollock, p. 171; H. Biddulph, pp. 171-172; William Hoste, pp. 172-173)]

Leslie Elmer Fuller, "What the Old Testament Gave to the New," *MR* 111 (1928) 622-625.

*J. Rendel Harris, "Tobit and the New Testament," *ET* 40 (1928-29) 315-319.

Alexander Ross, "Old Testament Quotations in the New Testament," *EQ* 1 (1929) 241-251.

(Miss) M. D. R. Willink, "The Exodus in the New Testament," *Theo* 30 (1935) 105-109.

Alexander Sperber, "The 'Bible' of the New Testament," *JBL* 57 (1938) vi-vii.

Richard Davidson, "The Old Testament Preparation for the New Testament Doctrine of the Church," *R&E* 38 (1941) 49-56.

*C. P. Coffin, "An Old Testament Prophecy and Some New Testament Miracle Stories," *JAAR* 11 (1943) 162-166.

*Allen Wikgren, "The Targum and the New Testament," *JR* 24 (1944) 89-95.

James T. Hudson, "Edifying Stories (Midrash) in the New Testament," *LQHR* 169 (1944) 305-310.

*J. C. Fenton, "The Promises of Haggai and the Yea of Christ," *Theo* 49 (1946) 47-51.

Hugo Odeberg, "The New Testament Concerning the Old Testament," *CTM* 18 (1947) 607-610.

B. F. C. Atkinson, "The Textual Background of the Use of the Old Testament by the New," *JTVI* 79 (1947) 39-60, 68-69. [Communications by F. F. Bruce, pp. 60-62; P. J. Wiseman, pp. 62-63; E. H. Betts, pp. 63-65; H. Biddulph, pp. 65-66; W. F. Spanner, pp. 66-67; B. B. Knopp, pp. 67-68]

Floyd V. Filson, "The Focus of History," *Interp* 2 (1948) 24-38. *[NT use of OT]*

*John A. T. Robinson, "Hosea and the Virgin Birth," *Theo* 51 (1948) 373-375.

*Terence Y. Mullins, "Jewish Wisdom Literature in the New Testament," *JBL* 68 (1949) 335-339.

*Arvid S. Kapelrud, "The Gates of Hell and the Guardian Angels of Paradise," *JAOS* 70 (1950) 151-156.

S. H. Hooke, "What has Christianity Inherited from Judaism?" *MC* 40 (1950) 216-226.

*Charles T. Fritsch, "The Gospel in the Book of Proverbs," *TT* 7 (1950-51) 169-183.

*Bruce M. Metzger, "The Formulas Introducing Quotations of Scripture in the NT and the Mishnah," *JBL* 70 (1951) 297-307.

*A. W. Argyle, "The Influence of the Testaments of the Twelve Patriarchs upon the New Testament," *ET* 43 (1951-52) 256-258.

*F. W. Grosheide, "The Translation of Quotations from the Old Testament in the New," *BTr* 6 (1955) 16-20.

Roger Nicole, "Old Testament Quotations in the New Testament," *GR* 1 (1955) 7-12, 63-68.

Martin Rist, "Old Testament Heroes of Jewish Legend in the New Testament," *IR* 13 (1956) #1, 3-14.

*John Hoad, "Some New Testament References to Isaiah 53," *ET* 68 (1956-57) 254-255.

*Edward F. Siegman, "The Blood of the Covenant," *AER* 136 (1957) 167-174.

Otto A. Piper, "Unchanging Promises. *Exodus in the New Testament*," *Interp* 11 (1957) 3-22.

*R. E. Brown, "The Semitic Background of the NT *Mysterion*," *B* 39 (1958) 426-448; 40 (1959) 70-87.

John L. Cheek, "The Apocrypha in Christian Scripture," *JAAR* 26 (1958) 207-212.

*R. McL. Wilson, "Genesis 1.26 and the New Testament," *BTPT* 20 (1959) 117-125.

*Manfred R. Lehmann, "Gen. 2:24 as the Basis for Divorce in Halakhah and the New Testament," *ZAW* 72 (1960) 263-267.

*J. A. Fitzmyer, "The Use of Explicit Old Testament Quotations in Qumran Literature and in the New Testament," *NTS* 7 (1960-61) 297-333.

Henry J. Boekhoven, "The Influence of Jeremiah Upon New Testament Literature," *RefR* 14 (1960-61) #1, 37-43.

Richard C. Oudersluys, "Old Testament Quotations in the New Testament," *RefR* 14 (1960-61) #3, 1-12.

K. V. Mathew, "The Hebrew Thought and the New Testament," *IJT* 11 (1962) 29-32.

*Samuel Sandmel, "Paralleomania," *JBL* 81 (1962) 1-13.

M. Gertner, "Midrashim in the New Testament," *JSS* 7 (1962) 267-292.

S. L. Edgar, "Respect for Context in Quotations from the Old Testament," *NTS* 9 (1962-63) 55-62.

*Jose Ramon Diaz, "Palestinian Targum and New Testament," *NT* 6 (1963) 75-80.

R. T. Mead, "A Dissenting Opinion about Respect for Context in Old Testament Quotations," *NTS* 10 (1963-64) 279-289.

Robert Rendall, "Quotation in Scripture as an Index of Wider Reference," *EQ* 36 (1964) 214-221.

*F. Hecht, "The Theological Interpretation of the Old Testament: An Act of Deliberation," *NGTT* 5 (1964) 93-98.

F. Muliyil, "The Idea of Fulfillment in the New Testament," *SBSB* 1 (1964) 35-42.

*J. Grassi, "Ezekiel xxxvii. 1-14 and the New Testament," *NTS* 11 (1964-65) 162-164.

*John F. X. Sheehan, "The Septuagint and the New Testament," *BibT* #17 (1965) 1133-1136.

S. Marion Smith, "New Testament Writers Use of the Old Testament," *SQ/E* 26 (1965) 239-250.

K. Runia, "The Interpretation of the Old Testament by the New Testament," *VR* #5 (1965) 1-12.

*R[obert] M. Grant, "The Book of Wisdom at Alexandria. Reflections on the History of the Canon and Theology," *StP* 7 (1966) 462-472.

G. W. Grogan, "The New Testament Interpretation of the Old Testament," *TB* #18 (1967) 54-76.

Lester J. Kuyper, "The Old Testament Used by New Testament Writers," *RefR* 21 (1967-68) #1, 2-13.

Harold S. Aonger, "Isaiah and the New Testament," *R&E* 65 (1968) 459-470.

T. L. Wilkinson, "The Role of Elijah in the New Testament," *VR* #10 (1968) 1-10.

James Flamming, "The New Testament Use of Isaiah," *SWJT, N.S.,* 11 (1968-69) #1, 89-104.

J. T. E. Renner, "The Old Testament in the New," *LTJ* 3 (1969) 41-50.

§1041 *5.5.1 The Use of the Old Testament in the Teachings of Jesus*

'Mosaicus', "On the Connexion between Faith in the Divine Mission of Christ, and that of Moses and the Prophets," *TRep* 6 (1788) 49-59.

*W. F., "Scripture Parallelisms. The Messias Prophet: with Remarks on the Parallelistic Form of His Discourses," *JSL, 1st Ser.,* 6 (1850) 179-188.

D. Gotthard Victor Lechler, "The Old Testament in the Discourses of Jesus," *CRB* 24 (1859) 368-390, 543-574.

*J. J. Oosterzee, "The Citations from the Old Testament by our Lord and His Apostles," *ThE* 4 (1867) 45-53. *(Trans. from the Dutch)*

Edgar C. S. Gibson, "Our Lord's Use of the Old Testament," *Exp, 2nd Ser.,* 1 (1881) 292-304.

Joseph John Murphy, "Christ's Use of Scripture," *Exp, 2nd Ser.,* 4 (1882) 101-110.

Alex B. Bruce, "The Kingdom of God. 2. *Christ's Attitude towards the Mosaic Age,*" *MI* 1 (1884-85) 81-97.

Howard Osgood, "Jesus Christ the Final Test of Biblical Criticism," *BQR* 9 (1887) 357-369.

*R. F. Horton, "Christ's Use of the Book of Proverbs," *Exp, 3rd Ser.,* 7 (1888) 105-123.

S. R. Driver, "Christ's Appeal to the Old Testament," *ET* 3 (1891-92) 17.

C. J. Ellicott, "The Teaching of Our Lord as to the Authority of the Old Testament," *ET* 3 (1891-92) 157-163, 256-259, 359-362, 457-463, 538-545; 4 (1892-93) 169-172, 218-222, 362-369, 450-458.

Buchanan Blake, "Christ and the Old Testament," *ET* 3 (1891-92) 518-519.

William Coven, "The Testimony of Christ to the Old Testament," *PRR* 3 (1892) 401-420.

A. R. Cocke, "The Old Testament Christ's Sword of the Spirit," *USR* 4 (1892-93) 278-286.

W. Sanday, "Christ and the Old Testament," *ET* 5 (1893-94) 228-229.

John P. Peters, "Christ's Treatment of the Old Testament," *JBL* 15 (1896) 87-105.

*Marshall B. Lang, "The Beatitudes in the Twenty-Third Psalm," *ET* 10 (1898-99) 46-47.

*G. Currie Martin, "Our Lord's use of the Book of Hosea," *ET* 10 (1898-99) 281.

W. M. McPheeters, "Bible Study," *CFL, O.S.,* 3 (1899) 258-262. [Christ's Bible; Christ the First Critic; Christ and the Law]

E. Fitch Burr, "Jesus Probator," *HR* 38 (1899) 305-309.

Herbert W. Horwill, "Christ and the Old Testament," *ET* 11 (1899-1900) 477.

Andrew Baird, "Jesus and the Prophets," *GUOST* 2 (1901-97) 54-56.

John J. Young, "Christ and the Old Testament," *LQ* 33 (1903) 554-565.

Winstead Paine Bone, "Jesus and the Old Testament According to the Critics," *CFL, 3rd Ser.,* 1 (1904) 626-630.

*Benjamin W. Robinson, "Some Elements of Forcefulness in Jesus' Comparisons," *JBL* 23 (1904) 106-179. [Section IV. Two Tables Comparing Deutero-Isaiah, Jesus, and Paul]

*David Smith, "Our Lord's Reductio ad Absurdum of the Rabbinical Interpretation of Psalm CX. (Matthew xxii. 41-46 = Mark xii. 35-37 = Luke xx. 41-44)," *ET* 16 (1904-05) 256-258.

Anonymous, "Notes and Comments. Our Lord and the Old Testament," *ICMM* 1 (1905) 2-4.

R[obert] H. Kennett, "Our Lord's Reference to Jonah," *ICMM* 1 (1905) 22-30.

C. S., "Correspondence. Our Lord's Reference to Jonah," *ICMM* 1 (1905) 275-276.

Robert H. Kennett, "Christ the Interpreter of Prophecy," *ICMM* 2 (1905-06) 127-138.

H. M. Scott, "Christ and the Old Testament," *CFL, 3rd Ser.,* 6 (1907) 26-27.

M. Wilson Cunningham, "Did Christ Preach from a Text?" *ET* 19 (1907-08) 187-188. *[Psa. 15 // Matt. 5:1-7:27]*

Frank Grant Lewis, "Jesus' Attitude to the Old Testament. An Exposition of Mark 7:1-23," *BW* 31 (1908) 131-137.

George Soltau, "Our Lord's Use of the Scriptures," *CFL, 3rd Ser.,* 9 (1908) 42-46.

Willis J. Beecher, "Does Jesus Teach a Doctrine Concerning the Scriptures?" *ASRec* 4 (1908-09) 155-177.

Ernest DeWitt Burton, "Jesus and the Old Testament Law," *BW* 35 (1910) 147-150. *(Editorial)*

Willis J. Beecher, "Harnack Concerning Jesus and the Old Testament," *CFL, 3rd Ser.,* 12 (1910) 253-257.

Edward E. Nourse, "Some Aspects of Jesus' relation to the Culture and Extra-Canonical Literature of the Last Two Centuries B.C.," *HSR* 20 (1910) 231-246.

Cyril W. Emmet, "The Apocalyptic Hope and the Teaching of Jesus," *IJA* #21 (1910) 34-36.

*J. F. Pollock, "The Inspiration and Interpretation of Scriptures," *LQ* 40 (1910) 479-498. [How Jesus Made Use of the Old Testament, pp. 495-498]

F. W. Klingensmith, "The Mind of Christ and the Old Testament," *LCR* 30 (1911) 458-480.

A. C. Bouquet, "The Parables of Our Lord: Sources and Parallels," *ICMM* 9 (1912-13) 384-397.

Robert H. Kennett, "Our Lord's Interpretation of Prophecy," *ICMM* 10 (1913-14) 359-374.

G. B. Strickler, "The Testimony of Christ to the Old Testament," *USR* 25 (1913-14) 86-96.

*Ernst von Dobschütz, "The Attitude of Jesus and St. Paul Toward the Bible," *BM* 2 (1914) 619-636.

Leander S. Keyser, "Christ's Witness to the Old Testament. Another Chapter on Biblical Criticism," *LQ* 44 (1914) 40-65.

T. P. Stafford, "The Relation of the Ethical Teaching of Jesus to that of the Old Testament," *R&E* 14 (1917) 466-478.

Alexander Mackenzie Lamb, "The Pentateuch in the Hands of Christ," *BR* 3 (1918) 395-408.

*Edward Chauncey Baldwin, "Jesus and the Testament of Solomon," *HR* 80 (1920) 189-190.

Henry J. Cadbury, "Jesus and the Prophets," *JR* 5 (1925) 607-622.

William S. Bishop, "Jesus and the God of the Old Testament," *ACM* 19 (1926) 284-291.

R[obert] D[ick] Wilson, "Jesus and the Old Testament," *PTR* 24 (1926) 632-661.

Parke P. Flournoy, "Christ and the Scriptures: What may We Gather from His Attitude and Instruction?" *JTVI* 60 (1928) 45-70, 76. [(Discussion, pp. 70-73) (Communications by A. T. Schofield, pp. 73-74; J. W. Thirtle, pp. 74-76)]

Willis J. Beecher, "Does Jesus Teach a Doctrine Concerning the Scriptures?" *CFL, 3rd Ser.,* 35 (1929) 590-599.

F. W. Pitt, "Christ and the Scriptures. The Old Testament: The Implications," *JTVI* 62 (1930) 38-55, 61. (Discussion, pp. 55-61)

*T. C. Skinner, "The Significance of the Old Testament Scriptures to Our Lord Jesus Christ," *JTVI* 62 (1930) 134-144, 161-163. [(Discussion, pp. 145-155) (Communications by L. M. Davies, pp. 155-157; William Hoste, pp. 157-158; J. J. B. Coles, p. 158; A. G. Secrett, pp. 158-160; W. P. Rowlatt-Jones, pp. 160-161)]

H. E. Dana, "Jesus' Use of the Old Testament," *BR* 16 (1931) 389-399.

*John Torrance, "Ps. XXII.—as Used by Christ and St. Paul," *ET* 44 (1932-33) 382.

S. C. Ylvisaker, "Christ's Use of the Old Testament in His Prophetic Ministry," *WLQ* 32 (1935) 119-141.

Lionel E. H. Stephens-Hodge, "Christ and the Old-Testament," *EQ* 10 (1938) 367-373.

Walter H. Gutbrod, "Notes. Jesus and the Law—Some Considerations," *Theo* 39 (1939) 123-127.

Louis Matthews Sweet, "The Relationship of Jesus to the Old Testament," *USR* 53 (1941-42) 109-124.

*Ernest Findlay Scott, "The Conception of God's Law in the Prophets and in Jesus," *JAAR* 11 (1943) 152-155.

Robert E. Speer, "Jesus and His Bible," *USR* 57 (1945-46) 111-120.

William C. Berkemeyer, "Jesus' Use of Scriptures and Ours," *LCQ* 20 (1947) 31-46.

David M. G. Stalker, "Ezekiel and Jesus," *GUOST* 13 (1947-49) 16-18.

Lowell E. Roberts, "Jesus' Use of the Old Testament," *ASW* 5 (1950) 15-21.

*J. Stanley Glen, "Jesus Christ and the Unity of the Bible," *Interp* 5 (1951) 259-267.

T. W. Manson, "The Old Testament in the Teaching of Jesus," *BJRL* 34 (1951-52) 312-332.

'Senex', "Christ's Method of Exegesis," *LofS* 8 (1953-54) 392-397.

S. Clive Thexton, "Jesus's Use of the Scriptures," *LQHR* 179 (1954) 102-108.

J. G. S. S. Thompson, "Christ and the Old Testament," *ET* 67 (1955-56) 18-20.

A. E. Turlington, "Jesus and the Law," *R&E* 53 (1956) 34-45.

*Paul Winter, "Genesis 1:27 and Jesus Saying on Divorce," *ZAW* 70 (1958) 260-261.

Morris Bender, "Christ's use of the Old Testament," *CCBQ* 2 (1959) #2, 33-35.

E. F. F. Bishop, "'Scripture Says'," *EQ* 37 (1965) 218-220.

Victor A. Bartling, "Christ's Use of the Old Testament with Special Reference to the Pentateuch," *CTM* 36 (1965) 567-576.

Eugene M. Skibbe, "Pentateuchal Themes in the Sermon on the Mount," *LQ* 20 (1968) 44-51.

S. C. Ylvisaker, "Christ's Use of the Old Testament in His Prophetic Ministry," *LSQ* 9 (1968-69) #4, 1-39.

§1042 *5.5.2 The Use of the Old Testament in the Gospels*

'Pamphilus', "Observations on the Quotation of Isaiah, ix. 1, 2. by the Evangelist Matthew," *TRep* 5 (1786) 123-128.

*J. C. K., "The Smoking Flax," *JSL, 3rd Ser.,* 6 (1857-58) 438-441. *[Isa. 42:3, 4 as cited in Matt. 12:20, 21]*

*W. R. B., "Zechariah XI. 13; Matthew XXVII. 9," *JSL, 3rd Ser.,* 12 (1860-61) 459-460.

*A. H. W., "Exegesis of Difficult Texts. Mark XV. 15, compared with Leviticus XVI. 5," *JSL, 4th Ser.,* 1 (1862) 350-358.

*Anonymous, "Micah's Prophecy of Christ," *BFER* 13 (1864) 195-240. *[Micah 5:1 as quoted in Matt. 2:6]*

*J. M. Stifler, "The Relation of the Gospels and the Pentateuch," *BFER* 34 (1885) 305-319.

Hugh Ross Hatch, "The Old Testament Quotation in Matthew 27:9, 10," *BW* 1 (1893) 345-354.

*J. A. Selbie, "The Apocalypse of Zecharias and the Gospel of Luke," *ET* 7 (1895-96) 497.

*Eb. Nestle, "The Genealogy in St. Matthew and the Septuagint of Chronicles," *ET* 11 (1899-1900) 191.

W. C. Allen, "The Old Testament Quotations in St. Matthew and St. Mark," *ET* 12 (1900-01) 187-189, 281-285.

*Paul Haupt, "The Prototype of the Magnificat," *ZDMG* 58 (1904) 617-632.

J. Rendel Harris, "Spoken by Jeremy the Prophet," *Exp, 6th Ser.,* 12 (1905) 161-171.

R. H. Kennett, "Old Testament Parallels to Christ and the Gospels," *OSHTP* (1905-06) 40-50.

*Eb. Nestle, "'The Times of the Gentiles'," *ET* 20 (1908-09) 279-280. *[Tobit 14:5 // Luke 21:24]*

*H. McLachlan, "Was St. Luke influenced by the Book of Wisdom?" *IJA* #30 (1912) 60.

*Henry A. Sanders, "The New Testament Quotation of a Twice-Repeated Prophecy," *BS* 71 (1914) 275-282. *[Isa. 40:3-8; Mal. 3:1]*

*L. W. Grensted, "The Use of Enoch in St. Luke XVI. 19-31," *ET* 26 (1914-15) 333-334.

*T. Herbert Bindley, "Concerning 'Testimony Books'," *ICMM* 14 (1917-18) 210-219.

*R. K. Yerkes, "The Lucian Version of the Old Testament as Illustrated from Jeremiah 1-3," *JBL* 37 (1918) 163-192.

*Robert A. Aytoun, "'Himself He Cannot Save,' (Ps. xxii 29 and Mark xv 31)," *JTS* 21 (1919-20) 245-248.

V. T. Kirby, "Did S. Luke Know the Old Testament?" *ET* 33 (1921-22) 227-229.

*A. O. Standen, "The Parable of Dives and Lazarus, and Enoch 22," *ET* 33 (1921-22) 523.

J. P. Naish, "The Semitic Background of the Gospels," *ICMM* 19 (1922-23) 288-297.

Paul P. Levertoff, "The Deuteronomic Background of the Logia," *Theo* 14 (1927) 65-72, 212-219.

*Charles C. Torrey, "B The Influence of Second Isaiah in the Gospels and Acts," *JBL* 48 (1929) 24-36.

*Godfrey Curnock, "A Neglected Parallel (Mt. XI. 28 and Ex. XXXIII. 14)," *ET* 44 (1932-33) 141.

*Leo Jung, "Mis-Translations a Source in Jewish and Christian Lore," *PAAJR* 5 (1933-34) 55-67. [VII. Some Cases of Theological Bias. (Zech. 9:9 as quoted in Matt. 21:2-7), pp. 66-67]

M. Black, "The Problem of the O.T. Quotations in the Gospels," *JMUEOS* 23 (1942) 4.

Sherman E. Johnson, "The Biblical Quotations in Matthew," *HTR* 36 (1943) 135-153.

*Lambert Nolle, "Old Testament Laws of Inheritance and St. Luke's Genealogy of Christ," *Scrip* 2 (1947) 38-42.

*H. F. D. Sparks, "St. Matthew's References to Jeremiah," *JTS, N.S.,* 1 (1950) 155-156.

A. G. Hebert, "The Virgin Mary as the Daughter of Zion," *Theo* 53 (1950) 403-410.

A. Guillaume, "Mt. xxvii, 46 in the Light of the Dead Sea Scroll of Isaiah," *PEQ* 83 (1951) 78-80.

H. J. M. Turner, "The Daughter of Zion," *Theo* 54 (1951) 27-28.

A. G. Hebert, "The Daughter of Zion," *Theo* 54 (1951) 71.

H. J. M. Turner and A. G. Hebert, "The Daughter of Zion," *Theo* 54 (1951) 150-151.

*A. W. Argyle, "A Parallel Between Luke II. 51 and Genesis XXXVII. 11," *ET* 65 (1953-54) 29.

*Jacob Z. Lauterbach, "The Talmud and the Gospels," *CCARJ* #12 (1956) 8-13, 17.

Hans Kosmala, "Matthew xxvi 52—A Quotation from the Targum," *NT* 4 (1960) 3-5.

Morton Smith, "The Jewish Elements in the Gospels," *JAAR* 24 (1956) 90-96.

*Ivor Buse, "The Markan Account of the Baptism of Jesus and Isaiah LXIII," *JTS, N.S.,* 7 (1956) 74-75.

T. Francis Glasson, "Mark XIII. and the Greek Old Testament," *ET* 69 (1957-58) 213-215.

P. Hadfield, "Matthew the Apocalyptic Editor," *LQHR* 184 (1959) 128-132.

Myles M. Bourke, "The Literary Genus of Matthew 1-2," *CBQ* 22 (1960) 160-175.

Arch. B. Taylor, "Decision in the Desert. *The Temptation of Jesus in the Light of Deuteronomy*," *Interp* 14 (1960) 300-309.

*Cecil Roth, "The Cleansing of the Temple and Zechariah xiv 21," *NT* 4 (1960) 174-181.

W. G. Essame, "Sowing and Plowing," *ET* 72 (1960-61) 54. *[Parables of Jesus and Jubilees 11:11]*

*O. Linton, "The Trial of Jesus and the Interpretation of Psalm CX," *NTS* 7 (1960-61) 258-262.

*J. A. Fitzmyer, "The Use of Explicit Old Testament Quotations in Qumran Literature and in the New Testament," *NTS* 7 (1960-61) 297-333.

John J. O'Rourke, "The Fulfillment Texts in Matthew," *CBQ* 24 (1962) 394-403.

*Charles de Santo, "The Assumption of Moses and the Christian Gospel. *A Survey*," *Interp* 16 (1962) 305-310.

Robert O. Coleman, "Matthew's Use of the Old Testament," *SWJT, N.S.*, 5 (1962-63) #1, 29-40.

Homer A. Kent Jr., "Matthew's Use of the Old Testament," *BS* 121 (1964) 34-43.

Norman Hillyer, "Matthew's Use of the Old Testament," *EQ* 36 (1964) 12-26.

*J. A. Emerton, "Mark XIV. 24 and the Targum to the Psalter," *JTS, N.S.*, 15 (1964) 58-59.

John J. O'Rourke, "Explicit Old Testament citations in the Gospels," *SMR* 7 (1964) 37-60.

John S. Roberts, "The Old Testament and the Historicity of the Gospels," *LQHR* 190 (1965) 44-49.

Robert W. Funk, "The Old Testament in Parable. *A Study of Luke 10:25-37*," *SQ/E* 26 (1965) 251-267.

*Stuart D. Currie, "Isaiah 63, 9 and the transfiguration in Mark," *ASBFE* 72 (Nov., 1966) #3, 7-34.

Jay B. Stern, "Jesus' Citation of Dt 6,5 and Lv 19,18 in the Light of Jewish Tradition," *CBQ* 28 (1966) 312-316.

L. Crockett, "Luke iv. 16-30 and the Jewish Lectionary Cycle: A Word of Caution," *JJS* 17 (1966) 13-46.

*S. Aalen, "St. Luke's Gospel and the Last Chapters of I Enoch," *NTS* 13 (1966-67) 1-13.

John F. Craghan, "A Redactional Study of Lk 7,21 in the Light of Dt 19,15," *CBQ* 29 (1967) 353-367.

William A. Beardslee, "The Wisdom Tradition and the Synoptic Gospels," *JAAR* 35 (1967) 231-240.

*Bruce Malina, "Matthew 2 and Is 41, 2-3: a possible relationship?" *SBFLA* 17 (1967) 290-302.

*Hugh J. Blair, "Putting One's Hand to the Plough. Luke ix. 62 in the Light of 1 Kings xix. 19-21," *ET* 79 (1967-68) 342-343.

*F. H. Borsch, "Mark xiv. 62 and I Enoch lxii. 5," *NTS* 14 (1967-68) 565-567.

C. H. Cave, "Lazarus and the Lukan Deuteronomy," *NTS* 15 (1968-69) 319-325.

*P. Grech, "Interprophetic Re-interpretation and Old Testament Eschatology," *Aug* 9 (1969) 235-265.

*Brevard Childs, "Psalm 8 in the Context of the Christian Canon," *Interp* 23 (1969) 20-31.

C. T. Ruddick Jr., "Behold, I Send My Messenger," *JBL* 88 (1969) 381-417.

§1043 *5.5.2.1 The Use of the Old Testament in the Gospel of John (specifically)*

*Samuel Davidson, "Irenæus, Polycarp and the Testaments of the Twelve Patriarchs, in Relation to the Fourth Gospel," *TRL* 7 (1870) 297-331.

*Edward B. Pollard, "Two Poems of Beginnings: Gen 1:1-15; John 1:1-18," *BW* 17 (1901) 107-110.

G. H. Box, "Some Jewish Affinities of the Phraseology of the Fourth Gospel," *OSHTP* (1905-06) 51-61.

*Eb. Nestle, "'Abraham Rejoiced'," *ET* 20 (1908-09) 477.

*James Hope Moulton, "'Abraham Rejoiced', etc.," *ET* 20 (1908-09) 523-524. *[John 8:56 // Gen. 17:17]*

R. H. Strachan, "The Newly Discovered Odes of Solomon, and their Bearing on the Problem of the Fourth Gospel," *ET* 22 (1910-11) 7-14.

*Robert A. Aytoun, "'No One Shall Snatch Them Out of My Hand'," *ET* 31 (1919-20) 475-476. *[John 10:28-30 // Isaiah 43:13]*

*E. C. Hoyskyns, "Genesis I-III and St. John's Gospel," *JTS* 21 (1919-20) 210-218.

C. F. Burney, "Our Lord's Old Testament Reference in St. John vii. 37, 38," *Exp, 8th Ser.,* 20 (1920) 385-388.

*D. J. Whitney, "In the Image of God—Genesis 1:27; John 4:24," *CFL, 3rd Ser.,* 32 (1926) 217.

A. Zimmerman, "John I: 1-18, and Genesis I," *RChR, 5th Ser.,* 5 (1926) 265-275.

*Charles C. Torrey, "**B** The Influence of Second Isaiah in the Gospels and Acts," *JBL* 48 (1929) 24-36.

Chaim Kaplan, "Some New Testament Problems in the Light of Rabbinics and the Pseudepigrapha. The Cosmological Similes in John 3, 5," *JSOR* 15 (1931) 64-66.

Otto W. Heick, "The Gospel According to St. John: A Missionary Tract Addressed to Israel?" *LCQ* 8 (1935) 173-190.

*C. A. Phillips, "The Use of John I. 9 in the 'Rest of the Words of Baruch'," *ET* 47 (1935-36) 431.

*Robert J. Drummond, "Genesis I. and John I. 1-14," *ET* 49 (1937-38) 568.

*A. Cowper Field, "Let there be Light: A Comparison of Genesis I, 3-5, and John I, with Root-Meanings of certain very Ancient Words," *JTVI* 74 (1942) 54-64, 69-71. (Communications by Charles Marston, p. 64; H. S. Curr, pp. 64-66; W. H. Molesworth, pp. 66-68; Leslie I. Moser, pp. 68-69)

*R. E. Wolfe, "Continuity of Thought between Proverbs and the Fourth Gospel as regards the *Logos*," *JBL* 64 (1945) x.

C. K. Barrett, "The Old Testament in the Fourth Gospel," *JTS* 48 (1947) 155-169.

*David R. Griffiths, "Deutero-Isaiah and the Fourth Gospel: Some Points of Comparison," *ET* 65 (1953-54) 355-360.

Richard Morgan, "Fulfillment in the Fourth Gospel. *The Old Testament Foundations,*" *Interp* 11 (1957) 155-165.

Jacob J. Enz, "The Book of Exodus as a Literary Type for the Gospel of John," *JBL* 76 (1957) 208-215.

W. C. Van Unnik, "The Quotation from the Old Testament in John 12:34," *NT* 3 (1959) 174-179.

P. Alexander Kerrigan, "Jn. 19, 25-27 in the Light of Johannine Theology and the Old Testament," *Anton* 35 (1960) 369-416.

Raymond E. Brown, "Three Quotations from John the Baptist in the Gospel of John," *CBQ* 22 (1960) 292-298.

Merrill C. Tenney, "The Old Testament and the Fourth Gospel," *BS* 120 (1963) 300-308.

*J. Edgar Bruns, "Some Reflections on Coheleth and John," *CBQ* 25 (1963) 414-416.

*Elizabeth R. Achtemeier, "Jesus Christ, the Light of the World, The Biblical Understanding of Light and Darkness," *Interp* 17 (1963) 439-449.

*Bruce Vawter, "Ezekiel and John," *CBQ* 26 (1964) 450-458.

*Lester J. Kuyper, "Grace and Truth. *An Old Testament Description of God, and its Use in the Johannine Gospel,*" *Interp* 18 (1964) 3-19.

*A. T. Hanson, "John's Citation of Psalm lxxxii," *NTS* 11 (1964-65) 158-162.

*James S. Ackerman, "The Rabbinic Interpretation of Psalm 82 and the Gospel of John: John 10:34," *HTR* 59 (1966) 186-191.

*A. T. Hanson, "John's Citation of Psalm lxxxii Reconsidered," *NTS* 13 (1966-67) 363-367.

*Martin McNamra, "*Logos* of the Fourth Gospel and *Memra* of the Palestinian Targum (Ex. 12^{42})," *ET* 79 (1967-68) 115-117.

*C. T. Ruddick Jr., "Feeding and Sacrifice. The Old Testament Background of the Fourth Gospel," *ET* 79 (1967-68) 340-341.

Arthur Wood, "The Adoption of the 'Logos' Idea," *PQL* 14 (1968) 273-278.

§1044 *5.5.3 The Use of the Old Testament in the Book of Acts*

*Meade C. Williams, "Reference of Isaiah liii. and Acts viii. to Jesus Christ, the Crucified," *CFL, 3rd Ser.,* 3 (1905) 135-138.

*W. H. Bass, "Acts II. 28 and Psalm XVI. 11," *ET* 29 (1917-18) 522.

*Charles C. Torrey, "**B** The Influence of Second Isaiah in the Gospels and Acts," *JBL* 48 (1929) 24-36.

Jacques Dupont, "The Use of the Old Testament in Acts," *TD* 3 (1955) 61-64.

M. Wilcox, "The Old Testament in Acts 1-15," *ABR* 5 (1956) 1-41.

*William A. Beardslee, "The Casting of Lots at Qumran and in the Book of Acts," *NT* 5 (1960) 245-252.

*Dale Goldsmith, "Acts 13:33-37: A *Pesher* on II Samuel 7," *JBL* 87 (1968) 321-324.

§1045 *5.5.4 The Use of the Old Testament in the New Testament Epistles - General Studies*

*George F. Moore, "Biblical Notes," *JBL* 16 (1897) 155-165. ["The Last Adam": Alleged Jewish Parallels, pp. 158-161]

James Hardy Ropes, "**C** The Influence of Second Isaiah on the Epistles," *JBL* 48 (1929) 37-39.

§1046 *5.5.5 The Use of the Old Testament in the Pauline Epistles*

Anonymous, "Are the Words of Eph. v. 14 to be Regarded as a Quotation from the Old Testament Scriptures?" *JSL, 1st Ser.,* 7 (1851) 447-449.

*Churchill Babington, "St. Paul and Philo: A Passage in 1 Cor., illustrated from Philo Judæus," *JCSP* 1 (1854) 47-51.

*P. S., "Dr. Maitland on Rom. xi. 25; and Genesis xlviii. 19," *JSL, 2nd Ser.,* 7 (1854-55) 199-204.

Howard Crosby, "Paul's Allegorical Use of the Mosaic Narrative," *AThR, N.S.,* 2 (1864) 303-311.

*E. H. Plumptre, "The Potter and the Clay. Jer. XVIII. 1-10; Rom. IX.. 19-24," *Exp, 1st Ser.,* 4 (1876) 369-480.

Edgar C. S. Gibson, "Sources of St. Paul's Teaching," *Exp, 2nd Ser.,* 4 (1882) 33-45,121-132, 209-220, 278-293, 343-355, 421-429. *[OT specifically, pp. 121-132]*

*James Scott, "Genesis XVII., 6-8 and Galatians III., 16," *ONTS* 4 (1884-85) 103-105.

E. G. King, "St. Paul's Method of Quotation," *Exp, 3rd Ser.,* 10 (1889) 233-238.

B[enjamin] B. Warfield, "Paul's Doctrine of the Old Testament," *PQ* 3 (1889) 389-406.

G. Emlen Hare, "The Soul and the Spirit," *PER* 3 (1889-90) 201-202.

*Eb. Nestle, "Eph. V. 14 and the Secrets of Enoch," *ET* 9 (1897-98) 376-377.

*C. G. Montefiore, "Rabbinic Judaism and the Epistles of St. Paul," *JQR* 13 (1900-01) 161-217.

*J. H. Ropes, "'Righteousness' and 'The Righteousness of God' in the Old Testament and in St. Paul," *JBL* 22 (1903) 211-227.

*Benjamin W. Robinson, "Some Elements of Forcefulness in Jesus' Comparisons," *JBL* 23 (1904) 106-179. [Section IV. Two Tables Comparing Deutero-Isaiah, Jesus, and Paul]

Franklin N. Jewett, "Questions from the Pew. Paul's Doctrine of Faith from the Old Testament," *OC* 21 (1907) 420-427.

*Richard Roberts, "St. Paul and the Book of Wisdom," *IJA* #18 (1909) 58-62; #19 (1909) 74-76.

*H. Bulcock, "The possible relation between the Pauline 'Christ' and the figure of Wisdom in the 'Wisdom of Solomon'," *IJA* #22 (1910) 61-63.

*Robert Paterson, "Scientific Difficulties in a Section of Paul's Teaching. I. *Evolution: Creation in Genesis*," *HR* 62 (1911) 15-21.

*Charles Johnston, "Paul and Philo," *ConstrQ* 1 (1913) 810-825.

*Ernst von Dobschütz, "The Attitude of Jesus and St. Paul Toward the Bible," *BM* 2 (1914) 619-636.

*[J.] Rendel Harris, "A Quotation from Judith in the Pauline Epistles," *ET* 27 (1915-16) 13-15. *[Judith 8:14 // 1 Cor. 2:10]*

*C. W. Emmet, "The Fourth Book of Esdras and St. Paul," *ET* 27 (1915-16) 551-556.

*Rendel Harris, "Enoch and 2 Corinthians," *ET* 33 (1921-22) 423-424.

Elmer E. Flack, "The Apostle Paul and the Old Testament," *LQ* 53 (1923) 330-356.

*J. Hugh Michael, "Paul and Job: A Neglected Analogy," *ET* 36 (1924-25) 67-70.

J. G. Tasker, "St. Paul's Use of the Old Testament," *ET* 41 (1929-30) 563-565. *(Review)*

*John Torrance, "Psalm XXII.—as Used by Christ and St. Paul," *ET* 44 (1932-33) 382.

Philip Carrington, "A Christian Midrash on the Pentateuch?" *ATR* 16 (1934) 206-209.

F. A. Schilling, "St. Paul's Knowledge and Use of the Book of Wisdom," *JBL* 53 (1934) xiii-xiv.

*Mary E. Andrews, "Paul, Philo and the Intellectuals," *JBL* 53 (1934) 150-166.

Thomas Houghton, "The Testimony of the Epistle to the Romans to the Old Testament," *EQ* 7 (1935) 419-426.

*James P. Wilson, "A Comparative Study of Exodus xxxiv. 29-35, and 2nd Cor. iii. 12-18, with Regard to the Veil on Moses' Face," *GUOST* 9 (1938-39) 1821.

*J. B. Orchard, "St Paul and the Book of Daniel," *B* 20 (1939) 172-179.

*John J. Collins, "Rabbinic Exegesis and Pauline Exegesis," *CBQ* 3 (1941) 15-26, 145-158.

Charles J. Costello, "The Old Testament in St. Paul's Epistles," *CBQ* 4 (1942) 141-145.

*Richard Hanson, "Moses in the Typology of St Paul," *Theo* 48 (1945) 174-177.

David Daube, "Paul and Rabbinic Judaism," *CQR* 147 (1948-49) 80-83. *(Review)*

A. T. Hanson, "The Interpretation of the Second Person Singular in Quotations from the Psalms in the New Testament. A Note on Romans xv, 3," *Herm* #73 (1949) 69-72.

*Robert A, Bartels, "Law and Sin in Fourth Esdras and Saint Paul," *LQ, N.S.,* 1 (1949) 319-330.

R. P. C. Hanson, "St. Paul's Quotations of the Book of Job," *Theo* 53 (1950) 250-253.

*Felix Gryglewicz, "Traces of the First Book of Maccabees in the Epistles of St Paul," *Scrip* 5 (1952-53) 149-152.

Peter Blaser, "Paul's Use of the Old Testament," *TD* 2 (1954) 49-52.

Mitchell J. Dahood, "Two Pauline Quotations from the Old Testament," *CBQ* 17 (1955) 19-24. *[Prov. 25:22(?); Psa. 116:10(?)]*

*Douglas Jones, "ἀνάμνησις in the LXX and the Interpretation of 1 Cor. XI. 25," *JTS, N.S.,* 6 (1955) 183-191.

Walter M. Abbott, "St. Paul's Use of Exodus in 1st Corinthians 10:1-13," *MH* 12 (1956-57) #1, 30-44.

*Neal Flanagan, "Messianic Fulfillment in St. Paul," *CBQ* 19 (1957) 474-484.

E. Earle Ellis, "'Saith the Lord'," *EQ* 29 (1957) 23-28.

John J. Donohue, "Sin and Sacrifice: The Old Testament Background of Pauline Thought," *MH* 14 (1958-59) #2, 1-19.

Raymond O. Zorn, "The Apostle Paul's Use of the Old Testament in Romans 10:5-8," *GR* 5 (1959) 29-34.

Richard C. Oudersluys, "Paul's Use of the Adam Typology," *RefR* 13 (1959-60) #4, 1-10.

*John Bowman, "The Doctrine of Creation, Fall of Man and Original Sin in Samaritan and Pauline Theology," *RTRM* 19 (1960) 65-72.

John W. Montgomery, "Some Comments on Paul's Use of Genesis in His Epistle to the Romans," *BETS* 4 (1961) 4-11.

*Krister Stendahl, "Hate, Non-Retaliation, and Love, 1QS x, 17-20 and Romans, 12:19-21," *HTR* 55 (1962) 343-355.

Ernst Bammel, "Paul and Judaism," *MC, N.S.,* 6 (1962-63) 279-285.

Henri Clavier, "Pauline Thought on the Old Testament," *Mwa-M* #3 (1963) 38-46.

Myles M. Bourke, "St. Paul and the Justification of Abraham," *BibT* #10 (1964) 643-649.

L. C. Allen, "The Old Testament in Romans I-VIII," *VE* 3 (1964) 6-41.

J. Massingberd Ford, "The Rabbinic Background of St. Paul's Use of ὑπέρακμος (1 *Cor.* vii. 36)," *JJS* 17 (1966) 89-91.

*A. J. Campbell, "Adam," *Theo* 69 (1966) 215-222.

Mathias Rissi, "The Brighter Splendor—Paul and the Old Testament According to II Corinthians 3," *Aff* 1 (1967) #2, 58-87.

S[olomon] Zeitlin, "Israelites, Jews in the Pauline Epistles," *JQR, N.S.,* 58 (1967-68) 72-74.

*Barbara Thiering, "St. Paul's Self-Understanding compared with that of the Qumran Sectarian," *Coll* 3 (1968-70) 293-306.

*T. Francis Glasson, "Colossians I 18, 15 and Sirach XXIV," *NT* 11 (1969) 154-156.

Allan M. Harmon, "Aspects of Paul's Use of the Psalms," *WTJ* 32 (1969-70) 1-23.

§1047 *5.5.6 The Use of the Old Testament in the Non-Pauline Epistles*

*Geo. Chr. Knapp, "Dissertation of 2 Pet. I. 19-21; as Exhibiting the Nature and Use of Old Testament Prophecies; Especially Those which Relate to the Messiah," *BibR* 2 (1826) 207-238. *(Trans. by E. N. K.)*

*E. Paret, "James iv. 5, in Connection with Genesis iv. 7," *AThR, N.S.,* 4 (1866) 292-298.

*J. Estlin Carpenter, "The Epistle of Jude and the Prophecy and Assumption of Moses," *TRL* 5 (1868) 259-276.

*Edward G. King, "Ῐς λουσαμέμνη εἰς κυλισμὸν βορπόρου," *JP* 7 (1876-77) 134-137. *[II Peter quotation of Prov. 26:11]*

*J. Rendel Harris, "An Unobserved Quotation from the Book of Enoch," *Exp, 6th Ser.,* 4 (1901) 194-199. *[Enoch 1:2 = 1 Peter 1:12]*

*J. Rendel Harris, "A Further Note on the Use of Enoch in 1 Peter," *Exp, 6th Ser.,* 4 (1901) 346-349. *[1 Peter 3:19, 20 = Enoch 10:4, 5, 12, 13]*

*C. Taylor, "I Peter and Enoch," *ET* 13 (1901-02) 40. *[1 Peter 1:12 // Enoch 1:2, 9:1; 1 Peter 1:10, 12 // Enoch 103:2, 106:19]*

*Carl Clemen, "The First Epistle of St. Peter and the Book of Enoch," *Exp, 6th Ser.,* 6 (1902) 316-320.

De Lacy O'Leary, "Rabbinical Illustrations of the Epistle of St. James," *ET* 15 (1903-04) 334-335.

[J.] Rendel Harris, "Jesus and the Exodus," *Exp, 8th Ser.,* 18(1919) 64-72.

*J. P. Wilson, "Is Genesis I. 2 the Scripture Cited in James IV. 5?" *GUOST* 6 (1929-33) 8-9.

*L. E. Elliott-Binns, "James I. 21 and Ezekiel XVI. 36: an Odd Coincidence," *ET* 66 (1954-55) 273.

*Frederick W. Danker, "II Peter 3:10 and Psalm of Solomon 17:10," *ZNW* 53 (1962) 82-86.

M. Gertner, "Midrashic Terms and Techniques in the New Testament and the Epistle of James, a Midrash on a Psalm," *StEv* 3 (1964) 463.

*P. J. Thompson, "Psalm 119: a possible Clue to the First Epistle of John," *StEv* 2 (1964) 487-492.

*Birger A. Pearson, "A Reminiscence of Classical Myth at *II Peter* 2.4," *GRBS* 10 (1969) 71-80.

§1048 *5.5.6.1 The Use of the Old Testament in the Epistle to the Hebrews*

*J. J. Stewart Perowne, "Wind and Fire Ministers of God, Psalm civ. 4; Hebrews i. 7," *Exp, 1st Ser.,* 8 (1878) 461-467.

*James Robertson, "Requests and Replies," *ET* 3 (1891-93) 68. *[Gen. 47:31 and Heb. 11:21]*

Emil Lund, "Quotations from the Old Testament in the Epistle to the Hebrews," *TTKF* 16 (1914) 36-59.

*J. Wilcock, "1 Samuel XII. 11; Hebrews XI. 32," *ET* 28 (1916-17) 41-42.

*[J.] Rendel Harris, "Some Notes on 4 Maccabees," *ET* 32 (1920-21) 183-184. *[Parallel to Hebrews]*

Edward B. Pollard, "Notes on the Old Testament Citations in the Epistle to the Hebrews," *CQ* 1 (1924) 447-452.

Anthony Hanson, "The Gospel in the Old Testament According to Hebrews," *Theo* 52 (1949) 248-252.

*Paul Leo., "Melchizedek and Christ," *WSQ* 12 (1948-49) #1, 3-9.

G. A. Turner, "Old Testament Exegesis in the Epistle to the Hebrews," *JBL* 70 (1951) xvi.

Robert Rendall, "The Method of the Writer to the Hebrews in Using Old Testament Quotations," *EQ* 27 (1955) 214-220.

*Eric Fredius, "The Priesthood of Christ and the Old Testament Priesthood: An Interpretation of Hebrews," *ACQ* 2 (1962) 162-165.

A. T. Hanson, "Christ in the Old Testament according to Hebrews," *StEv* 2 (1964) 393-407.

Kenneth J. Thomas, "The Old Testament Citations in Hebrews," *NTS* 11 (1964-65) 303-325.

George Howard, "Hebrews and the Old Testament Quotations," *NT* 10 (1968) 208-216.

§1049   5.5.7 The Use of the Old Testament in the Apocalypse

*(   ) G., "The Burial of Moses: With Remarks on Mal. IV. 5, 6, and the Reappearance of Enoch and Elijah as the Apocalyptic Witnesses," *JSL, 2nd Ser.,* 6 (1854) 135-165.

*(   ) G., "The Burial of Moses; with Remarks on Mal. IV. 5, 6, and the Reappearance of Enoch and Elijah as the Apocalyptic Witnesses," *MQR* 8 (1854) 394-427.

*Charles W. Cooper, "Some of the Precious Stones of the Bible, with Special Reference to the High Priest's Breastplate and the Jasper of Rev. IV. 3," *JTVI* 61 (1929) 60-74, 83-85. (Discussion, pp. 75-83)

*Martin Rist, "The Common Source of Revelation 16:17-22:5 and the Apocalypse of Elijah," *IR* 12 (1955) #1, 27-34.

*Richard L. Twomey, "Imagery in Isaiah and the Apocalypse," *MH* 12 (1956-57) #3, 13-21.

Martin Rist, "The Use of the Old Testament by the Author of Revelation," *IR* 17 (1960) #2, 3-10.

*D. R. Hillers, "Revelation 13:18 and a Scroll from Murabba'at," *BASOR* #170 (1963) 65.

L. P. Trudinger, "Some Observations Concerning the Text of the Old Testament in the Book of Revelation," *JTS, N.S.,* 17 (1966) 82-88.

§1050 5.6 Studies on Old Testament Prophecy as Used in the New Testament

*Geo. Chr. Knapp, "Dissertation of 2 Pet. I. 19-21; as Exhibiting the Nature and Use of Old Testament Prophecies; Especially Those which Relate to the Messiah," *BibR* 2 (1826) 207-238. *(Trans. by E. N. K.)*

*James Strong, *"Quotation of the Prophecy of Christ's Transfixion.—* Zech. xii, 10; John xix, 37," *MR* 32 (1850) 338-339.

Anonymous, "The Fulfillment of Prediction," *ONTS* 4 (1884-85) 426-427.

*R. H. Charles, "Messianic Doctrine in the Book of Enoch, and Its Influence on the New Testament," *ET* 4 (1892-93) 301-303.

*G. H. Gwilliam, "Interpretation of Messianic Prophecy. A Sermon Preached at the Church of St. Mary-the-Virgin, Oxford, on Sunday Afternoon, 11th March, 1900," *ET* 11 (1899-1900) 392-398.

Walter F. Adeney, "New Testament Revision of Old Testament Prophecy," *ICMM* 2 (1905-06) 178-183.

G. E. Ffrench, "The Interpretation of Prophecy," *HJ* 10 (1911-12) 861-874.

F. H. Woods, "The Messianic Interpretation of Prophecy," *ET* 24 (1912-13) 320-324.

*A. Nairne, "The Transformation of the Messianic Hope by Our Lord and His Apostles," *ICMM* 9 (1912-13) 17-35.

W. R. Inge, "The Transformation of Messianic Hope in the New Testament," *ConstrQ* 1 (1913) 306-320.

Theo. Labouré, "The Argument from the Messianic Prophecies," *AER* 56 (1917) 337-348.

H. D. A. Major, "Messianic Prophecy and the Gospels," *ICMM* 19 (1922-23) 179-187.

*C. P. Coffin, "An Old Testament Prophecy and Some New Testament Miracle Stories," *JAAR* 11 (1943) 162-166.

Gabriel Hebert, "Hope Looking Forward. *The Old Testament Passages used by the New Testament as Prophetic of the Resurrection of Jesus Christ,*" *Interp* 10 (1956) 259-269.

*J. C. G. Greig, "Gospel Messianism and the Qumran Use of Prophecy," *StEv* 1 (1959) 593-599.

Edmund F. Sutcliffe, "The Plenary Sense, Original or Superimposed," *HeyJ* 1 (1960) 68-70.

*P. Grech, "Interprophetic Re-Interpretation and Old Testament Eschatology," *Aug* 9 (1969) 235-265.

§1051 *5.7 Studies on the Old Testament in the Early Church*

Edward Reuss, "History of the Canon of the Holy Scriptures in the Christian Church," *ER* 18 (1867) 502-523. [Chapter I. Use of the Old Testament, in the Apostolic Church, pp. 502-513] *(Trans. by L W. Heydenreich)*

Anonymous, "Christianity and the Old Testament," *CR* 24 (1872) 256-273.

James Orr, "The Old Testament Question in the Early Church," *Exp, 5th Ser.,* 1 (1895) 346-361.

*E. P. Boys-Smith, "Apostolic and Critical Teaching on the Position of the Pentateuch," *ET* 7 (1895-96) 295-303.

H. M. Scott, "How the Apostles Regarded the Old Testament," *CFL, N.S.,* 1 (1900) 321-328.

J. A. Selbie, "Among the Periodicals. The Use of the 'Apocrypha' in the Early Church," *ET* 12 (1900-01) 70-71.

*Henry A. Poels, "History and Inspiration. Saint Jerome," *CUB* 12 (1906) 182-218.

*H. B. Swete, "The Old Testament in Greek. II. The Greek Old Testament in the Christian Church," *ICMM* 5 (1908-09) 129-146.

Frank C. Porter, "The Place of the Sacred Book in the Christian Religion," *YDQ* 5 (1908-09) 257-266.

Carl Clemen, "The Dependence of Early Christianity upon Judaism," *Exp, 7th Ser.,* 8 (1909) 289-307.

*G. H. Box, "Survey of Recent Literature Concerned with Judaism in Its Relation to Christian Origins and Early Development," *RTP* 6 (1910-11) 65-87.

*J. Rendel Harris, "Two Flood-Hymns of the Early Church," *Exp, 8th Ser.,* 2 (1911) 405-417.

Gerald Friedlander, "The Influence of the Jewish Hellenistic Literature on Christianity," *IJA* #29 (1912) 24-25.

*Herbert Lee Newman, "Influence of the Book of Wisdom on Early Christian Writings," *CQ* 8 (1931) 361-372.

H. E. Dana, "The Old Testament in the Apostolic Age," *BR* 17 (1932) 227-243.

*L. H. Brockington, "The Christian Approach to the Old Testament," *BQL* 11 (1942-45) 264-269. [1. The Old Testament as the Scripture of the Early Church, pp. 264-265]

*Robert M. Grant, "Historical Criticism in the Ancient Church," *JR* 25 (1945) 183-196. [IV. Greek Criticism of the Old Testament, p. 186; V. Christian Criticism of the Old Testament, pp. 186-188]

Robert M. Grant, "The Bible in the Ancient Church," *JR* 26 (1946) 190-202.

S. MacLean Gilmour, "The Bible of the Early Church," *IR* 7 (1950) 50-58.

*Leo Baeck, "Haggadah and Christian Doctrine," *HUCA* 23 (1950-51) Part 1, 549-560.

*E. C. Burleigh, "The Influence of Hebrew Wisdom Literature Upon Early Christian Doctrine," *ABR* 1 (1951) 75-87.

Robert M. Grant, "The Place of the Old Testament in Early Christianity," *Interp* 5 (1951) 186-202.

Loren E. Arnett, "The Significance of the Old Testament in the New Testament Church," *SQ/E* 12 (1951) 126-132.

Robert Smith, "The Relevance of the Old Testament for the Doctrine of the Church," *SJT* 5 (1952) 14-23.

*Albert C. Sundberg Jr., "The Old Testament of the Early Church (Study in Canon)," *HTR* 51 (1958) 205-226.

C. S. Mann, "The Old Testament—New Testament Problem in Preaching and Teaching," *StEv* 3 (1964) 483-487.

Ernst Hammerschmidt, "Jewish Elements in the Cult of the Ethiopian Church," *JES* 3 (1965) #2, 1-12.

Basil Hall, "The Old Testament in the History of the Church," *LQHR* 190 (1965) 30-36.

E. Bammel, "Christian Origins in Jewish Tradition," *NTS* 13 (1966-67) 317-335.

Herbert T. Mayer, "Scripture, Tradition and Authority in the Life of the Early Church," *CTM* 38 (1967) 19-23. [II. The Sacred Writings, pp. 20-21]

*G. Gerald Harrop, "The Bible Cover to Cover," *TBMDC* #4 (1968) 1-19. [The Problem of the Old Testament as Christian Scripture, pp. 7-10]

§1052 *5.8 Studies on Symbolism and Typology (includes Old Testament and Ancient Near East)*

'Ereunetes', "On the Oblation of Isaac, as figurative of the Death of Christ," *TRep* 6 (1788) 60-78.

Anonymous, "Abraham Offering His Son Isaac, a Type of Christ," *TRGR* 1 (1822) 553-557.

†( ) C., "On the Egyptian Tau, or Crux Ansata," *MMBR* 56 (1823-24) 21-24, 302-306.

†Anonymous, "Historical Types contained in the Old Testament," *BCQTR, 4th Ser.,* 2 (1827) 433-443. *(Review)*

*Joseph Muenscher, "On Types and the Typical Interpretation of Scripture," *BRCR, N.S.,* 5 (1841) 92-113.

Anonymous, "Symbology of the Old Testament, and Rules for its Interpretation," *CRB* 10 (1845) 113-137.

*[David N. Lord], "Analysis of the Principle Figures of the Scriptures and Statement of their Laws," *TLJ* 1 (1848-49) 353-399.

*[David N. Lord], "Objections to the Laws of Symbolization," *TLJ* 2 (1849-50) 596-632; 8 (1855-56) 1-50.

L. M., "Letter and Spirit in the Old Testament Scriptures," *JSL, 1st Ser.,* 6 (1850) 156-178.

( ) Davies, "Symbolic Rods," *JSL, 1st Ser.,* 7 (1851) 458-459.

*[David N. Lord], "Objections to the Laws of Figures," *TLJ* 3 (1850-51) 102-113.

*[David N. Lord(?)], "Objections to the Laws of Figurative Language," *TLJ* 3 (1850-51) 613-642.

J. F., "Typical Representations of the Godhead," *JSL, 2nd Ser.*, 1 (1851-52) 220-221.

†Anonymous, "Fairbairn's Typology of Scripture," *TLJ* 4 (1851-52) 353-395. *(Review)*

J. W. N., "Fairbairn's Typology," *RChR* 4 (1852) 76-80. *(Review)*

*[David N. Lord(?)], "Objections to the Laws of Figurative Language," *TLJ* 3 (1850-51) 613-642.

T. Apple, "The Typical Character of the Old Testament Church," *RChR* 8 (1856) 615-629.

†Anonymous, "Sacred Typology," *LQHR* 10 (1858) 381-416. *(Review)*

*Anonymous, "Jewish Sacrifices, with Particular Reference to the Sacrifice of Christ," *BS* 16 (1859) 1-56.

*(   ) Q., "The Typical Character of David: with a Digression concerning certain words," *JSL, 4th Ser.*, 5 (1864) 14-27.

T. T. Titus, "Was Isaac, on Mount Moriah, a Type of Christ?" *ER* 19 (1868) 447-460.

†Anonymous, "The Prechristian Cross," *ERCJ* 131 (1870) 222-255. *(Review)*

W. M. Thomson, "The Natural Basis of our Spiritual Language: Types and Symbols," *DTQ* 1 (1875) 250-259.

W. M. Thomson, "Natural Basis of Our Spiritual Language, No. IV. Types and Symbols," *BS* 32 (1875) 19-35.

Addison P. Foster, "The Types of Scripture," *CongQB* 18 (1876) 510-536.

W. G. Keady, "The Typical Significance of Elijah and Elisha.—2 Kings ii," *PQPR* 6 (1877) 745-754.

*M. C. Read, "The Symbolism of the Garden of Eden," *AAOJ* 3 (1880-81) 131-134.

*O. D. Miller, "Solar Symbolism in Ancient Religions," *AAOJ* 3 (1880-81) 218-227.

*O. D. Miller, "Symbolical Geography of the Ancients," *AAOJ* 3 (1880-81) 307-319.

*F. Rendall, "The Scriptural Idea of Priesthood Embodied in Successive Types," *Exp, 3rd Ser.,* 9 (1889) 24-55.

William W. McLane, "The Relation of Old Testament Types to Revelation," *HR* 19 (1890) 491-498.

Horace L. Singleton, "Scriptural Symbolism," *HR* 38 (1899) 170-172.

*Morris Jastrow Jr., "Dust, Earth, and Ashes as Symbols of Mourning among the Ancient Hebrews," *JAOS* 20 (1899) 133-150.

*John D. Davis, "The Symbolism of the Lamb," *CFL, N.S.,* 1 (1900) 71-72.

Ben-Ezra Stiles Ely Jr., "The Symbolism of the Deliverance," *CFL, N.S.,* 4 (1901) 336-347.

Hiram King, "The Sacrificial Types of Christ the Exponents of the Atonement," *RChR, 4th Ser.,* 9 (1905) 321-336.

Frank B. Tarbell, "The Palm of Victory," *AJA* 12 (1908) 69-70.

Anonymous, "Types in Scripture: The Importance of Studying Them," *CFL, 3rd Ser.,* 8 (1908) 113-115. *(Editorial Note)*

*Henry Proctor, "Symbolism of the Hebrew Alphabet," *AAOJ* 31 (1909) 16-18.

A. J. Maclean, "The Symbolical and Figurative Language of the Bible," *HR* 60 (1910) 348-352.

J[ames] F[rederick] M[etch] Ffrench, "The Use of Sun and Fire Symbols in Prehistoric Times," *ICQ* 5 (1912) 44-59.

L. W. King, "Origin of Animal Symbolism in Babylonia, Assyria and Persia," *SBAP* 34 (1912) 276-278.

[L. W. King], "Origin of Animal Symbolism in Babylonia, Assyria and Persia," *RP* 12 (1913) 100-101.

*Jacob Nacht, "The Symbolism of the Shoe with Special Reference to the Jewish Sources," *JQR, N.S.,* 6 (1915-16) 1-22.

G. B. G[ordon], "The Double Axe and Some Other Symbols," *MJ* 7 (1916) 46-68.

*Anonymous, "The Symbolism of Ancient Jewish Coins," *HR* 73 (1917) 25.

*Stephen Langdon, "A Tablet on the Mysteries of Babylonian Symbolism," *MJ* 9 (1918) 152-157.

H. Northcote, "The Eternal Waters," *ICMM* 15 (1918-19) 258-263.

H. W. Congdon, "The Symbolism of Scripture," *CRL, 3rd Ser.,* 26 (1920) 425-427.

Donald A. Mackenzie, "Colour Symbolism," *Folk* 33 (1922) 136-169.

*Eugene S. McCartney, "The Symbolism of Pegasus on Aera Signata," *AJA* 28 (1924) 66.

*Charles B. Warring, "Miracle, Law, Evolution," *BS* 60 (1903) 750-764.

[T. H.] Bindley, "Symbolism in the Old and New Testaments," *ET* 40 (1928-29) 548-550.

A. H. Finn, "Types in Scripture," *JTVI* 63 (1931) 198-213, 220-221. [(Discussion, pp. 213-219) (Communication by J. J. B. Coles, pp. 219-220)]

*G. D. Hornblower, "Blue and Green in Ancient Egypt," *AEE* 17 (1932) 47-53.

*M. Narkiss, "The Snuff-Shovel as a Jewish Symbol. (A Contribution to the problem of Jewish decorative motifs)," *JPOS* 15 (1935) 14-28.

R. F. Rattray, "The History of Symbols," *QRL* 267 (1936) 333-346. *(Review)*

*John Vernon McGee, "Theology of the Tabernacle," *BS* 94 (1937) 153-175, 295-320, 409-429; 95 (1938) 22-39.

Cameron Mackay, "The Sign of the Palm Tree," *CQR* 126 (1938) 187-212.

Zofja Ameisenowa, "The Tree of Life in Jewish Iconography," *JWCI* 2 (1938-39) 326-345.

*Harold C. Rowse, "Symbolism and Revelation," *BQL* 10 (1940-41) 5-11.

*Paul Romanoff, "Jewish Symbols on Ancient Coins," *JQR, N.S.,* 33 (1942-43) 435-444.

*P. Paschal Parente, "Ascetical and Mystical Traits of Moses and Elias," *CBQ* 5 (1943) 183-190.

*Paul Romanoff, "Jewish Symbols on Ancient Jewish Coins," *JQR, N.S.,* 34 (1943-44) 161-177, 299-312, 425-440.

*Lily Ross Taylor, "Symbols of the Augurate on Coins of the Caecilii Metelli," *AJA* 48 (1944) 352-356.

J. McG. Dawkins, "The Seal of Solomon," *JRAS* (1944) 145-150.

Carl Armerding, "The Brazen Serpent," *BS* 102 (1945) 110-117.

*Arthur Darby Nock, "Sarcophagi and Symbolism," *AJA* 50 (1946) 14-170. [Note by J. D. Beazley, p. 170]

Charles T. Fritsch, "Biblical Typology. New Trends in Old Testament Theology," *BS* 103 (1946) 293-305.

Charles T. Fritsch, "Biblical Typology. The Bible as Redemptive History," *BS* 103 (1946) 418-430.

Charles T. Fritsch, "Biblical Typology. Principles of Biblical Typology," *BS* 104 (1947) 214-222.

Harry J. Leon, "Symbolic Representations in the Jewish Catacombs of Rome," *AJA* 52 (1948) 374.

*Sydney P. Noe, "Symbols for Cities," *Arch* 1 (1948) 188-189.

John F. Walvoord, "The Incarnation of the Son of God. II. Christological Typology," *BS* 105 (1948) 286-296, 404-417.

P. J. Heather, "Colour Symbolism: Part I," *Folk* 59&60 (1948-49) 165-183. *[Part II not applicable]*

*E. Douglas Van Buren, "The Rod and Ring," *ArOr* 17 (1949) Part 2, 434-450.

John F. Walvoord, "Christological Typology," *BS* 106 (1949) 27-33.

George A. F. Knight, "Are we returning to typology?" *RTRM* 8 (1949) #2, 1-5.

E. R. Goodenough, "Stages in the Development of Jewish Symbolism," *JBL* 69 (1950) iii-iv.

*B. Ph. Lozinski, "Eagle Symbols in Metal Work," *AJA* 56 (1952) 175-176.

Robert C. Dentan, "Typology—Its Use and Abuse," *ATR* 34 (1952) 211-216.

Henri de Reidmatten, "Typology in the Scriptures," *NB* 33 (1952) 132-141. *(Trans. by Kathleen Pond)*

H. L. Ellison, "Typology," *EQ* 25 (1953) 158-166.

*G. W. H. Lampe, "Typological Exegesis," *Theo* 56 (1953) 201-208.

E. C. Blackman, "Return of Typology?" *CongQL* 32 (1954) 53-59.

Donald K. Campbell, "The Interpretation of Types," *BS* 112 (1955) 248-255.

*G. W. H. Lampe, "Hermeneutics and Typology," *LQHR* 190 (1955) 17-25.

*Cecil Roth, "Messianic Symbols in Palestine Archaeology," *PEQ* 87 (1955) 151-164.

Austin Farrer, "Important Hypotheses Reconsidered. VIII. Typology," *ET* 67 (1955-56) 228-231.

G. A. Wainwright, "The Cappadocian Symbol," *AS* 6 (1956) 137-143.

Arthur J. Crosmer, "Marriage, a Type of God's Relationship to His People," *CTM* 27 (1956) 370-382.

Chaim W. Reines, "Symbolism in Judaism," *Jud* 5 (1956) 13-21.

J. van der Ploeg, "Old Testament Signs," *Scrip* 8 (1956) 33-44.

*Mebrure Tosun, "The Significance of the Symbols of Gods in the Mesopotamian Cylinder Seals," *TTKB* 20 (1956) 49-59.

E. L. Wenger, "The Typological Hypothesis," *ET* 68 (1956-57) 222-223.

*J. Meyshan, "The Canopy Symbol on the Coins of Agrippa I," *BIES* 22 (1958) #3/4, n.p.n.

*H. W. Wolff, "The Old Testament in Controversy. *Interpretive Principles and Illustration,*" *Interp* 12 (1958) 281-290. *(Trans. by James L. Mays)*

Gabriel Vahanian, "Biblical Symbolism and Man's Religious Quest," *JR* 38 (1958) 226-239.

*G. A. Wainwright, "The 'Signet Royal' or Cappadocian Symbol," *Or, N.S.,* 27 (1958) 287.

*Andrew Alföldi, "Hasta—Summa Imperii. The Spear as Embodiment of Sovereignty in Rome," *AJA* 63 (1959) 1-27.

*Josef Meyshan (Mestschanski), "The Symbols on the Coinage of Herod the Great and Their Meanings," *PEQ* 91 (1959) 109-121.

*S. H. Hooke, "Symbolism in the Dead Sea Scrolls," *StEv* 1 (1959) 600-612.

G. B. Sarfatti, "The Tables of the Covenant as a Symbol of Judaism," *Tarbiz* 29 (1959-60) #4, IV-V.

Warren Vanhetloo, "God's Teaching Pictures," *CCBQ* 3 (1960) #1, 15-20.

*William L. Reed, "Symbolism and the Theology of the Psalms," *CollBQ* 37 (1960) #3, 35-43.

*Cecil Roth, "Star and Anchor: Coin Symbolism and the End of Days," *EI* 6 (1960) 13*-15*.

*Oscar J. F. Seitz, "'What Do These Stones Mean?'," *JBL* 79 (1960) 247-254.

Mary Francis Thelen, "Jewish Symbols and 'Normative Judaism'. A Review Article," *JAAR* 32 (1964) 361-363. *(Review)*

*James D. Roche, "Light as a Figure and Symbol in St. John and in the Old Testament," *MH* 15 (1960) #2, 18-29.

S. H. Hooke, "Fish Symbolism," *Folk* 72 (1961) 535-538.

*Gerhard von Rad, "The Interpretation of the Old Testament. II. Typological Interpretation of the Old Testament," *Interp* 15 (1961) 174-192.

Herbert Musurillo, "Shadow and Reality: Thoughts on the Problem of Typology," *ThSt* 22 (1961) 455-460.

*Isabel Speyart Van Woerden, "The Iconography of the Sacrifice of Abraham," *VC* 15 (1961) 214-255.

*W. Wirgin, "The Menorah as a Symbol of Judaism," *IEJ* 12 (1962) 140-142.

P. A. Verhoef, "Some Notes on Typological Exegesis," *OTW* 5 (1962) 58-63.

R. H. Beatty, "Tradition-history and Typology," *ACQ* 3 (1963) 231-246.

*Jacob Neusner, "Jewish Use of Pagan Symbols After 70 C.E.," *JR* 43 (1963) 303-314.

*Francis Foulkes, "Typology or Allegory?" *Them* 2 (1963-64) #2, 8-15.

W. Hartner and R. Ettinghausen, "The Conquering Lion, the Life Cycle of a Symbol," *Oriens* 17 (1964) 161-171.

J. A. Zeisler, "The Problem of Discrimination in Typology," *Coll* 1 (1964-66) 67-73.

Leroy Davis, "Typology in Barth's Doctrine of Scripture," *ATR* 47 (1965) 33-49.

*J. Massingberd Ford, "'You are "Abraham" and upon this rock' (A study of stone symbolism)," *HeyJ* 6 (1965) 289-301.

*Phyllis W. Lehmann, "The Meander Door: A Labyrinthine Symbol," *AJA* 70 (1966) 192.

M. Rosalie [Ryan?], "Yahweh is My Rock," *BibT* #23 (1966) 1515-1521.

Pierre Grelot, "Biblical figures; a definition and a criterion," *TD* 14 (1966) 8-13.

J. Massingberd Ford, "The Jewel of Discernment. (A study of stone symbolism)," *BZ, N.S.,* 11 (1967) 109-116.

J. Murtagh, "Sun Symbolism in the Old Testament," *IER, 5th Ser.,* 108 (1967) 243-253.

Morton Smith, "Goodenough's *Jewish Symbols* in Retrospect," *JBL* 86 (1967) 53-68.

Nobuaki Kuniya, "The Gammadiae, the Swastika, and the Divine Fluid—A Study on the Ancient Symbolism," *Orient* 4 (1967) 17-36.

*J. Massingberd Ford, "'You are "Abraham" and upon this rock' (A study of stone symbolism)," *TD* 15 (1967) 134-137.

*H. L. Ellison, "The Prophecy of Jeremiah," *EQ* 40 (1968) 34-40, 157-164. [XXX. Jeremiah's Symbolism, pp. 34-40]

*Jack M. Sasson, "Bovine Symbolism in the Exodus Narrative," *VT* 18 (1968) 380-387.

*Stanley N. Gundry, "Typology as a Means of Interpretation: Past and Present," *BETS* 12 (1969) 233-240.

*Melford E. Spiro, "Religious Symbolism and Social Behavior," *PAPS* 113 (1969) 341-349.

§1053 *5.9 Studies on Numbers and Numerology [See also: Mathematics and Numbering Systems §122 ←]*

Josiah W. Gibbs, "Biblical Criticisms and Remarks: A Peculiar Use of the Number Forty," *BRCR, N.S.,* 2 (1839) 480-483.

John W. Donaldson, "On Plato's Number," *TPS* (1842-44) 81-92.

Anonymous, "Arithmetical Criticism," *BFER* 15 (1866) 60-90. *(Review)*

*Robinson Thornton, "On the Numerical System of the Old Testament," *JTVI* 5 (1870-71) 105-120, 139-140. [(Discussion, pp. 120-138) (Remarks by C. Graham, pp. 141-145)]

*P. H. Gosse, "On the High Numbers in the Pentateuch: Are they Trustworthy?" *JTVI* 5 (1870-71) 349-377.

Anonymous, "The Numerical Figures of the Bible," *SPR* 26 (1875) 735-748.

J. F. Garrision, "The Symbolism of Numbers in the Bible and in the Ancient Religions and Philosophies," *CR* 28 (1876) 517-552. *(Review)*

S. M. Drach, "Why is Forty-three a Basal Biblical Number?" *SBAT* 5 (1876-77) 313-317, 597.

T. J. Dodd, "The Explanation of Numerical Difficulties," *ONTS* 4 (1884-85) 171-174.

John P. Peters, "Hebrew Use of Numbers," *AJSL* 2 (1885-86) 174.

*John P. Peters, "The Use of Numbers in Hebrew," *AJSL* 3 (1886-87) 113-114.

Joseph E. Walker, "Duality," *BS* 49 (1892) 560-595.

Joseph H. Rockwell, "The Meaning of Scriptural Numbers," *ACQR* 22 (1897) 178-196.

Paul Carus, "Seven," *OC* 15 (1901) 335-340, 412-427.

W. D. Kersill, "Numerical Errors in the Old Testament—the Explanation," *CFL, 3rd Ser.,* 1 (1904) 217-221.

*Ivan Panin, "The Old Testament Women in the New," *BN* 1 (1904) #5, 139-149.

Ivan Panin, "Old Testament Notes," *BN* 1 (1904) #6, 165-169.

Ivan Panin, "Verses in the Psalms," *BN* 1 (1904) #6, 170-177.

*Ivan Panin, "The Titles of the Psalms," *BN* 1 (1904) #6, 178-184.

Ivan Panin, "Persons After Whom the Old Testament Books are Named," *BN* 1 (1904) #6, 190-194.

*Ivan Panin, "Old Testament Writers Named in the Bible," *BN* 1 (1904) #8, 273-275.

W. B. Stevenson, "The Use of Artificial or Illustrative Numbers in the Old Testament," *GUOST* 3 (1907-12) 22-23.

Enno Littmann, "'23' and Other Numerical Expressions," *OC* 22 (1908) 119-124.

*C. F. Burney, "Four and Seven as Divine Titles," *JTS* 12 (1910-11) 118-120.

J. P. Peters, "Some Uses of Numbers," *JBL* 38 (1919) 15-23.

Lawrence Parmly Brown, "The Cosmic Five, Seven and Twelve," *OC* 37 (1923) 307-320, 373-383, 431-448, 488-509.

Phineas Mordel, "Note on the Theory of the Kabbalistic Origin of 'Arabic' Numerals," *JQR, N.S.,* 16 (1925-26) 207.

*Warren R. Dawson, "The number 'Seven' in Egyptian Texts," *Aeg* 8 (1927) 97-107.

Anonymous, "Symbolical and Sacred Numbers in Scripture," *MR* 110 (1927) 974-977.

J. A. Fleming, "Number in Nature and in the Biblical Literature indicating a Common Origin in a Supreme Intelligence," *JTVI* 60 (1928) 11-31, 42-44. [(Discussion, pp. 31-40) (Communications by A. T. Schofield, p. 40, G. Mackinlay, p. 40, R. McCormack, pp. 40-42)]

Campbell Bonner, "The Numerical Value of a Magical Formula," *JEA* 16 (1930) 6-9.

*Conrad Henry Moehlman, "The Apocalyptic Mind," *CRDSB* 3 (1930-31) 114-128.

Eric Burrows, "The Number Seventy in Semitic," *Or, N.S.,* 5 (1936) 389-392.

Robert Gordis, "The Heptad as an Element of Biblical and Rabbinic Style," *JBL* 62 (1943) 17-26.

Oswald T. Allis, "Biblical Numerics," *BTr* 3 (1952) 117-124.

*R. E. D. Clark, "The Large Numbers of the Old Testament—Especially in Connexion with the Exodus," *JTVI* 87 (1955) 82-93, 151-152. [(Discussion, pp. 145-149) (Communications by F. F. Bruce, pp. 149-150, J. W. Wenham, pp. 150-151, D. C. Mandeville, 151)]

Gerald T. Kennedy, "The Use of Numbers in Sacred Scriptures," *AER* 139 (1958) 22-35.

*Benjamin B. Dayton, "Numerical Codes in Bible Prophecy," *JASA* 11 (1959) #3, 6-11.

F. Rosenthal, "Nineteen," *SBO* 3 (1959) 304-318.

O. H. Lehmann, "Number-symbolism as a Vehicle of Religious Experience in the Gospels, Contemporary Rabbinic Literature and the Dead Sea Scrolls," *StP* 4 (1961) 125-135.

*G. Nádor, "Some Numerical Categories in Ancient Rabbinical Literature: The Numbers *Ten, Seven* and *Four,*" *AOASH* 14 (1962) 301-315.

W. M. W. Roth, "The Numerical Sequence x/x + 1 in the Old Testament," *VT* 12 (1962) 300-311.

John J. Davis, "Biblical Numerics," *GJ* 5 (1964) #3, 30-44.

J. B. Segal, "Numerals in the Old Testament," *JSS* 10 (1965) 2-20.

*D. Flusser, "The *Pesher* of Isaiah and the Twelve Apostles," *EI* 8 (1967) 69*-70*.

John J. Davis, "The Rhetorical Use of Numbers in the Old Testament," *GJ* 8 (1967) #2, 40-48.

J.W.Wenham, "Large Numbers in the Old Testament,"*TB* #18 (1967) 19-53.

A.S.Kapelrud,"The Number Seven in Ugaritic Texts,"*VT* 18 (1968) 494-499.

*S. Gevirtz, "Abram's 318," *IEJ* 19 (1969) 110-113.

§1054 *5.10 Studies on Dispensationalism*

( ) L., "The Jewish and Christian Dispensations," *QCS* 5 (1823) 233-240.

†Anonymous, "Faber on the Three Dispensations," *BCQTR, 3rd Ser.,* 2 (1826) 462-481. *(Review)*

Anonymous, "The Jewish and Christian Dispensation Historically Considered," *CR* 11 (1858-59) 193-217. *(Review)*

J. B., "The Mosaic Dispensation compared with the Christian," *JSL, 3rd Ser.,* 9 (1859) 79-88.

Anonymous, "The Mosaic Dispensation as Introduction to Christianity," *ThE* 4 (1867) 248-277. *(Review)*

Lewis Sperry Chafer, "Dispensationalism," *BS* 93 (1936) 390-449.

*O[swald] T. Allis, "Modern Dispensationalism and the Doctrine of the Unity of Scripture," *EQ* 8 (1936) 22-35.

*O[swald] T. Allis, "Modern Dispensationalism and the Law of God," *EQ* 8 (1936) 272-289.

*Elias Newman, "Is the Time of Jacob's Trouble Past or Future? *A Study in the Misleading Conceptions of Present-Day Millennialists," JTALC* 1 (1936) #2, 11-30.

F. E. Mayer, "Dispensationalism Examined and Found Wanting," *CTM* 17 (1946) 89-94.

Roy L. Aldrich, "An Apologetic for Dispensationalism," *BS* 112 (1955) 46-54.

John Wick Bowman, "The Bible in Modern Religions. II. Dispensationalism," *Interp* 10 (1956) 170-187.

‡Arnold D. Ehlert, "A Bibliography of Dispensationalism," *BS* 101 (1944) 95-101, 199-209, 319-328, 447-460; 102 (1945) 84-92, 207-219, 322-334, 445-467; 103 (1946) 57-67.

Clarence E. Mason Jr., "A Review of 'Dispensationalism' by John Wick Bowman," *BS* 114 (1957) 10-22, 102-122.

R. L. Aldrich, "An Outline Study of Dispensationalism," *BS* 118 (1961) 133-141.

R. L. Aldrich, "A New Look at Dispensationalism," *BS* 120 (1963) 42-49.

§1055 *5.11 Studies on Apologetics*

Anonymous, "On the Study of Divinity. Chapter V. On the Sacred Scriptures," *MR* 2 (1819) 281-284.

Anonymous, "On the Study of Divinity. Chapter IX. On the Elegance and Dignity of the Sacred Scripture," *MR* 2 (1819) 403-406.

J. G. Herder, "Herder, and His Letters Relating to the Study of Divinity," *CD, N.S.,* 2 (1820) 233-237. *(Trans. from the German)*

J. G. Herder, "Herder's Letters Relating to the Study of Divinity," *CD, N.S.,* 2 (1820) 417-429; 3 (1821) 1-11. *(Trans. from the German)*

J. G. Herder, "Herder's Letters," *CD, N.S.,* 3 (1821) 81-88, 171-176, 239-254. *(Trans. from the German)*

J. R. B., "The Bible.—its uses and abuses," *CTPR* 3 (1837) 448-459.

*Edward Robinson, "The Bible and its Literature," *BRCR, N.S.,* 5 (1841) 334-359.

Henry P. Tappan, "The Bible Its Own Interpreter," *BRCR, 3rd Ser.,* 3 (1847) 95-110.

James Rowland, "The Philosophy of the Bible," *BRCR, 3rd Ser.,* 4 (1848) 510-521.

T. H. Skinner, "A Short Homily on the Greatness of the Scriptures," *BRCR, 3rd Ser.,* 5 (1849) 551-558.

*Henry Burgess, "Is Biblical Criticism Unfavorable to Piety?" *JSL, 1st Ser.,* 4 (1849) 111-124.

Brewen Grant, "Is the Bible from God?" *BRCM* 6 (1849-60) 103-123.

L. M. Lee, "Restoration of the Jews," *MQR* 5 (1851) 284-299. *(Review)*

L. Eichelberger, "Bible Influence Indispensable to Society and the Institutions of Life," *ER* 3 (1851-52) 1-33.

C. Porterfield Krauth, "The Bible a Perfect Book," *ER* 4 (1852-53) 110-138.

W. S., "The Bible a sufficient Revelation from God to Man," *UQGR* 11 (1854) 5-26.

W. A. McSwain, "Searching the Scriptures," *MQR* 10 (1856) 265-274.

†Anonymous, "Foundation of Faith in the Word of God," *PQR* 7 (1858-59) 454-484. *(Review)*

Anonymous, "Internal Evidences that the Bible is the Word of God," *CRB* 24 (1859) 420-432.

†[Samuel Wilberforce], "Essays and Reviews," *QRL* 109 (1861) 248-305. *(Review)*

†[Samuel Wilberforce], "Aids to Faith," *QRL* 112 (1862) 445-499, 662. *(Review)*

Anonymous, "The Bible the Book of God.—An Argument," *ERG, 4th Ser.,* 1 (1866-67) 241-250.

David Oliphant, "The Bible a Book of Facts, not of Modes and Philosophies," *CongR* 7 (1867) 231-243.

Alvah Hovey, "Religion and Astronomy," *BQ* 5 (1871) 58-78.

Giles Bailey, "The Bible," *UQGR, N.S.,* 13 (1876) 23-34.

*W. Gray Elmslie, "The Place of the Psalms in Modern Apologetic," *BFER* 26 (1877) 726-755.

T. G. Apple, "The Permanence of Old Testament Revelation," *RChR* 24 (1877) 314-324.

I[srael] E. Dwinell, "The Formal and the Vital in the Bible," *BFER* 29 (1880) 140-161.

E. V. Gerhart, "Truth of the Old Testament," *RChR* 27 (1880) 173-194.

Anonymous, "The Written Word of God," *BWR* 3 (1881) 351-382.

Thos. Longley, "The Bible," *ERG, 8th Ser.,* 1 (1882-83) 164-176.

W. F. Adeney, "Why do we Believe in the Bible?" *CongL* 11 (1882) 887-897.

Lyman Abbott, "What is the Bible? And Why I Believe It," *JCP* 2 (1882-83) 390-413.

R. J. Bowman, "The Bible Epic: Messiad," *MQR, 2nd Ser.,* 5 (1883) 281-288.

G. T. Flaunders, "The Bible," *UQGR, N.S.,* 20 (1883) 464-481.

L. D. Temple, "The Preacher a Prophet," *ONTS* 4 (1884-85) 413-416.

*Talbot W. Chambers, "Sun Images and the Sun of Righteousness," *ONTS* 5 (1884-85) 193-203.

S. H. McCollester, "Our Scriptures and the Greek Language," *UQGR, N.S.,* 22 (1885) 202-212.

A. A. Pfanstiehl, "The Study of the Bible in its Entirety," *ONTS* 5 (1885-86) 83-84.

Eml. V. Gerhart, "The Light of the Holy Scripture. Negative Aspect," *RChR* 33 (1886) 207-222.

E[ml.] V. Gerhart, "The Light of the Holy Scripture. Positive Aspect," *RChR* 33 (1886) 285-300.

Joseph Rabinowitcz, "An Evangelical View of the Old Testament Scriptures," *HR* 13 (1887) 426-430. *(Trans. by Geo. H. Schodde)*

Anonymous, "What of the Bible?" *MR* 69 (1887) 603-608.

E. L. Curtis, "The Old Testament for Our Times," *ONTS* 7 (1887-88) 49-52, 85-89.

J. L. Lynch, "The Bible—Its Friends and Foes," *IER, 3rd Ser.,* 9 (1888) 22-30.

Anonymous, "The Relation of the Old Testament to Christian Faith," *MR* 72 (1890) 891-897.

G. Beesley Austin, "The Questions of the Bible," *TML* 4 (1890) 181-193.

L. B. Fisher, "On Popular Study of the Old Testament," *UQGR, N.S.,* 27 (1890) 41-52.

W. W. Moore, "Fresh Light for Bible Students," *USR* 2 (1890-91) 17-19.

W. W. Moore, "Facts versus Fancies," *USR* 2 (1890-91) 241-250.

Walter Lloyd, "Bibliolatry," *WR* 137 (1892) 113-122.

S. R. Driver, "The Moral and Devotional Value of the Old Testament," *ET* 4 (1892-93) 110-113.

W. S. Blackstock, "The Bible, the church, and the reason," *CMR* 5 (1893) 61-74. *(Review)*

*Anonymous, "'Is Christianity Progressing?' Is Judaism Progressing?" *MR* 75 (1893) 785-794.

John S. Vaughan, "The Creation: A Revelation of the Creator," *IER, 3rd Ser.,* 16 (1895) 124-136.

[A. A. Berle], "The Jewish and Christian Scriptures," *BS* 53 (1896) 161-163.

*C. C. Hersman, "The Bible Divine in Its Unity of Plan—In Its Evidences Cumulative," *USR* 8 (1896-97) 176-185.

*W. J. Beecher, "Messianic Prophecy: Its Apologetic Value," *AubSRev* 1 (1897) 13-27.

J. McIntyre, "Modern Faith and the Bible," *DR* 120 (1897) 38-55.

Anonymous, "The Meaning and Supremacy of the Bible," *LQHR* 89 (1897-98) 112-129. *(Review)*

J. Hogan, "The Apologetic Study of the Bible," *AER* 18 (1898) 604-619.

*Geo. H. Schodde, "The Bible of the Old and the Bible of the New Theology," *ColTM* 18 (1898) 321-327.

M. B. Lambdin, "Modern Discoveries in Bible Lands. Their Value for the Preacher," *USR* 10 (1898-99) 111-117.

Paul Carus, "The Bible," *Monist* 10 (1899-1900) 41-61.

[Hermann] Guthe, "What Great Men Think of the Bible," *ColTM* 20 (1900) 229-253.

Alexander Brown, "How Does it Stand with the Bible?" *LQHR* 94 (1900) 71-82. *(Review)*

E. V. Gerhart, "The Book of God," *RChR, 4th Ser.,* 4 (1900) 433-452.

Rudolph Grossmann, "The Rabbi as a Scholar," *YCCAR* 10 (1900) 133-147.

Camden M. Cobern, "What the Bible is and What it is Not," *BW* 18 (1901) 105-113.

[J. A. Selbie], "The Abiding Value of the Old Testament," *ET* 13 (1901-02) 455.

A. T. Burbridge, "The Divine Method of Inquiry," *BW* 20 (1902) 450-456.

D. S. Gregory, "The Bible or No Bible?" *HR* 43 (1902) 84-89.

Carl S. Patton, "The Religious Value of the Hebrew Prophets," *HSR* 13 (1902-03) 197-204.

A. F. Kirkpatrick, "Christianity and Judaism," *Exp, 6th Ser.,* 7 (1903) 241-258.

H. Hensley Henson, "The Future of the Bible," *ContR* 85 (1904) 565-576.

U. L. Ullman, "The Religious Value of the Old Testament," *TTKF* 6 (1904) 40-50, 87-97. *(Trans. by N. F[osander])*

George Macloskie, "The Human Side of the Old Testament," *USR* 16 (1904-05) 343-351.

*William H. Bennett, "The Apologetical Value of Modern Criticism, with Special Reference to the Old Testament," *BW* 25 (1905) 427-435.

*Hector Hall, "Grounds for Maintaining the Integrity and Inspiration of the Scriptures," *CFL, 3rd Ser.,* 2 (1905) 179-189.

J. Gray McAllister, "The Book Pre-Eminent," *USR* 17 (1905-06) 101-111.

*Henry B. Master, "The Value of Facts to the Historian," *CFL, 3rd Ser.,* 4 (1906) 111-119.

William H. Bates, "'The Bible in the Light of Modern Thought'," *CFL, 3rd Ser.,* 4 (1906) 181-191.

*Matthew Leitch, "Unscientific Criticism of the Bible," *CFL, 3rd Ser.,* 5 (1906) 3-6. [III. Unscientific Criticism of the Bible as a Book of Religion, pp. 5-6]

Charles Porterfield Krauth, "The Bible a Perfect Book," *LCR* 25 (1906) 425-443.

C[harles] P[orterfield] Krauth, "The Bible a Perfect Book. II," *LCR* 25 (1906) 665-679.

Lawrence Mills, "The Bible, the Persian Inscriptions, and the Avesta," *Monist* 16 (1906) 383-387.

Ed. König, "The True and Permanent Significance of the Old Testament," *BW* 29 (1907) 97-110.

William M. McPheeters, "'The Origin and Permanent Value of the Old Testament'—A Criticism," *CFL, 3rd Ser.,* 6 (1907) 423-430. *(Editorial)*

W. H. Fitchett, "'The Imperishable Bible'," *CFL, 3rd Ser.,* 7 (1907) 360-364.

Luther A. Fox, "Christian Faith and the Bible," *LQ* 37 (1907) 508-527.

E. C. Caldwell, "The Permanent Value of the Old Testament," *USR* 19 (1907-08) 40-52.

*T. McK. Stuart, "Critical Theories and the Old Testament Sabbath School Lessons," *CFL, 3rd Ser.,* 9 (1908) 164-168.

Charles H. Waller, "The Right Attitude Towards the Bible," *CFL, 3rd Ser.,* 9 (1908) 237-240.

*Julian Morgenstern, "Significance of the Bible for Reform Judaism in the Light of Modern Scientific Research," *YCCAR* 18 (1908) 217-238. [Responses by N. Krass, pp. 239-242; W. H. Ettelson, pp. 243-248]

E. M. Milligan, "Is it Reasonable to Believe the Bible?" *CFL, 3rd Ser.,* 10 (1909) 46-51.

John M. Thomas, "Faith and Old-Testament Criticism," *HR* 57 (1909) 183-186.

W. G. Jordan, "Israel's Second Exodus," *MQR, 3rd Ser.,* 35 (1909) 98-107.

Wm. J. Hinke, "The Religious Value of the Old Testament," *ASRec* 5 (1909-10) 464-478.

Thomas Robinson, "'The Two Bibles'—A Review of 'The Bible, Have We Lost It?'," *CFL, 3rd Ser.,* 12 (1910) 208-211.

George Milligan, "The Attitude of the Church Toward Recent Criticism of the Scriptures," *HR* 59 (1910) 24-26.

A. P. Drucker, "The Old Testament as a Text-Book," *OC* 24 (1910) 222-229. [Editorial Comment, 229]

C. Parez, "The Bible and the Clergy," *MC* 1 (1911-12) 690-695.

Ernest DeWitt Burton, "The Significance of the Old Testament for Today," *BW* 39 (1912) 75-79. *(Editorial)*

T. E. Rankin, "The Bible and Other Books," *HR* 64 (1912) 91-96.

Christopher G. Hazard, "The Oracles of God," *HR* 64 (1912) 264-269.

Andrew Wingate, "'Modern Unrest and the Bible'," *JTVI* 44 (1912) 339-352. (Discussion, pp. 352-354)

Amos Kidder Fiske, "Literary Genius of Ancient Israel," *OC* 26 (1912) 654-661.

Henry Preserved Smith, "The Present Value of the Old Testament," *BW* 41 (1913) 40-53.

J. M. Powis Smith, "The Old Testament and Vital Religion," *BW* 41 (1913) 373-381.

Charles S. Lobingier, "The Bible and a Law Book," *OC* 27 (1913) 738-742.

H. Mayne Young, "Doctrinal Reconstruction and the Bible," *MC* 3 (1913-14) 539-545.

J. Gray McAllister, "Teachings of Great Features of the Bible," *USR* 25 (1913-14) 97-112.

J. E. McFadyen, "The Old Testament and the Modern World," *Exp, 8th Ser.,* 7 (1914) 1-19.

C[arl] A. Blomgren, "The Great Problem," *TTKF* 16 (1914) 104-119.

Eugene Caldwell, "The Message of the Old Testament for the Modern Man," *USR* 26 (1914-15) 322-332.

Adolf Hult, "Scripture Meditation and Theological Study," *TTKF* 18 (1916) 178-191.

*H. W. Magoun, "A Lacuna in Scholarship," *BS* 74 (1917) 71-100, 284-311, 425-445, 553-580.

*J. B. Tannehill, "Unbelievable Stories," *CFL, 3rd Ser.,* 23 (1917) 312-314.

*H. T. Andrews, "The Message of the Apocalyptic for Modern Times," *Exp, 8th Ser.,* 14 (1917) 58-71.

George H. Schodde, "What is the Bible?" *TZTM* 7 (1917) 94-96. *(Editorial)*

H. W. Magoun, "The 'Mistakes of Moses'," *CFL, 3rd Ser.,* 24 (1918) 19-23.

William Barry, "Rome and Jerusalem," *DR* 162 (1918) 177-199.

Wilbur L. Caswell, "Why the Old Testament?" *ACM* 4 (1918-19) 307-315.

C. B. Wilmer, "The Value of the Old Testament," *ACM* 4 (1918-19) 505-519.

Francis J. Hall, "The Old Testament Why," *ACM* 5 (1919) 598-608.

G. Frederick Wright, "Some supposed unnecessary portions of the Bible," *CFL, 3rd Ser.,* 25 (1919) 14-15.

Charles Roads, "Shall the Best in the Bible now be Surrendered," *CFL, 3rd Ser.,* 25 (1919) 106-107.

Anonymous, "'Theology without Germany'," *CFL, 3rd Ser.,* 25 (1919) 190-192.

Wilbur P. Thirkield, "Theological Conservatism," *CFL, 3rd Ser.*, 25 (1919) 200.

M. Carrie Moore, "'In the Beginning God—'," *CFL, 3rd Ser.*, 25 (1919) 239.

G. H. Box, "The Permanent Value of the Old Testament in the Light of Criticism," *Exp, 8th Ser.*, 18 (1919) 1-23.

Anonymous, "Cropping the Old and New Testament," *CFL, 3rd Ser.*, 26 (1920) 16-17.

[Frank J. Boyer], "Evolution of Elimination," *CFL, 3rd Ser.*, 26 (1920) 43-44.

Leander S. Keyser, "Let us be Just and Fair," *CFL, 3rd Ser.*, 26 (1920) 51-54.

George McCredy Price, "'Theology Made in Germany'," *CFL, 3rd Ser.*, 26 (1920) 54-57.

[Frank J. Boyer], "The Hun, The Horror of History," *CFL, 3rd Ser.*, 26 (1920) 58-59.

C. C. Martindale, "The Bible and Magic," *DR* 167 (1920) 89-93.

Edward Shillito, "The Sequel to Job," *Exp, 8th Ser.*, 21 (1921) 417-424.

James H. Snowden, "The Written Word," *BR* 7 (1922) 232-245.

Albert L. Copeland, "The Bible—All or Part?" *CFL, 3rd Ser.*, 28 (1922) 81-84.

Henry F. Cope, "Will Children Read the Bible," *HR* 84 (1922) 443-446.

John H. Ritson, "The Bible: An Unfettered Missionary," *IRM* 11 (1922) 390-400.

Loyol H. Larimer, "How Shall we Judge the Old Testament?" *LCR* 41 (1922) 220-233.

Francis E. Powell, "Modernism and the Bible," *MC* 12 (1922-23) 260-268.

L[eander] S. K[eyser], "The Conflict over the Old Testament," *CFL, 3rd Ser.*, 29 (1923) 251-252.

W. Henderson-Begg, "The Place of the Old Testament in Modern Christian Teaching," *Exp, 8th Ser.,* 26 (1923) 93-99.

[Gilbert T. Rowe], "The Case of the Old Testament," *MQR, 3rd Ser.,* 50 (1924) 317-327. *(Review)*

Anonymous, "Our Bible," *CFL, 3rd Ser.,* 32 (1926) 581-583.

J. Parton Milum, "Egypt, Israel, and the Christ in the Light of the New Anthropology," *LQHR* 145 (1926) 206-217.

E. Edmund Seyzinger, "The Bible: Its Nature and Purpose," *ACM* 20 (1926-27) 229-239.

*W. S. Urquhart, "The Old Testament of the Indian Church," *CJRT* 5 (1928) 350-354.

G. L. Young, "Modernism or Biblicism—Which?" *CFL, 3rd Ser.,* 35 (1929) 529-534, 605-607, 650-652.

Kenneth S. Wuest, "The Reasonableness of the Bible," *CFL, 3rd Ser.,* 35 (1929) 537-539.

W. E. Beck, "The Spiritual Value of the Bible," *CQR* 109 (1929-30) 324-328.

F. C. Burkitt, "A Corpus of Sacred Writings," *MC* 19 (1929-30) 395-408.

Frederick Carl Eiselen, "The Purpose and Use of the Scriptures," *MR* 113 (1930) 639-648.

John Alfred Faulkner, "No Apology for Old Testament Needed," *MR* 113 (1930) 764-766.

Bernard J. Heller, "The Modernists Revolt Against God," *YCCAR* 40 (1930) 323-357. *[Table of Contents title:* "The God Idea That Should Be Taught in the Jewish Religious School"]

H[arold] P[aul] S[loan], "The Holy Bible," *CFL, 3rd Ser.,* 38 (1932) 8-12.

*George McCready Price, "Some Scientific Aspects of Apologetics," *EQ* 4 (1932) 234-243.

W. R. Inge, "The Use and Misuse of the Bible," *MC* 24 (1934-35) 245-258.

E. W. Barnes, "The Old Testament and Modern Man," *MC* 24 (1934-35) 295-308.

J. W. Newton, "Science, Scholarship and Scripture," *CFL, 3rd Ser.,* 42 (1936) 289-294.

A. R. Siebens, "The Scholar's Part in Upholding the Bible Today," *JBL* 55 (1936) xvii.

Douglas V. Duff, "Guardians of the Holy Sepulchre," *DR* 201 (1937) 193-220.

W. J. Blyton, "Some Moderns and the Bible," *QRL* 271 (1938) 245-264.

John Bright, "The Preacher's Old Testament: Recent Developments and Continuing Realities," *USR* 52 (1940-41) 195-222.

Richard R. Syre, "The Bible and Our Culture Mentality," *LCQ* 14 (1941) 243-261.

S[tanley] A. Cook, "The Modernity of the Bible," *MC* 32 (1942-43) 220-227.

Donald G. Miller, "Neglected Emphasis in Biblical Criticism," *USR* 56 (1944-45) 327-358.

A. C. Bouquet, "The Value of the Bible," *MC* 37 (1947-48) 246-263.

John Paterson, "The Living Word," *RL* 17 (1948) 258-267.

Paul L. Lehmann, "The Bible and the Significance of Civilization," *TT* 5 (1948-49) 350-357.

Merrill F. Unger, "The Uniqueness of the Old Testament," *BS* 107 (1950) 291-297.

Bernard J. Bamberger, "Jewish Universalism," *RL* 20 (1950-51) 362-373.

G. Ernest Wright, "The Old Testament: A Bulwark of the Church Against Paganism," *IRM* 40 (1951) 265-276.

Ian Hislop, "Themes of the Bible," *LofS* 6 (1951-52) 316-319.

Bede Griffiths, "The Mystery of the Scriptures," *LofS* 7 (1952-53) 67-75.

W. J. Platt, "The Place of the Bible in Evangelism," *IRM* 42 (1953) 184-193.

Arthur A. Vogel, "Stace, Time, and Deity," *JR* 33 (1953) 278-286.

Robert Francis Johnson, "The Old Testament in the Church," *CollBQ* 31 (1954) 69-71.

*M. F. Wiles, "The Old Testament in Controversy with the Jews," *SJT* 8 (1955) 113-126.

G. Ch. Aalders, "The Truth of the Old Testament," *RefmR* 3 (1955-56) 5-15.

*James H. Gailey Jr., "The Beginning of Wisdom," *CTSB* 49 (1956) #1, 1-9. *[Inaugural Address]*

*Elizabeth [Rice] Achtemeier, "The Old Testament in the Church," *USQR* 12 (1956-57) #3, 45-49.

*Roland E. Murphy, "Notes on Old Testament Messianism and Apologetics," *CBQ* 19 (1957) 5-15.

E. Garfield Evans, "A Queer Book for a Queer People," *PQL* 3 (1957) 161-166.

T. A. Roberts, "The Sacred and the Secular in the Bible," *MC, N.S.,* 1 (1957-58) 82-92.

Bernard Ramm, "The Apologetic of the Old Testament: The Basis of a Biblical and Christian Apologetic," *BETS* 1 (1958) #4, 15-20.

E. K. Taylor, "The Eloquence of Sacred Scriptures," *ClR* 43 (1958) 719-726.

Jakob J. Petuchowski, "The Grip of the Past—A Study in the Dynamics of Religion," *Jud* 8 (1958) 132-141.

Jakob J. Petuchowski, "Not by Bread Alone," *Jud* 7 (1958) 229-234.

Alex. Jones, "The Bible: News of God," *Scrip* 10 (1958) 17-21.

*T. Worden, "Questions and Answers. Similarities with Pagan Religions. What attitude ought we to adopt to the parallels so frequently adduced from extra-biblical sources in support of a denial that the Bible is the revealed word of God?," *Scrip* 10 (1958) 58-60.

Claude Saverbrei, "Why Teach the Old Testament?" *StLJ* 2 (1958-59) #3, 19-25.

George A. Turner, "The Emancipating Word of God," *ASW* 13 (1959) #1, 20-28. *[OT Refs., pp. 24-26]*

*Bruce Vawter, "In Many Fragmentary and Varying Utterances: The Use of Messianic Prophecy in Apologetics," *CTSP* 14 (1959) 97-119.

*K. V. Mathew, "Ancient Religions of the Fertile Crescent—and the Sanathana Dharma," *IJT* 8 (1959) 83-90.

B[ernard] M. G. Reardon, "The Bible and Criticism To-day," *QRL* 297 (1959) 208-218.

*Erwin I. J. Rosenthal, "Anti-Christian polemic in medieval Bible commentaries," *JJS* 11 (1960) 115-135.

*Harold Forshey, "Apologetics and Historical Criticism," *RestQ* 6 (1962) 217-228. [I. Julius Wellhausen and Israel's History; II. Gunkel and Tradition History; III. Albright and Archaeology; IV. Conclusions]

Joseph Goldschmidt, "The Eternal Validity of the Torah," *Trad* 5 (1962-63) 18-28.

David Stacey, "Clues from the Old Testament," *PQL* 10 (1964) 334-340.

Horace D. Hummel, "The Permanent Significance of the Old Testament for the Christian Church," *DJT* 4 (1965) 275-282.

*Patrick D. Miller Jr., "God the Warrior. *A Problem in Biblical Interpretation and Apologetics*," *Interp* 19 (1965) 39-46.

Abraham Joshua Heschel, "No Religion is an Island," *USQR* 21 (1965-66) 117-133.

D. Howard Smith, "Is the Old Testament Necessary?" *MC, N.S.,* 10 (1966-67) 19-27.

Paul G. Schrotenboer, "The Bible, Word of Power," *IRB* #32&33 (1968) 1-4.

J. A. Motyer, "Dead Prey of Living Oracles?" *Them* 5 (1968) #1, 44-47.

*James A. Wharton, "The Occasion of the word of God: An unguarded essay on the character of the Old Testament as the memory of God's story with Israel," *ASBFE* 84 (1968-69) #1, 5-54.

Henry Wansbrough, "Change and Revaluation of the Bible," *NB* 49 (1968-69) 174-179.

Norman Shepherd, "God's Word of Power," *IRB* #38 (1969) 17-20.

Paul G. Schrotenboer, "A Reply to Professor Shepherd," *IRB* #38 (1969) 21-26.

Bernhard W. Anderson, "The Contemporaneity of the Bible," *PSB* 62 (1969) #2, 38-50.

Bernhard W. Anderson, "The Contemporaneity of the Bible," *MTSB* (1970) 5-18.

§1056 *5.11.1 Studies on Anti-Semitism*

†Anonymous, "The Jewish Question," *LQHR* 59 (1882-83) 94-119. *(Review)*

G[eorge] H. Schodde, "The Anti-Semitic Agitation," *ColTM* 10 (1890) 10-18.

Albert A. Isaacs, "Jacob's Trouble," *EN* 2 (1890) 289-293.

Felix L. Oswald, "The Mask of Anti-Semitism," *OC* 7 (1893) 3907-3908.

*Anonymous, "Zionism and Anti-Semitism," *QRL* 195 (1902) 385-407. *(Review)*

*James Oscar Boyd, "Esther and Anti-Semitism," *CFL, N.S.,* 8 (1903) 298-300.

Ernst von Dobschütz, "Jews and Anti-Semites in Ancient Alexandria," *AJT* 8 (1904) 728-755.

Ed. König, "Biblical Anti-Semitism," *LCR* 40 (1921) 374-382. *(Trans. by C. Theodore Benze)*

Dudley Wright, "The Burnings of the Talmud," *OC* 39 (1925) 193-217.

'Dybbuk', "The Menorah Conference—A Critique," *JIQ* 3 (1926-27) #3, 12-14.

Israel Cohen, "The Jewish Tragedy," *QRL* 263 (1934) 252-268.

William Harbutt Dawson, "Cromwell and the Jews," *QRL* 263 (1934) 269-286.

Elias Newman, "The Fundamentalists' Resuscitation of the Anti-Semitic Protocol Forgery," *TF* 6 (1934) 212-229.

Adolf Pilger, "Anti-Semitism," *TF* 7 (1935) 28-41. [Reply by Elias Newman, pp. 33-41]

I[saak] Heinemann, "The Attitude of the Ancients toward Judaism," *Zion* 4 (1938-39) #4, I.

*A. H. Dirksen, "The Talmud and Anti-Semitism," *AER* 100 (1939) 33-44.

*N. W. Goldstein, "Cultivated Pagans and Ancient Anti-Semitism," *JR* 19 (1939) 346-364.

Isaak Heinemann, "The Attitude of the Ancient World Toward Judaism," *RR* 4 (1939-40) 385-400.

Hans Lewy, "Cicero on the Jews in His Speech for the Defense of Flaccus," *Zion* 7 (1941-42) #4, I.

Israel Cohen, "Polish Jewry under Nazi Tyranny," *QRL* 278 (1942) 48-61.

*T. E. N. Pennell, "Esther and Antisemitism," *ET* 55 (1943-44) 237-240.

Julian Franklyn, "Anti-Semitism: The Barometer of Social Decay," *ContR* 165 (1944) 159-163.

Roy Pascal, "Anti-Semitism in Germany before 1914," *ContR* 168 (1945) 214-218.

W. D. Davies, "Chosen People: The Approach to Anti-Semitism," *CongQL* 26 (1948) 327-341.

Israel Cohen, "The Plague of Anti-Semitism," *QRL* 287 (1949) 175-188.

Edmund Silberner, "Two Studies in Modern Anti-Semitism," *HJud* 14 (1952) 93-188.

Charles I. Glicksberg, "Antisemitism and the Jewish Novelist," *Jud* 1 (1952) 238-245.

Edmund Silberner, "Anti-Semitism and Philo-Semitism in the Socialist International," *Jud* 2 (1953) 117-122.

Dennis H. Wrong, "The Psychology of Prejudice and the Future of Anti-Semitism in America," *EJS* 6 (1956) 311-328.

George L. Mosse, "Culture, Civilization and German Anti-Semitism," *Jud* 7 (1958) 256-266.

Norman Pollack, "The Myth of Populist Anti-Semitism," *AmHR* 68 (1962-63) 76-80.

Richard L. Rubenstein, "The Protestant Establishment and the Jews," *Jud* 14 (1965) 131-145.

Edward H. Flannery, "Anti-Semitism: A Spiritual Disease," *TFUQ* 41 (1966) 33-44.

Robin M. Williams Jr., Andrew M. Greeley, and Daniel J. Levinson, "Review Symposium: Charles Y. Glock and Rodney Stark, *Christian Beliefs* and *Anti-Semitism*," *AmSR* 32 (1967) 1004-1013.

Harold H. Ditmanson, "Christian Declarations on Anti-Semitism," *DJT* 6 (1967) 168-175.

Allan Cutler, "The Origins of Modern Anti-Semitism: A New Hypothesis," *Jud* 17 (1968) 469-474.

§1057 **5.11.2 Studies on "Judaism" and Jewish-Christian Dialogue**

'Monitor', "The Jews," *CongML* 12 (1829) 16-20.

Anonymous, "The Future of the Jewish Nation," *BFER* 4 (1855) 146-216.

[Joann Andreæ Eisenmengers], "'Judaism Unveiled'," *MQR* 8 (1854) 565-583.

E. W. Hooker, "The Condition of the Jewish Mind relative to the Scriptures of the Old and New Testament," *AThR* 1 (1859) 61-81, 618-642.

E. W. Hooker, "The Condition of the Jewish Mind Relative to the Scriptures," *AThR* 2 (1860) 633-655.

Anonymous, "What Judaism Has Done," *ONTS* 2 (1882-83) 117.

Robert Flint, "The Relationship of Christianity to Judaism," *ONTS* 2 (1882-83) 276-277.

Samuel Kellogg, "Influence of the Jews in the History of Mankind," *ONTS* 3 (1883-84) 21-23.

Claude G. Montefiore, "A Justification of Judaism," *URRM* 24 (1885) 97-116, 207-228.

Charles A. Allen, "Why Not Turn Jew?" *URRM* 32 (1889) 123-130.

W. Bacher, "Judaeo-Christian Polemics in the Zohar," *JQR* 3 (1890-91) 781-784.

*Joseph William Reynolds, "Messianic Prophecy, *or Reasoning with the Jews*," *TML* 5 (1891) 73-84.

Julian Cohen, "The Jews and the Bible," *WR* 136 (1891) 66-75.

M. Gudemann, "Spirit and Letter in Judaism and Christianity," *JQR* 4 (1891-92) 345-356.

Thomas Pryde, "Characteristics of the Jewish Race," *ONTS* 14 (1892) 206-215.

K. Kohler, "Is Reform Judaism Destructive or Constructive?" *YCCAR* 3 (1892-93) 101-114.

Isaacs Moses, "The Meaning of the Survival of Israel," *YCCAR* 4&5 (1892-95) 14-22.

Julia Wedgwood, "The Message of Israel," *ContR* 62 (1893) 579-589.

*Anonymous, "'Is Christianity Progressing?' Is Judaism Progressing?" *MR* 75 (1893) 785-794.

C. G. Montefiore, "Mr. Smith: A Possibility," *JQR* 6 (1893-94) 100-110.

I. Abrahams, "Miss Smith: An Argument," *JQR* 6 (1893-94) 111-118.

D. Fay, "Miss Smith: A Protest," *JQR* 6 (1893-94) 299-305.

I. Abrahams and C. G. Montefiore, "Miss Smith: Notes in Reply," *JQR* 6 (1893-94) 306-316.

A. B. Bruce, "The Message of Israel," *ContR* 66 (1894) 77-90.

C. G. Montefiore, "Misconceptions of Judaism and Christianity by Each Other," *JQR* 8 (1895-96) 193-216.

Emil G. Hirsch, "The Philosophy of the Reform Movement in American Judaism," *YCCAR* 6 (1895-96) 90-112.

A. A. Berle, "A Jew on the Mission of Judaism," *BS* 54 (1897) 577-579.

E. N. Heimann, "A Study in Apologetics. Correspondence Between a Jew and a Jewish Christian Concerning Christianity," *LCR* 16 (1897) 166-179.

Oswald John Simon, "Jews and Modern Thought," *JQR* 11 (1898-99) 387-399.

J. Silverman, "The Achievements and the Possibilities of Judaism," *YCCAR* 9 (1898-99) 91-97.

Julius W. Walden, "Salvation is of the Jews," *PQ* 13 (1899) 298-312.

Adolph Guttmacher, "Modern Thought—Tendencies in Judaism," *YCCAR* 8*[sic]* (1899) 192-201. *[Bound between vols. 9 and 10]*

Felix Perles, "What Jews May Learn from Harnack," *JQR* 14 (1901-02) 517-543.

Tobias Schanfarber, "Judaism's Perplexities. Conference Lecture before the Central Conference of American Rabbis," *YCCAR* 13 (1903) 365-373.

Hugh Macdonald Scott, "The Modern Jew: His Whence and Whither," *BS* 61 (1904) 443-465.

Alexander H. Japp, "A Revived Judaism: is it Possible," *LQHR* 104 (1905) 136-154. *(Review)*

G. E. Biddle, "A Theist's Impression of Judaism," *JQR* 19 (1906-07) 209-228.

Geo. S. Hitchcock, "Modern Judaism," *IER, 4th Ser.,* 24 (1908) 43-67.

*Julian Morgenstern, "The Significance of the Bible for Reform Judaism in the Light of Modern Scientific Research," *YCCAR* 18 (1908) 217-238. [Responses by N. Krass, pp. 239-242; H. W. Ettelson, pp. 243-248]

Max. C. Currick, "Some Aspects of Jewish Apologetics," *YCCAR* 21 (1911) 271-305.

*G. H. Box, "The Christian Messiah in the Light of Judaism Ancient and Modern," *JTS* 13 (1911-12) 321-328.

Jacob H. Kaplan, "Some Fundamental Jewish Religious Problems and their Relation to Liberal Christian Sects: Sabbath-Sunday; Reform Judaism and Unitarianism; Pulpit and Stage; Race-Religion," *AJRPE* 5 (1912) 402-417.

Jacob H. Kaplan, "Modern Judaism (Questionnaire)," *AJRPE* 5 (1912) 348-349.

A. R. Simpson, "The Unconsumed People," *Exp, 8th Ser.,* 4 (1912) 147-158.

*C. G. Montefiore, "Modern Judaism and the Messianic Hope. A Reply to a Recent Indictment of Judaism," *HJ* 11 (1912-13) 366-377.

*G. H. Box, J. Albert Goldsmid, J. T. Turner, "'Modern Judaism and Messianic Hope'," *HJ* 11 (1912-13) 885-889.

Edward M. Merrins, "The Jews and Race Survival," *BS* 71 (1914) 64-79, 192-217, 434-457.

William Hudson, "The Jews of To-day and To-morrow," *LQHR* 121 (1914) 268-283. *(Review)*

J. Sumner Stone, "The Wandering Jew," *JR* 96 (1914) 267-270.

W. T. Davison, "The Future of Judaism," *LQHR* 123 (1915) 124-128.

W. J. Sparrow Simpson, "Liberal Judaism and the Christian Faith," *CQR* 81 (1915-16) 44-63.

H. D. A. M[ajor], "The Future of Judaism," *MC* 8 (1918-19) 391-393. *(Review)*

Claude G. Montefiore, "Modern Judaism," *HJ* 17 (1918-19) 642-656.

*David Capell Simpson, "Messianic Prophecy and the Jewish Problem," *CQR* 88 (1919) 109-122.

‡Horace J. Wolf (ed.), "Bibliography of Jewish Problems of the Reconstruction Period," *YCCAR* 29 (1919) 386-398.

[Count de] Soissons, "The Jews as a Revolutionary Leaven," *QRL* 233 (1920) 172-187.

Anonymous, "The Jews as a Revolutionary Leaven: A Reply," *QRL* 233 (1920) 401-410.

C. G. Montefiore, "Has Judaism a Future?" *HJ* 19 (1920-21) 28-41.

Hamilton Schuyler, "Is There a Jewish Menace?" *ACM* 10 (1921-22) 322-335.

C. G. Montefiore, "A Jewish Christian Symposium: I. Jewish Conceptions of Christianity," *HJ* 28 (1929-30) 246-260.

F. C. Burkitt, "A Jewish Christian Symposium: II. What Christians Think of Jews," *HJ* 28 (1929-30) 261-272.

Leo M. Franklin, "The Jew Whom Nobody Knows," *CQ* 7 (1930) 294-301.

John Stuart Conning, "Religion and Irreligion in Israel," *IRM* 19 (1930) 538-549.

C. G. Montefiore, "The Old Testament and the Modern Jew," *HJ* 30 (1931-32) 561-569.

W. R. Taylor, "The Jews and the Church," *CJRT* 9 (1932) 174-182.

Solomon Goldman, "The Task of Judaism," *JR* 14 (1934) 85-95.

Claude G. Montefiore, "What a Jew Thinks about Jesus," *HJ* 33 (1934-35) 511-520.

Samuel Schulman, "Israel," *YCCAR* 45 (1935) 260-311.

Abba Hillel Silver, "Israel," *YCCAR* 45 (1935) 312-342, 353-354. [Discussion by: James G. Heller, pp. 342, 347-348; [Samuel] Goldenson, pp. 343-344; [Zevi] Diesendruck, pp. 344-345; [Harry W.] Ettelson, pp. 345-347; Samuel S. Cohon, pp. 348-351; [Barnett R.] Brickner, pp. 351-352; [William H.] Fineshriber, pp. 352-353]

S. P. T. Pridequx, "A Reply to Mr. Montefiore," *HJ* 34 (1935-36) 125-129.

*Solomon Zeitlin, "The Jews: Race, Nation or Religion—Which?" *JQR, N.S.,* 26 (1935-36) 313-347.

James Moffatt, "The Old Testament and the New Jews," *ET* 48 (1936-37) 182-183. *(Review)*

C. G. Montefiore, "Liberal Christianity and Liberal Judaism," *HJ* 35 (1936-37) 497-509.

Sigmund Livingston, "Facts About Fictions Concerning the Jew," *CFL, 3rd Ser.,* 44 (1938) 291-302.

Frederick A. Aston, "Some Present-day Tendencies in Jewish Thought," *EQ* 10 (1938) 380-389.

Floyd V. Filson, "The Separation of Christianity from Judaism," *ATR* 21 (1939) 171-185.

Gerald Vann, "The Jews," *NB* 20 (1939) 414-419.

*Michael J. Gruenthaner, "The Jews as a Race," *TFUQ* 14 (1939) 36-51.

Aug. F. Zich, "The Wandering Jew," *WLQ* 36 (1939) 14-23.

Abba Hillel Silver, "The World Crisis and Jewish Survival," *YCCAR* 49 (1939) 309-330.

George Ricker Berry, "A Neglected Approach to the Jewish Problem," *CRDSB* 12 (1939-40) 121-126.

Philip E. Hughes, "The Jewish Problem in the Ancient World," *EQ* 12 (1940) 247-274.

Hans Kosmala, "Jews in Their New Environment. Intellectual and Spiritual Trends," *IRM* 29 (1940) 497-505.

Anonymous, "From the Jewish Viewpoint," *SQ/E* 1 (1940) 33-41.

Julius Gordon, "Palestine in Jewish Life and Literature," *YCCAR* 50 (1940) 261-276.

Willard Johnson, "Christian Solutions of the Jewish Problem," *CRDSB* 13 (1940-41) 77-84.

Hans Kosmala, "Judaism, and Christianity: The Jewish Point of View," *IRM* 30 (1941) 374-388.

Hans Kosmala, "Judaism, and Christianity: The Summons to the Christian Church," *IRM* 30 (1941) 521-530.

E. Gomann, "Life and Salvation—The Common Basis for Jews and Gentiles," *LCQ* 15 (1942) 174-180.

E. Lampert, "The Paths of Israel," *NB* 23 (1942) 142-148.

Gordon Cumming, "The Human Interest in the Ancient Hebrews," *BTSAB* 17 (1942) #4, 1-3, 8; 18 (1943) #1, 6-7; #2, 5-6.

*Hans Kosmala, "Two Judaisms," *IRM* 32 (1943) 420-426.

Alfred Martin, "Judaism: A Restatement," *BS* 101 (1944) 108-116, 227-231.

Edward Quinn, "What is a Jew?" *NB* 25 (1944) 46-53.

A. F. Day, "The Root of Bitterness," *NB* 25 (1944) 53-57.

Norman Bentwich, "Children of Israel," *ContR* 168 (1945) 167-170.

Charles S. Braden, "Christian-Jewish Relations Today," *JAAR* 13 (1945) 94-105.

Hans Kosmala, "What is Judaism?" *IRM* 35 (1946) 416-421.

A. F. Day, "Post-War Jewry," *NB* 27 (1946) 54-57.

Solomon B. Freehof, "Reform Judaism and the Halacha," *YCCAR* 56 (1946) 276-292. [Discussion by: Irving M. Levey, pp. 292-298; Max Raisin, pp. 299-300; Samuel S. Cohon, pp. 301-306; Frederick A. Doppelt, pp. 307-308; Julius Gordon, pp. 309-310; Max Reichler, pp. 311-312; Joseph Klein, pp. 312-313; Emanuel Gamoran, pp. 313-315; Reply by Solomon B. Freehof, pp. 315-317]

Julian Franklyn, "Israel: State or Religion?" *ContR* 172 (1947) 35-39.

Frederick A. Aston, "The Christian Church and the Modern Jew," *TT* 4 (1947-48) 230-237.

W. Burnet Easton Jr., "The Strategy of the Remnant," *TT* 5 (1948-49) 199-220.

James Parkes, "Jewry, Judaism, Israel," *CongQL* 27 (1949) 218-226.

Leo Baeck, "Judaism on Old and New Paths," *IRM* 39 (1950) 190-200.

A. Roy Eckardt, "Christian Faith and the Jews," *JR* 30 (1950) 235-245.

J. J. W. Murphy, "The Origins of Israel: Two Views," *IER, 5th Ser.,* 75 (1951) 39-49, 109-117. *(Review)*

Robert Gordis, "Reform and Conservative Judaism—Their Mutual Relationship," *YCCAR* 61 (1951) 259-283.

James G. Heller, "Conservatism and Reform," *YCCAR* 61 (1951) 283-293.

Ira Eisenstein, "Reform and Conservative Judaism," *YCCAR* 61 (1951) 293-301.

Leon I. Feuer, "Conservatism and Reform—Shall They Merge?" *YCCAR* 61 (1951) 302-318.

Ellis Rivkin, "Some Historical Aspects of Authority in Judaism," *YCCAR* 61 (1951) 365-377. [Discussion by: Solomon B. Freehof, pp. 378-379; Samuel S. Cohon, pp. 380-383]

Paul Tillich, "Is there a Judeo-Christian Tradition?" *Jud* 1 (1952) 106-109.

Bernhard Heller, "About the Judeo-Christian Traditions. *Some Comments on Paul Tillich's Article, Jud* 1 (1952) 257-261.

Emil L Fackenheim, "Self-Realization and the Search for God. *A Critique of Modern Humanism and a Defence of Jewish Supernaturalism,"* Jud 1 (1952) 291-306.

Maria Fuerth Sulzbach, "Karl Barth and the Jews," *RL* 21 (1952) 585-593.

Henry E[noch] Kagan, "The 'Judeo-Christian Heritage'—A Psychological Revaluation and a New Approach," *YCCAR* 63 (1953) 253-281.

Bernard Heller, "The Judeo-Christian Tradition Concept: Aid or Deterrent to Goodwill?" *Jud* 2 (1953) 133-139.

James Parkes, "Israel and the Diaspora," *Jud* 2 (1953) 291-306.

Israel I. Mattuck, "Judaism and the Future," *HJ* 52 (1953-54) 23-30.

Emile Marmorstein, "Judaism's Prospects," *HJ* 52 (1953-54) 31-39.

E. La B. Cherbonnier, "Jerusalem and Athens," *ATR* 36 (1954) 251-271.

Leon Fram, "'The Judeo-Christian Tradition'," *Jud* 3 (1954) 77-79.

Eugene Mihaly, "Reform Judaism and Halacha: The Contemporary Relevance of the *Mishneh Torah* of Maimonides," *YCCAR* 64 (1954) 214-226.

F. Loisky, "Christian-Jewish Relations: Some French Points of View," *IRM* 44 (1955) 274-291.

Ephraim Frisch, "Judaism, Distortion and Reality," *JAAR* 23 (1955) 38-41.

Eliezer Berkovits, "The Galut of Judaism," *Jud* 4 (1955) 225-234.

I. N. Steinberg, "Yavneh or Jerusalem?" *Jud* 4 (1955) 235-242.

*M. F. Wiles, "The Old Testament in Controversy with the Jews," *SJT* 8 (1955) 113-126.

Hans-Joachim Schoeps, "Philosemitism in the Baroque Period," *HJ* 54 (1955-56) 380-383.

Frank E. Gaebelein, "Arnold Toynbee and the Jews," *BS* 113 (1956) 308-321.

Ephraim Frisch, "Judaism—Fiction and Fact," *HJ* 55 (1956-57) 159-166.

Solomon Zeitlin, "Are Judaism and Christianity Fossil Religions?" *JQR, N.S.,* 47 (1956-57) 187-195.

R. J. Zwi Werblowsky, "Some Observations on the Renewal of the Dialogue between the Church and Israel," *HJ* 56 (1956-58) 273-282.

*E. Flesseman-van Leer, "The Significance of the Mystery of Israel for the Church," *CJT* 3 (1957) 5-14.

David W. Hay, "The Mystery of Israel: A Reply to E. Flesseman-van Leer," *CJT* 3 (1957) 97-101.

E. Flesseman-van Leer, "Jew and Gentile: Some Considerations Suggested by Dr. Hay's Reply," *CJT* 3 (1957) 235-240.

*Eric S. Gabe, "Atonement in Judaism and the Missionary Approach," *IRM* 46 (1957) 276-282, 394-400.

Natan Rotenstreich, "Kant's Interpretation of Judaism," *Tarbiz* 27 (1957-58) #2/3, XIX-XX.

Donald D. Evans, "The Mystery of Israel: A Reply to E. Flesseman-van Leer and David W. Hay," *CJT* 4 (1958) 30-36.

Herbert H. Rose, "Freedom Without a Framework," *Jud* 7 (1958) 320-328.

Frederic Thieberger, "The Problem of Religion in Israel," *Jud* 7 (1958) 329-336.

G. A. F. Knight, "Israel—A Theological Problem," *RTR* 17 (1958) 33-43.

Solomon Zeitlin, "Who is a Jew? A Halachic-Historic Study," *JQR, N.S.,* 49 (1958-59) 241-270.

Horace M. Kallen, "Who is a Jew? A Symposium," *Jud* 8 (1959) 3-6.

Eliezer Berkovits, "Who is a Jew? A Symposium," *Jud* 8 (1959) 6-9.

Levi A. Olan, "Who is a Jew? A Symposium," *Jud* 8 (1959) 9-12.

Abraham Menes, "Who is a Jew? A Symposium," *Jud* 8 (1959) 12-15.

David Max Eichorn, "Who is a Jew?" *YCCAR* 69 (1959) 240-247.

Joachim Prinz, "Who is a Jew?" *YCCAR* 69 (1959) 248-256. [Discussion by: Maurice J. Bloom, p. 257; Joseph I. Weiss, p. 257; Jerome R. Malino, pp. 257-258; Emanuel Gamoran, p. 258; Samuel S. Cohon, pp. 258-260; Martin Freedman, p. 260; Abraham I. Jacobson, pp. 260-261; Joel C. Dobin, p. 261; Ernst J. Conrad, pp. 261-262; [David Max] Eichhorn, p. 262]

*S. Lowy, "The Confutation of Judaism in the Epistle of Barnabas," *JJS* 11 (1960) 1-33.

*Erwin I. J. Rosenthal, "Anti-Christian polemic in medieval Bible commentaries," *JJS* 11 (1960) 115-135.

Frank R. Snavely, "Athens or Jerusalem?" *Person* 41 (1960) 32-37.

Morton S. Enslin, "The Parting of the Ways," *JQR, N.S.,* 51 (1960-61) 177-197.

James Parkes, "A Reappraisal of the Christian Attitude of Judaism," *JAAR* 29 (1961) 299-307.

George A. F. Knight, "Newly Developing Tensions Between Jews and Christians," *T&L* 5 (1962) 240-247.

Arthur Gilbert, "Religious Pluralism: A Jewish View," *TT* 19 (1962-63) 510-523.

Bruce L. Button, "The Jew," *GJ* 4 (1963) #3, 16-27.

J. Coert Rylaarsdam, "Common Ground and Difference," *JR* 43 (1963) 261-270.

Norman Bentwich, "Judaism & Israel," *HJ* 62 (1963-64) 186-188.

Harry M. Orlinksy, "Who is the Ideal Jew: The Biblical View," *Jud* 13 (1964) 19-28.

‡Max Celnik and Isaac Celnik, "Judaism and Jewish-Christian Relations," *JAAR* 33 (1965) 156-165.

*David Berger, "St. Peter Damian. His Attitude Toward the Jews and the Old Testament," *YR* 4 (1965) 80-112.

Barbara R. Krasner, "Torah and Daily Life. Report of a Jewish-Christian Debate," *Found* 9 (1966) 118-132.

Eugene B. Borowitz, "On the 'Commentary' Symposium: Alternatives in Creating a Jewish Apologetic," *Jud* 15 (1966) 458-465.

Augustine Cardinal Bea, "The Jewish People in the Divine Plan of Salvation," *TFUQ* 41 (1966) 9-32.

J. Coert Rylaarsdam, "Is Dialogue Between Jew and Christian Possible?" *Crit* 6 (1967) 33-35.

Arthur Gilbert, "A Jewish Response to the Recent Declarations of the Protestants and Catholics with Regard to the Jews," *DJT* 6 (1967) 176-183.

Richard L. Tubenstin, "Should Jews Talk to Christians?" *DJT* 6 (1967) 184-190.

J. Coert Rylaarsdam, "The Disavowal of the Curse: A New Beginning?" *DJT* 6 (1967) 190-199.

Gregory Baum, "The Doctrine Basis For Jewish-Christian Dialogue," *DJT* 6 (1967) 200-209.

Wendell W. Frerichs, "Christians and the People of the Book," *DJT* 6 (1967) 210-217.

Saphir P. Athyal, "Israel Amid the Nations: A Confrontation of Faiths," *R&S* 14 (1967) #1, 21-30.

David Flusser, "A New Sensitivity in Judaism and the Christian Message," *HTR* 61 (1968) 107-127.

Willis F. Erickson, "A Parish Pastor's Reflections on Christian-Jewish Relations," *LQ, N.S.,* 20 (1968) 229-237.

Richard L. Rubenstein, "Did Christians Fail Israel?" *LQ, N.S.,* 20 (1968) 251-254.

Jacob Neusner, "Tensions in Jewish-Christian Relations," *LQ, N.S.,* 20 (1968) 434-436.

Robert L. Wilken, "Is Christian-Jewish Dialog Possible?" *LTSB* 48 (1968) #2, 4-6.

Ben Zion Bokser, "The Bible, Rabbinic Tradition And Modern Judaism," *LTSB* 48 (1968) #2, 7-17.

Lowell D. Streiker, "Two Peoples of God—A Response to Bokser," *LTSB* 48 (1968) #2, 18-23.

Solomon S. Bernards, "Where Do We Go From Here?" *LTSB* 48 (1968) #2, 45-46.

Yitzhak Rabin, "What Can Israel Say to Us?" *YCCAR* 78 (1968) 237-247.

Herbert B. Huffmon, "The Israel of God," *Interp* 23 (1969) 66-77.

Nils A. Dahl, "Election and the People of God. Some Comments," *LQ, N.S.,* 21 (1969) 430-436.

Seymour Siegel, "Election and the People of God—a Jewish Perspective," *LQ, N.S.,* 21 (1969) 437-450.

Randall M. Fal, "The Tasks Ahead in Jewish-Christian Relationships," *VDR* 1 (1970) #2, 10-15.

§1058 *5.11.3 Studies on Zionism*

E. P., "Remarks on the Return of the Jews to Palestine," *CongML* 18 (1835) 89-94, 152-156, 217-221.

[David N. Lord], "The Restoration of the Israelites," *TLJ* 2 (1849-50) 15-60, 240-288, 453-478.

Anonymous, "Will the Jews, as a Nation, be Restored to Their Own Land?" *BFER* 6 (1857) 811-843.

Anonymous, "Will the Jews, as a Nation, be Restored to their own Land?" *PQR* 6 (1857-58) 46-85.

J. S. Foulk, "Restoration and Conversion of the Jews," *RChR* 18 (1871) 386-405.

*Anonymous, "Uzzen-Sherah; and Israel's Right to Canaan," *CongR* 1 (1861) 472-489.

A. C. George, "The Regeneration of Palestine," *MR* 62 (1880) 646-667.

William Wells, "The Regeneration of Palestine," *BFER* 30 (1881) 144-165.

A. W. Miller, "The Restoration of the Jews," *PQ* 1 (1887-88) 61-86, 249-279.

J. H. Scott, "The Jewish Nation," *EN* 2 (1890) 28-29.

John Cumming, "The Future of the Jews and Judæa," *EN* 2 (1890) 337-341.

Arthur W. Heidel, "The Semitic Question," *MR* 72 (1890) 238-246.

Anonymous, "Palestine for the Hebrews," *EN* 3 (1891) 276-277.

Anonymous, "Palestine," *EN* 3 (1891) 371-374.

[A.] Ben-Oliel, "Jerusalem Reviving: The Land, People, and Book," *EN* 4 (1892) 518-522.

G. H. Schodde, "The Zionite Movement," *ColTM* 15 (1895) 237-243.

M. Gaster, "The Return of the Jews to Palestine, and the Zionist Movement," *IAQR, 3rd Ser.,* 4 (1897) 301-311.

C. Walker, "Zionism," *PER* 12 (1898-99) 321-334.

I. Zangwill, "Zionism," *ContR* 76 (1899) 500-511.

Josephine Lazarus, "Zionism," *NW* 8 (1899) 228-242.

Gotthard Deutsch, "The National Movement amongst the Jews," *NW* 8 (1899) 242-255.

K. Kohler, "A United Israel," *YCCAR* 9 (1898-99) 81-90.

Henry Berkowitz, "Why I am not a Zionist," *YCCAR* 8*[sic]* (1899) 167-173. *[Bound between vols. 9 and 10]*

S. Sale, "Address on Zionism," *YCCAR* 8*[sic]* (1899) 174-178. *[Bound between vols. 9 and 10]*

C. Levias, "The Justification of Zionism," *YCCAR* 8*[sic]* (1899) 179-191. *[Bound between vols. 9 and 10]*

D. H. Geissinger, "Will the Jews be Restored to Palestine?" *LCR* 21 (1901) 1-9.

*Anonymous, "Zionism and Anti-Semitism," *QRL* 195 (1902) 385-407. *(Review)*

Paul Goodman, "Jewish Nationalism," *WR* 169 (1908) 276-282.

Louis Meyer, "Zionism," *BRec* 5 (1908) 186-200.

P. M. Raskin, "Jewish Ideals and Political Zionism," *WR* 175 (1911) 658-664.

P. M. Raskin, "Modern Jewish Nationalism. A Study in National Jewish Psychology," *WR* 178 (1912) 264-269.

Anonymous, "The Modern Jews and Palestine," *MR* 98 (1916) 466-472.

Albert M. Hyamson, "Egypt and Palestine," *QRL* 226 (1916) 411-432. *(Review)*

Joseph Cowen, "The Jewish Claim to Palestine," *ContR* 111 (1917) 709-714.

Lucien Wolf, "The Jewish National Movement," *ERCJ* 225 (1917) 303-318.

Anonymous, "Zionism," *MR* 99 (1917) 295-300.

Ernest W. G. Masterman, "The Deliverance of Jerusalem and the Future of Palestine," *CQR* 85 (1917-18) 315-327.

M. J. Landa, "The Restoration of Palestine," *HJ* 16 (1917-18) 223-233.

Israel Abrahams, "Palestine and Jewish Nationality. A Reply," *HJ* 16 (1917-18) 455-466.

William Barry, "Zionism," *DR* 163 (1918) 80-100.

Charles Cleveland Cohan, "'Are You Going Back to Jerusalem?'," *OC* 32 (1918) 441-448.

Lewis Bayles Paton, "Zionism," *HR* 77 (1919) 7-11.

P. S. Cannon, "Some Notes on Zionism," *IAQR* 15 (1919) 674.

Albert M. Hyamson, "Problems of the New Palestine," *QRL* 231 (1919) 318-332. *(Review)*

O. P. Eaches, "Do the Scriptures Foretell the Return of the Jews to Palestine?" *R&E* 16 (1919) 143-154.

D. S. Margoliouth, "The Prospects of Zionism," *IAQR* 16 (1920) 296-307.

P. S. Cannon, "Is Zionism a Fallacy?" *IAQR* 16 (1920) 680-687.

Herbert C. Alleman, "World Re-Construction and the Near East," *LQ* 50 (1920) 1-15.

Preston A. De Long, "Some Aspects of Zionism," *RChR, 4th Ser.,* 24 (1920) 316-330.

Thomas Cullen Roberts, "Who are the Rightful Proprietors of Palestine," *CFL, 3rd Ser.,* 27 (1921) 199. [Anonymous reply, pp. 199-200]

Anonymous, "Who are the Rightful Proprietors of Palestine?" *CFL, 3rd Ser.,* 27 (1921) 89-90.

Edwin J. Kissane, "The Political Status of Palestine," *ITQ* 16 (1921) 377-381.

Morris Jastrow, "Zionism," *IAQR* 17 (1921) 159.

Reginald Ginns, "The Position in Palestine," *NB* 2 (1921-22) 360-365.

J. Ramsay MacDonald, "Zionism and Palestine," *ContR* 121 (1922) 434-440.

Vivian Gabriel, "The Troubles of the Holy Land," *ERCJ* 235 (1922) 1-25.

John E. McFadyen, "Zionism," *ET* 35 (1923-24) 343-348. [Zionism a Religious Question; Difference in Old Testament Ideals; Prophetic Religion; Priestly Religion; The Prophetic Conception of the Future; The Earthly Zion; The City of God]

Wyndham Deedes, "Great Britain and the Palestine Mandate," *JTVI* 57 (1924) 33-40. [Discussion, pp. 41-46]

Theo. Hjerpe, "The Restoration of the Jewish Nation," *AQ* 4 (1925) 207-214.

J. M. Rowland, "Zionism," *MQR, 3rd Ser.,* 51 (1925) 102-113.

*Paul A. Bloomhardt, "Zionism in the Sixth Century B.C.," *LQ* 55 (1925) 13-28.

Reginald Ginns, "Lord Balfour and Palestine," *NB* 6 (1925) 280-287.

D. L. Adler Hobman, "The Zionist Contribution to Palestine," *ContR* 129 (1926) 357-362.

F. H. Tyrrell, "Zionism and Palestine," *IAQR* 22 (1926) 37-45.

Paul Goodman, "The Palestine Venture," *ContR* 132 (1927) 629-637.

J. A. Huffman, "The Jew and Arab Controversy Over Palestine," *CFL, 3rd Ser.,* 36 (1930) 551-553.

I. G. Matthews, "Zionism," *CQ* 7 (1930) 79-90.

W. ten Boom, "Zionism," *IRM* 19 (1930) 231-240.

W. M. Christie, "Arabs and Jews in Palestine," *JTVI* 62 (1930) 96-106, 115-116. [Discussion and Communications, pp. 106-115]

Israel Cohen, "The Jews under the Palestine Mandate," *JTVI* 62 (1930) 241-260, 265. [Discussion, pp. 260-264]

Sidney Dark, "Zionism and the Jews," *QRL* 254 (1930) 74-91 *(Review)*

Ryland Knight, "Palestine—A Problem," *R&E* 27 (1930) 11-23.

Joseph Rauch, "Contemporary Palestine," *R&E* 27 (1930) 24-31.

H. Danby, "The Cultural Aims of Zionism," *CQR* 111 (1930-31) 238-339.

W. R. Taylor, "The Present Political Situation in Palestine," *CJRT* 8 (1931) 19-30.

H. Charles Woods, "The Palestine Conflict," *QRL* 257 (1931) 157-172. *(Review)*

Jacob Rader Marcus, "Jewish Palestine: A Study in 'Becoming'," *OC* 46 (1932) 497-520.

Millar Burrows, "Jew and Arab in Palestine," *JR* 13 (1933) 269-278.

Douglas V. Duff, "The Mandates in Syria and Palestine," *QRL* 260 (1933) 71-83.

Douglas V. Duff, "The Arabs and the Jewish National Home," *QRL* 261 (1933) 112-129.

Edward Mack, "Zionism and Prophecy. *First-hand Impressions of Some Weeks in Palestine,*" *USR* 45 (1933-34) 214-224.

Douglas V. Duff, "The New Zion and the Old Sepulchre," *DR* 195 (1934) 256-266.

George Ricker Berry, "Zionism," *CRDSB* 8 (1935-36) 5-16.

*W. Leonard, "Sionism in the Psalter," *ACR* 13 (1936) 118-134.

M. Gaster, "The Present Position of the Jews in Relation to World Events," *JTVI* 68 (1936) 146-156, 168-171. [Discussion and Communications, pp. 156-168]

Julius Braunthal, "Arabs and Jews in Palestine," *ContR* 149 (1936) 466-474.

J. N. Schofield, "The Arab and the Jews in Palestine," *BQL* 8 (1936-37) 241-250.

Norman Bentwich and H. St. J. B. Philby, "The Palestine Problem," *ContR* 152 (1937) 257-269.

Douglas V. Duff, "The Future in Palestine," *DR* 200 (1937) 21-41.

E. M. E. Blyth, "The Palestine Report," *QRL* 269 (1937) 341-358. *(Review)*

Frederic C. Spurr, "The Jewish Problem," *ET* 49 (1937-38) 541-545.

Rollin Thomas Chafer, "The Boundaries of Greater Canaan," *BS* 95 (1938) 231-236.

A. N. Awab Zada, "Palestine: A Rational View," *ContR* 154 (1938) 69-74.

*A. Hiorth, "From the River of Egypt unto the Great River, The River of Euphrates. *A Suggested Solution of the Arab-Israel Problem in the Promised Land,*" *JTVI* 70 (1938) 126-145, 150-152. [Discussion, pp. 146-149]

N[athan] M. Gelber, "A Pre-Zionist Plan for Colonizing Palestine. The Proposal of a Non-Jewish German-American in 1852," *HJud* 1 (1938-39) 81-90.

Viscount Samuel, "Palestine: The Present Position," *ContR* 156 (1939) 9-17.

Arthur Merton, "The Arab-Jew Conference on Palestine," *ContR* 155 (1939) 205-212.

Viscount Samuel, "Palestine Today," *ContR* 157 (1940) 532-535.

Israel Cohen, "Palestine Today: The New Land Policy," *ContR* 157 (1940) 536-542.

Nathan M. Gelber, "The Palestine Question and the Congress of Berlin," *HJud* 2 (1940) 39-48.

Werner J. Cahnman, "Munich and the First Zionist Congress," *HJud* 3 (1941) 7-23.

John C. Mattes, "The Background of the Jewish Question," *KZ* 65 (1941) 472-473.

Israel Cohen, "Palestine, the Jews, and the War," *ContR* 161 (1942) 158-163.

David Goldstein, "A Semitic Problem," *AER* 109 (1943) 241-248.

Cecil Roth, "Zionism and the Jewish Problem," *ContR* 164 (1943) 337-342.

William W. Simpson, "The Jewish National Home," *NB* 25 (1944) 63-67.

Israel Cohen, "Palestine and the Jewish Future," *QRL* 282 (1944) 269-284.

E. B. Castle, "Reconciliation in Palestine," *HJ* 43 (1944-45) 140-147.

Wyndham Deeds, "Reconciliation in Palestine. A Comment," *HJ* 43 (1944-45) 265-269.

A. L. Warnshuis, L. S. Albright, Almon R. Pepper, Mark A. Dawber, Wilbert B. Smith, Mrs. Orrin R. Judd, Gloria M. Wysner, and F. Ernst Johnson, "The Palestine Question. A Christian Position," *CollBQ* 23 (1946) #3, 14-25.

Israel Cohen, "The Palestine Problem," *ContR* 169 (1946) 14-19.

A. M. Chirgwin, "Who Gets Palestine?" *LQHR* 171 (1946) 341-344.

Charles R. Watson, "Jew and Arab in the Holy Land," *PSB* 39 (1946) #4, 2-11.

Raphael Loewe, "A Jewish Answer to Zionism," *HJ* 45 (1946-47) 137-143.

Lessing J. Rosenwald, "'What is it We Have Got to Solve? Are the Jews a State or are They a Religion?'" *PAPS* 91 (1947) 274-280.

Albert M. Hyamson, "Palestine," *QRL* 285 (1947) 399-408.

G. Ernest Wright, "Palestinian Dilemma," *McQ* 1 (1947-48) #7, 12-13.

S. Wolf and Edward Atiyah, "Palestine," *ContR* 174 (1948) 1-8.

R. Travers Herford, "The Survival of Israel," *JJS* 1 (1948-49) 5-11.

S. Vernon McCasland, "The Jews and Palestine," *CQ* 26 (1949) 115-126, 246.

Edwin E. Calverley, "Palestine and Israel: A Review-Article," *RL* 18 (1949) 503-507. *(Review)*

S. F. Hunter, "The Return of the Jews to Palestine," *ET* 61 (1949-50) 313-316.

Ovid R. Seller, "Politics and Religion in the Holy Land," *McQ* 3 (1949-50) #2, 3-6.

Raphael Straus, "The Jewish Question as a Problem of Nationalism," *HJud* 12 (1950) 3-20.

Constantine Rackauskas, "The Jerusalem Problem: A Note on Legality," *TFUQ* 25 (1950) 100-114.

R. Mahler, "American Jewry and the Idea of the Return to Zion in the Period of the American Revolution," *Zion* 15 (1950) IX-X.

Henrik F. Infield, "The Concept of Jewish Culture and the State of Israel," *AmSR* 16 (1951) 506-513.

Ralph E. Knudsen, "Palestine in the Light of Contemporary Events," *R&E* 49 (1952) 167-174.

Simon Rawidowicz, "Israel *The People-The State,*" *Jud* 2 (1953) 31-40.

Norman Bentwich, "Spiritual Aspects of the Creation of the State of Israel," *HJ* 52 (1953-54) 127-133.

Robert Gordis, "Israel and the Diaspora in the Light of Tradition, History and Reality," *Jud* 3 (1954) 118-131.

Anton T. Pearson, "Israel, Land of Miracles," *BSQ* 3 (1954-55) #1, 44-56; #2, 38-49; #3, 36-44.

David O. Moberg and Norris A. Magnuson, "Israel, Land of Miracles—Part II," *BSQ* 3 (1954-55) #2, 50-58.

E. L. Mallalieu, "Israel and the Negev," *ContR* 186 (1955) 6-9.

Irene Mazinoff, "Israel—A People in the Making," *ContR* 186 (1955) 204-207.

S. Marion Smith, "The Arab-Jewish Problem in Palestine," *SQ/E* 17 (1956) 19-25. *(Correction, p. 215)*

Yves M-J. Congar, "The State of Israel in Biblical Perspective," *NB* 38 (1957) 244-249.

Theodore N. Lewis, "The Idea of Israel," *YCCAR* 67 (1957) 187-200.

Anonymous, "Will the Jews, as a Nation, be Restored to their own Land?" *PQR* 6 (1857-58) 46-85.

Eugene Hinterhoff, "Israel After Ten Years," *CNI* 9 (1958) #1/2, 30-33.

Helmut Gollwitzer, "What is the Theological Implication?" *CNI* 9 (1958) #1/2, 33-38.

Pinhas H. Peli, "Where Historical Science and Religion Converge," *Jud* 7 (1958) 23-25.

Itzhak Ben-Zvi, "The Ishmaelite Diaspora and the Building of the State of Israel," *Jud* 7 (1958) 99-105.

W. W. Simpson, "Israel's Tenth Anniversary," *LQHR* 183 (1958) 131-135.

*Jakob J. Petuchowski, "Diaspora Judaism—An Abnormality? The Testimony of History," *Jud* 9 (1960) 17-28.

Melvin A. Stuckey, "Some Characteristic Features of the Modern State of Israel," *TUSR* 7 (1960-63) 41-56.

Richard Sneed, "Palestine: Yahweh's Gift," *BibT* #1 (1962) 45-51.

Gerhard Jasper, "The State of Israel: A Study in Interpretation," *IRM* 50 (1962) 189-195.

Norman Bentwich, "The First Years of Political Zionism," *HT* 13 (1963) 260-266.

J. K. Mikliszanski, "The Question of Aliyah in Jewish Law," *Jud* 12 (1963) 131-141.

D. Alan Keighley, "Israel as an Ecumenical Question," *LQHR* 188 (1963) 38-46.

Eliezer Livneh, "Does Zionism have a Future?" *Trad* 6 (1963-64) #2, 30-41.

David Polish, "Israel—The Meeting of Prophecy and Power," *YCCAR* 74 (1964) 161-186. [Discussion by: Abraham J. Feldman, p. 187; Jay Kaufman, pp. 187-188; Jerome R. Malino, pp. 188-189; Morris N. Kertzer, pp. 189-190; Robert Bergman, p. 190]

Anonymous, "The Jews and Their Land.   As the Jewish people return to Israel, the prosperity of the land, described in the Old Testament, is being seen once again," *BH* 2 (1965) #1, 15-18.

Hillyer H. Straton, "Israel and Jordan Revisited," *ANQ, N.S.,* 6 (1965-66) #1, 2-28.

L. E. Travener, "Dilemma in Israel," *F&T* 94 (1965-66) 105-112.

Christopher Sykes, "The Protocols of the Elders of Zion," *HT* 17 (1967) 81-88.

Philip Charper, "Israel the Modern State and Contemporary Points of View," *ANQ, N.S.*, 8 (1967-68) 241-245.

Balfour Brickner, "Israel the Modern State and Contemporary Points of View," *ANQ, N.S.*, 8 (1967-68) 246-251.

Philip Scharper, "Israel the Modern State and Contemporary Christian Points of View," *LQ, N.S.*, 20 (1968) 255-259.

Ezra Spicehandler, "What Can We Say to Israel?" *YCCAR* 78 (1968) 227-236.

John W. Hollenbach, "The Christian Stance on the Arab-Israeli Conflict," *RefR* 22 (1968-69) #2, 10-17.

George A. Turner, "Tensions in the Holy Land," *ASW* 23 (1969) #3, 3-8.

Herbert B. Huffmon, "The Israel of God," *Interp* 23 (1969) 66-77.

Michael Wyschogrod, "The Law, Jews and Gentiles—A Jewish Perspective," *LQ, N.S.*, 21 (1969) 405-415.

Nils A. Dahl, "Election and the People of God. Some Comments," *LQ, N.S.*, 21 (1969) 430-436.

Seymour Siegel, "Election and the People of God—a Jewish Perspective," *LQ, N.S.*, 21 (1969) 437-450.

§1059 **6. Studies on the Influence and Interpretation of the Old Testament and Ancient Near East in the Fine Arts, Worship, and Contemporary Culture in General**

A. P. P., "The Bible," *CE* 33 (1842-43) 151-168. *[The influence of the Bible upon science, art and poetry]*

J. Few Smith, "The Silent Influence of the Bible," *ER* 2 (1850-51) 353-371.

Anonymous, "The Secondary and Collateral Influences of the Sacred Scriptures," *SPR* 7 (1853-54) 103-127.

*George M. Towle, "International and Ancient Law," *CongR* 5 (1865) 142-161.

S. S. Rahn, "The Bible the World-Book," *LQ* 21 (1891) 496-505.

*William H. Arnoux, "The Influence of the Bible on Modern Jurisprudence," *CT* 10 (1892-93) 21-30.

Owen H. Gates, "The Sociological Value of the Old Testament," *BS* 52 (1895) 587-606.

P., "The Bible as a Means of Culture," *ColTM* 15 (1895) 257-270.

George Adam Smith, "The Service of the Old Testament in the Education of the Race," *BW* 8 (1896) 91-100.

*†Anonymous, "The Psalms in History," *QRL* 185 (1897) 305-330. *(Review)*

A. B. Davidson, "The Uses of the Old Testament for Edification," *Exp, 6th Ser.,* 1 (1900) 1-18.

Henry Churchill King, "The Bible as an Aid to Self-Discovery," *HR* 50 (1905) 24-26.

W. G. Thomson, "Apocrypha Tapestries," *IJA* #4 (1905) 7-8.

G. Harford, "The Higher Criticism as it Affects Faith and Spiritual Life," *Exp, 7th Ser.,* 1 (1906) 246-257.

*John Hendrick de Vries, "Higher Criticism and the Sunday School," *CFL, 3rd Ser.,*8 (1908) 209-212.

Calvin K. Staudt, "The Contribution of the Hebrews to Civilization," *RChR, 4th Ser.,* 13 (1909) 1-15.

Wallace MacMullen, "The Civic Value of the Old Testament," *MR* 92 (1910) 44-54.

Gross Alexander, "The English Bible and the Anglo-Saxon People," *MQR* 38 (1912) 720-747.

George R. Grose, "The Bible in Modern Life," *BM* 1 (1913) 568-570.

N. F. Hoggson, "Current Notes and News. The Heritage of Greece," *A&A* 6 (1917) 217-218.

J. W. Crowder, "The Educational Value of the English Bible," *SWJT* 1 (1917) #1, 44-49.

J. E. Whitteker, "The Old Testament in Doctrine and Life," *LCR* 36 (1917) 201-206.

S. G. Hägglund, "The Biblical Aspect of the Woman Emancipation Question," *TTKF* 19 (1917) 51-56.

George Yeisley Rusk, "Modern Lessons from Ancient Israelites," *MR* 110 (1927) 301-305. [Editorial Proem, p. 301]

Julian Morgenstern, "American Culture and Oriental Studies," *JAOS* 48 (1928) 97-108.

Frank W. Clelland, "What is the Function of the Bible in Religious Education?—A Question and a Warning—," *ABBTS* 9 (1934-35) #1, 3, 6-7; #2, 3, 6.

*S. H. Hooke, "The Cultural Value of the Old Testament," *CQR* 120 (1935) 189-204.

A. Bruce Curry, "The Bible for Our Times," *RL* 4 (1935) 52-61.

G. S. Johnstone, "The Contribution of Judaism and Christianity to the Drama," *ET* 47 (1935-36) 377-379.

C[yrus] H. Gordon, "The Hebrew Scriptures in Aramean Magic," *JBL* 55 (1936) xvii.

A. E. Garvie, "The Value of the Old Testament for the Christian Church," *ET* 48 (1936-37) 374-378.

Frank Glenn Lankard, "Can An Ancient Book Teach Any Lessons to a Modern Machine Age?" *JAAR* 6 (1938) 3-15.

W. R. Matthews, "The Influence of the Bible Upon the English Nation," *JAAR* 7 (1939) 23-26.

Stanley Cook, "The Cultural Problem and the Bible," *MC* 31 (1941-42) 406-411.

George B. Hatfield, "The Bible in Mediaeval Civilization: The Saxon Code of Law in Illustration," *HJud* 5 (1943) 63-72.

Warren N. Nevius, "The Bible as a Religious Guide for College Students," *JAAR* 11 (1943) 22-27.

Muriel Streibert Curtis, "The Relevance of the Old Testament Today," *JAAR* 11 (1943) 81-87.

George H. Hartwig, "The English Bible and the Teacher of English. Personal Experience of an American Teacher," *HJ* 44 (1945-46) 226-230.

E. A. Speiser, "Oriental Studies and Society," *JAOS* 66 (1946) 193-197.

Mary Aquin, "The Vulgate and the Eve-concept in English Cycles," *CBQ* 9 (1947) 409-435.

Robert Gordis, "The Biblical Basis of Democracy," *CJ* 4 (1948) #4, 1-12.

Paul L. Lehmann, "The Bible and the Significance of Civilization," *TT* 5 (1948-49) 350-357.

Hans Rost, "The Cultural Influence of the Bible," *CBQ* 11 (1949) 126-132.

H. H. Huxley, "The Psalms in Heraldry," *EQ* 21 (1949) 297-302.

H. H. Huxley, "Heraldic Mottos from the Old Testament," *Theo* 52 (1949) 216-218.

John A. F. Gregg, "The Old Testament and the Approach to Religion," *ET* 62 (1950-51) 332-336.

‡Wilbur M. Smith, "A Bibliography of the Influence of the Bible on English Literature (and in part on Fine Arts)," *FLB* #9&10 (1951) 1-15.

Charles S. Braden, "The Bible in Contemporary Drama," *JAAR* 19 (1951) 177-182.

J. M. Larkin, "Old Testament Themes in Early Jesuit Drama," *MH* 8 (Winter, 1952) 22-31.

F. B. Elkisch, "The Old Testament and Modern Psychology," *LofS* 8 (1953-54) 382-391.

Frederick C. Grant, "The Bible and Civilization. Ad Clerum," *RL* 22 (1952-53) 431-437.

E. H. Robertson, "The Use of the Bible in Broadcasting," *LQHR* 179 (1954) 130-133.

*Sheldon H. Blank, "The Relevance of Prophetic Thought for the American Rabbi," *YCCAR* 65 (1955) 163-177.

Norman Lamm, "The Fifth Amendment and its Equivalent in Halkhah," *Jud* 5 (1956) 53-59.

William D. Reyburn, "The Message of the Old Testament and the African Church—I," *PA* 7 (1960) 152-156.

William D. Reyburn, "Sickness, Sin, and the Curse: The Old Testament and the African Church—II," *PA* 7 (1960) 217-222.

Charles E. Schulman, "Job on Broadway," *CCARJ* 8 (1960-61) #3, 22-26.

George Henderson, "Cain's Jaw-Bone," *JWCI* 24 (1961) 108-114.

Stephen Szikszai, "The Place of the Old Testament," *T&L* 7 (1964) 26-36.

*Robert Gordis, "Biblical Wisdom and Modern Existentialism," *CJ* 21 (1966-67) #4, 1-10.

*Norman Lamm, "The Fourth Amendment and Its Equivalent in the Halachah," *Jud* 16 (1967) 300-312.

Michael Walzer, "The Exodus and Revolution: An Exercise in Comparative History," *Mosaic* 8 (1967) #1, 6-21.

Wesley J. Fuerst, "Secularization—Legacy from the Old Testament?" *ContextC* 1 (1967-68) #3, 15-26.

§1060 *6.1 Studies on the Old Testament and Ancient Near East in Art*

†Anonymous, "Martin's *Illustrations of the Bible*," *WR* 20 (1834) 453-465. *(Review)*

C., "The Moses of Michael Angelo," *CongML* 28 (1845) 109-111.

Robert Seton, "Old Testament Subjects in Early Christian Art," *ACQR* 20 (1895) 501-509.

*D. Kaufmann, "Art in the Synagogue," *JQR* 9 (1896-97) 254-269.

D. Kaufmann, "Errors in the Septuagint and the Vulgate from which Illustrations and Sculptures Derived Their Origin," *JQR* 11 (1898-99) 163-166.

Walter Lowrie, "A Jonah Monument in the New York Metropolitan Museum," *AJA* 5 (1901) 51-57.

*Joseph Jacobs, "Earliest Representation of the Ark of the Law," *JQR* 14 (1901-02) 737-739.

Clifton Harby Levy, "The Old Testament Illustrated to the Life," *BW* 24 (1904) 431-442.

*G. Margoliouth, "An Ancient Illuminated Hebrew MS. at the British Museum," *JQR* 17 (1904-05) 193-197.

W. G. Thomson, "Apocrypha Tapestries," *IJA* #4 (1905) 7-8.

*G. Margoliouth, "Hebrew Illuminated Manuscripts," *JQR* 20 (1907-08) 118-144.

W. G. Thomson, "The Apocrypha in Continental Tapestries," *IJA* #14 (1908) 15-16.

Charles C. Torrey, "An Old Jewish Picture of the Sacrifice of Isaac," *AJA* 13 (1909) 50-51.

W. G. Thomson, "The Tobit Tapestry at Bisham Abbey," *IJA* #26 (1911) 43-45.

Allan Marquand, "A Note on Brunelleschi's Sacrifice of Isaac," *AJA* 18 (1914) 81.

Margaret MacLean, "The Horns of Michelangelo's Moses," *A&A* 6 (1917) 97-99.

*John K. Bonnell, "The Serpent with a Human Head in Art and in Mystery Play," *AJA* 21 (1917) 255-291.

Anonymous, "Tobit-Glass of the Sixteenth Century in English Churches," *IJA* #48 (1917) 4-5.

Frank Owen Payne, "The Angel in American Art," *A&A* 11 (1921) 155-161.

Herbert Adams, "The Debt of Modern Sculpture to Ancient Greece," *A&A* 12 (1921) 218-221.

Alison Moore Smith, "The Iconography of the Sacrifice of Isaac in Early Christian Art," *AJA* 26 (1922) 159-173.

*Rachel Vishnitzer, "Illuminated Haggadahs," *JQR, N.S.,* 13 (1922-23) 193-218.

F. C. Burkitt, "Note on the Pictures in 'the Pentateuch of Tours'," *JTS* 24 (1922-23) 414-415.

Paul V. C. Baur, "David and Goliath on an Early Christian Lamp," *YCS* 1 (1928) 43-51.

*Alexander Marx, "The Darmstadt Haggadah, with Notes on Illuminated Haggadah MSS.," *JQR, N.S,.* 19 (1928-29) 1-16.

Harold R. Willoughby, "The Reconstruction of Lost Rockefeller McCormick Miniatures," *JBL* 51 (1932) 253-262. [Miniatures in the Psalter Section of Suppl. Gr. 1335 - I. The Psalms; II. The Odes and Canticles]

Joseph C. Slaone Jr., "The Torah Shrine in the Ashburnham Pentateuch," *JQR, N.S.,* 25 (1934-35) 1-12.

B. Aquila Barber, "An Artist Among the Prophets," *LQHR* 160 (1935) 41-52.

Paul Romanoff, "A Family of Illuminators in the Time of the Second Temple," *JQR, N.S.,* 26 (1935-36) 29-35.

Erwin R. Goodenough, "Symbolism in Hellenistic Jewish Art: The Problem of Method," *JBL* 56 (1937) 103-114.

E. Gombrich, "A Classical Quotation in Michael Angelo's 'Sacrifice of Noah'," *JWCI* 1 (1937-38) 69.

Ernst Kitzinger, "The Story of Joseph on a Coptic Tapestry," *JWCI* 1 (1937-38) 226-268.

Adelheid Heimann, "The Six Days of Creation in a Twelfth Century Manuscript," *JWCI* 1 (1837-38) 269-275.

*E. L. Sukenik, "The Ezekiel Panel in the Wall Decoration of the Synagogue of Dura-Europos," *JPOS* 18 (1938) 57-62.

Anthony Blunt, "Blake's 'Ancient of Days': The Symbolism of the Compasses," *JWCI* 2 (1938-39) 53-63.

*Emil G. Kraeling, "The Meaning of the Ezekiel Panel in the Synagogue at Dura," *BASOR* #78 (1940) 12-18.

Rachel Wischnitzer-Bernstein, "The Messianic Fox," *RR* 5 (1940-41) 257-263.

*Rachel Wischnitzer-Bernstein, "The Conception of the Resurrection in the Ezekiel Panel of the Dura Synagogue," *JBL* 60 (1941) 43-55.

*Rachel Wischnitzer-Bernstein, "The Samuel Cycle in the Wall Decoration of the Synagogue at Dura-Europos," *PAAJR* 11 (1941) 85-103.

Erwin R. Goodenough, "Early Christian and Jewish Art," *JQR, N.S.,* 33 (1942-43) 403-417.

A[nthony] Blunt, "Blake's 'Brazen Serpent'," *JWCI* 6 (1943) 225-227.

Rachel Wischnitzer-Bernstein, "Studies in Jewish Art," *JQR, N.S.,* 36 (1945-46) 47-59.

S. Yeivin, "The Sacrifice of Isaac in the Beth Alpha Mosaic," *BIES* 12 (1946) I-II.

Franz Landsberger, "The Origin of the Winged Angel in Jewish Art," *HUCA* 20 (1947) 227-254.

Isaiah Sonne, "The Paintings of the Dura Synagogue," *HUCA* 20 (1947) 255-362.

Rachel Wischnitzer, "The Hebrew Bible in Art," *JQR, N.S.,* 38 (1947-48) 107-108.

Piloo Nanavutty, "A Title-Page in Blake's Illustrated Genesis Manuscript," *JWCI* 10 (1947) 114-122.

*Harald Riesenfield, "The Resurrection in Ezekiel XXXVII and in the Dura-Europos Paintings," *UUA* #11 (1948) 1-40.

Franz Landsberger, "The Origin of the European Torah Decorations," *HUCA* 24 (1952-53) 133-150.

*Sergio J. Sierra, "Hebrew Codices with Miniatures Belonging to the University of Bologna," *JQR, N.S.*, 63 (1952-53) 229-248.

S. Renov, "The Relation of Helios and the Quadriga to the Rest of the Beth Alpha Mosaic," *BIES* 18 (1953-54) #3/4, VIII. *[Dura Europos]*

Joseph Gutmann, "The Jewish Origin of the Ashburnham Pentatuech Miniatures," *JQR, N.S.*, 44 (1953-54) 55-72.

J. Pächt and O. Pächt, "An unknown cycle of illustrations of the Life of Joseph," *CAAMA* 7 (1954) 35-50.

James A. Rischer, "The Synagogue Paintings at Dura-Europos," *CBQ* 17 (1955) 189-195.

Helen Rosenau, "Contributions to the Study of Jewish Iconography," *BJRL* 38 (1955-56) 466-482.

Franz Landsberger, "A German Torah Ornamentation," *HUCA* 29 (1958) 315-330.

Carl-Otto Nordström, "The Water Miracles of Moses in Jewish Legend and Byzantine Art," *OrS* 7 (1958) 78-109.

Baruch Kanael, "Notes on Jewish Art in the Period of the Second Temple," *ALUOS* 1 (1958-59) 61-73.

Charles Carter, "In the Beginning: The Old Testament in Medieval Art," *PQL* 5 (1959) 151-156.

Francis R. Walton, "Adam's Ancestor," *Arch* 13 (1960) 253-258.

*Bluma L. Trell, "The Naophoroi of Greek Imperial Coins," *AJA* 66 (1962) 200.

*Zvi Keren, "The Influence of the Hebrew Language on Contemporary Israeli Art Music," *BSOAS* 25 (1962) 209-224.

Adelheid Heimann, "Jeremiah and his Girdle," *JWCI* 25 (1962) 1-8.

Mendel Metzger, "A Study of Some Unknown Hand-Painted Megilloth of the Seventeenth and Eighteenth Centuries," *BJRL* 46 (1963-64) 84-126.

Mendel Metzger, "The Earliest Engraved Italian Megilloth," *BJRL* 48 (1965-66) 381-432.

Carl-Otto Nordström, "Rabbinic features in Byzantine and Catalan art," *CAAMA* 15 (1965) 179-205.

John W. Williams, "A Castilian Tradition of Bible Illustration: The Romanesque Bible from San Millán," *JWCI* 28 (1965) 66-85.

Madlyn Kahr, "A Rembrandt Problem: Haman or Uriah?" *JWCI* 28 (1965) 258-273.

Jerry Clapsaddle, "Beginnings," *Resp* 7 (1965-66) 171-177.

Madlyn Kahr, "Titan's Old Testament Cycle," *JWCI* 29 (1966) 193-205.

T. S. R. Boase, "Biblical Illustration in Nineteenth-Century English Art," *JWCI* 29 (1966) 349-367.

Hubert L. Kessler, "An unnoticed Scene in the Granval Bible," *CAAMA* 17 (1967) 113-120.

*Bezalel Narkiss, "Towards a further Study of the Ashburnham Pentateuch (Pentateuque de Tours) Paris, Bibliothèque Nationale, Nouv. Acq. Lat 2334," *CAAMA* 19 (1969) 45-60.

§1061 *6.2 Studies on the Old Testament in Music*

†David Kay, "Old Opera on the Deluge," *MMBR* 29 (1810) 107.

H. R. Haweis, "Mendelssohn's 'Elijah'," *ContR* 14 (1870) 363-376.

Anonymous, "Handel's Oratio-'Susanna'," *IJA* #9 (1907) 10-11.

Anonymous, "Handel's Oratorios from I. Maccabees," *IJA* #10 (1907) 17-18.

Anonymous, "The Methodist Hymn-Book and the Apocrypha," *IJA* #10 (1907) 19-20.

Anonymous, "Roman Catholic Humnas and the Deutero-Canonical Books," *IJA* #47 (1916) 61-62.

Anonymous, "Dr. Arne's Oratorio 'Judith'," *IJA* #48 (1917) 12-13.

Louis F. Benson, "The Relation of Our Hymns to the Bible," *BR* 6 (1921) 334-351.

Willis J. King, "The Negro Spirituals and the Hebrew Psalms," *MR* 114 (1931) 318-326.

Robert B. Lee, "The Sacrament of Music," *USQR* 4 (1948-49) #2, 19-21.

Charles Goodwin, "Psalm 139 and Robert Bridges' Paraphrase," *JBL* 68 (1949) xvi.

§1062 *6.3 Studies on the Old Testament in Literature*

†J. B., "Outline of a Poem on the Deluge," *MMBR* 28 (1809-10) 469-471.

†Anonymous, "Lord Byron's Hebrew Melodies," *BCQTR, N.S.,* 3 (1815) 602-611. *(Review)*

John Ffraser, "Jephtha's Vow," *DUM* 12 (1838) 273-287. *[a poem]*

Anonymous, "Sketches in Verse from the Old Testament," *CTPR* 4 (1838) 337-342. *(Review)*

Anonymous, "Paradise after the Fall," *CTPR, N.S.,* 3 (1841) 348-352.

Anonymous, "Helen Lowe—The Prophecy of Balaam and Other Poems," *DUM* 19 (1842) 504-516. *(Review)*

Anonymous, "Misquotations of Scripture," *BRCM* 3 (1847) 268-272, 429-433.

M., "Jephtha's Daughter," *DUM* 34 (1849) 39-44.

*Edward Wilton, "A Parallel Between David and Titus Manilus Torquatus," *JSL, 1st Ser.,* 4 (1849) 374-378.

J. A. Seiss, "The Influence of the Bible on Literature," *ER* 5 (1853-54) 1-17.

Anonymous, "The Bible," *SPR* 7 (1853-54) 374-390.

Anonymous, "Sacred Poetry," *JSL, 2nd Ser.,* 6 (1854) 197-201; *3rd Ser.,* 1 (1855) 17-32.

Lemuel S. Potwin, "A Shakespearian Glossary for Our English Bible," *BS* 19 (1862) 551-563.

Anonymous, "Demonic Ideals in Poetry," *DUM* 63 (1864) 29-32.

W. T., "Shakespeare and the Bible," *BFER* 14 (1865) 236-256. *(Review)*

Anonymous, "Spanish Orientalisms Compared with Scripture," *CE* 87 (1869) 65-71. *(Review)*

Alvah Hovey, "The Song of God: A Didactic Poem by Julius Köbner," *BQ* 11 (1877) 352-377.

Anonymous, "Mr. Swinburne's Debt to the Bible," *SRL* 3 (1883-84) 266-285.

R. DeWitt Mallary, "Macaulay's Use of Scripture in His Essays," *ONTS* 7 (1887-88) 212-216, 246-249.

T. W. Hunt, "The Bible and the Homily in Old English," *HR* 17 (1889) 97-102.

Albert S. Cook, "Metrical Observations on a Northumbrianized Version of the Old English Judith," *TAPA* 20 (1889) 172-174.

Henry J. Van Dyke, "The Bible in Tennyson," *ET* 1 (1889-90) 15-19, 38-41.

*Alexander Kohut, "Parsic and Jewish Literature of the First Man," *JQR* 3 (1890-91) 231-250.

George S. Goodspeed, "Shakespeare and the Bible," *ONTS* 14 (1892) 218-224, 271-275.

Hudor Genone, "Chapters from the New Apocrypha. In the Beginning," *OC* 7 (1893) 3776-3777.

Hudor Genone, "Chapters from the New Apocrypha. Lamor on Mount Sinai," *OC* 7 (1893) 3884-3885.

Anonymous, "Judaism in Fiction," *CQR* 37 (1893-94) 364-376.

P[aul] C[arus], "Oneiros and Harpax," *OC* 8 (1894) 4100-4101.

Bernhard Pick, "Emperor Julian's Acquaintance with the Old Testament," *HR* 34 (1897) 403-404.

Chauncey Marvin Cady, "The English Bible and the English Writers," *BW* 9 (1897) 185-193.

George Lester, "Concerning Lord Tennyson's Knowledge and Use of the Bible," *MQR, 3rd Ser.*, 22 (1897) 163-170.

Francis Hindes Groome, "Tobit and Jack the Giant-Killer," *Folk* 9 (1898) 226-244.

Augustus C. Thompson, "Misquotation of Scripture," *HSR* 9 (1898-99) 210-222.

*W. Bacher, "Four Quotations from the Hebrew Ben Sira," *JQR* 11 (1898-99) 344.

A. Feldman, "The Bible in Neo-Hebraic Poetry," *JQR* 11 (1898-99) 569-584.

Theodore W. Hunt, "Hebraism and Hellenism in Literature," *HR* 38 (1899) 403-409.

W. C. Clark, "Macbeth and the Bible," *PQ* 13 (1899) 102-115.

James Mudge, "The Bible and the Poets," *MQR, 3rd Ser.*, 26 (1900) 75-96.

M. Kaufmann, "Psalms of the East and West," *Exp, 6th Ser.*, 5 (1902) 446-458; 6 (1902) 57-69.

Caroline A. Watters, "Elements of Hebrew Literature in Browning's 'Saul'," *MR* 84 (1902) 219-222.

Winfred C. Rhoades, "Job and Faust," *MR* 85 (1903) 373-387.

James Moffatt, "Literary Illustrations of the Bible. I. The Book of Ecclesiastes," *Exp, 6th Ser.*, 10 (1904) 388-400, 432-439.

John Franklin Cowan, "Fictions Based on the Bible," *HR* 48 (1904) 43-44.

John C. Hawkins, "The Use of Dante as an Illustrator of Scripture," *ET* 16 (1904-05) 393-396, 496-500, 547-553; 17 (1905-06) 37-42.

James Moffatt, "Literary Illustrations of Ecclesiastes," *Exp, 6th Ser.*, 11 (1905) 77-80.

James Moffatt, "Literary Illustrations of the Book of Daniel," *Exp, 6th Ser.,* 11 (1905) 237-240, 389-400, 469-472; 12 (1905) 74-80.

Thomas Carter, "Shakespeare's use of the Apocrypha," *IJA* #5 (1906) 6-8.

Anonymous, "'Shamone," *IJA* # 5 (1906) 8-9. *[From a Midrāsāh of Ephrem - Ref. 2 Macc. 7]*

A. J. Coultas, "Browning's Saul," *MR* 88 (1906) 784-795.

D. S. Margoliouth, "Ecclesiasticus in Arabic Literature," *ET* 18 (1906-07) 476-477.

Harry W. Ettelson, "Ecclesiastes: Some Quatrains," *HUCA* (1904) 267-281.

J. B. Mayor, "Virgil and Isaiah: an Inquiry into the Sources of the Fourth Ecologue of Virgil," *Exp, 7th Ser.,* 3 (1907) 289-311.

James Moffatt, "Literary Illustrations of the Book of Ecclesiasticus," *Exp, 7th Ser.,* 4 (1907) 279-288, 473-480.

W. H. Daubney, "The Apocrypha in English Fiction," *IJA* #6 (1907) 9-10.

Anonymous, "Chaucer and the Apocrypha," *IJA* #8 (1907) 6-7; #9 (1907) 11.

A. W. Hands, "Dante's Use of the Apocrypha," *IJA* #8 (1907) 12-13.

Anonymous, Professor Blackie's 'Benedictie'," *IJA* #8 (1907) 11. *[Song of the Three Children]*

Anonymous, "The Apocrypha in the Day-Hours," *IJA* #10 (1907) 5-6.

Anonymous, "Longfellow, on Bel and the Dragon, verses 33-39," *IJA* #10 (1907) 7-8.

T. Gregory Foster, "The Old English Poem of Judith," *IJA* #10 (1907) 10-12.

Anonymous, "Ruskin and the Apocrypha," *IJA* #10 (1907) 14.

'Dean of Llandaff', "Bishop Andrewes and the Apocrypha," *IJA* #11 (1907) 5-7.

W. W. Gibbings, "The 16th Century Esdras-Play," *IJA* #11 (1907) 13-15.

E. Hamilton Moore, "The Apocryphal Element in Mediaeval Drama," *IJA* #11 (1907) 15-16.

R. C. Jebb, "Samson Agonistes and the Hellenic Drama," *PBA* 3 (1907-08) 341-348.

Anonymous, "The Apocrypha in the Homilies," *IJA* #12 (1908) 9-11.

'Dean of Llandaff', "Allusions to the Apocrypha during the reign of Queen Elizabeth," *IJA* #13 (1908) 9-10.

Anonymous, "John Fitzgerald Pennie's Judith-Play," *IJA* #13 (1908) 12-13.

Anonymous, "Lord Byron's 'Hebrew Melodies'," *IJA* #13 (1908) 13.

C. G. Cartwright, "Ecclesiasticus in Salimbene's Chronicle," *IJA* #13 (1908) 15-16.

Anonymous, "The black-letter Ballad of Tobias," *IJA* #14 (1908) 9-11. *[16th Century translation in metred verse]*

Anonymous, "George Wither's 'Benedicite,' 1623," *IJA* #14 (1908) 12-13. *[Song of the Three Children]*

Anonymous, "The Elizabethan Ballad of Susanna," *IJA* #15 (1908) 12-13. *[16th Century metred poem of Susanna]*

Anonymous, "'Godly Queene Hester,' 1561," *IJA* #15 (1908) 16. *[16th Century metred Play]*

J. Lindskog, "The Swedish 'Tobiae Comedia,' 1550," *IJA* #16 (1909) 11-14.

Anonymous, "Milton and the Apocrypha," *IJA* #17 (1909) 31-33.

Anonymous, "Longfellow's 'Judas Maccabaeus'," *IJA* #18 (1909) 62-63.

*F. A. Blackburn, "The Use of the Old English Literature of the Apocryphal Passage in the Third Chapter of the Book of Daniel," *IJA* #19 (1909) 69-73. *[Vulgate - 3:24-90; Chap. 13 & 14 from Theodotion]*

Anonymous, "A Ballad on the Wisdom of the Son of Sirach, 1585-6," *IJA* #19 (1909) 73-74.

Edward Dowden, "The 'Judith' of Du Bartas," *IJA* #19 (1909) 76-77.

James Moffatt, "Ecclesiasticus in Literature," *IJA* #19 (1909) 79-83.

Calvin Thomas, "German Playwrights and the Apocrypha," *IJA* #21 (1910) 33-34.

Anonymous, "Wilton's 'Benedicite'," *IJA* #21 (1910) 38-40. *[Song of the Three Children]*

G. F. Cartwright, "George Eliot's 'Legend of Jubal'," *IJA* #22 (1910) 50-52. *[cf. Gen. 4:21]*

Anonymous, "Dr. Booker's Tobit-Poem, 1805," *IJA* #22 (1910) 59-60.

J. M. Potter, "Browning's Saul," *BWTS* 3 (1910-11) #4, 10-16.

B. A. Greene, "The Influence of the Authorized Version on English Literature," *BW* 37 (1911) 391-401.

James Moffatt, "Literary Illustrations of the Book of Ecclesiasticus," *Exp,* *8th Ser.,* 1 (1911) 84-96; 8 (1914) 379-384.

Anonymous, "A Woman's Tobit-Poem, 1787," *IJA* #25 (1911) 37.

Anonymous, "Shakespeare and the Apocrypha," *IJA* #26 (1911) 48-49.

John Calvin Metcalf, "The English Bible in English Literature," *R&E* 8 (1911) 511-523.

Anonymous, "Dr. Schutze's 'Judith'," *IJA* #28 (1912) 17-18.

T. Hudson-Williams, "Notes on the Apocrypha in Modern Literature," *IJA* #29 (1912) 26-27.

Anonymous, "The History of Daniel and the Dragon," *IJA* #29 (1912) 35-36.

*E. H. Holthouse, "Dante and Ben Sira: A Comparison," *CQR* 75 (1912-13) 395-415.

Anonymous, "Pell's 'Judas Maccabaeus'," *IJA* #32 (1913) 5-6.

Anonymous, "Southey and the Apocrypha," *IJA* #32 (1913) 8-9.

Anonymous, "Dr. Kenealy's 'Book of Enoch'," *IJA* #32 (1913) 14-15.

Anonymous, "17th Century Histories of Judith, Susanna, etc.," *IJA* #32 (1913) 17-18.

Albert S. Cook, "Ruskin's use of the Apocrypha," *IJA* #33 (1913) 30-33.

Anonymous, "Antiochus Epiphanes and the Maccabees," *IJA* #34 (1913) 52-53.

Anonymous, "The 14th Century Scottish Alliterative Poem of Susanna," *IJA* #36 (1914) 9-10.

Israel Abrahams, "The Tobit Drama in the 16th Century," *IJA* #37 (1914) 27-29.

Anonymous, "Mr. Sturge Moore's Dramatic Poem 'Judith'," *IJA* #37 (1914) 31-32.

W. Jentsch, "Shakespeare's Attitude Toward the Bible," *LCR* 33 (1914) 59-67.

*E. von Dobschütz, "A Collection of Old Latin Bible Quotations: Somnium Neronis," *JTS* 16 (1914-15) 1-27.

James Moffatt, "Literary Illustrations of Amos," *Exp, 8th Ser.,* 9 (1915) 272-288.

*James Moffatt, "Literary Illustrations of the Book of Numbers," *Exp, 8th Ser.,* 10 (1915) 374-384.

Clayton Haverstick Ranck, "Prose Fiction Relating to Old Testament Times," *HR* 69 (1915) 19-21.

Reed Taft Bayne, "The Proverbs of Thirdly, the Superannuated," *HR* 75 (1915) 366-367.

Geo. H. Willett, "Browning's 'Saul' and Wesley's 'Wrestling Jacob'," *MR* 97 (1915) 450-454.

Anonymous, "The Apocryphan in Henry VIII's Primer, 1546," *IJA* #40 (1915) 16-17.

Anonymous, "Michael Drayton and the Apocrypha," *IJA* #41 (1915) 26-27.

Anonymous, "Florian's Poem on Tobit," *IJA* #43 (1915) 59-61.

*Anonymous, "John Milton on I. Esdras iii.1- iv. 41," *IJA* #43 (1915) 71-72.

Paul Carus, "The Creation of Eve," *OC* 29 (1915) 674-677. *[poem]*

William Sanday, "A Short Sermon on Shakespeare," *ET* 37 (1915-16) 441-443. *[Gen. 1:21]*

Maurice G[arland] Fulton, "Browning and the Bible," *USR* 26 (1915-16) 1-17.

Maurice Garland Fulton, "Shakespeare and Holy Writ," *USR* 27 (1915-16) 329-346.

Edward Bagby Pollard, "How Shakespeare Got His Bible," *HR* 71 (1916) 278-283.

Edward M. Chapman, "The Bible and English Literature," *HR* 71 (1916) 438-444.

D. S. Margoliouth, "The Use of the Apocrypha by Moslem Writers," *IJA* #44 (1916) 10-12.

H. Temple Robins, "The Apocrypha in La Divine Commedia," *IJA* #46 (1916) 36-37.

Anonymous, "Caswall's 'Benedicite'," *IJA* #47 (1916) 53-55.

Edward J. Thompson, "Samson Agonistes," *LQHR* 125 (1916) 244-254.

*John K. Bonnell, "The Serpent with a Human Head in Art and in Mystery Play," *AJA* 21 (1917) 255-291.

James Moffatt, "Literary Illustrations of the Song of Solomon," *Exp, 8th Ser.,* 13 (1917) 391-400, 461-472.

M. Gaster, "The Apocrypha and the Jewish Chap-Books," *IJA* #48 (1917) 13-16.

Anonymous, "Sylvester's 'Judith' of Du Bartas, 1614," *IJA* #49 (1917) 31-32.

*Thomas E. Barr, "The Bible and Literature," *BS* 75 (1918) 213-236.

Charles L. Williams, "What Literature in English Owes to the Bible," *BCTS* 10 (1918) 114-137.

Charles Edward Locke, "The Influence of the English Bible on the Literature of the World," *CFL, 3rd Ser.,* 24 (1918) 117-120.

Carl Holliday, "English Literature's Debt to the Bible," *MQR, 3rd Ser.,* 45 (1919) 32-45.

James Moffatt, "Twisted Sayings—Mizpah," *HR* 78 (1919) 27.

Arthur C. Boggess, "The Old Testament in Longfellow's Poems," *MR* 103 (1920) 263-271.

C. Alphonso Smith, "Poe and the Bible," *BR* 5 (1920) 354-365.

Daniel E. Jenkins, "The Bible in Shakespeare," *PTR* 19 (1921) 309-328.

Clayton Haverstick Ranck, "Recent Fiction Touching Bible Lands and Times," *HR* 84 (1922) 433-436.

Henry T. Carley, "Immortality: The Basis of Hope in Browning's 'Saul'," *MQR, 3rd Ser.,* 47 (1922) 425-435.

*Maurice Bloomfield, "Joseph and Potiphar in Hindu Fiction," *PAPA* 54 (1923) 141-167.

G. W. Wade, "Biblical Phrases in Context and Currency," *ContR* 125 (1924) 216-224.

Fred Smith, "Fictionizing the Bible," *HR* 98 (1929) 188-190.

*(Mrs.) J. W. Kilgo, "The Hebrew Samson and Milton's Samson," *MQR, 3rd Ser.* 50 (1924) 312-316.

*Alexander Haggerty Krappe, "The Story of Eriphyle in Arabic Legend," *AJSL* 41 (1924-25) 194-197.

Jacob Philip Rudin, "The Fall of Jericho," *JIQ* 2 (1925-26) #2, 18-23. *[Imaginary Story regarding]*

George Yeisley Rusk, "An Unauthorized Bible: or the Prophets Speak Again," *MR* 111 (1928) 249-267.

H. Kamphausen, "That 'Unauthorized Bible'," *MR* 111 (1928) 761.

W. H. Hatten, "Dante and Jerusalem," *CQR* 110 (1930) 252-270.

Joshua Finkel, "Old Israelitish Tradition in the Koran," *PAAJR* 2 (1930-31) 7-21.

C. H. Coker, "The Influence of the Bible Upon the Koran," *MR* 114 (1931) 94-99.

Dom Ethelbert Horne, "The Dream of Gerontius and the Fall of Man," *DownsR* 50 (1932) 278-283.

John Lendrum, "Shakespeare and Miracle," *ET* 44 (1932-33) 316-319.

A. S. Tritton, "The Bible Text of Theodore Abu Kurra," *JTS* 34 (1933) 52-54.

H. J. Schick, "Shakespeare and the Bible," *TZDES* 62 (1934) 93-100.

Marbury Bladen Ogle, "Bible Quotations in the *de Nugis Curialim* of Walter Map," *PAPA* 66 (1935) xlii.

A. V. Williams Jackson, "Traces of Biblical Influence in the Turan Pahlavi Fragment M. 173," *JAOS* 56 (1936) 198-207.

Muriel S. Curtis, "The Vision of Isaiah," *JAAR* 5 (1937) 159-161.

*Bernard Lewis, "An Ismaili Interpretation of the Fall of Adam," *BSOAS* 9 (1937-39) 691-704.

Robert B. Pattison, "Bible Words as Book Titles," *RL* 7 (1938) 439-450.

E. H. Blakeney, "The English Bible as Literature," *Theo* 36 (1938) 325-337.

Margaret O. Becker, "Some Significant Elements in the Tales of Isaac," *JAAR* 7 (1939) 75-78.

Charles S. Braden, "The Bible in Contemporary Literature," *RL* 9 (1940) 113-127.

S. Vernon McCasland, "Gabriel's Trumpet," *JAAR* 9 (1941) 159-161.

W. Bardsley Brash, "The Hebrew Prophet and Poet," *LQHR* 167 (1942) 241-250.

Ivar Lou Myhr, "Milton and the Scriptures," *SQ/E* 3 (1942) 49-53.

*Toyozo W. Nakarai, "Columbus in the Genoa Psalter," *SQ/E* 3 (1942) 171-182.

Robert E. Fitch, "John Dewey and Jahweh," *JR* 23 (1943) 12-22.

A. S. Tritton, "The Bible in Early Muslim Literature," *GUOST* 11 (1942-44) 47-49.

William K. Prentice, "The Classics and the Bible," *CQ* 20 (1943) 12-17.

Richard Bell, "Muhammad's Knowledge of the Old Testament," *SSO* 2 (1945) 1-20.

Watson Kirkconnell, "Avitus' Epoch of the Fall," *LTP* 3 (1947) 222-242.

John Hennig, "The Literary Tradition of Moses in Ireland," *Tr* 7 (1949-51) 233-261.

Charles S. Braden, "The Bible in Contemporary Poetry," *RL* 19 (1950) 91-105.

Louis H. Feldman, "Jewish 'Sympathizers' in Classical Literature and Inscriptions," *TAPA* 81 (1950) 200-208.

‡Wilbur M. Smith, "Supplement to the Bibliography of the Influence of the Bible in English Literature," *FLB* #11 (1951) 5.

Allen Cabaniss, "The Harrowing of Hell, Psalm 24, and Pliny the Younger: A Note," *VC* 7 (1953) 65-74.

Richard M. Frank, "A 'Citation' from the Prophet Jeremias in Ibn Qutaiba and Tabari," *CBQ* 17 (1955) 379-402.

Sholom J. Kahn, "The Samuel-Saul Story as Drama," *Jud* 4 (1955) 3-12.

David C. Fowler, "Some Biblical Influences on Geoffrey of Monmouth's Historiography," *Tr* 14 (1958) 378-385.

Alfred L. Kellogg, "Langland and Two Scriptural Texts," *Tr* 14 (1958) 385-398.

H. Keith Beebe, "Biblical Adventures in an American Novel," *JAAR* 27 (1959) 133-138.

*Mary Frances Thelen, "*J.B.,* Job, and the Biblical Doctrine of Man," *JAAR* 27 (1959) 201-205.

M. H. Levine, "A Note to the 'Cain and Abel Passage' in *Sefer Ham-Mebaqqesh,*" *PAAJR* 28 (1959) 93-94.

John W. Brush, "The Dialect of Canaan," *ANQ, N.S.,* 1 (1960-61) #2, 35-42.

Carlos Baker, "The Place of the Bible in American Fiction," *TT* 17 (1960-61) 53-76.

*Edward Ullendorff, "The 'Death of Moses' in the Literature of the Falashas," *BSOAS* 24 (1961) 419-443.

C. S. Lewis, "The Literary Impact of the Authorized Version," *LQHR* 186 (1961) 100-108.

Keith Beebe, "Biblical Motifs in *All the King's Men*," *JAAR* 30 (1962) 123-130.

S[tanislav] Segert, "A Novel on the Qumran Cave," *NOP* 3 (1962) 60-61. *(Review)*

Edward J. Rose, "The Structure of Blake's *Jerusalem*," *BUS* 11 (1962-63) #3, 35-54.

Howard Sergeant, "Modern Poetry and the Bible," *ContR* 203 (1963) 93-95.

*Maurice Friedman, "The Modern Job. On Melville, Destoiesky, and Kafka," *Jud* 12 (1963) 436-455.

Ralph J. Mills Jr., "Eden's Gate: The Later Poetry of Edwin Muir," *Person* 44 (1963) 58-78.

Abraham Cronbach, "'Manner for Manner' in Dante," *HUCA* 35 (1964) 193-212.

Richard A. Hasler, "The Influence of David and the Psalms upon John Calvin's Life and Thought," *HQ* 5 (1964-65) #2, 7-18.

Abraham J. Feldman, "Shakespeare and the Bible," *HQ* 5 (1964-65) #4, 27-32.

T. R. Henn, "The Bible in relation to the study of English literature today," *Herm* #100 (1965) 29-43.

*Abraham Cronbach, "Unmeant Meanings of Scripture," *HUCA* 36 (1965) 99-123.

Merrill Lewis, "Organic Metaphor and Edenic Myth in George Bancroft's *History of the United States*," *JHI* 26 (1965) 587-592.

Martin Buber, "Elijah: A Mystery Play (Selections)," *Jud* 14 (1965) 260-266. *(Trans. by Maurice Friedman)*

A. D. Hallam, "Milton's Knowledge and Use of Hebrew," *Mwa-M* #5 (1965) 18-22.

Sheila Ralphs, "Dante, Poet of the Exodus," *Theo* 68 (1965) 479-485.

Esther Casier Quinn, "The Quest of Seth, Solomon's Ship and the Grail," *Tr* 21 (1965) 185-222.

B. Davie Naiper, "Come Sweet Death: A Quartet from Genesis. No. 1. The Garden," *MQ* 21 (1965) #1, 1-7.

B. Davie Naiper, "Come Sweet Death: A Quartet from Genesis. The Brothers," *MQ* 21 (1965) #2, 1-7.

B. Davie Naiper, "Come Sweet Death: A Quartet from Genesis." *MQ* 21 (1965) #3, 7-13. *[The Flood]*

B. Davie Naiper, "Come Sweet Death: A Quartet from Genesis. No. 4. 'The Tower'," *MQ* 21 (1965-66) #4, 10-16.

Eric F. F. Bishop, "The Bible in 'Arabia Deserta'," *PEQ* 98 (1966) 103-113.

*A. Crepin, "The Names of God in the Church Fathers and in Old English Poetry," *StP* 9 (1966) 525-531.

Z. Zinger, "The Bible Quotations in the Pesiktta de Rav Kahana," *Text* 5 (1966) 114-124.

N. F. Blake, "The Biblical Additions in Caxton's 'Golden Legend'," *Tr* 25 (1969) 231-247.

*Jefim Schirmann, "The Battle Between Behemoth and Leviathan According to an Ancient Hebrew *Piyyuṭ*," *PIASH* 4 (1969-70) 327-369.

§1063 **6.4 *Studies on the Use of the Old Testament in Preaching***

*C. E. Stowe, "On Expository Preaching and the Principles which should guide us in the Exposition of Scripture," *BRCR* 5 (1835) 384-402.

Stephen M. Vail, "Hermeneutics and Homiletics; or the Study of the Original Scriptures and Preaching. [Article First.]," *MR* 48 (1866) 37-50.

Stephen M. Vail, "Hermeneutics and Homiletics; or the Study of the Original Scriptures and Preaching. [Article Second.]," *MR* 48 (1866) 371-386.

Charles H. Waller, "The Use of the Old Testament in Preaching," *CM* 9 (1879) 1-15.

Archibald Duff, "Isaiah: A Study for Preachers," *BS* 39 (1882) 270-291.

S. Burnham, "The Value of the Old Testament for the Work of the Pastor," *ONTS* 4 (1884-85) 97-103, 151-156, 257-261.

R. S. MacArthur, "Old Testament Study for Homiletic Use," *ONTS* 4 (1884-85) 289-294.

Revere F. Weidner, "Letter I.—To a Pastor Who Wishes to Know How He May Study the Book of Psalms to His Own Best Advantage and that of His Congregation," *ONTS* 6 (1886-87) 235-237.

Wm. Elliot Griffis, "Homiletical Uses of the Song of Songs," *HR* 19 (1890) 221-227.

Charles E. Knox, "Biblical Homiletics.—No. I.—Advantages. Can the Bible be Wrought More Fully into the Science and Art of Preaching?" *HR* 20 (1890) 99-106.

Charles E. Knox, "Biblical Homiletics. II. Objections," *HR* 20 (1890) 319-325.

Charles E. Knox, "Biblical Homiletics. III.—To What Extent can the Scriptures be Used?" *HR* 21 (1891) 23-30; 22 (1891) 504-508.

Philip A. Nordell, "How to Prepare an Expository Sermon on Psalms XLII, and XLIII," *ONTS* 12 (1891) 216-220.

T. D. Witherspoon, "The Homiletic Value of the Book of Leviticus," *HR* 29 (1895) 264-268.

R. A. Lapsley, "The Study of the English Bible with a View to Preaching It," *USR* 7 (1895-96) 260-268.

T. R. English, "The Text: Its Use and Abuse," *USR* 8 (1896-97) 256-262.

F. W. Farrar, "The Importance of Presenting the Bible in Complete Books from the Pulpit," *HR* 33 (1897) 1-9.

Cunningham Geikie, "How Best to Present Bible Characters from the Pulpit," *HR* 34 (1897) 387-391.

J. F. McCurdy, "Light on Scriptural Texts from Recent Discoveries. How Oriental Discoveries are Helpful to the Preacher," *HR* 35 (1898) 217-220.

*E. H. Dewart, "'Modern Criticism and the Preaching of the Old Testament.'," *HR* 43 (1902) 118-124.

Herbert Edward Ryle, "The Old Testament in Teaching and Preaching, as Affected by the more Assured Results of Research," *ET* 15 (1903-04) 177-180.

Thomas Chalmer Straus, "The Homiletic Use of Hosea," *HR* 48 (1904) 199-201.

*Theodore G. Soares, "Old Testament Criticism and the Pulpit," *BW* 25 (1905) 267-273.

M. Joseph, "Biblical Criticism and the Pulpit," *JQR* 18 (1905-06) 291-301.

C. G. Montefiore, "Should Biblical Criticism be Spoken of in Jewish Pulpits?" *JQR* 18 (1905-06) 302-316.

Edward G. Andrews, "The Pastor and His Bible," *MR* 88 (1906) 523-544.

Frederick W. Eberhardt, "The Preacher as Prophet," *R&E* 3 (1906) 68-81.

Robert E. Vinson, "The Modern Pulpit and the Bible Teaching," *USR* 21 (1909-10) 167-174.

Marshall Dawson, "The Relation of Amos and Hosea to Present-Day Preaching," *BW* 39 (1912) 109-124.

George Arthur Andrews, "How Should the Bible be Used in Preaching?" *HR* 64 (1912) 365-368.

Harland Creelman, "The Value of the Old Testament to the Preacher," *ASRec* 8 (1912-13) 13-20.

*J. E. Compton, "The Preacher's Use of the Apocrypha," *HR* 65 (1913) 138-140.

E. E. Fischer, "Homiletical Uses of the Old Testament," *LCR* 34 (1915) May, 25-34.

*W. Ernest Beet, "The Map as an Aid to the Preaching of the Old Testament," *Exp, 8th Ser.,* 11 (1916) 56-66.

*J. E. Compton, "The Preacher's Use of the Apocrypha," *IJA* #46 (1916) 41-42.

Edward Mack, "The Homiletic Value of the Old Testament," *USR* 28 (1916-17) 298-307.

Harry Emerson Fosdick, "A Modern Preacher's Problem in His Use of the Scriptures," *MSTQB* 13 (1918-19) #3, 3-18.

Anonymous, "A Text from the Apocrypha," *HR* 78 (1919) 31.

Harry H. Mayer, "The History of Jewish Preaching with Special Reference to Adolph Jellinek," *YCCAR* 31 (1921) 158-179. [Discussion by: Felix A. Levy, pp. 179-180. [William] Rosenau, pp. 180-181; [Samuel] Goldenson, pp. 181-182; Max Heller, pp. 182-183; [David] Philipson, pp. 183-184; [Louis] Gross, pp. 184-185; Jonah B. Wise, p. 185]

Alexander Reid Gordon, "The Preacher and the Old Testament. I. The Historical Narrative," *HR* 84 (1922) 363-367.

Alexander Reid Gordon, "The Preacher and the Old Testament. II. The Poetry of Religion," *HR* 85 (1923) 93-98.

Alexander Reid Gordon, "The Preacher and the Old Testament. III. Moral Development," *HR* 85 (1923) 179-184.

Alexander Reid Gordon, "The Preacher and the Old Testament. IV. The Social Outlook," *HR* 85 (1923) 438-443.

Edward Mack, "The Preacher's Old Testament," *PSB* 17 (1923) #1, 8-18.

H. A. Kent, "The Preacher and the Old Testament," *CJRT* 1 (1924) 413-419.

John E. McFadyen, "The Preacher's Use of Jeremiah," *HR* 88 (1924) 361-365.

*John E. McFayden, "The Historical Method and the Preacher," *ET* 40 (1928-29) 36-40, 77-81.

J. S. MacArthur, "On Preaching from Texts," *ET* 40 (1928-29) 212-214.

*H. J. Lewis, "Theology in Relation to Preaching," *ET* 41 (1929-30) 458-462.

Albert Edgar Wardner, "The Preaching Values of the Psalms," *HR* 99 (1930) 114-117.

Julius A. Bewer, "The Christian Minister and the Old Testament," *JR* 10 (1930) 16-21.

George Manning, "Graphic Preaching and the Bible," *SS* 4 (1930) 66-74.

Dom. Hugh Bevenot, "Esther. A Scriptural Key to Preaching," *ClR* 4 (1932) 287-296.

Mordecai M. Kaplan, "The Jewish Method in Homiletics," *HR* 103 (1932) 111-116.

J. J. Murray, "The Preacher's Use of Ezekiel," *ET* 50 (1938-39) 314-316.

C. Ryder Smith, "The Bible and Preaching," *LQHR* 167 (1942) 127-133.

*R. G. Finch, "A Synagogue Sermon," *Theo* 45 (1942) 164-168.

*David Daube, "A Modern Synagogue Sermon," *Theo* 46 (1943) 106-108. *[Sidrah / Mikketz]*

James Muilenburg, "The Old Testament and the Christian Minister," *USQR* 1 (1945-46) #1, 10-18.

Samuel L. Terrien, "The Old Testament and the Christian Preacher Today," *RL* 15 (1946) 262-271.

James Stewart, "The Preacher and the Maxims of *Proverbs*," *CongQL* 26 (1948) 342-347.

Corwin C. Roach, "The Purpose of the Past. The Preacher's Use of the Biblical Story," *Interp* 2 (1948) 39-62.

Andrew W. Wood, "Servants of the Word. How to Preach from the Prophets," *Interp* 2 (1948) 158-171.

Herbert C. Alleman, "Personal Religion. How to Preach from the Wisdom Books and the Psalms," *Interp* 2 (1948) 299-312.

Raymond Calkins, "Militant Message. How to Preach from the Apocalyptic Messages of the Bible," *Interp* 2 (1948) 444-450.

James Stewart, "*Ecclesiastes* and the Christian Preacher. An Exercise in Sermon-Preparation," *CongQL* 29 (1951) 120-127.

Paul Gorin, "The Use of the Midrash in Preaching," *YCCAR* 62 (1952) 532-537.

William A. Irwin, "Symposium: The Bible and Preaching. The Old Testament," *PSTJ* 7 (1953-54) #2, 4-8.

Corwin C. Roach, "Preaching and the New Versions," *ATR* 36 (1954) 181-190.

*R. B. Y. Scott, "Is Preaching Prophecy?" *CJT* 1 (1955) 11-18.

Richard R. Caemmerer, "'Preaching from Isaiah'," *CTM* 26 (1955) 360-364. *(Review)*

Ray Branton, "Symposium: The Contemporary Minister and His Message. III. The Minister as Biblical Interpreter," *PSTJ* 10 (1956-57) #3, 10-12.

David H. C. Read, "The Old Testament and Modern Preaching," *USQR* 12 (1956-57) #2, 11-16.

D. K. Andrews, "Preaching from Proverbs," *CJT* 4 (1958) 120-126.

James D. Smart, "The Christian Ministry in the Light of the Old Testament," *R&E* 55 (1958) 235-254.

Reidar B. Bjornard, "Christian Preaching from the Old Testament," *R&E* 56 (1959) 8-19.

George M. Alexander, "The Use of the Psalter in Preaching," *StLJ* 3 (1959-60) #1, 24-31.

*William H. Rossell, "Preaching Values in Hebrew Words," *SWJT, N.S.,* 2 (1959-60) #1, 19-25.

Jesse J. Northcutt, "How to Prepare a Biblical Sermon," *SWJT, N.S.,* 2 (1959-60) #2, 33-48.

Paul Scherer, "The History That Becomes History: Preaching from the Old Testament," *USQR* 15 (1959-60) 273-280.

J. Y. Muckle, "The Preacher and the Old Testament," *PQL* 6 (1960) 165-172, 213-219.

H. Jackson Forstman, "What Does It Mean 'To Preach from the Bible'," *SQ/E* 21 (1960) 218-231.

*John H. Scammon, "The Minister and the Psalms," *ANQ, N.S.,* 1 (1960-61) #1, 28-38.

H. Jackson Forstman, "What Does It Mean 'To Preach from the Bible'," *ESS* 5 (1960-61) 59-74.

*Gerhard von Rad, "Ancient Word and Living Word. *The Preaching of Deuteronomy and Our Preaching,*" *Interp* 15 (1961) 3-13.

V. L. Stanfield, "Preaching Values in Jeremiah," *SWJT, N.S.,* 4 (1961-62) #1 69-80.

Louis H. Gunnemann, "The Old Testament and the Present," *MHSB* 7 (1962) #1, 21-25.

Herbert C. Brichto, "Resources for Preaching: Using the Bible," *YCCAR* 72 (1962) 149-150.

William G. Braude, "Resources for Preaching: The Rabbinic Sources," *YCCAR* 72 (1962) 151-152.

W. A. Markowicz, "Chrysostom's Sermons on Genesis: A Problem," *ThSt* 24 (1963) 652-664.

Herbert T. Mayer, "The Old Testament in the Pulpit," *CTM* 35 (1964) 603-608.

J. C. L. Gibson, "Preaching the Old Testament," *NCB* 2 (1964-65) #1, 21-25.

T. Miles Bennett, "Preaching Values in Deuteronomy," *SWJT, N.S.,* 7 (1964-65) #1, 41-53.

Charlotte Lee, "Reading the Word of God," *P* (Convention Issue 1965) 26-40. (Discussion, pp. 41-42)

Arthur Candeland, "Psalms and the Preacher," *PQL* 11 (1965) 31-36. [III. Preaching from the Psalms]

David Stacey, "Clues from the Old Testament," *PQL* 11 (1965) 110-117. [III. Preaching]

Alfred [E.] McBride, "How the Bible Helps the Preacher," *P* 1 (1966) #1,1-6.

*Alfred E. McBride, "The Preaching Technique of Isaiah," *P* 1 (1966) #3,1-4.

John O. Strange, "Preaching from Amos," *SWJT, N.S.,* 9 (1966-67) #1, 69-80.

Michael Maher, "Reflections on Jewish and Christian Preaching," *IER, 5th Ser.,* 108 (1967) 227-242.

Carl Graesser Jr., "Preaching from the Old Testament," *CTM* 38 (1967) 525-534.

*Ross Snyder, "Bible Study for Preaching Preparation," *P* 2 (1967) #1, 16-24.

Lawrence E. Toombs, "The Old Testament in the Christian Pulpit," *HQ* 8 (1968) #2, 7-14.

Max Warren, "Preaching from the Bible," *PQL* 14 (1968) 185-196.

F. N. Jasper, "Preaching in the Old Testament," *ET* 80 (1968-69) 356-361.

Lawrence E. Toombs, "The Problematic of Preaching from the Old Testament," *Interp* 23 (1969) 302-314.

§1064 6.5 Studies on the Old Testament in Worship and Liturgy

*Anonymous, "Spirit of the Hebrew Scriptures.—No. III. Public Worship: Social Crime, and its Retribution," *CE* 17 (1834) 78-92.

John T. Pressly, "Review of Letters on Psalmody," *UPQR* 1 (1860) 17-44, 204-223. *(Review)*

David Chandler Gilmore, "An Outline of the History of Psalmody," *BQR* 11 (1889) 166-177.

Wm. M. Lawrence, J. C. Goddard, S. M. Newman, Arthur Little, Lyman Abbott, F. M. Ellis, B. B. Tyler, Geo. Dana Boardman, W. E. Griffis, A. H. Plumb, "A 'Symposium' on Commenting in the Public Reading of the Scriptures," *ONTS* 12 (1891) 112-118.

James M. Garnett, "Why the Revised Version Should be 'Appointed to be Read in Churches'," *PER* 5 (1891-92) 321-336.

Edward Abbott, "The Revised Version in Public Worship," *PER* 6 (1892-93) 169-186.

Anton de Waal, "The Psalms in the Catacombs," *AER* 16 (1897) 113-125.

Edward T. Horn, "The Word of God in Christian Worship," *LQ* 27 (1897) 377-406.

W. Robertson Smith, "On the Translation and Use of the Psalms for the Public Worship of the Church," *ET* 16 (1904-05) 58-65, 105-110.

Anonymous, "The Apocrypha in the Lectionary," *IJA* #4 (1905) 6.

W. Taylor, "The Reading of Holy Scripture. Its Place in the Service of Christian Worship, and the Principles which should Regulate its Order," *ET* 17 (1905-06) 31-34.

Anonymous, "The Reading of Holy Scriptures," *ET* 17 (1905-06) 133-136.

James B. Grant, "I. The Reading of the Scriptures," *ET* 17 (1905-06) 136-137.

George Ferries, "II. The Reading of the Holy Scripture in the Service of Christian Worship," *ET* 17 (1905-06) 137-138.

Joseph Mitchell, William Brand, George Thompson, John Haggart, John Mack, C. S. Burdon, John C. Walker, John Wallace, Alexander Ross, Marshall B. Lang, J. R. Strachan, G. Marjoribanks, Peter Adam, "The Reading of the Holy Scripture. I. Should the Reading be Consecutive or Selected?" *ET* 17 (1905-06) 186-188.

R. Goodwillie, J. Milne Anderson, W. D. Morris, W. B. Kennedy, W. T. P. Macdonald, George Wight, Alexander MacLeod, John Oliver, John M. Dickie, Kenneth D. M'Laren, J. Ewing Wallace, John Henderson, Robert G. Forrest, Norman Macleod Caie, J. S. W. Irvine, "The Reading of the Holy Scripture. II. Should the Bible be read right through?" *ET* 17 (1905-06) 188-190.

Lauchlan MacLean Watt, George C. Watt, Andrew Mutch, William John, James Kirk, "The Reading of the Holy Scripture. III. Some Men's Methods," *ET* 17 (1905-06) 190-191.

David Hunter, "The Reading of Scripture in Public Worship. I. The Points in Question," *ET* 17 (1905-06) 235-236.

David A. Rollo, Wm. Johnston, D. Lamont, George W. Sprott, "The Reading of Scripture in Public Worship. II. Should we use a Table of Lessons?" *ET* 17 (1905-06) 236-237.

W. A. Mowat, "John Paterson, E. Sherwood Gunson, Charles M. Short, J. G. Lyon, Robt. J. Kyd, "The Reading of Scripture in Public Worship. III. Should there be a Unity or Variety in the Parts of Public Worship?" *ET* 17 (1905-06) 237-238.

James Millar, A. W. Wotherspoon, James Nicoll, T. E. S. Clarke, A. J. Campbell, J. M. Frazer, A. Irvine Robertson, Thomas Pryde, Hector Mackinnon, R. Montgomerie Hardie, Robert Howie, "The Reading of Scripture in Public Worship," *ET* 17 (1905-06) 310-315.

W. R. Adeney, William Adamson, James Adam, Martin Anstey, J. Bodvan Anwyl, R. F. Bracey, Arthur Baker, E. R. Barrett, Walter Baxendale, Alex. Cossar, R. J. Campbell, "The Reading of Scripture in Public Worship," *ET* 17 (1905-06) 471-476.

Cynfig Davies, J. Evans, J. Mathieson Forson, P. T. Forsyth, R. Augustus Foster, D. Z. Haig Forson, S. C. Gordon, Alfred E. Garvie, William Hamilton, J. A. Hopgood, F. D. Humphreys, J. Holden, George L. Hurst," The Reading of Holy Scripture in Public Worship," *ET* 17 (1905-06) 512-517.

J. Charteris Johnston, J. Knowles, D. C. Lloyd, Samuel A. Latham, Charles Leach, A. D. Martin, G. Currie Martin, Robert Mackintosh, "The Reading of Holy Scripture in Public Worship," *ET* 18 (1906-07) 30-34.

Frederick J. Feltham, "The Reading of Holy Scripture in Public Worship. The Intimacy between the Lesson and the Sermon," *ET* 18 (1906-07) 184-185.

T. W. Medhurst, "The Reading of Holy Scripture in Public Worship. Mr. Spurgeon's Practice," *ET* 18 (1906-07) 185.

Frederic C. Spurr, "The Reading of Holy Scripture in Public Worship. Itching Ears," *ET* 18 (1906-07) 185.

L. J. Havard, "The Reading of Holy Scripture in Public Worship. Dr. Hunter's Lectionary," *ET* 18 (1906-07) 185-186.

F. Goldsmith French, "The Reading of Holy Scripture in Public Worship. The Weakness of the Lectionary," *ET* 18 (1906-07) 186.

David Rowlands, "The Reading of Holy Scripture in Public Worship. The Central Figure," *ET* 18 (1906-07) 186.

Stanley Rogers, "The Reading of Holy Scripture in Public Worship. Worship," *ET* 18 (1906-07) 186-187.

George M'Hardy, "The Reading of Holy Scripture in Public Worship. The Atmosphere and Tone of Mind," *ET* 18 (1906-07) 187.

Henry Moulson, "The Reading of Holy Scripture in Public Worship. The Exact Opposite of the Text," *ET* 18 (1906-07) 187.

A. Norman Rowland, "The Reading of Holy Scripture in Public Worship. A Cycle of Old Testament Revelation," *ET* 18 (1906-07) 329-330.

D. W. Simon, Charles Spurgeon, J. Bryan Marshall, Edward Medley, Thomas Williams, E. H. Titchmarsh, W. L. Walker, W. T. Whitley, "The Reading of Holy Scripture in Public Worship," *ET* 18 (1906-07) 373-377.

*I. Elbogen, "Studies in the Jewish Liturgy," *JQR* 19 (1906-07) 229-249; 704-720. [I. B, C, פרס על שמע II. A, B, C, התיבה לפני [עבר

W. Emery Barnes, "The Use of the Psalter in the Services of the Church of England," *ICMM* 4 (1907-08) 18-32.

*John Allan Fitzgerald Gregg, "The First and Second Commandments in their relation to Jewish and Christian Worship," *ICQ* 3 (1910) 199-212.

Margaret G. Dampier, "The use of the Apocrypha in the Greek Service Books," *IJA* #21 (1910) 37-38.

H. F. B. Compston, "The Apocrypha in the Greek and Russian Churches," *IJA* #22 (1910) 46-48.

C. I. Gramah, "The Irish Lectionary and the Apocrypha," *IJA* #23 (1910) 78-79.

H. T. Knight, "The Public Reading of the Old Testament," *ICMM* 7 (1910-11) 187-194.

Edward Chauncey Baldwin, "The Debt of the Modern World to Israel's Priests," *BW* 40 (1912) 54-64.

'Lord Bishop of Moray', "The Apocrypha in the East Syrian (Nestorian) Daily Offices," *IJA* #28 (1912) 12-13.

John Neale Dalton, "Three Suggested forms for the Benedicite," *IJA* #32 (1913) 6-8.

Anonymous, "The Apocrypha in the proposed New Lectionary," *IJA* #33 (1913) 24-26.

Emery Barnes, "The Psalter as an Aid to Worship in the Twentieth Century," *Exp, 8th Ser.,* 9 (1915) 36-46.

J. A. MacCulloch, "The Apocrypha in the New Scottish Lectionary," *IJA* #40 (1915) 10-11.

Winifred Austin, "An 'Apocryphal' Service held in America," *IJA* #41 (1915) 39.

Anonymous, "A Jewish Sermon on the Books of the Maccabees," *IJA* #42 (1915) 53-56.

Anonymous, "Oxford Lectionary for College Use," *IJA* #42 (1915) 56.

Sidney Cooper, "A Plea for Lections from the Pseudepigrapha," *IJA* #44 (1916) 9-10.

*Sidney S. Tedesche, "Prayers of the Apocrypha and their Importance in the Study of Jewish Liturgy," *YCCAR* 26 (1916) 376-398.

Gilbert Clive Binyon, "The Church's Use of the Psalms," *ICMM* 13 (1916-17) 63-67.

*Robert Wallace Boyd, "The Psalter and the Lectionary in Public Worship," *ICQ* 10 (1917) 106-116.

E. J. D. Hellier, "Some Devotional Thoughts on the Benedicite," *IJA* #49 (1917) 25-30.

Alfred Plummer, "The Devotional Use of the Benedicite," *IJA* #50 (1917) 34-37.

E. J. D. Hellier, "The Devotional Use of the Benedicite," *IJA* #50 (1917) 37-40.

Anonymous, "The revised Revision of the Lectionary," *IJA* #51 (1917) 55-56.

G. A. Cooke, "The Bible and the Church," *CQR* 88 (1919) 15-26.

Herbert M. Denslow, "The Use of the Bible in Public Worship," *ACM* 6 (1919-20) 169-185.

Samuel A. B. Mercer, "The Old Testament and Religious Life," *ATR* 2 (1919-20) 118-121.

Anonymous, "Must the Old Testament Go?" *CFL, 3rd Ser.,* 26 (1920) 163.

J. G. Drummond, "The Problem of United Worship," *ET* 32 (1920-21) 296-299. *[The Use of the Psalms in Public Worship]*

*A. Z. Idelson, "Hebrew Music with special reference to Musical Intonations in the Recital of the Pentateuch," *JPOS* 1 (1920-21) 80-94.

W. H. Griffith Thomas, "The Church and the Old Testament," *CFL, 3rd Ser.,* 28 (1922) 398-403.

Gerson B. Levi, "The Place of the Sermon in Jewish Worship," *YCCAR* 34 (1924) 181-197. [Discussion by: Max Heller, pp. 197-199; [Solomon] Freehof, pp. 199-200; [Hyman G.] Enelow, pp. 200-202; Reply by Gerson B. Levi, p. 202]

David B. Alpert, "Torah Readings," *JIQ* 1 (1924-25) 125-126.

Alexander MacMillan, "The Twenty-third Psalm in Christian Worship," *CJRT* 2 (1925) 423-426.

A. Hastings Kelk, "The Psalms in Public Worship," *CQR* 102 (1926-27) 30-44.

Clement F. Rogers, "Sitting for the Psalms," *Theo* 15 (1927) 341-343.

Richard Davidson, "The Bible the Church's Book," *CJRT* 6 (1929) 6-15.

Clement F. Rogers, "Standing for the Psalms," *Theo* 29 (1934) 208-218.

F. L. Cross, "'Standing for the Psalms'," *Theo* 29 (1934) 360-361.

Francis Davidson, "The Scriptural Doctrine of Worship," *EQ* 7 (1935) 54-61.

Godfrey E. Phillips, "The Old Testament in the Life of the Younger Churches," *IRM* 27 (1938) 662-666.

Joh. Lindblom, "The Old Testament in the Christian Church," *ET* 51 (1939-40) 374-379.

William J. Lallou, "The Bible and Liturgy," *CBQ* 4 (1942) 210-217.

J. M. T. Winther, "The Old Testament Background of the Sacraments," *JTALC* 7 (1942) 721-739, 831-852.

Romanus Rois, "A Liturgical Hexameron," *ClR* 26 (1946) 393-401.

Robert E. Keighton, "The Bible and the Worship Service," *CQ* 24 (1947) 97-112.

Charles Slaughter, "The Prophet Zacharias in the Liturgy of the Holy Week," *ClR* 29 (1948) 160-168.

*John Hennig, "The First Chapter of Genesis in the Liturgy," *CBQ* 10 (1948) 360-375.

A. G. Herbert, "The Bible in the Church," *SJT* 1 (1948) 225-232.

A. H. Wilkinson, "The Bible in the Church," *IRM* 38 (1949) 145-148.

E. G. P. Wyatt, "The Liturgical Psalter," *Theo* 52 (1949) 305.

John Hennig, "The Book of Judith in the Liturgy," *ITQ* 18 (1951) 187-189.

John Hennig, "The Book of Wisdom in the Liturgy," *CBQ* 14 (1952) 233-235.

*John Wick Bowman, "Response and Fellowship. Devotional Life in the Bible," *Interp* 6 (1952) 279-289.

John Hennig, "The Book of Tobias in the Liturgy," *ITQ* 19 (1952) 84-90.

John Henning, "Psalm 116 in the Liturgy," *ITQ* 19 (1952) 192-195.

L. Johnston, "Scripture Occurring," *ClR* 38 (1953) 662-671.

C. E. Abraham, "The Place of the Bible in the Church," *IRM* 42 (1953) 194-199.

Frederick C. Grant, "Modern Study of the Jewish Liturgy," *ZAW* 65 (1953-54) 59-77.

E. F. F. Bishop, "'What is the Place of the Old Testament in Christian Worship?'" *HJ* 52 (1953-54) 134-140.

Sebastiano Pagano, "Public Bible Readings," *CBQ* 16 (1954) 20-32.

*N[aphtali] Wieder, "The Term קץ in the Dead Sea Scrolls and in Hebrew Liturgical Poetry," *JJS* 5 (1954) 22-31.

*S. Stein, "The Liturgy of Hanukkah and the First Two Books of Maccabees," *JJS* 5 (1954) 100-106, 148-155.

H. W. Newell, "The Psalter in the Parish Worship of the Church of England," *ET* 66 (1954-55) 323-325.

*John Fearon, "The Psalms and Prayer," *C&C* 7 (1955) 330-336.

Norman Adcock, "The Psalter in the Parish Worship of the Church of England," *ET* 67 (1955-56) 41.

W. G. E. Squire, "The Psalter in the Parish Worship of the Church of England," *ET* 67 (1955-56) 247.

G. E. Selwyn, "The Bible in Church," *QRL* 294 (1956) 297-304.

Illtud Evans, The Bible in Worship," *LofS* 11 (1956-57) 4-9.

Hubert J. Richards, "The Old Testament Readings of Holy Week," *ClR* 42 (1957) 129-137, 199-209.

*John MacDonald, "The Tetragrammaton in Samaritan Liturgical Compositions," *GUOST* 17 (1957-58) 37-47.

*John H. Scammon, "The Minister and the Psalms," *ANQ, N.S.,* 1 (1960-61) #1, 28-38.

Francis Lightbourn, "Getting the Old Testament into Liturgy," *ATR* 43 (1961) 370-374.

*Peter R. Ackroyd, "The Place of the Old Testament in the Church's Teaching and Worship," *ET* 74 (1962-63) 164-167.

*Solomon Zeitlin, "The Hallel: A Historical Study of Canonization of the Hebrew Liturgy," *JQR, N.S.,* 53 (1962-63) 22-29.

Louis Bouyer, "Jewish and Christian Liturgies," *CC* 13 (1963) 335-348.

*Vilmos Vajta, "Creation and Worship," *SL* 2 (1963) 29-46.

*Regin Prenter, "Worship and Creation," *SL* 2 (1963) 82-95.

Solomon Zeitlin, "The Tefillah, the Shemoneh Esreh: An Historical Study of the First Canonization of the Hebrew Liturgy," *JQR, N.S.,* 54 (1963-64) 208-249.

C. A. Simpson, "A consideration of the principles which should govern the making of a Lectionary," *OSHTP* (1963-64) 1-17.

*Arthur Candeland, "Psalms and the Preacher," *PQL* 10 (1964) 256-263. [I. The Psalms in Worship]

John A. Lamb, "The Liturgical Use of the Psalter: its ecumenical significance," *SL* 3 (1964) 65-87.

A. Gregory Murray, "A Popular Revival," *AfER* 7 (1965) 209-214. *[Hebrew Psalms in Liturgy]*

Carroll Stuhlmueller, "The Psalms and the Liturgy: The Heart and Heartbeat of Life," *BibT* #17 (1965) 1117-1125.

*Thomas Smith, "Cursing Psalms: can we still pray them?" *AfER* 8 (1966) 324-328.

*E. Wiesenberg, "Gleanings of the Liturgical Term *Melekh Ha-'Olam*," *JJS* 17 (1966) 47-72.

'Fisher of Lambert', "Manipulating the Old Testament," *Theo* 69 (1966) 412.

Ezra Fleisher, "*Havdalah-Shiv'atot* according to Palestinian Ritual," *Tarbiz* 36 (1966-67) #4, III-IV.

Sidney B. Hoenig, "Origins of the Rosh Hashanah Liturgy," *JQR, 75th* (1967) 312-331.

*Leon J. Liebreich, "The Term Miqra'qodesh in the Synagogue Liturgy," *JQR, 75th* (1967) 381-397.

Athanase Negoista, "The Psalter in the Orthodox Church," *SEÅ* 32 (1967) 55-68.

Lester J. Kuyper, "The Old Testament in the Church," *RefR* 21 (1967-68) #3, 9-25.

John Hennig, "The Martyrological Tradition of the Prophets," *IER, 5th Ser.*, 109 (1968) 209-225.

*G. Gerald Harrop, "The Bible Cover to Cover," *TBMDC* #4 (1968) 1-19. [The Rehabilitation of the Old Testament in the Church, pp. 11-15]

Franklin M. Segler, "Devotional Values of Isaiah," *SWTJ, N.S.*, 11 (1968-69) #1, 59-72.

*Naphtali Wieder, "Genizah-Studies in Babylonian Liturgy," *Tarbiz* 37 (1967-68) #2, II; #3 II.

John Van Seters, "The Psalms and Pastoral Theology," *ANQ, N.S.*, 10 (1969-70) 66-74.

*Alan D. Crown, "Theology, Eschatology and Law in Samaritan Funeral Rites and Liturgy," *GUOST* 23 (1969-70) 86-101.

Joseph P. Sanders, "Amos Speaks At Communion Service," *WSR* 62 (1969-70) 13-17.

§1065 *6.6 Studies on Methods of Studying the Old Testament*

C. E. Stowe, "Importance of Studying the Bible in Connexion with the Classics," *BRCR* 2 (1832) 724-743.

Nelson Rounds, "Biblical Knowledge," *MR* 24 (1842) 112.

Anonymous, "Practical Hints for Students of Biblical Literature," *MR* 38 (1856) 288-297.

Anonymous, "The Professional Study of the Bible," *SPR* 27 (1876) 353-382.

R. F. Weidner, "On the Study of the Bible," *PAPA* 12 (1879-80) 21-22. *[Bound with Transactions, but paged separately]*

C. J. H. Ropes, "The Importance and the Method of Bible Study," *DTQ, N.S.,* 2 (1883) 1-16.

R.. F. Weidner, "On the Study of the Old Testament," *ONTS* 3 (1883-84) 152-153.

H. A. Becker, "How to Read the Bible," *ColTM* 4 (1884) 107-116.

R.. F. Weidner, "On the Study of the Old Testament," *ONTS* 3 (1883-84) 152-153.

H. A. Becker, "How to Read the Bible," *ColTM* 4 (1884) 107-116.

Tayler Lewis, "Dr. Tayler Lewis on Biblical Study," *ONTS* 5 (1885-86) 303-304.

William R. Harper, "A Book-Study: First Samuel," *ONTS* 5 (1885-86) 312-317.

William R. Harper, "A Book Study: Second Samuel," *ONTS* 5 (1885-86) 343-347.

William R. Harper, "A Book Study: First and Second Samuel," *ONTS* 5 (1885-86) 376-380, 407-411.

George Dana Boardman, "How We Should Study the Bible," *ONTS* 5 (1884-85) 394-397.

Wm. G. Ballantine, "A Book-Study: Isaiah XL.-LXVI.," *ONTS* 6 (1886-87) 51-54.

William R. Harper, "A Chapter-Study. Jacob's Blessing (Gen. XLIX.)," *ONTS* 6 (1886-87) 79-83.

William R. Harper, "A Book Study. Part I. (Gen. I.-XI.)," *ONTS* 6 (1886-87) 117-122.

William R. Harper, "A Book-Study: Part II. (Gen. XII.-L.)," *ONTS* 6 (1886-87) 164-166.

William R. Harper, "A Book-Study: Exodus," *ONTS* 6 (1886-87) 196-202.

Revere F. Weidner, "Letter I.—To a Pastor Who Wishes to Know How He May Study the Book of Psalms to His Own Best Advantage and that of His Congregation," *ONTS* 6 (1886-87) 235-237.

F. B. Denio, "A Book-Study: Hosea," *ONTS* 6 (1886-87) 270-273.

*Franklin Carter, "The Study of the Hebrew Theocracy in the College," *ONTS* 2 (1887-88) 11-15.

W[illiam] R. Harper, W. G. Ballantine, Willis J. Beecher and G. S. Burroughs, "Inductive Bible Studies. Introductory," *ONTS* 7 (1887-88) 21-23.

Willis J. Beecher and W[illiam] R. Harper, "Books of Samuel, Kings and Chronicles. Second Inductive Bible-study," *ONTS* 7 (1887-88) 24-26.

Willis J. Beecher and G. S. Burroughs, "The Times Before the Administration of Samuel. Third Inductive Bible-study," *ONTS* 7 (1887-88) 27-30.

Willis J. Beecher and G. S. Burroughs, "Administration of Samuel. Fourth Inductive Bible-study," *ONTS* 7 (1887-88) 30-33.

Willis J. Beecher and G. S. Burroughs, "The Reign of Saul. Fifth Inductive Bible-study," *ONTS* 7 (1887-88) 53-57.

Willis J. Beecher, "Prophets, Religion and Scriptures of Israel in the Times of Eli, Samuel and Saul. Sixth Inductive Bible-study," *ONTS* 7 (1887-88) 57-61.

Willis J. Beecher and G. S. Burroughs, "The Rise of David's Empire. Seventh Inductive Bible-study," *ONTS* 7 (1887-88) 61-64.

Willis J. Beecher and G. S. Burroughs, "David's Reign from the Completion of his Conquests. Eighth Inductive Bible-study," *ONTS* 7 (1887-88) 64-67.

Willis J. Beecher, "Civilization in Israel in the Times from Eli to David. Ninth Inductive Bible-study," *ONTS* 7 (1887-88) 90-93.

William R. Harper, "The Psalms of David—First Period. Tenth Inductive Bible-study," *ONTS* 7 (1887-88) 93-96.

William R. Harper, "The Psalms of David—Second Period. Eleventh Inductive Bible-study," *ONTS* 7 (1887-88) 96-99.

William R. Harper, "The Psalms of David—Third Period. Twelfth Inductive Bible-study," *ONTS* 7 (1887-88) 99-102.

Willis J. Beecher, "Reign of Solomon. Thirteenth Inductive Bible-study," *ONTS* 7 (1887-88) 122-124.

J. L. Hurlburt, "The Temple of Solomon. Fourteenth Inductive Bible-study," *ONTS* 7 (1887-88) 125-127.

W[illiam] R. Harper, "Proverbs I.-XXIV. Fifteenth Inductive Bible-study," *ONTS* 7 (1887-88) 128-130.

W[illiam] R. Harper, "Proverbs XXV.-XXXI. and the Book as a Whole. Sixteenth Inductive Bible-study," *ONTS* 7 (1887-88) 130-133.

Willis J. Beecher and W[illiam] R. Harper, "Israel and Judah During the Dynasties of Jeroboam and Baasha. Seventeenth Inductive Bible-study," *ONTS* 7 (1887-88) 153-156.

Willis J. Beecher and W[illiam] R. Harper, "Israel and Judah During Omri's Dynasty. Eighteenth Inductive Bible-study," *ONTS* 7 (1887-88) 156-160.

Willis J. Beecher and W[illiam] R. Harper, "Elijah, Elisha, and Their Fellow Prophets. Nineteenth Inductive Bible-study," *ONTS* 7 (1887-88) 161-164.

Willis J. Beecher and W[illiam] R. Harper, " Israel and Judah During the First Reigns of the Dynasty of Jehu. Twentieth Inductive Bible-study," *ONTS* 7 (1887-88) 164-167.

Willis J. Beecher and W[illiam] R. Harper, "Israel and Judah in the Reigns of Jerobam II. and Menaham. Twenty-first Inductive Bible-study," *ONTS* 7 (1887-88) 195-198.

G. S. Burroughs, "The Book of Jonah. Twenty-second Inductive Bible-study," *ONTS* 7 (1887-88) 198-201.

G. S. Burroughs, "The Prophecy of Amos. Twenty-third Inductive Bible-study," *ONTS* 7 (1887-88) 201-204.

G. S. Burroughs, "The Prophecy of Hosea. Twenty-fourth Inductive Bible-study," *ONTS* 7 (1887-88) 204-207.

G. S. Burroughs, "The Prophecy of Joel. Twenty-fifth Inductive Bible-study," *ONTS* 7 (1887-88) 226-228.

Willis J. Beecher, "Israel and Judah During the Reigns of Pekahiah, Pekah and Hoshea. Twenty-sixth Inductive Bible-study," *ONTS* 7 (1887-88) 229-232.

Willis J. Beecher, "Hezekiah's Reign. Twenty-seventh and Twenty-eighth Inductive Bible-studies (in one)," *ONTS* 7 (1887-88) 233-237.

G. S. Burroughs, "The Prophecy of Micah. Twenty-ninth Inductive Bible-study," *ONTS* 7 (1887-88) 261-264.

G. S. Burroughs, "The Prophecy of Nahum. Thirtieth Inductive Bible-study," *ONTS* 7 (1887-88) 264-267.

W[illiam] R. Harper, "Isaiah 1-12. Thirty-first and thirty-second Inductive Bible-studies," *ONTS* 7 (1887-88) 290-296.

William R. Harper (ed.), "The Psalms of Asaph. Thirty-third Inductive Bible-study," *ONTS* 7 (1887-88) 296-298.

William R. Harper (ed.), "The Psalms of the Sons of Korah. Thirty-fourth Inductive Bible-study," *ONTS* 7 (1887-88) 298-299.

Willis J. Beecher, "Reigns of Manasseh, Amon and Josiah. Thirty-fifth Inductive Bible-study," *ONTS* 7 (1887-88) 300-301.

G. S. Burroughs, "The Prophecies of Zephaniah and Habakkuk. Thirty-sixth Inductive Bible-study," *ONTS* 7 (1887-88) 323-326.

Willis J. Beecher, "The Reigns of Jehoiakim and Zedekiah. Thirty-seventh Inductive Bible-study," *ONTS* 7 (1887-88) 326-328.

W[illiam] R. Harper, "Jeremiah. Thirty-eighth and Thirty-ninth Inductive Bible-studies (in one)," *ONTS* 7 (1887-88) 328-330.

Willis J. Beecher, "Judah and Israel in Exile. Fortieth Inductive Bible-study," *ONTS* 7 (1887-88) 330-333.

J. B. Shearer, "Bible Study in College—The Methods," *PQ* 2 (1888) 282-286.

*W[illiam] E. Chancellor, "The Literary Study of the Bible: Its Methods and Purposes Illustrated in a Criticism of the Book of Amos," *ONTS* 8 (1888-89) 10-19.

J. F. McCurdy, "Proportion and Method in Old Testament Study," *ONTS* 8 (1888-89) 325-331.

George F. Moore, "The Minister's Study of the Old Testament," *AR* 12 (1889) 341-355.

William R. Harper, "Samuel, Saul, David and Solomon. (Inductive Bible Studies, Third Series)," *ONTS* 9 (1889) 37-50, 103-111, 178-186. [Samuel's Early Life; The Close of the Theocracy; Saul Appointed, Elected and Established; Saul's Reign Till his Rejection; David Introduced and Banished; David's Outlaw-Life; Saul's Last Days; David's Reign over Judah and in Jerusalem; David's Reign; Absalom's Rebellion; David Restored; Some Appendices]

William R. Harper, "Samuel, Saul, David and Solomon. (Inductive Bible Studies, Third Series) The Psalms of David," *ONTS* 9 (1889) 233-242.

William R. Harper, "Samuel, Saul, David and Solomon. (Inductive Bible Studies, Third Series)," *ONTS* 9 (1889) 298-307. [Special Topics Connected with 2 Samuel 1-12; Special Topics Connected with 2 Samuel 13-24; David and his Reign; The Times and Reign of Solomon]

William R. Harper, "Samuel, Saul, David and Solomon. (Inductive Bible Studies, Third Series)," *ONTS* 9 (1889) 353-364. [The Temple of Solomon; The Higher Criticism of the Books of Samuel; Israelitish Civilization before the Division of the Kingdom; The Prophetic Element connected with Samuel, David and Solomon]

Jesse Bowman Young, "On the Study of the Books of the Bible," *MR* 73 (1891) 133-135.

R. G. Moulton, "The Study of the English Bible as a Classic," *HR* 24 (1892) 195-200.

Thomas Cary Johnson, "The Study of the English Bible," *PQ* 6 (1892) 360-384.

J. L. Withrow and O. P. Gifford, "How Much Do I Study the Bible, and How?" *BW* 3 (1894) 260-263.

S. Burnham and W. H. P. Faunce, "How Much Do I Study the Bible, and How?" *BW* 3 (1894) 417-419.

Luther A. Fox, "The Bible and its Expositors," *LQ* 25 (1895) 541-546.

D. S. Gregory, "School of Bible Study," *HR* 31 (1896) 61-65, 161-164, 260-263, 350-354, 446-451, 538-544.

Theodore E. Schmauk, "Concordance and Other Mechanical Apparatus for Bible Study," *LCR* 17 (1898) 454-467.

Willis J. Beecher, "A Few Hints as to the Method in Old Testament Study," *AubSRev* 3 (1899) 7-14.

Jas. Lewis Howe, "A Layman's Bible Reading," *CFL, O.S.,* 3 (1899) 455-459.

W. Emery Barnes, "A Devotional Reading of Isaiah," *Exp, 5th Ser.,* 9 (1899) 311-317.

Willis J. Beecher, "Three Ways of Studying a Biblical Narrative," *HR* 38 (1899) 99-104.

T. R. English, "A Plea for the Inductive Study of the Bible," *USR* 11 (1899-1900) 165-171.

Paul C. Kegan, "The Bible for Home Reading," *DownsR* 19 (1900) 27-32. *(Review)*

J. T. Gibson, "How to Read the Book of Job," *CFL, N.S.,* 3 (1901) 110-114.

D. S. Gregory, "A Suggestive Study in Genesis," *HR* 42 (1901) 180-186.

Edward Hooker Knight, "The Study of the English Bible," *HSR* 13 (1902-03) 32-49.

Lewis B. Paton, "The Prophets of Israel and Their Writings. Outline of a Course of Study for Advanced Classes. Part I. From Moses to Elisha," *HSR* 13 (1902-03) 112-142.

Lewis B. Paton, "The Prophets of Israel and Their Writings. Outline of a Course of Study for Advanced Classes. Part II. From Amos to the Fall of Babylon," *HSR* 13 (1902-03) 205-251.

W. A. Lambert, "Is Higher Criticism Satisfactory as a Method of Biblical Study?" *CFL, N.S.,* 8 (1903) 166-169.

D[aniel] S. Gregory, "A Year in Reading the Bible," *HR* 45 (1903) 158-160, 361-364, 537-539.

Anonymous, "General Questions on 'Bible League Primer No. I.' For the Study of the Outline of the Old Testament," *CFL, 3rd Ser.,* 1 (1904) 445-448.

Anonymous, "Bible League Course on the Pentateuch. Introductory View," *CFL, 3rd Ser.,* 1 (1904) 693-701.

Wilbert Webster White, "The Divine Library—Its Abuse and Use, or How to Study the Bible," *BRec* 2 (1905) 26-38.

Jean de Visme, "How One Should Read the Bible," *CFL, 3rd Ser.,* 3 (1905) 462-468.

A. E. Garvie, "The New Method of Studying the Bible," *ET* 17 (1905-06) 344-346, 403-405, 444-446, 510-511.

Edwin H. Hughes, "The Bible and Education," *MR* 88 (1906) 765-772.

Lewis B. Paton, "Three Ways of Studying the Bible," *HR* 55 (1908) 97-100. *[Some issues read: pp. 186-189]*

Daniel S. Gregory, "Method of Bible Study for Permanent Results," *CFL, 3rd Ser.,* 9 (1908) 375-380; 10 (1909) 40-46, 342-346, 403-409.

[Daniel S. Gregory], " Method of Bible Study for Permanent Results," *CFL, 3rd Ser.,* 11 (1909) 30-38.

Theron H. Rice, "An Ideal Course in the English Bible," *USR* 21 (1909-10) 11-18.

Clayton Sedgwick Cooper, "Why Should Men Study the Bible?" *HR* 60 (1910) 181-185.

Henry N. Snyder, "The Religious Value of Bible Study," *MQR, 3rd Ser.,* 36 (1910) 523-535.

James M. Mullan, "The Bible Viewed Devotionally," *RChR, 4th Ser.,* 14 (1910) 216-224.

Daniel S. Gregory, "Method of Bible Study for Permanent Results and Use," *CFL, 3rd Ser.* 15 (1912) 88-119.

Anonymous, "Introductory Suggestions to the Study of Genesis," *CFL, 3rd Ser.,* 15 (1912) 219-224. [I. Place of the Book of Genesis in the Five Books of Moses; II. Outline View and Plan of the Book of Genesis; III. Some Suggestions on Graded Lessons on the Book of Genesis]

Louis M. Sweet, "The Study of the English Bible," *BM* 1 (1913) 8-20, 129-135, 201-211, 288-302, 442-459, 529-539, 621-635, 695-703, 775-795.

Wilbert W. White, "Bible Study Programs. The Book of Genesis," *BM* 1 (1913) 66-80, 158-160, 231-232, 317-318, 480.

Wilbert W. White, "Bible Study Programs. The Book of Exodus," *BM* 1 (1913) 151-157.

Wilbert W. White, "Bible Study Programs. The Book of Leviticus," *BM* 1 (1913) 222-230.

Wilbert W. White, "Bible Study Programs. The Book of Numbers," *BM* 1 (1913) 475-479.

Wilbert W. White, "Bible Study Programs. The Book of Jeremiah," *BM* 1 (1913) 636-640.

Wilbert W. White, "Bible Study Programs. The Book of Jeremiah (Second Study)," *BM* 1 (1913) 715-720.

Wilbert W. White, "Bible Study Programs. The Book of Deuteronomy," *BM* 1 (1913) 954-957; 2 (1914) 959.

*Andrew C. Zenos, "Apocryphal Literature and Bible Study," *IJA* #47 (1916) 58-59.

Fleming James, "The Indispensableness of Bible Study," *ACM* 3 (1918) 401-415.

P. T. Forsyth, "A Few Hints about Reading the Bible," *BR* 3 (1918) 530-544.

N. A. Barr, "How to Use the Bible," *CFL, 3rd Ser.,* 26 (1920) 247-248.

W. K. Lowther Clarke, "In the Study V.—An Old Testament Book," *Theo* 3 (1921) 290-291.

Anonymous, "How should we Read the Bible?" *CFL, 3rd Ser.,* 28 (1922) 250-253.

Delco C. Grover, "The Psychological Approach to the Study of the Bible," *Person* 4 (1923) 39-45.

*Edourard Naville, "The Historical Method in the Study of the Old Testament," *PTR* 22 (1924) 353-376.

M. Ryerson Turnbull, "Studying the Bible by Books," *USR* 36 (1924-25) 138-147.

Joseph B. Matthews, "The Study of the Old Testament," *MQR, 3rd Ser.,* 52 (1926) 247-260.

Wm. Janzow, "'Wrong Uses of the Bible'," *AusTR* 1 (1930) 43-55.

Frederick C. Grant, "The Beginnings of Our Religion: Outline of a Study Course," *ATR* 14 (1932) 314-339.

Henry S. Gehman, "Some Present-Day Values of Old Testament Studies," *PSB* 28 (1934) #3, 5-20.

H. Hamann, "'The Bible Designed to be Read as Literature'," *AusTR* 9 (1938) 58-59.

*Ernest Williams Parsons, "The Use of the Bible To-day," *CRDSB* 11 (1938-39) 53-66.

Donald W. Riddle, "Why Study the Bible Today?" *JAAR* 8 (1940) 67-71.

Roger Hazelton, "Why Study the Bible Today?" *JAAR* 8 (1940) 149.

Dwight M. Beck, "Why Study the Bible Today?" *JAAR* 8 (1940) 149-150.

Walter W. Sikes, "Objectives and Method in Studying the Bible," *JAAR* 8 (1940) 188-192.

Morton S. Enslin, "'Why Study the Bible Today?'" *JAAR* 8 (1940) 211, 228.

Howard Tillman Kuist, "How to Enjoy Nehemiah," *AQ* 20 (1941) 289-305.

Daniel Duffy, "On Reading the Old Testament," *IER, 5th Ser.,* 63 (1944) 39-47.

Edwin C. Munson, "Sunday Evenings with Isaiah," *AQ* 24 (1945) 129-137.

Kenneth J. Foreman, "Approaches to Bible Study," *SQ/E* 9 (1948) 166-173.

B. C. G. Widdowson, "Scheme of Reading the Psalter," *CBQ* 12 (1950) 327-330.

Floyd V. Filson, "Method in Studying Biblical History," *JBL* 69 (1950) 1-18.

Reginald Ginns, "On Reading the Scriptures," *LofS* 6 (1951-52) 320-327.

Nicolette Gray, "On Reading the Bible with One's Children," *LofS* 6 (1951-52) 348-351.

T. Worden, "Why Study the Old Testament?" *ClR* 39 (1954) 341-349.

Duncan Campbell, "On Reading the Bible: I," *LofS* 12 (1957-58) 5-15.

Duncan Campbell, "On Reading the Bible: II," *LofS* 12 (1957-58) 53-58.

Nicolette Gray, "Bible Reading," *LofS* 13 (1958-59) 69-76.

C. Dennis Phippen, "A Method of Bible Study: 1. Amos," *PQL* 5 (1959) 315-320. *[Part 2 not applicable]*

C. Dennis Phippen, "A Method of Bible Study: 3—The Psalms," *PQL* 6 (1960) 152-160.

*Ivan Engnell, "Methodological aspects of Old Testament study," *VTS* 7 (1960) 13-30.

Edmund Hill, "Bible Reading Made Easy," *LofS* 15 (1960-61) 513-516.

*Peter R. Ackroyd, "The Place of the Old Testament in the Church's Teaching and Worship," *ET* 74 (1962-63) 164-167.

Pius Parsch, "Learning to Read the Bible," *BibT* #8 (1963) 511-526.

P. D. Pahl, "Do We Neglect the Old Testament?" *AusTR* 35 (1964) 66-67.

Joseph Blenkinsopp, "The Bible and the People. Reading Deuteronomy," *ClR* 50 (1965) 778-783.

David Lieber, "Modern Trends in Bible Study," *CJ* 20 (1965-66) #2, 37-46.

L. P. Fitzgerald, "The Study of Sacred Scripture," *AER* 43 (1966) 194-205.

E. Reim, "How to Read the Psalter with Profit," *JTLC* 7 (1967) #1, 1-11.

*Ross Snyder, "Bible Study for Preaching Preparation," *P* 2 (1967) #6, 16-24.

Holland H. Jones, "Old Testament Introduction," *CTM* 40 (1969) 612-618.

Herbert B. Huffmon and Paul A Riemann, "Pointing the Way: Some Suggestions for Old Testament Study," *DG* 40 (1969-70) 135-142.

§1066 *6.6.1 Studies concerning Research Tools for Old Testament Study*

Anonymous, "Smith's Bible Dictionary," *CE* 76 (1864) 223-231. *(Review)*

†Anonymous, "Dr. William Smith's Dictionary of the Bible," *QRL* 116 (1864) 383-413. *(Review)*

†Anonymous, *"Dictionaries of the Bible* (Smith *and* Kitto)," *ERCJ* 121 (1865) 42-73. *(Review)*

†Anonymous, "The Speaker's Commentary," *BQRL* 55 (1872) 135-166. *(Review)*

†Anonymous, "The Speaker's Bible," *ERCJ* 140 (1874) 32-71. *(Review)*

†Anonymous, "The Speaker's Commentary on the Old Testament," *QRL* 147 (1879) 293-336. *(Review)*

O. S. Stearns, "Some Practical Hints," *ONTS* 4 (1884-85) 30-32. [What Commentaries to Buy? How to Use a Commentary]

Anonymous," Dr. Hasting's Dictionary of the Bible," *LQHR* 102 (1904) 287-294. *(Review)*

Shailer Mathews, "The Jewish Encyclopedia," *HR* 52 (1906) 264-267.

Bernard M. G. Reardon, "The Church and the Scriptures," *QRL* 302 (1964) 200-205. *(Review) [Cambridge History of the Bible]*

§1067 **6.7 *Studies on Teaching the Old Testament***

Anonymous, "The Bible as a Distinctive Branch of Education in Our Literary Institutions," *FBQ* 5 (1857) 408-419.

†Anonymous, "Education, Secularism, and Non-conformity," *QRL* 132 (1872) 509-535. *[Teaching the Bible in Public Schools]*

Samuel T. Spear, "The Bible and the Public School," *PRev* 54 (1878) Part 1, 361-394.

J. B. Burne, "The Old Testament: its Place in the Religious Instruction of Elementary School," *CM* 19 (1884) 305-310.

Anonymous, "Old Testament History in the Sunday School," *ONTS* 4 (1884-85) 88-89.

Anonymous, "Prophecy and Poetry," *ONTS* 4 (1884-85) 89.

Anonymous, "The Department of the Old Testament in the Seminary," *ONTS* 4 (1884-85) 136-138.

E. C. Bissell, Henry Green, Herrick Johnson, J. H. Vincent, G. H. Schodde, E. F. Williams, E. V. Gerhart, W. F. Crafts, C. R. Blackall, M. S. Terry, H. Clay Trumbull, W. J. Beecher, Howard Crosby, "The Old Testament in the Sunday School," *ONTS* 4 (1884-85) 299-309.

Anonymous, "The Opposition to Old Testament Study in the Sunday School," *ONTS* 4 (1884-85) 326.

Bernard Pick, "The Old Testament in the Sunday School," *ONTS* 4 (1884-85) 368-370.

†Talbot W. Chambers, "The Old Testament in the Sunday School," *ONTS* 4 (1884-85) 370-371. *[Untitled Article]*

Anonymous, "The Duty of the Theological Seminary in Reference to Bible-Study," *ONTS* 5 (1885-86) 234-235.

Lyman Abbott, A. J. F. Behrends, Joseph Cook, Howard Crosby, Wayland Hoyt, G. W. Lasher, F. N. Peloubet, Arthur T. Pierson, J. A. Smith, W[illia]m Hayes Ward, "A Symposium on Bible-Study in the Theological Seminaries," *ONTS* 5 (1885-86) 325-334.

Henry Dexter, Isaac Errett, Samuel Fallows, O. P. Gifford, R. Heber Newton, C. E. Robinson, A. J. Rowland, Wm. M. Taylor, H. L. Wayland, "A Symposium on Bible-Study in the Theological Seminaries. II," *ONTS* 5 (1885-86) 356-365.

E. Schreiber, "How to Teach Biblical History in our Sabbath-Schools," *YCCAR* 1 (1890-91) 59-61.

George S. Burroughs, "The Bible in the College," *AR* 18 (1892) 253-262.

F. H. Gaines, "The Bible in the College Curriculum," *PQ* 9 (1895) 211-233.

Philip S. Moxom, "How Should the Bible be Studied in the Sunday School," *BW* 8 (1896) 229-232.

Owen H. Gates, "The Relation of the Seminary to Previous Bible Study," *BW* 8 (1896) 265-271.

J. Sheatsley, "A Plea for a More Extended Use of the Old Testament," *ColTM* 16 (1896) 293-303.

J. Hogan, "The Different Kinds of Bible Study," *AER* 18 (1898) 502-512.

F. H. Gaines, "The Bible in Education," *USR* 10 (1898-99) 202-209.

*D. S. Margoliouth, "Old-Testament Criticism in its Relation to Teaching," *HR* 41 (1901) 8-13.

Anonymous, "Teaching the Old Testament," *CQR* 54 (1902) 120-143.

Irving F. Wood, "What Shall the Adult Bible Class Do with Modern Biblical Scholarship?" *BW* 21 (1903) 375-378.

Edward L. Curtis, "The Old Testament in Religious Education," *BW* 22 (1903) 424-435.

Charles Foster Kent, "Certain Problems of the Modern Bible Teacher," *AubSRev* 7 (1903-04) 198-204.

Abram Simon, "A Curriculum for a Jewish Sabbath School," *BW* 24 (1904) 122-125.

J. T. Bergen, "Teaching the Pentateuch to the Young," *CFL, 3rd Ser.,* 1 (1904) 692-693.

William H. P. Faunce, "Coordination of the Bible with Other Subjects of Study," *HR* 47 (1904) 344-348.

Dorothea Beale, "Some Hints on Teaching the Old Testament," *ICMM* 1 (1905) 352-359.

Lee McCrae, "Watch. A Blackboard Trellis for a Bible Reading," *HR* 51 (1906) 211.

*Ernest G. Loosey, "Jewish Home Teaching and Old Testament Criticism," *LQHR* 106 (1906) 288-298.

Felix Coblenz, "Biblical Criticism in Religious Instruction," *JQR* 19 (1906-07) 1-23.

Holmes Dysinger, "The Hebrew Scriptures: Their Place and Function in Ministerial Teaching." *LQ* 37 (1907) 22-43.

Joseph S. Kornfeld, "The Bible in the Sunday School," *OC* 23 (1909) 476-483.

[Paul Carus], "How to Teach the Bible in Schools," *OC* 23 (1909) 484-488.

Moses Buttenwieser, "The Presentation of Biblical Stories to Children," *BW* 35 (1910) 387-395.

Theodore F. Herman, "The Value of the Old Testament in a Theological Curriculum," *RChR, 4th Ser.,* 14 (1910) 24-27.

Willis J. Beecher, "Agnostic Criticism and the Sunday School Lessons," *CFL, 3rd Ser.,* 14 (1911-12) 39-45.

Barnard C. Taylor, "The Place of Old Testament Study in a Theological Curriculum," *BCTS* 4 (1912) 133-150.

H. F. B. Compston, "Greek Catechisms and the Apocrypha," *IJA* #28 (1912) 10-12.

Herbert C. Alleman, "The Study of the Old Testament in the Theological Curriculum," *LQ* 42 (1912) 13-25.

Wm. J. Hinke, "The Place of the Old Testament in the Theological Curriculum," *ASRec* 8 (1912-13) 6-13.

S. De Bath, "Bible Teaching in Schools. An Attempt at Reconstruction," *MC* 3 (1913-14) 233-243.

Anonymous, "Bible Teaching in Schools," *MC* 3 (1913-14) 303-308.

Jesse F. Steiner, "The Message of the Bible as Material for Religious Education of the Japanese," *RChR, 4th Ser.,* 18 (1914) 353-372.

Ephraim Frisch, "The Use of the Bible as a Text-book in the Religious School," *YCCAR* 24 (1914) 339-345.

William James Mutch, "The Bible and the Children," *HR* 69 (1915) 105-108.

William James Mutch, "The Aims of Elementary Bible Teaching," *HR* 69 (1915) 191-196.

William James Mutch, "Organization of Elementary Bible Material," *HR* 69 (1915) 268-271.

William James Mutch, "The Oral Method of Elementary Bible Teaching," *HR* 69 (1915) 362-366.

Samuel Schulman, "Round Table on Bible Reading in Public Schools," *YCCAR* 25 (1915) 423-427. [Discussion by [David] Lefkowitz, p. 427; [David] Philipson, p. 427; [Moses] Gries, p. 427 [William] Rosenau, p. 427; [Max.] Heller, pp. 427-428; Reply by Samuel Schulman, pp. 428-429]

Alfred Fawkes, "The Old Testament in Pulpit and Parish," *MC* 5 (1915-16) 340-350.

(   ) Glazenbrook, "The Old Testament in Secondary Schools," *MC* 5 (1915-16) 351-361.

J. M. Powis Smith, "The Value of the Old Testament in the Theological Curriculum," *BW* 53 (1919) 372-382.

E. C. Wilm, "The Bible and the Child," *MR* 103 (1920) 44-51.

Henry F. Cope, "The Bible and Public Instruction," *OC* 34 (1920) 513-519.

Max Reichler, "Religious Education Program: The Instruction of Hebrew in Our Sunday Schools," *YCCAR* 33 (1923) 281-285.

T. Grigg-Smith, "The Presentation of the Old Testament to Children," *ICMM* 20 (1923-24) 215-222.

J. G. H. Barry, "First Aid to Intelligent Religion. II. Children and the Bible," *ACM* 15 (1924) 540-549. *[Part I not applicable]*

George Jackson, "The Church and the Old Testament," *HR* 87 (1924) 37.

E. Basil Redlich, "The Bible and the Child," *ET* 36 (1924-25) 200-204.

Edgar W. Thompson, "The Bible in the Religious Education of Africa," *IRM* 16 (1927) 394-404.

Edward A. Annett, "The Use of the Old Testament in Schools for Non-Christians," *IRM* 17 (1928) 366-374.

*W. S. Urquhart, "The Old Testament of the Indian Church," *CJRT* 5 (1928) 350-354.

Henry B. Robinson, "The Undergraduate Curriculum of Biblical Courses. Their Integration and Teaching," *CSQC* 4 (1928) #2, 19-31.

Allen H. Godbey, "Some Relations of Semitic Studies to Divinity School Courses," *MQR, 3rd Ser.,* 54 (1928) 227-245.

F. J. Rae, "Teaching the Child," *ET* 40 (1928-29) 412-416.

Andrew Macphail, "The Bible in Scotland," *QRL* 257 (1931) 15-36. *(Review)*

Florence Mary Fitch, "Symposium: The Bible in Modern Education. The Historical Approach to the Study of the Bible," *JAAR* 1 (1933) #2, 11-14.

Henry T. Fowler, "Symposium: The Bible in Modern Education. The Place of the Bible in the College Curriculum," *JAAR* 1 (1933) #2, 25-28.

Earle Bennett Cross, "The Old Testament in Modern Education," *CRDSB* 6 (1933-34) 5-21.

Alvin S. Luchs, "Teaching Jewish Personalities to Young Children," *YCCAR* 44 (1934) 270-271.

Millar Burrows, "The Bible in the Theological Curriculum," *JR* 15 (1935) 379-388.

Thornton W. Merriam, "Religion in the College Curriculum Today," *JR* 15 (1935) 462-470.

F. J. Rae, "The Teacher and the Old Testament," *ET* 47 (1935-36) 454-458.

Sophia Lyon Fahs, "A Plea to Biblical Scholars and Archaeologists," *JAAR* 5 (1937) 176-178.

*Beatrice L. Goff, "Books Suitable for Use in Undergraduate Courses in the Old Testament," *JAAR* 6 (1938) 140-143, 171.

P. Gardner-Smith, "The Teaching of the Old Testament," *MC* 28 (1938-39) 321-331.

Godfrey E. Phillips, "The Use of the Old Testament in India," *IRM* 29 (1940) 382-390.

H. StJ. Hart, "The Future of Bible Reading," *Theo* 40 (1940) 332-340.

*Toyozo W. Nakarai, "Some Problems in Teaching the Old Testament in Relation to the Critical Approach," *SQ/E* 3 (1942) 288-297.

Erdman Harris, "Should the Study of the Bible Be Required in Preparatory Schools?" *JAAR* 11 (1943) 28-30.

Rolland Emerson Wolfe, "Problems in Teaching the Old Testament to College Students," *JAAR* 11 (1943) 107-112.

Margaret B. Crook, "Presentation of Job in the Classroom," *JAAR* 11 (1943) 113-116.

Adelaide Teague Case, "The Bible and Christian Education," *RL* 13 (1944) 71-76.

Joseph M. Gettys, "The Bible in Christian Education," *USR* 56 (1944-45) 182-197.

Matthew P. Stapleton, "The Seminary Viewpoint," *JAAR* 13 (1945) 149-151, 176.

Chester Warren Quimby, "The Use of Costumes, Objects and Models in Teaching the Bible," *JAAR* 13 (1945) 152-154, 176.

John J. Dougherty, "Teaching the Bible," *AER* 117 (1947) 112-116.

Lowell B. Hazzard, "Conduct Objectives in Teaching the Old Testament," *JAAR* 15 (1947) 206-209.

R. Gladstone Griffith, "How to Teach the Bible," *MC* 37 (1947-48) 263-270.

Edward F. Siegman, "The Use of Sacred Scripture in Textbooks of Dogmatic Theology," *CBQ* 11 (1949) 151-164.

James P. Berkeley, "Forty Years with the Bible," *ANQ* 42 (1949-50) #3, 1-11.

August J. Engelbrecht, "Responsibilities of the Old Testament Department at Wartburg Seminary," *WSQ* 13 (1949-50) #1, 3-10.

Willis W. Fisher, "Evaluating the Teaching Significance of Biblical Literature," *JAAR* 18 (1950) 178-181.

Virginia Corwin, "The Teaching Situation and the Bible," *JAAR* 19 (1951) 57-62.

John A. Hutchison, "On Hearing the Word of God," *JAAR* 19 (1951) 67-70.

Zelda Jeanne Ryan, "The Use of the Bible in Public Schools," *RL* 21 (1952) 603-612.

S. B. Frost, "Religious Education. Visual Aids to the Teaching of the Old Testament," *ET* 65 (1953-54) 252-253.

Eugene Maly, Edward Siegman, and John Whealon, "Methods of Teaching Sacred Scripture," *CBQ* 16 (1954) 46-51.

Lawrence E. Porter, "Teaching the Old Testament Prophets: Their Place in the Agreed Syllabus," *EQ* 26 (1954) 130-145.

A. Victor Murray, "The Use of the Bible in Schools," *LQHR* 179 (1954) 126-129.

Margaret Avery, "Religious Education. Neglected Treasures of the Old Testament," *ET* 66 (1954-55) 227-229.

J. W. D. Smith, "Religious Education. Moses at the Bush: Exodus iii. 1-12. A Study in Teaching Method," *ET* 66 (1954-55) 382-383.

David M. Stanley, Barnabas Mary Ahern, and Richard T. Murphy, "Panel Discussion on the Methods of Teaching Scripture," *CBQ* 17 (1955) 35-53.

Eugene Kevane, "Sacred Scripture in the Catholic High School," *CBQ* 17 (1955) 136-153.

F. S. Leahy, "The Song of Solomon in Pastoral Teaching," *EQ* 27 (1955) 205-213.

Charles Smith, "Religious Education. Conveying the Truth of the Bible," *ET* 67 (1955-56) 67-69.

*James H. Gailey Jr., "The Beginning of Wisdom," *CTSB* 49 (1956) #1, 1-9. *[Inaugural Address]*

M. H. Harrison, "The Place of the Old Testament Studies in Indian Theological Education," *IJT* 5 (1956) #1, 1-8.

Rosemary Heddon, "The Use of Mime in Scripture Teaching," *LofS* 11 (1956-57) 34-38.

J. J. Twomey, "Genesis for Juniors," *ClR* 42 (1957) 65-76.

A Victor Murray, "The Bible in Education," *LQHR* 182 (1957) 52-59.

Merrill C. Tenney, "Some Basic Theological Assumptions of Christian Education," *JCE* 1 (1958) 7-12.

L. Wigney, "Provision for Religious Education in the State School Systems of Australia and in the Territory of Papua and New Guinea," *JCE* 1 (1958) 69-80.

Margaret E. Fewtrell, "Some Aspects of Teaching Scripture in the Primary School," *JCE* 1 (1958) 105-108.

W. R. England, "Some Principles of Teaching Scripture," *JCE* 1 (1958) 147-152.

W. P. B. Gamlen, "Provisions for Religious Instruction in New Zealand Schools," *JCE* 2 (1959) 32-37.

D. G. Davis, "A Dual System?" *JCE* 2 (1959) 76-81.

P. D. Davis, "The Revised Scripture Syllabus for New South Wales Primary Schools," *JCE* 2 (1959) 135-140.

W. R. England, "The Teacher—And the Bible as Literature: III. Bringing the Bible into the Classroom," *JCE* 3 (1960) 95-103.

W. R. Niblett, "Religious Education in English Schools," *JCE* 3 (1960) 57-61.

D. H. Monro, "The Case Against Religion in Secondary Schools," *JCE* 3 (1960) 62-71.

W. E. Andersen, "Religion in State Secondary Schools: The Issues," *JCE* 3 (1960) 72-79.

*Bernice Strack, "The Temple-Model as a Visual Aid in the Study of Scripture," *Scotist* 16 (1960) 60-73.

*John H. Scammon, "The Minister and the Psalms," *ANQ, N.S.,* 1 (1960-61) #1, 28-38.

*Edward Lee Beavin, "The Dead Sea Scrolls and the Teaching of the Old Testament to Undergraduates," *JAAR* 29 (1961) 39-43.

J. Stanley Chestnut, "Problems in Teaching the Old Testament," *JAAR* 30 (1962) 284-290.

Geoffrey Peterson, "Theory and Practice in Theological Education," *JCE* 5 (1962) 77-83.

E. Roberts-Thomson, "The Training of Theological Students," *JCE* 5 (1962) 84-92.

D. W. B. Robinson, "College for Theological Knowledge," *JCE* 5 (1962) 110-116.

J. Daniel Joyce, "The Biblical Basis of the Teaching Ministry. *The Heritage of the Religious Teacher,*" *SQ/E* 23 (1962) 170-180.

John Batsel and Roy Wells, "Case Study: Biblical Criticism and the Local Church," *VDR* 6 (1962) #1, 10-12.

Vincent M. Novak, "Teaching the Old Testament," *BibT* #6 (1963) 268-371, 374-377.

John V. Leach, "The Historical Approach to the Bible as Literature in College Teaching," *IR* 20 (1963) #2, 11-16.

D. Hickman, "Intellect and the Knowledge of God. I," *JCE* 6 (1963) 154-158.

*Henry Cohen, "The Idea of God in Jewish Education," *Jud* 12 (1963) 165-178.

Zvi Adar, "The Teaching of the Bible in Israel and the Problems of Religious Education," *SH* 13 (1963) 77-104.

Edward J. Young, "Some Thoughts on Old Testament Scholarship," *F&T* 93 (1963-64) 74-87.

Roy L. Honeycutt, "Deuteronomy and the Church Teaching," *R&E* 61 (1964) 284-295.

M. H. Harrison, "Some Notes on the teaching of the Old Testament in Indian Theological Education," *SBSB* 1 (1964) 10-19.

*Colin F. Gauld, "The Impact of Science on Christianity with Special Reference to the Doctrine of Man," *JCE* 8 (1965) 5-12.

Clyde T. Francisco, "Teaching Amos in the Churches," *R&E* 63 (1966) 413-426.

Brian E. Colles, "The Divine Teacher Figure in Biblical Theology," *JCE* 10 (1967) 24-38. *[Parts I-II]*

Brian E. Colles, "The Divine Teacher Figure in Biblical Theology. Parts III and IV," *JCE* 10 (1967) 112-123.

Brian E. Colles, "The Divine Teacher Figure in Biblical Theology. V. The Divine Educational Programme," *JCE* 10 (1967) 151-162.

William E. Andersen, "Education and the Biblical Concept of a Person," *JCE* 12 (1969) 169-184.

*F. N. Jasper, "Old Testament theology: a problem of ministerial training," *Min* 9 (1969) #2, 58-61.

*Fritz A. Rothschild, "The Concept of God in Jewish Education," *CJ* 24 (1969-70) #2, 2-20.

§1068　*7. Studies on the Discoveries at Qumran - General Studies*

J. Philip Hyatt, "The Dead Sea Discoveries: Retrospect and Challenge," *JBL* 76 (1957) 1-12.

Joseph M. Baumgarten, "Qumran Studies," *JBL* 77 (1958) 249-257.

G. G. Garner, *"The Dead Sea Scrolls:* Excavations at Qumran," *AT* 4 (1959-60) #3, 3-6.

*Edward Lee Beavin, "The Dead Sea Scrolls and the Teaching of the Old Testament to Undergraduates," *JAAR* 29 (1961) 39-43.

William A. Beardslee, "The Dead Sea Scrolls and the Teaching of the New Testament to Undergraduates," *JAAR* 29 (1961) 44-47.

John E. Steinmueller, "Qumran: Its Geography and History," *BibT* #12 (1964) 775-779.

Père Roland De Vaux, "The Qumran Story," *BibT* #22 (1966) 1437-1450.

Stanislav Segert, "Some Trends in Qumran Research," *ArOr* 35 (1967) 128-144.

Solomon Zeitlin, "Judaism and Professors of Religion," *JQR, N.S.,* 60 (1969-70) 187-196.

§1069　*7.1 Studies on Bibliographical Material of the Dead Sea Scrolls*

*Raymond F. Surburg, "Intertestamental Studies 1946-1955," *CTM* 27 (1956) 95-114. [III. The Dead Sea Scrolls and the Essenes, pp. 101-105]

Solomon Zeitlin, "Recent Literature on the Dead Sea Scrolls," *JQR, N.S.,* 47 (1956-57) 196-213.

William Sanford LaSor, "Bibliography of the Dead Sea Scrolls, 1948-1957," *FLB* #31 (1958) 1-92.

Christoph Burchard, "Bibliographie," *RdQ* 1 (1958-59) 149-160, 309-320, 461-479, 547-626; 2 (1959-60) 117-151, 299-312.

R. Busa, "Index of all non Biblical Dead Sea Scrolls published up to December 1957," *RdQ* 1 (1958-59) 187-198.

William Sanford LaSor, "Bibliography," *RdQ* 2 (1959-60) 459-472, 587-601; 3 (1961-62) 149-160, 313-320, 467-480, 593-602; 4 (1963-64) 139-159, 311-320, 467-480; 5 (1964-66) 149-160, 293-320.

Solomon Zeitlin, "More Literature on the Dead Sea Scrolls—More Pseudo-Scholarship," *JQR, N.S.,* 49 (1958-59) 221-238.

Stanislav Segert, "New Books on the Dead Sea Scrolls," *ArOr* 27 (1959) 447-462.

Patrick W. Skehan, "Two Books on Qumrân Studies," *CBQ* 21 (1959) 71-78. *(Review)*

Anonymous, "Bibliography of the Dead Sea Scrolls in Japanese Journals," *NOGG* 2 (1959) #7, 10-12. *[Text in Japanese]*

Simon [E.] Smith, "The Dead Sea Scrolls: A Bibliographical Orientation," *MH* 15 (1960) #1, 34-40.

Simon E. Smith, "The Dead Sea Scrolls: a bibliographical orientation," *TD* 8 (1960) 186-188.

Solomon Zeitlin, "Recent Literature on the Dead Sea Scrolls: The Sicarii and the Zealots," *JQR, N.S.,* 51 (1960-61) 156-169, 254-261.

Anonymous, "Bibliographie," *RdQ* 4 (1963-64) 597-606.

Jean Carmignac, "Bibliographie," *RdQ* 5 (1964-66) 463-479; 6 (1967-69) 301-320, 457-479; 7 (1969-71) 131-159, 305-319, 463-480.

R. A. Martin, "Selected Bibliography of the Dead Sea Scrolls (1957 and Later)," *IJT* 14 (1965) 116-125.

Anonymous, "Qumran Bibliography," *BibT* #22 (1966) 1482-1483.

*J. A. Sanders, "Palestinian Manuscripts, 1947-1967," *JBL* 86 (1967) 431-440.

Edward F. Campbell Jr., and Robert G. Boling, "Bookshelf on the Dead Sea Scrolls," *McQ* 21 (1967-68) 318-320.

Joseph A. Fitzmyer, "A Bibliographical Aid to the Study of the Qumran Cave IV Texts, 158-186," *CBQ* 31 (1969) 59-71.

§1070 *7.2 Studies on the Community of Qumran - General Studies*

J. L. Teicher, "The Damascus Fragments and the Origin of the Jewish Christian Sect," *JJS* 2 (1950-51) 115-143. [1. The Literary Form and Contents of the Fragments, 2. The Clue to the Date, 3. The Church in Jerusalem, 4. The Origin of the Jewish-Christian Sect, 5. The Messiah from Aaron and Israel, 6. A Difficulty and its Solution, 7. Conclusions]

P. Kahle, "The Karaites and the Manuscripts from the Cave," *VT* 3 (1953) 82-84.

S. Esh, "Three Short Notes on Prof. Segal's 'On the History of the *Yahad* Sect'," *Tarbiz* 24 (1954-55) #1 IX.

*Robert J. North, "The Qumran 'Sadducees'," *CBQ* 17 (1955) 164-188.

James Muilenburg, "The New Covenant," *ANQ* 49 (1956) #1, 3-4.

*J. M. Allegro, "Further Light on the History of the Qumran Sect," *JBL* 75 (1956) 89-95.

Stanley G. Luff, "The Monks of Qumran and St Benedict's Rule. The Continuity of Monastic Tradition," *DR* 231 (1957) 313-321.

Harold H. Rowley, "Some Traces of the Qumran Sect," *TZ* 13 (1957) 530-540.

Norman Bentwich, "Dead Sea Citadels," *ContR* 193 (1958) 71-74.

B. Kanael, "Some Observations on the Chronology of Khirbet Qumran," *EI* 5 (1958) 93*.

Roland Potter, "The Quest for God in the Judean Desert. I. The Men of Qumran," *LofS* 13 (1958-59) 115-122.

J. T. Milik, "Who lived at Qumran?" *TD* 7 (1959) 8-10.

G. G. Garner, "*The Dead Sea Scrolls:* The People of Qumran," *AT* 4 (1959-60) #4, 17-19.

*G. Vermes, "Essenes—Therapeutai—Qumran," *DUJ, N.S.,* 21 (1959-60) 97-115.

K. Greenleaf Pedley, "The Library at Qumran," *RdQ* 2 (1959-60) 21-42. *[The Building]*

*Everett Ferguson, "Ordination in the Ancient Church (I)," *RestQ* 4 (1960) 117-138. [Functionaries in the Qumran Community, pp. 122-136]

C. Roth, "Qumran and Masadah: A Final Clarification Regarding the Dead Sea Sect," *RdQ* 5 (1964-66) 81-88.

Roland de Vaux, "Essenes or Zealots? *Some Thoughts on a recent Book,*" *NB* 47 (1965-66) 396-410. *(Review)*

H. H. Rowley, "The History of the Qumran Covenanters," *BibT* #22 (1966) 1475-1481.

G. R. Driver, "Myths of Qumran," *ALUOS* 6 (1966-68) 23-48.

H. H. Rowley, "The History of the Qumran Sect," *BJRL* 49 (1966-67) 203-232.

A. Negoitsa, "Did the Essenes Survive the 66-71 War?" *RdQ* 6 (1967-69) 517-530.

Frank M. Cross Jr., "The Early History of the Qumran Community," *McQ* 21 (1967-68) 249-264.

E. J. Pryke, "The Identity of the Qumran Sect: a Reconsideration," *NT* 10 (1968) 42-61.

David G. Flusser, "The Social Message from Qumran," *JWH* 11 (1968-69) 107-115.

Samuel Iwry, "Was There a Migration to Damascus? The Problem of שבי ישראל," *EI* 9 (1969) 80-88. *[Non-Hebrew Section]*

*David Noel Freedman, "The Flowering of Apocalyptic," *JTC* 6 (1969) 166-174. [III. Qumran, an Apocalyptic Community, pp. 170-173]

*I. H. Eybers, "The *pèšèr-* Commentaries on Habakkuk and Nahum and the Origin of the Qumran Sect," *OTW* 12 (1969) 75-90.

§1071 *7.2.1 Studies on the Archaeological Discoveries at Qumran (including artifacts, other than Scrolls)*

*E. W. G. Masterman, "'Ain el-Feshkhah, el-Ḥajar el-Aṣbaḥ, and Khurbet Kumrân," *PEFQS* 34 (1902) 160-167-, 297-299.

*E. W. G. Masterman, "Notes on Some Ruins and a Rock-cut Aqueduct in the Wady Kumran," *PEFQS* 35 (1903) 264-267.

G. Ernest Wright, "The Cave Excavated," *BA* 12 (1949) 32-33. *[Cave 1]*

G. Ernest Wright, "Additional Comments on the Scroll Cave," *BA* 12 (1949) 64-65.

O. R. Sellers, "Excavation of the 'Manuscript' Cave at 'Ain Fashkha," *BASOR* #114 (1949) 5-9.

Anonymous, "Report Upon a Fragment of Cloth from the Dead Sea Scroll Cave," *BASOR* #118 (1950) 9-11.

O. R. Sellers, "Date of Cloth from the 'Ain Fashkha Cave," *BA* 14 (1951) 29.

O. R. Sellers, "Radiocarbon Dating of the Cloth from 'Ain Fashkha Cave," *BASOR* #123 (1951) 24-26.

Robert North, "Qumran and its Archaeology," *CBQ* 16 (1954) 426-437.

G. M. Crowfoot, "Linen Textiles from the Cave of Ain Feshkha in the Jordan Valley," *PEQ* 83 (1951) 5-31.

Carl H. Kraeling, "A Dead Sea Scroll Jar at the Oriental Institute," *BASOR* #125 (1952) 5-7.

Anonymous, "Qumran Excavations," *BA* 16 (1953) 18.

J. M. Allegro, "Some Archaeological Sites and the Old Testament. Qumrân," *ET* 66 (1954-55) 259-262.

Frank M. Cross Jr., "Archaeological News and Views," *BA* 18 (1955) 79-80. *[Qumran]*

James L. Kelso, "The Archaeology of Qumran," *JBL* 74 (1955) 141-146.

*Anonymous, "Excavations in Jordan, 1953-1954," *ADAJ* 3 (1956) 74-87. [Khirbet Qumran, pp. 75-77].

Immanuel Ben-Dor, "The Jars of the Dead Sea Scrolls," *AJA* 61 (1957) 181-182.

B[ruce] M. Metzger, "The Furniture in the Scriptorium at Qumran," *RdQ* 1 (1958-59) 509-515.

F. E. Zeuner, "Notes on Qumran," *PEQ* 92 (1960) 27-36. {I. Radiocarbon Age; II. The Animal Bones; III. Pottery Clay and Cistern Fillings; IV. The Basins of 'Ain Feshkha]

J. B. Poole and R. Reed, "The 'Tannery' of 'Ain Feshkha," *PEQ* 93 (1961) 114-123.

*R. R. Williams, "An Early Coin from Qumran," *NTS* 8 (1961-62) 334-335.

John C. Trever, "When was Qumran Cave I Discovered?" *RdQ* 3 (1961-62) 135-141.

*R. A. Martin, "Some Recent Developments in the Study of Discoveries near the Dead Sea," *IJT* 14 (1965) 102-116. [I. Survey of the Archaeological Exploration of the Dead Sea Area, pp. 103-108]

Robert G. Boling, "Twenty Years of Discovery," *McQ* 21 (1967-68) 265-271.

*N. Hass and H. Nathan, "Anthropological Survey on the Human Skeletal Remains in Qumran," *RdQ* 6 (1967-69) 345-352.

S[olomon] H. Steckoll, "Preliminary Excavation Report in the Qumran Cemetery," *RdQ* 6 (1967-69) 323-344.

Solomon H. Steckoll, "Marginal Notes on the Qumran Excavations," *RdQ* 7 (1969-71) 33-44.

§1072 *7.2.2 Studies on the Organization of the Qumran Community*

William R. Farmer, "The Economic Basis of the Qumran Community," *TZ* 11 (1955) 295-308.

L. E. Toombs, "The Early History of the Qumran Sect," *JSS* 1 (1956) 367-381.

William R. Farmer, "Postscript to 'The Economic Basis of the Qumran Community'," *TZ* 12 (1956) 56-58.

*J. A. Thompson, "Education in the Qumran Community," *JCE* 1 (1958) 13-20.

E[dmund] F. Sutcliffe, "The General Council of the Qumran Community," *B* 40 (1959) 971-984.

*Edmund F. Sutcliffe, "The First Fifteen Members of the Qumran Community: A Note on 1QS 8:1ff.," *JSS* 4 (1959) 134-139.

E[dmund] F. Sutcliffe, "The General Council of the Qumran Community," *SBO* 2 (1959) 403-415.

Bill J. Humble, "The *Mebaqqer* in the Dead Sea Scrolls," *RestQ* 7 (1963) 33-38.

§1073 *7.2.3 Studies on the Practices of the Qumran Community*

Joseph M. Baumgarten, "Sacrifice and Worship Among the Jewish Sectarians of the Dead Sea (Qumran) Scrolls," *HTR* 46 (1953) 141-159.

*D. Flusser, "The Apocryphal Book of *Ascensio Isaiae* and the Dead Sea Sect," *IEJ* 3 (1953) 30-47.

*J. L. Teicher, "Priests and Sacrifices in the Dead Sea Scrolls," *JJS* 5 (1954) 93-99.

D. Flusser, "Healing through the Laying-on of Hands in a Dead Sea Scroll," *IEJ* 7 (1957) 107-108.

J. van der Ploeg, "The Meals of the Essenes," *JSS* 2 (1957) 163-175.

Sylvio J. Scorza, "Praise and Music in the Qumran Community," *RefR* 11 (1957-58) #3, 32-36.

*J. Bowman, "Did the Qumran Sect Burn the Red Heifer?" *RdQ* 1 (1958-59) 73-84.

E[dmund] F. Sutcliffe, "Hatred at Qumran," *RdQ* 2 (1959-60) 345-356.

E[dmund] F. Sutcliffe, "Sacred Meals at Qumran?" *HeyJ* 1 (1960) 48-65.

Edmund F. Sutcliffe, "Baptism and Baptismal Rites at Qumran," *HeyJ* 1 (1960) 179-188.

*William A. Beardslee, "The Casting of Lots at Qumran and in the Book of Acts," *NT* 5(1960) 245-252.

Judah Rosenthal, "The Sabbath Laws of the Qumranites or the Damascus Covenanters," *BRes* 6 (1961) 10-17.

Manfred R. Lehmann, "'Yom Kippur' in Qumran," *RdQ* 3 (1961-62) 117-124.

*J. Liver, "The Half-Shekel in the Scrolls of the Judean Desert Sect," *Tarbiz* 31 (1961-62) #1, III-IV.

M. Beer, "The Sects of the Half-Sheqel," *Tarbiz* 31 (1961-62) #3, IV.

*B. Noack, "The Day of Pentecost in Jubilees, Qumran, and Acts," *ASTI* 1 (1962) 73-95.

George Wesley Buchanan, "The Role of Purity in the Structure of the Essene Sect," *RdQ* 4 (1962-63) 397-406.

J. G. Harris, "Aspects of the Ethical Teaching of the Qumran Covenanters," *EQ* 37 (1965) 142-146.

E. J. Pryke, "Beliefs and Practices of the Qumran Community," *CQR* 168 (1967) 314-325.

K. H. Rengstorf, "The Concept *'Goral'* (גורל) in the Dead-Sea Scrolls," *Tarbiz* 35 (1965-66) #2,II-III.

J. M. Baumgarten, "The Essene Avoidance of Oil and the Laws of Purity," *RdQ* 6 (1967-69) 183-192.

S. T. Kimbrough, "The Ethic of the Qumran Community," *RdQ* 6 (1967-69) 483-498.

Sidney B. Hoenig, "Qumran Rules of Impurities," *RdQ* 6 (1967-69) 559-567.

*Menachem M. Brayer, "Psychosomatics, Hermetic Medicine, and Dream Interpretation in the Qumran Literature," *JQR, N.S.,* 60 (1969-70) 112-127, 213-230.

*Roger T. Beckwith, "The Qumran Calendar and the sacrifices of the Essenes," *RdQ* 7 (1969-71) 587-591.

§1074 *7.2.4 Studies on the Doctrines of the Qumran Community - General Studies*

Matthew Black, "Theological Conceptions in the Dead Sea Scrolls," *SEÅ* 18&19 (1953-54) 72-99.

D. Flusser, "The Religious Ideas of the Judean Desert Sect," *Zion* 19 (1954) #3/4, I.

N. Golb, "Literary and Doctrinal Aspects of the Damascus Covenant in the Light of Karaite Literature," *JQR, N.S.,* 47 (1956-57) 354-374.

*Menahem Mansoor, "Studies in the *Hodayot*— IV," *JBL* 76 (1957) 139-148. *[Qumran Angelology]*

*J. A. Fitzmyer, "A Feature of Qumran Angelology and the Angels of I Cor. xi. 10," *NTS* 4 (1957-58)48-57.

John C. Trever, "The Qumran Covenanters and Their Use of Scripture," *Person* 39 (1958) 127-138.

*Theodor H. Gaster, "A Curious Qumran Tradition," *BASOR* #151 (1958) 33.

*Jacob Neusner, "Qumran and Jerusalem: Two Jewish Roads to Utopia," *JAAR* 27 (1959) 284-290.

*S. H. Hooke, "Symbolism in the Dead Sea Scrolls," *StEv* 1 (1959) 600-612.

Paul Winter, "The Wicked Priest," *HJ* 58 (1959-60) 53-60.

Shemaryahu Talmon, "The Order of Prayers of the Sect from the Judaean Desert," *Tarbiz* 29 (1959-60) #1, I.

*Everett Ferguson, "Ordination in the Ancient Church (I)," *RestQ* 4 (1960) 117-138. [Functionaries in the Qumran Community, pp. 122-136]

*J. van der Ploeg, "The Belief in Immortality in the Writings of Qumrān," *BO* 18 (1961) 118-124.

*F. F. Bruce, "Preparation in the Wilderness. *At Qumran and in the New Testament,*" *Interp* 16 (1962) 280-291.

E. F. F. Bishop, "Qumran and the Preserved Tablet(s)," *RdQ* 5 (1964-66) 253-256.

*S. T. Kimbrough Jr., "The Concept of Sabbath at Qumran," *RdQ* 5 (1964-66) 483-502.

John Bligh, "The 'Two Ways' at Qumran and in the Early Church," *BibT* #22 (1966) 1470-1474.

J. Liver, "The 'Sons of Zadok the Priest' in the Dead Sea Scrolls," *EI* 8 (1967) 70*.

J. Licht, "The Doctrine of 'Times' According to the Sect of Qumran and Other 'Computers of Seasons'," *EI* 8 (1967) 70*.

J. G. Harris, "The Covenant Concept Among the Qumran Sectaries," *EQ* 39 (1967) 86-92.

*J. Liver, "The Sons of Zadok the Priests' in the Dead Sea Sect," *RdQ* 6 (1967-69) 3-30.

§1075 *7.2.4.1 Studies on the Doctrine of God at Qumran*

*P. Peters, "The Divine Name YHWH in the Dead Sea Scrolls," *WLQ* 48 (1951) 148.

S. J. De Vries, "Note Concerning the Fear of God in the Qumran Scrolls," *RdQ* 5 (1964-66) 233-238.

F. F. Bruce, "Holy Spirit in the Qumran Texts," *ALUOS* 6 (1966-68) 49-55.

§1076 *7.2.4.2 Studies on the Doctrine of Man and His Salvation at Qumran*

Wallace I. Wolverton, "The Double-Minded Man in the Light of Essene Psychology," *ATR* 38 (1956) 166-175.

*Robert Gordis, "The Knowledge of Good and Evil in the Old Testament and the Qumran Scrolls," *JBL* 76 (1957) 123-138.

David Flusser, "The Dualism of 'Flesh and Spirit' in the DSS and the NT," *Tarbiz* 27 (1957-58) #2/3, V.

John V. Chamberlain, "Toward a Qumran Soteriology," *NT* 3 (1959) 305-313.

Oscar J. F. Seitz, "Two Spirits in Man: An Essay in Biblical Exegesis," *NTS* 6 (1959-60) 82-95.

*Barbara Thiering, "St. Paul's Self-Understanding compared with that of the Qumran Sectarian," *Coll* 3 (1968-70) 293-306.

§1077 *7.2.4.3 Studies on Qumran and the Calendar*

Julian Obermann, "Calendaric Elements in the Dead Sea Scrolls," *JBL* 75 (1956) 285-297.

Shemaryahu Talmon, "The Calendar Reckoning of the Sect from the Judean Desert," *SH* 4 (1957) 162-199.

*Theodor H. Gaster, "A Curious Qumran Tradition," *BASOR* #151 (1958) 33.

*C. S. Mann, "The Chronology of the Passion and the Qumran Calendar," *CQR* 160 (1959) 446-456.

*John Bowman, "Is the Samaritan Calendar the Old Zadokite One?" *PEQ* 91 (1959) 23-37.

Roger T. Beckwith, "The modern attempt to reconcile the Qumran calendar with the true solar year," *RdQ* 7 (1969-71) 379-396.

*Roger T. Beckwith, "The Qumran Calender and the sacrifices of the Essenes," *RdQ* 7 (1969-71) 587-591.

§1078 *7.2.4.4 Studies on Qumran and Messianic Ideas*

Millar Burrows, "The Messiahs of Aaron and Israel," *ATR* 34 (1952) 202-205.

*Wm. H. Brownlee, "The Servant of the Lord in the Qumran Scrolls I.," *BASOR* #132 (1953) 8-15.

*Wm. H. Brownlee, "The Servant of the Lord in the Qumran Scrolls II.," *BASOR* #135 (1954) 33-38.

N. Wieder, "The 'Law-Interpreter' of the Sect of the Dead Sea Scrolls: The Second Moses," *JJS* 4 (1953) 158-175.

*Solomon Zeitlin, "The Essenes and the Messianic Expectations. A Historical Study of the Sects and Ideas During the Second Jewish Commonwealth," *JQR, N.S.,* 45 (1954-55) 83-119.

N. Wieder, "The Doctrine of the Two Messiahs among the Karaites," *JJS* 6 (1955) 14-25.

L. H. Silberman, "The Two 'Messiahs' of the Manual of Discipline," *VT* 5 (1955) 77-82.

*J. V. Chamberlain, "The Functions of God as Messianic Titles in the Complete Qumran Isaiah Scroll," *VT* 5 (1955) 365-372.

*J. M. Allegro, "Further Messianic References in Qumran Literature," *JBL* 75 (1956) 174-187.

W[illiam] S[anford] LaSor, "The Messiahs of Aaron and Israel," *VT* 6 (1956) 425-429.

W[illiam] H. Brownlee, "Messianic Motifs of Qumran and the New Testament," *NTS* 3 (1956-57) 12-30, 195-210.

*Raymond E. Brown, "The Messianism of Qumran," *CBQ* 19 (1957) 53-82.

M. Black, "Messianic Doctrine in the Qumran Scrolls," *StP* 1 (1957) 441-459.

R[obert] Gordis, "The 'Begotten' Messiah in the Qumran Scrolls," *VT* 7 (1957) 191-194.

J. Liver, "The Doctrine of Two Messiahs in Sectarian Literature in the Time of the Second Commonwealth," *HTR* 52 (1959) 149-185.

Morton Smith, "What is Implied by the Variety of Messianic Figures?" *JBL* 78 (1959) 66-72.

*Glenn Hinson, "Hodayoth III, 6-18: In What Sense Messianic?" *RdQ* 2 (1959-60) 183-204.

John F. Priest, "Mebaqqer, Paqid, and the Messiah," *JBL* 81 (1962) 55-61.

R. B. Laurin, "The Problem of Two Messiahs in the Qumran Scrolls," *RdQ* 4 (1962-63) 39-52.

John F. Priest, "The Messiah and the Meal in 1QSa," *JBL* 82 (1963) 95-100.

Charles T. Fritsch, "The so-called 'priestly Messiah' of the Essenes," *JEOL* #17 (1963) 242-248.

Emil A. Wcela, "The Messiah(s) of Qumran," *CBQ* 26 (1964) 340-349.

*E[dward] L. Bode, "The Baptist, The Messiah and the Monks of Qumran," *BibT* #17 (1965) 1111-1116.

Raymond E. Brown, "J. Starcky's Theory of Qumran Messianic Development," *CBQ* 28 (1966) 51-57.

*N. Wieder, "The 'Land of Damascus' and Messianic Redemption," *JJS* 20 (1969) 86-88.

§1079 *7.2.4.5 Studies on Qumran and Eschatology*

*Millar Burrows, "The Ascent From Acco in 4Q p Isa^a," *VT* 7 (1957) 104-105.

*J. Allegro, "Addendum to Professor Millar Burrow's note on the Ascent from Accho in 4QpIsa ^{a}," *VT* 7 (1957) 183.

*Otto A. Piper, "The 'Book of Mysteries' (Qumran I 27)   A Study in Eschatology," *JR* 38 (1958) 95-106.

*J. C. G. Greig, "Gospel Messianism and the Qumran Use of Prophecy," *StEv* 1 (1959) 593-599.

*Cecil Roth, "Star and Anchor: Coin Symbolism and the End of Days," *EI* 6 (1960) 13*-15*.

*Max Wilcox, "Qumran Eschatology: Some Observations on 1QS," *ABR* 9 (1961) 37-42.

*J. P. Thorndike, "The Apocalypse of Weeks and the Qumran Sect," *RdQ* 3 (1961-62) 163-184.

*A. R. C. Leaney, "The Eschatological Significance of Human Suffering in the Old Testament and the Dead Sea Scrolls," *SJT* 16 (1963) 286-296.

*J. Licht, "Time and Eschatology in Apocalyptic Literature and in Qumran," *JJS* 16 (1965) 177-182.

*O. Betz, "The Eschatological Interpretation of the Sinai-Tradition in Qumran and in the New Testament," *RdQ* 6 (1967-69) 89-107.

E. J. Pryke, "Some Aspects of Eschatology in the Dead Sea Scrolls," *StEv* 5 (1968) 296-302.

§1080 *7.2.4.6 Studies on the Teacher of Righteousness*

*C. Rabin, "The 'Teacher of Righteousness' in the 'Testaments of the Twelve Patriarchs'?" *JJS* 3 (1952) 127-128.

*O. R. Sellers, "A Possible Old Testament Reference to the Teacher of Righteousness," *IEJ* 5 (1955) 93-95.

*William R. Farmer, "The Teacher of Righteousness and Jesus the Christ," *DG* 26 (1955-56) 183-194.

J. C. G. Greig, "The Teacher of Righteousness and the Qumran Community," *NTS* 2 (1955-56) 119-126.

*Edward J. Young, "The Teacher of Righteousness and Jesus Christ. Some Reflections Upon the Dead Sea Scrolls," *WTJ* 18 (1955-56) 121-145.

James Muilenburg, "The Teacher of Righteousness," *ANQ* 49 (1956) #1,1-14.

*H. H. Rowley, "4QpNahum and the Teacher of Righteousness," *JBL* 75 (1956) 188-193.

*H. H. Rowley, "The Kittim and the Dead Sea Scrolls," *PEQ* 88 (1956) 92-109.

Kevin Smyth, "The Teacher of Righteousness," *ET* 69 (1957-58) 340-342.

James Muilenburg, "The Teacher of Righteousness," *RefR* 11 (1957-58) #2, 1-10.

*I. Rabinowitz, "The Guides of Righteousness," *VT* 8 (1958) 391-404.

*Paul Winter, "Back to the Caves," *PEQ* 91 (1959) 132-134. [I. Prophecy in the Ṣadoqite Fragments? II. The Moreh Hassedeq in the Toledoth Yeshu?]

J. Weingreen, "The Title Moreh Sedek," *JSS* 6 (1961) 162-174.

*C. Roth, "The Teacher of Righteousness and the Prophecy of Joel," *VT* 13 (1963) 91-95.

G. W. Buchanan, "The Priestly Teacher of Righteousness," *RdQ* 6 (1967-69) 553-558.

*Barbara Thiering, "The Teacher of Righteousness and the Messiah in the Damascus Document," *AJBA* 1 (1968-71) #4, 74-81.

§1081   ***7.2.4.7 Studies on Qumran and the Conflict of***
                              Light and Darkness

*M. Avi-Yonah, "The 'War of the Sons of Light and the Sons of Darkness'
and the Maccabean Warfare," *IEJ* 2 (1952) 1-5.

*K. M. T. Atkinson, "The Historical Setting of the 'War of the Sons of Light
and the Sons of Darkness'," *BJRL* 40 (1957-58) 272-297.

Herbert G. May, "Cosmological Reference in the Qumran Doctrine of the
Two Spirits and in Old Testament Imagery," *JBL* 82 (1963) 1-14.

§1082   ***7.2.4.8 Studies on the Qumran Community and***
                              Its Interpretation of Scripture

*William H. Brownlee, "Biblical Interpretation Among the Sectaries of the
Dead Sea Scrolls," *BA* 14 (1951) 54-76.

J. C. G. Greig, "Gospel Messianism and the Qumran Use of Prophecy," *StEv*
1 (1959) 593-599.

C. Roth, "The Subject Matter of Qumran Exegesis," *VT* 10 (1960) 51-68.

*I. H. Eybers, "The Book of Ezekiel and the Sect of Qumran," *OTW* 4
(1961) 1-9.

David Noel Freedman, "The Old Testament at Qumran," *McQ* 21 (1967-68)
299-306.

G. Vermes, "The Qumran Interpretation of Scripture in its Historical
Setting," *ALUOS* 6 (1966-68) 84-97.

Elieser Slomovic, "Toward an Understanding of the Exegesis in the Dead
Sea Scrolls," *RdQ* 7 (1969-71) 3-15.

§1083 ***7.2.5 Studies on the Qumran Community and Its Relation***
                    to the Outside World

William H. Brownlee, "A Comparison of the Covenanters of the Dead Sea
Scrolls with Pre-Christian Jewish Sects," *BA* 13 (1950) 49-72. [I.
Comparison with the Covenanters of Damascus; II. Comparison with
the Essenes; III. Comparison with the Therapeutae; IV. Comparison
with John the Baptist and His Movement]

*Ralph Marcus, "Philo, Josephus and the Dead Sea *Yaḥad,*" *JBL* 71 (1952) 207-209.

*H. F. D. Sparks, "The Books of the Qumran Community," *JTS, N.S.,* 6 (1955) 226-229.

*H. H. Rowley, "The Kittim and the Dead Sea Scrolls," *PEQ* 88 (1956) 92-109.

*J. R. Rosenbloom, "Notes on historical identification in the Dead Sea Scrolls," *RdQ* 1 (1958-59) 265-272.

*Cecil Roth, "Did Vespasian Capture Qumran?" *PEQ* 91 (1959) 122-129.

C[ecil] Roth, "A Talmudic Reference to the Qumran Sect?" *RdQ* 2 (1959-60) 261-265.

Richard Nelson Frye, "Reitzenstein and Qumran Revisited by an Iranian," *HTR* 55 (1962) 261-268.

S. H. Steckoll, "The Qumran Sect in Relation to the Temple of Leontopolis," *RdQ* 6 (1967-69) 55-69.

*L. W. Barnard, "Hadrian and Judaism," *JRelH* 5 (1968-69) 285-298. [Appendix: The Second Jewish Revolt and the Discoveries by the Dead Sea, p. 295-298]

§1084 *7.2.5.1 Studies on Qumran and Its Relation to the Essenes*

M. H. Gottstein, "Anti-Essene Traits in the Dead Sea Scrolls," *VT* 4 (1954) 141-147.

B. J. Roberts, "The Qumran Scrolls and the Essenes," *NTS* 3 (1956-57) 58-64.

C[ecil] Roth, "Why the Qumran Sect Cannot have been the Essenes," *RdQ* 1 (1958-59) 417-422.

Cecil Roth, "Were the Qumran Sectaries Essenes? A Re-examination of some Evidences," *JTS, N.S.,* 10 (1959) 87-93.

G. Vermes, "The Etymology of 'Essenes'," *RdQ* 2 (1959-60) 427-443.

G. Vermes, "Essenes and Therapeutai," *RdQ* 3 (1961-62) 495-504.

Shermaryahu Talmon, "A Further Link Between the Judean Covenanters and the Essenes," *HTR* 56 (1963) 313-319.

§1085 **7.2.5.2 Studies on Qumran and Its Relation to Christianity [See also: The Qumran Scrolls and the New Testament §1155 →]**

J. L. Teicher, "The Teaching of the Pre-Pauline Church in the Dead Sea Scrolls," *JJS* 3 (1952) 111-118, 139-150; 4 (1953) 1-13, 49-58, 93-103, 139-153.

J. L. Teicher, "'Jesus' Sayings in the Dead Sea Scrolls," *JJS* 5 (1954) 38.

Oscar Cullmann, "The Significance of the Qumran Texts for Research into the Beginnings of Christianity," *JBL* 74 (1955) 213-226.

F. F. Bruce, "Qumran and Early Christianity," *NTS* 2 (1955-56) 176-190.

Melville Chaning-Pearce, "The Christian Significance of the Dead Sea Scrolls," *HJ* 55 (1956-57) 43-48.

Henry J. Cadbury, "New Light from Old Scrolls," *UC* 11 (1955-56) #2, 9-12.

Geoffrey Graystone, "Qumran and Christianity: A recent Book on the Dead Sea Scrolls," *IER, 5th Ser.,* 85 (1956) 233-242. *(Review)*

Alex. Jones, "Qumran and Christianity," *Scrip* 8 (1956) 82-95.

Morris Ashcraft, "The Dead Sea Scrolls and Early Christianity," *R&E* 54 (1957) 7-22.

W. D. Davies, "The Dead Sea Scrolls and Christian Origins," *RL* 26 (1957) 246-263.

David Flusser, "The Dead Sea Sect and Pre-Pauline Christianity," *SH* 4 (1957) 215-266.

Dennis J. McCarthy, "Qumran and Christian Beginnings," *TD* 5 (1957) 39-47.

C. S. Mann, "The Scrolls, The Lord, and the Primitive Church," *CQR* 159 (1958) 512-531.

Barnabas Lindars, "Qumran and the Christian Ministry," *CQR* 160 (1959) 335-344.

J.-D. Barthelemy, "Essenism and Christianity," *Scrip* 12 (1960) 119-126.

J.-D. Barthelemy, "Essenism and Christianity—II," *Scrip* 13 (1961) 20-24.

H. H. Rowley, "The Qumran Sect and Christian Origins," *BJRL* 44 (1961-62) 119-156.

William Sanford LaSor, "The Dead Sea Scrolls and the Beginnings of Christianity," *CNI* 13 (1962) #2, 8-13.

H. H. Rowley, "Comparison and Contrast. *Qumran and the Early Church*," *Interp* 16 (1962) 292-304.

J. C. L. Gibson, "From Qumran to Edessa: *or* The Aramaic Speaking Church before and after 70 A.D.," *ALUOS* 5 (1963-65) 24-39.

J. C. L. Gibson, "From Qumran to Edessa: *or* The Aramaic Speaking Church before and after 70 A.D.," *NCB* 2 (1964-65) #2, 9-20.

Lucetta Mowry, "The Dead Sea Scrolls and the Early Church," *TFUQ* 40 (1965) 515-528.

Patrick W. Skehan, "The Dead Sea Scrolls and the Christian Church," *BibT* #22 (1966) 1451-1461.

W. D. Davies, "The Dead Sea Scrolls and Christian Origins," *BibT* #25 (1966) 1749-1762.

Matthew Black, "The Dead Sea Scrolls and Christian Doctrine," *CNI* 17 (1966) #2/3, 27-30.

F. F. Bruce, "The Dead Sea Scrolls and Early Christianity," *BJRL* 49 (1966-67) 69-90.

A. R. C. Leaney, "The Dead Sea Scrolls and Christianity," *Coll* 2 (1966-68) 3-14.

§1086   *7.2.5.3 Studies on Qumran and Its Relation to "Main-Stream Judaism" and the Reconstruction of Early Judaism*

Charles T. Fritsch, "Herod the Great and the Qumran Community," *JBL* 74 (1955) 173-181.

Ralph Marcus, "The Qumran Scrolls and Early Judaism," *BRes* 1 (1956) 9-47.

Melvin G. Nida, "'Sectarian' Judaism," *IR* 14 (1957) #2, 33-38.

*Cecil Roth, "The Jewish Revolt Against the Romans (66-73) in the Light of the Dead Sea Scrolls," *PEQ* 90 (1958) 104-121.

Morton Smith, "The Dead Sea Sect in Relation to Ancient Judaism," *NTS* 7 (1960-61) 347-360.

*C[ecil] Roth, "The Era of the Habakkuk Commentary," *VT* 11 (1961) 451-455.

§1087   *7.2.5.4 Studies on Qumran and Other Jewish Sects*

J. L. Teicher, "The Dead Sea Scrolls—Documents of the Jewish Christian Sect of Ebionites," *JJS* 2 (1950-51) 67-99.

Joseph A. Fitzmyer, "The Qumran Scrolls, the Ebionites and Their Literature," *ThSt* 16 (1955) 335-372.

N. Weider, "The Qumran Sectaries and the Karaites," *JQR, N.S.,* 47 (1956-57) 97-113, 269-292.

J. Bowman, "Contact Between Samaritan Sects and Qumran?" *VT* 7 (1957) 184-189.

*L. E. Toombs, "Barcosiba and Qumran," *NTS* 4 (1957-58) 65-71.

H. H. Rowley, "The Qumran Sectaries and the Zealots, an Examination of a Recent Theory," *VT* 9 (1959) 379-392.

C[ecil] Roth, "The Zealots and Qumran: The Basic Issue," *RdQ* 2 (1959-60) 81-84.

H. H. Rowley, "The Qumran Sectaries: A Rejoinder," *VT* 10 (1960) 227-229.

Norman Golb, "The Qumran Covenanters and the Later Jewish Sects," *JR* 41 (1961) 38-50.

*E. E. Ellis, "Jesus, the Sadducees and Qumran," *NTS* 10 (1963-64) 274-279.

H. Nibley, "Qumran and 'The Companions of the Cave'," *RdQ* 5 (1964-66) 177-198.

J. Massingberd Ford, "Can We Exclude Samaritan Influence from Qumran?" *RdQ* 6 (1967-69) 109-129.

§1088   ***7.2.5.5 Studies on Qumran and Gnosticism***

Bo Reicke, "Traces of Gnosticism in the Dead Sea Scrolls?" *NTS* 1 (1954-55) 137-141.

*Hans Jonas, "The Secret Books of Egyptian Gnostics," *JR* 42 (1962) 262-273. *[Short section at end on Qumran and Gnosticism]*

Edward Yamauchi, "Qumran and Colosse," *BS* 121 (1964) 141-152.

John Painter, "Gnosticism and the Qumran Texts," *ABR* 17 (1969) 1-6.

§1089 ***7.3 General Studies on the Dead Sea Scrolls***

Anonymous, "Discovery of Biblical Manuscripts," *Antiq* 22 (1948) 159-160.

P. Peters, "The Greatest Manuscript Find of Modern Time," *AusTR* 19 (1948) 74-75.

Millar Burrows, "The Newly Discovered Jerusalem Scrolls, II. The Contents and Significance of the Manuscripts," *BA* 11 (1948) 57-61.

Bleddyn J. Roberts, "Recent Discoveries of Hebrew Manuscripts," *ET* 60 (1948-49) 305-308.

H. Hamann, "More Ancient Hebrew Manuscripts," *AusTR* 20 (1949) 87-88.

Mar Athanasius Y. Samuel, "The Purchase of the Jerusalem Scrolls," *BA* 12 (1949) 26-31.

G. Ernest Wright, "The Extent of the Total Discovery," *BA* 12 (1949) 33-35.

O. R. Sellers, "Archaeological News from Palestine. Study of Finds in the Ain Fashkha Cave," *BA* 12 (1949) 53-56.

John C. Trever, "The Bible Comes Alive," *JAAR* 17 (1949) 98-101.

H. Darby, *"Megilloth Genuzoth* ['Scrolls Hidden Away']," *JTS* 50 (1949) 169-173. *(Review)*

R. T. O'Callaghan, "The Scrolls Newly Discovered in Palestine," *Scrip* 4 (1949-51) 41-46.

G. B. Elhardt, "Ancient Hebrew Manuscripts to be Exhibited at Duke, February 12-17, 1950," *DDSR* 14 (1949-50) 115-116.

Bleddyn J. Roberts, "The Dead Sea Scrolls: Publications and Review," *ET* 61 (1949-50) 323-327.

W[illiam] F[oxwell] Albright, "Are the 'Ain Feshkha Scrolls a Hoax," *JQR, N.S.,* 40 (1949-50) 41-49.

Millar Burrows, "A Note on the Recently Discovered Manuscripts," *JQR, N.S.,* 40 (1949-50) 51-56.

G. R. Driver, "The Hebrew Manuscripts," *JQR, N.S.,* 40 (1949-50) 127-134.

G. R. Driver, "New Hebrew Manuscripts," *JQR, N.S.,* 40 (1949-50) 359-372.

William A. Irwin, "Before Christ Was—These Were!" *PSTJ* 3 (1949-50) #2, 4-7.

Bleddyn J. Roberts, "The Jerusalem Scrolls," *ZAW* 62 (1949-50) 224-245.

Edward P. Arbez, "The New Hebrew Manuscripts," *AER* 122 (1950) 25-36, 137-145, 196-206.

P. Peters, "The Dead Sea Scrolls," *WLQ* 47 (1950) 321-323.

G. R. Driver, "New Hebrew Scrolls," *HJ* 49 (1950-51) 11-21.

J. L. Teicher, "The Dead Sea Scrolls—Documents of the Jewish-Christian Sect of Ebionites," *JJS* 2 (1950-51) 67-99. [A. Preliminary Clearance, 1. The Jars, 2. The Scroll of "Haftaroth", 3. Arguments from Palæography and Orthography for late date of the Scrolls derived from their contents and Language; B. The Three Essential Issues, 1. The Archæological Evidence, 2. The Palæographical Evidence, 3. "Zadokite" Writings in the Ninth and Tenth Centuries; C. The Solution of the Problem of the Origin of the Scrolls]

Joseph Reider, "The Dead Sea Scrolls," *JQR, N.S.*, 41 (1950-51) 59-70.

John C. Trever, "The 'Suppressed' Scroll of the Haftarot," *JQR, N.S.*, 41 (1950-51) 71-81.

F. F. Bruce, "Recent Discoveries in Biblical Manuscripts," *JTVI* 82 (1950) 131-144, 148-149. [Discussion, pp. 144-148]

G. R. Driver, "The Hebrew Scrolls from the Neighbourhood of Jericho and the Dead Sea," *FDWL* #4 (1951) 1-51.

John C. Trever, "Scrolls from a Dead Sea Cave," *BTr* 2 (1951) 75-79.

John A. O'Flynn, "The Dead Sea Manuscripts," *ITQ* 18 (1951) 177-182.

Solomon A. Birnbaum, "Notes on the Internal and Archaeological Evidence Concerning the Cave Scrolls," *JBL* 70 (1951) 227-232.

Saul Lieberman, "Light on the Cave Scrolls from Rabbinic Sources," *PAAJR* 20 (1951) 395-404.

B[leddyn] J. Roberts, "Some Observations on the Damascus Document and the Dead Sea Scrolls," *BJRL* 34 (1951-52) 366-387.

Millar Burrows, "Concerning the Dead Sea Scrolls," *JQR, N.S.*, 42 (1951-52) 105-132.

G. Ernest Wright, "More Cave Manuscripts," *BA* 15 (1952) 44-45.

John A. O'Flynn, "New Finds in the Holy Land," *ITQ* 19 (1952) 386-388.

H. F. D. Sparks, "The Dead Sea Scrolls," *MC* 42 (1952) 334-337.

*G. Lankester Harding, "Khirbet Qumran and Wady Muraba'at. *Fresh Light on the Dead Sea Scrolls and the New Manuscript Discoveries in Jordan*," *PEQ* 84 (1952) 104-109.

G. Graystone, "The Dead Sea Scrolls," *Scrip* 5 (1952-53) 112-122.

D. Winton Thomas, "The Dead Sea Scrolls," *Theo* 55 (1952) 321-324.

Anonymous, "Another Find of Manuscripts in Palestine," *Antiq* 27 (1953) 39-40.

Anonymous, "More News on the Manuscript Search," *BA* 16 (1953) 17-18.

Anonymous, "The Dead Sea Scrolls," *TD* 1 (1953) 103.

G. R. Driver, "Once Again the Judaean Scrolls," *JQR, N.S.,* 44 (1953-54) 1-20.

G. Graystone, "Further Notes on the Dead Sea Scrolls," *Scrip* 6 (1953-54) 17-21.

G. Graystone, "The Dead Sea Scrolls—New Discoveries and Conclusions. I. Khirbet Qumran: Its Caves and MSS," *Scrip* 6 (1953-54) 131-143.

Frank M[oore] Cross Jr., "The Manuscripts of the Dead Sea Caves," *BA* 17 (1954) 2-21. [The Manuscripts of Cave 1; The Search for More Material; The Murabba'at Caves; Two Additional Groups; Work on the Fragments from Cave Four; The Contents of Cave Four; The Date of the Scrolls]

R. B. Y. Scott, "Acquisition of Dead Sea Scroll Fragments by McGill University," *BASOR* #135 (1954) 8.

William L. Reed, "The Qumran Caves Expedition of March, 1952," *BASOR* #135 (1954) 8-13.

Bleddyn J. Roberts, "The Qumran (Dead Sea) Scrolls: A Survey," *CongQL* 32 (1954) 114-124.

Joseph S. Considine, "The Dead Sea Scrolls," *CBQ* 16 (1954) 41-45.

H. F. D. Sparks, "Professor Dupont Sommer on the Discoveries by the Dead Sea," *MC* 44 (1954) 300-305. *(Review)*

*H. F. D. Sparks, "The Books of the Qumran Community," *JTS, N.S.,* 6 (1955) 226-229.

G. Graystone, "The Dead Sea Scrolls—III. Wadi en-Nar," *Scrip* 7 (1955) 106-108.

Henri de Contenson, "In the Footsteps of St. John the Baptist: Notes on the Rolls of the Dead Sea," *A&S* 1 (1955-56) 37-55.

James Muilenburg, "The Significance of the Scrolls," *DG* 26 (1955-56) 171-183.

John M. Allegro, "The Latest News of the Dead Sea Scrolls," *GUOST* 16 (1955-56) 17-21.

James Muilenburg, "The Significance of the Scrolls," *USQR* 11 (1955-56) #3, 3-12.

Ignatius [J.] Hunt, "The Meaning of the Dead Sea Scrolls," *ABenR* 7 (1956) 31-53.

Roland E. Murphy, "'Those Dead Sea Scrolls...'," *AER* 134 (1956) 361-373.

Frank M[oore] Cross Jr., "The Scrolls from the Judaean Desert," *Arch* 9 (1956) 41-53.

Millar Burrows, "The Implications of the Dead Sea Scrolls," *CCARJ* #12 (1956) 14-17.

William H. Brownlee, "My Eight Years of Scroll Research," *DDSR* 21 (1956) 68-81.

Frank M[oore] Cross Jr., "Qumran Cave I," *JBL* 75 (1956) 121-125.

A. M. Haberman, "The Dead Sea Scrolls—A Survey and a New Interpretation," *Jud* 5 (1956) 306-315.

Ralph Tyler Flewelling, "'Sea-Scroll Madness'," *Person* 37 (1956) 341-349.

Charles T. Fritsch, "The Dead Sea Scrolls—1956," *PSB* 50 (1956) #2, 20-26.

P. Peters, "The Qumran Manuscripts," *WLQ* 53 (1956) 152-153.

Norm Wente, "The Qumran Scrolls," *Amb* 5 (1956-57) #2, 14-15, 25.

Anonymous, "Seventh Dead Sea Scroll Unrolled," *AT* 1 (1956-57) #1, 9.

Frank M[oore] Cross Jr., "McCormick's Rehnborg Collection of Dead Sea Scrolls," *McQ* 10 (1956-57) #4, 7-10.

Bruce M. Metzger, "New Light from Old Manuscripts," *TT* 13 (1956-57) 72-86.

M. A. Stuckey, "A Brief Account of the History, Contents, and Significance of the Qumran Manuscripts of the Judean Desert," *TUSR* 5 (1956-58) 1-15.

William Leonard, "The Dead Sea Scrolls: A Brief Review," *ACR* 34 (1957) 304-312.

Norman Bentwich, "The Dead Sea Scrolls," *ContR* 192 (1957) 311-315.

Walter G. Williams, "The Importance of the Dead Sea Scrolls for Christian Scholars," *IR* 14 (1957) #1, 1-14.

Norman Snaith, "The Dead Sea Scrolls," *PQL* 3 (1957) 201-206.

Alex. Jones, "Apropos Four Recent Books on the Scrolls," *Scrip* 9 (1957) 21-26. *(Review)*

P. Peters, "The Qumran Scrolls," *WLQ* 54 (1957) 62-63.

Ralph Tyler Flewelling, "The Battle of the Scrolls," *Person* 39 (1958) 5-14.

G. D. Griffith, "The Dead Sea Scrolls," *StMR* #13 (1958) 10-23.

A. N. Poliak, "The Dead Sea Scrolls: A New Approach," *JQR, N.S.,* 49 (1958-59) 89-107.

*Sidney B. Hoenig, "Scroll Idolization," *Trad* 1 (1958-59) 222-226.

D. Winton Thomas, "The Dead Sea Scrolls," *Antiq* 33 (1959) 189-194.

Joseph Bourke, "The Qumran Scrolls: A General Survey," *CC* 9 (1959) 255-266.

Joseph Bourke, "The Qumrân Scrolls: A General Survey," *NB* 40 (1959) 154-169.

G. G. Garner, "*The Dead Sea Scrolls:* An Amazing Modern Discovery," *AT* 4 (1959-60) #2, 2-5.

Frank M[oore] Cross Jr., "Report from the Dead Sea 'Scrollery'," *McQ* 13 (1959-60) #2, 20-23.

John Reumann, "The Dead Seal Scrolls in America," *LQ, N.S.,* 12 (1960) 91-110.

Anonymous, "More Dead Sea Scroll Discoveries," *AT* 5 (1960-61) #3, 16.

Sidney B. Hoenig, "Megillath Midbar Yehuda," *JQR, N.S.,* 51 (1960-61) 72-78. *(Review)*

F. F. Bruce, "The Dead Sea Scrolls," *MC, N.S.,* 4 (1960-61) 45-55.

Cecil Roth, "The Historian and the Dead Sea Scrolls," *HT* 11 (1961) 90-97.

W. H. Gispen, "The Dead Sea Scrolls," *FUQ* 8 (1961-62) 117-131.

William Sanford LaSor, "Historical Framework. *The Present Status of the Dead Sea Scroll Study,"* Interp 16 (1962) 259-279.

J. P. Kabel, "New Light from Qumran," *PJT* #1 (1961) 4-12; #3 (1962) 11-18.

Norman Bentwich, "More History from Jerusalem and the Judean Desert," *QRL* 300 (1962) 310-317.

Patrick W. Skehan, "A New Translation of Qumran Texts," *CBQ* 25 (1963) 119-123. *(Review)*

Kevin Smith, "The Dead Sea Scrolls," *DR* 237 (1963-64) 335-360.

*J. C. Trever, "Completion of the Publication of Some Fragments from Qumran Cave I," *RdQ* 5 (1964-66) 323-344. [I. Treatment, pp. 323-326; II. Historical Background, pp. 326-327; III. Notes on the Texts, pp. 327-331; A. The Liturgical Prayer Scroll, 1 Q Prayers (Pl. IV), pp. 328-329; B. The Daniel Fragments, 1 Q Dan[ab] (Plates V and VI), 329-331; C. The Smaller Fragments (Pl. VII), p. 331; IV. The Relation of Dan[a] to 1 Q Dan[b], pp. 331-332; V. Paleography, pp. 332-334]

*R. A. Martin, "Some Recent Developments in the Study of Discoveries near the Dead Sea," *IJT* 14 (1965) 102-116. [II. Aspects of the Study of the Scroll Material, pp. 108-116]

*Solomon Zeitlin, "The Judean Calendar during the Second Commonwealth and the Scrolls," *JQR, N.S.,* 57 (1966-67) 28-45.

Alfred v. R. Sauer, "The Dead Sea Scrolls," *CTM* 38 (1967) 258-262.

*Anonymous, "The Dead Sea Scrolls, and a New Book on Masada," *BH* 3 (1967) #1, 12-13. *(Review)*

E. M. Blaiklock, "The Real Significance of the Dead Sea Scrolls," *BH* 3 (1967) #4, 3-13.

Edward F. Campbell Jr., "Editorial—*The Dead Sea Scrolls Today*," *McQ* 21 (1967-68) 247-248.

Jonas C. Greenfield, "The Small Caves of Qumran," *JAOS* 89 (1969) 128-141. *(Review)*

§1090 *7.3.1 Literary Criticism of the Scrolls - General Studies*

*John C. Trever, "Preliminary Observations on the Jerusalem Scrolls," *BASOR* #111 (1948) 3-16. [A. The Jerusalem Isaiah Scroll, pp. 4-9; B. The 'Sectarian Document', pp. 9-12; C. The Habakkuk Commentary, pp. 12-14; D. The Unidentified Fourth Scroll, pp. 14-16]

Solomon Zeitlin, "Scholarship and the Hoax of the Recent Discoveries," *JQR, N.S.,* 39 (1948-49) 337-363.

*Frank M[oore] Cross Jr., "The Newly Discovered Scrolls in the Hebrew University in Jerusalem," *BA* 12 (1949) 36-46. [The Scroll of the War Between the Children of Light and the Children of Darkness, pp. 40-43; The Hymns of Thanksgiving, pp. 43-46]

*J. M. Paul Bauchet, "The Newly Discovered Scrolls of the Judean Desert," *CBQ* 11 (1949) 308-315. [I. Text of the Newly Found Is. 42-43 Compared with Masoretic, pp. 310-312; II. A Song of Thanksgiving (1QH)]

*J.-M. P. Bauchet, "Notes on the Recently-Found Hebrew Manuscripts," *Scrip* 4 (1949-51) 115-117.

Solomon Zeitlin, "Where is the Scroll of the Haftarot?" *JQR, N.S.,* 40 (1949-50) 291-296.

Solomon Zeitlin, "When Were the Hebrew Scrolls 'Discovered'—in 1947 or 1907?" *JQR, N.S.,* 40 (1949-50) 373-378.

Floyd V. Filson, "Some Recent Study of the Dead Sea Scrolls," *BA* 13 (1950) 96-99.

F[loyd] V. F[ilson], "New Fragments of the Dead Sea Scrolls," *BA* 13 (1950) 99-100. [The Lamech Scroll; Isaiah Fragments; The Manual of Disciple]

Solomon Zeitlin, "The Mystery of the Hebrew Scrolls," *CQ* 27 (1950) 35-42.

Solomon Zeitlin, "The Mystery of the Hebrew Scrolls," *JBL* 69 (1950) vi-vii.

Solomon Zeitlin, "The Hebrew Scrolls: Once More and Finally," *JQR, N.S.,* 41 (1950-51) 1-58.

Tovia Weschsler, "The 'Hidden Geniza' Once More or Mr. Trever *versus* Mr. Trever," *JQR, N.S.,* 41 (1950-51) 247-250.

Solomon Zeitlin, "The Hebrew Scrolls: A Challenge to Scholarship," *JQR, N.S.,* 41 (1950-51) 251-275.

Isaiah Sonne, "Final Verdict on the Scrolls?" *JBL* 70 (1951) 37-44.

H. H. Rowley, "The Historical Background of the Dead Sea Scrolls," *ET* 63 (1951-52) 378-384.

Solomon Zeitlin, "The Hebrew Scrolls and the Status of Biblical Scholarship," *JQR, N.S.,* 42 (1951-52) 133-192.

Isaac Rabinowitz, "The Authorship, Audience and Date of the De Vaux Fragment of an Unknown Work," *JBL* 71 (1952) 19-32. [1QpHab; 1QH; CD]

J. L. Teicher, "Material Evidence of the Christian Origin of the Dead Sea Scrolls," *JJS* 3 (1952) 128-132.

Bleddyn J. Roberts, "The Dead Sea Scrolls—Towards a Perspective," *JTVI* 84 (1952) 163-180, 185-186. (Discussion, pp. 180-184)

H. H. Rowley, "The Covenanters of Damascus and the Dead Sea Scrolls," *BJRL* 35 (1952-53) 111-154.

Tovia Wechsler, "The Origin of the So Called Dead Sea Scrolls," *JQR, N.S.,* 43 (1952-53) 121-139.

Solomon Zeitlin, "The Hebron Pogrom and the Hebrew Scrolls," *JQR, N.S.,* 43 (1952-53) 140-152.

Solomon Zeitlin, "More Hebrew Scrolls," *JQR, N.S.,* 43 (1952-53) 406-408.

*Peben Wernberg-Møller, "צדק, צדיק and צדוק in the Zadokite Fragments (CDC), the Manual of Discipline (DSD), and the Habakkuk-Commentary (DSH)," *VT* 3 (1953) 310-315.

Solomon Zeitlin, "The Fiction of the Recent Discoveries near the Dead Sea," *JQR, N.S.*, 44 (1953-54) 85-115.

Solomon Zeitlin, "The Antiquity of the Hebrew Scrolls and the Piltdown Hoax: A Parallel," *JQR, N.S.*, 45 (1954-55) 1-29.

Frank M[oore] Cross Jr., "The Oldest Manuscripts from Qumran," *JBL* 74 (1955) 147-172. *[Studies on scrolls from 4Q]*

*Solomon Zeitlin, "The Propaganda of the Hebrew Scrolls and the Falsification of History," *JQR, N.S.*, 46 (1955-56) 1-39. [I. The War Between the Sons of Light and the Sons of Darkness; II. The Thanksgiving Hymns; III. The So called Letter of Bar Kokba; IV. Phylacteries]

Solomon Zeitlin, "The Propaganda of the Hebrew Scrolls and the Falsification of History," *JQR, N.S.*, 46 (1955-56) 116-180. [V. Other Finds; VI. Scrolls Purchased by the Hebrew University, Commentary of Habakkuk, The So Called Manual of Disciple, The Zadokite Fragments; An Explanation Is Desideratum; VII. The Essenes and the Sadducees; VIII. Paleography, Archaeology and Propaganda, Nash Papyrus; IX. Distortions and Falsifications]

Solomon Zeitlin, "The Propaganda of the Hebrew Scrolls and the Falsification of History," *JQR, N.S.*, 46 (1955-56) 209-258. [X. The Beginnings of Christianity and the Hebrew Scrolls; XI. Where is the Fifth Scroll?; XII. Qumran Cave I; XIII. Recent Literature; XIV. The Mystery of the Discovery of the Scrolls]

Solomon Zeitlin, "The Dead Sea Scrolls," *JQR, N.S.*, 46 (1955-56) 389-400.

P. Benoi, Maurice Baille, Jozef T Milik, Frank M. Cross, Jr, Patrick W. Skehan, John M. Allegro, John Strugnell, Jean Starkey, Calus-Hunna Hunzinger, "Editing the Manuscript Fragments from Qumran," *BA* 19 (1956) 75-96. [The Minor Caves of Qumran (2Q, 3Q, 6Q, 5Q); Cave 4 of Qumran (4Q)] *(Trans. from the French by Jules L. Moreau)*

Solomon Zeitlin, "The Dead Sea Scrolls: A Travesty on Scholarship," *JQR, N.S.*, 47 (1956-57) 1-36.

Solomon Zeitlin, "Revealing Date on the So-called Discovery of the Dead Sea Scrolls," *JQR, N.S.*, 47 (1956-57) 183-186.

*Solomon Zeitlin, "The Dead Sea Scrolls: 1. The Lamech Scroll—A Medieval Midrash; 2. The Copper Scrolls; 3. Was Kando the Owner of the Scrolls?" *JQR, N.S.,* 47 (1956-57) 245-268.

Solomon Zeitlin, "The Dead Sea Scrolls: Fantasies and Mistranslations," *JQR, N.S.,* 48 (1957-58) 71-85.

Solomon Zeitlin, "The Idolatry of the Dead Sea Scrolls," *JQR, N.S.,* 48 (1957-58) 243-278. [Correction, p. 399]

Patrick W. Skehan, "Professor Zeitlin and the Dead Sea Scrolls," *CBQ* 20 (1958) 228-229.

J. L. Teicher and J. M. Allegro, "Spurious Texts from Qumran?" *PEQ* 90 (1958) 61-64.

Solomon Zeitlin, "The Medieval Mind and the Theological Speculation on the Dead Sea Scrolls," *JQR, N.S.,* 49 (1958-59) 1-34.

*Solomon Zeitlin, "The Masora and the Dead Sea Scrolls," *JQR, N.S.,* 49 (1958-59) 161-163.

*W. Wirgin, "Numismatics and the Dead Sea Scrolls," *RdQ* 2 (1959-60) 69-74.

John A. O'Flynn, "Recent Discussions on the Dead Sea Scrolls," *ITQ* 26 (1959) 275-277.

Jerry Vardaman, "Significant Developments in Scroll Research," *R&E* 58 (1961) 181-199.

Solomon Zeitlin, "The Fallacy of the Antiquity of the Hebrew Scrolls Once More Exposed," *JQR, N.S.,* 52 (1961-62) 346-366.

A. Murtonen, "A Historico-Philological Survey of the Main Dead Sea Scrolls and Related Documents," *ABR-N* 4 (1963-64) 56-95.

H. L. Ellison, "Evaluation of the Qumran Manuscripts," *F&T* 93 (1963-64) 19-22.

Solomon Zeitlin, "History, Historians and the Dead Sea Scrolls," *JQR, N.S.,* 55 (1964-65) 97-117.

Solomon Zeitlin, "Were There Three Torah-Scrolls in the Azarah?" *JQR, N.S.,* 56 (1965-66) 269-272.

D. Winton Thomas, "The Dead Sea Scrolls: What may we Believe?" *ALUOS* 6 (1966-68) 7-20.

Joachim Jeremias, "The Theological Significance of the Dead Sea Scrolls," *CTM* 39 (1968) 557-571. *(Trans. by David Zersen)*

Fred L. Horton Jr., "Formulas of introduction in the Qumran Literature," *RdQ* 7 (1969-71) 505-514.

§1091 *7.3.2 Relation of the Dead Sea Scrolls to Other Literature*

*M. H. Goshen-Gottstein, "The Shapira Forgery and the Qumran Scrolls," *JJS* 7 (1956) 187-194.

*M. R. Lehmann, "Talmudic Material Relating to the Dead Sea Scrolls," *RdQ* 1 (1958-59) 391-404.

Sidney B. Hoenig, "Halakhic Implications in the Dead Sea Scrolls," *Trad* 1 (1958-59) 64-76.

Joseph M. Baumgarten, "The Dead Sea Scrolls: a Threat to Halakhah?" *Trad* 1 (1958-59) 209-221.

*Sidney B. Hoenig, "Scroll Idolization," *Trad* 1 (1958-59) 222-226.

*A. A. T. Ehrhardt, "A Penitentiary Psalm from the Dead Sea Scrolls and its Allies," *StEv* 1 (1959) 582-592.

*M. R. Lehmann, "Midrashic Parallels to Selected Qumran Texts," *RdQ* 3 (1961-62) 546-552.

*David Winston, "The Iranian Component in the Bible, Apocrypha, and Qumran: A Review of the Evidence," *HRel* 5 (1965-66) 183-216.

*Solomon Zeitlin, "The Slavonic Josephus and the Dead Sea Scrolls: An Expose of Recent Fairy Tales," *JQR, N.S.,* 58 (1967-68) 173-203.

*H. G. Jefferson, "The Shapira Manuscript and the Dead Sea Scrolls," *RdQ* 6 (1967-69) 391-399.

§1092 *7.3.3 Studies on the Discovery of the Scrolls*

John C. Trever, "The Newly Discovered Jerusalem Scrolls, I. The Discovery of the Scrolls," *BA* 11 (1948) 45-57.

G. Lankester Harding, "The Dead Sea Scrolls," *PEQ* 81 (1949) 112-116.

Frank M[oore] Cross Jr., "A Report on the Biblical Fragments of Cave Four in Wadi Qumran," *BASOR* #141 (1956) 9-13.

Sherman E. Johnson, "The Finding of the Scrolls," *ATR* 39 (1957) 208-217.

William H. Brownlee, "Muhammad ed-Deeb's Own Story of His Scroll Discovery," *JNES* 16 (1957) 236-239.

James Albertson, "An Application of Mathematical Probability to Manuscript Discoveries," *JBL* 78 (1959) 133-141.

Herbert E. Robbins, "Comments on a Paper by James Albertson," *JBL* 78 (1958) 347-350.

W[illiam] H. Brownlee, "Edh-Dheeb's Story of His Scroll Discovery," *RdQ* 3 (1961-62) 483-494.

W[illiam] H. Brownlee, "Some New Facts Concerning the Discovery of the Scrolls of 1 Q," *RdQ* 4 (1962-63) 417-420.

J. L. Teicher, "Archaeology and the Dead Sea Scrolls," *Antiq* 37 (1963) 25-30.

Père de Vaux, "Archaeology and the Dead Sea Scrolls," *Antiq* 37 (1963) 126-127.

§1093 *7.3.4 Studies on Dating the Scrolls, Paleography, and Related Studies*

M. Black, "The Dating of the New Hebrew Scrolls on Internal Evidence," *JJS* 1 (1948-49) 199.

John C. Trever, "A Paleographic Study of the Scrolls," *BASOR* #113 (1949) 6-23.

*W[illiam] F[oxwell] Albright, "On the Date of the Scrolls from 'Ain Feshkha and the Nash Papyrus," *BASOR* #115 (1949) 10-19.

Solomon A. Birnbaum, "The Dates of the Cave Scrolls," *BASOR* #115 (1949) 20-22.

Ernest R. Lacheman, "Reply to the Editor," *BASOR* #116 (1949) 16-17. [Ref. Albright, *BASOR* #115 (1949) pp. 10-19]

W[illiam] F[oxwell] Albright, "Comments on Dr. Lacheman's Reply and the Scrolls," *BASOR* #116 (1949) 17-18.

J. M. Myers, "The Discovery of New Hebrew Manuscripts," *LQ, N.S.,* 1 (1949) 195-200.

Solomon Zeitlin, "The Alleged Antiquity of the Scrolls," *JQR, N.S.,* 40 (1949-50) 57-78.

J. M. Paul Bauchet, "A Note on the Orthography of the Dead Sea MSS," *CBQ* 12 (1950) 68.

John C. Trever, "Some Comments on the Palæography of the Dead Sea Scrolls," *JJS* 2 (1950-51) 195-199.

*J. L. Teicher, "Method in Hebrew Palæography," *JJS* 2 (1950-51) 200-202.

Millar Burrows, "The Dating of the Dead Sea Scrolls," *BASOR* #122 (1951) 4-6.

B. Kanael, "Notes on the Ancient Hebrew Script in the Judean Scrolls," *BIES* #16 (1951) #1/2, III.

N. H. Tur-Sinai, "The Development of the Letters and the Date of the Dead Sea Scrolls," *BIES* #16 (1951) #3/4, I-II.

William G. Guindon, "Radio-active Carbon and the Dead Sea Scrolls," *CBQ* 13 (1951) 268-275.

*O. H. Lehmann, "Materials Concerning the Dating of the Dead Sea Scrolls: I: Habakkuk," *PEQ* 83 (1951) 32-54.

P. Kahle, "The Age of the Scrolls," *VT* 1 (1951) 38-48.

Solomon A. Birnbaum, "How Old are the Cave Manuscripts? A Palaeographical Discussion," *VT* 1 (1951) 91-109.

I. Rabinowitz, "Internal Evidence on the Sequence and Dates of the Extra-Biblical Dead Sea Scroll-Texts and Damascus Fragments," *JBL* 71 (1952) iv-v.

H. H. Rowley, "The Internal Dating of the Dead Sea Scrolls," *ETL* 28 (1952) 257-276.

John C. Trever, "Studies in the Problem of Dating the Dead Sea Scrolls," *PAPS* 97 (1953) 184-193.

*S. A. Birnbaum, "An Unknown Aramaic Cursive," *PEQ* 85 (1953) 23-41.

John C. Trever, "The Problem of Dating the Dead Sea Scrolls," *SIR* (1953) 425-435.

Ernest R. Lacheman, "Hebrew Paleography Once More," *JQR, N.S.,* 44 (1953-54) 116-123.

Frank M[oore] Cross Jr., "The Oldest Manuscripts from Qumran," *JBL* 74 (1955) 147-172.

Solomon Zeitlin, "How Ancient are the Hebrew Scrolls from the Dead Sea?" *Jud* 6 (1957) 55-58.

*Patrick W. Skehan, "The Period of the Biblical Texts from Khirbet Qumran," *CBQ* 19 (1957) 435-440.

N. Avigad, "The Palaeography of the Dead Sea Scrolls and Related Documents," *SH* 4 (1957) 56-87.

*J. R. Rosenbloom, "Notes on Historical Identification in the Dead Sea Scrolls," *RdQ* 1 (1958-59) 265-272.

E. Hammershaimb, "On the Method, applied in the Copying of the Manuscripts in Qumran," *VT* 9 (1959) 415-418.

H. A. Butler, "The Chronological Sequence of the Scrolls of Qumran Cave One," *RdQ* 2 (1959-60) 533-540.

*Solomon Zeitlin, "The Expression B^etalmud in the Scrolls Militates Against the Views of the Protagonists on their Antiquity," *JQR, N.S.,* 54 (1963) 89-98.

Richard S. Hanson, "Paleo-Hebrew Scripts in the Hasmonean Age," *BASOR* #175 (1964) 26-42.

*J. C. Trever, "Completion of the Publication of Some Fragments from Qumran Cave I," *RdQ* 5 (1964-66) 323-344. [V. Paleography, pp. 332-334]

§1094 *7.3.5 Studies on the Relation of the Biblical Scrolls to the Masoretic Text and the Old Testament Canon*

William H. Morton, "The Jerusalem Scrolls: Their Significance for Biblical Studies," *R&E* 46 (1949) 427-453.

Bleddyn J. Roberts, "The Dead Sea Scrolls and the Old Testament Scriptures," *BJRL* 36 (1953-54) 75-96.

M. H. Gottstein, "Bible Studies in the Light of the Dead Sea Scrolls. A lecture given on the occasion of the 30th anniversary of the Institute of Jewish Studies," *Tarbiz* 24 (1954-55) #3, II-III.

*R. Laird Harris, "The Evidence for the Canon from the Dead Sea Scrolls," *RefmR* 3 (1955-56) 139-153.

Merrill F. Unger, "The Significance for Biblical Studies of the New Manuscript Finds," *BS* 113 (1956) 24-29, 117-122.

*Moshe Greenberg, "The Stabilization of the Text of the Hebrew Bible, Reviewed in the Light of the Biblical Materials from the Judean Desert," *JAOS* 76 (1956) 157-167.

*Dewey M. Beegle, "The Meaning of the Qumran Scrolls for Translators of the Bible," *BTr* 8 (1957) 1-8.

*George W. Frey Jr., "Archaeology and Biblical Manuscripts," *UTSB* 57 (1957-58) #2, 9-13.

*Francis I. Andersen, "The Dead Sea Scrolls and the Formation of the Canon," *BETS* 1 (1958) #3, 1-7.

F. F. Bruce, "Qumran and the Old Testament," *F&T* 91 (1959-60) 9-27.

*J. A. Fitzmyer, "The Use of Explicit Old Testament Quotations in Qumran Literature and in the New Testament," *NTS* 7 (1960-61) 297-333.

Howard M. Teeple, "Qumran and the Old Testament," *WSR* 53 (1960-61) #6, 13-17.

*Walter G. Williams, "Text, Canon and Qumran," *IR* 18 (1961) #1, 23-28.

*I. H. Eybers, "Some Light on the Canon of the Qumran Sect," *OTW* 5 (1962) 1-14.

S. Talmon, "Aspects of the Textual Transmission of the Bible in the Light of Qumran Manuscripts," *Text* 4 (1964) 95-132.

Norman Bentwich, "The Dead Sea Scrolls and the Bible," *ContR* 209 (1966) 78-81.

F[rank] M[oore] Cross Jr., "The Contribution of the Qumran Discoveries to the Study of the Biblical Text," *IEJ* 16 (1966) 81-95.

*Shemaryahu Talmon, "The 'Desert Motif' in the Bible and in Qumran Literature," *LIST* 3 (1966) 31-63.

*James A. Sanders, "Cave 11 Surprises and the Question of Canon," *McQ* 21 (1967-68) 284-298.

*Peter R. Ackroyd, "The Open Canon," *Coll* 3 (1968-70) 279-292.

§1095 *7.3.6 Studies on the Dead Sea Scrolls and the Septuagint*

*Harry M. Orlinsky, "Qumran and the Present State of the Old Testament Text Studies: The Septuagint Text," *JBL* 78 (1959) 26-33.

*P. Kahle, "The Greek Bible and the Gospels. Fragments from the Judaean Desert," *StEv* 1 (1959) 613-621.

(§1096) *7.3.7 Studies on Specific Biblical Books found at Qumran*

§1097 *7.3.7.1 Studies on the Book of Exodus from Qumran (4QEx[a] 4QpaleoEx[m] 4QEx[f])*

Patrick W. Skehan, "Exodus in the Samaritan Recension from Qumran," *JBL* 74 (1955) 182-187.

§1098 *7.3.7.2 Studies on the Book of Leviticus from Qumran (4QLXXLev[a])*

S. Yeivin, "The Leviticus Fragments in the Hidden Scrolls Find," *BIES* 15 (1949-50) #3/4, IV.

Solomon A. Birnbaum, "The Leviticus Fragments from the Cave," *BASOR* #118 (1950) 20-27.

S. Yeivin, "The Date and Attribution of the Leviticus Fragments from the Cache in the Judaean Desert," *BASOR* #118 (1950) 28-30.

§1099   *7.3.7.3 Studies on the Book of Numbers from Qumran
          (4QLXXNu)*

*P[atrick] W. Skehan, "The Qumran Manuscripts and Textual Criticism,"
   VTS 4 (1957) 148-160. *[4Q LXX Numbers 3:40-42; 4:6-9]*

§1100   *7.3.7.4 Studies on the Book of Deuteronomy from Qumran
          (4QDt^m 4QDt^q = Deut 32)*

*Patrick W. Skehan, "A Fragment of the 'Song of Moses' (Deut. 32) from
   Qumran," *BASOR* #136 (1954) 12-15.

Theodore H. Gaster, "A Qumran Reading of Deuteronomy XXXIII 10," *VT* 8
   (1958) 217-219.

§1101   *7.3.7.5 Studies on the Books of Samuel from Qumran
          (4QSam)*

Frank M. Cross Jr., "A New Qumran Biblical Fragment Related to the
   Original Hebrew Underlying the Septuagint," *BASOR* #132 (1953) 15-
   26. *[1 Samuel]*

I. H. Eybers, "Notes on the Texts of Samuel found in Qumran Cave 4,"
   OTW 3 (1960) 1-17.

§1102   *7.3.7.6 Studies on the Isaiah Scroll A (1QIs^a)*

Anonymous, "An Early Hebrew Manuscript," *AusTR* 19 (1948) 74.

G. Ernest Wright, "A Phenomenal Discovery," *BA* 11 (1948) 21-23.

Millar Burrows, "Variant Readings in the Isaiah Manuscript," *BASOR* #111
   (1948) 16-24; #113 (1949) 24-32.

*John C. Trever, "Preliminary Observations on the Jerusalem Scrolls,"
   BASOR #111 (1948) 3-16. [A. The Jerusalem Isaiah Scroll, pp. 4-9]

Solomon A. Birnbaum, "The Date of the Isaiah Scroll," *BASOR* #113 (1949)
   33-35.

*J. M. Paul Bauchet, "The Newly Discovered Scrolls of the Judean Desert,"
   CBQ 11 (1949) 308-315. [I. Text of the Newly Found Is. 42-43
   Compared with Masoretic, pp. 310-312]

Millar Burrows, "Orthography, Morphology, and Syntax of the St. Mark's Isaiah Manuscript," *JBL* 68 (1949) 195-211.

*P. Peters, "The Masoretic Text and the Newly Discovered Isaiah Manuscript," *WLQ* 46 (1949) 49-59.

W[illiam] F[oxwell] Albright, "The Dead Sea Scrolls of St. Mark's Monastery," *BASOR* #118 (1950) 5-6.

H[arry] M. Orlinsky, "The St. Mark's Isaiah Scroll in the Light of Lower Textual Criticism," *JBL* 69 (1950) vi.

Harry M. Orlinsky, "Studies in the St. Mark's Isaiah Scroll," *JBL* 69 (1950) 149-166.

*Harry M. Orlinsky, "Studies in the St. Mark's Isaiah Scroll,. III. חמה in Isaiah XLII, 25" *JJS* 2 (1950-51) 151-154.

M. D. Goldman, "The Isaiah MSS of the Dead Sea Scrolls," *ABR* 1 (1951) 1-22.

*John C. Trever, "Isaiah 43:19 According to the First Isaiah Scroll (DSIa)," *BASOR* #121 (1951) 13-16.

Dewey M. Beegle, "Proper Names in the New Isaiah Scroll," *BASOR* #123 (1951) 26-30.

Harry M. Orlinsky, "Photography and Paleography in the Textual Criticism of St. Mark's Isaiah Scroll, 43:19," *BASOR* #123 (1951) 33-35.

*Millar Burrows, "Waw and Yodh in the Isaiah Dead Sea Scroll (DSIa)," *BASOR* #124 (1951) 18-20.

G. R. Driver, "Hebrew Scrolls," *JTS, N.S.,* 2 (1951) 17-30.

P. A. H. De Boer, "A Mistranscription," *VT* 1 (1951) 68. *[Isa. 43:19-1QIsa]*

Elwyn R. Rowlands, "Mistranscription in the Isaiah Scroll," *VT* 1 (1951) 226-229. *[Isa. 43:19-1QIsa]*

M. D. Goldman, "Addendum to 'Dead Sea Scrolls'," *ABR* 2 (1952) 129.

*John C. Trever, "Some Corrections Regarding Isaiah 43:19 in the Isaiah Scroll," *BASOR* #126 (1952) 26-27.

William Hugh Brownlee, "The Manuscripts of Isaiah from Which DSIa Was Copied," *BASOR* #127 (1952) 16-21.

Harry M. Orlinsky, "Studies in the St. Mark's Isaiah Scroll, II. Masoretic *Yiṣwāḥū* in 42:11," *JNES* 11 (1952) 153-156.

Harry M. Orlinsky, "Studies in the St. Mark's Isaiah Scroll, IV," *JQR, N.S.,* 43 (1952-53) 329-340.

H[arry] M. Orlinsky, "The Textual Criticism of the St. Mark's Isaiah Scroll," *JBL* 72 (1953) xiii.

D[ewey] M. Beegle, "Proper Names in the Dead Sea Scroll (DSIa)," *JBL* 72 (1953) xiii-xiv.

*Arie Rubinstein, "Notes on the Use of the Tenses in the Variant Readings of the Isaiah Scroll," *VT* 3 (1953) 92-95.

*A[rie] Rubinstein, "Isaiah LII 14 מִשְׁחַת and the DSIa Variant," *B* 35 (1954) 475-479.

Harry M. Orlinsky, "Studies in the St. Mark's Isaiah Scroll, VI," *HUCA* 25 (1954) 85-92.

Harry M. Orlinsky, "Studies in the St. Mark's Scroll - V," *IEJ* 4 (1954) 5-8.

Samuel Loewinger, "New Corrections to the Variae Lectiones of O. Eissfeldt," *VT* 4 (1954) 80-87.

Isaiah Sonne, "The X-Sign in the Isaiah Scroll," *VT* 4 (1954) 90-94.

*Arie Rubinstein, "Formal Agreement of Parallel Clauses in the Isaiah Scroll," *VT* 4 (1954) 316-321.

H. M. Orlinsky, "Studies in St. Mark's Isaiah Scroll VII," *Tarbiz* 24 (1954-55) #1, I-III.

Patrick W. Skehan, "The Text of Isaias at Qumran," *CBQ* 17 (1955) 158-163.

Arie Rubinstein, "The Theological Aspect of Some Variant Readings in the Isaiah Scroll," *JJS* 6 (1955) 187-200.

*A[rie] Rubinstein, "Singularities in the Consecutive-tense Constructions in the Isaiah Scroll," *VT* 5 (1955) 180-188.

J. L. Teicher, "The Christian Interpretation of the Sign X in the Isaiah Scroll," *VT* 5 (1955) 189-198.

*A[rie] Rubinstein, "Conditional Constructions in the Isaiah Scroll (DSI$_a$)," *VT* 6 (1956) 69-79.

*Samuel Iwry, "The Qumran Isaiah and the End of the Dial of Ahaz," *BASOR* #147 (1957) 27-33.

Alfred Guillaume, "Some Readings in the Dead Sea Scroll of Isaiah," *JBL* 76 (1957) 40-43.

Samuel Iwry, "*maṣṣēbah* and *bāmāh* in 1Q ISAIAHa 6:13," *JBL* 76 (1957) 225-232.

*Martin J. Wyngaarden, "The Servant of Jehovah in Isaiah and the Dead Sea Scrolls," *BETS* 1 (1958) #3, 20-24.

P. Wernberg-Møller, "Studies in the Defective Spellings in the Isaiah-Scroll of St. Mark's Monastery," *JSS* 3 (1958) 244-264.

*Arie Rubinstein, "A Kethib-Qere Problem in the Light of the Isaiah Scroll," *JSS* 4 (1959) 127-133.

*R. H. Gundry, "למטלים. 1 Q Isaiah A 50, 6 and Mark 14, 65," *RdQ* 2 (1959-60) 559-567.

*S. Talmon, "DSIa as a Witness to Ancient Exegesis of the Book of Isaiah," *ASTI* 1 (1962) 62-72.

*D. Flusser, "The Text of Isa. xlix, 17 in the DSS," *Text* 2 (1962) 140-142.

K. H. Richards, "A Note on the Bisection of Isaiah," *RdQ* 5 (1964-66) 257-258. *[1QIsa A col. 27 & 28]*

*S[amuel] Iwry, "והנמצא—A Striking Variant Reading in 1QIs^a," *Text* 5 (1966) 34-43.

§1103 *7.3.7.7 Studies on the Isaiah Scroll B (1QIs ^{b})*

Samuel Loewinger, "The Variants of DSI II," *VT* 4 (1954) 155-163.

Bleddyn J. Roberts, "The Second Isaiah Scroll from Qumran (1QIsb)," *BJRL* 42 (1959-60) 132-144.

S. A. Birnbaum, "The Date of the Incomplete Isaiah Scroll from Qumran," *PEQ* 92 (1960) 19-26.

§1104 *7.3.7.8 Studies on Other Isaiah Scrolls (4QIsªᵃ)*

O. H. Lehmann, "A Third Dead Sea Scroll of Isaiah," *JJS* 4 (1953) 38-40.

§1105 *7.3.7.9 Studies on the Book of Ezekiel from Qumran (11QEz)*

W[illiam] H. Brownlee, "The Scroll of Ezekiel from the Eleventh Qumran Cave," *RdQ* 4 (1962-63) 11-28.

*B. Thiering, "The Qumran Interpretation of Ezekiel 4:5-6," *AJBA* 1 (1968-71) #2, 30-34.

§1106 *7.3.7.10 Studies on the Books of the Minor Prophets*
   from Qumran (4QXII?)

*P. Peters, "A Missing Link in the History of the Septuagint," *WLQ* 51 (1954) 146.

§1107 *7.3.7.11 Studies on the Books of Psalms from Qumran*
   (4QPsª⁻ᑫ 4QPsᵇ 4QPsᶠ cols vii-x 4QPsᑫ
   4QPs89 11QPsª 11QPsApª = 11QPsᵉ?)

J. A. Sanders, "The Scroll of Psalms (11QPss) from Cave 11: A Preliminary Report," *BASOR* #165 (1962) 11-15.

*W[illiam] H. Brownlee, "The 11 Q Counterpart to Psalm 151, 1-5," *RdQ* 4 (1962-63) 379-388.

*J. A. Sanders, "Ps. 151 in 11QPss," *ZAW* 75 (1963) 73-86.

Patrick W. Skehan, "A Psalm Manuscript from Qumran (4Q Psᵇ)," *CBQ* 26 (1964) 313-322.

J. A. Sanders, "Two Non-Canonical Psalms in 11 QPsª," *ZAW* 76 (1964) 57-75.

*Isaac Rabinowitz, "The Alleged Orphism of 11 QPss 28:3-12," *ZAW* 76 (1964) 193-200. (Response by J. A. Sanders, p. 200)

A. Hurvitz, "Observations on the Language of the Third Apocryphal Psalm from Qumran," *RdQ* 5 (1964-66) 225-232.

W[illiam] H. Brownlee, "The Significance of 'David's Compositions'," *RdQ* 5 (1964-66) 569-574. *[11Q Psᵃ]*

J. A. Sanders, "Pre-Masoretic Psalter Texts," *CBQ* 27 (1965) 114-123.

Shemaryahu Talmon, "Hebrew Apocryphal Psalm from Qumran," *Tarbiẕ* 35 (1965-66) #3, II-III.

John Strugnell, "More Psalms of 'David'," *CBQ* 27 (1965) 207-216. *[11QPsᵃ]*

*M[itchell] Dahood, "Ugaritic *ušn,* Job 12, 10 and 11QPsᵃPlea 3-4," *B* 47 (1966) 207-208.

*J. A. Sanders, "The Psalter at the Time of Christ," *BibT* #22 (1966) 1462-1469.

J. A. Sanders, "*Variorum* in Psalms Scroll (11QPsᵃ)," *HTR* 59 (1966) 83-94.

John Strugnell, "Notes on the Text and Transmission of the Apocryphal Psalms 151, 154 (= Syr. II) and 155 (= Syr. III)," *HTR* 59 (1966) 257-281.

Y. Yadin, "Another Fragment (E) of the Psalms Scroll from Qumran Cave 11 (11QPsᵃ)," *Text* 5(1966) 1-10.

S. Talmon, "Pisqah Be'emṣa' Pasuq and 11QPsᵃ," *Text* 5 (1966) 11-21.

*M. H. Goshen-Gottstein, "The Psalm Scroll (11QPsᵃ). A Problem of Canon and Text," *Text* 5 (1966) 22-33.

Sidney B. Hoenig, "The Qumran Liturgic Psalms," *JQR, N.S.,* 57 (1966-67) 327-332. *(Review)*

S. B. Gurewicz, "Hebrew Apocryphal Psalms from Qumran," *ABR* 15 (1967) 13-20. *[11QPsᵃ]*

Conrad E. L'Heureux, "The Biblical Sources of the 'Apostrophe to Zion'," *CBQ* 29 (1967) 60-74. *[11Q Psᵃ, col. XXII]*

A. Hurwitz, "The Language and Date of Psalm 151 from Qumran," *EI* 8 (1967) 70*-71*.

Robert Polzin, "Notes on the Dating of the Non-Massoretic Psalms of 11QPs^a," *HTR* 60 (1967) 468-476.

Jonathan P. Siegel, "Grammar or *Gematria* ?" *JQR, N.S.,* 59 (1968-69) 161-162. *[11QPs^a]*

§1108   **7.3.7.12 Studies on the Book of Ecclesiastes from Qumran (4QQoh^a)**

James Muilenburg, "A Qoheleth Scroll from Qumran," *BASOR* #135 (1954) 20-28.

§1109   **7.3.7.13 Studies on the Book of Daniel from Qumran (4QDan^a 4QDan^b 1QDan^{ab})**

G. Ernest Wright, "Fragments of the Book of Daniel Found," *BA* 12 (1949) 33.

W. Wegner, "The Book of Daniel and the Dead Sea Scrolls," *WLQ* 55 (1958) 103-116.

*J. C. Trever, "Completion of the Publication of Some Fragments from Qumran Cave I," *RdQ* 5 (1964-66) 323-344. [III. Notes on the Texts, pp. 327-331; B. The Daniel Fragments, 1 Q Dan^{ab} (Plates V and VI), 329-331; IV. The Relation of Dan ^{a} to 1 Q Dan^b, pp. 331-332]

John C. Trever, "1 Q Dan^a, the latest of the Qumran Manuscripts," *RdQ* 7 (1969-71) 277-286.

(§1110) **7.3.8 Studies on Apocryphal and Pseudepigraphal Books Found at Qumran**

*David Flusser, "The Connection between the Apocryphal *Ascensio Isaiae* and the Dead Sea Scrolls," *BIES* 17 (1952-53) #1/2, I & II.

*B. J. Roberts, "The Dead Sea Scrolls and Apocalyptic Literature," *OSHTP* (1952-53) 29-35.

*J. Allegro, "Some Unpublished Fragments of Pseudepigraphal Literature from Qumran's Fourth Cave," *ALOUS* 4 (1962-63) 3-5.

§1111 *7.3.8.1 Studies on the Genesis Apocryphon /*
        The Lamech Scroll (1QapGen)

*John C. Trever, "Preliminary Observations on the Jerusalem Scrolls,"
    BASOR #111 (1948) 3-16. [The Unidentified Fourth Scroll, pp. 14-16]

John C. Trever, "Identification of the Aramaic Fourth Scroll from 'Ain
    Feshkha," *BASOR* #115 (1949) 8-10.

N. Avigad, "Last of the Dead Sea Scrolls Unrolled," *BA* 19 (1956) 22-24.

Anonymous, "The Seventh Dead Sea Scroll," *CNI* 7 (1956) #1/2, 36-38.

P. Peters, "The Lamech Scroll," *WLQ* 53 (1956) 153-156.

N. Avigad, "An Apocryphal Genesis Scroll in Aramaic," *A&S* 2 (1957) #2/3,
    237-243.

E. Y. Kutscher, "Dating the Language of the Genesis Apocryphon," *JBL* 76
    (1957) 288-292.

E. Y. Kutscher, "The Language of the Genesis Apocryphon: a Preliminary
    Study," *SH* 4 (1957) 1-35.

Paul Winter, "Note on Salem-Jerusalem," *NT* 2 (1957-58) 151-152.

Solomon Zeitlin, "Dating the Genesis Apocryphon," *JBL* 77 (1958) 75-76.

L. Rabinowitz, "A Note to the Genesis Apocryphon," *JSS* 3 (1958) 55-57.

H. Lignée, "Concordance de *1 Q Genesis Apocryphon,*" *RdQ* 1 (1958-59)
    163-186.

*M.-R. Lehmann, "*1 Q Genesis Apocryphon* in the Light of Targumim and
    Midrashim," *RdQ* 1 (1958-59) 249-263.

G. Sarfatti, "Notes on the Genesis Apocryphon," *Tarbiz* 28 (1958-59) #3/4,
    I-II.

*H. L Ginsberg, "Notes on Some Old Aramaic Texts," *JNES* 18 (1959) 143-
    149. [II. The Genesis Apocryphon, A. The Third Person Plural of the
    Perfect, B. Miscellaneous Observations on GA, pp. 149-149]

Joseph A. Fitzmyer, "Some Observations on the *Genesis Apocryphon,*" *CBQ*
    22 (1960) 277-291.

*D[avid] N[oel] Freedman and A. Ritterspach, "The Use of Aleph as a Vowel Letter in the Genesis Apocryphon," *RdQ* 6 (1967-69) 293-300.

R. Weiss, "Fragments of a Midrash on Genesis from Qumran Cave 4," *Text* 7 (1969) 132-134.

§1112 *7.3.8.2 Studies on the Books of Enoch from Qumran (4QHen ar 1Q19)*

J. T. Milik, "The Dead Sea Scrolls Fragment of the Book of Enoch," *B* 32 (1951) 393-400.

*J. P. Thorndike, "The Apocalypse of Weeks and the Qumran Sect," *RdQ* 3 (1961-62) 163-184. *[1 Enoch 93:1-10; 91:12-17]*

§1113 *7.3.8.3 Studies on the Book of Jubilees from Qumran (4QJub f 1Q17 1Q18)*

*Bent Noack, "Qumran and the Book of Jubilees," *SEÅ* 22&23 (1957-58) 191-207.

E. Wiesenberg, "The Jubilee of Jubilees," *RdQ* 3 (1961-62) 3-40.

Alexander Rofé (Roifer), "Further Manuscript Fragments of Jubilees in the Third Cave of Qumran," *Tarbiz* 34 (1964-65) #4, IV.

§1114 *7.3.8.4 Studies on the Testament of Levi from Qumran (4QTLevi ar b 1Q21)*

*D. Flusser, "Qumran and Jewish 'Apotropaic' Prayers," *IEJ* 16 (1966) 194-205.

§1115 *7.3.8.5 Studies on the Prayer of Nabonidus from Qumran (4QPrNab ar)*

David Noel Freedman, "The Prayer of Nabonidus," *BASOR* #145 (1957) 31-32.

Anonymous, "The Prayer of Nabonidus," *AT* 2 (1957-58) #2, 11-12.

§1116   **7.3.8.6 Studies on the Ben Sira / Ecclesiasticus from Qumran**

*M. R. Lehmann, "Ben Sira and the Qumran Literature," *RdQ* 3 (1961-62) 103-116.

*Alexander A. Di Lella, "Qumrân and the Geniza Fragments of Sirach," *CBQ* 24 (1962) 245-267.

*R. Gordis, "Qoheleth and Qumran—A Study of Style," *B* 41 (1960) 395-410.

M. H. Segal, "Ben-Sira in Qumran," *Tarbiz* 33 (1963-64) #3, II-III.

J. Priest, "Ben Sira 45, 25 in the Light of Qumran Literatures," *RdQ* 5 (1964-65) 111-118.

§1117 **7.3.9 Studies on Pesharim / Commentaries from Qumran - General Studies**

J. G. Harris, "Early Trends in Biblical Commentaries as Reflected in Some Qumran Texts," *EQ* 36 (1964) 100-105.

*Sidney B. Hoenig, "The New Qumran Pesher on Azazel," *JQR, N.S.,* 56 (1965-66) 248-253.

J. D. Amoussine, "The Qumran Commentaries," *VDI* (1968) #4, 108.

§1118   **7.3.9.1 Studies on Commentaries of Isaiah from Qumran (4QpIs a 4QpIs b-d)**

James Muilenburg, "Fragments of Another Qumran Isaiah Scroll," *BASOR* #135 (1954) 28-32.

J. M. Allegro, "Further Messianic References in Qumran Literature," *JBL* 75 (1956) 174-187. [4QIsª, pp. 177-182]

*Y. Yadin, "Some Notes on Commentaries on Genesis xlix and Isaiah from Qumran Cave 4," *IEJ* 7 (1957) 66-68.

*Millar Burrows, "The Ascent from Acco in 4QpIsaª," *VT* 7 (1957) 104-105.

*John [M.] Allegro, "Addendum to Professor Millar Burrow's note on the Ascent from Accho in 4QpIsaᵃ," *VT* 7 (1957) 183.

J[ohn] M. Allegro, "More Isaiah Commentaries from Qumran's Fourth Cave," *JBL* 76 (1958) 215-221. [4QpIsaᵇ, Pap4QpIsaᶜ, 4QpIsaᵈ fgt.1]

Y. Yadin, "Some Notes on the Newly Published *Pesharim* of Isaiah," *IEJ* 9 (1959) 39-42.

W. R. Lane, "Pešer Style as a Reconstruction Tool in 4 Q Pešer Isaiah B," *RdQ* 2 (1959-60) 281-283.

*D. Flusser, "The *Pesher* of Isaiah and the Twelve Apostles," *EI* 8 (1967) 69*-70*.

Judah M. Rosenthal, "Biblical Exegesis of 4QpIs," *JQR, N.S.,* 60 (1969-70) 27-36.

§1119 *7.3.9.2 Studies on Commentaries of Hosea from Qumran (4QpIsᵃ 4QpIsᵇ⁻ᵈ)*

J. M. Allegro, "A Recently Discovered Fragment of a Commentary on Hosea from Qumran's Fourth Cave," *JBL* 78 (1959) 142-147.

J. D. Amussin, "A Qumran Commentary on Hosea (4QHosᵇ II) Historical Background and Date," *VDI* (1969) #3, 87-88.

§1120 *7.3.9.3 Studies on Commentaries of Nahum from Qumran (4QpNah)*

*J. M. Allegro, "Further Light on the History of the Qumran Sect," *JBL* 75 (1956) 89-95. [4QpNahum, pp. 90-93]

H. H. Rowley, "4QpNahum and the Teacher of Righteousness," *JBL* 75 (1956) 188-193.

Daniel Leibel, "Some Remarks on the 'Commentary on the Book of Nahum'," *Tarbiz* 27 (1957-58) #1, II-III.

J. M. Allegro, "More Unpublished Pieces of a Qumran Commentary on Nahum (4Q pNah)," *JSS* 7 (1962) 304-308.

Sidney B. Hoenig, "*Dorshé Ḥalaḳot* in the Pesher Nahum Scrolls," *JBL* 83 (1964) 119-138. *[4QpNah]*

Ben Zion Wacholder, "A Qumran Attack on the Oral Exegesis? The Phrase *'šr btlmwd šqrm* in 4 Q Pesher Nahum," *RdQ* 5 (1964-66) 575-578.

*Sidney B. Hoenig, "The Pesher Nahum 'Talmud'," *JBL* 86 (1967) 441-445. *[Nah. 3:4 and 4QpNah]*

*I. H. Eybers, "The *pèšèr*-Commentaries on Habakkuk and Nahum and the Origin of the Qumran Sect," *OTW* 12 (1969) 75-90.

§1121 7.3.9.4 Studies on Commentaries of Habakkuk from Qumran (1QpHab)

*John C. Trever, "Preliminary Observations on the Jerusalem Scrolls," *BASOR* #111 (1948) 3-16. [C. The Habakkuk Commentary, pp. 12-14]

W[illiam] H. Brownlee, "The Jerusalem Habakkuk Scroll," *BASOR* #112 (1948) 8-18.

Solomon Zeitlin, "'A Commentary on the Book of Habakkuk' Important Discovery or Hoax?" *JQR, N.S.,* 39 (1948-49) 235-247.

W[illia]m H. Brownlee, "Further Light on Habakkuk," *BASOR* #114 (1949) 9-10.

David Noel Freedman, "The 'House of Absalom' in the Habakkuk Scroll," *BASOR* #114 (1949) 11-12.

W[illia]m H. Brownlee, "Further Corrections of the Translation of the Habakkuk Scroll," *BASOR* #116 (1949) 14-16.

S. A. Birnbaum, "The Date of the Habakkuk Cave Scroll," *JBL* 68 (1949) 161-168.

P. Peters, "The Midrash on Habakkuk," *WLQ* 46 (1949) 140-141.

W[illiam] H. Brownlee, "The Original Height of the Dead Sea Habakkuk Scroll," *BASOR* #118 (1950) 7-9.

*S. M. Stern, "Notes on the New Manuscript Find," *JBL* 69 (1950) 19-30. [Notes on the translation of the Exposition of Habakkuk, pp. 25-28; Notes on the text of Habakkuk in the Exposition, pp. 28-29]

*Isaac Rabinowitz, "The Second and Third Columns of the Habakkuk Interpretation Scroll," *JBL* 69 (1950) 31-49.

J. L. Teicher, "Jesus in the Habakkuk Scroll," *JJS* 3 (1950-51) 53-55.

P. R. Weis, "The Date of the Habakkuk Scroll," *JQR, N.S.*, 41 (1950-51) 125-154.

*Yehuda Ratzaby, "Remarks Concerning the Distinction between *waw* and *yodh* in the Habakkuk Scroll," *JQR, N.S.*, 41 (1950-51) 155-157.

*M. B. Dagut, "The Habakkuk Scrolls and Pompey's Capture of Jerusalem," *B* 32 (1951) 542-548.

S. Talmon, "Yom Hakkippurim in the Habakkuk Scrolls," *B* 32 (1951) 549-563.

*M. H. Segal, "The Habakkuk 'Commentary' on the Damascus Fragments," *JBL* 70 (1951) 131-147.

*O. H. Lehmann, "Materials Concerning the Dating of the Dead Sea Scrolls: I: Habakkuk," *PEQ* 83 (1951) 32-54.

S. Talmon, "Notes on the Habakkuk Scroll," *VT* 1 (1951) 33-37.

William H. Brownlee, "The Historical Allusions of the Dead Sea Habakkuk Midrash," *BASOR* #126 (1952) 10-20.

R. Tamisier, "A Prototype of Christ?" *Scrip* 5 (1952-53) 35-39. *[1QpHab]*

Ed. Nielsen, "The Righteous and the Wicked in Habaqquq," *ST* 6 (1952) 54-78.

Frederick L. Moriarty, "The Habakkuk Scroll and a Controversy," *ThSt* 13 (1952) 228-233.

Millar Burrows, "The Meaning of '*šr 'mr* in DSH," *VT* 2 (1952) 255-260.

*N. Weider, "The Habakkuk Scroll and the Targum," *JJS* 4 (1953) 14-18.

*A. M. Honeyman, "Notes on a Teacher and a Book," *JJS* 4 (1953) 131-132. [1. Moreh Haṣṣedeq; 2. Sefer Hahagu]

*H. H. Gottstein, "A DSS Biblical Variant in a Medieval Treatise," *VT* 3 (1953) 187-188. *[1QpHab and Hab. 1:13]*

*W[illiam] H. Brownlee, "Emendations of the Dead Sea Manual of Discipline and Some Notes Concerning the Habakkuk Midrash," *JQR, N.S.*, 45 (1953-54) 141-158, 198-217.

J. L. Teicher, "The Habakkuk Scroll," *JJS* 5 (1954) 47-59.

Bertil Gartner, "The Habakkuk Commentary (DSH) and the Gospel of Matthew," *ST* 8 (1954) 1-24.

*J. R. Brown, "Pesher in the Habakkuk Scroll," *ET* 66 (1954-55) 125.

*Solomon Zeitlin, "Additional Remarks," *JQR, N.S.,* 45 (1954-55) 218-229. [Ref. Brownlee, *JQR, N.S.,* 45 (1953-54) 141ff., 198ff.]

*C. Rabin, "Notes on the Habakkuk Scroll and the Zadokite Documents," *VT* 5 (1955) 148-162.

*W[illiam] H. Brownlee, "The Habakkuk Midrash and the Targum of Jonathan," *JJS* 7 (1956) 169-186.

F. F. Bruce, "The Dead Sea Habakkuk Scroll," *ALUOS* 1 (1958-59) 5-24.

*J. A. Sanders, "Habakkuk in Qumran, Paul, and the Old Testament," *JR* 39 (1959) 323-244.

K. M. T. Atkinson, "The Historical Setting of the Habakkuk Commentary," *JSS* 4 (1959) 238-263.

Lou H. Silberman, "Unriddling the Riddle. A Study in the Structure and Language of the Habakkuk Pesher," *RdQ* 3 (1961-62) 323-364.

E. Sjoberg, "The Restoration of Col. II of the Habakkuk Commentary of the Dead Sea Scrolls," *ST* 4 (1950) 120-128.

*C[ecil] Roth, "The Era of the Habakkuk Commentary," *VT* 11 (1961) 451-455.

A. Finkel, "The Pesher of Dreams and Scriptures," *RdQ* 4 (1962-63) 357-370.

*I. H. Eybers, "The *pèšèr*-Commentaries on Habakkuk and Nahum and the Origin of the Qumran Sect," *OTW* 12 (1969) 75-90.

Y. Baer, "'Pesher Habakkuk' and its Period," *Zion* 34 (1969) #1/2, I-III.

§1122 *7.3.9.5 Studies on Commentaries of Books of Psalms from Qumran (4QpPs37)*

*Isaac Rabinowitz, "The Existence of a Hitherto Unknown Interpretation of Psalm 107 Among the Dead Sea Scrolls," *BA* 14 (1951) 50-52.

J. M. Allegro, "A Newly Discovered Fragment of a Commentary on Psalm XXXVII from Qumran," *PEQ* 86 (1954) 69-75.

J. M. Allegro, "Further Light on the History of the Qumran Sect," *JBL* 75 (1956) 89-95. [pPs37:32-33, p. 94; pPs37:14-15, pp. 94-95]

Sidney B. Hoenig, "Qumran Pesher on 'Taanit'," *JQR, N.S.,* 57 (1966-67) 71-73.

§1123 *7.3.10 Studies on Sectarian Works from Qumran*

H. L. Ginsberg, "The Hebrew University Scrolls from the Sectarian Cache," *BASOR* #112 (1948) 19-23.

M. H. Gottstein, "Bible Quotations in the Sectarian Dead Sea Scrolls," *VT* 3 (1953) 79-82.

M. Wallenstein, "Some Aspects of the Vocabulary and Morphology of the Hymns of the Judean Scrolls," *VT* 7 (1957) 209-213.

*Sidney B. Hoenig, "The Sectarian Scrolls and Rabbinic Research," *JQR, N.S.,* 59 (1968-69) 24-70. *[Review and Commentary]*

§1124   *7.3.10.1 Studies on the Zadokite Documents - The Damascus Document (CD 4QCDa)*
[See also: Literary Criticism, and Exegetical Studies on the Zadokite Document §777 and §803 ←]

*John C. Trever, "Preliminary Observations on the Jerusalem Scrolls," *BASOR* #111 (1948) 3-16. [B. The 'Sectarian Document', pp. 9-12]

M. H. Segal, "The Habakkuk 'Commentary' and the Damascus Fragments," *JBL* 70 (1951) 131-147.

S. A. Birnbaum, "The Date of the Covenant Scroll," *PEQ* 81 (1949) 140-147.

Paul J. M. Bauchet, "Transcription and Translation of *Megilloth Genuzoth* B, Plate VI," *CBQ* 12 (1950) 458-459.

B. B. Bamberger, "The Date of the Zadokite Document," *JBL* 71 (1952) iv.

J. L. Teicher, "Restoration of the 'Damascus Fragments': XIV, 12-16," *JJS* 3 (1952) 87-88.

I. Rabinowitz, "The '390 Years' of the 'Damascus' ('Zadokite') Fragments 1:5-6," *JBL* 72 (1953) ix.

*A. M. Honeyman, "Notes on a Teacher and a Book," *JJS* 4 (1953) 131-132.

Isaac Rabinowitz, "Sequence and Dates of the Extra-Biblical Dead Sea Scroll Texts and 'Damascus Fragments'," *VT* 3 (1953) 175-185.

Isaac Rabinowitz, "A Reconsideration of 'Damascus' and '390 Years' in the 'Damascus' ('Zadokite') Fragments," *JBL* 73 (1954) 11-35.

J. L. Teicher, "Puzzling Passages in the Damascus Fragments," *JJS* 5 (1954) 139-147. [1. Page II (MS. A); 2. Page XII (MS. A)]

Paul Winter, "Notes on Wieder's Observations on the דורש התורה in the Book of the Covenanters of Damascus," *JQR, N.S.,* 45 (1954-55) 39-47.

C. Rabin and J. L. Teicher, "On a Puzzling Passage in the Damascus Fragments," *JJS* 6 (1955) 53-55. *[CDC ii, 12]*

*C. Rabin, "Notes on the Habakkuk Scroll and the Zadokite Documents," *VT* 5 (1955) 148-162.

C. Rabin, "On a Puzzling Passage in the Damascus Fragments, A Reply," *JJS* 6 (1955) 111. *[CDC ii, 12]*

*P[aul] Winter, "Ben Sira and the Teaching of the 'Two Ways'," *VT* 5 (1955) 315-138.

*E. Wiesenberg, "Chronological Data in the Zadokite Fragments," *VT* 5 (1955) 284-308.

*Y. Yadin, "Three Notes on the Dead Sea Scrolls," *IEJ* 6 (1956) 158-162. [1. The Damascus Document, 2:12-13, pp. 158-159]

Ralph Marcus, "בפרתיה in the Damascus Covenant XII. 7-8," *JNES* 15 (1956) 184-187.

*P[reben] Wernberg-Møller, "Some Passages in the 'Zadokite' Fragments and Their Parallels in the *Manual of Discipline*," *JSS* 1 (1956) 110-128.

Norman Walker, "Concerning the 390 Years and the 20 Years of the Damascus Document," *JBL* 76 (1957) 57-58.

Jacob Licht, "An Analysis of the Treatise of the Two Spirits in DSD," *SH* 4 (1957) 88-100.

A. Rubinstein, "Notes on Some Syntactical Irregularities in text B of the Zadokite Documents," *VT* 7 (1957) 356-361.

J. Brand, "The Scroll of the Covenant of Damascus and the Date of Composition," *Tarbiẕ* 28 (1958-59) #1, II-III.

*Paul Winter, "Back to the Caves," *PEQ* 91 (1959) 132-134. [I. Prophecy in the Sadoqite Fragments? II. The Moreh Hassedeq in the Toledoth Yeshu?]

Norman Walker, "An Awkward Reading in the Damascus Document," *JBL* 79 (1960) 169-170.

E. F. Sutcliffe, "The Translation of CDC 5:5-6," *VT* 11 (1961) 91-94.

*Y. Baer, "The Manual of Discipline; A Jewish-Christian Document from the Beginning of the Second Century C.E. (Including a Discussion of the Damascus Document)," *Zion* 29 (1964) #1/2, I-II.

P[aul] Winter, "Ṣadoquite Fragments IX, 1," *RdQ* 6 (1967-69) 131-136.

I. Rabinowitz, "The Meaning and Date of *'Damascus'* Document IX, 1," *RdQ* 6 (1967-69) 433-435.

Z. W. Falk, "*Beḥuqey Hagoyim* in Damascus Document IX, 1," *RdQ* 6 (1967-69) 569.

Jerome Murphy-O'Connor, "The translation of *Damascus Document* VI, 11-14," *RdQ* 7 (1969-71) 553-556.

§1125 *7.3.10.2 Studies on the Manual of Discipline (DSD 1QS 4QS variants)*

J.-M. P. Bauchet and E. F. Sutcliffe, "The 'Sectarian Document'," *Scrip* 4 (1949-51) 76-79.

Millar Burrows, "The Discipline Manual of the Judaean Covenanters," *OTS* 8 (1950) 156-192.

Solomon Zeitlin, "A Note on 'The Manual of Discipline'," *JQR, N.S.,* 41 (1950-51) 449.

W[illia]m H. Brownlee, "Excerpts From the Translation of the Dead Sea Manual of Discipline," *BASOR* #121 (1951) 8-12.

*William H. Brownlee, "Light on the Manual of Discipline (DSD) From The Book of Jubilees," *BASOR* #123 (1951) 30-32.

*F. W. Young, "The Discipline Scroll and The Gospel of John," *JBL* 70 (1951) x-xi.

Saul Lieberman, "The Discipline in the So-Called Dead Sea Manual of Discipline," *JBL* 71 (1952) 199-206.

Ralph Marcus, "Textual Notes on the Dead Sea Manual of Discipline," *JNES* 11 (1952) 205-211.

*Sherman E. Johnson, "The Jerusalem Church of the Book of Acts and the Community of the Dead Sea Manual of Discipline," *JBL* 72 (1953) xix.

Preben Wernberg-Møller, "Observations on the Interchange of ע and ח in the Manual of Discipline (DSD)," *VT* 3 (1953) 104-107.

Preben Wernberg-Møller, "Notes on the Manual of Discipline (DSD) I 18, II 9, III 1-4, 9 VII 10-12, and XI 21-22," *VT* 3 (1953) 195-202.

*W[illiam] H. Brownlee, "Emendations of the Dead Sea Manual of Discipline and Some Notes Concerning the Habakkuk Midrash," *JQR, N.S.,* 45 (1953-54) 141-158, 198-217.

J. R. Mantey, "Baptism in the Dead Sea Manual of Discipline," *R&E* 51 (1954) 422-427.

M. H. Gottstein, "A Supposed Dittography in DSD," *VT* 4 (1954) 422-424.

*Solomon Zeitlin, "Additional Remarks," *JQR, N.S.,* 45 (1954-55) 218-229. [Ref. Brownlee, *JQR, N.S.,* 45 (1953-54) 141ff.]

*James Muilenburg, "The Beginning of the Gospels and the Qumran Manual of Discipline," *USQR* 10 (1954-55) #2, 23-29.

*Sherman E. Johnson, "The Dead Sea Manual of Discipline and the Jerusalem Church of Acts," *ZAW* 66 (1954) 106-120.

*Sherman E. Johnson, "Paul and the Manual of Discipline," *HTR* 48 (1955) 157-165.

Yigael Yadin, "A Note on DSD IV 20," *JBL* 74 (1955) 40-43.

P[reben] Wernberg-Møller, "Some Reflections on the Biblical Material in the Manual of Discipline," *ST* 9 (1955) 40-66.

*Y. Yadin, "Three Notes on the Dead Sea Scrolls," *IEJ* 6 (1956) 158-162. [2 The Title of the Manual of Discipline, p. 159; 3. The Manual of Discipline 10:4, pp.160-162]

Ralph Marcus, "*Mebaqqer* and *Rabbim* in the Manual of Discipline vi. 11-13," *JBL* 75 (1956) 298-302.

*P[reben] Wernberg-Møller, "Some Passages in the 'Zadokite' Fragments and Their Parallels in the *Manual of Discipline*," *JSS* 1 (1956) 110-128.

Ralph Marcus, "On the Text of the Qumran Manual of Discipline *I-IX*," *JNES* 16 (1957) 24-38.

G. R. Driver, "Three Difficult Words in *Discipline* (iii. 3-4, vii. 5-6, 11)," *JSS* 2 (1957) 247-250.

Benedikt Otzen, "Some Text-problems in 1QS," *ST* 11 (1957) 89-98. [V, 7; III, 2; VII, 15; VIII, 7; VI, 12f.; IV, 6; IV, 7; IV, 7f.; IV, 8]

I. Sonne, "Remarks on 'Manual of Discipline', col VI, 6-7," *VT* 7 (1957) 405-408.

Israel Renov, "A Proposed Reading of the *Manual of Discipline*, X, 4," *JSS* 3 (1958) 356-362.

*Edmund F. Sutcliffe, "The First Fifteen Members of the Qumran Community: A Note on 1QS 8:1ff.," *JSS* 4 (1959) 134-139.

*P[reben] Wernberg-Møller, "*waw* and *yod* in the Rule of the Community (1 Q S)," *RdQ* 2 (1959-60) 223-236.

T. Leahy, "Studies in the Syntax of 1QS," *B* 41 (1960) 135-157.

*Max Wilcox, "Qumran Eschatology: Some Observations on 1QS," *ABR* 9 (1961) 37-42.

P[reben] Wernberg-Møller, "A Reconsideration of the Two Spirits in the Rule of the Community *(1 Q Serek III, 13 - IV, 26)*," *RdQ* 3 (1961-62) 413-441.

E. J. Revell, "The Order of the Elements in the Verbal Statement Clause of I Q Serek," *RdQ* 3 (1961-62) 559-569.

*Krister Stendahl, "Hate, Non-Retaliation, and Love, 1QS x, 17-20 and Romans 12:19-21," *HTR* 55 (1962) 343-355.

*Y. Baer, "The Manual of Discipline; A Jewish-Christian Document from the Beginning of the Second Century C.E. (Including a Discussion of the Damascus Document)," *Zion* 29 (1964) #1/2, I-II.

Bruno W. Dombrowski, "חיחד in 1QS and τὸ κοινόν: An Instance of Early Greek and Jewish Synthesis," *HTR* 59 (1966) 293-307.

*P[reben] Wernberg-Møller, "The Nature of the *yahad* according to the *Manual of Discipline* and Related Documents," *ALUOS* 6 (1966-68) 56-81.

*John Strugnell, "Notes on 1QS 1,17-18; 8,3-4 and 1QM 17,8-9," *CBQ* 29 (1967) 580-582.

J. M. Baumgarten, "The Meaning of 1 Q Serek III, 2-3," *RdQ* 6 (1967-69) 287-288.

*James H. Charlesworth, "A Critical Comparison of the Dualism in 1QS iii, 13-14, 26 and the 'Dualism' contained in the Fourth Gospel," *NTS* 15 (1968-69) 389-418.

B[runo] W. Dombrowski, "The idea of God in 1 Q Serek," *RdQ* 7 (1969-71) 515-531.

§1126 *7.3.10.3 Studies on the Rule of the Congregation (1QSa)*

R. North, "Qumran 'Serek a' and Related Fragments," *Or, N.S.*, 25 (1956) 90-99.

H. Neil Richardson, "Some Notes on 1QSA," *JBL* 76 (1957) 108-122.

Joseph M. Baumgarten, "On the Testimony of Women in 1QSA," *JBL* 76 (1957) 266-269.

Sidney B. Hoenig, "On the Age of Mature Responsibility in 1QSa," *JQR, N.S.*, 48 (1957-58) 371-375.

*Henry J. Cadbury," A Qumran Parallel to Paul," *HTR* 51 (1958) 1-2. [1QSa and 1 Cor. 11:2-6]

Joseph M. Baumgarten, "IQSa 1.11—Age of Testimony or Responsibility?" *JQR, N.S.*, 49 (1958-59) 157-161.

Joseph M. Baumgarten, "IQSa 1.11—Age of Testimony or Responsibility?" *JQR, N.S.,* 49 (1958-59) 157-161.

*Sidney B. Hoenig, "The Age of Twenty in Rabbinic Tradition and 1QSa," *JQR, N.S.,* 49 (1958-59) 209-214.

Patrick W. Skehan, "Two Infinitives and Their Orthography in *1QSᵃ*," *CBQ* 21 (1959) 220.

Yigael Yadin, "A Crucial Passage in the Dead Sea Scrolls. 1QSa ii. 11-17," *JBL* 78 (1959) 238-241.

*Morton Smith, "'God's Begetting the Messiah' in 1QSa," *NTS* 5 (1959-60) 218-224.

E. F. Sutcliffe, "The Rule of the Congregation (1 Q S a) II, 11-12: Text and Meaning," *RdQ* 2 (1959-60) 541-547.

P. Borgen, "'At the Age of Twenty' in 1 Q S a," *RdQ* 3 (1961-62) 267-277.

M. Treves, "The Two Spirits of the Rule of the Community," *RdQ* 3 (1961-62) 449-452.

S. H. Levey, "The Rule of the Community III, 2," *RdQ* 5 (1964-66) 239-244.

§1127 *7.3.10.4 Studies on the War Scroll (1QM 4QMᵃ ᵇ⁻ᵉ pap 4QMᵉᶠ)*

*Frank M[oore] Cross Jr., "The Newly Discovered Scrolls in the Hebrew University in Jerusalem," *BA* 12 (1949) 36-46. [The Scroll of the War Between the Children of Light and the Children of Darkness, pp. 40-43]

J.-M. Paul Bauchet, "A Newly Discovered Hebrew Manuscript," *Scrip* 4 (1949-51) 21-22.

*Paul Winter, "Twenty-six Priestly Courses," *VT* 6 (1956) 215-217.

M. H. Segal, "The Qumran War Scroll and the Date of its Composition," *SH* 4 (1957) 138-143.

*K. M. T. Atkinson, "The Historical Setting of the 'War of the Sons of Light and the Sons of Darkness'," *BJRL* 40 (1957-58) 272-297.

M. Treves, "The Date of the War of the Sons of Light," *VT* 8 (1958) 419-424.

J. L. Teicher, "A Spurious Version of the War Scroll," *ZAW* 70 (1958) 257-258.

Edmund F. Sutcliffe, "A Note on Milḥamah 9:1 and 16:8 יחלו ידם להפיל בחללים," *B* 41 (1960) 61-69.

Anatole M. Gazov-Ginzberg, "The Structure of the Army of the Sons of Light," *RdQ* 5 (1964-66) 163-176.

*John Strugnell, "Notes on 1QS 1,17-18; 8,3-4 and 1QM 17,8-9," *CBQ* 29 (1967) 58-582.

§1128 *7.3.10.5 Studies on the Thanksgiving Hymns (1QH)*

*Frank M[oore] Cross Jr., "The Newly Discovered Scrolls in the Hebrew University in Jerusalem," *BA* 12 (1949) 36-46. [The Hymns of Thanksgiving, pp. 43-46]

*J. M. Paul Bauchet, "The Newly Discovered Scrolls of the Judean Desert," *CBQ* 11 (1949) 308-315. [II. A Song of Thanksgiving, pp. 312-315]

J.-M. Paul Bauchet, "A Note on the Scroll of Thanksgiving Songs," *Scrip* 4 (1949-51) 277-278.

*E. F. F. Bishop, "Qumran and the Preserved Tablet(s)," *RdQ* 5 (1964-66) 253-256. *[1 QHodayot I 23-24]*

Paul J. M. Bauchet*[sic]*, "Transcription and Translation of a Psalm from Sukenik's Dead Sea Scroll," *CBQ* 12 (1950) 331-335.

Isaiah Sonne, "A Sectarian Psalm Against Heretics and False Prophets in the Newly Discovered Scrolls," *JBL* 69 (1950) vi.

Isaiah Sonne, "A Hymn Against Heretics in the Newly Discovered Scrolls and [Its Gnostic Background]," *HUCA* 23 (1950-51) Part 1, 275-313.

Solomon A. Birnbaum, "The Date of the Hymns Scroll," *PEQ* 84 (1952) 94-103.

George S. Glanzman, "Sectarian Psalms from the Dead Sea," *ThSt* 13 (1952) 487-524.

Joseph Baumgarten and Menahem Mansoor, "Studies in the New *Hodayot* (Thanksgiving Hymns)—I," *JBL* 74 (1955) 115-124.

Joseph Baumgarten and Menahem Mansoor, "Studies in the New *Hodayot* (Thanksgiving Hymns)—II," *JBL* 74 (1955) 188-195.

John V. Chamberlain, "Another Qumran Thanksgiving Psalm," *JNES* 14 (1955) 32-41. *[1QH6 = 1QHiii]*

John V. Chamberlain, "Further Elucidation of a Messianic Thanksgiving Psalm from Qumran," *JNES* 14 (1955) 181-182. *[1QH6 = 1QHiii]*

M[eir] Wallenstein, "A Hymn from the Scrolls," *VT* 5 (1955) 277-283.

Meir Wallenstein, "A Striking Hymn from the Dead Sea Scrolls," *BJRL* 38 (1955) 241-265.

J. P. Hyatt, "The View of Man in the Qumran 'Hodayot'," *NTS* 2 (1955-56) 276-284.

Lou H. Silberman, "Language and Structure in the *Hodayot* (1QH3)," *JBL* 75 (1956) 96-106.

Joseph Baumgarten and Menahem Mansoor, "Studies in the New *Hodayot* (Thanksgiving Hymns)—III," *JBL* 75 (1956) 107-113.

Sigmund Mowinckel, "Some Remarks on *Hodayot* 39.5-20," *JBL* 75 (1956) 265-276.

J. Licht, "The Doctrine of the Thanksgiving Scroll," *IEJ* 6 (1956) 1-13, 89-101.

Charles F. Kraft, "Petic Structure in the Qumran Thanksgiving Psalms," *BRes* 2 (1957) 1-18.

*Menahem Mansoor, "Studies in the *Hodayot*—IV,' *JBL* 76 (1957) 139-148.

Robert B. Laurin, "The Question of Immortality in the Qumran 'Hodayot'," *JSS* 3 (1958) 344-355.

*A. A. T. Ehrhardt, "A Penitentiary Psalm from the Dead Sea Scrolls and its Allies," *StEv* 1 (1959) 582-592.

Meir Wallenstein, "The Palaeography of the *zayin* in the Hymns Scroll with Special Reference to the Interpretation of Related Obscure Passages," *VT* 9 (1959) 101-107.

*Glenn Hinson, "Hodayth III, 6-18: In What Sense Messianic?" *RdQ* 2 (1959-60) 183-204.

Menahem Mansoor, "Studies in the New *Hadayot* (Thanksgiving Hymns) —V: Some Theological Doctrines," *BRes* 5 (1960) 1-21.

Helmer Riggren, "The Branch and the Plantation in the Hodayot," *BRes* 6 (1961) 3-9.

*M. Mansoor, "The Thanksgiving Hymns and the Massoretic Text," *RdQ* 3 (1961-62) 259-266, 387-394.

Barbara Thiering, "The Poetic Forms of the Hodayot," *JSS* 8 (1963) 189-209.

*P. Wernberg-Moller, "The Contribution of the *Hadayot* to Biblical Textual Criticism," *Text* 4 (1964) 133-175.

*S. J. De Vries, "The Syntax of Tenses and Interpretation in the Hodayoth," *RdQ* 5 (1964-66) 375-414.

Sidney B. Hoenig, "Textual Readings and Meanings in Hodayot (1QH)," *JQR, N.S.,* 58 (1967-68) 309-316.

Schuyler Brown, "Deliverance from the Crucible: Some further reflexions on 1QH iii. 1-18," *NTS* 14 (1967-68) 247-259.

E. P. Sanders, "Chiasmus and the Translation of *1 Q Hodayot* VII, 26-27," *RdQ* 6 (1967-69) 427-431.

N. Fried, "Some Further Notes on *Haftaroth* Scrolls," *Text* 6 (1968) 118-126.

§1129 *7.3.10.6 Studies on the Sayings of Moses (1QDM)*

Theodore H. Gaster, "A Curious Qumran Tradition," *BASOR* #151 (1958) 33.

§1130 *7.3.10.7 Studies on the Midrash on Melchizedek (11QMelch)*

*Y. Yadin, "A Note on Malchizedek and Qumran," *IEJ* 15 (1965) 152-154.

*M. de Jonge and A. S. van der Woude, "11Q Melchizedek and the New Testament," *NTS* 12 (1965-66) 301-326.

David Flusser, "Melchizedek and the Son of Man (A preliminary note on a new fragment from Qumran)," *CNI* 17 (1966) #1, 23-29.

*Joseph A. Fitzmyer, "Further Light on Melchizedek from Qumran Cave 11," *JBL* 86 (1967) 10-24.

J. D. Amusin, "A New Eschatological Text from Qumran (11QMelchisedek)," *VDI* (1967) #3, 62.

*Merrill P. Miller, "The Function of Isa. 61:1-2 in 11Q Melchizedek," *JBL* 88 (1969) 467-469.

§1131 *7.3.10.8 Studies on 4QFloriglegium (4QEschMidr)*

*J. M. Allegro, "Further Messianic References in Qumran Literature," *JBL* 75 (1956) 174-187. [4QFlorilegium, pp. 182-187]

J. M. Allegro, "Fragments of a Qumran Scroll of Eschatological *Midrāšîm*," *JBL* 77 (1958) 350-354.

Y. Yadin, "A Midrash on 2 Sam. vii and Ps. i-ii: (4Q Florilegium)," *IEJ* 9 (1959) 95-98.

D. Flusser, "Two Notes on the Midrash on 2 Sam. vii," *IEJ* 9 (1959) 99-109.

Lou H. Silberman, "A Note on 4Q Florilegium," *JBL* 78 (1959) 158-159.

William R. Lane, "A New Commentary Structure in 4Q Florilegium," *JBL* 58 (1959) 343-347.

§1132 *7.3.10.9 Studies on 4QBless (?pGen 49)*

*J. M. Allegro, "Further Messianic References in Qumran Literature," *JBL* 75 (1956) 174-187. [4QPatriarchalBless, pp. 174-176]

*Y. Yadin, "Some Notes on Commentaries on Genesis xlix and Isaiah, from Qumran Cave 4," *IEJ* 7 (1957) 66-68.

§1133 *7.3.10.10 Studies on the Angelic Liturgy (1QS1 39-40)*

J[ohn] Strugnell, "The angelic liturgy at Qumrân, 4Q Serek Šîrôt ʿÔlat Haššabbāt," *VTS* 7 (1960) 318-345.

§1134 *7.3.10.11 Studies on the Three Tongues of Fire (4QDidHam 1Q29)*

M. R. Lehmann, "A Re-Interpretation of *4 Q Dibrê Ham-me'oroth*," *RdQ* 5 (1964-66) 106-110. *[4 Q Luminaries]*

§1135 *7.3.10.12 Studies on "Ordinances" (4QOrd)*

J. M. Allegro, "An Unpublished Fragment of Essene Halakhah (4Q Ordinances)," *JSS* 6 (1961) 71-73.

Y. Yadin, "A Note on 4Q 159 (Ordinances)," *IEJ* 18 (1968) 250-252.

§1136 *7.3.10.13 Studies on the Wiles of a Harlot (4QWiles - Harlot)*

J. M. Allegro, "The Wiles of the Wicked Woman," *PEQ* 96 (1964) 53-55.

Sidney B. Hoenig, "Another Satirical Qumran Fragment," *JQR, N.S.,* 55 (1964-65) 256-259.

A. M. Gazov-Ginzberg, "Double Meaning in Qumran Work ('The Wiles of the Wicked Woman')," *RdQ* 6 (1967-69) 279-285.

§1137 *7.3.10.14 Studies on 4QMess ar*

Joseph [A.] Fitzmyer, "The Aramaic 'Elect of God' Text from Qumran Cave IV," *CBQ* 27 (1965) 348-372.

§1138 *7.3.10.15 Studies on 4QCryptic*

J. M. Allegro, "An Astrological Cryptic Document from Qumran," *JSS* 9 (1964) 291-294.

Jacob Licht, "Legs as Signs of Election," *Tarbiz* 35 (1965-66) #1, II-III.

R. Gordis, "A Document in Code from Qumran—Some Observations," *JSS* 11 (1966) 37-39.

§1139 *7.3.10.16 Studies on Prayers (1QPrayers, 4QPrs)*

*J. Allegro, "Some Unpublished Fragments of Pseudepigraphal Literature from Qumran's Fourth Cave," *ALUOS* 4 (1962-63) 3-5.

*J. C. Trever, "Completion of the Publication of Some Fragments from Qumran Cave I," *RdQ* 5 (1964-66) 323-344. [III. Notes on the Texts, pp. 327-331; A. The Liturgical Prayer Scroll, 1 Q Prayers (Pl. IV), pp. 328-329]

John C. Trever, "A Further Note About 1 Q Prayers," *RdQ* 6 (1967-69) 137-138.

§1140 *7.3.10.17 Studies on a Targum of Job (11QtgJob)*

A. S. van der Woude, "The Targum of Job from Qumran Cave Eleven," *AJBA* 1 (1968-71) #2, 19-29. *(Trans. by B. Thiering)*

§1141 *7.3.10.18 Studies on the Copper Scrolls (3Q15)*

H. Wright Baker, "Notes on the Opening of the 'Bronze' Scrolls from Qumran," *BJRL* 39 (1956-57) 45-56.

Sigmond Mowinckel, "The Copper Scroll—An Apocryphon?" *JBL* 76 (1957) 261-265.

P. Peters, "A Bronze Scroll in Hebrew," *WLQ* 49 (1952) 215-217.

J. Jeremias, "The Copper Scroll from Qumran," *ET* 61 (1959-60) 227-228.

J. T. Milik, "The Copper Document from Cave III," *BA* 19 (1956) 60-64.

John M. Allegro, "The Copper Scroll from Qumran," *GUOST* 18 (1959-60) 56-65.

J. T. Milik, "The Copper Document from Cave III of Qumran: Translation and Commentary," *ADAJ* 4&5 (1960) 137-155.

L. H. Silberman, "A Note on the Copper Scroll," *VT* 10 (1960) 77-79.

E. Ullendorff, "The Greek Letters of the Copper Scroll," *VT* 11 (1961) 223-227.

Kevin Smyth, "The Dead Sea Scrolls. The Fragments and the Treasure Scroll From Jordan," *ITQ* 30 (1963) 326-339.

M. R. Lehmann, "Identification of the *Copper Scroll* Based on Its Technical Terms," *RdQ* 5 (1964-66) 97-105.

§1142 **7.3.10.19 Studies on the Phylacteries (4QPhyl a-d)**

G. Vermes, "Pre-Mishnaic Jewish Worship and the Phylacteries from the Dead Sea," *VT* 9 (1959) 65-72.

§1143 **7.3.10.20 Studies on the Testimonia (4QTestimonia)**

*J. M. Allegro, "Further Messianic Reference to Qumran Literature," *JBL* 75 (1956) 174-187. [4QTestimonia, pp. 176-177]

*N. Wieder, "Notes on the New Documents from the Fourth Cave of Qumran," *JJS* 7 (1956) 71-76. [The Messianic Testimonia and the Rebuilding of Jericho, pp. 75-76]

*J. A. Fitzmyer, "'4Q Testimonia' and the New Testament," *ThSt* 18 (1957) 513-537.

M. Treves, "On the Meaning of the Qumran Testimonia," *RdQ* 2 (1959-60) 569-571.

Barnabas Lindars, "Second Thoughts. IV. Books of Testimonies," *ET* 75 (1963-64) 173-175.

§1144 **7.3.10.21 Studies on the Temple Scroll / Mishmarot / "Courses"**

Yigael Yadin, "The Temple Scroll," *BA* 30 (1967) 135-139.

Yigael Yadin, "The Temple Scroll," *CNI* 18 (1967) #3/4, 41-48.

Anonymous, "The New Temple Scroll," *BH* 4 (1968) 28-30.

§1145 **7.3.10.22 Studies on Miscellaneous Scrolls from Qumran**

*Frederic William Bush, "Evidence from Milḥamah and the Masoretic Text for a Penultimate Accent in Hebrew Verbal Forms," *RdQ* 2 (1959-60) 501-514. *[1 Q Milḥamah]*

*Theodor H. Gaster, "A Curious Qumran Tradition," *BASOR* #151 (1958) 33. *[The Oration of Moses]*

*Otto A. Piper, "The 'Book of Mysteries' (Qumran I 27) A Study in Eschatology," *JR* 38 (1958) 95-106. [The Document; Eschatology; Abstract and Dramatic Eschatology]

S. Talmon, "'Manual of Benedictions' of the Sect of the Judaean Desert," *RdQ* 2 (1959-60) 475-500.

*F. Charles Fensham, "'Camp' in the New Testament and Milḥamah," *RdQ* 4 (1962-63) 557-562.

§1146 *7.3.11 Studies on Other Palestinian Finds - General Studies*

*G. Lankester Harding, "Khirbet Qumran and Wady Muraba'at. *Fresh Light on the Dead Sea Scrolls and New Manuscript Discoveries in Jordan*," *PEQ* 84 (1952) 104-109.

M. R. Lehmann, "Studies in the Murabba'ât and Naḥal Ḥever Documents," *RdQ* 4 (1962-63) 53-81.

§1147   *7.3.11.1 Studies concerning Bar Kochba's Revolt*

Ernest Renan, "The Last Jewish Revolt," *ContR* 35 (1879) 595-607.

*Samuel Raffaeli, "Jewish Coinage and the Date of the Bar-Kokhbah Revolt," *JPOS* 3 (1923) 193-196.

F. M. Heichelheim, "New Light on the End of Bar Kokba's War," *JQR, N.S.,* 34 (1943-44) 61-63.

*Solomon Zeitlin, "The Assumption of Moses and the Revolt of Bar Kokba," *JQR, N.S.,* 38 (1947-48) 1-45.

*Leo Mildenberg, "The Eleazar Coins of the Bar Kochba Rebellion," *HJud* 11 (1949) 77-108.

Solomon Zeitlin, "Bar Kokba and Bar Kozeba," *JQR, N.S.,* 43 (1952-53) 77-82.

Isaac Rabinowitz, "A Hebrew Letter of the Second Century from Beth Mashko," *BASOR* #131 (1953) 21-24.

H. L. Ginsberg, "Notes on the Two Published Letters to Jeshua ben Galgolah," *BASOR* #131 (1953) 25-27.

J. L. Teicher, "Documents of the Bar-Kochba Period," *JJS* 4 (1953) 132-134.

*S. A. Birnbaum, "An Unknown Aramaic Cursive," *PEQ* 85 (1953) 23-41.

Ernest R. Lacheman, "The So-Called Bar Kokba Letter," *JQR, N.S.,* 44 (1953-54) 285-290.

J. L. Teicher, "Are the Bar Kokhba Documents Genuine?" *JJS* 5 (1954) 39-40.

Ralph Marcus, "A Note on the Bar Kokeba Letter from Murabbaʻat," *JNES* 13 (1954) 51.

Isaiah Sonne, "The Newly Discovered Bar Kokeba Letters," *PAAJR* 23 (1954) 75-108.

S. A. Birnbaum, "Bar Kokhba and Akiba," *PEQ* 86 (1954) 23-32.

Solomon Zeitlin, "A Note on the Fiction of the 'Bar Kokba' Letter," *JQR, N.S.,* 45 (1954-55) 171-180.

*Arie Rubinstein, "The Appellation 'Galileans' in Ben Kosebah's Letter to Ben Galgola," *JJS* 6 (1955) 26-34.

G. Graystone, "The Dead Sea Scrolls—II. Wadi Murabbaʻat," *Scrip* 7 (1955) 66-76.

Josef Meyshan (Mestschanski), "The Legion which Reconquered Jerusalem in the War of Bar Kochba (A.D. 132-135)," *PEQ* 90 (1958) 19-26.

*L. E. Toombs, "Barcosiba and Qumran," *NTS* 4 (1957-58) 65-71.

Yigael Yadin, "The Newly-Found Bar Kochba Letters," *CNI* 11 (1960) #3, 12-16.

Reuven Yaron, "The Murabbaʻat Documents," *JJS* 11 (1960) 157-171.

Anonymous, "*Dead Sea Scrolls:* New Light on Bar Cochba Revolt," *AT* 5 (1960-61) #2, 15-17, cont. on p. 14.

Yigael Yadin, "New Discoveries in the Judean Desert," *BA* 24 (1961) 34-50.

Yigael Yadin, "More on the Letter of Bar Kochba," *BA* 24 (1961) 86-95.

S[olomon] Zeitlin, "The Fiction of the Bar Kokba Letters," *JQR, N.S.,* 51 (1960-61) 265-274.

Joshua Brand, "Some Notes on the Bar Kokhba Letters," *Tarbiz* 32 (1962-63) #3, II-III.

*Z. W. Falk, "The Kethubbah of Murabba'at," *JJS* 15 (1964) 157.

David Rokeaḥ, "Comments on the Revolt of Bar Kokhba," *Tarbiz* 35 (1965-66) #2, III-IV.

S. Applebaum, "The Agrarian Question and the Revolt of Bar Kokhba," *EI* 8 (1967) 77*.

Hugo Mantel, "The Causes of the Bar Kokba Revolt," *JQR, N.S.,* 58 (1967-68) 224-242, 274-296.

S. A. Birnbaum, "Akiba and Bar-Kosba," *PEQ* 100 (1968) 137-138.

§1148   ***7.3.11.2 Studies on the Ben Sira Scroll from Masada***

*Solomon Zeitlin, "The Ben Sira Scroll from Masada," *JQR, N.S.,* 56 (1965-66) 185-190.

*Joseph M. Baumgarten, "Some Notes on the Ben Sira Scroll from Masada," *JQR, N.S.,* 58 (1867-68) 323-327.

Y. Yadin, "The Ben Sira Scroll from Masada," *EI* 8 (1967) 69*.

John Strugnell, "Notes and Queries on 'The Ben Sira Scroll from Masada'," *EI* 9 (1969) 109-119. *[Non- Hebrew Section]*

§1149 ***7.3.12 Philological Studies on the Qumran Literature***

Robert Gordis, "'Naᶜalam' and Other Observations on the Ain Feshka Scrolls," *JNES* 9 (1950) 44-47.

Harris Birkeland, "Some Linguistic Remarks on the Dead Sea Scrolls," *NTTO* 56 (1955) 24-35.

Chaim Rabin, "The Historical Background to Qumran Hebrew," *SH* 4 (1957) 144-161.

*Z. Ben-Hayyim, "Traditions in the Hebrew Language, with Special Reference to the Dead Sea Scrolls," *SH* 4 (1957) 200-214.

Menahem Mansoor, "Some Linguistic Aspects of the Qumran Texts," *JSS* 3 (1958) 40-54.

Sydney B. Hoenig, "What is the Explanation for the Term 'Beᵗalmud' in the Scrolls?" *JQR, N.S.,* 53 (1962-63) 274-276.

*Solomon Zeitlin, "The Expression BeTalmud in the Scrolls Militates Against the Views of the Protagonists on Their Antiquity," *JQR, N.S.,* 54 (1963-64) 89-98.

Nathan Drazin, "What Can 'Betalmud' Prove?" *JQR, N.S.,* 54 (1963-64) 333.

Sidney B. Hoenig, "BeTalmud and Talmud," *JQR, N.S.,* 54 (1963-64) 334-339.

S[olomon] Z[eitlin], "Asher BeTalmud," *JQR, N.S.,* 54 (1963-64) 340-341.

Solomon Zeitlin, "The Word beᵗalmud and the Method of Congruity of Words," *JQR, N.S.,* 58 (1967-68) 78-80.

§1150 *7.3.12.1 Lexicographical Studies on the Dead Sea Scrolls*

Edward P. Arbez, "Notes on the New Hebrew MSS," *CBQ* 12 (1950) 173-189.

Dewey M. Beegle, "Ligatures with Waw and Yodh in the Dead Sea Scrolls," *BASOR* #129 (1953) 11-14.

§1151   *7.3.12.1.1 Studies on Specific Hebrew Words in the Qumran Texts (Alphabetical Listing)*

P. Peters, "The First Published Extra-Biblical Occurrence of the Old Testament Word for Covenant," *WLQ* 48 (1951) 149. [ברית]

*J. C. Greenfield, "The Root 'GBL' in Mishnaic Hebrew and the Hymnic Literature of Qumran," *RdQ* 2 (1959-60) 155-162. [גבל]

*Hans Kosmala, "The term *geber* in the Old Testament and in the Scrolls," *VTS* 17 (1969) 159-169. [גבר]

*J. Neusner, "ḤBR and N'MN," *RBQ* 5 (1964-66) 119-122. [חבר]

J. J. Glück, "Ḥalālîm (ḥalāl), 'carnage, massacre'," *RdQ* 7 (1969-71) 417-419. [חלל]

*M. Wallenstein, "Some Lexical Material in the Judean Scrolls," *VT* 4 (1954) 211-214. [חלכה]

R. E. Murphy, "*Yeṣer* in the Qumran Literature," *B* 39 (1958) 334-344. [יצר]

*B. W. Dombrowski, "The meaning of the Qumran terms TWDH and MDH," *RdQ* 7 (1969-71) 567-574.[מדה]

*M. Wallenstein, "Some Lexical Material in the Judean Scrolls," *VT* 4 (1954) 211-214. [מקוה]

Joseph Reider, "On Mšḥty in the Qumran Scrolls," *BASOR* #134 (1954) 26-27. (Additional remarks by Wm. H. Brownlee, pp. 27-28; W. F. Albright, p. 28; J. Reider, p. 28; Carl H. Kraeling, p. 28) [משחתי]

*J. Neusner, "ḤBR and N'MN," *RdQ* 5 (1964-66) 119-122. [נאמן]

G. Sarfatti, "The Forms פעלהו, יפעלהו and the Expression of Impersonal Subject in the Manual of Discipline (1QS, 1QSa, 1QSb)," *Lěš* 32 (1967-68) #1/2, IV.

*J. J. Glück, "The Verb PRṢ in the Bible and in the Qumran Literature," *RdQ* 5 (1964-66) 123-127. [פרץ]

R. Weiss, "On ספרתי in DS IsA," *Lěš* 30 (1965-66) #3, n.p.n.

*S. Kogut, "Does the form *Qětol* = *qotel* Exist in the Bible?" *Lěš* 34 (1969-70) #1/2, 3 [קוטל] *[English Supplement]*

*N[aphtali] Wieder, "The Term קץ in the Dead Sea Scrolls and in Hebrew Liturgical Poetry," *JJS* 5 (1954) 22-31.

*M. Wallenstein, "Some Lexical Material in the Judean Scrolls," *VT* 4 (1954) 211-214. [מֶקֶץ, קֵץ]

A. A. Anderson, "The Use of 'Ruaḥ' in 1QS, 1QH and 1QM," *JSS* 7 (1962) 293-303. [רוח]

R. E. Murphy, "*Šaḥat* in the Qumran Literature," *B* 39 (1958) 61-66.[שחת]

M. Z. Kaddari, "The Root TKN in the Qumran Texts," *RdQ* 5 (1964-66) 219-224. [תכן]

*B. W. Dombrowski, "The meaning of the Qumran terms TWDH and MDH," *RdQ* 7 (1969-71) 567-574.[תעודה]

§1152 *7.3.12.1.2 Studies on Hebrew Phrases in the Qumran Literature*

M. H. Goshen-Gottstein, "'Sefer-Hagu'—The end of a puzzle," *VT* 8 (1958) 286-288.

Paul Winter, "Two Non-Allegorical Expressions in the Dead Sea Scrolls," *PEQ* 91 (1959) 38-46.

*John M. Allegro, *"Thrakidan,* The 'Lion of Wrath' and Alexander Jannaeus," *PEQ* 91 (1959) 47-51. [כפיר החרון]

*I. Rabinowitz, "The Guides of Righteousness," *VT* 8 (1958) 391-404. [מורה הצדק]

Isaac Rabinowitz, "The Qumran Authors' *SPR HHGW/Y," JNES* 20 (1961) 109-114. [ספר ההגוי]

§1153 *7.3.12.1.3 Studies on Hebrew Grammar and Syntax in the Qumran Literature*

Isaac Rabinowitz, "Trever's taw and Orlinsky's Argument," *BASOR* #124 (1951) 29.

M. H. Gottstein, "Studies in the Language of the Dead Sea Scrolls," *JJS* 4 (1953) 104-107. [1. The Interchange of Final *Yod* and *He;* 2. The Imperfect Patterns]

Shlomo Morag, "The Pronouns of the Third Person Singular in the Dead Sea Scrolls," *EI* 3 (1954) X.

M. H. Goshen-Gottstein, "Linguistic Structure and Tradition in the Qumran Documents," *SH* 4 (1957) 101-137.

*P. Wernberg-Møller, *"Waw* and *yod* in the Rule of the Community (1 Q S)," *RdQ* 2 (1959-60) 223-236.

*F. W. Bush, "Evidence from Milḥamah and the Masoretic Text for a Penultimate Accent in Hebrew Verbal Forms," *RdQ* 2 (1959-60) 501-514.

E. J. Revell, "Clause Structure in the Prose Documents of Qumran Cave I," *RdQ* 5 (1964-66) 3-22.

*S. J. De Vries, "The Syntax of Tenses and Interpretation in the Hodayoth," *RdQ* 5 (1964-66) 375-414.

D[avid] N[oel] Freedman and A. Ritterspach, "The Use of Aleph as a Vowel Letter in the Genesis Apocryphon," *RdQ* 6 (1967-69) 293-300.

Jonathan P. Siegel, "Final *mem* in medial position and medial *mem* in final position in *11 Q Ps a* Some Observations," *RdQ* 7 (1969-71) 125-130.

§1154 *7.3.12.1.4 Studies on Hebrew Grammar and Syntax in Specific Books of the Qumran Literature*

*Yehuda Ratzaby, "Remarks Concerning the Distinction Between *waw* and *yodh* in the Habakkuk Scroll," *JQR, N.S.*, 41 (1950-51) 155-157.

*Millar Burrows, "Waw and Yodh in the Isaiah Dead Sea Scroll (DSIa)," *BASOR* #124 (1951) 18-20.

*Arie Rubinstein, "Notes on the Use of the Tenses in the Variant Readings of the Isaiah Scroll," *VT* 3 (1953) 92-95.

*Arie Rubinstein, "Formal Agreement of Parallel Clauses in Isaiah Scroll," *VT* 4 (1954) 316-321.

*A[rie] Rubinstein, "Conditional Constructions in the Isaiah Scroll (DSIa)," *VT* 6 (1956) 69-79.

*A[rie] Rubinstein, "Singularities in the Consecutive-Tense Constructions in the Isaiah Scroll," *VT* 5 (1955) 180-188.

Einar Brønno, "The Isaiah Scroll DSIa and the Greek Transliterations of Hebrew," *ZDMG* 106 (1956) 252-258.

*P. Wernberg-Møller, "Pronouns and Suffixes in the Scrolls and the Masoretic Text," *JBL* 76 (1957) 44-49.

*Malachi Martin, "The Use of Second Person Singular Suffixes in 1QIs[a]," *Muséon* 70 (1957) 125-144.

§1155 **7.3.13 *Studies on the Qumran Scrolls and Their Relation to the New Testament [See also: Studies on Qumran and Its Relation to Christianity §1085←]***

*F. W. Young, "The Discipline Scroll and the Gospel of John," *JBL* 70 (1951) x-xi.

A. Guillaume, "Matt. XXVII, 46 in the Light of the Dead Sea Scroll of Isaiah," *PEQ* 83 (1951) 78-80.

W. D. Davies, "'Knowledge' in the Dead Sea Scrolls and Matthew 11:25-30," *HTR* 46 (1953) 113-139.

*Sherman E. Johnson, "The Jerusalem Church of the Book of Acts and the Community of the Dead Sea Manual of Discipline," *JBL* 72 (1953) xix.

W. D. Davies, "'Knowledge' in the Dead Sea Scrolls and Matthew 11:25-30," *JBL* 72 (1953) xx.

Lucetta Mowry, "The Dead Sea Scrolls and the Background for the Gospel of John," *BA* 17 (1954) 78-97.

*Bertil Gartner, "The Habakkuk Commentary (DSH) and the Gospel of Matthew," *ST* 8 (1954) 1-24.

*Sherman E. Johnson, "The Dead Sea Manual of Discipline and the Jerusalem Church of Acts," *ZAW* 66 (1954) 106-120.

*James Muilenburg, "The Beginning of the Gospels and the Qumran Manual of Discipline," *USQR* 10 (1954-55) #2, 23-29.

Raymond E. Brown, "The Qumran Scrolls and the Johannine Gospels and Epistles," *CBQ* 17 (1955) 403-419, 559-574.

*Sherman E. Johnson, "Paul and the Manual of Discipline," *HTR* 48 (1955) 157-165.

W. H. Brownlee, "John the Baptist in the New Light of Ancient Scrolls," *Interp* 9 (1955) 71-90.

Geoffrey Graystone, "The Dead Sea Scrolls and the New Testament," *ITQ* 22 (1955) 214-230, 329-346; 23 (1956) 25-48; 24 (1957) 238-258.

*William R. Farmer, "The Teacher of Righteousness and Jesus the Christ," *DG* 26 (1955-56) 183-194.

*Edward J. Young, "The Teacher of Righteousness and Jesus Christ. Some Reflections Upon the Dead Sea Scrolls," *WTJ* 18 (1955-56) 121-145.

Roland E. Murphy, "Insights into the New Testament from the Dead Sea Scrolls," *AER* 135 (1956) 9-22.

Roland E. Murphy, "The Dead Sea Scrolls and New Testament Comparisons," *CBQ* 18 (1956) 263-272.

John A. T. Robinson, "The Baptism of John and the Qumran Community," *HTR* 50 (1957) 175-191.

Yigael Yadin, "The Dead Sea Scrolls and the Epistle to the Hebrews," *SH* 4 (1957) 36-55.

*J[oseph] A. Fitzmyer, "'4Q Testimonia' and the New Testament," *ThSt* 18 (1957) 513-537.

*J[oseph] A. Fitzmyer, "A Feature of Qumran Angelology and the Angels of I Cor. xi. 10," *NTS* 4 (1957-58)48-57.

Joseph H. Dampier, "The Scrolls and the Scribes of the New Testament," *BETS* 1 (1958) #3, 8-19.

F. F. Bruce, "Qumran and the New Testament," *F&T* 90 (1958) 92-102.

Martin Rist, "Modern Manuscript Discoveries and the New Testament," *IR* 15 (1958) #2, 3-10.

Joachim Jeremias, "The Qumran Texts and the New Testament," *ET* 70 (1958-59) 68-69.

B. Hjerl-Hansen, "Did Christ Know the Qumran Sect?" *RdQ* 1 (1958-59) 495-508.

J. Howard [W.] Rhys, "The Impact of the Dead Sea Scrolls on New Testament Teaching," *StLJ* 2 (1958-59) #1, 9-18.

*C. S. Mann, "The Chronology of the Passion and the Qumran Calendar," *CQR* 160 (1959) 446-456.

David Noel Freedman, "The Scrolls and the New Testament," *JBL* 78 (1959) 326-334. *(Review)*

*J. A. Sanders, "Habakkuk in Qumran, Paul, and the Old Testament," *JR* 39 (1959) 232-244.

M. Black, "The Gospels and the Scrolls," *StEv* 1 (1959) 565-579.

*R. H. Gundry, "למטלים 1 Q Isaiah A 50, 6 and Mark 14, 65," *RdQ* 2 (1959-60) 559-567.

D. Flusser, "Blessed Are the Poor in Spirit," *IEJ* 10 (1960) 1-14.

Howard M. Teeple, "Qumran and the origin of the Fourth Gospel," *NT* 4 (1960) 6-25.

John McRay, "John the Baptist and the Dead Sea Scrolls," *RestQ* 4 (1960) 80-88.

*G. H. P. Thompson, "The Son of Man: The Evidence of the Dead Sea Scrolls," *ET* 72 (1960-61) 125.

Joseph A. Fitzmyer, "Qumran and the Interpolated Paragraph in 2 Cor 6,14-7,1," *CBQ* 23 (1961) 271-280.

Henry A. Gustafson, "The Sons of Light," *CovQ* 19 (1961) #1, 1-12.

David Flusser, "Matthew XVII, 24-27 and the Dead Sea Sect," *Tarbiz* 31 (1961-62) #2, III.

Homer A. Kent Jr., "The Qumran Community and New Testament Backgrounds," *GJ* 3 (1962) #2, 35-44.

*Krister Stendahl, "Hate, Non-Retaliation, and Love 1QS x, 17-20 and Romans 12:19-21," *HTR* 55 (1962) 343-355.

*F. F. Bruce, "Preparation in the Wilderness. *At Qumran and in the New Testament,*" *Interp* 16 (1962) 280-291.

John Pryke, "John the Baptist and the Qumran Community," *RdQ* 4 (1962-63) 483-496.

*F. Charles Fensham, "'Camp' in the New Testament and Milḥamah," *RdQ* 4 (1962-63) 557-562.

Pierre Benoit, "Qumran and the New Testament," *TD* 11 (1963) 167-172.

H. Kosmala, "The Parable of the Unjust Steward in the Light of Qumran," *ASTI* 3 (1964) 114-121.

R. E. Osborne, "Did Paul Go to Qumran?" *CJT* 10 (1964) 15-24.

O. Betz, "The Dichotomized Servant and the End of Judas Iscariot," *RdQ* 5 (1964-65) 43-58.

F. C[harles] Fensham, "Judas' Hand in the Bowl and Qumran," *RdQ* 5 (1964-66) 259-261.

J[ohn] Pryke, "'Spirit' and 'Flesh' in the Qumran Documents and Some New Testament Texts," *RdQ* 5 (1964-66) 345-360.

J[ohn] Pryke, "The Sacraments of Holy Baptism and Holy Communion in the Light of the Ritual Washings and Sacred Meals at Qumran," *RdQ* 5 (1964-66) 543-552.

H. Kosmala, "The Three Nets of Belial (A Study in the Terminology of Qumran and the New Testament," *ASTI* 4 (1965) 91-113.

*E[dward] L. Bode, "The Baptist, the Messiah and the Monks of Qumran," *BibT* #17 (1965) 1111-1116.

*M. de Jonge and A. S. van der Woude, "11Q Melchizedek and the New Testament," *NTS* 12 (1965-66) 301-326.

Raymond E. Brown, "Second Thoughts. X. The Dead Sea Scrolls and the New Testament," *ET* 78 (1966-67) 19-23.

J. E. Wood, "Pauline Studies and the Dead Sea Scrolls," *ET* 78 (1966-67) 308-311.

*D. Flusser, "The *Pesher* of Isaiah and the Twelve Apostles," *EI* 8 (1967) 69*-70*.

Floyd V. Filson, "The Dead Sea Scrolls and the New Testament," *McQ* 21 (1967-68) 307-317.

*O. Betz, "The Eschatological Interpretation of the Sinai-Tradition in Qumran and in the New Testament," *RdQ* 6 (1967-69) 89-107.

William R. Stegner, "Wilderness and Testing in the Scrolls and in Matthew 4:1-11," *BRes* 12 (1967) 18-27.

A. R. C. Leaney, "The Experience of God in Qumran and in Paul," *BJRL* 51 (1968-69) 431-452.

*James H. Charlesworth, "A Critical Comparison of the Dualism in 1QS iii, 13-iv, 26 and 'Dualism' contained in the Fourth Gospel," *NTS* 15 (1968-69) 389-418.

A. G. McL. Pearce Higgins, "A Few Thoughts on the Dead Sea Scrolls," *MC, N.S.,* 13 (1969-70) 198-201.

§1156 *7.3.14 Studies on the Qumran Scrolls and Their Relation to the New Testament Apocryphal and Pseudepigraphal Writings*

David Flusser, "The Connection Between the Apocryphal *Ascensio Isaiae* and the Dead Sea Scrolls," *BIES* 17 (1952-53) #1/2 I-II.

J. O'Dell, "The Religious Background of the Psalms of Solomon (Re-evaluated in the light of the Qumran Texts)," *RdQ* 3 (1961-62) 241-258.

J. Massingberd Ford, "A Possible Liturgical Background to the Shepherd of Hermas," *RdQ* 6 (1967-69) 531-551.

§1157 *7.3.15 Studies on the Qumran Scrolls and Their Relation to the Early Church Fathers*

Edward Rochie Hardy, "The Dead Sea Discipline and the Rule of St. Benedict," *JAAR* 25 (1957) 183-186.

L. W. Barnard, "The Epistle of Barnabas and the Dead Sea Scrolls," *SJT* 13 (1960) 33-42.

H. Avenary, "Pseudo-Jerome Writings and the Qumran Tradition," *RdQ* 4 (1962-63) 3-10.

About the Author

William G. Hupper studied at Florida Beacon College and Gordon College. He has continued scholarly pursuits in Ancient Near Eastern studies and biblical languages, as an avocation, studying Hebrew under a private tutor. Software developed by him for Macintosh™ computers to produce Egyptian hieroglyphics on screen and in print is available commercially. Articles by Mr. Hupper appear in theological journals, as well as official government documents related to his vocation. He has been a member of the Society of Biblical Literature for over twenty-five years. Presently residing in Torrance, CA, he is employed in the traffic department of a multinational manufacturing firm.